T0180310

Communications in Computer and Information Science 1254

Commenced Publication in 2007
Founding and Former Series Editors:
Simone Diniz Junqueira Barbosa, Phoebe Chen, Alfredo Cuzzocrea,
Xiaoyong Du, Orhun Kara, Ting Liu, Krishna M. Sivalingam,
Dominik Ślęzak, Takashi Washio, Xiaokang Yang, and Junsong Yuan

More information about this series at http://www.springer.com/series/7899

Communications in Computer and Information Science 1254

Commenced Publication in 2007
Founding and Former Series Editors:
Simone Diniz Junqueira Barbosa, Phoebe Chen, Alfredo Cuzzocrea,
Xiaoyong Du, Orhun Kara, Ting Liu, Krishna M. Sivalingam,
Dominik Ślęzak, Takashi Washio, Xiaokang Yang, and Junsong Yuan

More information about this series at http://www.springer.com/series/7899

Xingming Sun · Jinwei Wang ·
Elisa Bertino (Eds.)

Artificial Intelligence and Security

6th International Conference, ICAIS 2020
Hohhot, China, July 17–20, 2020
Proceedings, Part III

 Springer

Editors
Xingming Sun (iD)
Nanjing University of Information Science
and Technology
Nanjing, China

Jinwei Wang (iD)
Nanjing University of Information Science
and Technology
Nanjing, China

Elisa Bertino (iD)
Purdue University
West Lafayette, IN, USA

ISSN 1865-0929   ISSN 1865-0937 (electronic)
Communications in Computer and Information Science
ISBN 978-981-15-8100-7   ISBN 978-981-15-8101-4 (eBook)
https://doi.org/10.1007/978-981-15-8101-4

This Springer imprint is published by the registered company Springer Nature Singapore Pte Ltd.
The registered company address is: 152 Beach Road, #21-01/04 Gateway East, Singapore 189721, Singapore

Preface

The 6th International Conference on Artificial Intelligence and Security (ICAIS 2020), formerly called the International Conference on Cloud Computing and Security (ICCCS), was held during July 17–20, 2020, in Hohhot, China. Over the past five years, ICAIS has become a leading conference for researchers and engineers to share their latest results of research, development, and applications in the fields of artificial intelligence and information security.

We used the Microsoft Conference Management Toolkits (CMT) system to manage the submission and review processes of ICAIS 2020. We received 1,064 submissions from 20 countries and regions, including Canada, Italy, Ireland, Japan, Russia, France, Australia, South Korea, South Africa, Iraq, Kazakhstan, Indonesia, Vietnam, Ghana, China, Taiwan, Macao, the USA, and the UK. The submissions cover the areas of artificial intelligence, big data, cloud computing and security, information hiding, IoT security, multimedia forensics, encryption, cybersecurity, and so on. We thank our Technical Program Committee (PC) members and external reviewers for their efforts in reviewing papers and providing valuable comments to the authors. From the total of 1,064 submissions, and based on at least three reviews per submission, the program chairs decided to accept 186 papers, yielding an acceptance rate of 17%. The volume of the conference proceedings contains all the regular, poster, and workshop papers.

The conference program was enriched by a series of keynote presentations, and the keynote speakers included: Xiang-Yang Li, University of Science and Technology of China, China; Hai Jin, Huazhong University of Science and Technology (HUST), China; and Jie Tang, Tsinghua University, China. We look forward to their wonderful speeches.

There were 56 workshops organized in ICAIS 2020 which covered all hot topics in artificial intelligence and security. We would like to take this moment to express our sincere appreciation for the contribution of all the workshop chairs and their participants. We would like to extend our sincere thanks to all authors who submitted papers to ICAIS 2020 and to all PC members. It was a truly great experience to work with such talented and hard-working researchers. We also appreciate the external reviewers for assisting the PC members in their particular areas of expertise. Moreover, we want to thank our sponsors: Nanjing University of Information Science and Technology, New York University, ACM China, Michigan State University, University of Central Arkansas, Université Bretagne Sud, National Natural Science Foundation of China, Tech Science Press, Nanjing Normal University, Inner Mongolia University, and Northeastern State University.

May 2020

Xingming Sun
Jinwei Wang
Elisa Bertino

Organization

General Chairs

Yun Q. Shi	New Jersey Institute of Technology, USA
Mauro Barni	University of Siena, Italy
Elisa Bertino	Purdue University, USA
Guanglai Gao	Inner Mongolia University, China
Xingming Sun	Nanjing University of Information Science and Technology, China

Technical Program Chairs

Aniello Castiglione	University of Salerno, Italy
Yunbiao Guo	China Information Technology Security Evaluation Center, China
Suzanne K. McIntosh	New York University, USA
Jinwei Wang	Nanjing University of Information Science and Technology, China
Q. M. Jonathan Wu	University of Windsor, Canada

Publication Chair

Zhaoqing Pan	Nanjing University of Information Science and Technology, China

Workshop Chair

Baowei Wang	Nanjing University of Information Science and Technology, China

Organization Chairs

Zhangjie Fu	Nanjing University of Information Science and Technology, China
Xiaorui Zhang	Nanjing University of Information Science and Technology, China
Wuyungerile Li	Inner Mongolia University, China

Technical Program Committee Members

Saeed Arif	University of Algeria, Algeria
Anthony Ayodele	University of Maryland, USA

Zhifeng Bao	Royal Melbourne Institute of Technology University, Australia
Zhiping Cai	National University of Defense Technology, China
Ning Cao	Qingdao Binhai University, China
Paolina Centonze	Iona College, USA
Chin-chen Chang	Feng Chia University, Taiwan, China
Han-Chieh Chao	Taiwan Dong Hwa University, Taiwan, China
Bing Chen	Nanjing University of Aeronautics and Astronautics, China
Hanhua Chen	Huazhong University of Science and Technology, China
Xiaofeng Chen	Xidian University, China
Jieren Cheng	Hainan University, China
Lianhua Chi	IBM Research Center, Australia
Kim-Kwang Raymond Choo	The University of Texas at San Antonio, USA
Ilyong Chung	Chosun University, South Korea
Robert H. Deng	Singapore Management University, Singapore
Jintai Ding	University of Cincinnati, USA
Xinwen Fu	University of Central Florida, USA
Zhangjie Fu	Nanjing University of Information Science and Technology, China
Moncef Gabbouj	Tampere University of Technology, Finland
Ruili Geng	Spectral MD, USA
Song Guo	Hong Kong Polytechnic University, Hong Kong, China
Mohammad Mehedi Hassan	King Saud University, Saudi Arabia
Russell Higgs	University College Dublin, Ireland
Dinh Thai Hoang	University Technology Sydney, Australia
Wien Hong	Sun Yat-sen University, China
Chih-Hsien Hsia	National Ilan University, Taiwan, China
Robert Hsu	Chung Hua University, Taiwan, China
Xinyi Huang	Fujian Normal University, China
Yongfeng Huang	Tsinghua University, China
Zhiqiu Huang	Nanjing University of Aeronautics and Astronautics, China
Patrick C. K. Hung	Ontario Tech University, Canada
Farookh Hussain	University of Technology Sydney, Australia
Genlin Ji	Nanjing Normal University, China
Hai Jin	Huazhong University of Science and Technology, China
Sam Tak Wu Kwong	City University of Hong Kong, Hong Kong, China
Chin-Feng Lai	National Cheng Kung University, Taiwan, China
Loukas Lazos	University of Arizona, USA
Sungyoung Lee	Kyung Hee University, South Korea
Chengcheng Li	University of Cincinnati, USA
Feifei Li	Utah State University, USA

Jin Li	Guangzhou University, China
Jing Li	Rutgers University, USA
Kuan-Ching Li	Providence University, Taiwan, China
Peng Li	University of Aizu, Japan
Yangming Li	University of Washington, USA
Luming Liang	Uber Technology, USA
Haixiang Lin	Leiden University, The Netherlands
Xiaodong Lin	Ontario Tech University, Canada
Zhenyi Lin	Verizon Wireless, USA
Alex Liu	Michigan State University, USA
Guangchi Liu	Stratifyd Inc., USA
Guohua Liu	Donghua University, China
Joseph Liu	Monash University, Australia
Quansheng Liu	University of South Brittanny, France
Xiaodong Liu	Edinburgh Napier University, UK
Yuling Liu	Hunan University, China
Zhe Liu	University of Waterloo, Canada
Daniel Xiapu Luo	The Hong Kong Polytechnic University, Hong Kong, China
Xiangyang Luo	Zhengzhou Science and Technology Institute, China
Tom Masino	TradeWeb LLC, USA
Suzanne K. McIntosh	New York University, USA
Nasir Memon	New York University, USA
Sangman Moh	Chosun University, South Korea
Yi Mu	University of Wollongong, Australia
Elie Naufal	Applied Deep Learning LLC, USA
Jiangqun Ni	Sun Yat-sen University, China
Rafal Niemiec	University of Information Technology and Management, Poland
Zemin Ning	Wellcome Trust Sanger Institute, UK
Shaozhang Niu	Beijing University of Posts and Telecommunications, China
Srikant Ojha	Sharda University, India
Jeff Z. Pan	University of Aberdeen, UK
Wei Pang	University of Aberdeen, UK
Chen Qian	University of California, Santa Cruz, USA
Zhenxing Qian	Fudan University, China
Chuan Qin	University of Shanghai for Science and Technology, China
Jiaohua Qin	Central South University of Forestry and Technology, China
Yanzhen Qu	Colorado Technical University, USA
Zhiguo Qu	Nanjing University of Information Science and Technology, China
Yongjun Ren	Nanjing University of Information Science and Technology, China

Arun Kumar Sangaiah	VIT University, India
Di Shang	Long Island University, USA
Victor S. Sheng	University of Central Arkansas, USA
Zheng-guo Sheng	University of Sussex, UK
Robert Simon Sherratt	University of Reading, UK
Yun Q. Shi	New Jersey Institute of Technology, USA
Frank Y. Shih	New Jersey Institute of Technology, USA
Biao Song	King Saud University, Saudi Arabia
Guang Sun	Hunan University of Finance and Economics, China
Jianguo Sun	Harbin University of Engineering, China
Krzysztof Szczypiorski	Warsaw University of Technology, Poland
Tsuyoshi Takagi	Kyushu University, Japan
Shanyu Tang	University of West London, UK
Jing Tian	National University of Singapore, Singapore
Yoshito Tobe	Aoyang University, Japan
Cezhong Tong	Washington University in St. Louis, USA
Pengjun Wan	Illinois Institute of Technology, USA
Cai-Zhuang Wang	Ames Laboratory, USA
Ding Wang	Peking University, China
Guiling Wang	New Jersey Institute of Technology, USA
Honggang Wang	University of Massachusetts-Dartmouth, USA
Jian Wang	Nanjing University of Aeronautics and Astronautics, China
Jie Wang	University of Massachusetts Lowell, USA
Jin Wang	Changsha University of Science and Technology, China
Liangmin Wang	Jiangsu University, China
Ruili Wang	Massey University, New Zealand
Xiaojun Wang	Dublin City University, Ireland
Xiaokang Wang	St. Francis Xavier University, Canada
Zhaoxia Wang	A*STAR, Singapore
Sheng Wen	Swinburne University of Technology, Australia
Jian Weng	Jinan University, China
Edward Wong	New York University, USA
Eric Wong	The University of Texas at Dallas, USA
Shaoen Wu	Ball State University, USA
Shuangkui Xia	Beijing Institute of Electronics Technology and Application, China
Lingyun Xiang	Changsha University of Science and Technology, China
Yang Xiang	Deakin University, Australia
Yang Xiao	The University of Alabama, USA
Haoran Xie	The Education University of Hong Kong, Hong Kong, China
Naixue Xiong	Northeastern State University, USA
Wei Qi Yan	Auckland University of Technology, New Zealand

Aimin Yang	Guangdong University of Foreign Studies, China
Ching-Nung Yang	Taiwan Dong Hwa University, Taiwan, China
Chunfang Yang	Zhengzhou Science and Technology Institute, China
Fan Yang	University of Maryland, USA
Guomin Yang	University of Wollongong, Australia
Qing Yang	University of North Texas, USA
Yimin Yang	Lakehead University, Canada
Ming Yin	Purdue University, USA
Shaodi You	The Australian National University, Australia
Kun-Ming Yu	Chung Hua University, Taiwan, China
Weiming Zhang	University of Science and Technology of China, China
Xinpeng Zhang	Fudan University, China
Yan Zhang	Simula Research Laboratory, Norway
Yanchun Zhang	Victoria University, Australia
Yao Zhao	Beijing Jiaotong University, China

Organization Committee Members

Xianyi Chen	Nanjing University of Information Science and Technology, China
Yadang Chen	Nanjing University of Information Science and Technology, China
Beijing Chen	Nanjing University of Information Science and Technology, China
Baoqi Huang	Inner Mongolia University, China
Bing Jia	Inner Mongolia University, China
Jielin Jiang	Nanjing University of Information Science and Technology, China
Zilong Jin	Nanjing University of Information Science and Technology, China
Yan Kong	Nanjing University of Information Science and Technology, China
Yiwei Li	Columbia University, USA
Yuling Liu	Hunan University, China
Zhiguo Qu	Nanjing University of Information Science and Technology, China
Huiyu Sun	New York University, USA
Le Sun	Nanjing University of Information Science and Technology, China
Jian Su	Nanjing University of Information Science and Technology, China
Qing Tian	Nanjing University of Information Science and Technology, China
Yuan Tian	King Saud University, Saudi Arabia
Qi Wang	Nanjing University of Information Science and Technology, China

Lingyun Xiang	Changsha University of Science and Technology, China
Zhihua Xia	Nanjing University of Information Science and Technology, China
Lizhi Xiong	Nanjing University of Information Science and Technology, China
Leiming Yan	Nanjing University of Information Science and Technology, China
Li Yu	Nanjing University of Information Science and Technology, China
Zhili Zhou	Nanjing University of Information Science and Technology, China

Contents – Part III

Big Data and Cloud Computing

Information Processing

Information Security

Security Protocol for Cloud Storage Based on Block-Chain

Congdong Lv[✉]

Nanjing Audit University, Nanjing 211815, China
lvcongdonglv@163.com

Abstract. With the development of cloud storage, it is more and more import to ensure the security of clout storage. Many professors and researchers have done a lot of valuable works. Block-chain has the characteristics of "unforgeability", "whole process trace", "traceability", "openness and transparency" and "collective maintenance". Based on these characteristics, block-chain technology has laid a solid "trust" foundation, created a reliable "cooperation" mechanism, and has broad application prospects. In this paper, we design two protocol based on block-chain to keep the security of cloud storage. One is for enterprises, which generally have large amount of data access, so it is necessary to solve the problem of fast encryption and decryption of large-scale data. The other is for individuals. Generally, the amount of personal data access is relatively small, but the operation is frequent, so the frequent encryption and decryption of small-scale data should be solved. The protocols are designed to make the data can only been attach by the one who hold them.

Keywords: Cloud storage · Block-chain · Storage · Security module

1 Introduction

There are two definitions about cloud storage. In technology, the definition is that cloud storage is a model of networked online storage where data is stored on multiple virtual servers, generally hosted by third parties, rather than being hosted on dedicated servers. Hosting companies operate large data centers [1]; and people who require their data to be hosted buy or lease storage capacity from them and use it for their storage needs. The data center operators, in the background, virtualize the resources according to the requirements of the customer and expose them as storage pools, which the customers can themselves use to store files or data objects [2]. Physically, the resource may span across multiple servers [3]. The other definition is given by SNIA (Storage Networking Industry Association) [4]. Cloud storage is a service that provides virtual storage and related data that can be configured [5]. On the other way, cloud storage is virtual and automatic storage [6]. The definition given by SNIA is on the sight of service and usage [7]. Through these two definitions, we can conclude three character of cloud storage [8]. The first is that cloud storage is based on the internet. The second is that cloud storage can be configured and distributed by need. The last is that cloud storage is a kind of virtual storage and data management.

© Springer Nature Singapore Pte Ltd. 2020
X. Sun et al. (Eds.): ICAIS 2020, CCIS 1254, pp. 3–12, 2020.
https://doi.org/10.1007/978-981-15-8101-4_1

With the development of the society, the demand of energy is growing. But resources are limited. So today's research focus is how to conserve resources. With advances in storage technology, now we can use a small amount of money to get any size of storage. But we may need more money to use it. And sometimes, most of storages are unused. It is a waste of money and resources. Cloud storage can save most of the problems. We can use the storage as we need. We can save money because we don't need to manage them and we don't need to prepare a place to store them. We just need the network to connect them.

Cloud storage has advantages as following.

First, Have Redundant Hardwares and Automatic Failover
Cloud storage solves a potential problem of hardware damage by copying the files to a different server. It knows the location where files stored. When the hardware is damaged, the system will guid reading and writing commands to the file stored on another server to maintain the service to continue.

Second, Storage Upgrades Without Service Interruption
When the traditional storage system upgrade, we need to backup the old files out of the storage. Then stop the machine and put on new storage equipment, which will lead the service to stop.

Cloud storage does not only rely on one storage server. When update and upgrade storage hardwares, it will not effect on providing storage service. The system will move old files to storage. After the new storage provides service, the file will be moved back.

Third, Large Capacity, Capacity Expansion and Save Electricity
When adding a new service project, we may make a wrong decision with the growth of the data, which causes a waste of storage devices which was bought based on the decision.

The extension of cloud storage is very simple. The storage capacity assigned to echo project can exceed the actual storage capacity. For example, the total hard disk capacity is only 1000 TB, but the provider can set 2000 TB or 3000 TB to the system. Then provide them to the project. When the capacity is running out, the provider buys the servers. This will benefit the storage service provider.

Fourth, Massively Parallel Expansion
The traditional storage uses serial expansion. No matter how much expansion box connected, there is always a limit.

Cloud storage is a parallel infrastructure for the expansion. When capacity is not enough, as long as you can purchase new storage servers, the capacity will increase immediately, which is almost no limit.

Fifth, Use Common External Name
The traditional storage is based on the physical volume for mapping. If the application side needs to read several sets of storage, all the storage must be mounted to the application. This will be very difficult to the application which needs to see all the data and make the index at the same time.

Cloud storage provides a unified name. It allows applications to access the data of the entire storage pool with the name. It is very convenient for the development of the application.

Sixth, Load Balancing
In past, when there were several sets of storage devices, inevitably, there would be uneven distribution of workload. Some devices were not used, but others were excessive load at the same time. This would lead to a bottleneck to the performance for the storage.

Seventh, Manage Easily
Storage management is very complex. Different manufacturers have different storage management interface. Data center staff often faces a variety of storage products, in which case, to understand the usage of the storage (capacity, load, etc.) becomes very complex.

Cloud storage is very simple. All storage servers are only one set of storage in the eyes of the manager. The manager purchase new servers when the capacity of the hard disk is running out. Each storage server usage can be seen in an administration interface.

Eighth, Have No Waste of Storage
The traditional storage has demanding requirements to the consistency of the hard disk. They must be the same brand, same capacity, and same model. Otherwise, the system is very easy to go wrong. With the rapid changes in the IT industry, it hard to find the same type of hard disk to replace, when the system is used for 2 to 3 years and the hard disk is damaged.

The security problem of cloud storage is also very clear.

Howard Marks said goodbye to Dropbox on his blog [9]. The reason is that he knows the first stories about how Dropbox's employees actually had access to users' encryption keys and could decypt users' data or even worse, deliver it to anyone with a count order [10].

Maybe it is just a story. However, the security risk is real. How to sovle the problem is what we really care about [11].

In this paper, we give two modules to solve the security problems of cloud storage. In Sect. 2, we will introduce related works. And in Sect. 3, we will describe the module in detail. We will conclude our work and talk about the future work in Sect. 4.

2 Related Works

As we have mentioned in Sect. 1, many experts and cholars research in this area.

Huang Jianzhong and his colaborators give a security protocol about the third-party storage [12]. They proposed a security storage service model combining storage mechanism and security policy and designed a set of scalable third-party security protocols [13–15]. Another method to ensure data storage security is given by Cong Wang and his partners. They proposed an effective and flexible distributed scheme with two salient features, opposing to its predecessors [16–18].

In the paper written by Jun Feng and his partners, they revealed the vulnerability in the Amazon's AWS cloud [19–21].

There are also other papers discussing about the security of cloud storage [22–26].

Papers above all talk about the storage security. The point how to protect the data from storage providers has not been mentioned. In this paper, models are used to solve this problem. We also talk about the integrity and other properties of the data security.

3 Design Security Protocol

3.1 Basic Theory

A. Private (Symmetric) Key Cryptosystem

Advantages:
High data throughput;
Relatively short key size;
Primitives to construct various cryptographic mechanisms.
Disadvantages:
The key must remain secret at both ends;
O (n2) keys to be managed;
Relatively short life time of the key;
Now we assume as follow:
M is the cleartext;
Mk is the ciphertext; K is the key;
E () is the encryption algorithm;
D () is the decryption algorithm.
Encryption:

$$Mk = E\ (M,\ K).$$

Decryption:

$$M = D\ (Mk,\ K);$$

B. Public (Asymmetric) Key Cryptosystem

Advantages:
Only the private key must be kept secret;
Relatively long life time of the key;
Relatively efficient digital signature mechanisms;
O (n) keys to be managed.
Disadvantages:
Low data throughput;
Have much larger key size.
Now we assume as follow:
M is the cleartext;
Mk is the ciphertext;
Kpri is the private key;

Kpub is the public key;
E () is the encryption algorithm;
D () is the decryption algorithm.
Encryption:

$$Mk = E\,(M, Kpub).$$

Decryption:

$$M = D\,(Mk, Kpri);$$

3.2 Security Protocol

Figure 1 is a description of the enterprise user model. The Staff uses cloud storage through the server of the enterprise. They don't need to care about the security of communications between the server and cloud storage.

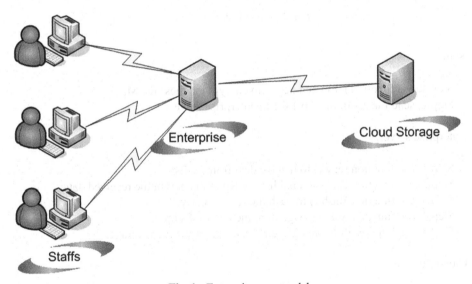

Fig. 1. Enterprise user model

Now we will describe the details of these models.

Figure 2 is a description of the individual user model. Individual users communicate with cloud storage directly. They should ensure the security of the data when they communicate with cloud storage.

Figure 3 is specific processes of the enterprise model.

The following is the process from staffs to cloud storage.

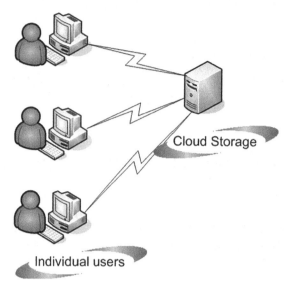

Fig. 2. Individual user model

Staffs:

Step 1, use function E1 () and key K to encrypt the message M;
Step 2, send the result of step 1 C1 to enterprise servers.

Enterprise server:

Step 1, use function recv () to receive data from staffs;
Step 2, use function E2 () and public key Kpub to encrypt the received data;
Step 3, use function Hash () to hash the result of step 2;
Step 4, use function Sig () to signature the result of step 3;
Step 5, send the result of step 2, step 3, and step 4 to client storage.

Cloud Storage

Step 1, use function recv () to receive data from enterprise servers;
Step 2, use function ver () to verificate the data;
Step 3, use funcion store () to store the data on the storage.

The following is the process from cloud storage to staffs.
Cloud Storage:

Step 1, use function get () to get the data C2;
Step 2, use function ver () to verificate the date C2;
Step 3, send data C2 to enterprise servers.

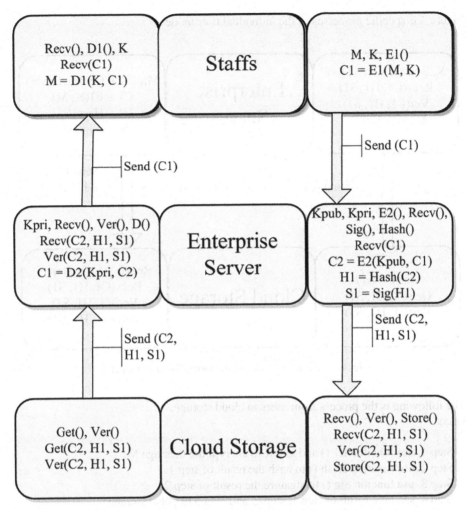

Fig. 3. Specific processes of the enterprise model

Enterprise Server:

Step 1, use function recv () to receive data from cloud storage;
Step 2, use function ver () to verificate the data received from cloud storage;
Step 3, use function D2 () and private key Kpri to decrypt data;
Step 4, send data got in step 3 to staffs.

Staffs:

Step 1, use function recv () to receive data from enterprise servers;
Step 2, use function D1 () and key K to descrypt data.

Figure 4 is specific processes of the individual user model.

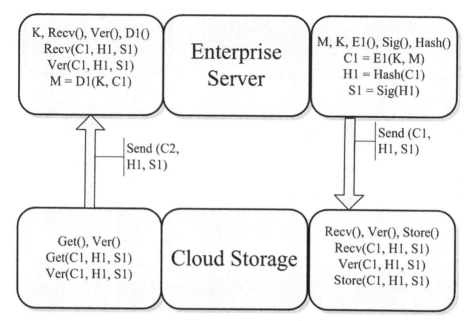

Fig. 4. Specific processes of the individual user model

The following is the process from users to cloud storage.
Users:

Step 1, use function E1 () and key K to encrypt the message M;
Step 2, use function Hash () to hash the result of step 1;
Step 3, use funcion Sig () to sigature the result of step 2;
Step 4, send the result of step 1, step 2, and step 3 to client storage.

Cloud Storage

Step 1, use function recv () to receive data from users;
Step 2, use function ver () to verificate the data;
Step 3, use funcion store () to store the data on the storage.

The following is the process from cloud storage to users.
Cloud Storage:

Step 1, use function get () to get the data C1;
Step 2, use function ver () to verificate the date C1;
Step 3, send data C1 to users.

Users:

Step 1, use function recv () to receive data from cloud storage;
Step 2, use function ver () to verificate the data received from cloud storage;
Step 3, use function D1 () and key K to decrypt data;

3.3 Analysis Models

Both of the two models share some common features. The others include cloud storage providers don't know the encryption key. It can keep the security of the data when they are stored in cloud storage. The hash value is used to ensure then integity of the data. The signature is used to explan who the data is belonging to.

They also have some differences. In the enterprise model, the encrytion algorithm is an asymmetric algorithm. But in the individual user model, the algorithm is a symmetric algorithm. For individuals, the computing power is limited. And requirements of symmetric algorithms for computing power are not very great. The enterprise server has a great computing power. It can fit the need of asymmetirc algorithms.

4   Conclusions and Future Work

Saving energy is a major trend today. Sustainable development is very important to the whole society. Cloud storage is very convenient and very efficient. But compared to the traditional storage, cloud storage has some security issues. In this paper, we give two modules to solve the problem. In the future, how to make the modules work effectively is what we will research on.

References

1. Bacis, E., De Capitani di Vimercati, S., Foresti, S., Paraboschi, S., Rosa, M., Samarati, P.: Protecting resources and regulating access in cloud-based object storage. In: Samarati, P., Ray, I., Ray, I. (eds.) From Database to Cyber Security. LNCS, vol. 11170, pp. 125–142. Springer, Cham (2018). https://doi.org/10.1007/978-3-030-04834-1_7
2. Rawal, B.S., Vijayakumar, V., Manogaran, G., et al.: Secure disintegration protocol for privacy preserving cloud storage. Wirel. Pers. Commun. 103(2), 1161–1177 (2018)
3. Zhong, H., Zhu, W., Xu, Y., et al.: Multi-authority attribute-based encryption access control scheme with policy hidden for cloud storage. Soft. Comput. 22(1), 243–251 (2018)
4. Huang, J., Xie, C., Zhong, H.: Design and analysis of a scalable thrid-party storage security protocal; networking, architecture, and storage. In: International Conference on NAS' 08, pp. 20–27 (2008)
5. Wang, C., Wang, Q., Ren, K., Lou, W.: Ensuring data storage securtiy in cloud computing; quality of service. In: 17th International Workshop on IWQoS, pp. 1–9 (2009)
6. Feng, J., Chen, Y., Liu, P.: Bridging the missing link of cloud data storage security in AWS. In: 2010 7th IEEE Consumer Communications and Networking Conference (CCNC), pp. 1–2 (2010)
7. Wang, C., Wang, Q., Ren, K., Lou, W.: Privacy-preserving public auditing for data storage security in cloud computing. In: INFOCOM, 2010 Proceeding IEEE, pp. 1–9 (2010)

8. Wang, Q., Wang, C., Ren, K., Lou, W., Li, J.: Enabling public auditability and data dynamics for storage security in cloud computing; parallel and distributed systems. IEEE Trans. **22**(5), 847–859 (2011)

9. Tribuwan, M.R., Bhuyar, V.A., Pirzade, S.: Ensuring data storage security in cloud computing through two-way handshake based on token management. In: 2010 International Conference on Advances in Recent Technologies in Communication and Computing (ARTCom), pp. 386–389 (2010)

10. Yang, C., Chen, X., Xiang, Y.: Blockchain-based publicly verifiable data deletion scheme for cloud storage. J. Netw. Comput. Appl. **103**, 185–193 (2018)

11. Du, M., Wang, Q., He, M., et al.: Privacy-preserving indexing and query processing for secure dynamic cloud storage. IEEE Trans. Inf. Forensics Secur. **13**(9), 2320–2332 (2018)

12. Pooranian, Z., Chen, K.C., Yu, C.M., et al.: RARE: defeating side channels based on data-deduplication in cloud storage. In: IEEE INFOCOM 2018-IEEE Conference on Computer Communications Workshops (INFOCOM WKSHPS), pp. 444–449. IEEE (2018)

13. Guo, C., Luo, N., Bhuiyan, M.Z.A., et al.: Key-aggregate authentication cryptosystem for data sharing in dynamic cloud storage. Future Gen. Comput. Syst. **84**, 190–199 (2018)

14. Xue, K., Chen, W., Li, W., et al.: Combining data owner-side and cloud-side access control for encrypted cloud storage. IEEE Trans. Inf. Forensics Secur. **13**(8), 2062–2074 (2018)

15. Li, J., Wu, J., Chen, L.: Block-secure: blockchain based scheme for secure P2P cloud storage. Inf. Sci. **465**, 219–231 (2018)

16. Shen, W., Qin, J., Yu, J., et al.: Enabling identity-based integrity auditing and data sharing with sensitive information hiding for secure cloud storage. IEEE Trans. Inf. Forensics Secur. **14**(2), 331–346 (2018)

17. Wang, T., Zhou, J., Chen, X., et al.: A three-layer privacy preserving cloud storage scheme based on computational intelligence in fog computing. IEEE Trans. Emerg. Topics Comput. Intell. **2**(1), 3–12 (2018)

18. Zhang, X., Wang, H., Xu, C.: Identity-based key-exposure resilient cloud storage public auditing scheme from lattices. Inf. Sci. **472**, 223–234 (2019)

19. Wang, F., Xu, L., Wang, H., et al.: Identity-based non-repudiable dynamic provable data possession in cloud storage. Comput. Electr. Eng. **69**, 521–533 (2018)

20. Zhang, X., Tang, Y., Wang, H., et al.: Lattice-based proxy-oriented identity-based encryption with keyword search for cloud storage. Inf. Sci. **494**, 193–207 (2019)

21. Li, H., Huang, Q., Ma, S., et al.: Authorized equality test on identity-based ciphertexts for secret data sharing via cloud storage. IEEE Access **7**, 25409–25421 (2019)

22. Teing, Y.-Y.: Private cloud storage forensics: seafile as a case study. In: Dehghantanha, A., Choo, K.-K.R. (eds.) Handbook of Big Data and IoT Security, pp. 73–127. Springer, Cham (2019). https://doi.org/10.1007/978-3-030-10543-3_5

23. Bobba, R., Grov, J., Gupta, I., et al.: Survivability: design, formal modeling, and validation of cloud storage systems using Maude. In: Assured Cloud Computing, pp. 10–48 (2018)

24. Xia, Z., Lu, L., Qiu, T., Shim, H.J., Chen, X., Jeon, B.: A privacy-preserving image retrieval based on AC-coefficients and color histograms in cloud environment. Comput. Mater. Continua **58**(1), 27–43 (2019)

25. Deng, Z., Ren, Y., Liu, Y., Yin, X., Shen, Z., Kim, H.-J.: Blockchain-based trusted electronic records preservation in cloud storage. Comput. Mater. Continua **58**(1), 135–151 (2019)

26. Han, S., Seo, J., Kim, D.-Y., Kim, S., Lee, H.: Development of cloud based air pollution information system using visualization. Comput. Mater. Continua **59**(3), 697–711 (2019)

A New Pairing-Based Scheme for Anonymous Communication System

Meichen Xia[✉][iD] and Zhimin Chen[iD]

School of Computer and Software Engineering, Xihua University,
Chengdu 610039, China
xiameichen123@gmail.com

Abstract. Anonymous technology is a critical tool to preserve privacy. In some communication systems, users of one communication group want to verify that they are the legal members without exposing their identities. Some identity-based cryptographic solutions have been proposed for anonymous communications. However, these approaches assume that a centralized trust authority is in charge of the private key generation, so the communications are not anonymous to the trust authority. We present a pairing-based anonymous scheme to realize encryption/decryption, digital signature, key exchange, and key revocation solutions for communications system. In our scheme, users can self-choose their private keys and they can also prove that they are the legal members of one group. Our approach is simple and feasible and it can be applied to some anonymous services.

Keywords: Anonymous system · Identity-based cryptographic · Weil paring

1 Introduction

Preserving-privacy communication systems are very important. On the one side, users in the communication need to prove to the peers that they are legal [1,2]. On the other side, they do not want to leak their identities during this conversation. For the anonymous communication, there are always these kinds of ways to follow. (1) Using the pseudonym to hide the actual identity. Zhang et al. [3] proposed the identity-based key management approach [4] for anonymous communications. In their approach, a trust authority (TA) administrates the anonymous communication system in broadcasting wireless environment. TA can also serve as an organizer who generates the publicly known system parameters and distribute the keys for anonymous users. Users use each other's identity (i.e., a pseudonym) as the public key to set up anonymous communication sessions.

Supported by the Sichuan education department research project (no. 16226483), Sichuan Science and Technology Program (2018GZDZX0008), Chengdu Science and Technology Program (2018-YF08-00007-GX), the National Natural Science Foundation of China (61872087).

Based on the identity-based solution, the ciphertext sender just simply uses the receivers' pseudonyms as the public key to encrypt the plaintext. This approach has one drawback, the anonymous communications are not blind to the TA. To resolve the problem in Zhang's scheme, Huang [5] proposed a pseudonym based scheme to achieve the goal that it is blind to TA. (2) Using the ring/group signatures to hide the actual identity of the sender in a set. Zeng et al. [6] proposed a privacy-preserving protocol for VANETs communication based on the ring signature. In their scheme, the actual sender chooses other members to form a ring. The generated signature is verified under these members' public keys. Therefore the sender's identity will not be exposure to the public. (3) Using the deniable authentication to deny the involvement of one conversation. Li et al. [7] proposed an ID-based deniable authentication for ad hoc networks. In their scheme, the sender's output is not verified publicly. Instead, only the conversation peer can verify this authentication. Therefore, the sender can deny as his peer can generate the whole communication transcript by his own. We propose a pairing-based scheme to achieve the anonymous communication. Comparing to traditional identity-based cryptography, our approach does not depend on the TA to generate a user's private key, but TA signs for each user's identity (who are legal). On the one hand, we want to protect users' identities from being exposed; on the other hand, we expect to create a manageable and admissible communication environment for users. Some conclusions in [4,8,9] will be applied in our scheme to realize encryption/decryption, digital signature, key exchange, and revocation solutions for communications system.

2   The Weil Pairing

2.1   The Properties of Weil Pairing

In this section we shall summarize the properties we require of the Weil pairing, much of the details can be found in [4,10]. The major pairing-based construction is the bilinear map. We denote E being an elliptic curve over the field F. Considering two groups G_1 and G_2 of prime order p. G_1 is an additive group and G_2 is a multiplicative group. The bilinear mapping can be denoted by $e : G_1 \times G_1 \rightarrow G_2$ and the mapping has three properties:

1. Bilinear:

$$e(P_1 + P_2, Q) = e(P_1, Q) \bullet e(P_2, Q)$$
$$e(P, Q_1 + Q_2) = e(P, Q_1) \bullet e(P, Q_2)$$
$$e(aP, bQ) = e(P, Q)^{(a+b)}$$

For$(P, Q, P_1, P_2, Q_1, Q_2) \in G_1, (a, b) \in Z_P^*$
2. Non-degenerate: There exists $P \in G_1$ such that $e(P, P) \neq 1$.
3. Computable: One can compute $e(P, Q)$ in polynomial time.

2.2 Some Hard Problems in Elliptic Curve

There are some hard problems in Elliptic Curve Cryptology (ECC), we describe them as follows:

Elliptic Curve Discrete Logarithm Problem (ECDLP Problem): Given P, mP in G_1 with $m \in Z_P^*$, compute m.

Computational Diffie-Hellman Problem (CDH Problem): Give P, aP, bP in G_1 with $a, b \in Z_P^*$ compute abP.

Bilinear Diffie-Hellman Problem (BDH Problem): For a bilinear pairing $e : G_1 \times G_1 \rightarrow G_2$ defined as follows: $\text{given}(P, aP, bP, cP) \in G_1$, compute $e(P, P)^{abc} \in G_2$ where $(a, b, c) \in Z_P^*$.

Bilinear Diffie-Hellman Assumption: We assume that the BDH problem is hard, which means there is no polynomial time algorithm to solve BDH problem with non-negligible probability.

Pairing Inversion Problem: Given P and s, find Q such that $e(P, Q) = s$.

The details of the pairing algorithms are out of the scope of our paper. The interested reader may study them from [11]. The remainder of this paper we will use the Weil pairing and take advantage of these hard problems in ECC to ensure our scheme's security.

3 Our Scheme

In our scheme, we propose a pairing-based public key infrastructure. Our scheme includes following steps: Setup, Extract, Encryption/Decryption, Digital Signature, Key Exchange, and Key Revocation.

3.1 Parameters Setup and Key Extract

Similar to the IBC, our scheme also needs TA to setup the system parameters, and some parameters (denoted as *params*) should be publicly known to all users. There are many ways to publish the *params*. For example, it can be published on some trusted web sites, and thus all the users can download it; some publicly well-known trusted party can generate a certificate for the *params*, and thus the certificate can be broadcasted during the anonymous communication and all users can verify the *params*:

The key generate center (KGC and here we denote it as TA) runs BDH *params* generator to generate two groups G_1 and G_2 whose orders are prime p, and a bilinear pairing $e : G_1 \times G_1 \rightarrow G_2$, which are described above. KGC also choose an arbitrary generator $P \in G_1$ and defines three cryptographic hash functions:

$$H : \{0,1\}^n \rightarrow G_1;$$

$$H_1 : \{0,1\}^n \times G_1 \rightarrow Z_p^*;$$

$$H_2 : G_2 \rightarrow \{0,1\}^n;$$

KGC chooses a random number $s \in Z_P^*$ and set $P_{pub} = sP$. Then the KGC publishes system parameters $params = \{G_1, G_2, p, P, P_{pub}, H, H_1, H_2\}$, and keep s as master-key.

A user M_i chooses a random value $a_i \in Z_P^*$ as his private key, and submits his identity ID_i to the KGC. KGC computes $Q_i = s \cdot H(ID_i)$ and returns Q_i to M_i. M_i computes $P_i = a_i Q_i$. a_i is kept as a secret and P_i is public to everyone. $<a_i, P_i>$ is a key pair of M_i.

3.2   Encryption and Decryption

To encrypt the plaintext $M \rightarrow \{0,1\}^n$ for M_i with M_i's public key P_i, M_j performs the following steps:

1. M_j chooses a random value $r_j \in Z_P^*$;
2. M_j computes $g = e(P_i, r_j P)$, the ciphertext

$$C = (M \oplus H_2(g), r_j P_{pub}) = (V, U) \tag{1}$$

3. M_i uses his private key a_i to decrypt:

$$V \oplus H_2(e(a_i H(ID_i), U)) \tag{2}$$

3.3   Digital Signature

Given a message M, M_i needs to sign it for M_j. If M_j computing the following equation comes into existence, M_i will be considered the signer and M_i also will be considered the legal user of one group. Our description is as follows:

Sign: assuming M_i as a signer, M_i chooses a random value $r_i \in Z_P^*$, and computes:

$$U_i = r_i P_i \tag{3}$$
$$h_i = H_1(M, U_i) \tag{4}$$
$$V_i = (r_i + h_i) \cdot a_i \cdot H(ID_i) \tag{5}$$

Sends (U_i, V_i) to receiver M_j.

Verify: M_j computes:

$$h_i = H_1(M, U_i) \tag{6}$$
$$Q_i = U_i + h_i \cdot P_i \tag{7}$$

and performs the following test:

$$e(V_i, P_{pub}) = e(Q_i, P) \tag{8}$$

3.4 Key Exchange

Suppose two users M_i and M_j wish to agree a key. We denote the private keys of the two users as a_i and a_j, their public keys are P_i and P_j, and both of them choose $random(r_i, r_j) \in Z_P^*$, they broadcast: $r_i P_{pub}$ and $r_j P_{pub}$.

M_i computes:

$$k_{ij} = e(r_i P_j, P)e(a_i H(ID_i), r_j P_{pub})$$
$$= e(H(ID_j), P_{pub})^{a_j r_i} e(H(ID_i), P_{pub})^{a_i r_j} \qquad (9)$$

M_j computes:

$$k_{ji} = e(r_j P_i, P)e(a_j H(ID_j), r_i P_{pub})$$
$$= e(H(ID_i), P_{pub})^{a_i r_j} e(H(ID_j), P_{pub})^{a_j r_i} \qquad (10)$$

Obviously that $k_{ij} = k_{ji}$.

3.5 Key Revocation

Our scheme is simple for TA to revoke the key of users when users leave the group. If a user M_i leaves the group, the TA takes charge of the revocation event. TA adds the public key P_i corresponding to M_i into the public key revocation list, and TA maintains the list. Thus, before encrypting a message or manipulating the other events, M_i should check the revocation list in order to validate the corresponding public key.

If a user whose public key has already added into the revocation list, and he will want to join the group again, it only needs to choose a new a_i to construct $a_i \cdot Q_i$ as his public key. The proposed IBC schemes have difficulty in key renewal. After revocation, new ID-based keys are difficult in issuing for the same identity. This scheme which we propose introduces a new format for public keys such new public key can be used for the same identity after the previous key has been revoked. M_i only needs to choose a new a_i to construct his new public key after being revoked.

4 Analysis of Our Scheme

4.1 Comparison Between Our Scheme and IBC

Our scheme is similar to IBC scheme, however, they are fundamentally different. We describe their difference as follows.

Firstly, the duty of KGC is different. In IBC scheme, the KGC (TA) takes charge of generating the user's private key. But in our scheme, KGC signs for user's identity to make user legal.

Secondly, the ways of key generation are different. In IBC scheme, users' pairwise of keys is generated by KGC. It means that KGC knows all the keys of users so that KGC can decrypt all ciphertexts which users deliver and KGC can sign messages by imitating legal users. In other words, the way of key generation in IBC scheme is not blind to KGC. But in our scheme, the private key of user is generated by user himself, nobody except himself knows the private key. User's public key is based on signature of KGC and the user's private key so that he can verify his legality. Our scheme is suit for anonymous communication system.

Thirdly, in IBC scheme, the users can use the identities of others as their public key, in other words, the identities of users are not anonymous in communications. In our scheme, the identities of users are blind to anyone, and the public key of M_i is masked by the corresponding private key $a_i \in Z_P^*$. Both the public key and the private key cannot be derived by other users.

Finally, in IBC scheme, there is no simple way to renew the identity of M_i if his public key has been revoked. But in our scheme, we present a new form that the KGC signs for ID_i, if M_i wants to join the group again after his public key being revoked, he only needs to choose a new value a_i to construct the public key. Notice, KGC should maintain a revocation list which all the users can avail it.

4.2 Security Analysis of Our Scheme

In our scheme, private key a_i is chosen by M_i himself, and the public key of M_i is $a_i s H(ID_i)$. It is a one-way function from private key to public key under ECDLP problem, which is presented in Sect. 2.2.

Theorem 1. *Our Encryption\Decryption scheme is secure.*

Here, we analyze our scheme presented in Sect. 3.2. To see how it works, we demonstrate the correctness in the Encryption\Decryption algorithm. When decrypts the ciphertext, he performs as follow:

$$
\begin{aligned}
V \oplus H_2(e(a_i H(ID_i)), U) &= V \oplus H_2(e(a_i H(ID_i)), r_i P_{pub}) \\
&= V \oplus H_2(e(a_i s H(ID_i)), r_i P) \\
&= V \oplus H_2(e(P_i, r_i P)) \\
&= M \oplus H_2(g) \oplus H_2(g) \\
&= M
\end{aligned}
$$

Proof. We assume that the IBE scheme is secure due to the proof presented by Boneh et al. [4,12]. To prove our scheme is secure, we should prove the modification introduced by our scheme will not affect the security of the original IBE scheme. In our scheme, everyone including KGC cannot derive $a_j H(ID_j)$ from $P_j = a_j s H(ID_j)$, though he knows $s H(ID_j)$. Because it is at least as hard as to solve ECDLP problem. In encryption, M_j can compute $g = e(P_i, r_j P) = e(a_i H(ID_i), r_j P_{pub})$. To find $a_i H(ID_i)$ and satisfy $g = e(a_i H(ID_i), r_j P_{pub})$ is believed to be a pairing inversion problem (see Sect. 2.2).

IBE scheme is proved in choosing ciphertext attack secure under **Random Oracle** model by Boneh et al. [4,12]. There is no polynomial bounded algorithm having a non-negligible advantage in solving the BDH problem. Based on the above analysis, we claim that our scheme is also secure.

Theorem 2. *Our signature scheme is secure.*

Firstly, we also present the correctness of our signature scheme.

$$
\begin{aligned}
e(V_j, P_{pub}) &= e((r_i + h_i)a_i H(ID_i), P_{pub}) \\
&= e((r_i + h_i)a_i s H(ID_i), P) \\
&= e(U_i + h_i P_i, P) \\
&= e(Q_i, P)
\end{aligned}
$$

Proof. M_i uses private key a_i to sign the message M. The adversary cannot solve $a_i H(ID_i)$ from $U_i = r_i s a_i H(ID_i)$, which is equivalent to solving ECDLP problem as presented above. Thus the adversary cannot forge the signature $V_i = (r_i + h_i)a_i H(ID_i)$. So adversary cannot modify the (U_i, V_i) to satisfy the equation $e(V_i, P_{pub}) = e(Q_i, P)$.

The correctness of key exchange has been presented in Sect. 3.4, and here we present the secure properties in our key exchange scheme.

(1) **Known Key Security:** The key exchange of every times, M_i would choose a different random value, and the adversary cannot deduce the future session keys from the past session keys.

(2) **Forward Secrecy:** If a long term secret key, such as a_i has disclosed, at some point in the future does not lead to the compromise of communications in the past, as though the private key of KGC is compromised.

(3) **Key Control:** Neither party can control the outcome of the session keys, everyone should contribute the equal share to the key exchange.

4.3   Anonymity Analysis of Our Scheme

In our scheme, the private key a_i of M_i is chosen by M_i himself, and identity of M_i is masked by private key a_i. Both of pairwise keys cannot be derived by other users. And the adversary needs to know the private information a_i. Given a point $sH(ID_i)$ and $P_i = a_i s H(ID_i)$, the adversary cannot derive the value a_i which is equivalent to solving ECDLP problem. The KGC only knows users' identities when he verifies the users' legality. This kind of hidden identity just suits for anonymous communication system.

5   Conclusion

We propose a paring-based scheme for anonymous communication system. In our scheme, pairs of keys are generated by users themselves. KGC takes charge of signing the identities of users. If a user is legal, (it means he is signed by KGC) they can communicate with others including encryption/decryption, digital signature, key exchange and so on. In our scheme, key revocation is simple because the key renewal is easy to realize. We present the correctness and the security analysis of our algorithm. Our scheme is simple and feasible and it is suitable for anonymous communication system.

References

1. Kou, L., Shi, Y., Zhang, L., et al.: A lightweight three-factor user authentication protocol for the information perception of IoT. CMC-Comput. Mater. Continua **58**(2), 545–565 (2019)
2. Jiang, X., Liu, M., Yang, C., et al.: A blockchain-based authentication protocol for WLAN mesh security access. CMC-Comput. Mater. Continua **58**(1), 45–59 (2019)
3. Zhang, Y., Liu, W., Lou, W.: Anonymous communications in mobile ad hoc networks. In: 24th Annual Joint Conference of the IEEE Computer and Communications Societies. Proceedings of IEEE **3**, 1940–1951 (2005)
4. Boneh, D., Franklin, M.: Identity-based encryption from the weil pairing. In: Kilian, J. (ed.) CRYPTO 2001. LNCS, vol. 2139, pp. 213–229. Springer, Heidelberg (2001). https://doi.org/10.1007/3-540-44647-8_13
5. Huang, D.: Pseudonym-based cryptography for anonymous communications in mobile ad-hoc networks. Int. J. Secur. Netw. **2**, 272–283 (2007)
6. Zeng, S., Huang, Y., Liu, X.: Privacy-preserving communication for VANETs with conditionally anonymous ring signature. Int. J. Netw. Secur. **17**(2), 135–141 (2015)
7. Li, F., Xiong, P., Jin, C.: Identity-based deniable authentication for ad hoc network. Computing **96**, 843–853 (2014)
8. Choon, J.C., Hee Cheon, J.: An identity-based signature from gap Diffie-Hellman groups. In: Desmedt, Y.G. (ed.) PKC 2003. LNCS, vol. 2567, pp. 18–30. Springer, Heidelberg (2003). https://doi.org/10.1007/3-540-36288-6_2
9. Smart, N.P.: Identity-based authenticated key agreement protocol based on weil pairing. Electron. Lett. **38**(13), 630–632 (2002)
10. Menezes, A.J., Okamoto, T., Vanstone, S.: Reducing elliptic curve logarithms to logarithms in a finite field. IEEE Trans. Info. Th. **39**, 1639–1646 (1993)
11. Bao, F., Deng, R.H., Zhu, H.F.: Variations of Diffie-Hellman problem. In: Qing, S., Gollmann, D., Zhou, J. (eds.) ICICS 2003. LNCS, vol. 2836, pp. 301–312. Springer, Heidelberg (2003). https://doi.org/10.1007/978-3-540-39927-8_28
12. Li, D., Luo, M., Zhao, B., Che, X.: Provably secure APK redevelopment authorization scheme in the standard model. CMC-Comput. Mater. Continua **56**(3), 447–465 (2018)

A Two-Way Quantum Key Distribution Based on Two Different States

Shihuan Xu, Zhi Qin[(✉)], Yan Chang, Shibin Zhang, and Lili Yan

School of Cybersecurity, Chengdu University of Information
Technology, Chengdu 610225, China
xsf12315tt@163.com, cuitqz@qq.com

Abstract. In this paper, we propose a two-way quantum key distribution protocol based on two different states (Single photon and Bell-states). It is a two-way communication protocol. There is a correspondence between the Single photon and the Bell-states. The participants both are honest. Through this protocol participants can obtain the secret key. The secret key is generated by half of participants' key, the reason for the secret key is generated by this way is to prevent the outside attackers attacking just once that can obtain the secret key that the participant wants to distribute. And so the can establish communication by the key. We take into account the diversity of attack patterns, so the participants in our protocol are both have ability to detect attackers. In the security analysis, for the security of the whole protocol, we introduce twice eavesdropping detection in the protocol process, the analyse results show that the protocol can resistant to several well-known attacks.

Keywords: Quantum · Two-way · Single photon · Bell-states · Eavesdropping detection · Secret key

1 Introduction

With the emergence of quantum computing technology, the traditional cryptography has been greatly impacted. It is important for both participants to establish a secure secret key for message communication. Therefore, quantum secret key distribution has always been one of the basic researches in the field of quantum communication. Since the first quantum secret key distribution protocol was proposed by Bennett in 1984 (BB84) [1], more quantum information schemes have been proposed, such as, quantum secret sharing (QSS) [2–6], semi-quantum QKD(SQKD) [7–9], and also have a good development prospect in another domain [11, 12]. All make use of the fundamental principles of quantum physics to ensure its safety [13].

The QSS (quantum secret sharing) is an important part of quantum communication. It encodes the secrets of the secret owner and breaks it up, then sends the information to a group of participants. Participants must cooperate to get the original information, And none of them can obtain the initial information by themselves. Because of there are different kinds of information to share, one is to share classical information [14],

© Springer Nature Singapore Pte Ltd. 2020
X. Sun et al. (Eds.): ICAIS 2020, CCIS 1254, pp. 21–27, 2020.
https://doi.org/10.1007/978-981-15-8101-4_3

the other is to share quantum information. Quantum secret sharing scheme proposed by Hillery et al. in 1999 is called HBB, which realizes secret sharing through the entangled state of GHZ. After the HBB was proposed, After the HBB was proposed, there are so many QSS protocols have been proposed.

The SQKD (semi-quantum quantum key distribution) is an extension of QKD. It reduced the operating cost of QKD by combining classical channel with quantum channel. Such protocols are easier to implement. For example, in 2007, Boyer et al. proposed SQKD protocol [7], which is called BKM07 protocol. In 2009, Zou simplified the protocol [15], reduced the number of quantum states used in the protocol, It reduces Alice's quantum operations and reduces the distance between SQKD and reality.

The QKD (quantum key distribution), it enables both parties to communicate to generate a random and secure key to encrypt and decrypt messages. Quantum uncertainty principle is the most important Property, for example, in BB84 Alice prepare four polarization states of the photon, Bob doesn't know use which base to measure it, so he will randomly use Z-base or the X-base to measure the photon. If there has a outsider attacker, he also doesn't knows the correct base, so he will measure photons by his own strategy, after he finished the measuring operation he will prepare a new particle and sends it to Bob. Through these operations, the initial of photons maybe have been changed. In the protocol, the participants have a high probability of detecting attackers. And in 1992, Bennett improved BB84 and proposed B92 [16]. In 2000, Phoenix et al. proposed a QKD protocol [7] that is easier to implement than BB84 protocol, called PBC00. PBC00 adds a third non-orthogonal polarization state, which is more secure than B92 and can detect eavesdroppers more effectively. In 2004, Renes et al. [17] improved the PBC00, and the improved protocol called R04, the protocol adopt spherical coding technique that can let the utilization rate of the key are improved. Many scholars have demonstrated his unconditional security.

Most protocols in the field of quantum secret key distribution are one-way. However, in our protocol, the two parties to the protocol are both the sender and receiver of the key, it is a two-way protocol. Each participant gives half of the classical sequence to generate the final secret key. In real life, communication between two organizations is based on equality of status, the secret key should be generated by mutual decision. And participants generate different bases, it can increase the difficulty for external attackers to make a attack in transmission.

The rest of this paper is organized as follows. Our QKD protocols is presented in Sect. 2, the security analysis is discussed in Sect. 3, and a conclusion is drawn in Sect. 4.

2 The Proposed Protocol

The proposed protocol allows two participants, Alice and Bob, to get a secret key by themselves. In this protocol participants both are honest. Participants must follow the rules of the protocol. The processes of proposed protocol are described as follows.

Step1: Alice generates n-bit classical sequences randomly, $SA = \{Sa_1, Sa_2, \ldots, Sa_i\}$, $i = 4n$ and $Sa_i \in \{0, 1\}$. If $Sa_i = 0$ it means that the Alice's the ith particle is $|0\rangle$, so if $Sa_i = 1$ Alice prepares $|1\rangle$.

Step2: Alice prepares quantum states according to SA, when Alice get these qubits, Alice performs H ($|0\rangle \rightarrow |+\rangle$, $|1\rangle \rightarrow |-\rangle$) or I operation on these qubits(equal probability), and then sends them to Bob.

Step3: After Bob receives the particle, Bob performs H or I operation and measures it on Z-basis. And then Bob and Alice begin a public discussion, Bob and Alice discuss their operations. They keep the particles that they had performed the same operation. Bob generates SB, $SB = \{Sb_1, Sb_2, \ldots, Sb_j\}$, the value of j is the number of they kept particles, and the $Sb_i \in \{0, 1\}$. Also Alice will update the SA(Removes discard bits), let the i = j. Bob knows the measurements of Alice's particles, so Bob also can know Sa_i. Bob prepares particles based on Sb_j and Sa_i. There are four situations 00, 01, 10, 11 ($|\varphi^+\rangle$, $|\psi^+\rangle$, $|\varphi^-\rangle$, $|\psi^-\rangle$).

Step4: According to the measured results, Bob will prepare in one of four states $|\varphi^+\rangle$, $|\psi^+\rangle$, $|\varphi^-\rangle$, $|\psi^-\rangle$. For example, if Bob measurement result of Alice's particle is $|0\rangle$ and $Sb_j = 0$, Bob will prepares $|\varphi^+\rangle$. How to prepare the Bell-states show in Table 1. Bob performs H operation on these states and sends to Alice. In this case Alice knows the value of the Sa_i and Alice has to receive $|\varphi^+\rangle$ or $|\varphi^-\rangle$ if Alice received another states the protocol will be restart.

Table 1. The strategy of Bob how to prepare the Bell-states.

Alice's states	The value of Sa_i	The value of Sb_j	Prepare
$|0\rangle$	0	0	$|\varphi^+\rangle$
$|0\rangle$	0	1	$|\varphi^-\rangle$
$|1\rangle$	1	0	$|\psi^+\rangle$
$|1\rangle$	1	1	$|\psi^-\rangle$

Step5: When Alice gets the particle, he will know Sb_j. For example, if Alice received particle is $|\varphi^+\rangle$, and Alice always knows Sa_i, so he knows that the value of Sb_j must be 0. If they complete the above steps, Bob will know SA, Alice will obtain SB.

Step6: Alice and Bob begin to have a public discussion whether there have attackers during the second transmission. Alice randomly announce a half of SB(value and location), call it SB', Bob compares SB with SB'. If it is as not same as his own, the protocol will be restart.

Step7: If the SB' is as same as SB, Alice will use the other half of the SB and SA to generate a new secret key. Bob does the same operation to get the new key.

After the above steps, in the ideal case of the quantum channel, Alice obtains get the SB, Bob obtains the SA. So they can be able to establish a communication. Alice obtains get the SB, Bob obtains the SA.

3 Security Analyses

3.1 Modification Attack

Under the circumstances, the outsider attacker Eve will perform some unitary operation to let participants share a incorrect secret key. In this protocol, there are two transfers of quantum information in the protocol. Therefore, Eve has three different attack strategies. Eve can attack either of two transfers or attack both two transfers. The outsider attacker Eve can use the unitary operation $i\sigma_y$ to modify the states.

$$i\sigma_y = -|1\rangle\langle 0| + |0\rangle\langle 1| = \begin{bmatrix} 0 & 1 \\ -1 & 0 \end{bmatrix} \tag{1}$$

If Eve attacks at the first transmission (step2), Eve performs the $i\sigma_y$ operation ($|0\rangle \leftrightarrow |1\rangle$, $|+\rangle \leftrightarrow |-\rangle$) and he will send the particle to Bob. Eve wants to Alice and Bob get an incorrect secret key. In the step1 to step3, There's $\frac{1}{4}$ chance of keeping the particle. In step5, Alice begins to eavesdropping detection, the probability that Eve not being detected is 0 because Alice knows the initial states. So Eve modify the particle in step2, The probability that Alice finds an attacker is 1.

If Eve attacks at the second transmission (in step 4), Eve performs $i\sigma_y$ to modify the particle, The specific operation is shown below Table 2. Alice also can detect an attacker. Table 1 shows that there are three cases in which the attacker modifies states successfully. Eve preforms $i\sigma_y$ on the second particle and the probability not being detected by Alice's eavesdropping detection is 1, but in the step6 the probability of Bob can detect the attacker is $\frac{1}{2}$ (in step6), so the probability of he modifies n bits and can't be detected is $1-\left(\frac{1}{2}\right)^n$. If the value of the n is large enough, Eve is hard to miss. Due to the protocol process there are twice eavesdropping detection. Hence, if the outsider attackers modify the initial states, participants can find out attackers easily.

Table 2. Eve performs $i\sigma_y$ to modify the particle.

Intercepted states	Eve's operation	Result	Alice's state
$|\varphi^+\rangle H$	$(|\varphi^+\rangle H)i\sigma_y$	$\frac{1}{2}(|01\rangle + |00\rangle + |11\rangle + |10\rangle)$	$|\varphi^-\rangle$
$|\psi^+\rangle H$	$(|\psi^+\rangle H)i\sigma_y$	$\frac{1}{2}(|01\rangle - |00\rangle + |11\rangle + |10\rangle)$	$|\psi^-\rangle$
$|\varphi^-\rangle H$	$(|\varphi^-\rangle H)i\sigma_y$	$\frac{1}{2}(|01\rangle + |00\rangle - |11\rangle + |10\rangle)$	$|\varphi^+\rangle$
$|\psi^-\rangle H$	$(|\psi^-\rangle H)i\sigma_y$	$\frac{1}{2}(|01\rangle - |00\rangle - |11\rangle - |10\rangle)$	$|\psi^+\rangle$

And Eve also can attack both two transfers, in this case, Eve also will be detected. Because he modifies the Alice's states, In step4 Alice can detect attackers. Therefore the probability of Eve can't be detected is 0.

3.2 Intercept-and-Resend Attack

In this attack mode, the outsider attacker, Eve want to get the complete secret key(SA and SB), he may try to intercept the transmitted qubits, measures these qubits, and generates fake qubits depending on his measurement results. And then Eve Sends the fake qudits to Bob or Alice. If the participants cannot detect the fake qubits, Eve will obtain the information about the secret key bits of the participants.

In our protocol, there are twice transfers and twice eavesdropping detection. Eve wants to get as much information as possible without being discovered, so he has to pass eavesdropping detection.

In the step 2, Eve intercepts qubits and measures them by Z-basis. And if he measures result is $|0\rangle$ he will prepare a $|+\rangle (|1\rangle \rightarrow |-\rangle)$. The probability that the participant chooses the same basis is $\frac{1}{4}$. The specific situation is shown in Table 3. The probability of he can obtain one bit is $\frac{1}{8}$, and the probability of he can obtain n bits is $\left(\frac{1}{8}\right)^n$, and the probability of the attack can be detected is $1 - \left(\frac{1}{8}\right)^n$. If the n is large enough Alice can detect the attack.

Table 3. Eve intercepts the qubits in the first transfer

Alice's operation	Bob's operation	The probability of Eve knows one bit
I	I	$\frac{1}{8}$
H	H	$\frac{1}{8}$

In the step 4, Eve intercepts particles and measures it by Bell-basis. The specific situation is shown in Table 4. He will measure it and send the measurement to Alice, the probability of Eve can't be detected the attack by Alice is $\frac{1}{2}$(in step4). And he gets the information is also wrong. The probability of he obtain one bit and can not be detected by Bob is $\frac{1}{4}$(in step6). So the probability of Eve obtain n bits and can be detected is $1 - \left(\frac{1}{4}\right)^n$. If the n is large enough Bob can detect the attack.

Table 4. Eve intercepts the particles in the second transfer

Intercepts particles	Eve's result
$\frac{1}{2}(|00\rangle + |01\rangle + |10\rangle - |11\rangle)$	$|\varphi^-\rangle / |\psi^+\rangle$
$\frac{1}{2}(|00\rangle - |01\rangle + |10\rangle + |11\rangle)$	$|\varphi^+\rangle / |\psi^-\rangle$
$\frac{1}{2}(|01\rangle + |00\rangle - |11\rangle + |10\rangle)$	$|\varphi^+\rangle / |\psi^-\rangle$
$\frac{1}{2}(|01\rangle - |00\rangle - |11\rangle - |10\rangle)$	$|\varphi^-\rangle / |\psi^+\rangle$

Eve wants to have the complete secret key. He have to attack twice, so after two eavesdropping detection, if n is large enough, the probability of the Intercept-and-Resend attack obtain the secret key and not being detected is close to 0.

3.3 Trojan-Horse Attack

The Trojan-horse attack is a common attack, in which outsider Eve can prepares Trojan-horse photons. The Trojan photons can be inserted into particles sent from the participants. In the process of our protocol, there are two communication. Eve try to obtain SA in step 2 and obtain SB in step 4. However, in our protocol, Alice and Bob send different particles, and they infer information from the particles they received. Eve can insert Trojan-horse photons into the particles, but she can't extract any information about the participants' secret key because Eve can't retrieve the Trojan-horse photons. Hence, our protocol be able to defense the Trojan-horse attack.

4 Conclusions

In this paper, we proposed a two-party QKD, which can be used between two quantum organizations. In the ideal quantum channel environment, the participants can generate 4n-bits of classical sequence to get n-bits secret key, it has good efficiency. Security analyse shows that the proposed protocol are resistant to the Modification attack, the Intercept-and-resend attack, and the Trojan-horse attack. Because in our protocol there are tow eavesdropping detection, Alice checks SA, Bob checks SB. If the results are not as same as the initial value both two participants can restart the protocol. Therefore, our protocol has good security.

Acknowledgments. The authors would like to thank for who have helped improve the quality of this paper. This work is supported by NSFC (Grant Nos.61572086, 61402058), Sichuan Science and Technology Program (Grant Nos. 2017JY0168, 2018TJPT0012, 2018GZ0232, 2018CC0060, 2017GFW0119, 2017GZ0006, 2016GFW0127), the National Key Research and Development Program (No. 2017YFB0802302), Sichuan innovation team of quantum security communication (No. 17TD0009), Sichuan academic and technical leaders training funding support projects (No. 2016120080102643).

References

1. Bennett, C.H., Brassard, G.: Public key distribution and coin tossing. In: Proceedings of the IEEE International Conference on Computers, Systems and Signal Processing, Bangalore, pp. 175–179. IEEE, New York (1984)
2. Hillery, M., Buoek, V., Berthiaume, A.: Quantum secret sharing. Phys. Rev. A **59**, 1829 (1999)
3. Guo, G.P., Guo, G.C.: Quantum secret sharing without entanglement. Phys. Lett. A **310**(4), 247–251 (2002)
4. Cleve, R., Gottesman, D., Lo, H.-K.: How to share a quantum secret. Phys. Rev. Lett. **83**(3), 648–651 (1999)
5. Zhang, Z.J., Li, Y., Man, Z.X.: Multiparty quantum secret sharing. Phys. Lett. A (2004)
6. Dou, Z., Gang, X., Chen, X., Yuan, K.: Rational non-hierarchical quantum state sharing protocol. Comput. Mater. Continua **58**(2), 335–347 (2019)
7. Zou, X., Qiu, D., Li, L., et al.: Semiquantum-key distribution using less than four quantum states. Phys. Rev. A **79**(5), 052312 (2009)

8. Li, C.M., Yu, K.F., Kao, S.H., et al.: Authenticated semi-quantum key distributions without classical channel. Quantum Inf. Process. **15**(7), 2881–2893 (2016)

9. Xiao, H., Zhang, J., Huang, W., Zhou, M., Wencheng, H.: An efficient quantum key distribution protocol with dense coding on single photons. Comput. Mater. Continua **61**(2), 759–775 (2019)

10. Gisin, N., Ribordy, G., Tittel, W., Zbinden, H.: Quantum cryptography. Rev. Mod. Phys. **74**, 145–195 (2002)

11. Shang, T, Pei, Z, Chen, R, Liu, J.: Quantum homomorphic signature with repeatable verification. Comput. Mater. Continua **59**(1), 149–165 (2019)

12. Ying, C.: A Controllable Quantum Sequential Signature and Vote Scheme (2012)

13. He, X.L., Yang, C.P.: Deterministic transfer of multiqubit GHZ entangled states and quantum secret sharing between different cavities. Quantum Inf. Process. **14**(12), 4461–4474 (2015)

14. Boyer, M., Kenigsberg, D., Mor, T.: Quantum key distribution with classical bob. Phys. Rev. Lett. **99**(14), 140501 (2007)

15. Bennett, C.H.: Quantum cryptography using any two nonorthogonal states. Phys. Rev. Lett. 68 (1992)

16. Phoenix, S.J.D., Barnett, S.M., Chefles, A.: Three-state quantum cryptography. J. Modern Opt. **47**(2/3), 507–516 (2000)

17. Renes, J.M.: Spherical-code key-distribution protocols for qubits. Phys. Rev. A **70**(5), 052314 (2004)

Fault-Tolerant Semi-quantum Secure Direct Communication Scheme in Noisy Environment

Chi Qiu, Shibin Zhang$^{(\boxtimes)}$, Yan Chang, and Lili Yan

School of Cybersecurity, Chengdu University of Information Technology, Chengdu 610225, China
550135878@qq.com, 498251651@qq.com

Abstract. We present an anti-noise quantum states, which is $|\varphi^1> = \frac{1}{\sqrt{2}}(|0_L 0_L>$ $+ |1_L 1_L>)$ or $|\Psi^2> = \frac{1}{\sqrt{2}}(|0_L 1_L> + |1_L 0_L>)$ to resist collective dephasing noise and $|\varphi^3> = \frac{1}{\sqrt{2}}(|0_R 0_R> + |1_R 1_R>)$ or $|\Psi^4> = \frac{1}{\sqrt{2}}(|0_R 1_R> + |1_R 0_R>)$ to resist collective rotation noise. With the anti-noise quantum states, Alice encode her information. She keep the first qubit and send the second qubit to Bob. Bob can choose to measure which means measure the second qubit by the basis $\{|0_L>, |1_L>\}$ or $\{|0_R>, |1_R>\}$, or can choose to reflect which means send the qubit with undisturbed. About the transmission efficiency, when Alice transfers the information of 2n bits, Bob can get the information of n bits. Moreover, the security analysis of our scheme is also given.

Keywords: Anti-noise quantum states · Semi-quantum · Secure direct communication

1 Introduction

Nowadays, quantum information science has many different branches of research. Quantum information science include quantum key distribution (QKD) [1, 2], quantum teleportation [3] and quantum secret sharing (QSS) [4, 5]. One of the research directions of quantum information science is quantum secure direct communication (QSDC). The first QSDC protocol called the efficient QSDC protocol [6, 7] was proposed in 2002 by Long and Liu.

Quantum direct communication is different from quantum key distribution. Quantum key distribution requires the transmission of key through quantum channel, and then the transmission of information through key encryption. However, quantum secure direct communication can directly transmit information through quantum channel, which is more efficient than quantum key distribution.

During the transmission, the polarization DOF of photons is incident to be influenced by the thermal fluctuation, vibration and the imperfection of the fiber, which we call them noise in total [8]. At present, we always suppose the noise in a quantum channel is a collective one [9]. With this kind of noise, several methods have been proposed to cancel or reduce the noise effect, such as entanglement purification [10], quantum error correct

© Springer Nature Singapore Pte Ltd. 2020
X. Sun et al. (Eds.): ICAIS 2020, CCIS 1254, pp. 28–36, 2020.
https://doi.org/10.1007/978-981-15-8101-4_4

code (QECC) [11], single-photon error rejection [12] and decoherence-free subspace (DFS) [13, 14]. This paper is based on decoherence-free subspace.

This paper is based on Semi-quantum Secure Direct Communication Scheme Based on Bell States [15]. On this basis, the optimization is improved and the anti-noise function is added. The optimized part is to stop eavesdropping at the location Bob chooses to measure. Because this part of the eavesdropping detection can not find eavesdropping. The eavesdropper can measure the second qubit and send the results to Alice. Then remake this qubit and send to Bob. In this way Alice does not know whether the measurement operation was performed for Bob. So Alice can't find the eavesdropper. Removing this step of eavesdropping detection can save the cost and improve efficiency.

In this scheme, on the basis of Bell state, Alice prepare two kinds of anti-noise quantum states, namely, anti-phase-shift noise quantum state $|\varphi^+> = \frac{1}{\sqrt{2}}(|0_L0_L> + |1_L1_L>)$ or $|\Psi^+> = \frac{1}{\sqrt{2}}(|0_L1_L> + |1_L0_L>)$ and anti-rotation noise quantum state $|\varphi^+> = \frac{1}{\sqrt{2}}(|0_R0_R> + |1_R1_R>)$ or $|\Psi^+> = \frac{1}{\sqrt{2}}(|0_R1_R> + |1_R0_R>)$. Then, Alice keep the first qubit and send the second qubit to Bob. Bob can choose reflect or measure the second qubit in the basis $\{|0_L>, |1_L>\}$ or $\{|0_R>, |1_R>\}$, and record the measurement in r_b. After that, Alice will do some operations to detect the eavesdropping. If no eavesdropping, Alice will publish her measurement of the first qubit r_a. Bob can recover the message that Alice want to give she based on r_a and r_b.

2 About Collective Noise

In decoherence-free subspace, suppose a qubit undergoes a dephasing process. Namely, qubit j undergoes the transformation

$$|0\rangle_j \longrightarrow |0\rangle_j \tag{1}$$

$$|1\rangle_j \longrightarrow e^{i\varphi}|1\rangle_j \tag{2}$$

which puts a random phase φ between the basis states $|0>$ and $|1>$ (eigenstates of σ_z with respective eigenvalues $+1$ and -1) [11]. This can also be described by the matrix $R_z(\varphi) = \text{diag}(1, e^{i\varphi})$ acting on the $\{|0>, |1>\}$ basis. In the two-qubit Hilbert space,

$$|0\rangle_1 \otimes |0\rangle_2 \longrightarrow |0\rangle_1 \otimes |0\rangle_2 \tag{3}$$

$$|0\rangle_1 \otimes |1\rangle_2 \longrightarrow |0\rangle_1 \otimes e^{i\varphi}|1\rangle_2 \tag{4}$$

$$|1\rangle_1 \otimes |0\rangle_2 \longrightarrow e^{i\varphi}|1\rangle_1 \otimes |0\rangle_2 \tag{5}$$

$$|1\rangle_1 \otimes |1\rangle_2 \longrightarrow e^{i\varphi}|1\rangle_1 \otimes e^{i\varphi}|1\rangle_2 \tag{6}$$

We can see the state $|0>_1 \otimes |1>_2$ and $|1>_1 \otimes |0>_2$ acquire the same phase. So there has suggestion that a simple encoding trick can solve the problem. We can define encoded states by $|0_L> = |01>$ and $|1_L> = |10>$.

In our scheme, I want transfer a Bell state in the dephasing noise environment. I can use the encoded Bell state to transfer the information.

$$\left|\varphi^+\right\rangle = \frac{1}{\sqrt{2}}(|00\rangle + |11\rangle)) \longrightarrow \left|\varphi^1\right\rangle = \frac{1}{\sqrt{2}}(|0_L0_L\rangle + |1_L1_L\rangle)) \tag{7}$$

$$\left|\varphi^-\right\rangle = \frac{1}{\sqrt{2}}(|00\rangle - |11\rangle)) \longrightarrow \left|\varphi^2\right\rangle = \frac{1}{\sqrt{2}}(|0_L0_L\rangle - |1_L1_L\rangle)) \tag{8}$$

$$\left|\psi^+\right\rangle = \frac{1}{\sqrt{2}}(|01\rangle + |10\rangle)) \longrightarrow \left|\psi^1\right\rangle = \frac{1}{\sqrt{2}}(|0_L1_L\rangle + |1_L0_L\rangle)) \tag{9}$$

$$\left|\psi^-\right\rangle = \frac{1}{\sqrt{2}}(|01\rangle - |10\rangle)) \longrightarrow \left|\psi^2\right\rangle = \frac{1}{\sqrt{2}}(|0_L1_L\rangle - |1_L0_L\rangle)) \tag{10}$$

Namely, a qubit r undergoes the collective rotation noise.

$$|0\rangle_r \longrightarrow \cos\theta|0\rangle + \sin\theta|1\rangle \tag{11}$$

$$|1\rangle_r \longrightarrow -\sin\theta|0\rangle + \cos\theta|1\rangle \tag{12}$$

Where the parameter θ depends on the noise and fluctuates with time. The same, in the two-qubit Hilbert space,

$$|0\rangle_1 \otimes |0\rangle_2 \longrightarrow (\cos\theta|0\rangle + \sin\theta|1>) \otimes (\cos\theta|0\rangle + \sin\theta|1>) \tag{13}$$

$$|0\rangle_1 \otimes |1\rangle_2 \longrightarrow (\cos\theta|0\rangle + \sin\theta|1>) \otimes (-\sin\theta|0\rangle + \cos\theta|1>) \tag{14}$$

$$|1\rangle_1 \otimes |0\rangle_2 \longrightarrow (-\sin\theta|0\rangle + \cos\theta|1>) \otimes (\cos\theta|0\rangle + \sin\theta|1>) \tag{15}$$

$$|1\rangle_1 \otimes |1\rangle_2 \longrightarrow (-\sin\theta|0\rangle + \cos\theta|1>) \otimes (-\sin\theta|0\rangle + \cos\theta|1>) \tag{16}$$

similar to the dephasing noise, We can see the state $|0>_1 \otimes |1>_2$ and $|1>_1 \otimes |0>_2$ acquire the same phase. So there has suggestion that a simple encoding trick can solve the problem. We can define encoded states by $|0_r> = |\varphi^+>$ and $|1_r> = |\Psi^->$.

In our scheme, I want transfer a Bell state in the dephasing noise environment. I can use the encoded Bell state to transfer the information.

$$\left|\varphi^+\right\rangle = \frac{1}{\sqrt{2}}(|00\rangle + |11\rangle)) \longrightarrow \left|\varphi^3\right\rangle = \frac{1}{\sqrt{2}}(|0_R0_R\rangle + |1_R1_R\rangle)) \tag{17}$$

$$\left|\varphi^-\right\rangle = \frac{1}{\sqrt{2}}(|00\rangle - |11\rangle)) \longrightarrow \left|\varphi^4\right\rangle = \frac{1}{\sqrt{2}}(|0_R0_R\rangle - |1_R1_R\rangle)) \tag{18}$$

$$\left|\psi^+\right\rangle = \frac{1}{\sqrt{2}}(|01\rangle + |10\rangle)) \longrightarrow \left|\psi^3\right\rangle = \frac{1}{\sqrt{2}}(|0_R1_R\rangle + |1_R0_R\rangle)) \tag{19}$$

$$\left|\psi^-\right\rangle = \frac{1}{\sqrt{2}}(|01\rangle - |10\rangle)) \longrightarrow \left|\psi^4\right\rangle = \frac{1}{\sqrt{2}}(|0_R1_R\rangle - |1_R0_R\rangle)) \tag{20}$$

3   The Scheme

In both collective phase shift noise and collective rotation noise, our protocol steps are shown in Fig.1.

3.1   In the Collective Phase Shift Noise

1.   Alice prepares one of the two quantum anti-noise state to transmit the information:

$$\left| \varphi^1 \right\rangle = \frac{1}{\sqrt{2}} (|0_L 0_L\rangle + |1_L 1_L\rangle) \tag{21}$$

$$\left| \psi^1 \right\rangle = \frac{1}{\sqrt{2}} (|0_L 1_L\rangle + |1_L 0_L\rangle) \tag{22}$$

Alice keeps the first qubit and transfer the second qubit to Bob. $|\varphi^1\rangle$ is used to encode bit 0. $|\psi^2\rangle$ is used to encode bit 1.

2.   When the qubit arrives, Bob chooses randomly either to MEASURE, or to REFLECT. When Bob chooses is measurement, Bob will use the basis $\{|0_L\rangle, |1_L\rangle\}$ to measure the qubit and record the measurement in r_b.
3.   After the qubit comes back to Alice, Alice tells Bob that she has got the qubit. The bits carried by the lost photons are disregarded. After that, Bob will tell Alice what operation she has chosen. Alice will conduct eavesdropping detection based on this result.

If Bob's choices is REFLECT, Alice will use the basis $\{|\varphi^1\rangle, |\varphi^2\rangle, |\psi^1\rangle, |\psi^2\rangle\}$ to measure the state. This base is the same as described in the previous background section. If Alice transfer a $|\varphi^1\rangle$ to encode her information of bit 0, when Alice' measurement has $|\varphi^2\rangle, |\psi^1\rangle$ or $|\psi^2\rangle$, and she will know there have some eavesdroppers. If Alice transfer a $|\psi^1\rangle$ to encode her information of bit 1, when Alice's measurement has $|\varphi^1\rangle, |\varphi^2\rangle$ or $|\psi^2\rangle$, and she will know there have some eavesdroppers. If there is any eavesdropping, Alice will shut down the quantum channel, establishes another secure quantum channel and re-execute the above process.

If Bob's choices is MEASURE, Alice will use the basis $\{|0_L\rangle, |1_L\rangle\}$ to measure the first qubit. When Alice's measurement is $|01\rangle$, and she will record a bit 0 in r_a. When Alice's measurement is $|10\rangle$, and she will record a bit 1 in r_a. Only when Bob chooses measure, Alice will record bit 0 or bit 1 in r_a. When Bob chooses reflect, Alice just do eavesdropping detection and don't record anything.

4.   When all the information has been transmitted, Alice publishes her measurement result r_a for all of the first bits. Then Bob uses r_b and the measurement result r_a for all of the first bits to recover the message by $S = r_a \oplus r_b$, that is, perform the XOR operation for each bit pair in r_a and r_b. The results are shown in Table 1.

Table 1. The transmitted information is in the collective rotation noise

Alice's measurement	Operation	Bob's measurement	Results
$|0_L\rangle$	XOR	$|0_L\rangle$	0
$|1_L\rangle$	XOR	$|1_L\rangle$	0

3.2 In the Collective Rotation Noise

1. Alice prepares one of the two quantum anti-noise state to transmit the information:

$$\left|\varphi^3\right\rangle = \frac{1}{\sqrt{2}}(|0_R0_R\rangle + |1_R1_R\rangle) \tag{23}$$

$$\left|\psi^4\right\rangle = \frac{1}{\sqrt{2}}(|0_R1_R\rangle + |1_R0_R\rangle) \tag{24}$$

Alice keeps the first qubit and transfer the second qubit to Bob. $|\varphi^+\rangle$ is used to encode bit 0. $|\Psi^+\rangle$ is used to encode bit 1.

2. When the qubit arrives, Bob chooses randomly either to MEASURE, or to REFLECT. When Bob chooses is measurement, Bob will use the basis $\{|0_R\rangle, |1_R\rangle\}$ to measure the qubit and record the measurement in r_b.
3. After the qubit comes back to Alice, Alice tells Bob that she has got the qubit. The bits carried by the lost photons are disregarded. After that, Bob will tell Alice what operation she has chosen. Alice will conduct eavesdropping detection based on this result.

If Bob's choices is REFLECT, Alice will use the basis $\{|\varphi^3\rangle, |\varphi^4\rangle, |\Psi^3\rangle, |\Psi^4\rangle\}$ to measure the state. This base is the same as described in the previous background section. If Alice transfer a $|\varphi^3\rangle$ to encode her information of bit 0, when Alice' measurement has $|\varphi^4\rangle, |\Psi^3\rangle$ or $|\Psi^4\rangle$, and she will know there have some eavesdroppers. If Alice transfer a $|\Psi^3\rangle$ to encode her information of bit 1, when Alice's measurement has $|\varphi^3\rangle, |\varphi^4\rangle$ or $|\Psi^4\rangle$, and she will know there have some eavesdroppers. If there is any eavesdropping, Alice will shut down the quantum channel, establishes another secure quantum channel and re-execute the above process.

If Bob's choices is MEASURE, Alice will use the basis $\{|0_R\rangle, |1_R\rangle\}$ to measure the first qubit. When Alice's measurement is $|01\rangle$, and she will record a bit 0 in r_a. When Alice's measurement is $|10\rangle$, and she will record a bit 1 in r_a. Only when Bob chooses measure, Alice will record bit 0 or bit 1 in r_a. When Bob chooses reflect, Alice just do eavesdropping detection and don't record anything.

5. When all the information has been transmitted, Alice publishes her measurement result r_a for all of the first bits. Then Bob uses r_b and the measurement result r_a for

all of the first bits to recover the message by $S = r_a \oplus r_b$, that is, perform the XOR operation for each bit pair in r_a and r_b. The results are shown in Table 2.

Table 2. The transmitted information is in the collective rotation noise

Alice's measurement	Operation	Bob's measurement	Results
$|0_R>$	XOR	$|1_R>$	1
$|1_R>$	XOR	$|0_R>$	1

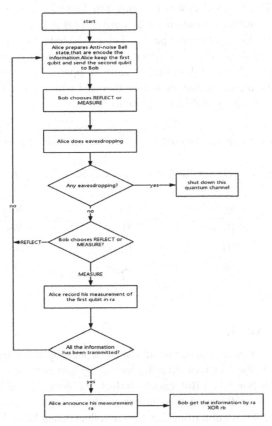

Fig. 1. Flow-process diagram of our scheme

4   Security Analysis

4.1   Intercept - Measure - Refire attacks

The so-called intercept-measure-refire attack means that eavesdropping intercepts the quantum bits transmitted in the channel, measures them, and then sends the appropriate quantum state to the legitimate receiver. This is a relatively simple and common attack method.

For intercept-measure-refire attacks, Eve can obtain r_a easily. The important is the security of r_b. If Eve can't obtain r_b, he can't obtain the encode message. Because Eve don't know which operation Bob choose. He can only choose to measure or not measure the second qubit with a certain probability. When Eve choose measure the second qubit, while Bob choose reflect the second qubit. Alice will have a ½ chance of detecting eavesdropping. When Alice chooses to conduct eavesdropping detection, the probability of Eve being discovered is shown in Table 3. Table 3 lists the situation of dephasing noise, and the rotation noise is similar. That is to say, when Bob chooses reflection, the probability of eavesdropper Eve being detected is ½, and the probability of Bob choosing measurement is ½, which means that Alice does not conduct eavesdropper detection. So the probability of detecting an eavesdropper is $¼ = ½ * ½$. When Alice transfer enough bits, the eavesdropper will be detected with a probability of $1 - (¾)^n$. When n is big enough, the probability is close to 100%.

Table 3. Eavesdropping detection analysis in intercept - measure - refire attacks

A particle sent by Alice	The results of Eve measured	Bob chooses reflect	Detection of hacking
$|0_L>$	$|0_L>$	$|0_L>$	No
$|0_L>$	$|1_L>$	$|0_L>$	Yes
$|1_L>$	$|1_L>$	$|1_L>$	No
$|1_L>$	$|0_L>$	$|1_L>$	Yes

4.2   Modification Attack

Because the attack of eavesdropper is similar in dephasing noise and rotation noise, and we only analyze the attack of eavesdropper in dephasing noise. Alice only do the Eavesdropping detection when Bob choose reflect. As shown in Table 4, When Alice send a qubit $|0_L>$, Eve will modify this qubit from $|0_L>$ to $|1_L>$ and send the qubit $|1_L>$ to Bob. When Bob get this qubit from Eve, he will reflect this qubit to Alice. When Alice get this qubit $|1_L>$, she will know that there have eavesdroppers. Namely, When Alice send a qubit $|1_L>$, Eve will modify this qubit from $|1_L>$ to $|0_L>$ and send the qubit $|0_L>$ to Bob. When Bob get this qubit from Eve, he will reflect this qubit to Alice. When Alice get this qubit $|0_L>$, she will know that there have eavesdroppers. When Alice does eavesdropping, she has 100% to know the eavesdropper. So, the probability of detecting an eavesdropper is $½ = 1 * ½$.

Table 4. Eavesdropping detection analysis in modification attacks

The qubit of Alice send	The qubit of modification	Bob choose reflect	Detection of hacking
$|0_L>$	$|1_L>$	$|1_L>$	Yes
$|1_L>$	$|0_L>$	$|0_L>$	Yes

5 Conclusion

This paper is based on Semi-quantum Secure Direct Communication Scheme Based on Bell States [11]. In this scheme, we present anti-noise quantum states between two parts, which can ensure this scheme execute normally in noisy environment. Meanwhile, for the original protocol, We optimize it.

Acknowledgments. This work is supported by the National Natural Science Foundation of China (No. 61572086, No. 61402058), the Key Research and Development Project of Sichuan Province (No. 20ZDYF2324, No. 2019ZYD027, No. 2018TJPT0012), the Innovation Team of Quantum Security Communication of Sichuan Province (No. 17TD0009), the Academic and Technical Leaders Training Funding Support Projects of Sichuan Province (No. 2016120080102643), the Application Foundation Project of Sichuan Province (No. 2017JY0168), the Science and Technology Support Project of Sichuan Province (No. 2018GZ0204, No. 2016FZ0112).

References

1. Bennett, C.H., Brassard, G.: Public key distribution and coin tossing. In: Proceedings of the IEEE International Conference on Computers, Systems and Signal Processing, Bangalore, pp. 175–179. IEEE, New York (1984)
2. Xiao, H., Zhang, J., Huang, W., Zhou, M., Wencheng, H.: An efficient quantum key distribution protocol with dense coding on single photons. Comput. Mater. Continua **61**(2), 759–775 (2019)
3. Tan, X., Li, X., Yang, P.: Perfect quantum teleportation via bell states. Comput. Mater. Continua **57**(3), 495–503 (2018)
4. Chen, R., Zhang, Y., Shi, J., et al.: A multiparty error-correcting method for quantum secret sharing. Quantum Inf. Process. **13**(1), 21–31 (2014)
5. Chen, X., Tang, X., Xu, G., et al.: Cryptanalysis of secret sharing with a single d-level quantum system. Quantum Inf. Process. **17**(9) (2018)
6. Zhong, J., Liu, Z., Juan, X.: Analysis and improvement of an efficient controlled quantum secure direct communication and authentication protocol. Comput. Mater. Continua **57**(3), 621–633 (2018)
7. Long, G.L., Liu, X.S.: Theoretically efficient high-capacity quantum-key-distribution scheme. Phys. Rev. A **65**, 032302 (2002)
8. Li, X.H., Zhao, B.K., Sheng, Y.B., et al.: Fault tolerant quantum dense coding with collective noise. Microwave Opt. Technol. Lett. **49**(7), 1768–1772 (2009)
9. Zanardi, P., Rasetti, M.: Phys. Rev. Lett. **79**, 3306–3309 (1997)
10. Bennett, C.H., Brassard, G., Popescu, S., Schumacher, B., Smolin, J.A., Wootters, W.K.: Phys. Rev. Lett. **76**, 722–725 (1996)

11. Nielsen, M.A., Chuang, I.L.: Quantum Computation and Quantum Information. Cambridge University Press, Cambridge (2000)
12. Li, X.H., Deng, F.G., Zhou, H.Y.: Appl. Phys. Lett. **91**, 144101 (2007)
13. Walton, Z.D., Abouraddy, A.F., Sergienko, A.V., Saleh, B.E.A., Teich, M.C.: Phys. Rev. Lett. **91**, 087901 (2003)
14. Boileau, J.C., Gottesman, D., Laflamme, R., Poulin, D., Spekkens, R.W.: Phys. Rev. Lett. **92**, 017901 (2004)
15. Xie, Chen, Li, Lvzhou, Situ, Haozhen, He, Jianhao: Semi-quantum secure direct communication scheme based on bell states. Int. J. Theoret. Phys. **57**(6), 1881–1887 (2018). https://doi.org/10.1007/s10773-018-3713-7

Review on Variant Consensus Algorithms Based on PBFT

Chen Yang, Mingzhe Liu$^{(\boxtimes)}$, Kun Wang, Feixiang Zhao, and Xin Jiang

State Key Laboratory of Geohazard Prevention and Geoenvironment Protection,
Chengdu University of Technology, Chengdu 610059, China
`liumz@cdut.edu.cn`

Abstract. In the Block Chain (BC), all parties reach trust with each other by distributed network, non-tamperable cryptography ledger and consensus algorithm. The consensus algorithm is the core of the BC and many researchers make efforts for its improvement. The performamce of these consensus algorithms receive better improvement by making optimization for them. Besides, combining two or more consensus algorithms could apply to specific occasions. This paper introduces some variant consensus algorithms based on the Practical Byzantine Fault Tolerance and respectively discusses their implementation processes. Then we analyze their performance and make a conclusion for this paper.

Keywords: Blockchain · Consensus algorithm · Performance evaluation

1 Introduction

Indeed, the Block Chain (BC) was first defined as the virtual infrastructure that enables the mining and transfer of bitcoins [1, 2]. In recent years, the BC attains wide application in financial, credit, sharing economic and IoT. The features of BC includes: it maintains an increasing chain and data on this chain cannot be tampered; The parties in it can reach consensus without centralized control; It uses cryptography to ensure the transaction cannot be destroyed and protect the privacy of user. In the transaction process, the BC network may have malicious replicas tamper the request, then the consensus algorithm is necessary for ensuring consistency valid requests. Malicious attacks exist in various occasions, such as in WLAN mesh security access. Jiang et al. presented a blockchain-based authentication protocol. It effectively monitors malicious attacks in WLAN mesh while reducing the deployment cost [3]. Generally, this phenomenon of malicious replicas is called the Byzantine faults and this consensus algorithm is called the Byzantine Fault Tolerance (BFT) algorithm. The process of consensus is that many replicas do consistency check to the requests and submit the requests to the BC network in order. Consensus algorithms are divided into two types: Consensus algorithms based on proof, the PoX (the Proof of concept approach used in Block chains has elegantly emulated the leader-election function required in a BFT protocol to simulate the block proposal process [4]), such as PoW (Proof of Work) and PoS (Proof of Stake); Consensus algorithms based on vote such as Practical Byzantine Fault Tolerance

© Springer Nature Singapore Pte Ltd. 2020
X. Sun et al. (Eds.): ICAIS 2020, CCIS 1254, pp. 37–45, 2020.
https://doi.org/10.1007/978-981-15-8101-4_5

(PBFT).This paper summarizes some variant BFT consensus algorithms, respectively introducing their implementation processes and performances. Section 2 discusses the classical consensus algorithm PBFT. Section 3 introduces eight variant PBFT consensus algorithms and classifies them into four types. Section 4 describes the performance of these algorithms. Section 5 does a summary of this paper.

2 The Classical Consensus Algorithm

PBFT was proposed by Castro and Liskvo in 1999 [5]. It solves the problem that the original Byzantine Fault Tolerance algorithm is not efficient. It uses a three-phase protocol: Pre-Prepare, Prepare and Commit.

Pre-prepare
The primary orders the request from the client and broadcasts the pre-prepare message $<<PRE - PREPARE,$ v,n,d $>$, m $>$ to backup replicas. (v is the view number; m is the request form client; d is the digest of message)

Prepare
Backup replica validates the pre-prepare message from the primary. It validates the correctness of signature and digest at first, then it confirms the number of view if corresponding or not. After the pre-prepare message has been validated, the backup replica joins in the prepare phase and broadcasts to all replicas the prepare message $<PREPARE,$ v, n, di> (i is the number of replica). The pre-prepare and prepare messages are written into the local message log.

Commit
The replica checks the received prepare message and writes it to local message log after the message has no faults. If the replica receives 2f prepare messages from different replicas that matches the pre-prepare messages, the replica joins in the prepare phase and broadcasts to all replicas the commit message $<COMMIT,$ v, n, d, i>.

The above three steps determine the number of replicas in PBFT is 3f + 1. In Pre-Prepare phase, the primary broadcasts the pre-prepare message to all replicas, the number of communications is f − 1; In the Prepare phase, every replica broadcasts the prepare message after agrees on the request, the number of communications is $f * (f - 1) = f^2 - f$; In the Commit phase, every replica broadcasts the commit message after be in prepare state, the number of communications is also $f^2 - f$. The total number of communications is $f - 1 + f^2 - f + f^2 - f = 2f^2 - f - 1$. The communication complexity is $O(f^2)$.

3 Variant Consensus Algorithms Based on PBFT

According to Sect. 2, we can see several disadvantages of PBFT. At first, in any system a solution to the Byzantine fault tolerance is usually complex and assumed to require 3f + 1 active replication system to tolerate f failures [6]. In addition, the communication complexity $O(f^2)$ leads the large delay. Besides, the overload of PBFT is high because of cryptography and multicast operations (Fig. 1).

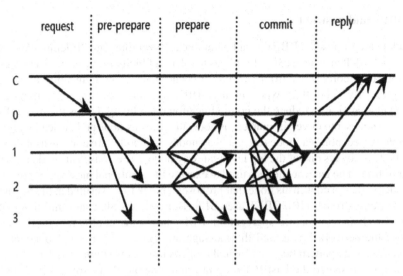

Fig. 1. PBFT algorithm flow chart

So variant consensus algorithms are presented to issue the shortcomings of PBFT. There are a considerable number of existing consensus protocols [7]. Many solutions for synchronization and co-ordination based problems in distributed systems use leader election as an integral part of their algorithm [8, 9]. We discuss eight algorithms and divide them into four types. The first algorithm is dedicated to reduce the communication complexity. The second tries to reduce the total number of replicas. The third aims to decrease the network resources cost. And the last is an optimization for public chains. The schematic is shown in Fig. 2.

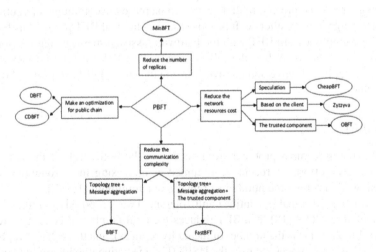

Fig. 2. The schematic of variant consensus algorithm

3.1 BBFT and FastBFT

ByStack team proposed a BBFT — a Hierarchical Byzantine Fault Tolerant Consensus Algorithm [10]. It also needs $3f + 1$ replicas to tolerant f faulty replicas, but it reduces the communication complexity from $O(f^2)$ to $O(f)$ and makes communication complexity growing linearly rather than exponentially. BBFT uses the topology tree structure and message aggregation to reduce the communication complexity. It lays the network and divides the nodes into three: the consensus node, the gateway node and the leader node. In the topology tree, non-leaf nodes are gateway nodes, leaf nodes are consensus nodes and leader node is always one of the top level gateway nodes. The consensus node is used to join consensus. The gateway node is used to execute the additional message aggregation. The leader node is a consensus node that proposes a block to be verified at the beginning of the consensus round [10]. BBFT uses BLS (Boneh-Lynn-Shacham) multi-signature scheme for efficient signature aggregation. BBFT has better configurability due to the model of the network laying and the message aggregation in it is independent. The message exchange pattern between logical replicas mimics is similar to PBFT [11].

Liu et al. presented the FastBFT — a fast and scalable BFT protocol in 2018. It's a novel message aggregation technique that combines hardware-based trust execution environments (TEES) with lightweight secret sharing [12]. Trying to improve these protocols allowing the decision to be taken in few communication steps, fast consensus protocols for crash [13] and byzantine [14] failure models are able to decide in two communication steps, matching the lower bounds for asynchronous distributed consensus [15]. FastBFT needs only $2f + 1$ replicas to tolerant f faulty replicas. In the normal case, it needs $f + 1$ active replicas agree and execute the request and the other f passive replicas do nothing but update their states. It's a technique based on secret sharing rather than multi-signature, that reduces the cost brought by the encryption process due to it not needs public key operation. This technology is suitable for hardware assistance protocol and reduces the communication complexity from $O(f^2)$ to $O(f)$. FastBFT also uses the topology tree structure and fault detection to increase the communication efficiency and improve algorithm resilience. It proposes a new classical BFT protocol as fall-back protocol and combines MinBFT with the hardware-assisted message aggregation technology described above. When the failure occurs, FastBFT triggers the view change protocol. All replicas (active and passive) execute the above fall-back protocol during a specific time.

3.2 MinBFT

To prevent the agreement protocol from becoming the bottleneck of the entire BFT system, research efforts in recent years aimed at increasing the throughput of BFT agreement while keeping the number of replicas at a minimum [16, 17].

The MinBFT (Minimal Byzantine Fault Tolerance) was proposed by Giuliana Santos Veronese et al. in 2009 [18]. MinBFT reduces the total number of consensus replicas from $3f + 1$ to $2f + 1$ (f is the number of the faulty replicas), and these $2f + 1$ replicas all join in the consensus process. It uses the USIG (Unique Sequential Identifier Generator) service to rule the behavior of the primary, thus it only needed $2f + 1$ replicas to agree and execute the requests.

Besides, it abandons the Pre-Prepare phase of PBFT. Instead, when a client sends a request to all servers, the primary uses the USIG service to assign a sequence number to the request and then sends it to all servers in a PREPARE message. When a primary is malicious, the view change triggered by timeout has to be executed and chooses a new primary. In addition, MinBFT also batches several requests in a single message to reduces the cost.

3.3 OBFT, CheapBFT and Zyzzyva

In 2012, Shoker et al. presented the OBFT (Obfuscated Byzantine Fault Tolerance), a variant PBFT algorithm based on clients [19]. It only needs $3f + 1$ replicas to reach consensus (f is the number of faulty replicas). In OBFT, message communication is not between replicas instead of replicas and clients. In OBFT message communication happens among clients and replicas, the overload on the replicas brought by cryptographic load and requests multicast has been reduced and the performance has been improved. OBFT is also a speculative algorithm. It includes two phases: Speculative phase and Recovery phase. At first, $2f + 1$ replicas are chosen to the Active set and the other replicas are in Passive set. In the Speculative phase, the primary assigns a sequence number to the request. When all the responses of the Active set match, the client commit the request. Otherwise, the Recovery phase is launched. After some steps in Recovery phase, the new $2f + 1$ active replicas are chosen to the updated Active and the Speculative phase is launched again.

The other algorithm, CheapBFT (Resource-efficient Byzantine Fault Tolerance), also reduces the total number of replicas from $3f + 1$ to $2f + 1$. It was presented by Rudiger Kaitza et al. in 2012 [20].

CheapBFT adopts the optimistic execution and it only needs $f + 1$ replicas to agree and execute requests of clients. It is a protocol based on a trusted component. The trusted component in the CheapBFT is a FPGA trusted device called CASH (Counter Assignment Service in Hardware), every replica all hosts a trusted CASH system. The CASH system has two parts, CREATE MC is used to create the message certificate and CHECK MC is used to check if messages were accepted or not.

CheapBFT does not adopt the traditional three-phase protocol instead of a composite protocol. In CheapBFT, only $f + 1$ active replicas participate in the consensus process and the other f passive replicas do nothing but update their own states. In the normal case CheapTiny only uses $f + 1$ replicas, if in faulty case it has no ability to tolerance the faults. CheapBFT uses the MinBFT to make use of $2f + 1$ replicas to tolerant f faults [20]. However, replicas must keep corresponding state in the protocol switch, then CheapBFT proposes the CheapSwitch protocol for the safe protocol switch [20]. The core of the CheapSwitch protocol is the operation of the Abort history by non-faulty replicas. The last protocol of CheapBFT is Fall-back protocol — MinBFT. In fact, every protocol which uses $2f + 1$ replicas to tolerant f faults can be adopted. As we except permanent replicas faults to be rare, CheapBFT executes MinBFT in a specific time and performs CheapTiny at other time.

Zyzzyva is a Speculative Byzantine Fault Tolerance which is proposed by Ramakrishna Kotla et al. Speculation is that replicas speculatively execute requests without running an expensive agreement protocol to definitively establish the order [21]. It also uses 3f + 1 replicas to tolerant f faulty replicas. Zyzzyva does not adopts the three-phase protocol in PBFT instead of agreement, view change and checkpoint three phases. Replicas speculatively receive the request order from the primary and response to the client immediately. In this speculative process, replicas could not stay corresponding states with each other, but clients will check and correct these states. An algorithm with speculative execution must keep its safety and liveness. The general method is that append the history information on the reply received by the client to help the client determine when it is appropriate to act on a reply. In addition, Zyzzyva also batches the requests as well as caches out of order request.

3.4 DBFT and CDBFT

HAO et al. proposed the CDBFT (Credit-Delegated Byzantine Fault Tolerance) [22]. It introduces the voting rewards and punishments scheme of DPoS (Delegated Proof of Stake) into the PBFT and reduces the participation probability of malicious replicas in the consensus process. CDBFT includes three parts, a credit evaluation system for displaying the states of replicas, a vote mechanism for increasing the enthusiasm of trusted replicas and a privilege classification mechanism for choosing the primary with the highest credit value. In addition, lots of communication resources are used in the periodicity-based checkpoint in PBFT, the CDBFT proposes time-stamp-based checkpoint protocol to reduce the communication cost.

Jeon et al. proposed the DBFT (Diversity of opinion Byzantine Fault Tolerance) [23]. It's also an optimization for the application of public blockchain, reducing the probability of collusion between malicious replicas. DBFT is a two layer consensus agreement algorithm. The first consensus process uses the classical BFT algorithm. The second consensus process groups the participants and randomly chooses a validator from every group to agree and execute the request.

4   The Performance of Variant Consensus Algorithm

Table 1 shows the performance of every variant consensus algorithms under different preconditions.

When answering a request with 1 KB payload, the speed of FastBFT is twice that of Zyzzyva. With the increase of replicas' number and request's overload, the performance is marginally affected [12]. In addition, FastBFT has a good balance between performance and resilience. When the faulty replicas are 10, the peak throughput is about 3,000 op/s and the latency is 1.5 ms.

In the communication steps and the total number of replicas of MinBFT are less than PBFT, so its throughput is higher than PBFT. Under the high load, the PBFT can batch up to 70 messages, however MinBFT can batch 200 messages in a single request. It presented the better latency results than PBFT when the network latency is greater than 2 ms. With the USIG service, the peak throughput is 23,404 op/s and the latency is 1,617 ms.

OBFT could deal with 240 requests from the client at the same time due to the existence of the primary. No matter which benchmark, the peak throughput is higher

Table 1. The performance of variant consensus algorithm

Protocol	Latency	(peak)throughput
MinBFT [18]	1,617 ms	23,404 op/s
CheapBFT [20]	1 ms	12,000 op/s
OBFT [19]	100 ms	2,193 op/s
Zyzzyva [21]	0.6 ms	86,000 op/s
FastBFT [12]	1.5 ms	3,000 op/s
DBFT [22]	—	10,000 op/s
CDBFT [23]	—	110 op/s

than PBFT and the response time and occupied CPU resources are less than MinBFT. With the increase of clients, the throughput is gradually decreasing. It scales 280 clients with a peak throughput equals to 2,193 op/s. In normal case, CheapBFT can process more than 12 k requests every second, an increase of 14% over MinBFT, so CheapBFT has higher throughput. Whether in batching or not, the throughput of Zyzzyva is better than PBFT. Because PBFT has higher cryptographic and message overload. Zyzzyva uses fast agreement to drive its latency near the optimal for an agreement protocol, 3 one-way message delays [21]. Zyzzyva has better fault scalability when the faulty replicas increases and as batching is used. When the batch size is increased to 10, the peak throughput increases to 86,000 op/s and the latency is about 0.6 ms.

Only a part of replicas chosen by a vote mechanism in CDBFT, when the number of replicas increases, the throughput of CDBFT still keeps increasing. With the number of error replicas is about 10, the throughput is 110 op/s. When the number of replicas is small, DBFT's throughput is similar to PBFT. In contrast, the performance of its is still higher. The peak throughput is about 10,000 op/s.

5 Conclusion

This paper provides a review of introduction and performance description of variant consensus algorithms based on PBFT. We could see not every consensus algorithm is perfect. For example, OBFT relies entirely on the client and cannot prevent the client from being malicious, so it can be applied on application where participants are trusted numbers of the same organization. Zyzzyva uses the speculative execution and it has bad fault tolerance. In the future, a consensus algorithm should also be used for a specific spot while improving its performance.

References

1. Brito, J., Castillo, A.: Bitcoin: A primer for policymakers. Mercatus Center at George Mason University (2013)
2. Ouattara, H.F., Ahmat, D., Ouédraogo, F.T., Bissyandé, T.F., Sié, O.: Blockchain consensus protocols. In: Odumuyiwa, V., Adegboyega, O., Uwadia, C. (eds.) AFRICOMM 2017. LNICST, vol. 250, pp. 304–314. Springer, Cham (2018). https://doi.org/10.1007/978-3-319-98827-6_29
3. Jiang, X., Liu, M., Yang, C., Liu, Y., Wang, R.: A blockchain-based authentication protocol for WLAN mesh security access. CMC-Comput. Mater. Continua **58**(1), 45–59 (2019)
4. Barhanpure, A., Belandor, P., Das, B.: Proof of stack consensus for blockchain networks. In: Thampi, S.M., Madria, S., Wang, G., Rawat, D.B., Alcaraz Calero, J.M. (eds.) SSCC 2018. CCIS, vol. 969, pp. 104–116. Springer, Singapore (2019). https://doi.org/10.1007/978-981-13-5826-5_8
5. Castro, M., Liskov, B., et al.: Practical byzantine fault tolerance. In: OSDI, vol. 99, pp. 173–186 (1999)
6. Duan, S., Peisert, S., Levitt, K.N.: hBFT: speculative byzantine fault tolerance with minimum cost. IEEE Trans. Dependable Secure Comput. **12**(1), 58–70 (2014)
7. Alzahrani, N., Bulusu, N.: Towards true decentralization: a blockchain consensus protocol based on game theory and randomness. In: Bushnell, L., Poovendran, R., Başar, T. (eds.) GameSec 2018. LNCS, vol. 11199, pp. 465–485. Springer, Cham (2018). https://doi.org/10.1007/978-3-030-01554-1_27
8. Srinivasan, S., Kandukoori, R.: A Paxos based algorithm to minimize the overhead of process recovery in consensus. Acta Informatica **56**, 433–446 (2019)
9. Ailijiang, A., Charapko, A., Demirbas, M.: Consensus in the cloud: Paxos systems demystified. In: IEEE 25th International Conference on Computer Communication and Networks (ICCCN), pp. 1–10 (2016)
10. https://github.com/bystackcom/BBFT-Whitepaper/blob/master/whitepaper.pdf
11. Thai, Q.T., Yim, J.C., Yoo, T.W., Yoo, H.K., Kwak, J.Y., Kim, S.M.: Hierarchical byzantine fault-tolerance protocol for permissioned blockchain systems. J. Supercomput. 1–29 (2019)
12. Liu, J., Li, W., Karame, G.O., Asokan, N.: Scalable byzantine consensus via hardware-assisted secret sharing. IEEE Trans. Comput. **68**(1), 139–151 (2018)
13. Lamport, L.: Fast paxos. Distrib. Comput. **19**(2), 79–103 (2006)
14. Lamport, L.: Lower bounds for asynchronous consensus. Distrib. Comput. **19**(2), 104–125 (2006)
15. Martin, J.P., Alvisi, L.: Fast byzantine consensus. IEEE Trans. Dependable Secure Comput. **3**(3), 202–215 (2006)
16. Behl, J., Distler, T., Kapitza, R.: Consensus-oriented parallelization: how to earn your first million. In: Proceedings of the 16th Annual Middleware Conference, pp. 173–184. ACM (2015)
17. Li, B., Xu, W., Abid, M.Z., Distler, T., Kapitza, R.: Sarek: optimistic parallel ordering in byzantine fault tolerance. In: 2016 12th European Dependable Computing Conference (EDCC), pp. 77–88. IEEE (2016)
18. Veronese, G.S., Correia, M., Lung, L.C., Bessani, A.N.: Minimal byzantine fault tolerance (2008)
19. Shoker, A., Bahsoun, J.P., Yabandeh, M.: Improving independence of failures in BFT. In: 2013 IEEE 12th International Symposium on Network Computing and Applications, pp. 227–234. IEEE (2013)
20. Kapitza, R., et al.: Cheapbft: resource-efficient byzantine fault tolerance. In: Proceedings of the 7th ACM European Conference on Computer Systems, pp. 295–308. ACM (2012)

21. Kotla, R., Alvisi, L., Dahlin, M., Clement, A., Wong, E.: Zyzzyva: speculative byzantine fault tolerance. In: ACM SIGOPS Operating Systems Review, vol. 41, pp. 45–58. ACM (2007)
22. Jeon, S., Doh, I., Chae, K.: RMBC: Randomized mesh blockchain using DBFT consensus algorithm. In: 2018 International Conference on Information Networking (ICOIN), pp. 712–717. IEEE (2018)
23. Wang, Y.: Study of blockchains's consensus mechanism based on credit. IEEE Access **7**, 10224–10231 (2019)

A New Network Intrusion Detection Method
Based on Deep Neural Network

Xingwang Li, Zhiwei Sheng$^{(\boxtimes)}$, Yuanyuan Huang, and Shibing Zhang

School of Cybersecurity, Chengdu University of Information Technology, Chengdu 610225,
China
Sg141sg141@163.com

Abstract. With the development and popularization of the Internet, Intrusion detection systems become indispensable. In view of the great achievements of deep neural network in many fields. In order to improve the validity and accuracy of network intrusion detection. A new intrusion detection method based on deep neural network is proposed to detect the characteristics of kdd99 dataset. This model adopts deep learning technology, including relu, full connection layer and cascade different level. The experiment on kdd99 data set shows that the model improves the performance of intrusion detection, reducing the training time and false alarm rate with an accuracy rate of 92.7%.

Keywords: IDS · Cascade different level · Densenet

1 Introduction

Intrusion detection system (ids) is a kind of network security equipment that monitors the network transmission in real time and gives an alarm or takes active response when suspicious transmission is found. The difference between it and other network security equipment is that IDS is a kind of active safety technology and is a kind of detection method based on the characteristics. It is the essence of a classification problem. To the problem of classification of machine learning, algorithm is regarded as one of the most efficient algorithm, which received a lot of application in intrusion detection in recent years. For example, Pervez et al. proposed a filtering algorithm based on support vector machine (SVM) [1]. Shapoorifard et al. proposed knn-aco method based on KNN [2]. Ingre and Bhupendra et al. proposed the intrusion detection method based on decision tree [3], Amjad Mehmood et al. proposed the intrusion detection system based on naive bayes [4], NabilaFarnaaz et al. proposed the intrusion detection system based on random forest [5], Traditional machine learning algorithms (such as random forest, support vector machine, KNN, naive bayes, decision tree, neural network, etc.). Yu proposed an intrusion detection algorithm based on feature graph [6], Ling made application of self-organizing feature map neural network based on K-means Clustering in network intrusion detection [7], Wu proposed a distributed intrusion detection model via non-destructive partitioning and balanced allocation for Big Data [8]. Although in terms of detection accuracy and the rate of false positives have good grades, a large amount of high

© Springer Nature Singapore Pte Ltd. 2020
X. Sun et al. (Eds.): ICAIS 2020, CCIS 1254, pp. 46–57, 2020.
https://doi.org/10.1007/978-981-15-8101-4_6

dimensional nonlinear network data without a label to the intrusion detection system has brought new challenges with the expansion of the network data, because the traditional methods of detection performance is dependent on the characteristics of [9], in the face of a large number of new network data and lower performance. With the development of deep learning, deep learning, a branch of machine learning, can automatically learn effective features from the original data, so as to improve the classification accuracy. Meanwhile, deep learning does not need feature engineering: classic ML algorithm usually needs complex feature engineering. Typically, exploratory data analysis needs to be performed first on the dataset. Then, lower the dimensions for processing. Finally, the best features must be carefully selected to be passed to the ML algorithm. When using deep learning, such feature engineering is not needed [10], because good performance can be achieved immediately simply by passing the data directly to the network. This completely eliminates the heavy and challenging feature engineering phases of the entire process.

At present, a large number of scholars have carried out researches on intrusion detection methods based on deep learning, and obtained better detection results in terms of accuracy and false alarm rate than traditional machine learning and shallow learning. Kang songlin et al. [11] proposed the Multiple Layer Extreme Learning Machine (ml-elm) algorithm based on the combination of deep neural network (DNN) and Extreme Learning Machine, which reduced data classification time. Kim [12] applied high persistent threat in intrusion detection based on Deep Belief Nets (DBN). Alom Zahangir et al. [13] used Deep Belief Nets, DBN and Extreme Learning Machine (ELM) to conduct intrusion detection, which greatly improved the accuracy of intrusion detection. Deep learning has achieved many excellent research results in computer image processing, including resnet, densenet, CNN, etc.

For example, densenet has the advantage of saving parameters and achieves the same accuracy in ImageNet classification dataset. The number of parameters required by densenet is less than half of ResNet. For industry, small models can significantly save bandwidth and reduce storage overhead [14]. Province is calculated. With a precision comparable to ResNet, DenseNet required only about half as much computation as ResNet. The demand of computational efficiency in the practical application of deep learning is very strong. Show DenseNet has very big potential for this type of application, even without the Depth Separable Convolution can achieve better results than existing methods. Anti-over-fitting, DenseNet has very good anti-over-fitting performance, especially suitable for the application where the training data is relatively scarce. There is a more intuitive explanation for DenseNet's anti-over-fitting: the features extracted at each layer of the neural network are equivalent to a nonlinear transformation of the input data, and the complexity of the transformation gradually increases as the depth increases (more composite of nonlinear functions). Compared with the classifier of general neural network, which is directly dependent on the features of the last layer of the network (with the highest complexity), DenseNet can comprehensively take advantage of the features with lower complexity of the shallow layer, so it is easier to obtain a smooth decision function with better generalization performance. However, due to the incompatibility between the dimension of intrusion detection data and the data structure of image network, the intrusion detection data is basically one-dimensional data, while the image is basically two-dimensional or three-dimensional data. The image processing network is less used in intrusion detection (Table 1).

Table 1. The deep learning algorithm commonly used in intrusion detection field.

dataset	Lstm	gru	cnn	resnet	densenet
Kdd99	√	√	√	√	

As can be seen from the figure above, densenet is still a blank in the field of intrusion detection.

At the same time, due to the great difference between current network environments and the traditional one, it puts forward higher requirements on the applicability of the intrusion detection. At present, there are vast amounts of data transmitted through the network every day, how to effectively deal with these data for intrusion detection speed and efficiency of the higher requirements are put forward. The accuracy of detection and false alarm rate has always been the research focus of intrusion detection, although a lot of research in this area has made significant progress, but there is still room for improvement. Intrusion detection as an online system, real-time is very heavy Although deep learning can improve the accuracy of detection, it is difficult to train due to too many parameters. Therefore, how to improve the training speed of the model and better meet the real-time requirements of intrusion detection is also an important problem to be solved.

Inspired by densenet, due to the network densenet is based on image processing, the input is a 2d and 3d, and intrusion detection system is basically a dimensional data, the correlation between the data is not large, forced data litres of d may increase the amount of calculation, under the inspiration of densenet, based on the depth of neural network, combined with relu, all connections, cross connection between cascade method puts forward a new intrusion detection method, and based on the model based on pytorch - gpu implemented code, the last is verified using kdd99 data set.

Intrusion detection system can be divided into three modules: data preprocessing module, feature learning module and intrusion type classification module. The ids model is shown in Fig. 2. First data input, data preprocessing, then feature learning, and finally classifier for detection. The details of these three modules are explained below (Fig. 1).

2 Data Pre-processing

In this paper, KDD99 datasets are used as our training and testing datasets, the data set is nine weeks of network connection data collected from a simulated U.S. air force local area network, divided into training data with identification and test data without identification. The test data and the training data have different probability distributions, and the test data contains some attack types that do not appear in the training data, which makes the intrusion detection more realistic. Each connection of the data set consists of 41 features and 1 attack type. The training data set contains 1 normal identification type

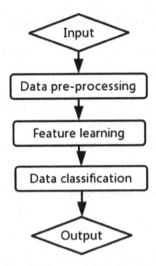

Fig. 1. Proposed IDS structure

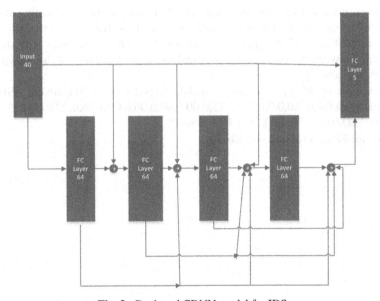

Fig. 2. Designed CDNN model for IDS

and 36 training attack types, among which 22 attack modes are in the training data and 14 attacks only appear in the test data set (Table 2).

TCP basic connection characteristics (total 9 types) basic connection characteristics include some basic connection attributes, such as continuous time, protocol type, number of bytes transferred, etc. The content characteristics of TCP connection (13 kinds in total) are extracted from the content characteristics of data content that may reflect

Table 2. Details of five labels

Intrusion category	Description	Details
Normal	Normal record	Normal
DOS	Denial of service attack	Back, land, neptune, pod, Smurf, teardrop
Probing	Scanning and detection	Ipswee, ap, portsweep, satan
R2L	Unauthorised remote access	ftp_write, guess_passwd, imap, multihop phf, spy, warezclient, warezmaster
U2R	Illegal access to local super users	buffer_overflow, loadmodule, perl, rootkit

the intrusion, such as the number of login failures. Statistical characteristics of network traffic based on time (a total of 9 types, 23 ~ 31). Since network attack events have a strong correlation in time, some connections between the current connection records and the previous connection records in a period of time can be statistically calculated to better reflect the relationship between connections. Host-based network traffic statistical characteristics (total 10 types, 32 ~ 41) time-based traffic statistics only show the relationship between the past two seconds and the current connection, as shown in the figure below (Table 3).

An example of the original intrusion data record is x = {0,icmp,ecr_i,SF,1032, 0,0,0,0,0,0,0,0,0,0,0,0,0,0,0,0,0,0,511,511,0.00,0.00,0.00,0.00,1.00,0.00,0.00,255,255, 1.00,0.00, 1.00,0.00,0.00,0.00,0.00, 0.00,smurf}

There are 41 features and one label.

Table 3. Details of forty one features

Description	Feature	Data attributes
Basic feature of individual	duration	continuous
TCP connections	protocol_type	symbolic
	service	symbolic
	flag	symbolic
	src_bytes	continuous
	dst_bytes	continuous
	land	symbolic
	wrong_fragment	continuous
	urgent	continuous
content features within a	hot	continuous
connection suggested by	num_failed_logins	continuous
domain knowledge	logged_in	symbolic
	num_compromised	continuous
	root_shell	continuous
	su_attempted	continuous
	num_root	continuous
	num_file_creations	continuous
	num_shells	continuous
	num_access_files	continuous
	num_outbound_cmds	continuous
	is_host_login	symbolic
	is_guest_login	symbolic
	count	continuous
	srv_count	continuous
	serror_rate	continuous
	srv_serror_rate	continuous
	rerror_rate	continuous
	srv_rerror_rate	continuous
	same_srv_rate	continuous
	diff_srv_rate	continuous
	srv_diff_host_rate	continuous
traffic features computed	dst_host_count	continuous
in and out a host	dst_host_srv_count	continuous
	dst_host_same_srv_rate	continuous
	dst_host_diff_srv_rate	continuous
	dst_host_same_src_port_rate	continuous
	dst_host_srv_diff_host_rate	continuous
	dst_host_serror_rate	continuous
	dst_host_srv_serror_rate	continuous
	dst_host_rerror_rate	continuous
	dst_host_srv_rerror_rate	continuous

2.1 Character Numeric

Firstly we should remove duplicate data. In the actual collected data, many intrusion records are the same, so duplicate data elimination technology can be used to reduce the amount of data entering ids and eliminate information redundancy. The kdd99 dataset has been de-duplicated and no filtering is required in this article. But some of the features in the kdd99 dataset are numeric and some are character. Standardization is then used to convert all the data captured from different ids sources into a digital format to simplify data processing. The symbolic characteristic numeric rule is as follows: the method of attribute mapping is adopted. For example, the attribute 2 is the protocol type protocol_type, which has three values: TCP, udp, icmp, and is expressed by its position, wherein TCP is 1, udp is 22, and icmp is 3. Similarly, the mapping relationship between symbol values and corresponding values can be established by 70 symbol values of attribute characteristic service and 11 symbol values of flag. Label is processed as follows (Table 4).

Table 4. Description of five labels

Intrusion type	Description	Label
Normal	Normal record	0
Dos	Denial of service attack	1
Probe	Scanning and detection	2
R2L	Unauthorised remote access	3
U2R	Illegal access to local super users	4

2.2 Normalization

Because the value of some features is 0 or 1, while the value of some other features has a wide range, in order to avoid the influence of a wide range of values is too large, and the influence of a small range of values disappears, normalization processing is needed to convert the values of each feature into between [0,1].

$$y = (x - xmin/xmax - xmin) \tag{1}$$

After normalisation,

x = {0.0,3.38921626955e-07,0.00128543131293,0.0,0.0,0.0,0.0,0.0,0.0,0.0,0.0,0.0, 0.0,0.0,0.00195694716243,0.00195694716243,0.0,0.0,0.0,0.0,0.0,1.0,0.0,0.0,0.0,0.12549019 6078,1.0,1.0,0.0,0.0,0.03,0.05,0.0,0.0,0.0,0.0,0.0,0.0}

3 CDNN Model Building

It can be seen that this model has 40 neurons in input layer and 5 neurons in output layer. There are four hidden layers, each with 64 neurons and cascade different level structure. The input of the latter layer is the output concat of all the previous layers.

3.1 The Activation Function

Select relu as the activation function. As a nonlinear element, Relu function can increase the nonlinearity of neural network and make the structure of convolutional neural network piecewise linear. When the activation function is calculated by using functions such as Sigmoid, the calculation amount is large. When the back propagation is used to calculate the error gradient, the derivation involves division, and the calculation amount is relatively large. Relu can make the output of some neurons 0, which leads to the sparsity of the network, reduces the interdependence of parameters, and alleviates the over-fitting problem.

3.2 The Loss Function

Select categorical_crossentropy, as the lossfunction, and its calculation formula is as follows:

$$loss(x, target) = -\log\left(\frac{\exp(x[target])}{\sum_j \exp(x[j])}\right) = x[target] + \log\left(\sum_j \exp(x[j])\right) \quad (2)$$

X and target represent the predicted output and label values, respectively, and j represents each category.

3.3 Hidden Layers and Neural

First of all, we default to 80 neurons per layer (Fig. 3). It can be seen from the figure that the accuracy of the model increases with the number of layers and reaches the highest point when the number of the hidden layers is 4 (Table 5).

On the basis that the number of hidden layers is 4. It can be seen from the figure that the accuracy of the model is on the rise from 40 to 64 nodes and on the decline from 64 to 100 nodes. The test finds that 64 nodes are the best.

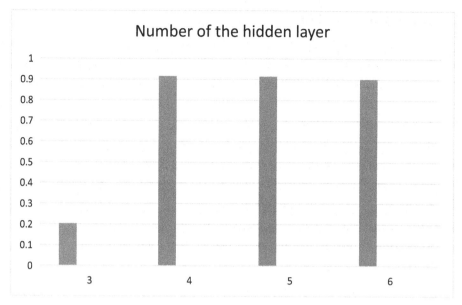

Fig. 3. Network layer number and detection accuracy test of the proposed NDNN on KDD99 dataset

Table 5. Number of neural and accuracy test on KDD99 dataset

Number of neural	Accuracy
40	0.503
60	0.917
63	0.923
64	0.927
65	0.920
80	0.916
100	0,904

4 Experiment

4.1 Experimental Environment

The experimental environment in this paper is windows10, Anaconda open source library, python programming language, pytorch for deep learning, etc. GTX950 graphics card is used as GPU for accelerated computing.

4.2 The Experimental Process

The evaluation indexes were accuracy, recall, precision and f-score are as follows (Table 6)

Table 6. The meanings of TP, FP, FN and TN

Actual class	Predicted class	
	Anomaly	Normal
Anomaly	TP	FN
Normal	FP	TN

$$\text{Accuracy} = \frac{TP + TN}{TP + TN + FP + FN} \qquad (3)$$

$$\text{Recall} = \frac{TP}{TP + FN} \qquad (4)$$

$$\text{PRECISION} = \frac{TP}{TP + FP} \qquad (5)$$

The classification problem is to classify instances into positive or negative classes. For a thing sub problem, hu hu four kinds of feelings appear. If an instance is positive and is predicted to be positive, it is True positive; if an instance is negative and is predicted to be positive, it is False positive. Accordingly, if the example is a negative class and is predicted to be a negative class, it is called True negative, and if the positive class is predicted to be a negative class, it is false negative (Table 7).

Table 7. Details of the KDD99 dataset

Intrusion category	Number of training data	Number of test data
Normal	97278	60593
Probe	4107	4166
Dos	391458	229853
U2R	52	228
U2L	1126	16189

In the experiment, the experiment results of KNN, decision tree, AdaBoost, random forest (RF) and CNN, RNN are compared, and the accuracy of the algorithm is shown in Fig. 3. The accuracy of KNN, decision tree, AdaBoost, random forest and CNN are respectively 76.6%, 80.4%, 79.7%, 76.6% and 77.7%. It can be seen that the algorithm

Table 8. Comparison of evaluation indexes of different algorithms

Model	Accuracy	Recall	F-score
Knn	0.766	0.610	0.748
Decision tree	0.804	0.695	0.791
Adaboost	0.797	0.698	0.796
Random Forest	0.766	0.605	0.744
Proposed	0.927	0.987	0.849

proposed in this paper has certain improvement in accuracy compared with traditional machine learning algorithm and deep neural network CNN, reaching 92.7% (Table 8).

Known from the analysis of above benchmark Recall value compared with the traditional algorithm has great improvement, because of IDS is designed to improve the Recall value, which reduced the abnormal samples miss as normal the number of samples. Compared with some algorithms, this paper has made great progress in this aspect. However, as a whole, the number of misjudgment accounts for a high proportion of the total sample size, so the precision has not been significantly improved.

5   Conclusion

Deep learning method is a new machine learning method in the field of intrusion detection. It has strong feature extraction ability for high-dimensional feature vectors and good classification performance. In this paper, cross-hierarchy connection is used in intrusion detection. Densenet network has made great achievements in image, which proves that it can perform the task of feature extraction excellently. This network can be used in intrusion detection and has good performance of feature extraction. In future work, this neural network needs further improvement to reduce training time, further improve classification accuracy and improve model generalization ability.

Acknowledgments. The authors would like to thank the reviewers for their detailed reviews and constructive comments, which have helped improve the quality of this paper. This work was supported in part by the National Key Research and Development Program of China (No. 2017YFB0802302), the Science and Technology Support Project of Sichuan Province (No. 2016FZ0112, No. 2017GZ0314, No. 2018GZ0204), the Academic and Technical Leaders Training Funding Support Projects of Sichuan Province (No. 2016120080102643), the Application Foundation Project of Sichuan Province (No. 2017JY0168), the Science and Technology Project of Chengdu (No. 2017-RK00-00103-ZF, No. 2016-HM01-00217-SF).

References

1. Pervez, M.S., Farid, D.M.: Feature selection and intrusion classification in NSL-KDD cup 99 dataset employing SVMs. In: International Conference on Software, Knowledge, Information Management and Applications. IEEE (2015)

2. Shapoorifard, H., Shamsinejad, P.: Intrusion detection using a novel hybrid method incorporating an improved KNN. Int. J. Comput. Appl. **173**(1) (2017)

3. Ingre, B., Yadav, A., Soni, A.K.: Decision tree based intrusion detection system for NSL-KDD dataset (2017). Author, F.: Contribution title. In: 9th International Proceedings on Proceedings, pp. 1–2. Publisher, Location (2010)

4. Mehmood, A., Mukherjee, M., Ahmed, S.H., et al.: J. Supercomput. **74**, 5156 (2018)

5. Farnaaz, N., Jabbar, M.A.: Random Forest Modeling for Network Intrusion Detection System Author links open overlay panel

6. Xiang, Yu., Tian, Z., Qiu, J., Shen, S., Yan, X.: An intrusion detection algorithm based on feature graph. Comput. Mater. Continua **61**(1), 255–274 (2019)

7. Ling, T., Chong, L., Jingming, X., Jun, C.: Application of self-organizing feature map neural network based on K-means clustering in network intrusion detection. Comput. Mater. Continua **61**(1), 275–288 (2019)

8. Xiaonian, W., Zhang, C., Zhang, R., Wang, Y., Cui, J.: A distributed intrusion detection model via nondestructive partitioning and balanced allocation for big data. Comput. Mater. Continua **56**(1), 61–72 (2018)

9. Shone, N., Ngoc, T.N., Phai, V.D., et al.: A deep learning approach to network intrusion detection. IEEE Trans. Emerg. Topics Comput. Intell. **2**(1), 41–50 (2018)

10. Lecun, Y., Bengio, Y., Hinton, G.: Deep learning. Nature **521**(7553), 436 (2015)

11. Kim, J., Shin, N., Jo, S.Y., et al.: Method of intrusion detection using deep neural network. In: 2017 IEEE International Conference on Big Data and Smart Computing (BigComp). IEEE (2017)

12. Kang, S., Liu, Le., Liu, C., et al.: Application of multi-layer extreme learning machine in intrusion detection. Comput. Appl. **35**(9), 2513–2518 (2015)

13. Alom, Z., Bontupalli, V.R., Taha, T.M.: Intrusion detection using deep belief network and extreme learning machine. Int. J. Monit. Surveillance Technol. Res. **3**(2), 35–56 (2015)

14. Gao, H., Zhuang, L., van der Maaten, L., Weinberger, K.Q.: Densely Connected Convolutional Networks. arXiv:1608.06993

Improved Single Target Tracking Learning Detection Algorithm

Hongjin Zhu, Jiawei Li, Congzhe You, Xiangjun Chen, and Honghui Fan[✉]

College of Computer Engineering, Jiangsu University of Technology, Changzhou 213001,
People's Republic of China
fanhonghui@jsut.edu.cn

Abstract. In order to improve the robustness and speed of single target tracking, this paper proposes an improved tracking learning method. The purpose is to improve the tracking module in the traditional tracking learning detection (TLD) algorithm. By introduced oriented fast and rotated brief (ORB) feature points and keep the original uniform distribution point to improve the robustness and speed up execution of tracking. The experiment shows that the improved TLD algorithm has strong robustness in different environments, and the feat can quickly and accurately track the single object. The proposed algorithm can overcome the tracking failures caused by objects with partial occlusion, fast motion and leave the tracking field of vision, and has better robustness. It is experimentally verified that it has the veracity and the execution speed, compared with the traditional TLD algorithm.

Keywords: Tracking learning detection · ORB feature points · Single-target tracking · Uniformed-distributed points

1 Introduction

With the rapid development of information technology, intelligent detection and tracking technology of moving objects has been widely applied in daily life. For example: in ITS, accurate detection of vehicles is a very important part; In the intelligent monitoring system, detection and tracking of moving objects such as humans, animals and vehicles is the key to the operation of the whole system. Moving target detection and tracking technology is becoming more and more mature. However, due to the impact of many adverse factors in the process of target detection and tracking and the high expectation of precision in the application process of the industry, this research direction is still a hot research topic.

In the process of detection and tracking of the moving target, the moving target and the background may change, such as rotation change, rapid movement, illumination change, scale change, background similar interference, motion blur, occlusion and beyond the field of vision [1, 2]. Moving object detection and tracking algorithms are mainly divided into two categories [3]. The first one is to detect moving objects directly from image sequences without relying on prior knowledge, and to identify target objects and track moving targets of interest [4]. The second one is the prior knowledge that

© Springer Nature Singapore Pte Ltd. 2020
X. Sun et al. (Eds.): ICAIS 2020, CCIS 1254, pp. 58–68, 2020.
https://doi.org/10.1007/978-981-15-8101-4_7

depends on the target. First, it models the moving objects, and then finds the matching moving targets in the image sequence in real time. The algorithm proposed in this paper belongs to second kinds of algorithms, and it is also suitable for long time tracking [5]. There is a common problem in the research of long time target tracking. After moving away from the camera's field of vision, the motion target will appear again, whether the system can detect it again, and start the new tracking. In addition, there are many problems to be solved in the process of long time tracking, such as the fusion of detection and tracking, the occlusion of the moving target and the feature selection of the detector. The tracking learning algorithm (Tracking Learning Detection), proposed by Dr. Kalal of the University of Surrey in 2013, is one of the most representative long - time tracking methods in recent years [6]. The TLD algorithm is composed of three modules, the tracker, the detector and the learning module. These three modules support each other, complement each other, run at the same time, and have high efficiency. It is a relatively complete tracking method. Although TLD has shown excellent performance in robustness and accuracy, there is still room for improvement. Wang et al. [7] uses the back projection algorithm to construct skin color classifier to transform the detection module in TLD. Medouakh et al. [8] introduces a new tracking and detection feedback mechanism by introducing color histogram feature and scale adaptation. These two papers have been modified for the traditional TLD algorithm, all of which have improved the robustness of the traditional TLD algorithm to a certain extent, but the speed of execution still needs to be improved.

This paper is mainly aimed at improving the tracker module of traditional TLD, and designing a new tracker. The new tracker introduces the ORB feature points, and preserves the original uniform distribution points. The improved algorithm has better robustness and execution speed. Experiments show that the algorithm proposed in this paper improves the execution speed of the traditional TLD algorithm, and solves the problem of tracking failure due to the occlusion or rapid movement of the moving target.

The traditional TLD algorithm is a long time tracking algorithm suitable for a single target in complex environment, which consists of three parts, the detector (detector), the tracker (tracker) and the learner (learning), which are composed. Unlike traditional tracking and detection methods, TLD algorithm has both detection module and tracking module, and they are not interfering with each other and run at the same time. The modular module of TLD algorithm mainly consists of three modules, and the algorithm structure is shown in Fig. 1. Tracking module: assuming that the tracking objects in the front and rear frames are tracking the field of vision, they are used as a precondition to track the motion of the target. Once the tracking target is lost in the tracking field, the tracking failure will happen. Detection module: assuming each video frame is independent of each other, according to the target model detected and learned, the full graph of each frame is searched to locate the area that the tracking target may appear. However, as with other simple target detection methods, there are also errors in the detection modules in TLD. The errors are divided into two cases, which are the positive sample as negative sample and the negative sample as the positive sample. Learning module: according to the results of the tracking module, the two errors of the detection module are evaluated, and the training samples are generated to update the target model of the detection module according to the results of the evaluation, and the key feature points of the tracking module are updated to avoid the similar mistakes.

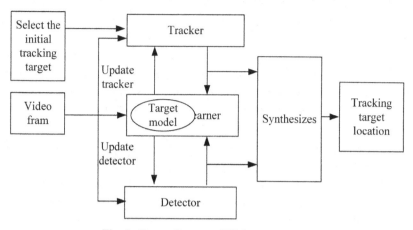

Fig. 1. Frame diagram of TLD components

2 Improved Tracking Learning Detection Algorithm

Feature point extraction is the key step in the process of target detection and tracking by feature matching algorithm. The quality of feature point extraction will directly affect the follow-up detection or tracking work [9, 10]. SURF, SIFT, BRISK, ORB and FREAK are common feature points extraction algorithms [11]. The ORB algorithm is proposed by Zhu and others in the article "Copy-move forgery detection based on scaled ORB" in 2016. Based on the well-known feature descriptor of Fast feature detection and the Brief descriptor proposed by Calonder et al. [13, 14]. In recent years, the feature points are directed to the feature points, and the feature points are rotated [15–17]. Based on meanwhile, we propose to solve the problem of scale invariance by constructing Pyramid method. The ORB feature matching algorithm steps are as follows:

Step 1: First of all, the scale Pyramid is built.
Pyramid has a total N level, which is different from SIFT, with only one image per layer. The scale of layer S is:

$$scale_s = Fator^s \tag{1}$$

The *Fator* is the initial scale (the default is 1.2), and the original is on the zeroth level. Layer s image size is:

$$Size_s = (H * \frac{1}{scale}) \times (W * \frac{1}{scale}) \tag{2}$$

Among them, H is the height of the initial image, and W is the width of the initial image.

Step 2: Using Faster to detect feature points on different scales.

On each layer, the feature points N need to be extracted by formula are calculated, and the Faster corner response values are sorted on this layer, $2N$ feature points are extracted before and then sorted according to the response value of Harris corner points, and the former N feature points are taken as the feature points of this layer.

$$N = \sum_{x \forall (circle(p))} |I(x) - I(P)| > \varepsilon_d \tag{3}$$

The P is the candidate point, and $I(X)$ is the gray value of any point on the circle of the circle with the P point. $I(P)$ is the gray value of the center P, the epsilon ε_d is the threshold, and if $N > \varepsilon_d$ determines that P is a feature point.

Step 3: Calculate the main direction of each feature point.

Taking the feature points obtained in step 2 as the center, the Cartesian coordinate system is set up. In this field, the center of mass is calculated in S, then the feature point is the starting point and the center of mass is the direction vector. The direction of the direction vector is the direction of the feature point. The moment of the region S is:

$$m_{p,q} = \sum_{x,y} x^p y^q I(x, y) \tag{4}$$

Regional centroid:

$$C = \left(\frac{m_{1,0}}{m_{0,0}}, \frac{m_{0,1}}{m_{0,0}} \right) \tag{5}$$

Characteristic point direction:

$$\theta = \arctan \left(\frac{m_{0,1}}{m_{1,0}} \right) \tag{6}$$

Including: X, y, $-[-R, R]$, R and P is at the center of the circle radius, P feature points, Q as the center point.

Step 4: Rotate the Patch of each feature point to the main direction, and use the 256 best descriptors selected by the above step 3 to account for 32 bytes.

Test criteria for τ:

$$\tau(P; x, y) = \begin{cases} 1, & P(x) < P(y) \\ 0, & P(x) \geq P(y) \end{cases} \tag{7}$$

N-dimensional binary bit strings:

$$f_n(P) = \sum_{1 \leq i \leq n} 2^{i-1} \tau(P; x_i, y_i) \tag{8}$$

Among them: P is the image domain of $S \times S$ size, $P(x)$ is the gray value of P at x in the image domain, $P(y)$ is the gray value of P in the y area of the image domain. (x_i, y_i) represents a test point pair, In formula (8) $n = 256$.

Step 5: Use the Hamming distance to match the feature points.

Suppose k_1, k_2 is the feature point obtained by the ORB algorithm:

$$k_1 = x_0x_1x_2 \cdots x_{255}, \quad k_2 = y_0y_1y_2 \cdots y_{255} \qquad (9)$$

Then, the Hamming distance of two 256 dimensional ORB feature points is calculated by calculation to get the similarity between them.

$$D(k_1, k_2) = \sum_0^{255} x_i \oplus y_i \qquad (10)$$

$D(k_1, k_2)$ represents similarity, a larger value indicates a lower similarity.

In order to verify the characteristics of ORB feature points, a group of experiments were carried out, and the experimental results were shown in Fig. 2 (the threshold in experiment is 2000). From Fig. 2(a) and Fig. 2(b), we can see that ORB feature points overcome the problem of rotation and noise better, and have good rotation invariant characteristics and anti noise characteristics.

(a) Rotation

(b) Noise

Fig. 2. ORB feature point matching effect

In order to further verify that the execution speed of the ORB algorithm is far superior to the previous SIFT and SURF algorithms, the data sets (mainly used for feature detection and matching) provided by Mikolajczyk and Schmid are used for experiments. The experimental results are shown in Table 1. By contrast, the execution speed of ORB is much better than that of other algorithms.

Table 1. Comparison of detection speed and matching speed between 5 feature points.

Algorithm	SIFT	SURF	ORB
Successful matching logarithm	5335	2809	446
Total time (s)	13.9123	4.17253	0.36394
Matching speed (ms)	2.6081	1.4849	0.7931

3   TLD Algorithm Based on ORB Feature Point Improvement

In the process of moving target tracking, the traditional TLD algorithm tends to track the drift due to the tracking target occluded or the moving speed is too fast, which leads to the failure of tracking. From the 2.1 section, we can see that ORB feature points are insensitive to noise, rotation invariance and fast execution speed, which satisfy the requirement of saliency feature points. Therefore, this algorithm combines traditional TLD algorithm and ORB feature points to transform the tracking module in traditional TLD algorithm. The ORB feature point and the uniform feature point are used in a mixed way, rather than using the ORB feature point alone, because the target tracking failure can be caused when the ORB feature point of the tracking target is not extracted or when it is very small. The algorithm of the improved tracker is as follows:

Input: I_{t-1}, I_t, b_{t-1}
Output: $b_t \leftarrow (b_{t-1}, T, S)$

Step1: The selected tracking target is uniformly sampled to get the initial tracking point $R_{t-1} = \left\{ x_1^{t-1}, x_2^{t-1}, \cdots, x_M^{t-1} \right\}$, R_{t-1} refers to 100 uniform feature points in b_{t-1}.

Step 2: Using the ORB algorithm, the feature point $K_t = \left\{ x_1^t, x_2^t, \cdots, x_m^t \right\}$ between I_{t-1} and I_t are obtained. Optimum matching is used to get the optimal feature point $\overline{K}_t = \left\{ x_1^t, x_2^t, \cdots, x_n^t \right\}$.

Step 3: If the feature point $\overline{R}_t$ found in Step2, $\overline{K}_t$ and R_{t-1} are combined into F as a reliable tracking point to predict.

Step 4: If the best feature points are not found in Step2, the optical flow method will be used, Calculate the trace points $R_t = \left\{ x_1^{t-1}, x_2^{t-1}, \cdots, x_M^{t-1} \right\}$ and $\overline{R_{t-1}} = \left\{ \overline{x_1^{t-1}}, \overline{x_2^{t-1}}, \cdots, \overline{x_M^{t-1}} \right\}$ from I_{t-1} to I_t.

Step 5: Evaluation of tracking error fb $= FB(R_{t-1}, \overline{R_{t-1}})$, ncc $= NCC(R_{t-1}, R_t)$, Among them, FB refers to the error of the forward and backward direction; NCC refers to a normalized cross-correlation.

Step 6: Filter out the peripheral points to $R = \{(R_{t-1}, R_t) | ncc > M\,ncc, fb < M\,fb\}$, Among them, $M\,fb = med(fb)$, $M\,ncc = med(ncc)$, med refers to an array for an intermediate value.

Step 7: The tracking points R and K_t feature points into a reliable point is $\overline{R}$.

Step 8: Using reliable $\overline{R}$ to evaluate scale transformation S and translation transform T:

$$S = \text{med}\left\{ \frac{\left\| x_i^t - x_j^t \right\|}{\left\| x_i^{t-1} - x_j^{t-1} \right\|}, i \neq j \right\} \tag{11}$$

$$T = \text{med}(d_x, d_y) \tag{12}$$

Among them, d_x, d_y respectively refer to R_t and R_{t-1}, which want to reduce the horizontal and vertical components.

4　Experimental Results and Analysis

In this paper, the traditional TLD algorithm and ORB based O-TLD algorithm are experimentation in the same complex environment respectively. Figure 3 is the tracking experiment result of the traditional TLD algorithm, and Fig. 4 is the tracking experiment result of O-TLD algorithm.

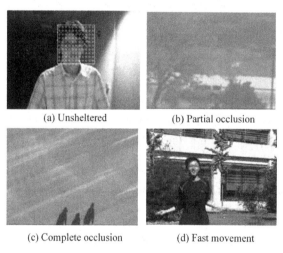

(a) Unsheltered　　　　　　　　(b) Partial occlusion

(c) Complete occlusion　　　　　(d) Fast movement

Fig. 3. The tracking results of the original TLD algorithm

Figure 3(a) and Fig. 4(a) show the tracking effect of the moving target under no occlusion. The TLD algorithm and the O-TLD algorithm all follow the success, but by contrast, the tracking effect of the O-TLD algorithm is better; Fig. 3(b) and Fig. 4(b) show the tracking effect of the moving target under partial occlusion, the TLD algorithm tracking failure, the O-TLD algorithm heel Fig. 3(c) and Fig. 4(c) show the tracking effect that the moving target has just left the camera field of vision (complete occlusion). The O-TLD algorithm is successfully traced to the position of the moving target to leave the camera field, while the TLD algorithm fails to track the target, Fig. 3(d) and Fig. 4(d) show the tracking effect of the fast motion of the moving target. The fast motion of the

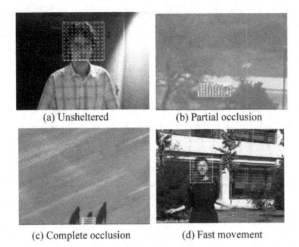

(a) Unsheltered   (b) Partial occlusion

(c) Complete occlusion   (d) Fast movement

Fig. 4. The tracking results of the improved TLD algorithm

moving target produces motion blur, the TLD algorithm fails to track, and the O-TLD algorithm tracks the moving target better. The following results are summarized, and two points are obtained. (1) when moving targets are not blocked, O-TLD algorithm has better tracking effect and higher accuracy. (2) when the tracking target appears partial occlusion, complete occlusion (just leaving the field of vision) and fast moving, the O-TLD algorithm can better overcome these problems, successfully track the moving target and have better robustness.

In order to verify the performance of the algorithm in different experimental environments, 15 test video sequences were selected in TB-100, and TLD algorithm and O-TLD algorithm were tested. 15 of the selected video sequences cover a variety of problems, such as fast moving, illumination change, scale change, background similar interference, motion blur, occlusion and beyond the field of vision. This experiment uses 2 performance indicators to evaluate the performance of tracking: (1) the success rate (Success Rate, SR): the ratio of the number of successful tracking frames to the total number of frames. (2) the average time consuming (Average Consumption Time, ACT): refers to the average time of processing each frame. Table 2 shows the average data of two algorithms on 15 test videos. Figure 5 shows the performance comparison between O-TLD and TLD algorithm.

Table 2. The test results of the video.

Item	SR/(%)		ACT/(ms)	
Algorithm	TLD method	O-TLD method	TLD method	O-TLD method
Mean value	52.1	67.6	14.23	12.38

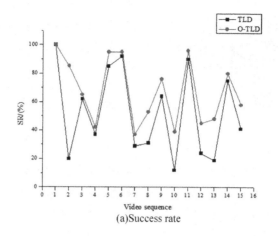

(a)Success rate

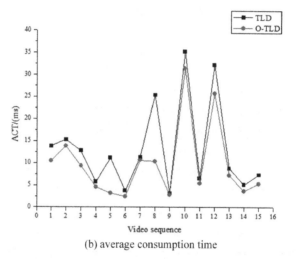

(b) average consumption time

Fig. 5. O-TLD algorithm and TLD algorithm

From the average data of Table 2, we know that the accuracy of O-TLD algorithm is about 15% higher than that of TLD algorithm, and the average consumption time is less than 2 ms. The analysis of Fig. 5(a) shows that the success rate of O-TLD algorithm is much higher than that of TLD algorithm. The analysis of Fig. 5(b) shows that the average consumption time of O-TLD algorithm is much lower than that of TLD algorithm. Therefore, the O-TLD algorithm proposed in this paper has better success rate and execution speed. The experimental results also prove that the O-TLD algorithm is more accurate and real-time.

5 Conclusion

This paper mainly improves the tracker in TLD, introduces the ORB feature points, and preserves the original uniform distribution point, and solves the problem of occlusion and fast moving of the moving target, and improves the robustness, accuracy and execution speed of the algorithm. The experimental results show that the improved TLD is better than the traditional TLD performance in terms of robustness and execution speed, but it is only a single target tracking, and further research is needed in the tracking of multiple targets. In the future work, we will further improve the TLD tracking algorithm to achieve multi-target motion tracking.

Acknowledgements. This work was supported in part by the his work was supported by National Natural Science Fund of China (61806088, 61603159), Qing Lan Project of Jiangsu Province and Natural Science Fund of Changzhou (CE20175026).

References

1. Lv, L., Fan, T., Li, Q., Sun, Z., Xu, L.: Object tracking with improved firefly algorithm. Int. J. Comput. Sci. Math. **9**(3), 219–231 (2018)
2. Chen, X., Zhong, H., Bao, Z.: A GLCM-feature-based approach for reversible image transformation. Comput. Mater. Contin. **59**(1), 239–255 (2019)
3. Kalal, Z., Mikolajczyk, K., Matas, J.: Tracking-learning-detection. IEEE Trans. Patten Anal. Mach. Intell. **34**(7), 1409–1422 (2012)
4. Maamar, A., Benahmed, K.: A hybrid model for anomalies detection in AMI system combining K-means clustering and deep neural network. Comput. Mater. Contin. **60**(1), 15–39 (2019)
5. Liu, J., Zhang, B., Cheng, X., Chen, Y., Zhao, L.: An adaptive superpixel tracker using multiple features. Comput. Mater. Contin. **60**(3), 1097–1108 (2019)
6. Hare, S., Saffari, A., Torr, P.H.S.: Struck: structured output tracking with kernels. IEEE Trans. Pattern Anal. Mach. Intell. **38**(10), 2096–2109 (2016)
7. Wang, J., Zhao, M., Zou, L., Hu, Y., Cheng, X., Liu, X.: Fish tracking based on improved TLD algorithm in real-world underwater environment. Mar. Technol. Soc. J. **53**(3), 80–89 (2019)
8. Medouakh, S., Boumehraz, M., Terki, N.: Improved object tracking via joint color-LPQ texture histogram based mean shift algorithm. Signal Image Video Process. **12**(3), 583–590 (2017). https://doi.org/10.1007/s11760-017-1196-2
9. He, Z., Li, X., You, X., Tao, D., Tang, Y.Y.: Connected component model for multi-object tracking. IEEE Trans. Image Process. **25**(8), 3698–3711 (2016)
10. Zhang, C., Huang, Y., Wang, Z., Jiang, H., Yan, D.: Cross-camera multi-person tracking by leveraging fast graph mining algorithm. J. Vis. Commun. Image Represent. **55**, 711–719 (2018)
11. Suo, C., Yang, D., Liu, Y.: Comparing SIFT, SURF, BRISK, ORB and FREAK in some different perspectives. Beijing Surv. Mapp. **4**, 23–26 (2014)
12. Zhu, Y., Shen, X., Chen, H.: Copy-move forgery detection based on scaled ORB. Multimedia Tools Appl. **75**(6), 3221–3233 (2015)
13. George, A., Joseph, X.F.: Object recognition algorithms for computer vision system: a survey. Int. J. Pure Appl. Math. **117**(21), 69–74 (2017)

14. Mur-Artal, R., Montiel, J.M.M., Tardos, J.D.: ORB-SLAM: a versatile and accurate monocular SLAM system. IEEE Trans. Robot. **31**(5), 1147–1163 (2015)
15. Xu, H.K., Qun, Y.Y., Chen, H.R.: Feature points matching in images based on improved ORB. Sci. Technol. Eng. **14**(18), 105–109 (2014)
16. Ozuysal, M., Calonder, M., Lepetit, V., Fua, P.: Fast keypoint recognition using random ferns. IEEE Trans. Pattern Anal. Mach. Intell. **32**(3), 448–461 (2009)
17. Zhuo, L., Geng, Z., Zhang, J., Li, X.G.: ORB feature based web pornographic image recognition. Neurocomputing **173**, 511–517 (2016)

Identity-Checking for Provable Data Possession Without Privacy Leakage

Jiaqi Wang[1(✉)], Shengke Zeng[2], and Shiliang Li[1]

[1] School of Computer and Software Engineering, Xihua University, Chengdu 610039, China
jerry_salvatore@qq.com
[2] School of Computer Science and Engineering, University of Electronic Science and Technology of China, Chengdu 611731, China

Abstract. The user data stored in remote server should be assured intact. Remote data integrity checking scheme (RDIC) allows a third party auditor (TPA) to examine the integrity of data in cloud server. As we know, the user authentication is necessary in the cloud storage. Obviously, the user identity is sensitive as the user can be identified when it requests integrity checking. In this paper, we employ zero-knowledge undeniable signature to RDIC to tackle the privacy leakage. There is no evidence to show the user checking, thus the user privacy is protected.

Keywords: Cloud storage · Privacy preserving · Data integrity · Provable data possession

1 Introduction

In the era of big data, due to the fact that everyone has a lot of data need to upload and download [6,15], the traditional remote data integrity checking is far from satisfying people's needs. Since cloud storage has huge memory and computing resources which breaks the restrictions of geography and storage for users, the original method by comparing hash value is not suit for current situation for the lack of local copy anymore. Thus, the paradigm of provable data possession (PDP) was first proposed by Giuseppe Ateniese et al. [1].

In the model of provable data possession, taking consideration of users' computation resource and the size of the file, generally speaking, a third party auditor (TPA) could be employed by data owners to check the integrity of the file with a high probability to prevent some malicious cloud servers delete or lost users' data, which could bring a good deal of benefits for data owners. For example, data owners can save more time and energy to manage their outsourced file [12,14]. However, the foundation of provable data possession lie in the truthful

This work is supported by the Ministry of Education "chunhui plan" (Z2016150), Sichuan Science and Technology Program (2018GZDZX0008) and Chengdu Science and Technology Program (2018-YF08-00007-GX).

© Springer Nature Singapore Pte Ltd. 2020
X. Sun et al. (Eds.): ICAIS 2020, CCIS 1254, pp. 69–80, 2020.
https://doi.org/10.1007/978-981-15-8101-4_8

interaction between users and cloud. Owning to the reason that the user purchase the server's service, for the general case, the cloud service should only be available to those honest and already paid users [10,18]. Therefore, in this circumstances, in order to ensure the legitimacy of the user's identity while not revealing the user's privacy, we proposed our scheme.

1.1 Motivation

In this paper, we would pay more attention to the contradiction between users and cloud. Considering such a scenario, suppose *Alice* needs to upload some private information to the cloud. What if other one pretends to be *Alice* uploading some junk file? It would lead to network congestion. Therefore, making an authentication before saving data from users directly is widely viewed indispensable to the cloud. In a common sense, *Alice* can make a digital signature on file block labels to convince cloud server the authenticity of her identity. Unfortunately, *Alice* worries her private information would be known to the server.

Several schemes that support identity authentication resorted to group signature or ring signature. But there are both important premises that group signature needs a trusted group manager which still not address the difficulty in essence. And for ring signature, getting the signature of the members of the group is in terms of forming a group. Thus, it is very essential to utilize undeniable signature [7,8] technology for help.

1.2 Related Work

To prevent some malicious cloud server delete data owners' files, a scheme which allow users to check the outsourced date without downloading the whole file was presented by Blum [3]. In 2007, a paradigm called PDP was first introduced by Ateniese et al. [1]. After that, Giuseppe Ateniese et al. continued to propose dynamic PDP notion and its related concrete scheme [2]. But it failed to realize inserting operation. Hence Erway et al. [9] utilized rank-based authenticated skip lists to make PDP model dynamic in 2009. Also the same work has been made by F. Sebé et al. [17] which dramatically reduced the I/O cost at a lower level. Then in 2012, Wang et al. [22] manipulated Merkel Hash Tree (MHT) to enhance the block tag authentication . But it could contribute to replace attack said by Liu et al. [13]. To deal with the problem, Yu et al. [25] picked a tag salt and appended it at the end of the file and they improved their scheme based on identity, filling the gap that no zero-knowledge stored data privacy had ever been realized [24]. At the meantime, to make the protocol more efficient and flexible, Wang et al. [21] distributed the PDP in multi cloud storage .

In other aspect, considering to provide anonymity for users, Yu et al. [26] let the users commonly share a secret key and all legal users could use it. But it subjects to the scale of group. Formally, Wang et al. [19] proposed the model of privacy-preserving for shared data which combines the property of ring signature [5,16]. Similar work has been done by [11,20]. Different from the previous one, [4,20] resorted to short group signature method in tag generation algorithm to meet the need of constant tag size. Although the tag size has already had nothing to do with scale of users, the composition of uploader's tag is still complex. Because the group $\mathbb{G}_1$ has four elements, $\mathbb{G}_2$ has one and other six elements are from $\mathbb{Z}_p^*$. Therefore, aimed at optimize both efficiency and privacy, Wu et al. [23] constructed a special three triples of tag. But the cloud still know the privacy is from one of the group members and the data owners need to form a group first before uploading.

1.3 Contributions

In this paper, we focus on eliminating the contradiction between identity verification and privacy preserving problem. We proposed the new model called privacy-preserving authentication for cloud audit (PPACA). We construct a 4-round interaction between user and cloud server by utilizing undeniable signature [7,8].

1.4 Paper Organization

The following part is organized as follows. Section 2 we review some preliminaries. Section 3 we formalize our model: PPACA. Section 4 concretes our PPACA protocol. Section 5 the soundness of our PPACA scheme will be formally proven and its performance will be analyzed. In the end, we conclude the paper in Section 6.

2 Preliminaries

2.1 Bilinear Map

A bilinear map is a function that generates an element of the third vector space from elements in two vector spaces, and the function is linear for each parameter. Specifically, let $\mathbb{G}_1$ and $\mathbb{G}_2$ be two cyclic group. The prime order is q. Typically, $e\colon \mathbb{G}_1 \times \mathbb{G}_1 \to \mathbb{G}_2$ is a bilinear pairing map function if it meets the following properties:

1) Bilinear: $\hat{e}(u^a, v^b) = \hat{e}(u, v)^{ab}$, for all $u, v \in \mathbb{G}_1$ and $a, b \in \mathbb{Z}_q$.
2) Non-degeneracy: $\hat{e}(g, g) \neq 1$, for generator g.
3) Computable: $\hat{e}(u^a, v^b)$ can be computed efficiently for any $u, v \in \mathbb{G}_1$ and $a, b \in \mathbb{Z}_q$.

2.2 Computational Diffie-Hellman (CDH) Problem

(CDH Problem). Let $\hat{e} : \mathbb{G}_1 \times \mathbb{G}_1 \to \mathbb{G}_2$ be a bilinear pairing map function. The following is the CDH problem: Given $(g, g^a, g^b) \in \mathbb{G}_1$ for randomly chosen $a, b \in \mathbb{Z}_q$, compute $g^{ab} \in \mathbb{G}_1$. We say a adversary has advantage ϵ in solving the problem if

$$\Pr[g^{ab} \leftarrow \mathcal{A}(g, g^a, g^b)] \geq \epsilon.$$

Definition 1. *(CDH Assumption). For any polynomial-time adversary, the advantage in solving the CDH problem is negligible in the CDH assumption.*

2.3 Syntax of Undeniable Signature

(Protocol). We suppose the prime order q and a primitive element g are public for any signers. x is signer's private key and g^x corresponds the public key. The message is m and the signature $z = m^x$. So the challenge is the form of

$$z^a(g^x)^b,$$

where the a and b are independently and uniformly selected by verifier from the group elements. Next, the signer needs to calculate the response as the form of

$$m^a g^b$$

to pass the verification.

A secure undeniable signature scheme should have the two properties such as confirmation and disavowal.

Confirmation. The signer S can convince the verifier that his signature is valid by providing a correct response.

Disavowal. Even the signer S has infinite computing power, S still cannot provide an incorrect response for his valid signature with exceeding q^{-1} probability.

3   The Model of PPACA Scheme

3.1   System Components of PPACA Scheme

As we can see in Fig. 1, the components of an PPACA consist of mainly three entities, namely the users, the cloud server and the third party auditor (TPA).

– Users: Any user can use his or her secret key to calculate the label of the message which is stored in a certain message block with index tag. Then, user can upload the index message tag tuple to the server.
– Cloud Server (CS): It is an entity which has huge memory space and significant computation resource to maintain files from data owners. Typically, the message block is the basic storage element and it is labeled by index. Each tag and the message are stored in corresponding message block.
– Third Party Auditor (TPA): The TPA receives audit requests from a set of users and challenges the server to perform audits by using some message block indexes and corresponding challenge values. It then, on behalf of user, checks the validity of the server response and notifies the user of the results.

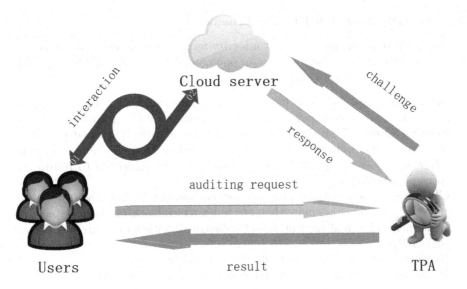

Fig. 1. Components of an PPACA system.

3.2 Syntax of PPACA Scheme

A PPACA model includes 6 algorithms. They are listed below: Setup, KeyGen, Sign, Interaction, Challenge, Respond and Verify. The following is the detail of each algorithm.

- **Setup**(1^k): Input the security parameter 1^k. Then it outputs some public parameter. Moreover, this algorithm still generates the public and the secret key pair (pk_j, sk_j) for the jth users.
- **Sign**(sk_j, i, m_i): Next, the jth user inputs sk_j, i and m_i to generate an index-message-tag $\sigma_{ij} = (i, m_i, \sigma_{ij})$. The index-message-tag will be uploaded in the cloud.
- **Authentication**(σ_{ij}): Upon receiving σ_{ij} from the user, the cloud need to confirm the validity of the tag. Hence, the user has to make an undeniable signature with the cloud.
- **Challenge**(pk_j, $\mathcal{P}$): The TPA takes the public keys and randomly select $\mathcal{P}$ from block sectors S to generate the challenge *chal*. After that, TPA sends the *chal* to the cloud.
- **Respond**(*chal*, M, Σ): Getting the challenge, the server calculates the message $M = \{m_i| \ i \in \mathcal{P}\}$ and the associated tags $\Sigma = \{\sigma_{ij}| \ i \in \mathcal{P}\}$ to generate the response(σ_{res}, μ). Then the cloud will reply it to TPA.
- **Verify**(σ_{res}, μ, *chal*): The TPA utilities the secret value s and the challenge *chal* to verify the response. Hence, the TPA outputs '1' when the verification correct and '0' for false.

3.3   Security Model of PPACA Scheme

We say a PPACA scheme can resist integrity forgery if there exists no IF adversary who can win the following game in polynomial time t with a non-negligible advantage $Adv_{\mathcal{A}}^{IF}$ against challenger $\mathcal{C}$.

- **Setup:** First, the challenger inputs the security parameter 1^k. Then it outputs some public parameter and public key pk_j which would be given to adversary.
- **Signing Query:** The signing oracle could be adaptively queried by adversary for the index-message pair (i, m_i). According to the public key pk_j the adversary chooses, the challenger utilities the sign algorithm to return the corresponding tag σ_{ij}.
- **Challenge:** The adversary randomly selects a subset $\mathcal{P}^*$ from the storage sector S as long as existing more than one index which has never been accessed to sign oracle. The challenger utilities Challenge algorithm to return a challenge chal of $\mathcal{P}^*$.
- **Respond:** The adversary outputs the respond (σ_{res}, μ).

We define the advantage of the adversary in winning the game as:

$$
Adv_{\mathcal{A}}^{IF} = \Pr \left\langle
\begin{array}{l}
\text{Verify}(\sigma_{res}, \mu, chal\,) \\
\quad = \text{'}1\text{'}
\end{array}
\middle|
\begin{array}{l}
(\text{parameter}, pk_j) \leftarrow Setup(1^k) \\
(pk_j, i, m_i) \leftarrow \mathcal{A}(1^k) \\
\sigma_{ij} \leftarrow Sign(sk_j, i, m_i) \\
\mathcal{P}^* \leftarrow \mathcal{A}(1^k) \\
chal \leftarrow Challenge(pk_j, \mathcal{P}^*) \\
(\sigma_{res}, \mu) \leftarrow \mathcal{A}(chal)
\end{array}
\right\rangle
$$

Definition 2. *For any polynomial time IF adversary $\mathcal{A}$, the advantage of adaptively integrity forgery Attack in PPACA scheme is negligible.*

3.4   Deniability Property of PPACA Scheme

We say a PPACA scheme can reach deniability property if there exists no adversary $\mathcal{A}'$ who can win the following game in polynomial time t with a non-negligible advantage against challenger $\mathcal{C}$.

- **Setup:** First, the challenger inputs the security parameter 1^k. Then it outputs some public parameter and secret key pairs $(sk_1, pk_1, \ldots, sk_n, pk_n)$ which would be given to adversary.
- **Signing Query:** The signing oracle could be adaptively queried by adversary for the index-message pair (i, m_i). According to the public key pk_j the adversary chooses, the challenger utilities the signing algorithm to return the corresponding tag σ_{ij} for $i \in \{1, \ldots, M\}$ and $j \in \{1, \ldots, N\}$.
- **Authentication:** The adversary can adaptively pick σ_{ij} to make an undeniable signature with the algorithm. The algorithm would return a commitment C_1.

- **Challenge:** The challenger randomly selects i' and j' to generate a tag $\sigma_{i'j'}$ through the signing oracle. Then the challenger utilities undeniable signature algorithm to generate a challenge commitment $C_{1'}$.
- **Guess:** The adversary selects a σ_{ij}.

We define the advantage of the adversary in winning the game as:

$$
\mathrm{Adv}_{\mathcal{A}'}^{IND} = \Pr \left\langle \begin{array}{c} i' = i \\ j' = j \end{array} \middle| \begin{array}{c} (\text{parameter}, (sk_1, pk_1), \ldots, (sk_n, pk_n)) \leftarrow \text{Setup}(1^k) \\ (sk_j, pk_j, i, m_i) \leftarrow \mathcal{A}'(1^k) \\ \sigma_{ij} \leftarrow \text{Sign}(sk_j, i, m_i) \\ C_{1'} \leftarrow \text{Authentication}(\sigma_{i'j'}) \\ (i, j) \leftarrow \mathcal{A}'(1^k) \end{array} \right\rangle - \frac{1}{MN}
$$

Definition 3. (Deniability). *The PPACA scheme reaches deniability property for any polynomial time IND adversary $\mathcal{A}'$. The advantage of $\mathrm{Adv}_{\mathcal{A}'}^{IND}$ is negligible.*

4 Construction of PPACA Scheme

4.1 Construction

- **Setup(1^k):** Input the security parameter 1^k. Then it outputs some public parameters $= \{\mathbb{G}_1, \mathbb{G}_2, e : \mathbb{G}_1 \times \mathbb{G}_1 \to \mathbb{G}_2, q, d, g \in \mathbb{G}_1, \text{H}:\{0, 1\}^* \to \mathbb{G}_1\}$. Moreover, this algorithm still generates the public and the secret key pair (pk_j, sk_j) for the jth user U_j. Pick $sk_j = x_j \in \mathbb{Z}_q^*$ and compute $pk_j = g^{x_j}$.
- **Sign(sk_j, i, m_i):** Assume that, the ith message block stores $m_i \in \mathbb{Z}_q$ and U_j can sign the message block like this:

$$
\sigma_{ij} = (\text{H}(i) \cdot d^{m_i})^{\frac{1}{x_j}}.
$$

Then, the tuple of index-message-tag (i, m_i, σ_{ij}) will be upload.
- **Authentication(σ_{ij}):**

  1) Upon receiving σ_{ij} from U_j, The cloud randomly select two number λ_1 and λ_2 to compute a commitment C_1 and send C_1 to user, where

  $$
  C_1 = (\text{H}(i) \cdot d^{m_i})^{\frac{1}{x_j} \cdot \lambda_1} \cdot g^{\lambda_2}.
  $$

  2) Then U_j also randomly selects $\beta \in \mathbb{G}_1$ to calculate a pair of commitments C_2 and C_3, where

  $$
  C_2 = (\text{H}(i) \cdot d^{m_i})^{\frac{1}{x_j} \cdot \beta} \cdot g^{b+\beta},
  $$
  $$
  C_3 = [(\text{H}(i) \cdot d^{m_i})^{\frac{1}{x_j} \cdot \beta} \cdot g^{b+\beta}]^{x_j}.
  $$

  3) Later, to confirm the commitment C_2 and C_3, the server gives user "λ_1" and "λ_2".

4) Next, U_j first checks if

$$C_1 \stackrel{?}{=} (\mathrm{H}(i) \cdot d^{m_i})^{\frac{1}{z_j} \cdot \lambda_1} \cdot g^{\lambda_2}.$$

If it holds, then U_j continues to tell server the value of "β"; Otherwise abort.

5) At last, the server examine the correctness of C_1 and C_2, if right then store U_j's data; Otherwise abort.

– **Challenge**(pk_j, $\mathcal{P}$): U_j recalls TPA to perform the verification. Consequently, TPA randomly selects a subset $\mathcal{P}$ from the storage sector S and randomly chooses $s_i \in \mathbb{Z}_q^*$ for $i \in \mathcal{P}$. $\mathrm{T} = \{(i, s_i) | \ i \in \mathcal{P}\}$. Therefore the challenge $chal = (pk_j, \mathrm{T})$.

– **Respond**(***chal***, ***M***, Σ): Then server calculates the response (σ_{res}, μ):

$$\sigma_{res} = \prod_{(i, \, s_i) \, \in \, \mathrm{T}} \hat{e}(\sigma_{ij}^{s_i}, pk_j) \quad \text{and} \quad \mu = \sum_{(i, \, s_i) \, \in \, \mathrm{T}} s_i \cdot m_i,$$

where $M = \{m_i | \ i \in \mathcal{P}\}$, $\Sigma = \{\sigma_{ij} | \ i \in \mathcal{P}\}$ and σ_{ij} represents the U_j's tag.

– **Verify**(σ_{res}, μ, *chal*): In the end, the TPA verifies whether

$$\sigma_{res} \stackrel{?}{=} \hat{e} \left(\prod_{(i, \, s_i) \, \in \, \mathrm{T}} \mathrm{H}(i)^{s_i} \cdot d^{\mu}, g \right).$$

If the equation holds, it means the message block is stored integrally; Otherwise, TPA does not accept it.

4.2   Comparison

Compared with Wu's scheme [23], our scheme achieves a lower cost of computation. To reach information-theoretical anonymity, their scheme needs to hide the user into a group. However, in our scheme, our privacy preserving solution relys on zero-knowledge undeniable signature. We avoid n pairs of bilinear pairing computation. Hence, the overhead is relatively low.

In other aspect, our scheme achieves a better security property than Wu's scheme. In our scheme, our privacy preserving solution is provided with deniability property. Even if the cloud leak users' data to the TPA, since the copy of authentication can be simulated by anyone, the TPA would not trust the authentication is real. Therefore, the privacy property is relatively better.

5   Security

5.1   Correctness

The verification can be always passed and the elaboration of correctness can be listed as follows.

$$\sigma_{res} = \prod_{(i \cdot s_i \in T)} \hat{e}\left(\sigma_{ij}^{s_i},\ pk_j\right)$$

$$= \prod_{(i \cdot s_i \in T)} \hat{e}\left((\mathrm{H}(i) \cdot d^{m_i})^{\frac{1}{x_j} \cdot s_i},\ g^{x_j}\right)$$

$$= \hat{e}\left(\prod_{(i \cdot s_i \in T)} \mathrm{H}(i)^{s_i} \cdot d^{\mu},\ g\right).$$

5.2   Soundness

Theorem 1. *If a verifier cannot confirm that a malicious server delete data, an instance of the CDH problem can be addressed.*

Proof. Suppose that, an adversary can adaptively access to hash oracle no more than p times and sign oracle within time t. Of course, the adversary may output a valid response with the advantage ϵ. Given the parameters=$\{\mathbb{G}_1, \mathbb{G}_2, q, g, g^a, g^b\}$. The simulator θ is aimed at computing $\hat{e}(g, g)^{ab}$. Thus, a challenger may have advantage over $\frac{\epsilon}{p}$ in addressing CDH problem within time $\mathcal{O}(t)$ by playing a game with adversary.

Setup: Randomly pick $l_0, l_j \in \mathbb{Z}_q^*$ and calculate

$$(g^a)^{l_0}, (g^a)^{l_j}$$

set $d = (g^a)^{l_0}$ and pick hash function H:$\{0, 1\}^* \to \mathbb{G}_1$ as random oracle. Then, give adversary the parameters $= \{\mathbb{G}_1, \mathbb{G}_2, q, \hat{e}, g, d, \mathrm{H}\}$ and U_j's public key

$$pk_j = (g^a)^{l_j}.$$

Hash Queries: For any query for the value of the index, the hash oracle will give adversary the answer. Then the simulator would keep a pre-test paper and he can randomly select $i^* \in \{1, \ldots, p\}$ and $\alpha^* \in \mathbb{Z}_q^*$. If the adversary require the hash value of i^*, then the $k_{i^*} = (g^b)^{\alpha^*}$ will be returned to adversary and (i^*, α^*) will be included in the pre-test paper. Otherwise, randomly choose $\alpha_i \in \mathbb{Z}_q^*$ and include (i, α_i) in the pre-test paper. Then, the adversary will have the value of $k_i = (g^a)^{\alpha_i}$.

Signing Queries: For any query for the ith data block m_i, assume the hash value of i has been hash queried, the oracle would always tell adversary the tag as long as $i \neq i^*$. Therefore here is a valid tag

$$\sigma_{ij} = g^{\frac{\alpha_i}{l_j}} \cdot g^{\frac{l_0 \cdot m_i}{l_j}}$$

$$= (g^{a \cdot \alpha_i})^{\frac{1}{a \cdot l_j}} \cdot (g^{a \cdot l_0 \cdot m_i})^{\frac{1}{a \cdot l_j}}$$

$$= (\mathrm{H}(i) \cdot d^{m_i})^{\frac{1}{sk_j}}$$

Authentication: The adversary can choose λ_1 and λ_2 at random to compute a commitment

$$C_1 = (H(i) \cdot d^{m_i})^{\frac{1}{sk_j} \cdot \lambda_1} \cdot g^{\lambda_2}.$$

And the simulator can choose $\beta \in \mathbb{G}_1$ at random to calculate a pair of commitments

$$C_2 = (H(i) \cdot d^{m_i})^{\frac{1}{sk_j} \cdot \beta} \cdot g^{b+\beta},$$

$$C_3 = [(H(i) \cdot d^{m_i})^{\frac{1}{sk_j} \cdot \beta} \cdot g^{b+\beta}]^{sk_j}.$$

Then, in order to pass the verification, the adversary need to give λ_1, λ_2 and the simulator need to give β.

Challenge: Now the adversary randomly selects a subset $\mathcal{P}^*$ from the storage sector S as long as existing more than one index which has never been accessed to signing oracle. Without loss of generality, suppose there is only one index called i'. Then the simulator would randomly choose s_i, for $i \in \mathcal{P}^*$ and $\gamma \in \mathbb{Z}_q^*$ if and only if $i' = i^*$. Compute

$$U_j = (g^a)^{l_j} \text{ and } T = \{(i, s_i) \mid i \in \mathcal{P}^*\}.$$

Finally, the simulator gives the challenge $chal = (T, U_j)$ to adversary.

Respond: The game will be ended with the response (σ_{res}, μ) calculated by adversary. If and only if

$$\sigma_{res} = \hat{e}\left(\prod_{(i, s_i) \in T} H(i)^{s_i} \cdot d^{\mu}, g \right),$$

the adversary would win the game.

Next, the simulator outputs

$$result = \left[\frac{\hat{e}\left(\displaystyle\prod_{(i, s_i) \in T} H(i)^{s_i} \cdot d^{\mu}, g \right)}{\left(\hat{e} \displaystyle\prod_{(i, s_i) \in T, i \neq i'} g^{\alpha_i}, g \right)^{s_i} \cdot \hat{e}(g^{l_0 \cdot \mu}, g)} \right]^{\frac{1}{(s_{i'} \cdot \alpha^*)}}$$

$$= \hat{e}(H(i')^{s_{i'}}, g^a)^{\frac{1}{(s_{i'} \cdot \alpha^*)}}$$

$$= \hat{e}(g, g)^{ab}.$$

From the above equation, we can make sure one point that whether the challenger can solve the CDH problem relies not only on the valid response the adversary calculate but also for the limitation factor that $i \neq i^*$ in the Signing Query phase and $i' = i^*$ in the Challenge phase. Therefore, with the help of adversary, the advantage of addressing CDH problem is:

$$Adv_{\mathcal{C}}^{CDH} \geq \Pr(\neg abort_\theta) \cdot Adv_{\mathcal{A}} \geq \frac{\epsilon}{p}.$$

Simultaneously, since the λ_1, λ_2 and β are respectively choosen by two parties at random, the process of authentication can be simulated by anyone. Therefore, the privacy leakage problem can be perfectly solved.

6   Conclusion

In this paper, we enhance the security and avoid the drawbacks of previous scheme. Thus, we formally propose our PPACA scheme aimed at checking the legality of user's identity while not revealing user's privacy. At the same time, the correctness and soundness of the scheme has been proved. Therefore, the risk of denial of service attack and privacy breach can be perfectly solved.

References

1. Ateniese, G., et al.: Provable data possession at untrusted stores. In: Proceedings of the 2007 ACM Conference on Computer and Communications Security, CCS 2007, Alexandria, Virginia, USA, 28–31 October 2007, pp. 598–609 (2007)
2. Ateniese, G., Di Pietro, R., Mancini, L.V., Tsudik, G.: Scalable and efficient provable data possession. In: 4th International ICST Conference on Security and Privacy in Communication Networks, SECURECOMM 2008, Istanbul, Turkey, 22–25 September 2008, p. 9 (2008)
3. Blum, M., Evans, W.S., Gemmell, P., Kannan, S., Naor, M.: Checking the correctness of memories. Algorithmica **12**(2/3), 225–244 (1994)
4. Boneh, D., Boyen, X., Shacham, H.: Short group signatures. In: Franklin, M. (ed.) CRYPTO 2004. LNCS, vol. 3152, pp. 41–55. Springer, Heidelberg (2004). https://doi.org/10.1007/978-3-540-28628-8_3
5. Boneh, D., Gentry, C., Lynn, B., Shacham, H.: Aggregate and verifiably encrypted signatures from bilinear maps. In: Biham, E. (ed.) EUROCRYPT 2003. LNCS, vol. 2656, pp. 416–432. Springer, Heidelberg (2003). https://doi.org/10.1007/3-540-39200-9_26
6. Centonze, P.: Security and privacy frameworks for access control big data systems. Comput. Mater. Continua **58**, 361–374 (2019)
7. Chaum, D.: Zero-knowledge undeniable signatures (extended abstract). In: Damgård, I.B. (ed.) EUROCRYPT 1990. LNCS, vol. 473, pp. 458–464. Springer, Heidelberg (1991). https://doi.org/10.1007/3-540-46877-3_41
8. Chaum, D., van Antwerpen, H.: Undeniable signatures. In: Brassard, G. (ed.) CRYPTO 1989. LNCS, vol. 435, pp. 212–216. Springer, New York (1990). https://doi.org/10.1007/0-387-34805-0_20
9. Erway, C.C., Küpçü, A., Papamanthou, C., Tamassia, R.: Dynamic provable data possession. In: Proceedings of the 2009 ACM Conference on Computer and Communications Security, CCS 2009, Chicago, Illinois, USA, 9–13 November 2009, pp. 213–222 (2009)
10. Fang, L., Changchun Yin, L., Zhou, Y.L., Chunhua, S., Xia, J.: A physiological and behavioral feature authentication scheme for medical cloud based on fuzzy-rough core vector machine. Inf. Sci. **507**, 143–160 (2020)
11. Feng, Y., Mu, Y., Yang, G., Liu, J.K.: A new public remote integrity checking scheme with user privacy. In: Foo, E., Stebila, D. (eds.) ACISP 2015. LNCS, vol. 9144, pp. 377–394. Springer, Cham (2015). https://doi.org/10.1007/978-3-319-19962-7_22

12. Li, C., Wang, P., Sun, C., Zhou, K., Huang, P.: Wibpa: an efficient data integrity auditing scheme without bilinear pairings. Comput. Mater. Continua **58**, 319–333 (2019)
13. Liu, C., Ranjan, R., Yang, C., Zhang, X., Wang, L., Chen, J.: Mur-dpa: top-down levelled multi-replica merkle hash tree based secure public auditing for dynamic big data storage on cloud. IEEE Trans. Comput. **64**(9), 2609–2622 (2015)
14. Ren, Y., Leng, Y., Zhu, F., Wang, J., Kim, H.-J.: Data storage mechanism based on blockchain with privacy protection in wireless body area network. Sensors **19**(10), 2395 (2019)
15. Ren, Y.: Data query mechanism based on hash computing power of blockchain in internet of things. Sensors **20**(1), 207 (2020)
16. Rivest, R.L., Shamir, A., Tauman, Y.: How to leak a secret. In: Boyd, C. (ed.) ASIACRYPT 2001. LNCS, vol. 2248, pp. 552–565. Springer, Heidelberg (2001). https://doi.org/10.1007/3-540-45682-1_32
17. Sebé, F., Domingo-Ferrer, J., Martínez-Ballesté, A., Deswarte, Y., Quisquater, J.-J.: Efficient remote data possession checking in critical information infrastructures. IEEE Trans. Knowl. Data Eng. **20**(8), 1034–1038 (2008)
18. Wang, B., Kong, W., Xiong, N.: A dual-chaining watermark scheme for data integrity protection in internet of things. Comput. Mater. Continua **58**, 679–695 (2019)
19. Wang, B., Li, B., Li, H.: Oruta: privacy-preserving public auditing for shared data in the cloud. In: 2012 IEEE Fifth International Conference on Cloud Computing, Honolulu, HI, USA, 24–29 June 2012, pp. 295–302 (2012)
20. Wang, B., Li, H., Li, M.: Privacy-preserving public auditing for shared cloud data supporting group dynamics. In: Proceedings of IEEE International Conference on Communications, ICC 2013, Budapest, Hungary, 9–13 June 2013, pp. 1946–1950 (2013)
21. Wang, H.: Identity-based distributed provable data possession in multicloud storage. IEEE Trans. Serv. Comput. **8**(2), 328–340 (2015)
22. Wang, Q., Wang, C., Li, J., Ren, K., Lou, W.: Enabling public verifiability and data dynamics for storage security in cloud computing. In: Backes, M., Ning, P. (eds.) ESORICS 2009. LNCS, vol. 5789, pp. 355–370. Springer, Heidelberg (2009). https://doi.org/10.1007/978-3-642-04444-1_22
23. Wu, G., Mu, Y., Susilo, W., Guo, F.: Privacy-preserving cloud auditing with multiple uploaders. In: Bao, F., Chen, L., Deng, R.H., Wang, G. (eds.) ISPEC 2016. LNCS, vol. 10060, pp. 224–237. Springer, Cham (2016). https://doi.org/10.1007/978-3-319-49151-6_16
24. Yu, Y.: Identity-based remote data integrity checking with perfect data privacy preserving for cloud storage. IEEE Trans. Inf. Forensics Secur. **12**(4), 767–778 (2017)
25. Yu, Y., et al.: Enhanced privacy of a remote data integrity-checking protocol for secure cloud storage. Int. J. Inf. Secr. **14**(4), 307–318 (2015)
26. Yu, Y., Mu, Y., Ni, J., Deng, J., Huang, K.: Identity privacy-preserving public auditing with dynamic group for secure mobile cloud storage. In: Au, M.H., Carminati, B., Kuo, C.C.J. (eds.) NSS 2014. LNCS, vol. 8792, pp. 28–40. Springer, Cham (2014). https://doi.org/10.1007/978-3-319-11698-3_3

Adversarial Examples Generation System Based on Gradient Shielding of Restricted Region

Weixiong Hu, Zhaoquan Gu[(⊠)], Chuanjing Zhang, Le Wang, and Keke Tang

Cyberspace Institute of Advanced Technology, Guangzhou University, Guangzhou 510006, China
zqgu@gzhu.edu.cn

Abstract. In recent years, deep neural networks have greatly facilitated machine learning tasks. However, emergence of adversarial examples revealed the vulnerability of neural networks. As a result, security of neural networks is drawing more research attention than before and a large number of attack methods have been proposed to generate adversarial examples to evaluate the robustness of neural networks. Furthermore, adversarial examples can be widely adopted in machine vision, natural language processing, and video recognition applications. In this paper, we study adversarial examples against image classification networks. Inspired by the method of detecting key regions in object detection tasks, we built a restrict region-based adversarial example generation system for image classification. We proposed a novel method called gradient mask to generate adversarial examples that have a high attack success rate and small disturbances. The experimental results also validated the method's performance.

Keywords: Adversarial examples · Gradient mask · Restricted region · Image classification

1 Introduction

Neural networks are seeing wider adoption in different fields including medical services, transportation management and control systems. With the development of deep learning in recent years, neural networks have indeed achieved great success. Neural networks are very effective in many complex machine learning tasks. In image recognition, the accuracy of neural networks has reached a level similar to that of human vision [1, 2]. Moreover, neural networks are also widely used in speech recognition [3] and natural language processing [4–6].

However, in 2014, Szegedy et al. [7] first discovered the existence of adversarial examples which imply the neural networks are easy to be fooled by small perturbations added onto the image. The existence of adversarial examples makes people aware of the vulnerability of neural networks. In some areas with high security requirements, such as self-driving, facial payment, financial risk control, the robustness of neural networks is emphasized. Adversarial examples can serve as an important surrogate to evaluate and improve the robustness of models [8]. Adversarial examples have been detected not

© Springer Nature Singapore Pte Ltd. 2020
X. Sun et al. (Eds.): ICAIS 2020, CCIS 1254, pp. 81–91, 2020.
https://doi.org/10.1007/978-981-15-8101-4_9

only in image classification tasks, but also in speech recognition [9], objection detection [10], natural language processing tasks [11] and many real-world applications [12].

In our paper, we focus on generating adversarial example for image classification tasks. Many methods have been proposed to generate adversarial examples in image classification. In 2015, Goodfellow et al. first proposed FGSM (fast gradient sign method) [13] to generate adversarial examples. After that, many gradient-based methods have been proposed, such as BIM (basic iterative method) [14], PGD (project gradient descent) [15] and MI-FGSM (momentum iterative FGSM) [16]. These methods, also known as white-box attacks, entail the gradient information of a given model. White-box attacks assume that the complete knowledge of the network is known beforehand. Black-box attacks are proposed without obtaining the network information in advance. Typical black-box methods include a genetic algorithm proposed in [17], UPSET (universal perturbations for steering to exact targets) and ANGRI (antagonistic network for generating rogue images) [18].

The contributions of the paper is summarized as follows:

1) We proposed a new method to generate adversarial examples, i.e. a restrict region-based gradient mask method.
2) We built a system that users can restrict the attack region by themselves.
3) Our method could have a higher attack success rate and a smaller perturbation range than existing methods.

The remainder of the paper is organized as follows. The next section high-lights the related work. Preliminaries are provided in Sect. 3. We describe our method for Gaussian Noise attacks to the restricted region and gradient mask attacks to the restricted region respectively in Sect. 4. We show the results and analysis in Sect. 5. We discuss about the advantages and disadvantages of the our method in Sect. 6. Finally, we conclude the paper in Sect. 7.

2   Related Work

Because neural networks are vulnerable and inexplicable, many adversarial example generation algorithms have been proposed in recent years to attack neural networks. These algorithms can be classified based on different standards. First, according to the target of attacks, they can be divided into targeted attacks and non-targeted attacks. These algorithms can also be divided into white-box attacks and black-box attacks based on the attacker's understanding of the model. There are also real-world attacks, which we call physical-domain attacks. Next, we will introduce the details.

2.1 Image Classification

Image classification is the process of taking an input (like a picture) and outputting a class (like a cat) or a probability that the input belongs to a particular class (there is a 90% probability that this input is a cat). When you look at a picture of your face, you will recognize it is you, and a computer can also recognize it. The convolutional neural network (CNN) is a class of deep learning neural networks. CNNs represent a huge breakthrough in image recognition. They are widely used to analyze visual imagery and are frequently working behind the scenes in image classification. In our paper, we generate adversarial examples for three CNN models, i.e. VGG16 [24], IncetionV3 [25], ResNet50 [26], to conduct image classification.

2.2 Adversarial Examples

Adversarial examples are specifically created examples that will make models misclassify the input. If an input example is a natural sample, such as a photo from the ImageNet dataset, we call it a clean example. If an input alters the image so that a model mis-classifies the image, we call it an adversarial example. Adversarial attack algorithms do not always succeed in attacking the model. Sometimes, an attacked model may still be able to classify adversarial examples correctly. We can measure the accuracy or error rate of different models on a particular set of adversarial examples.

White-Box Attack. The attacker has all the knowledge of the model, including the structure of the model, all the parameters and the values of trainable weights. If the attacker knows such information, a white-box attack algorithm will transform the problem of generating adversarial examples into an optimization problem. Its purpose is to ensure that the difference between the adversarial examples and the original images is as small as possible so that the adversarial examples can mislead the models.

The L-BFGS [22] algorithm is a commonly-used method to solve function optimization problems in machine learning. Szegedy et al. first proposed the term of "adversarial examples" in 2014. They used the L-BFGS white-box attack algorithm to solve the problem of adversarial example generation. After Szegedy et al. [7] first pointed out the existence of adversarial examples, Goodfellow et al. [13] analyzed the causes. They assumed that the linear behavior in the high-dimensional space is a cause for the generation of adversarial examples, and on that basis, they proposed a classical white-box attack algorithm based on gradient, i.e. the fast gradient sign method (FGSM). After the FGSM algorithm was proposed, a large number of white box attack algorithms based on gradient were proposed, such as the PGD attack, which was considered to be the strongest first-order iterative gradient attack. The mi-fgsm attack proposed in [16] is a gradient attack based on momentum and has won the 2017 NIPS adversarial examples challenge competition. In addition to gradient-based white box attack algorithms, there are many other white box attack algorithms. For example, the C&W attack [19], an optimization-based attack algorithm, realizes attacks mainly by adjusting the parameters c and k. It can adjust the confidence and generate small disturbances, but the speed is slow. There is also a DeepFool attack algorithm [23] based on the decision surface, which iteratively calculates the closest boundary to the original image to find adversarial examples.

Black-Box Attack. Black box attacks are divided into black box attacks with query and black box attacks without query. In black box attacks with query, the attacker does not know much about the model, but can query the model by, for instance, using some inputs and observing the model's outputs. In black box attacks without query, the attacker has limited or no knowledge about the model and is not allowed to use querying methods to build a specific adversarial example. In this case, the attacker must construct a generalized adversarial example that can fool many machine learning models. In [7], Szegedy et al. indicated that adversarial examples could be generalized between different models. In other words, if an adversarial example can fool one model, it can fool other models. In a black-box scenario, an attacker can train his model on the same dataset, or even on other datasets with the same distribution as the trained dataset. The adversarial examples of the model trained by the attacker is likely to be able to fool other unknown target models. We can improve the success rate of the attacking model based on transferability of adversarial examples by systematically designing the model instead of relying on mere luck.

If the attacker is not in a full black box scenario and the query is allowed to be used, a query can be made to train the attacker's own copy of the target model, which is called a "replacement". This approach is very powerful because the input examples as queries do not need to be real training examples; instead, they can be specific examples selected by the attacker to accurately locate the decision boundary of the target model. Therefore, the attacker's model can not only be trained to be a good classifier, but also can actually imitate the details of the target model, so the two models can have a high success rate based on transferability of adversarial examples. One strategy to increase the success rate of adversarial examples in a black-box scenario where the attacker cannot send queries is to combine multiple models into a set as the source model to generate adversarial examples. The basic idea here is that if an adversarial example can fool every model in the entire set, it is more likely to be generalized and fool other models.

3 Preliminaries

3.1 Notations

Neural Networks: A neural network can be regarded as a function $F(x) = y$ that accepts an input $x \in Rn$ and produces an output $y \in Rm$. The model F also implicitly depends on some model parameters θ; in our work, the model is fixed. We produce adversarial examples by constantly adjusting the input of the model. In this paper, we focus on neural networks used as an m-class classifier. The output of the network is computed using the softmax function, which ensures that the output vector y satisfies $0 \leq y_i \leq 1$ and $y_1 + \ldots + y_m = 1$. The output vector y is thus treated as a probability distribution, i.e., y_i is treated as the probability that input x belongs to class i. The classifier assigns the label $C(x) = \text{argmax}_i F(x)_i$ to the input x. Let $C(x)$ be the correct label of x.

Targeted Adversarial Examples: When given a valid input x and a target $t = C(x)$, it is often possible to find a similar input x' such that $C(x') = t$, yet x, x' are close according to some distance metric. An example x' with this property is known as a targeted adversarial example.

Non-targeted Adversarial Examples: Instead of classifying x into a given target class, we only search for an input x' such that $C(x') \neq C(x)$ and x, x' are close.

3.2   Adversarial Attack Algorithms

Fast Gradient Sign Method (FGSM):   In the white box, FGSM calculates the derivative of the model to the input, then obtains its specific gradient direction with the symbolic function, and then multiplies it by a step size, and the resulting "disturbance" is added to the original input to obtain the adversarial example x'.

$$x' = x + \varepsilon \cdot sign(\nabla_x J(x, y)) \tag{1}$$

In Eq. (1), ε is a hyperparameter which is used to control the size of perturbation; Sign($\cdot$) is a sign function to make the perturbation meet the L_{infty} norm bound; $\nabla x J$ is a gradient of the loss function.

Basic Iterative Method (BIM):   The Basic Iterative Method was first introduced in [14]. It is an iterative version of the one-step attack FGSM. In a non-targeted attack setting, it gives an iterative formulation to create x':

$$x_0 = x \tag{2}$$

$$x_{t+1} = Clip_{x,\varepsilon}(x_t + \alpha \cdot sign(\nabla_x L(\theta, x_t, y))) \tag{3}$$

This iterative attacking method is also known as Projected Gradient Method (PGD) if the algorithm is added by a random initialization on x, as used in [15].

Momentum Iterative Fast Gradient Sign Method (MI-FGSM):   This   method assumes that perturbation in every epoch is related not only to the current gradient, but also to the previously calculated gradient. The update procedure is:

$$g^{t+1} = \mu \cdot g^t + \frac{\nabla x J(x_t', y)}{||\nabla x J(x_t', y)||_1} \tag{4}$$

where g_t gathers the gradient information up to the t-th iteration with a decay factor μ.

Carlini & Wagner's method (C&W):   C&W method is a powerful optimization-based method, which solves

$$\arg\min_{x'} ||x' - x||_p - c \cdot J(x', y) \tag{5}$$

where the loss function J could be different from the cross-entropy loss. This method is based on two assumptions. First, adversarial examples generated by this method have the smallest perturbation. Second, adversarial examples generated by this method need to fool the model that is attacked.

4 Method

As we know, an adversarial attack algorithm modifies the pixels of the original image to generate adversarial examples. If the range of modification is large, it would lead to large perturbation to the original image. Our goal, however, is to minimize the perturbation. Although there are black-box attack algorithms that generate adversarial examples by modifying only one pixel in [17], its success rate is very low and its speed is very slow. We try to generate adversarial examples in restricted regions, which is inspired by the attention mechanism [20, 21]. We know that when people observe an image, they will quickly skim the whole image to find the target region of key information, and then complete identification of the image by understanding the key region. Based on this, we tried to generate adversarial examples that only modify the key-information region of an image. In our built system, the region could be selected by the user.

In our work, we designed a system that would allow users to choose the region that they wanted to attack. We used several attack algorithms for comparison, i.e. FGSM, PGD and restrict region attack methods.

Next, we introduce two steps to make restrict region attacks. One is the Gaussian noise perturbation method. To be specific, We produce a Gaussian noise matrix according to the region the user chooses. After that, we add the matrix to the corresponding region of the original image to obtain adversarial examples.

Figure 1 shows the architecture of our method. We initialize the adversarial example with the value of the original image. To select an image classification model that we want to attack, such as an inception model, we calculate the output using the forward function, obtain the gradient using the backpropagation algorithm, and then use the gradient mask method to ignore the gradient outside the restricted region. Finally, we use the PGD algorithm to update adversarial examples. We finish attacks until the number of iteration epochs reaches the preset maximum or until the adversarial example succeeds in fooling the model.

Fig. 1. The architecture of gradient mask method.

The gradient mask method is easy to implement. Figure 2 shows an image of a size of 299 × 299. The size of the restricted region is 229 × 229. We construct a matrix that the shape is the same as the gradient matrix. The value is 1 within the restricted region, while the value is 0 outside the restricted region. We use this matrix to modify the gradient.

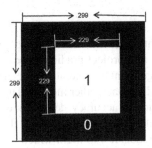

Fig. 2. Gradient mask.

5 Experiments

5.1 Experimental Setup

In our experiments, we use GPU 2080Ti to finish our experiments. We use Python 3.5 and keras 2.2.4 on ubuntu. We choose an ImageNet dataset comprised of 3000 images to conduct our experiments. This dataset is used in the CAAD 2019 CTF Image Adversarial competition. We use three typical models (InceptionV3, VGG16, ResNet50) to make image classification. We compare our algorithm with FGSM [13] and PGD [15], two typical white-box attack methods. For the setting of hyper-parameters, we set the maximum perturbation at $\epsilon = 16$ among all experiments with pixel values in [0,255]. For the iterative attack, we set the maximum number of iteration as 2000. If the number of iteration epochs reaches the maximum number, the algorithm will break forcibly. The learning rate is 1.0.

5.2 Image Classification

In our experiments, we used three models to recognize 3000 images used in the CAAD 2019 CTF Image Adversarial competition. Table 1 shows the recognition accuracy of the three models. We used the weights of Keras's built-in ImageNet dataset. As Table 1 shows, the accuracy of InceptionV3 is the highest.

Table 1. Accuracy of three models.

Model	Accuracy
InceptionV3	**99.866%**
VGG16	76.833%
ResNet50	92.100%

5.3   Gradient-Based Attack

We chose two different gradient-based attack methods to conduct our experiments: fast gradient sign method (FGSM) and project gradient descent (PGD). We use the InceptionV3 model to calculate the gradient to generate adversarial examples. The generated adversarial examples were used to attack other models. The results are shown in Table 2 and we can find that the prediction accuracy decreases dramatically by the gradient-based attack method against the InceptionV3 model. However, we can see that the prediction accuracy of some models is still high, which implies that the attacks are not very successful.

Table 2. Different gradient-based (InceptionV3) attacks on three models.

Model	InceptionV3	VGG16	ResNet50
FGSM	**36.066%**	42.566%	70.233%
PGD	**0.000%**	50.300%	87.700%

Figure 3 shows the adversarial examples generated by the FGSM method and the PGD method for InceptionV3. We use different gradient-based attack methods (FGSM, PGD, MIFGSM) and they are all depicted in Fig. 3. The first column shows the original images, the second column shows the images generated by the FGSM method, and the third column shows the images generated by the PGD method. The prediction accuracy of the models are listed in Table 2.

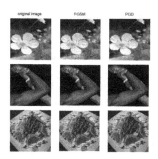

Fig. 3. Original images and adversarial images by FGSM and PGD.

5.4   Restrict Region Attack

In order to reduce perturbation between the adversarial examples and the original ones, We used a restrict region based gradient mask attack method to generate adversarial examples. To facilitate the calculation of the success rate of attacks, we chose a fixed region of a size of 229×229 in the middle of the original image. In our built system, the user can customize the location and size of the attack region.

Figure 4 shows the adversarial examples generated by two restrict region attack methods for InceptionV3, including the Gaussian noise attack and the gradient mask attack. The first column shows the original images, the second column shows the images generated by the Gaussian noise attack method, and the third column shows the images generated by our method. The recognition accuracy of the models is listed in Table 3.

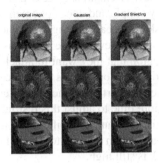

Fig. 4. Original images and adversarial images by Gaussian Noise Attack and our method.

Table 3. Restrict Region Attacks on three models.

Model	InceptionV3	VGG16	ResNet50
Gaussian Noise Attack	**96.366%**	72.333%	91.233%
Iterative Gradient Mask Attack (our)	**0.000%**	36.433%	80.333%

In our work, we find the selection of region is very important, and selecting a proper region can improve the success rate. Figure 5 shows images with different attack regions. The first column is the original image, and the second column is the image with a selected attack region of a size of 229 × 229 on the top left. The third image has a selected attack region of a size of 229 × 229 in the middle. We attacked the images with different attack regions, and found that images with an attack region closer to the image's edges were more difficult to attack successfully. Even when the attack succeeded, it took more time than the image with an attack region in the center. We selected 100 images for comparison and found that the average time for successful attack of the top left region was 92 s, and that for the middle region was 63 s. This indicates that selection of the attack region is very important. A properly selected region means a higher success rate and faster attacks. Hence, we built the system that enables users select any region to generate the adversarial examples.

Fig. 5. Images with different attack regions.

6 Advantages and Disadvantages

In this paper, we propose a method based on gradient mask to generate adversarial examples in restricted areas of images. The experimental results show that the effect is very good. First of all, we restrict the change region of an image so that the overall visual disturbance of an adversarial example is less than that of an original image. Secondly, our algorithm is very simple and does not entail many additional operations. It only implements partial mask of the backpropagation gradient in the restricted region through a mask matrix. There are, however, some problems in our method. Our system allows the user to select the region that they want to attack, but this step increases the processing time and requires additional operations. Then the time of our attack algorithm is unstable and the success rate is uncertain. If the user selects a small region, it means that our algorithm will need more time to adjust this restricted region. What's worse, if the region selected by the user is small and insignificant, or not the region that the model focuses on, it is likely that our algorithm will fail to attack. In general, based on gradient mask, the success rate of attack is still high.

7 Conclusion and Future Work

In this paper, we propose a method based on gradient mask to generate adversarial examples in restricted areas of images. This method alters a limited region of an image and generates smaller perturbation than other existing methods do. Based on the success of the idea of gradient mask, we also want to make similar attempts on the loss function in the future. For example, we can focus on the loss of a certain part of the key area in an image and hide the loss of other parts to generate adversarial examples. In the future, we will conduct more experiments to verity the feasibility of this idea.

Acknowledgement. This work was supported in part by the National Natural Science Foundation of China under Grant 61902082, Grant U1636215, and the National Key R&D Program of China 2019YFB1706003.

References

1. LeCnn, Y., Bottou, L., Bengio, Y., Haffner, P.: Gradientbased learning applied to document recognition. Proc. IEEE **86**(11), 2278–2324 (1998)
2. Krizhevsky, A., Sutskever, I., Hinton, G.E.: ImageNet classification with deep convolutional neural networks. In: Advances in Neural Information Processing Systems, pp. 1097–1105 (2012)
3. Hinton, G., et al.: Deep neural networks for acoustic modeling in speech recognition: the shared views of four research groups. IEEE Sig. Process. Mag. **29**(6), 82–97 (2012)
4. Andor, D., et al.: Globally normalized transition-based neural networks. arXiv preprint arXiv: 1603.06042 (2016)
5. Xu, F., Zhang, X., Xin, Z., Yang, A.: Investigation on the Chinese text sentiment analysis based on convolutional neural networks in deep learning. Comput. Mater. Continua **58**(3), 697–709 (2019)

6. Wang, M., Niu, S., Gao, Z.: A novel scene text recognition method based on deep learning. Comput. Mater. Continua **60**(2), 781–794 (2019)
7. Szegedy, C., et al.: Intriguing properties of neural networks. In: ICLR (2013)
8. Madry, A., Makelov, A., Schmidt, L., Tsipras, D., Vladu, A.: Towards deep learning models resistant to adversarial attacks. In: ICLR (2018)
9. Carlini, N., et al.: Hidden voice commands. In: 25th USENIX Security Symposium (USENIX Security 16), Austin, TX (2016)
10. Xie, C., Wang, J., Zhang, Z., Zhou, Y., Xie, L., Yuille, A.: Adversarial examples for semantic segmentation and object detection. arXiv preprint arXiv:1703.08603 (2017)
11. Ebrahimi, J., Rao, A., Lowd, D., Dou, D.: HotFlip: white-box adversarial examples for text classification. In: ACL (2018)
12. Kurakin, A., Goodfellow, I., Bengio, S.: Adversarial examples in the physical world. arXiv preprint arXiv:1607.02533 (2016)
13. Goodfellow, I., Shlens, J., Szegedy, C.: Explaining and harnessing adversarial examples. In: International Conference on Learning Representations (ICLR) (2015)
14. Kurakin, A., Goodfellow, I., Bengio, S.: Adversarial machine learning at scale. arXiv preprint arXiv:1611.01236 (2017)
15. Madry, A., Makelov, A., Schmidt, L., Tsipras, D., Vladu, A.: Towards deep learning models resistant to adversarial attacks. arXiv preprint arXiv:1706.06083 (2017)
16. Dong, Y., et al.: Boosting adversarial attacks with momentum. In: Proceedings of the IEEE Conference on Computer Vision and Pattern Recognition (CVPR) (2018)
17. Su, J., Vargas, D.V., Sakurai, K.: One pixel attack for fooling deep neural networks. https://arxiv.org/abs/1710.08864 (2017)
18. Sarkar, S., Bansal, A., Mahbub, U., Chellappa, R.: UPSET and ANGRI: Breaking High Performance Image Classifiers, arXiv preprint arXiv:1707.01159 (2017)
19. Carlini, N., Wagner, D.: Towards evaluating the robustness of neural networks. In: IEEE Symposium on Security and Privacy (SP) (2017)
20. Mnih, V., Heess, N., Graves, A., Kavukcuoglu, K.: Recurrent models of visual attention. In: Neural Information Processing Systems (NIPS) (2014)
21. Qiu, J., et al.: Dependency-based local attention approach to neural machine translation. Comput. Mater. Continua **59**(2), 547–562 (2019)
22. Nocedal, J., Wright, S.J.: Numerical Optimization, 2nd edn. Springer, New York (2006). https://doi.org/10.1007/978-0-387-40065-5
23. Moosavi-Dezfooli, S., Fawzi, A., Frossard, P.: DeepFool: a simple and accurate method to fool deep neural networks. In: IEEE Conference on Computer Vision and Pattern Recognition (CVPR) (2016)
24. Simonyan, K., Zisserman, A.: Very deep convolutional networks for large-scale image recognition. Comput. Sci. (2014)
25. Szegedy, C., Vanhoucke, V., Ioffe, S., Shlens, J., Wojna, Z.: Rethinking the inception architecture for computer vision. In: The IEEE Conference on Computer Vision and Pattern Recognition (CVPR) (2016)
26. He, K., Zhang, X., Ren, S., Sun, J.: Deep residual learning for image recognition. In: The IEEE Conference on Computer Vision and Pattern Recognition (CVPR) (2016)

Attribute Value Extraction Based on Rule Matching

Yue Han[1], Weihong Han[1(✉)], Shudong Li[1(✉)], and Zhen Wang[2]

[1] Cyberspace Institute of Advanced Technology,
Guangzhou University, Guangzhou 510006, China
1057894045@qq.com, {hanweihong,lishudong}@gzhu.edu.cn
[2] School of Mechanical Engineering and the Center for Optical Imagery Analysis and Learning
(OPTIMAL), Northwestern Polytechnical University, Xi'an 710072, China

Abstract. Faced with the explosive growth of Internet information today, the Internet is full of public opinion information, which contains rich and valuable data and covers a large amount of false information. How to extract key information from the information published on the Internet is the content of this paper. Since the accuracy of the factual information provided by the encyclopedic text on the Internet is higher than other texts, and for the resume text of the character, the encyclopedic knowledge covers a large amount of unstructured information, and the information has high accuracy. The work of this research is based on the knowledge of Chinese network encyclopedia to obtain key information. The main method is to conduct experiments based on the rule matching mode and the method of extracting attribute values by the language technology platform tool of Harbin Institute of Technology. The experimental results prove the feasibility and accuracy of the extraction effect.

Keywords: Attribute value extraction · Data processing · Rule matching

1 Introduction

In the past ten years, the data of the explosive growth of the information age has been promoted, making the information data of the Internet an important way for people to obtain information in daily life. However, there is a large amount of unstructured and semi-structured information and entity-attribute relationships, which brings certain difficulties to our use of network data to build a knowledge base. Earlier, Michael B and Michael J C [1] proposed an open information extraction technology, followed by Kedar B and Partha P T and others [2] proposed a weakly supervised entity attribute extraction method. Later, for unstructured information extraction, research and breakthroughs were made based on pattern matching methods [3, 4]. For the problem, we can use information extraction technology and entity and attribute relationship extraction technology to build high-quality and high-confidence knowledge base from network data.

The problem studied in this paper is based on the key research and development plan of Guangdong Province, "Large Space Search: Accurate Characters for Public Information". The preliminary purpose of the research is to provide the resume information of

© Springer Nature Singapore Pte Ltd. 2020
X. Sun et al. (Eds.): ICAIS 2020, CCIS 1254, pp. 92–104, 2020.
https://doi.org/10.1007/978-981-15-8101-4_10

the academicians of the Chinese Academy of Engineering and the academicians of the Chinese Academy of Sciences on the Chinese network encyclopedia, extract the attribute values, construct the structured resume information of all academicians, and provide support for the construction of the knowledge base of academicians of the Chinese Academy of Engineering and academicians of the Academy of Sciences.

The main contributions of this paper are as follows. First of all, in the realization process of precision resume engineering project, the attribute value technology mentioned in this paper has an important role in obtaining attribute value information. Then, the paper cleverly borrows the named entity recognition function of the LTP tool to handle part of the task of attribute value extraction.

The overall structure of this paper is as follows. The first part is an overview of the background of attribute value extraction and the overall flow of attribute value extraction. The second part introduces the related work and achievements made by researchers in the field of attribute value extraction in recent years. The third part details the specific algorithmic process of attribute value extraction in the resume project. The fourth part is based on the partial test display and effect analysis of the attribute value extraction in the resume project. The fifth part is a summary analysis of this article.

2 Related Work

Because Wikipedia is composed of a large number of manually labeled and structured information, a large number of researchers now use Wikipedia as a data source to study the automatic acquisition of attributes and attribute values. However, the Chinese network encyclopedia is different from the structure of Wikipedia. Therefore, if you want to apply the knowledge acquisition method for Wikipedia to the knowledge acquisition of Chinese network encyclopedia, the algorithm idea may have some reference, but the specific implementation process is Chinese. Network encyclopedia has certain limitations. The Chinese network encyclopedia covers a wider range of knowledge, and the number of entries and the number of users far exceed the scale of Wikipedia. Each entry article is an exact description of an instance, and the text contains a wealth of attributes and attribute value information. The content of the Chinese Network Encyclopedia is updated faster, and it can reflect the latest hot events in China as soon as possible.

As early as 2007, Fabian M.S et al. [5] proposed a technology called 'YAGO', which is a new ontology that combines high coverage and high quality. It makes effective use of the fact that Wikipedia has category pages, and the core is assembled by Wikipedia. The experiments in this article show the extraction technique, which extends YAGO from the facts of web documents. The more facts YAGO contains, the easier it is to expand through more facts. The result of a unified experiment on WordNet and the facts from Wikipedia was 95% accurate. Soren Auer et al. [6] subsequently studied the availability of structured information from Wikipedia that is highly usable, and it is also the text of Wikipedia that handles the demarcation of attributes and attribute values.

Wu [7], Weld [8] and others backed up the manually labeled Wikipedia text sentences, and obtained training corpus for extracting attribute values, which were used to train the extractor of each attribute. However, most Chinese encyclopedia texts have not been manually labeled. Jun [9] research shows that there are not many related features between different web pages, and most categories of attributes are scattered among the various article articles. Therefore, the more mature methods of dealing with Wikipedia cannot be directly used to process the text of the Chinese Network Encyclopedia.

In the field of extracting category attributes, Tokunago [10] uses large-scale web documents as data sources, using word frequency statistics, document patterns, and HTML tags to extract attributes related to attributes. Pasca [11], Han [12] and Durme [13] cleverly use the search engine to query the log and extract it as a data source. Through deep use of search engine query results, Kopliku [14], Han [15], Sanchez [16], Wei [17], Shudong [18], Wenjie [19] and others use seed instances or patterns as query requests to extract attributes. In the process of extracting attribute values, Yoshinago [20] uses the given attributes to extract attribute values from semi-structured web documents. Probst [21], Chen [22] and Bakalov [23] use semi-supervised learning, using a small number of seeds. Obtain trained data for the decimator that trains the attribute values. Jianyi [24] and Zheng [25] draw on the relevant methods of character attribute extraction, which is used to study the extraction of entity relations, and uses the support vector machine method in machine learning algorithm to judge the relationship.

Mintz [26], Yao [27], Hangfeng [28], Riedel [29], Surdeanu [30], Hoffmann [31], Qing [32], Libo [33], Daojian [34] etc. use the weak supervised method of the knowledge base to use the text of the existing relational instance as the data source and the unlabeled data. Training corpus, the performance of extracting attribute values depends on the size of the training corpus, which often determines the performance of general machine learning algorithms.

In the Chinese Internet Encyclopedia, the descriptions of the members of the Chinese Academy of Engineering and the Chinese Academy of Sciences contain a large amount of textual information, while a small amount of descriptions are incorrect or even wrong. The main work of this paper is to perform more perfect and accurate attribute value extraction tasks for the resume texts of 852 academicians of the Chinese Academy of Engineering and academicians of the Chinese Academy of Sciences in four Chinese online encyclopedias.

3 General Attribute Value Extraction Method

At present, there is a large amount of false information in the introduction part of the existing resume system on the network, which is inconsistent with the actual situation of the character. After the accurate character resume project of this topic is completed, we only need to input the name of a certain character we want to obtain in the system, and the system can automatically return a resume with a higher authenticity. Follow-up on the attribute value extraction task in the project is discussed.

3.1 Brief Description of the Entity Attribute Extraction Process

The overall process of attribute and attribute value extraction can be divided into the following five steps, as shown in Fig. 1 below.

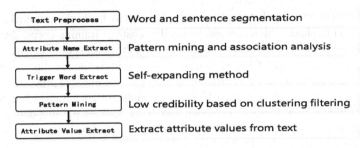

Fig. 1. Entity attribute extraction process

3.2 Overview of Entity Attributes and Attribute Value Extraction Methods

The traditional attribute value extraction method is based on the evolution of machine learning evolution. However, with the rapid growth of computer storage capacity in recent years, the computing speed of computers has increased, and the application of deep learning has become more and more extensive. For the field of attribute value extraction, a large number of researchers use the deep learning method to do the task of attribute value extraction. Figure 2 below is a classification representation of the attribute value extraction method.

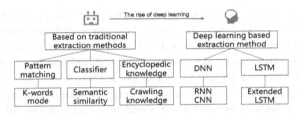

Fig. 2. Classification of attribute value extraction methods

In the traditional attribute value extraction method, the main methods can be divided into three categories, namely the pattern matching method, the classifier-based method and the encyclopedic knowledge method. Among them, for the method of pattern matching, K-words mode matching is commonly used, and the method needs to manually formulate a lexical syntax pattern or a dependency relationship mode. Therefore, the shortcomings of this method are obvious, its extraction performance is poor, the accuracy of the obtained attribute values is relatively low, and the robustness of the established model is weak.

A classifier-based method, which relies on semantic similarity between multiple texts, classifies texts with similar content into one class, and gives some common attribute trigger words for the text as a fixed extraction method for the category. Its shortcoming lies in the generation process of the classifier, which requires a large number of manually labeled training corpora. The quality of the extracted results depends not only on the scale of the manually labeled training corpus, but also on the accuracy of the manually labeled corpus.

The use of network encyclopedia knowledge belongs to the third traditional attribute value extraction method, which can automatically construct training corpus by means of information box knowledge in encyclopedia, saving the process of manually labeling corpus. However, the range of knowledge in encyclopedia is limited, the coverage of training corpus is not high, and it is difficult to cope with the massive processing needs.

In the work of Huanjian [35], the LSTM-based multi-instance multi-label attribute extraction method is used to train the model, and the large-scale training data is generated by the remote supervision method. The overall process of completing the attribute extraction task is as shown in Fig. 3 below.

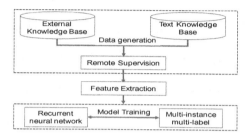

Fig. 3. Attribute extraction based on deep learning

The first step is the process of generating data. This paper uses the external knowledge base and the text knowledge base as the whole data source, and uses remote monitoring to convert the text into the format text needed in the later stage of the city. Then, the process of feature extraction of the standard input text, the learning acquired features will be used as the input of the next recursive neural network. The neural network will adjust the parameters and network structure during the learning and training process, and finally input to the layer of multi-instance and multi-label, which will give feedback to the recurrent neural network layer.

3.3 Overview of Entity Attributes and Attribute Value Extraction Methods

Firstly, the word segmentation work of the acquiring encyclopedia resume is done, and the word segmentation effect using the Boson segmentation is the best. Since the method of using rule matching is very demanding on the input data, it must be very regular. The most important point is to be able to match one of the rule sets written by the match. Therefore, a large amount of data preprocessing work is performed on the acquired webpage text, the data is cleaned, and data with high data quality is obtained as an input of the rule matching process.

In the entire accurate resume project, the flow chart of attribute value extraction is as follows (Fig. 4).

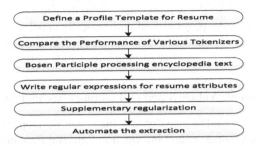

Fig. 4. Program flow chart for attribute value extraction

In the first part, the image below shows part of our attributes for the accurate resume attribute table (Fig. 5).

Fig. 5. Partial attribute display of the accurate resume attribute table

In the second part, the comparative experiments on the Jieba segmentation, the Language Technology Platform (LTP) tools created by Harbin Institute of Technology and the commonly used word segmentation tools show that most of the word segmentation tools are not accurate for the identification of names, while the Boson segmentation can identify the names of the people, and the effect of the participles is more accurate. Therefore, the third step is to use the Boson participle to carry out the preliminary work of text processing.

In the fourth part, we observe a large number of description languages and grammatical features based on the texts introduced by the encyclopedia, and summarize the common grammatical rules and common language patterns of some attributes. Then write the relevant regular expression as the core extraction algorithm of the rule matching algorithm. The fifth part is to improve the applicability of the whole program, manually check a large number of texts, and complete the regular rule set of each attribute, so that the whole program is very robust against various variable network texts.

In the sixth part, we will serialize the entire process of aquiring the encyclopedia text and extracting the attribute values to form a program that automatically extracts the attribute values and outputs the resume attributes of the characters. In this program, our input can be 852 Chinese Academy of Sciences. With the name of each academician in the engineering institute, the program will automatically crawl multiple encyclopedia information from the Internet, and then carry out the process of extracting each attribute value, thereby forming a more accurate resume information of the academician.

3.4 Extracting Attribute Values Based on Language Technology Platform

LTP is an open Chinese natural language processing system developed by Harbin Institute of Technology Social Computing and Information Retrieval Research Center for more than a decade. The tool contains a very important function is the named entity recognition function, which can be used for text segmentation. Partial identification is classified into entities and non-entities. For the entity part, the tool subdivides the three categories of adult name, place name, and organization name.

We took note of this feature of the tool and applied it to the attribute value extraction process of the accurate resume generation project. For the work of extracting attribute values of the sub-attribute part of the organizational unit in the work experience of the character, we abandon the method of using a large amount of human-generated rule set, and select the LTP named entity recognition function to identify the attribute value of the specific statement. For example, information on institutional units. Through programming experiments, we found that this method can more accurately find the attribute value of the organization unit than the original rule matching method, and can extract the name of the organization name appearing in the Chinese sentence. Therefore, it is efficient and accurate to use the method for the attribute value extraction work of the person's service unit.

4 Attribute Value Extraction Implementation Based on Accurate Resume Project

The subsequent experimental content is the practice process of the principle method described earlier. Through the experimental analysis, we can clearly see the partial display of the attribute value extraction, which enables us to have a deeper understanding and understanding of the natural language processing process. The process of natural language processing and the accumulation of experience in the process of code implementation. The experiment is mainly divided into two parts, which are based on rule extraction attribute values and LTP extraction attribute values.

4.1 Data Set

We have selected four common Chinese Internet encyclopedia texts as data sources, namely Baidu Encyclopedia, Sogou Encyclopedia, Interactive Encyclopedia and 360 Encyclopedia. In the realization of the engineering project, the selected objects are 852 academicians of the Chinese Academy of Engineering and academicians of the Chinese

Academy of Sciences. Then use web crawler technology to obtain its encyclopedic knowledge, and use the resume text as the text of the attribute value to be extracted. In the course of subsequent experiments, we only use the well-known biographical information of Obama as an example to briefly explain the experimental process.

4.2 Extracting Attribute Values Based on Rule Matching Method

4.2.1 Text Segmentation Preprocessing

After we fully investigate the performance of the existing multi-word segmentation tools, we choose the Boson segmentation as the word segmentation tool for the resume text. The Boson segmentation industry and business field are the most widely used tools with the best word segmentation.

The following is the pseudo code for the word segmentation process:

```
Define Text Segmentation:
    Input an Academician's Encyclopedia Resume Text;
    For each statement in the text:
        Introduce the Boson NLP tool and import the API;
        Boson NLP tool handles each statement;
   Word segmentation results are stored in plain text as output text.
```

Using the Boson word segmentation tool, we need to register an account with the Boson word segmentation. The account number corresponds to the API interface used by a tool. This API interface needs to be put into the function called the programming function, which is one of the parameters. In the process of running the code, the API password will be executed normally. We selected the resume information of Baidu Encyclopedia of Obama as an example to show the word segmentation (Fig. 6):

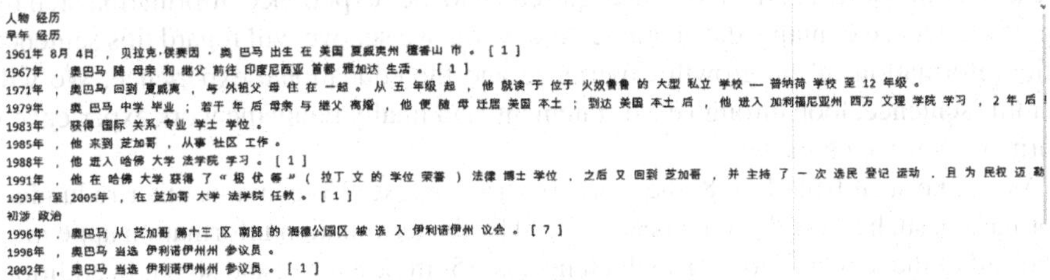
人物 经历
早年 经历
1961年 8月 4日 ， 贝拉克·侯赛因 · 奥 巴马 出生 在 美国 夏威夷州 檀香山 市 。 [1]
1967年 ， 奥巴马 随 母亲 和 继父 前往 印度尼西亚 首都 雅加达 生活 。 [1]
1971年 ， 奥巴马 回到 夏威夷 ， 与 外祖父 母 住 在 一起 。 从 五 年级 起 ， 他 就读 于 位于 火奴鲁鲁 的 大型 私立 学校 — 普纳荷 学校 至 12 年级 。
1979年 ， 奥 巴马 中学 毕业 ； 若干 年 后 母亲 与 继父 离婚 ， 他 便 随 母 迁居 美国 本土 ； 到达 美国 本土 后 ， 他 进入 加利福尼亚州 西方 文理 学院 学习 ， 2 年 后
1983年 ， 获得 国际 关系 专业 学士 学位 。
1985年 ， 他 来到 芝加哥 ， 从事 社区 工作 。
1988年 ， 他 进入 哈佛 大学 法学院 学习 。 [1]
1991年 ， 他 在 哈佛 大学 获得 了 “ 极 优 等 ” （ 拉丁 文 的 学位 荣誉 ） 法律 博士 学位 ， 之后 又 回到 芝加哥 ， 并 主持 了 一 次 选民 登记 活动 ， 且 为 民权 迈 勒
1993年 至 2005年 ， 在 芝加哥 大学 法学院 任教 。 [1]
初涉 政治
1996年 ， 奥巴马 从 芝加哥 第十三 区 南部 的 海德公园区 被 选 入 伊利诺伊州 议会 。 [7]
1998年 ， 奥巴马 当选 伊利诺伊州州 参议员 。
2002年 ， 奥巴马 当选 伊利诺伊州州 参议员 。 [1]

Fig. 6. Participle results display

4.2.2 Text Segmentation Preprocessing

According to the resume text of Obama, after observing and thinking, the text information of the part of the character experience contains a large amount of unstructured redundant information. This information is very confusing for the process of extracting attribute values using the rule matching method. Since the rule matching method requires a very uniform format for the input statement, we need to further filter the text after the word segmentation before using the method to extract the attribute value. The text of the character experience part is the most complicated, as shown in the following Fig. 7, we will elaborate on the information of this part.

竞选 总统
第一 任期
2007年 2月 ， 奥巴马 正式 宣布 竞选 总统 ， 他 在 竞选 中 以 " 变革 " 为 主题 ， 强调 结束 伊拉克 战争 、 实现 能源 自给 停止 减税 政策 和 普及 医疗 保险 等 ， 并 承诺
2008年 8月 27日 ， 他 在 民主党 全国 代表大会 上 获得 总统 候选人 提名 。
2008年 11月 4日 ， 他 在 美国 总统 大选 中 获胜 ， 当选 第44 任 （ 第56 届 ） 美国 总统 ， 并 成为 美国 历史 上 首 位 非洲 裔 总统 。
2009年 1月 20日 ， 奥巴马 正式 宣誓 就职 总统 ； 11月 15日 至 18日 ， 奥巴马 对 中国 进行 国事访问 ， 他 是 首任 就任 一 年 内 访问 中国 的 美国 总统 。 [1] [5]
第二 任期
2012年 11月 6日 ， 奥巴马 在 大选 中 击败 共和党 挑战者 罗姆尼 ， 成功 连任 。 [3]
2016年 5月 15日 ， 奥巴马 出席 罗格斯 大学 毕业 典礼 ， 并 被 授予 荣誉 博士 学位 [8]。
2017年 1月 10日 （ 当地 时间 ） ， 美国 总统 奥巴马 回到 芝加哥 ， 在 麦克考米克 广场 的 湖滨 会议 中心 发表 离任 告别 演说 。 [9 - 10]
离任 生活
2017年 1月 20日 ， 奥巴马 正式 卸任 美国 总统 。 [11]
2018年 5月 21日 ， 美国 在线 影片 租赁 提供 商 Netflix 电影 公司 宣 布巴拉克·奥巴马 和 他 的 妻子 米歇尔·奥巴马 与 该 公司 签署 长期 协议 ， 为 Netflix 公司 制作 电影

Fig. 7. Character experience of Obama

For the person to experience this part of the information, we define four attributes for the work experience, namely the starting time of the job, the termination time of the job, the name of the organization and the title of the job. The process of getting this part of the text from the entire resume text is shown below:

The explanation for the above figure is as follows. In the text we acquired, we defined four parts, namely basic information, character experience, social service and major achievements. Therefore, we use the character experience and social service as the identification words, and intercepting all the texts is the information about the experience of the characters we need. Then, for the information obtained, it also includes the person's growth experience and educational experience, and we only need to get the work experience of the character. Therefore, we have given some high-frequency vocabulary descriptions of the growth experience and the text of the educational experience as feature words, and check the acquired character experience information step by step. If a sentence contains the characteristic words we set, we will regard this sentence as the information of the growth experience and the educational experience. We will filter this sentence, loop through each statement, and finally retain the work experience's information of the character.

As can be seen from Fig. 8, the work experience text also contains other redundant information, such as the digital label "[1, 5, 11]", the termination information appearing at the end of the text "(第56 届)", which means '(56th Session)', and so on. In addition, there are multiple job information in some sentences, we need to extract the title of each job, so before designing the regular expression, we must also consider the structure of the statement, whether it contains multiple job information, split multiple job title information Then, the regular expression is used to extract the title of the job for each support information.

For the process of extracting multiple job information, we need to manually generate a job list, which needs to cover a large number of job titles. For each job statement, according to the expression convention of Chinese language, the job unit and job title are generally closely combined. For example, Professor of Harbin Institute of Technology. Therefore, the design algorithm checks whether the last four words of the statement are in the job list. If it exists in the job list, the word before the statement is regarded as

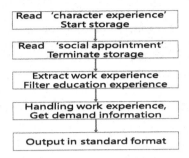

Fig. 8. Character experience of obama

the employer unit, otherwise it is further checked whether the last three words of the statement are in the job list. In turn, decide whether to distinguish between units and titles. If the last three words are still not on the list, use the last two words to check. If they are still not in the list, the last word will definitely appear in the list. Separate the unit of employment from the title of the job. The following figure is a set of selected attributes. The corresponding Chinese meaning is that Obama held the presidency of the United States from January 20, 2009 to January 10, 2017 (Fig. 9).

{'起始时间': '2009年1月20日', '终止时间': '2017年1月10日', '所在单位': '', '职称': '美国总统'},

Fig. 9. Extracted one piece of job attribute information

4.3   Based on LTP to Extract Some Attribute Values

Based on the named entity recognition function of the Harbin Institute of Technology LTP tool, the name, place name, and organization name appearing in the text can be identified and marked with different label symbols. We combine this function with the attribute value extraction task to realize the attribute value extraction task of the unit organization in the job experience.

4.3.1   Based on LTP to Extract Some Attribute Values

The installation process of the tool's pyltp version requires the computer to be configured with a python environment and installed using the pip install command. In addition, the tool also needs a model file, which can be downloaded from the LTP website. When using the tool in the program, you need to import the path of the model from the local folder to use the various functions of the tool. As shown below (Fig. 10):

4.3.2   Extracting the Attribute Values of the Organization Using LTP

The pseudo code to call the tool is as follows:

```
LTP_DATA_DIR = r'I:\Coding_Practice\LTP\ltp_data_v3.4.0'  # Path to the ltp model directory
cws_model_path = os.path.join(LTP_DATA_DIR, 'cws.model')  # Segmentation model path
pos_model_path = os.path.join(LTP_DATA_DIR, 'pos.model')  # Part of speech tagging model path
ner_model_path = os.path.join(LTP_DATA_DIR, 'ner.model')  # Named entity recognition model path
par_model_path = os.path.join(LTP_DATA_DIR, 'parser.model')  # Dependency Syntax Analysis Model Path
srl_model_path = os.path.join(LTP_DATA_DIR, 'srl')  # Semantic role labeling model directory path
```

Fig. 10. Importing a model file in a program

Import model files and paths;
Define named entity recognition function:
    Initialize the instance and import the named entity recognition model;
    Enter the statement into the model function;
    Function output statement with named entity annotation;
    Release the model to free up memory space.

The tool includes word segmentation, part-of-speech tagging, named entity recognition, dependency parsing and semantic role tagging. In combination with accurate resume projects, we only use named entity recognition.

The results of the extraction of the two statements are shown below (Fig. 11):

```
{'起始时间': '2002年', '终止时间': '', '所在单位': '伊利诺伊州', '职称': '州参议员'},
{'起始时间': '2004年', '终止时间': '', '所在单位': '联邦', '职称': '参议员'},
```

Fig. 11. Extracting the attribute values using LTP

Interpretation of the above Chinese: Obama has served as state senator in Illinois since 2002, and Obama has served in the federal Senate since 2004.

As can be seen from the extraction results, the statement is a text containing multiple job information. For the second result, the attribute of the unit is equivalent to the first result, so it is not displayed, only the change of the position is displayed. According to this method, the information of the unit organizations in all the experience is extracted. The results of the extraction of 852 academicians show that the accuracy and efficiency of the extraction results will be higher only on this attribute.

5   Conclusion

This paper is mainly based on the attribute value extraction task in the accurate resume generation system. The resume information of 852 academicians of the Chinese Academy of Sciences and the Chinese Academy of Sciences in four Chinese encyclopedias is used as a data source, word segmentation, and filtering of redundant information. Then use the regular matching method and Harbin Institute of Technology's language technology platform tools to jointly extract the attribute values, and finally get a more accurate 852 academician's resume text. Subsequent research work will focus on the study of deep learning. In the future, deep learning methods can be considered to extract the academician's resume information in order to further improve the efficiency and accuracy of the information.

Acknowledgement. This work was Funded by NSFC (No. 61972106, U1803263, U1636215, 61672020), National Key research and Development Plan (Grant No. 2019QY1406), Guangdong Province Key research and Development Plan (Grant No. 2019B010136003).

References

1. Banko, M.: Open information extraction for the web. University of Washington (2007)
2. Bellare, K., Partha Pratim, T., Kumaran, G.: Lightly-supervised attribute extraction (2007)
3. Na, F., Wan-Dong, C., Yu, Z.: Extraction of subjective relation in opinion sentences based on maximum entropy model. Comput. Eng. (2010)
4. Xiang, C.W., Ting, L., Sheng, L.I.: Automatic entity relation extraction. J. Chin. Inform. Process. **19**(2), 1–6 (2005)
5. Fabian, M.S., Gjergji, K., Gerhard, W.: Yago: a core of semantic knowledge unifying wordnet and Wikipedia. In: 16th International World Wide Web Conference. WWW, pp. 697–706 (2007)
6. Auer, Sören, Bizer, Christian, Kobilarov, Georgi, Lehmann, Jens, Cyganiak, Richard, Ives, Zachary: DBpedia: a nucleus for a web of open data. In: Aberer, Karl, et al. (eds.) ASWC/ISWC -2007. LNCS, vol. 4825, pp. 722–735. Springer, Heidelberg (2007). https://doi.org/10.1007/978-3-540-76298-0_52
7. Wu, F., Weld, DS.: Autonomously semantifying Wikipedia. In: Proceedings of the Sixteenth ACM Conference on Information and Knowledge Management, pp. 41–50. ACM (2007)
8. Wu, F., Weld, DS.: Automatically refining the Wikipedia infobox ontology. In: Proceedings of the 17th International Conference on World Wide Web, pp. 635–644. ACM (2008)
9. Zhao, J., Liu, K., Zhou, G.: Open text information extraction (2011)
10. Tokunaga, K., Kazama, J., Torisawa, K.: Automatic discovery of attribute words from web documents. In: Dale, R., Wong, K.-F., Su, J., Kwong, O.Y. (eds.) IJCNLP 2005. LNCS (LNAI), vol. 3651, pp. 106–118. Springer, Heidelberg (2005). https://doi.org/10.1007/11562214_10
11. Paşca, M.: Organizing and searching the world wide web of facts–step two: harnessing the wisdom of the crowds. In: Proceedings of the 16th International Conference on World Wide Web, pp. 101–110. ACM (2007)
12. Han, W.H., Tian, Z.H., Shi, W., Huang, Z.Z., Li, S.D.: Low-power distributed data flow anomaly-monitoring technology for industrial internet of things. Sensors **19**(12), 2804 (2019)
13. Paşca, M., Van Durme, B.: Weakly-supervised acquisition of open-domain classes and class attributes from web documents and query logs. In: Proceedings of ACL-08: HLT, pp. 19–27 (2008)
14. Kopliku, A., Pinel-Sauvagnat, K., Boughanem, M.: Retrieving attributes using web tables. In: Proceedings of the 11th Annual International ACM/IEEE Joint Conference on Digital Libraries, pp. 397–398. ACM (2011)
15. Han, W., Huang, Z., Li, S., Jia, Y.: Distribution-sensitive unbalanced data oversampling method for medical diagnosis. J. Med. Syst. **43**(2), 39 (2019)
16. Sánchez, D.: A methodology to learn ontological attributes from the web. Data Knowl. Eng. **69**(6), 573–597 (2010)
17. Kang, W., Sui, Z.: Synchronous extraction of ontology concepts and attributes based on web weak guidance. Chin. J. Inform. **24**(1), 54–59 (2010)
18. Li, S., Zhao, D., Wu, X., Tian, Z., Li, A., Wang, Z.: Functional immunization of networks based on message passing. Appl. Math. Comput. **366**, 124728 (2020)
19. Li, W., Sui, Z.: Synchronous extraction method for concept instances and attributes based on parallel structure. Chin. J. Inform. **26**(2), 82–87 (2012)

20. Yoshinaga, N., Torisawa, K.: Open-domain attribute-value acquisition from semi-structured texts. In: Proceedings of the 6th International Semantic Web Conference (ISWC-07), Workshop on Text to Knowledge: The Lexicon/Ontology Interface (OntoLex-2007), pp. 55–66 (2007)
21. Probst, K., Ghani, R., Krema, M., et al.: Semi-supervised learning of attribute-value pairs from product descriptions. In: IJCAI, vol. 7, pp. 2838–2843 (2007)
22. Liu, C., Guo, H., Li, Z., Gao, X., Li, S.: Coevolution of multi-game resolves social dilemma in network population. Appl. Math. Comput. **341**, 402–407 (2019)
23. Bakalov, A., Fuxman, A., Talukdar, P.P., et al.: Scad: collective discovery of attribute values. In: Proceedings of the 20th International Conference on World Wide Web, pp. 447–456. ACM (2011)
24. Guo, J., Li, Z., Zhengtao, Y.: Domain ontology concept instance, attribute and attribute value extraction and relationship prediction. J. Nanjing Univ. **48**(4), 383–389 (2012)
25. Ye, Z., Hongfei, L., Sui, S.: Character wake up extraction based on support vector machine. Comput. Res. Dev. **44**, 271–275 (2007)
26. Mintz, M., Bills, S., Snow, R., et al.: Distant supervision for relation extraction without labeled data. In: Proceedings of the Joint Conference of the 47th Annual Meeting of the ACL and the 4th International Joint Conference on Natural Language Processing of the AFNLP: Volume 2-Volume 2, pp. 1003–1011. Association for Computational Linguistics (2009)
27. Yao, L., Riedel, S., McCallum, A.: Collective cross-document relation extraction without labelled data. Proceedings of the 2010 Conference on Empirical Methods in Natural Language Processing, pp. 1013–1023. Association for Computational Linguistics (2010)
28. Yang, H., Li, S., Wu, X., Lu, H., Han, W.: A novel solution for malicious code detection and family clustering based on machine learning. IEEE Access **7**(1), 148853–148860
29. Riedel, S., Yao, L., McCallum, A.: Modeling Relations and Their Mentions without Labeled Text. In: Balcázar, J.L., Bonchi, F., Gionis, A., Sebag, M. (eds.) ECML PKDD 2010. LNCS (LNAI), vol. 6323, pp. 148–163. Springer, Heidelberg (2010). https://doi.org/10.1007/978-3-642-15939-8_10
30. Surdeanu, M., McClosky, D., Tibshirani, J., et al.: A simple distant supervision approach for the TAC-KBP slot filling task (2010)
31. Hoffmann, R., Zhang, C., Ling, X., et al.: Knowledge-based weak supervision for information extraction of overlapping relations. In: Proceedings of the 49th Annual Meeting of the Association for Computational Linguistics: Human Language Technologies-Volume 1. Association for Computational Linguistics, pp. 541–550 (2011)
32. Tian, Q., Cao, M., Ma, T.: Feature relationships learning incorporated age estimation assisted by cumulative attribute encoding. Comput. Mater. Continua **56**(3), 467–482 (2018)
33. Yin, L., Meng, X., Li, J., Sun, J.: Relation extraction for massive news texts. Comput. Mater. Continua **60**(1), 275–285 (2019)
34. Zeng, D., Xiao, Y., Wang, J., Dai, Y., Kumar Sangaiah, A.: Distant supervised relation extraction with cost-sensitive loss. Comput. Mater. Continua **60**(3), 1251–1261 (2019)
35. Jiang, H.: Research on attribute extraction technology based on deep learning. Zhejiang University (2017)

Research on Automated Vulnerability Mining
of Embedded System Firmware

Xiaoyi Li[1], Lijun Qiao[2], Yanbin Sun[1(✉)], and Quanlong Guan[3]

[1] Cyberspace Institute of Advanced Technology, Guangzhou University, Guangzhou, China
sunyanbin@gzhu.edu.cn
[2] The People's Armed Police Sergeant School, Beijing, China
[3] Jinan University, Guangzhou, China

Abstract. The development of the Internet of Things (IoT) makes people pay more and more attention to the security of embedded systems. The most important of it is the security issues brought by firmware. The threat posed by firmware vulnerabilities is fatal. Researching firmware vulnerability mining technology is a way to effectively protect embedded systems. However, it's not easy to move the software's vulnerability mining methods to firmware. The existing firmware vulnerability mining work can effectively solve some problems, but it still has some shortcomings. In this paper, we first summarize the main challenges of firmware research. Then we analyze the work related to firmware vulnerability mining. After that, we classify and analyze the existing firmware vulnerability mining work from two aspects of method and technology. At the same time, we have made some performance comparisons on the exiting work. Finally, we give some suggestions on the future direction of the firmware vulnerability mining work.

Keywords: Firmware · Embedded system · Vulnerability mining

1 Introduction

Nowadays, with the development of IoT, more and more embedded devices are connected to the Internet. In the trend of the IoT, embedded devices are almost everywhere. They penetrate into every aspect of our lives and play a decisive role in the future of IoT security. Today, the security of embedded systems is getting more and more attention, and the core of embedded system security is firmware.

The term firmware is defined as a layer of bonded microcode between the CPU instruction set and the actual hardware in a Datamation article written by Opler A [1] in 1967. However, this definition is gradually expanded to the level of computer data with the development of computer hardware devices. The firmware is given a new meaning in the IEEE Standard Glossary of Software Engineering Terminology, Std 610.12-1990 [2]: The combination of a hardware device and computer instructions and data that reside as read-only software on that device.

© Springer Nature Singapore Pte Ltd. 2020
X. Sun et al. (Eds.): ICAIS 2020, CCIS 1254, pp. 105–117, 2020.
https://doi.org/10.1007/978-981-15-8101-4_11

After that, the rise of the IoT has allowed the definition of firmware to be developed again. According to Zhang [3], firmware refers to a binary program stored in a non-volatile memory (e.g., FLASH, ROM) of an embedded device, which is non-volatile and solidified. Zaddach J et al. [4] generalize the firmware to all code sets (machine code and virtual machine code) running on the hardware processor. These definitions introduce the features of the firmware from different aspects, but their core content is actually the same: firmware is the set of software that makes an embedded system functional.

Embedded devices are mostly controlled by firmware, which is usually provided by the device vendor and has strong specificity and privacy. Unfortunately, these device vendors typically do not consider security when designing firmware. This makes millions of homes and small businesses face known and unknown threats on the network at all times. With these vulnerabilities, an attacker can easily control and destroy a device. Tor hidden services is also a new security issue. Q. Tan et al. [5] present practical Eclipse attacks on Tor HSs that allow an adversary with an extremely low cost to block arbitrary Tor HSs. A firmware vulnerability is fatal for some equipment related to social infrastructure, which seriously threatens people's lives and property. Therefore, we must accurately identify the vulnerability in the firmware. Although the existing firmware vulnerability mining research has achieved results in some aspects, there are still some limitations.

In summary this paper makes the following contributions:

- We point out the challenges brought by the firmware.
- We review and compare the work related to firmware vulnerability mining.
- We classify the related work from two aspects of method and technology.
- We analyze the technical route of the work including the simulator.
- We summarize the future work and development direction of firmware vulnerability mining.

2   Challenges

The reason why firmware has many security issues and is difficult to detect is that firmware is essentially different from traditional software. These differences hinder the security of the firmware, so that the original mature software security policies and detection methods can not be applied to the firmware. At the same time, these differences are also challenges that we must overcome in the security research process. We summarize some important firmware challenges as follows.

2.1   Complex Format

The format of the firmware is a very complicated problem. Unlike traditional software, the firmware does not have a standard file format. In today's embedded device market, the firmware formats used by different vendors are different. Although the exact format of the firmware is difficult to determine, Zaddach J et al. classify the firmware into the following three categories based on the components and functions of the firmware:

- Full-blown (full-OS/kernel + bootloader + libs + apps).
- Integrated (apps + OS-as-a-lib).
- Partial updates (apps or libs or resources or support).

In addition, these objects can be arbitrarily grouped and packaged into various archives or file system images. The combination of different firmware categories and different packaging methods allows the firmware format to be changed at will, which greatly increases the complexity of the firmware format.

2.2 Update Difficulty

For firmware vendors, it is important to consider how to obtain more profit, and the security of firmware is something that will be considered after that. On the other hand, the diversity of platforms and applications increases the difficulty of compiling and maintaining. In addition, since some firmware involves important infrastructure, special inspection standards are required for supervision.

For users, the process of updating the firmware is not as easy as the software update. Updating the firmware sometimes requires the user to have some knowledge of the hardware device, and even need to learn the knowledge of the specific update software. To make matters worse, if the update process fails, it may cause device crash. And updating the firmware does not bring new features.

2.3 Diverse Architecture

Different from the hardware architecture of traditional computers, embedded devices have many choice. These architectures have their own unique features in various fields, which are difficult to replace for each vendor. And it is difficult to achieve uniformity in one aspect.

In terms of processor architecture, embedded devices are more diverse than traditional computers. ARM and MIPS processors are the most widely distributed. The choice of architecture for simple devices is diverse, such as PowerPC, ARC and Motorola 6800/68000 with smaller memory.

The use of the operating system is equally diverse. Complex devices usually use a mature operating system (e.g., Linux, Windows NT), and Linux is currently the most popular operating system. And simple devices use a proprietary real-time operating system (e.g., VxWorks). It even includes some questions about Internet of Vehicles. Z. Tian et al. [6] propose to consider dynamical and diversity attacking strategies in the simulation of reputation management scheme evaluation.

3   Review of Firmware Vulnerability Mining

In recent years, people gradually realize the significance and value of firmware vulnerability research, and urgently want to apply software vulnerability mining methods to the firmware. However, research on firmware vulnerability mining is not as smooth as imagined. We study the existing firmware vulnerability mining methods. Hou et al. [7]

and Xie et al. [8] have some good classification of existing methods. Based on these efforts, we reclassify existing research into the following categories from the method level. And we compare them in Table 1.

3.1 Static Analysis

Static analysis is a way to directly analyze firmware content to discover bugs in a program without having to execute the program on the actual device or simulator.

Costin et al. [9] propose a static analysis framework for the process of firmware collection, filtering, unpacking, and large-scale analysis. The framework determines whether it contains a private encryption key or a string of known errors by studying the firmware information extracted from each firmware sample. This work is tested in approximately 32,356 firmware images collected. It proves that 693 firmware images are affected by at least one vulnerability. Of these, 38 are newly discovered vulnerabilities. However, this approach faces the classic trade-off of static analysis. That is, the analysis of the firmware is too broad or too specific.

3.2 Symbolic Execution

Instead of specific variables, symbolic values are used to simulate each path to produce the possibility of each execution. Solving the mathematical expression of a result gives the path to the result.

FIE [10] is a major concern for memory security issues and is used to automatically analyze firmware vulnerability detection systems that are widely used in MSP430 microcontrollers. It compiles the source code of the analysis firmware into LLVM bytecode for analysis as input to the symbol execution. It is based on the KLEE [11] symbolic execution engine. FIE significantly improves code coverage with state pruning and memory blur. It can be used to discover two types of vulnerabilities. However, FIE is limited to analyzing small firmware written in C and must obtain firmware source code. And for the vulnerability reported by the system, the user must manually verify.

Firmalice [12] is a symbolic analysis system for analyzing binary code in complex firmware on different hardware platforms. It is based on the angr [13] symbol execution engine. Firmalice generates a program dependency graph for the firmware from the static analysis module and uses this graph to create an authentication slice from the entry point to the privileged program point. It attempts to find the path to the privileged program point and performs a certificate bypass check on the successfully arrived symbol state. After testing, Firmalice can effectively detect a large number of complex backdoors without relying on the implementation details of the firmware itself. However, Firmalice requires manual operation when providing security policies for devices, so it cannot be used for large-scale analysis.

Avatar [14] is a dynamic analysis framework based on embedded device firmware. It acts as a software agent between the embedded device and the simulator based on the S2E [15]. The firmware instructions are executed in the simulator, and I/O operations are introduced into the embedded device. The state is passed between the simulator and the device while the firmware is running. And the state remains the same when it is passed. The experimental results show that Avatar can play a good supporting role for reverse engineering of firmware, vulnerability detection and hardcoded backdoor discovery. However, Avatar is much slower on the emulator than on the actual device. And Avatar relies on hardware devices.

3.3 Fuzzing

Fuzzing is to construct random and unintended malformed data as the input of the program, and monitor the abnormalities that may occur during the execution of the program.

Firmadyne [16] is a framework for dynamically analyzing vulnerabilities in Linux-based embedded firmware. It is an automated, scalable dynamic analysis technology. It collects firmware on the vendor's website. A binwalk script effectively implements the extraction of file systems and optional kernels. During the simulation phase, Firmadyne performed an initial simulation on the QEMU [17] simulator. This learning process, it will continually modify the network configuration for QEMU. Fimadyne provides three analysis channels to analyze firmware. Firmadyne can accurately simulate the firmware of network devices and has good versatility. However, Firmadyne uses a general-purpose kernel in the simulation process. This approach prevents it from analyzing vulnerabilities in kernel or kernel modules.

Dai et al. [18] propose a method based on using dynamic fuzzing and static taint tracing on the simulator to locate and exploit firmware vulnerabilities. This method uses risk weights to design a set of fuzzing cases, which improves code coverage and dynamic analysis capabilities. It constructs a taint propagation path graph by identifying and tracing tainted data sources for binary data. The taint path graph is then dynamically executed on the simulator and fuzzed to detect vulnerabilities in the firmware. However, this method also has certain limitations. The simulator cannot accurately simulate some firmware images that require hardware support.

3.4 Comprehensive Analysis

Comprehensive analysis refers to the use of several different methods for firmware vulnerability mining. And some tools are effectively integrated to provide more accurate analysis results.

Avatar2 [19] is a dynamic multi-target orchestration framework designed to support interoperability between any number of different dynamic binary analysis frameworks, debuggers, simulators, and physical devices. Avatar2 is a completely redesigned system compared to Avatar. It includes the Avatar2 kernel, targets, protocols, and endpoints. In the end, Avatar2 integrated five targets: GDB, OpenOCD [20], QEMU, PANDA [21], angr. These targets provide a large number of analytical combinations. However, the GDB stubs are highly dependent on the architecture of the analysis target and are difficult to abstract in a generic way.

3.5 Others

In addition to the above literature, the following literature also contributes to the firmware vulnerability mining and can be classified by the above methods, which is not described in detail here.

Bojinov et al. [22] propose a vulnerability scanning work for the embedded web interface of IoT devices. They scan a total of 21 devices. More than 40 new vulnerabilities are discovered and a new type of web vulnerability called XCS is discovered.

FEMU [23] proposes a simulation framework that mixes firmware and hardware. It implements consistent SoC verification by using the ported QEMU at the BIOS level. But this method requires the support of hardware devices.

Hu et al. [24] study embedded firmware without file system. They discuss the problems of library function identification and backdoor detection. This method successfully identify the main contents of a real firmware and detect multiple backdoors.

Shang et al. [25] design a vulnerability analysis system for industrial embedded devices, including multiple analysis modules. It provides a theoretical approach to the development of vulnerability analysis systems for industrial control systems.

Li et al. [26] aim at the recurrence of the same vulnerability in the development process of embedded device firmware. Finally, they perform vulnerability detection on similar firmware based on the analysis result.

Genius [27] is a vulnerability search system based on digital feature search technology. It learns advanced features from control flow graphs. Genius tests in 8126 firmware and averages the search in less than a second.

Table 1. Performance comparison of firmware vulnerability mining

Tool/method	Architecture	Vulnerability type	Support	Large-scale analysis	Simulator	Vulnerability mining
Costin et al.	–	Backdoor	Homology	✓	×	×
FIE	MSP430	Memory security	Source code	✓	×	✓
Firmalice	–	Backdoor	–	×	×	✓
Avatar	–	–	Device	×	✓	✓
Firmadyne	Linux (ARM, MIPS)	–	–	✓	✓	×
Dai et al.	ARM, MIPS	–	–	×	✓	✓
Avatar2	–	–	–	×	✓	✓

4   Technical Route

The above firmware vulnerability mining methods can be divided into two categories from the technical level: No-simulator and Simulator.

No-simulator usually rely on firmware source code (e.g., FIE). However, the firmware source code is usually not provided by the vendor. And it becomes the biggest bottleneck of this type of method. Methods that do not use firmware source code are also present (e.g., Firmalice), but such methods have poor analytical capabilities.

Simulator pays more attention to the execution of the firmware in the embedded device. It has no excessive restrictions on the input, and has relatively better analysis and expansion capabilities. It is suitable for firmware analysis without actual device or device without a debug interface. The technical route is clear. We design a framework for vulnerability mining with a simulator (see Fig. 1).

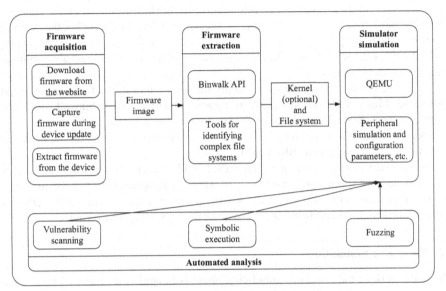

Fig. 1. The framework for vulnerability mining with a simulator

4.1 Firmware Acquisition

In the firmware acquisition phase, our main task is to accurately obtain the firmware to be analyzed and provide sufficient firmware information resources for the analysis. The technology of this process is relatively fixed.

The first method is the most ideal and the most common method. For some larger vendors, the firmware is usually posted on the official website. At the same time, the firmware released on the official website usually has a lot of firmware information. These firmware information plays a role in the later analysis. Some vendors' official websites do not provide firmware, but there are dedicated FTP download sites.

The second method is complicated. It requires us to find the firmware from the official website update package when the firmware is updated. We can capture it during the firmware transfer. This requires us to have some understanding of the firmware and the corresponding firmware update process.

The worst case is that we have to extract the firmware from the embedded device. At this time we have to understand part of the structure of the device, find the interface to extract the firmware, and use the professional tools and methods to extract the firmware. Among them edge computing is a new security issue. Z. Tian et al. [28] propose a method named CloudSEC meaning real time lateral movement detection for the edge-cloud environment.

4.2 Firmware Extraction

In the firmware extraction phase, we need to extract the parts we need from the complete, and identify the hardware architecture information that the firmware depends on. Binwalk [29] is the most common tool in the process. We only need to use the API of the binwalk to write analysis scripts according to the content we need. Besides binwalk, firmware-mod-kit [30], FRAK [31], and Binary Analysis Toolkit (BAT) [32] are also optional firmware extraction tools.

The content we want to extract is mainly the file system in the firmware. Normal compressed files and file systems can be recognized and extracted by binwalk, but some complex or packaged files modified by the vendor require special unpacking tools. They may need some digital technology. Z. Tian et al. [33] propose a secure digital evidence framework using blockchain (Block-DEF).

Another part worthy of our attention is the kernel in the firmware, which is the part that must be used during the simulation. However, it is optional during the firmware extraction process. This is because the kernel in the firmware usually only performs some of the device-related functions. So we can use a pre-prepared kernel.

4.3 Simulator Simulation

The main work of the simulator simulation phase is to apply the extracted parts from the firmware to the simulator and finally run the firmware. Traditional device emulation is roughly divided into three levels: complete hardware emulation, hardware over-approximate, and firmware adaptation.

We can see that the performance of the simulator is the key to the simulator simulation phase. What needs to be considered is how to simulate more accurately. Using the improved QEMU is a broad idea. QEMU is a machine simulator and virtualization platform. It has the ability to simulate a complete system and user-mode.

Although the performance of QEMU is good enough, its shortcomings are obvious. First of all, the architecture it supports is not enough, which makes it difficult to imitate dedicated complex devices. Secondly, in addition to the kernel and file system, QEMU needs to input the most basic parameters for system configuration. These parameters are not recognized by QEMU. In addition, QEMU is also helpless with the simulation of peripheral devices and memory mapping.

4.4 Automated Analysis

After the firmware has been run on the simulated device, our task is to analyze the virtual device using dynamic analysis. This process is usually targeted at a specific category or categories of vulnerabilities. It is limited by the analytical capabilities of the analysis tool. Here are some common firmware vulnerability mining methods.

At its simplest, you can scan the device for vulnerabilities. This method is based on a vulnerability database. Nmap [34] is an analysis tool that provides information about exploits that may exist on a device. However, this type of method cannot discover new vulnerabilities.

Symbolic execution (as described in Sect. 3.2) is a very efficient method of analysis that can reduce the difficulty of analysis and theoretically reveal all vulnerabilities. The commonly used symbolic execution engines are angr and KLEE, both of which are very powerful enough to enable in-depth vulnerability mining. An analytical framework based on the symbolic execution engine is also a good choice.

Fuzzing (as described in Sect. 3.3) is considered to be the most effective method of vulnerability analysis. However, in the current firmware vulnerability detection tools, there are few tools that use fuzzing. This is mainly limited by the difficulty of fuzzing and device interaction. AFL [35], LibFuzzer [36], Honggfuzz [37], etc. are simple and powerful fuzzing tools. These tools also provide more options for exploiting embedded devices.

In addition, analytical methods combining symbolic execution with fuzzing are also evolving, and Driller [38] is a typical example of this approach. It adds the dynamic symbolic execution engine angr to the AFL. Simulation of network devices may involve network routing decisions. Z. Tian et al. [39] present a prefix level route decision prediction model.

5 Future Work

The existing firmware vulnerability mining methods have formed a complete technical route. However, there are still many shortcomings in these methods. We can continue to find more versatile methods for the key issues in each step along this technical route. And we can even extend the new technology route. We believe that the future direction of firmware vulnerability mining should aim to achieve a large-scale automated firmware vulnerability mining tool with in-depth analysis capabilities. This paper proposes the following new ideas and suggestions.

5.1 Introducing Machine Learning Module

Since the firmware does not have a standard format (as described in Sect. 2.1), the firmware extraction phase relies too heavily on unpacking tools like binwalk. Existing methods are discussed in a single form in addition to binwalk, while binwalk often has false positives when dealing with complex formats, and scripts written using the API of the binwalk are less versatile. If there are multiple file systems in the firmware, then binwalk alone can't complete our needs. Some firmware may require trusted communication services. Vcash [40] is a reputation framework for identifying denial of traffic service.

We can consider adding a separate machine learning module. The module first needs to acquire a large number of different categories of firmware. After that, it is the work that machine learning needs to accomplish. We formatted a large number of different categories of firmware to select the main features of each part of the firmware, and vectorized these features to finally train the optimal firmware model. With this firmware model, we can identify the firmware and split the firmware more accurately and conveniently during the firmware extraction phase. It is no longer limited by the type and packaging of firmware.

5.2 Improve In-depth Analysis

Existing methods can take many approaches during the automated analysis phase (as described in Sect. 4.4). However, they generally have problems with insufficient analytical capabilities. Vulnerability scanning can only verify existing vulnerabilities; symbolic execution is generally detected for certain types of vulnerabilities; the use of fuzzing is almost always on the surface. This limits the ability of large-scale vulnerability mining to a certain extent.

We consider improving the software's fuzzing tools to adapt it to the firmware. The focus is on the interaction of the fuzzing process with the emulation device and how to run the scripts we need on the firmware of the different architectures. At the same time, symbolic execution needs to overcome the limitations of single vulnerability detection, which requires further study of the symbolic execution engine. This will greatly improve the analysis capabilities of firmware vulnerability mining and achieve large-scale in-depth analysis.

5.3 Integrate Existing Tools

A number of tools have been developed for different phases of analysis of different architectures that overlap in functionality but have their own analytical capabilities. We consider ways to integrate multiple tools. The work of Avatar2 is similar to ours, but the shortcomings of Avatar2 are obvious (as described in Sect. 3.4).

Our idea is not limited to the integration of tools at a certain stage, but the integration of stage tools with the overall tools. For example, by integrating Firmayne and Angr, firmware vulnerability exploitation of general network devices with good performance can be achieved; Costin's system can greatly improve the analysis capabilities of Firmalice as input from Firmalice. It should be noted that in the process of integrating tools, the synchronization of the running state of the devices and the memory data between different frameworks is crucial. Integrating existing frameworks is designed to enable large-scale, general-purpose analysis.

6 Conclusion

In this paper, we summarize the important firmware challenges. We divide the existing firmware vulnerability mining work into four categories: static analysis, symbolic execution, fuzzing, and comprehensive analysis. The contributions and deficiencies of the typical work in these four categories are analyzed in detail and compared. Then we divide them into No-simulator and Simulator technically. We notice the lack of No-simulator and detail analysis of the technical route of the Simulator. We divide this technical route into four stages: firmware acquisition, firmware extraction, simulator simulation, and automated analysis. At the same time, the techniques commonly used and the problems that should be paid attention to in each stage are summarized. Finally, we propose the future direction of the firmware vulnerability mining work for the above analysis. This includes three suggestions: introducing machine learning modules, improving in-depth analysis capabilities, and integrating existing tools. Our work is aimed at implementing a large-scale automated firmware vulnerability mining tool with in-depth analysis capabilities.

Acknowledgments. This work is funded by the National Key Research and Development Plan (Grant No. 2018YFB0803504), the National Natural Science Foundation of China (No. 61702223, 61702220, 61871140, 61602210, 61877029, U1636215), the Science and Technology Planning Project of Guangdong (2017A040405029), the Science and Technology Planning Project of Guangzhou (201902010041), the Fundamental Research Funds for the Central Universities (21617408, 21619404).

References

1. Opler, A.: Fourth generation software. Datamation **13**(1), 22–24 (1967)
2. IEEE Standards Coordinating Committee.: IEEE standard glossary of software engineering terminology (IEEE Std 610.12–1990). Los Alamitos. CA: IEEE Computer Society, 169 (1990)
3. Zhang, P.: Research on embedded operating system recognition technology for firmware. Inform. Eng. Univ (2012)
4. Zaddach, J., Costin, A.: Embedded devices security and firmware reverse engineering. Black-Hat USA (2013)
5. Tan, Q., Gao, Y., Shi, J., Wang, X., Fang, B., Tian, Z.: Toward a comprehensive insight to the eclipse attacks of tor hidden services. IEEE Internet Things J. **6**(2), 1584–1593 (2019)
6. Tian, Z., Gao, X., Su, S., Qiu, J., Du, X., Guizani, M.: Evaluating reputation management schemes of internet of vehicles based on evolutionary game theory. IEEE Trans. Veh. Technol. IEEE (2019)
7. Hou, J., Li, T., Chang, C.: Research for vulnerability detection of embedded system firmware. Procedia Comput. Sci. **107**, 814–818 (2017)
8. Xie, W., Jiang, Y., Tang, Y., et al.: Vulnerability detection in IoT firmware: a survey. In: 2017 IEEE 23rd International Conference on Parallel and Distributed Systems (ICPADS), pp. 769–772. IEEE (2017)
9. Costin, A., Zaddach, J., Francillon, A., et al.: A large-scale analysis of the security of embedded firmwares. In: 23rd {USENIX} Security Symposium ({USENIX} Security 14), pp. 95–110 (2014)
10. Davidson, D., Moench, B., Ristenpart, T., et al.: {FIE} on firmware: finding vulnerabilities in embedded systems using symbolic execution. In: 22nd {USENIX} Security Symposium ({USENIX} Security 13), pp. 463–478 (2013)
11. Michel, S., Triantafillou, P., Weikum, G.: Klee: a framework for distributed top-k query algorithms. In: Proceedings of 31st International Conference on Very Large Data Bases, pp. 637–648. VLDB Endowment (2005)
12. Shoshitaishvili, Y., Wang, R., Hauser, C., et al.: Firmalice-automatic detection of authentication bypass vulnerabilities in binary firmware. In: NDSS (2015)

13. Shoshitaishvili, Y., Wang, R., Salls, C., et al.: Sok: (state of) the art of war: offensive techniques in binary analysis. In: 2016 IEEE Symposium on Security and Privacy (SP), pp. 138–157. IEEE (2016)

14. Zaddach, J., Bruno, L., Francillon, A., et al.: Avatar: a framework to support dynamic security analysis of embedded systems' firmwares. In: NDSS, pp. 1–16 (2014)

15. Chipounov, V., Kuznetsov, V., Candea, G.: S2E: a platform for in-vivo multi-path analysis of software systems. In: ACM SIGARCH Computer Architecture News, vol. 39, no. 1, pp. 265–278. ACM (2011)

16. Chen, D.D., Woo, M., Brumley, D., et al.: Towards automated dynamic analysis for Linux-based embedded firmware. In: NDSS, pp. 1–16 (2016)

17. Bellard, F.: QEMU, a fast and portable dynamic translator. In: USENIX Annual Technical Conference, FREENIX Track, vol. 41, p. 46 (2005)

18. Dai, Z.: Research on the localization of firmware vulnerability based on stain tracking. J. Shandong Univ. (Nat. Sci.) **51**, 41–46 (2016)

19. Muench, M., Nisi, D., Francillon, A., et al.: Avatar 2: a multi-target orchestration platform. In: Workshop on Binary Analysis Research (colocated with NDSS Symposium) (February 2018), BAR vol. 18 (2018)

20. Högl, H., Rath, D.: Open on-chip debugger–openocd. Fakultat fur Informatik, Technical report (2006)

21. Dolan-Gavitt, B., Hodosh, J., Hulin, P., et al.: Repeatable reverse engineering with PANDA. In: Proceedings of the 5th Program Protection and Reverse Engineering Workshop, p. 4. ACM (2015)

22. Bojinov, H., Bursztein, E., Lovett, E., et al.: Embedded management interfaces: emerging massive insecurity. BlackHat USA **1**(8), 14 (2009)

23. Li, H., Tong, D., Huang, K., et al.: FEMU: a firmware-based emulation framework for SoC verification. In: Proceedings of the Eighth IEEE/ACM/IFIP International Conference on Hardware/Software Codesign and System Synthesis, pp. 257–266. ACM (2010)

24. Hu, C., Xue, Y., Zhao, L., et al.: Backdoor detection in embedded system firmware without file system. J. Commun. **34**(8), 140–145 (2013)

25. Wenli, S.: Study on the vulnerability analysis method for industrial embedded devices. Autom. Instrum. **36**(10), 63–67 (2015)

26. Lee, D.: Firmware vulnerability detection in embedded device based on homology analysis. Comput. Eng. (2016)

27. Feng, Q., Zhou, R., Xu, C., et al.: Scalable graph-based bug search for firmware images. In: Proceedings of the 2016 ACM SIGSAC Conference on Computer and Communications Security, pp. 480–491. ACM (2016)

28. Tian, Z., et al.: Real time lateral movement detection based on evidence reasoning network for edge computing environment. IEEE Trans. Industr. Inform. **15**(7), 4285–4294 (2019)

29. Heffner, C.: Binwalk: firmware analysis tool (2010). https://code.google.com/p/binwalk/. Accessed 03 Mar 2013

30. Heffner, C., Collake, J.: Firmware mod kit-modify firmware images without recompiling (2015)

31. Cui, A.: FRAK: firmware reverse analysis konsole. In: Proceedings of Black Hat USA, pp. 1–33 (2012)

32. Hemel, A., Coughlan, S.: BAT–Binary Analysis Toolkit. Accessed Jan 2017

33. Tian, Z., Li, M., Qiu, M., Sun, Y., Su, S.: Block-DEF: a secure digital evidence system using blockchain. Inform. Sci. **491**, 151–165 (2019)

34. Lyon, G.: Nmap–free security scanner for network exploration & security audits (2009)

35. Zalewski, M.: American fuzzy lop (2017). http://lcamtuf.coredump.cx/afl

36. Serebryany, K.: LibFuzzer a library for coverage-guided fuzz testing. LLVM project (2015)

37. Swiecki, R.: Honggfuzz: a general-purpose, easy-to-use fuzzer with interesting analysis options. https://github.com/google/honggfuzz. Accessed 21 June 2017
38. Stephens, N., Grosen, J., Salls, C., et al.: Driller: augmenting fuzzing through selective symbolic execution. NDSS **16**(2016), 1–16 (2016)
39. Tian, Z., Su, S., Shi, W., Du, X., Guizani, M., Yu, X.: A data-driven model for future internet route decision modeling. Future Gener. Comput. Syst. **95**, 212–220 (2019)
40. Tian, Z., Su, S., Yu, X., et al.: Vcash: a novel reputation framework for identifying denial of traffic service in internet of connected vehicles. IEEE Internet Things J. **7**(5), 3901–3909 (2019)

Attacking Naive Bayes Journal Recommendation Systems

Sheng Wang, Mohan Li, Yinyin Cai, and Zhaoquan Gu$^{(\boxtimes)}$

Cyberspace Institute of Advanced Technology, Guangzhou University, Guangzhou, China
zqgu@gzhu.edu.cn

Abstract. Recommendation systems have been extensively adopted in various applications. However, with the security concern of artificial intelligence, the robustness of such systems against malicious attacks has been studied in recent years. In this paper, we build a journal recommendation system based on the Naive Bayesian algorithm which helps recommend suitable journals for the authors. Since journal recommendation systems may also suffer from various attacks, we explore attack methods on the malicious data. We construct specific malicious data to attack the availability of training data, and such deviations in the training data could lead to poor recommendation accuracy. We also conduct extensive experiments and the results show that the recommendation accuracy could be dramatically reduced under such attacks.

Keywords: Naive Bayes · Journal recommendation systems · Malicious data attack

1 Introduction

The emergence of the Internet has brought a lot of information to users, which satisfies the demand for information in the information age. However, with the rapid development of the network, the amount of online information has increased dramatically. When facing a lot of information, users cannot get the information that is really useful to the users, which reduces the efficiency of using the information. This is the so-called information overload problem. The recommendation system could solve this problem well, which serves as an information filtering system recommending information and products interested by the users, according to the users' demands and interests.

Recommendation algorithms can be divided into several categories: content-based recommendations, collaborative filtering recommendations, recommendations based on social network analysis, and other recommendation methods. Among them, the recommendation for the text mainly includes content recommendation and collaborative filtering recommendation. Based on the data of the sample text, the content recommendation algorithm selects a text type with a similar feature from each text category as the recommendation result. This recommendation algorithm first extracts the key contents (or keywords) of the text, and then achieves the classification effect by calculating the difference between the categories. Collaborative filtering algorithm recommends by

© Springer Nature Singapore Pte Ltd. 2020
X. Sun et al. (Eds.): ICAIS 2020, CCIS 1254, pp. 118–128, 2020.
https://doi.org/10.1007/978-981-15-8101-4_12

categorizing users who like to read similar texts. Usually, the needs of users with the same interests are also highly similar. The recommended text is obtained by querying the selection of the same user group. This algorithm can be considered as recommending by the users' categories.

In the recommendation of texts, journal recommendation plays a very important role, because the recommendation system could efficiently recommend some journals with high matching rate of a submitting manuscript for academic service organizations. Then, the authors of the manuscript/paper could select the final journal from the recommended journals. The Naive Bayesian method is very suitable for this kind of recommendation scenario, because the Naive Bayesian method has been widely used in text categorization since the 1950s. In theory, it is assumed that the appearance of each word is independent of each other. We can calculate the frequency of occurrence of a single word, and then multiply all the words to obtain the result. The algorithm only needs to count the frequency of the words in the paper, so the data preprocessing process could be relatively simple, and the calculation process is similar when calculating the similarity between the paper and each candidate journal. The efficiency is also relatively high, and the method of recommending by the algorithm has practical application scenarios. However, there may be some competition between academic service organizations. Some organizations may deliberately pollute competitors training data for the purpose of malicious competition, with the intention of biasing the models trained by opponents.

For example, the amount of data in other journal articles is maliciously inserted into a normal journal article which interferes with the normal distribution of the original data, generating large errors in the results. Such attacks are often referred to as data poisoning attacks against usability. At present, there exists few work on journal recommendation scenarios to study attacks of poisoning data against usability. To this end, this paper has carried out the research work on attacking the journal recommendation system, which is depicted as Fig. 1.

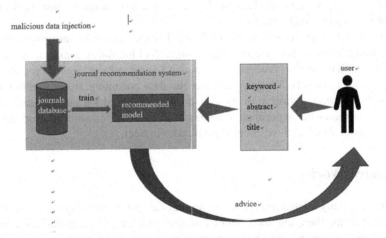

Fig. 1. The process of the journal recommendation system

The main contributions of this paper are as follow. In the first place, we implemented a Naive Bayesian-based journal recommendation and the recommendation accuracy has been quantitatively evaluated and analyzed. Secondly, we construct the data poisoning method to attack the system and we show some experimental results against the generated journal recommendation system. Finally, comparing the result of attacking, we show that the security of such system exists and should be considered when we design the recommendation system.

Specifically, we study the Naive Bayesian-based journal recommendation algorithm in this paper. We firstly collect the titles, abstracts and keywords of paper in each journal, and remove the pre-processing of the stop words in the paper. After becoming words to vectors, the TF-IDF value of the words in each category is counted, the word frequency of the statistical range in some limits can stay in keyword database, and the proportion of the same type of paper data in the total data is calculated, and the words of each category are compared with the same words of the target paper. Probability, descending and sorting the results, the larger the value, the more identical words appear, the higher the similarity, so that the journals with the top ranked recommendation results can be used as the journal recommendation reference.

Afterwards, we construct the data poisoning method of usability data. When training the test papers as example, it is not easy to find the specific and malicious data in amounts of training papers' data. However, these malicious data is too adequate to change the distinguish ability of model, and we can make the system finally produces error result to users. We add a small amount of specific interference data to the journal database and in this way the normal journal can get the more features including some features of other journals after training. Hence, we can affect the journal recommendation performance.

Finally, we conduct real experiments in journal recommendation system. The result indicates that when adding ten malicious papers including specific words to 50% journals, it can reduce the recommendation accuracy by 20% compared with the normal recommendation accuracy. With more malicious data, the recommendation accuracy could be much worse. Thus we can conclude the Naive Bayesian recommendation model is very vulnerability against such attacks.

The rest of the paper is organized as follows. The second section discusses is the journal recommendation system and the related research of journal system attacks. Section 3 shows the implementation process of the Naive Bayesian-based journal recommendation algorithm in details. Section 4 depicts the data poisoning attack method against the recommendation algorithm of the Naive Bayesian based journal recommendation. Section 5 compares the experimental results of the journal recommendation algorithm with or without attack and we conclude the paper in Sect. 6.

2 Related Work

There are not many related researches on journal recommendation systems, but in other application areas, there are some similar studies including content-based recommendations, collaborative filtering-based recommendations, and hybrid recommendations. In the work of G. Adomavicius et al. [1], there are three main methods for reviewing modern recommendation systems.

Content-Based Recommendations. M.J. Pazzan et al. [2] Pollock et al. [3] A. Gunawardana et al. [4] mentioned that the user U would be recommended to be similar to the item I1 bought in the past. The principle of the characteristic item I2, which solves the recommendation problem at the time of text retrieval, uses TF-IDF to judge keywords, and the methods include Naive Bayes, Decision tree, Neural network and other methods to construct the recommendation system. though independence of keywords does not seem to be true, but the accuracy of the Naive Bayesian algorithm is quite high. Of course, the method based on content recommendation is difficult to describe the item in detail because of the number of features that the system can extract from the item; It is impossible to distinguish the advantages and disadvantages of the items to be recommended; the recommended closed-loop problem is that the user will always be recommended for items similar to the items that have already been purchased, and it is difficult to find new items with different characteristics; the new user problem in cold start, one user must Purchase records for items can be recommended.

Collaborative Filtering-Based Recommendations. Such as P. Resnick et al. [5], B. Sarwar et al. [6], H. Kautz et al. [7], M. Cornor et al. [8] using user U will be recommended and similar to him. The principle of the item I purchased by the hobby user U1, which was first proposed by D. Goldberg et al. [14] in his work of 1992. Unlike content-based recommendations, it has two ways: user-based and item-based. Collaborative filtering algorithm, where the user-based algorithm is applicable to occasions where there are few users, and the timeliness is strong, and the user's personalized interest is not obvious, but the real-time performance is not strong, and the new item needs to be calculated after a period of time after going online. Push to the user, the second item-based algorithm is applicable to the occasion where the number of items is significantly smaller than the number of users, the long-tail items are abundant, and the user's personalized demand is strong. Real-time is very strong, once the user has new behavior, it will lead to real-time recommendation changes, but there is no way to recommend new items to the user without updating the item similarity table offline.

Hybrid Recommendations. There are P. Melville [9], BM Sarwar [10], and B. Burke [11]. The work of the model can be divided into four categories: (1) the two methods are implemented separately, and their predicted results are combined. (2) Add some features of the content in the content filtering to the collaborative filtering (3) Add some features of the collaborative filtering to the content filtering (4) Create a joint model and fuse the two methods together.

At the same time as the recommendation system emerged, attacks against the recommendation system also followed. Author Michael P.O'Mahony proposed two attacks in his work [12]: 1. Targeted attack strategy, recommended from the recommendation system. In the process, look for the eigenvalues that can influence the recommendation orientation, and then pretend that the normal users successfully guide the eigenvalues. The performance on the product, for example, the user's evaluation affects the product's rating, and the attacker creates a large number of malicious users to score. There is a gap between the orientation and the real result. Second, the probe attack strategy uses the seed user to understand the recommended weights, to refine the real structure of the recommendation system and then focus on the critical areas. Compared with the first method, it only needs a small amount of Resources can achieve mastery of the recommended structure.

In the work of author David J. Miller [13], a hybrid model for attacking data pollution based on naive Bayes is proposed. In the spam classification, the guiding factor for Naive Bayes is single factor, so you can use the classifier to increase the weight of certain specific words, the spam of the words with the same part of speech but not often appears can successfully attack the recipient.

From the above related work, there is not much research work on the journal recommendation system. This paper studies the security of the Naive Bayesian-based journal recommendation algorithm.

3   Naive Bayes Journal Recommendation Algorithm

3.1   An Overview of the Algorithm

When an author wants to submit a paper to a suitable journal after completing the manuscript, how can the author quickly select a number of journals that meet his requirements from so many journals? For this purpose, designing an efficient journal recommendation system can help the author solve the task. According to the manuscript's topic, the recommendation system can help the author identify several appropriate journals and the author could select the most appropriate one to submit. Hence, the author can save a lot of time in selecting journals and focus more on scientific research.

In the real experiment, it is assumed that there exists a journal recommendation system. The system includes some key information of the paper, such as the title T, abstract A, and the content of the keyword K. Suppose there are NUM journals from the journal publisher's website and we define the recommendation rate as RA, thus the number of recommended journals TAR = NUM * RA.

The training set is trained by extracting C% of the papers from each journal, and the remaining (1 − C%) papers are selected as test sets. In the test set, these papers are calculated by the similarity probability of journals according to the Naive Bayesian algorithm, and we denote the pre-TAR journals are selected as recommended journals according to the descending order of the similarity probability.

If the recommended journals of the manuscript contain the journal corresponding to the paper in the test set, the journal recommendation is considered successful. If the journal in which the paper is located is not available in all recommended journals, the recommendation is considered failed.

Finally, in order to prevent some journals due to having more test papers, the recommendation accuracy rate of the journals will be lowered. Therefore, the recommendation accuracy of the journal recommendation system is calculated according to the weighted of every journal's papers. The quantity is finally averaged for the total, and the correct rate is recommended by NUM journals.

3.2   Preprocessing Module

We use all words of the paper as a corpus, remove the stop words from the words in the corpus and merge the words in the singular and plural form. After that, we calculate the TF-IDF value for the remaining words. According to the TF-IDF value range of MAX(R1) and MIN(R2), we can filter some frequently or rare words to reduce the number of words, and then select the representative keywords according to the words' frequency of each journal. According to whether the position of words in the title, abstract and keyword, we can plus the different weights to count its word frequency, thus constructing a word frequency table containing keywords in each journal. We need to filter the test set papers of each journal to include the vector corresponding to the representative keyword in the corpus. In the statistics of the number of papers in each journal as a percentage of the total number of papers in the journal, we can calculate the Naive Bayes algorithm based on the data of the three tables. The following process is shown in Fig. 2.

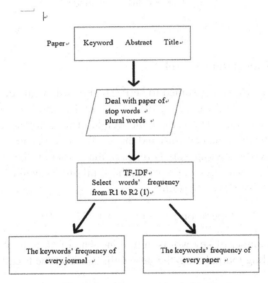

Fig. 2. Generate two data tables

3.3 Recommended Calculation Module

When the user submits the title, keyword and abstract of the paper to the recommendation system, the system first extracts the representative keyword according to the paper words provided by the user. Then the next steps include removing the stop word, merging the singular, plural forms of the word, and comparing the extract keyword with each representative keyword of journal. If there exists the same word, it can calculate the probability that the word frequency of the journal keyword occupied in the same corpus; otherwise, the system multiplies the reciprocal of the number of words in all the current corpus, the logarithm is added after each keyword is calculated and the total similarity probability is obtained by summing up them. The probability of each journal is different in principle. According to the similarity probability ranking from high to low, the journals of the former TAR (the number of recommended journals) are regarded as recommended journals. Then, we can verify whether the original papers are in the recommended journals by the test set. The details of Operation 1 and Operation 2 are introduced in Sect. 3.4, and the process is depicted in Fig. 3.

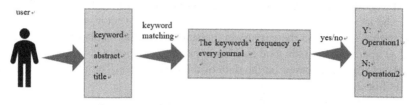

Fig. 3. Keyword match model.

3.4 Probability Calculation Module

The total number of words is assumed to be P. The P words in the paper database have P serial numbers. The word frequency of each journal's keyword number is recorded in the word frequency table. At this time, the weight of word frequency calculation can be considered by the title, the keyword and the abstract in descending order. Assuming that the specific keyword (X) appears N times in the journal, if the paper submitted by the user contains the corresponding X word, the similarity probability with a journal is calculated by the Naive Bayes algorithm.

$$\text{Operation 1}: \quad (1 + N)/(M + P)$$

M is the total number of key words in training data of all journals. If there is no X word in corresponding journal, then the probability at this time is calculated as:

$$\text{Operation 2}: \quad 1/(M + P)$$

Finally, each result is multiplied by the number of papers in the journal as a percentage of the total number of papers.

In order to facilitate the calculation, each calculation of the probability results takes the logarithm and adds the results of each logarithm of the entire journal to as the recommended value of the entire journal. Comparing the recommended values of each journal can produce the recommendation list.

4 Training Data of Poisoning Attack Against Naive Bayesian Journal Recommendation Algorithm

4.1 Attacking Target

The target of this attack is the availability of data whose destination is to disturb the training data. We select S% representative keyword from papers of journal, and these words can express the feature of journal. For example, if the journal belong to biology area, it may has knowledge including some specific words. When the model trains by the database, these malicious data disguised in the database can could affect the recommendation results. In addition, we can adjust the value of S to maintain the level of attack that decreases the recommendation accuracy.

4.2 Attacking Method

We calculate the word frequently to find the representative keyword in each journal and these words may consist the S% proportion of keyword database. We put the papers which include the keyword of other journals to every journal, the recommendation model may predict error result. When the rate of journals' keyword gets closer to the S%, the recommendation accuracy will be more decrease, we can analysis accuracy of different rate of journal keywords to conclude the attack effect.

4.3 Evaluation Metric

When keeping the number of recommendation journal, we evaluate the effect of the success recommendation rate. Then we can change the different proportion of malicious data to observe the change of the recommendation accuracy.

5 Experimental Results and Analysis

5.1 Experiment Setting

In our experiment, we select one hundred journals including the latest published papers and the number exceeds twenty thousand. These papers contain three section: the title (T), the abstract (A), and the keyword (K). We assume the recommendation rate is 5%; we select 90% papers of each journal as training data, and the remaining 10% papers are considered as test set. We use the TF-IDF to take out the words frequently over 1000 times and the remaining words consist the keywords database. Then we gain the statistic of keywords and table of every word frequency. According to the words in the title, abstract and keywords, the frequency of word multiply 5, 1, 3 to weight the frequency. In addition, we gain the statistic about the test set including corresponding keywords in database and the number of paper in each journal as a percentage of the total number of papers, using these three tables to calculate the recommendation probability through the Naive Bayesian algorithm.

The attack method is based on 50% of the random journals from 100 journals to simulate the injection of malicious data. In the selected journals, ten fake papers with specific malicious data are added which includes the title, abstract and keywords of each paper. The malicious data is about 5000 words located near the highest IDF value, and the recommended accuracy is calculated after retraining the entire model.

5.2 Accuracy Distribution of the Number of Different Recommended Journals Without Attack

Figure 4 shows the experimental results of the accuracy distribution of the number of different recommended journals without attack. The number of recommended journals on the x-axis is from 1 to 5. The recommendation accuracy is gradually increasing. The recommended growth rate is firstly fast and then slow, with the number of recommendations increasing, the recommendation accuracy gradually approaches the upper limit. When TAR = 5, the recommendation accuracy rate reached 84.3%.

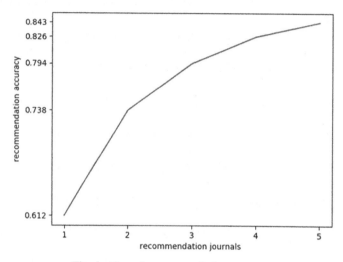

Fig. 4. Normal recommendation accuracy

5.3 Accuracy Distribution of the Number of Different Recommended Journals with Attack

Figure 5 shows the experimental results of the accuracy distribution of the number of different recommended journals under attack. When TAR = 5, the recommendation accuracy rate reaches 61.1% and when TAR = 1, the recommendation accuracy rate only reaches 43.3%, lower than the normal recommendation accuracy.

5.4 Comparison of Recommendation Accuracy Rate with or Without Attack

Figure 6 shows the results of a comparison of the accuracy distributions of different recommended journals with or without attack. It can be seen that the recommendation accuracy of the post-attack model is significantly reduced, and the accuracy relative to the number of recommended journals is reduced by about 20%.

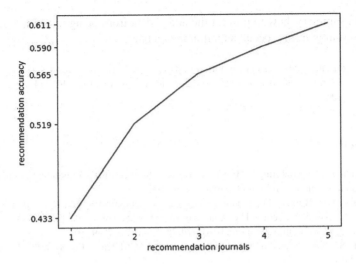

Fig. 5. Attacked recommendation accuracy

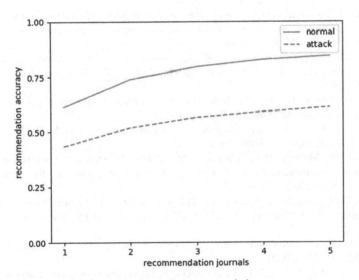

Fig. 6. Normal and attack recommendation accuracy

6 Conclusion

The Naive Bayesian-based journal recommendation system is fragile, and we can severely damage the recommendation system by attacking the availability of the training data. As long as we could find the keywords with high weight in the journal recommendation system, we can achieve good results by a small number of attack contents. As our experiment shows, only ten papers could reduce the recommendation accuracy rate by 20%. In summary, how to prevent the attack data from being mixed into the model through retraining needs special attention in practice.

Acknowledgement. This work is supported in part by the National Natural Science Foundation of China under Grant 61902082, Grant U1636215, and the National Key R&D Program of China 2018YFB1004003.

References

1. Adomavicius, G., Tuzhilin, A.: Toward the next generation of recommender systems: a survey of the state-of-the-art and possible extensions (2005)
2. Pazzani, M.J., Billsus, D.: Content-based recommendation systems. In: Brusilovsky, P., Kobsa, A., Nejdl, W. (eds.) The Adaptive Web. LNCS, vol. 4321, pp. 325–341. Springer, Heidelberg (2007). https://doi.org/10.1007/978-3-540-72079-9_10
3. Pollock, S.: A rule-based message filtering system. ACM Trans. Inf. Syst. (TOIS) **6**(3), 232–254 (1988)
4. Gunawardana, A., Shani, G.: A survey of accuracy evaluation metrics of recommendation tasks. J. Mach. Learn. **10**, 2935–2962 (2009)
5. Resnick, P., Iacovou, N., et al.: GroupLens: an open architecture for collaborative filtering of netnews. In: Proceedings of ACM Conference on Computer Supported Cooperative Work, CSCW 1994, pp. 175–186 (1994)
6. Sarwar, B., Karypis, G., Konstan, J., Riedl, J.: Item-based collaborative filtering recommendation algorithms. In: Proceeding of the 10th International Conference on World Wide Web, WWW (2001)
7. Kautz, H., Selman, B., Shah, M.: Referral web: combining social networks and collaborative filtering. Commun. ACM **40**(2), 63–65 (1997)
8. Cornor, M., Herlocker, J.: Clustering items for collaborative filtering. In: Proceedings of the ACM SIGIR Workshop, SIGIR (1999)
9. Melville, P., Mooney, R.J., Nagarajan, R.: Content-boosted collaborative filtering for improved recommendations. In: Proceedings of American Association for Artificial Intelligence, AAAI (2002)
10. Sarwar, B.M., Karypis, G., Konstan, J., Riedl, J.: Analysis of recommendation algorithms for E-commerce. In: Proceedings of the 2nd ACM conference on Electronic commerce, ACM EC (2000)
11. Burke, B.: Hybrid recommender systems: survey and experiments. User Model. User-Adap. Inter. **12**, 331–370 (2002)
12. O'Mahony, M.P., Hurley, N.J., Silvestre, G.C.M.: Recommender systems: attack types and strategies
13. Miller, D.J., Hu, X., Xiang, Z., Kesidis, G.: A mixture model based defense for data poisoning attacks against naive bayes spam filters
14. Goldberg, D., Nichols, D., Oki, B., Terry, D.: Using collaborative filtering to weave an information tapestry
15. Li, M., Sun, Y., Shen, S., Tian, Z., Wang, Y., Wang, X.: DPIF: a framework for distinguishing unintentional quality problems from potential shilling attacks. Comput. Mater. Cont. **59**(1), 331–344 (2019)
16. Hou, M., Wei, R., Wang, T., Cheng, Y., Qian, B.: Reliable medical recommendation based on privacy-preserving collaborative filtering. Comput. Mater. Cont. **56**(1), 137–149 (2018)
17. Bin, S., et al.: Collaborative filtering recommendation algorithm based on multi-relationship social network. Comput. Mater. Cont. **60**(2), 659–674 (2019)

Research on Intrusion Detection Technology of Industrial Control Systems

Dailing Xia[1], Yanbin Sun[1(✉)], and Quanlong Guan[2]

[1] Cyberspace Institute of Advanced Technology, Guangzhou University, Guangzhou, China
sunyanbin@gzhu.edu.cn
[2] Jinan University, Guangzhou, China

Abstract. The industrial control system is the core of various infrastructures. With the development of process technology and the development of computer network technology, industrial control systems are constantly integrating with the Internet, evolving into an open system, which also brings numerous threats to the industrial control systems. As an important security protection technology, many scholars have conducted a lot of research on industrial control system intrusion detection. The main work of this paper is to summarize the current intrusion detection technology. First part introduces the industrial control system and analyzing its threat and the main defense technologies. The second introduces the intrusion detection technology. followed by the current research on the different classification methods of intrusion detection technology to summarize, classify and compare the existing research. Finally, it summarizes and looks forward to intrusion detection technology of industrial control system.

Keywords: Industrial control systems · Intrusion detection · Safety protection

1 Introduction

Industrial control system is a general term for control systems of industrial production. It is widely used in petroleum, chemical, electric power, manufacturing and so on. In recent years, due to the development of process technology and the development of information technology, traditional physical isolation industrial control systems have been unable to meet the needs of modern industrial production, and have developed into a large number of open systems connected to the Internet. While it brings a lot of convenience and progress to the industrial control system, it also brings a lot of security threats. Because the traditional industrial control system is mainly for the safety of the system and it doesn't take into account the network information security of the system, so there are no corresponding security protection measures. In recent years, the security threats against industrial control systems have increased, and the degree of harm is quite large too.

The Stuxnet in 2010 caused huge losses to the Iranian nuclear power plant, it seriously affect the operation of nuclear reactors and it cause irreversible damage to nuclear reactor equipment [1]; in 2011, the emergence of a variant of the Stunet virus, Duqu virus,

X. Sun et al. (Eds.): ICAIS 2020, CCIS 1254, pp. 129–139, 2020.
https://doi.org/10.1007/978-981-15-8101-4_13

which could last for a long time lurk and collect relevant information, and launch an attack when necessary; In 2012, a flame virus was discovered, which is able to collect various sensitive information; a continuous high-level attack took in 2014 caused the production process of a German steel plant to shut down suddenly, causing irreversible damage to the entire production system; in 2015, the attackers attacked the Ukrainian power sector monitoring and management system, causing 42 substations in Ukraine to fail, causing power outages in many areas for several hours. These events made many countries gradually realize the importance of industrial control system safety. Along with the implementation of the German Industry 4.0 strategy, many countries have raised industrial control systems to national strategic security and taken various security protection methods for various malicious threats, such as vulnerability scanning, deep firewall defense, Intrusion detection, etc. As an important way of security protection, intrusion detection can detect the internal and external threats of the system, which has implications for the late defense of the system.

At present, the intrusion detection technology for industrial control systems has considerable more research, and the work of this paper is mainly about the overview of current research. First part mainly introduces the threat of industrial control system and Introduce the industrial control system and analyze its threats and current main defense technologies. The second introduce the related concepts and classification methods of intrusion detection technology. followed by the current research on the different classification methods of intrusion detection technology to summarize, classify and compare the existing research. Finally, it summarizes and looks forward to intrusion detection technology in its industrial control system.

2 Industrial Control System

2.1 Overview of Industrial Control System

Industrial control system is a general term for control systems in industrial production, which is widely used in petroleum, chemical, power, manufacturing, etc. From the emergence of computers and beginning to be used in industrial control systems, the development of industrial control systems has probably gone from direct digital Control system, distributed control system, and fieldbus control system. At the present, the industrial control system has changed from a traditional closed system to an open network interconnection system. The modern industrial control system includes enterprise office network and process control. And it consists of three parts: the monitoring network and the on-site control system. The corporate office network is mainly composed of the enterprise resource planning network and the manufacturing execution system, which is mainly responsible for receiving system information, network information and issuing decisions. The process control and monitoring network consists of various monitoring stations, engineer station, various historical database server and OPC server, which is mainly responsible for data collection. The field control system mainly includes remote control unit, programmable logic controller and various physical equipment. The structure of modern industrial control system brings great convenience in industrial production, which is also very vulnerable. Currently, the threats and attacks against industrial control systems involved in every level of the system.

2.2 The Threats to the Industrial Control Systems

Although many countries pay more and more attention to industrial control security and propose corresponding countermeasures. Plenty of the cyber-attack methods are constantly developing in these years. However, the current form of industrial control security is still in danger. So, some scholars have proposed the security threats faced by industrial control systems, which can be roughly divided into three categories: misuse of mobile media, the lack of network management awareness, and system security vulnerabilities [2]. There are two main aspects of security risks caused by misuse of mobile media. On the one hand, some related people have unintentionally or jointly leaked the system with external personnel. On the other hand, the mobile media used were infected with viruses, which made the stored information destroyed or stolen. The lack of network management awareness can be divided into two aspects. Firstly, it mainly refers to the lack of personnel management training in current enterprises. As a result, many system administrators lack enough security awareness who may directly publish confidential corporate information on the network or leading to the use of illegal elements. Secondly, some enterprises are short of enough management, which will cause huge losses to the enterprise. There is a security breach in the system. It mainly refers to the existence of system vulnerabilities in the design of industrial control systems, which provides relevant attackers with an opportunity. They can use the system's existing vulnerabilities to attack the system. The literature [3] takes advantage of the vulnerability of the existing decentralized structure used by hidden services in the Internet of things to launch Eclipse attacks on them, and demonstrates the great threat posed by these vulnerabilities. In response to these threats and attacks, the industrial and academic industries have proposed various protective measures.

2.3 Industrial Control System Safety Protection Technology

The architecture of the industrial control system is very different from the information network. First of all, in terms of security concepts, information technology follows the CIA principle, which is about the confidentiality, integrity, and availability. The first consideration is the confidentiality of information. However, industrial control systems follow the CIA principle and put safety on the first place. When considering safety solutions, they are due to the unique characteristics of industrial control systems. So we must consider new solutions that based on the characteristics of industrial control systems. At present, the main safety of industrial control systems protection methods includes industrial firewall technology, security audit technology, access control technology, intrusion detection technology, vulnerability scanning vulnerability mining technology, and situational awareness technology [4].

Access control technology is used to restrict the access to specific resources in the system, and ensure the security of the system by authorizing access. The typical access control method is by establishing a whitelist mechanism. The whitelist mechanism is the basic security policy of industrial control system security protection. By establishing a white list of software, system configuration, user connections, and identity authentication. Literature [5] proposed to improve the reliability of vehicle application level by deploying RSG, aiming at the problem of vehicle verification trust existing in the Internet of vehicles. In order to ensure the security of digital evidence in documents, literature [6] designed a block-DEF framework using Block chain technology, and proved through experiments that this design can well meet the needs.

The vulnerability scanning and mining technology identify some vulnerabilities in the system by scanning system devices, system software and then compare them with a network security vulnerability library. It can be divided into static vulnerability mining methods and dynamic vulnerability mining methods. Literature [7] designed the concept of network reference vulnerability association based on evidence reasoning, and built erns for network system vulnerability and environment information. In the literature [8], the game theory is used to model the attack of the attacker, and the experiment proves that this scheme plays an important role in the protection of Internet of vehicles.

Industrial firewall, intrusion detection and security audit together form the whole of the defense-in-depth system. As the outermost layer of defense-in-depth, industrial control firewalls should play a role about the function of intrusion from external networks. For industrial control firewall designing, industrial control firewalls must support industrial control. The analysis of unique protocols and the deep protection of industrial control systems must be combined with specific process information and intrusion detection. As the second step of defense in depth, which can not only detect threats outside the system, but also detect anomalies from inside the system. For the last link of defense in depth, security audit also plays an important role in the security protection in industrial control systems. It can perform in-depth analysis and analysis of the actual network topology and detection information and messages of industrial control systems. Analysis of malicious behavior, which strengthens the defense effect of the entire system in turn.

As a major way of security protection in industrial control systems, intrusion detection can detect abnormalities from inside and outside of the system. In next section, this paper will introduce the related concepts, classification and applications of industrial control system's intrusion detection technology.

3   Intrusion Detection Technology

Researchers draw on the traditional intrusion detection in the information field, and propose the intrusion detection of industrial control systems based on the characteristics of industrial control networks. As an important security protection technology, intrusion detection is mainly through security monitoring and abnormal alarms to ensure the industrial control system safety. The detection process can be described as firstly by collecting various devices and network information in the industrial control system, and then identifying and distinguishing the information in a specific manner, and finally determining the state of the system, that is, whether the system is normal or abnormal. In recent years, the industry and academia have conducted a lot of research on the intrusion detection of industrial control systems, and have achieved a lot of achievement.

At present, there is still no unified classification method for intrusion detection systems. The mainstream method still adopts two main classification methods [9]. One classification method is based on the detection technology, and the intrusion detection system is divided into a feature-based intrusion detection system and anomaly-based intrusion detection systems. The feature-based intrusion detection system establishes a model for abnormal behaviors and establishes an anomalous behavior library. When there are new behaviors, it compares with the feature behavior library to find anomalies. The anomaly-based intrusion detection is just opposite. it discovers anomalous behavior by establishing a model of normal behavior. Another classification method is to divide the intrusion detection system into network intrusion detection system and host intrusion detection system according to different data sources. network intrusion detection system can be summarized as setting detection points at different locations in the network to acquire traffic in the network, and excavating and analyzing the acquired network traffic; the host intrusion detection system can be summarized as mainly through monitoring and detecting host configuration, applications, and I/O in industrial control systems to detect anomalies. The following content mainly summarizes the existing research based on these two classification methods and compares the specific classification among them.

4 Classification of Intrusion Detection Based on Different Detection Techniques

4.1 Feature-Based Intrusion Detection

Feature-based intrusion detection mainly finds the abnormal behavior of the system by comparing the detection behavior with the existing abnormal behavior library. Therefore, the key and difficult point of this method is to accurately extract the description features of abnormal behavior. Because of the diversity and complexity of industrial control systems, when designing feature-based intrusion detection systems for specific industrial control systems. It is necessary to accurately extract features that reflect abnormal behaviors and to simplify other features. In this way, it can improve the accuracy of the intrusion detection system and reduce the time of intrusion detection.

At present, many scholars have done a lot of research on feature-based intrusion detection. The features selected to indicate anomalies in the current research are mainly network traffic, industrial control communication protocols, and system parameters. There are quite a few scholars use the change of network traffic as a feature to detect anomalies in the system. Reference [10] uses the network traffic of SCANDA system as a feature, and proves the effectiveness of the method from the concept of implementation. Reference [11] uses the size of network traffic to identify abnormalities in the system, and experimental results show that the method can effectively identify abnormal conditions in the system. In the research characterized by system parameters, literature [12] mainly uses various I/O data and registers of the system. The value is used as the characteristic value representing the abnormal behavior, and the abnormality of the system is detected by the way of supervised learning; Literature [13] uses the time parameter of the equipment, various communication information, etc. as the characteristic value to detect the abnormal intrusion of the substation. The method can detect anomalies in different locations and different substations. At the same time, a large number of scholars also specialize in industrial control communication protocols. Anomaly detection. Reference [14] is based on the Modbus RTU/ASCII protocol commonly used in industrial control systems, using intrusion detection based on Snort software to identify abnormalities in the system. For the redundancy and high latitude characteristics of data in industrial control systems, the optimization of feature selection improves the accuracy of detection algorithms and reduces the false alarm rate. Literature [15] propose the use of Fisher score and KPCA algorithm, and designed an intrusion detection model based on SVPSO-SVM. Through experiments and compare with other algorithm models proves the effectiveness of this algorithm.

4.2 Anomaly-Based Intrusion Detection

Anomaly intrusion detection technology is another important way to detect anomalies. Unlike feature-based detection, this detection method requires the establishment of a model of normal behavior. Anomalies in industrial control systems are identified based on the comparison of normal behavior.

Aiming at the detection of industrial control abnormal protocol behaviors, the literature [16] establishes an industrial control communication protocol data detection model through the SVM method, and compares the relevant parameters of the established model to identify abnormal phenomena in the system. Some scholars mainly focus on establishing an anomaly detection model for industrial control system model parameters. Literature [17] has carried out efficient path modeling for routing. Literature [18] established a multi-model based on industrial process automation system, and distinguished between faults and abnormalities through the HMM model, the simulation results show that the system has high detection accuracy and the false alarm rate is less than 1.6% high detection accuracy, and the false alarm rate is below 1.6%, and it also verifies that the system has little effect on the real-time performance of the system. At the same time, the literature [19] mainly establishes a system model for complex industrial control systems, and use the ant colony algorithm and unsupervised feature extraction to identify abnormal behaviors. Aiming at some problems in the detection of traditional machine learning algorithms, some scholars are committed to algorithm improvement to improve the level of intrusion detection in industrial control systems In literature [20], SSAE unsupervised learning algorithm is used to improve the traditional PNN model to solve the problem of slow convergence and high false positives of collaborative intrusion detection algorithm, and the feasibility of the algorithm was proved through experiments.

4.3 Comparison of Two Detection Methods

The detection method used in feature-based intrusion detection systems is to detect attacks in industrial control systems by extracting features that can indicate abnormal behavior, and then identify the features through feature recognition. Therefore, this detection method has high detection accuracy. However, its defects are also obvious. First of all, it is necessary to count a large number of characteristics of abnormal behavior, and there is another obvious defect is that it cannot detect unknown types of attacks. The detection method used by anomaly-based intrusion detection algorithms is by extracting features that can represent normal behavior, and according to the normal behavior model identifies and detects attacks in industrial control systems. One obvious advantage of this detection method is the ability to identify unknown types of attacks. However, due to the complexity of industrial control systems, it is difficult to establish a normal and universal model that can represent the normal system, and the performance of feature-based intrusion detection systems is not as good as that of feature-based intrusion detection systems.

On the whole, the application scope of anomaly-based intrusion detection is wider than that of feature-based intrusion detection. At present, a major research hotspot based on anomalies is mainly to improve its detection accuracy. There are related studies that combine the two methods together to detect anomalies in industrial control network.

5   Classification of Intrusion Detection Based on Data Sources

5.1   Network Intrusion Detection

The monitoring device in the Intrusion Detection System (IDS) based on the industrial control network is always located in the entire network, capturing communication packets between the master control center and the field site or field devices. The information in these captured data packets is evaluated to determine whether it constitutes a threat. If the packet is suspicious, an alert will be issued. This detection method is called network intrusion detection.

Network intrusion detection mainly focuses on the detection of network traffic and industrial control network protocol. In the research of network protocol detection, in literature [21], MODBUS RTU/ASCII Snort is used to simulate the use of snort rules to detect four exceptions: denial of service, command injection, response injection and system reconnaissance anomaly on Modbus network, and it focus on the implementation of this system and improve detection accuracy; the literature [22] uses neural network algorithms to detect attacks on commonly used industrial control protocols such as Modbus and OPC protocols. At the same time, many studies are devoted to the use of various algorithms to detect anomalies based on abnormal network traffic in industrial control networks. [23] uses probabilistic component analysis to detect traffic transmitted between networks; reference [24] models the network traffic of the industrial control network to detect anomalies in the network; reference; the literature [25] uses the K-neighborhood learning algorithm to detect network traffic.

Detection accuracy and false alarm rate are important evaluation indicators for industrial control system intrusion detection. Therefore, research on improving the detection accuracy of the algorithm and reducing the false alarm rate is particularly important. The literature [26] detects the known attack types by using information mining and semi-supervised learning algorithms, and simulates the network attack to detect the effectiveness of the algorithm. The experimental results show that the algorithm can avoid the semi-supervised K-means algorithm's shortcomings and it can improve the detection accuracy.

5.2   Host Intrusion Detection

The host intrusion detection system mainly extracts the information of the status of the host device, the login of the device, the operation of the device, the I/O of the device, and various operations performed on the device, and then performs detection according to the extracted features.

In terms of device input and output detection, In literature [27], the normal output of the system is modeled by the self-associative kernel regression model, and the anomalies in the system are identified according to the residuals of the normal model. Some research scholars mainly rely on System data is used to identify abnormal data. the literature [28] adopted Obtain all kinds of data of smart grid operation, and then use unsupervised learning to detect anomalies. In terms of system state parameters as features, reference [29] uses industry Control the various register values in the system to build a system model, and identify system anomalies based on the difference between the model output and the actual output. Literature [30] uses various system parameters and establishes a normal model of the system to implement anomaly detection based on the model. Anomaly detection can also be performed based on the input and output of the system, for example, the anomalies of data utilization and CPU utilization of the system are solved by the iterative data mining method in [31].

5.3   Comparison of Two Detection Methods

The network intrusion detection system identifies network anomalies in the system by detecting network packets in the industrial control network. It does not depend on specific hosts and configurations, so it has the characteristics of high portability. In addition, the network intrusion detection system can only detect and monitor a network area, which can greatly reduce the cost of detection. T Network intrusion detection system are main defects cannot detect the host internal attacks and unable to cope with Dos attack at the same time, it can't check all packets at the same time, can lead to packet loss, thus caused it weak in terms of accuracy, compared with the method of network intrusion detection, host intrusion detection method does not need to monitor the network data flow, it largely reduces the consumption of time and resources. However, due to the large differences between the system structure and functions of the industrial control system, the host intrusion detection system performs poorly in terms of portability. Also because the host needs to occupy system resources, it will affect the host performance. There is also a negative impact on host performance due to the host intrusion detection system need to occupy system resources.

6   Conclusion

The networking of modern industrial control systems has become an inevitable trend. However, when it brings great progress and convenience to the industrial control system, it also brings many security threats to the industrial control system. Intrusion detection technology as an important security protection method for the information network, it has been obtained extensive research in the security protection of industrial control systems. The mainstream method still adopts two main classification methods. One classification method is based on the detection technology, and the intrusion detection system is divided into a feature-based intrusion detection system and anomaly-based intrusion detection systems. Another classification method is to divide the intrusion detection system into network intrusion detection system and host intrusion detection system according to different data sources. This paper mainly reviews the research involved in this existing mainstream method, and summarizes the advantages and disadvantages of each detection method. These studies can improve the safety of industrial control systems to a certain extent, but for the moment, the whole. The research started late and it is mainly in the state of theoretical research. In the face of complex and specific industrial control systems, each industrial control system has its own unique characteristics in practical applications. It is necessary to study and adapt to different industrial control systems. With the continuous development of industrial control systems and the development of aggressive behavior, the corresponding intrusion detection must continue to develop.

As far as the current research is concerned, the intrusion detection technology should be further developed for the detection of more efficient anomaly intrusion detection features, continuous improvement of intrusion detection algorithms, and further application of machine learning and data mining methods to intrusion detection systems. Further strengthen the accuracy and real-time of the intrusion system, and must further strengthen the combination of theoretical research and practical application. As an important security protection method for industrial control system security, intrusion detection is of great significance to enhance the security of industrial control systems. At the same time, intrusion detection should be combined with other security protection methods to jointly protect the Industry Control System security.

Acknowledgments. This work is funded by the National Key Research and Development Plan (Grant No. 2018YFB0803504), the National Natural Science Foundation of China (No. 61702223, 61702220, 61871140, 61602210, 61877029, U1636215), the Science and Technology Planning Project of Guangdong (2017A040405029), the Science and Technology Planning Project of Guangzhou (201902010041), the Fundamental Research Funds for the Central Universities (21617408, 21619404).

References

1. Langner, R.: Stuxnet: dissecting a cyberwarfare weapon. IEEE Secur. Priv. Mag. **9**(3), 49–51 (2011)
2. Bai, X.: Discussion on industrial control system security threat and protection application. China information technology (2018)
3. Tan, Q., Gao, Y., Shi, J., Wang, X., Fang, B., Tian, Z.: Toward a comprehensive insight to the eclipse attacks of tor hidden services. IEEE Internet Things J. **6**(2), 1584–1593 (2019)
4. Qi, W.: Review on information security of industrial control systems. Commun. Power Technol. **36**(05), 225–226 (2019)
5. Tian, Z., Li, M., Qiu, M., Sun, Y., Su, S.: Block-DEF: a secure digital evidence system using blockchain. Inf. Sci. **491**, 151–165 (2019). https://doi.org/10.1016/j.ins.2019.04.011
6. Tian, Z., Su, S., Yu, X., et al.: Vcash: a novel reputation framework for identifying denial of traffic service in internet of connected vehicles. IEEE Internet Things J. **7**(5), 3901–3909 (2019)
7. Tian, Z., et al.: Real time lateral movement detection based on evidence reasoning network for edge computing environment. IEEE Trans. Ind. Inform. **15**(7), 4285–4294 (2019). https://doi.org/10.1109/TII.2019.2907754
8. Tian, Z., Gao, X., Su, S., Qiu, J., Du, X., Guizani, M.: Evaluating reputation management schemes of Internet of vehicles based on evolutionary game theory. IEEE Trans. Veh. Technol. **68**(6), 5971–5980 (2019). https://doi.org/10.1109/TVT.2019.2910217

9. Misra, S., Krishna, P.V., Abraharm, K.I.: Energy efficient learning solution for intrusion detection in wireless sensor network. In: Proceedings of the 2nd Communication System and Networks, pp. 1–6. IEEE (2010)

10. Barbosa, R.R.R., Sadre, R., Pras, A.: Towards periodicity based anomaly detection in SCADA networks. In: Proceedings of 2012 IEEE 17th International Conference on Emerging Technologies and Factory Automation (ETFA 2012). IEEE (2012)

11. Hou, C., et al.: A probabilistic principal component analysis approach for detecting traffic normaly in industrial networks. J. Xi'an Jiaotong Univ. **46**(2), 70–75 (2012)

12. Luo, Y.: Research and design on intrusion detection methods for industrial control system. Ph.D. Zhejiang University, Hangzhou, China (2013)

13. Ten, C.W., Hong, J., Liu, C.C.: Anomaly detection for cybersecurity of the substations. IEEE Trans. Smart Grid **2**(4), 865–873 (2011)

14. Morrist, T., Vaughnr, R., Dandassy, Y.: A retrofit network intrusion detection system for modbus RTU and ASCII industrial control systems. In: The 45th Hawaii International Conference on System Science, pp. 2338–2345 (2012)

15. Zhang, R., Chen, H.: SVPSO-SVM industrial control intrusion detection algorithm, pp. 1–17 (2019). Accessed 29 Nov 2019. https://doi.org/10.19678/j.issn.1000-3428.0054989

16. Vollmer, T., Manic, M.: Cyber-physical system security with deceptive virtual hosts for industrial control networks. IEEE Trans. Ind. Inf. **10**(2), 1337–1347 (2014)

17. Tian, Z., Su, S., Shi, W., Du, X., Guizani, M., Yu, X.: A data-driven model for future Internet route decision modeling. Future Gener. Comput. Syst. **95**, 212–220 (2019)

18. Shang, W., et al.: Industrial communication intrusion detection algorithm based on improved one-class SVM. In: 2015 World Congress on Industrial Control Systems Security (WCICSS). IEEE (2015)

19. Xiong, Y., Wang, H.: Research on network intrusion detection based on SSAE-PNN algorithm 019. J. Tianjin Univ. Technol. **35**(05), 6–11 (2015)

20. Morris, T., Vaughn, R., Dandass, Y.: A retrofit network intrusion detection system for MODBUS RTU and ASCII industrial control systems. In: 2012 45th Hawaii International Conference on System Sciences. IEEE (2012)

21. Wang, H.: On anomaly detection and defense resource allocation of industrial control networks. Diss. Zhejiang University (2014)

22. Hou, C.Y., Jiang, H.H., Rui, W.Z., Liu, L.: A probabilistic principal component analysis approach for detecting traffic anomaly in industrial network. J. Xi'an Jiao Tong Univ. **46**(2), 70–75 (2017)

23. Gao, C.M.: Network traffic anomaly detection based on industrial control network. Beijing University of Technology, Beijing (2014)

24. Shang, W.L., Sheng, S.Z., Ming, W.: Modbus/TCP communication anomaly detection based on PSO-SVM. In: Applied Mechanics and Materials. vol. 490. Trans Tech Publications (2014)

25. Yang, D., Usynin, A., Hines, J.W.: Anomaly-based intrusion detection for SCADA systems. In: 5th International Topical Meeting on Nuclear Plant Instrumentation, Control and Human Machine Interface Technologies (Npic & Hmit 2005) (2015)

26. Liu, C.C.: Research on intrusion detection technology of industrial control system. University of Electronic Science and Technology of China, Cheng Du (2017)

27. Khalili, A., Sami, A.: SysDetect: a systematic approach to critical state determination for industrial intrusion detection systems using Apriori algorithm. J. Process Control **32**, 154–160 (2015)

28. Ahmed, S., et al.: Unsupervised machine learning—based detection of covert data integrity assault in smart grid networks utilizing isolation forest. IEEE Trans. Inf. Forensics Secur. **14**(10), 2765–2777 (2019)

29. Huazhong, W., Zhihui, Y., et al.: Application of fusion PCA and PSO-SVM method in industrial control intrusion detection. Bull. Sci. Technol. **33**(1), 80–85 (2017)

30. Zhang, F., et al.: Multi-layer data-driven cyber-attack detection system for industrial control systems based on network, system and process data. IEEE Trans. Ind. Inf. **15**(7), 4362–4369 (2019)
31. Erez, N., Avishai, W.: Control variable classification, modeling and anomaly detection in Modbus/TCP SCADA systems. Int. J. Crit. Infrastruct. Prot. **10**, 59–70 (2015)

Resnet-Based Slide Puzzle Captcha Automatic Response System

Danni Wu[1], Jing Qiu[1], Huiwu Huang[2(✉)], Lihua Yin[1], Zhaoquan Gu[1],
and Zhihong Tian[1]

[1] Cyberspace Institute of Advanced Technology, Guangzhou University, Guangzhou 510006,
China
2111906090@gzhu.edu.cn
[2] Center of Campus Network and Modern Educational Technology,
Guangdong University of Technology, Guangzhou 510006, China
393575614@qq.com

Abstract. Slide puzzle captcha is a kind of dynamic cognitive game, which
requires users to pass a series of cognitive tasks to verify themselves. Compared to
boring text captcha, the user experience has been greatly improved, so slide puzzle
captcha has gradually replaced the text-based captcha on many large platforms.
In this paper, we divided slide puzzle captcha cracking into three steps: identifying the gap position, generating the sliding track, and implementing the browser
automation. For the location identification of the gap, we used residual network
based on object detection and yolov3-based object detection, establish Resnet-18
model and Yolov3 model, and in order to train the two models, we collect 1000
images from Bilibili, Netease Shield, Tik Tok, Jingdong, etcand estimated accuracy of gap identification; As for the generation of sliding trajectory, we analyze
the sliding trajectory of human and imitated the human slider trajectory by the
piecewise curve fitting of least-squares method; For the automatic implementation of browser, we calculate the offset position, use the TencentAPI, directly feed
the recognition result to the page. We choose the resnet-18 and Yolov3 model
to identify the location of the gap. We utilize the least-squares method to fit the
sliding trajectory segmentally, increasing the degree of simulation and avoiding
machine detection.

Keywords: Slide puzzle captcha · Resnet · Yolo neural network · Object
detection

1 Introduction

The basic principle of Captcha is a Turing test, which aims to distinguish a legitimate
human user from a computerized program in a simple and low-cost way, so it is also
called Human-Computer Interaction Verification (HIP), but the current captcha, no matter traditional text-based captcha, slide puzzle captcha, audio captcha or even spatial
reasoning captcha [1], there is a method of cracking, but since the cracking cost is high

© Springer Nature Singapore Pte Ltd. 2020
X. Sun et al. (Eds.): ICAIS 2020, CCIS 1254, pp. 140–153, 2020.
https://doi.org/10.1007/978-981-15-8101-4_14

and a certain basic technology is required, the captcha is now often used to block Automated scripting on the web for the abuse of online services, including walking spam and a lot of repetitive operations [2].

In order to realize the automatic response system of the slide puzzle captcha, we innovatively use the Resnet-based object detection and Yolov3-based object detection to identify the gap location, establish Resnet-18 model and Yolov3 [3] model, and in order to train the two models, we collect 1000 images from Bilibili, Netease Shield, Tik Tok, Jingdong, etc. As a result, the accuracy of the object detection model based on Resnet-18 can reach about 88% in the step of identifying the gap position, and the object detection model based on Yolov3 can reach 90%. By analyzing the human sliding trajectory, the segmental curve fitting of the least-squares method is used to simulate the human sliding trajectory to achieve the purpose of confusing the machine.

2 Related Research

Object detection is widely used in many scenarios such as intelligent navigation, medical examination, industrial inspection [4], etc. There is a lot of methods for improvement in the accuracy and efficiency of detection [5]. The machine learning method is adopted, wherein the main classifiers used are Support Vector Machine (SVM) [6] and convolutional neural networks. Among them, well-known algorithms include: R-CNN [7], Over Feat [8], Fast R-CNN [9], Faster R-CNN [10], Yolo [11], SSD [12], Yolov2 [13], AlexNet [14], GoogleNet, etc. These object detection algorithms based on convolutional neural networks are divided into candidate region-based object detection models (R-CNN, SPP-Net [15], Fast R-CNN, and Faster R-CNN) based on the difference in the way of target location. Regression object detection models and residual-based object detection models. Suphannee Sivakor el al. design a novel low-cost attack that leverages deep learning technologies for the semantic annotation of images. The success rates of their system range from 37% to 83%. Binbin Zhao and Raheem Beyah (2018) propose three generic attacks against selection captcha, slide puzzle captcha, and click-based captcha. their attacks are mainly built on object detection models including CNN, R-CNN and Faster R-CNN, The success rates of the recognition and captcha-solving services range from 41% to 90%.

At present, slide puzzle captcha are gradually being used by major websites and network service providers. theoretical research and verification of their security are still needed, and a lot of manpower and material resources are needed to realize them. How to improve the user recognition rate, prevent brute force attacks, prevent hackers from malicious attacks, improve security and reliability, this is the main content of this paper.

3 Resnet-Based Slide Puzzle Captcha Automatic Response System

3.1 System Functions

Data Set Collecting. Collecting the slide puzzle captcha images from Bilibili, Netease Shield, Tik Tok, Jingdong, etc., as a data set preparation.

Image Preprocessing. Normalize and grayscale the captured images, and expand the training set through various methods such as blurring and rotation, and finally convert to permanent storage of binary files.

Model Effect Test. The object detection effects of Resnet-18 model and Yolov3 model were tested separately.

Curve Fitting. Use the least-squares method to fit the drag track that best suits human habits.

Notch Position Identification. Select the picture and frame the gap.

Automated Response. Use the Flask web framework and the TencentAPI to directly report the recognition results to the page. Using the Flask template, and send a verification request to the Tencent server, driving the mouse to drag the control to achieve the purpose of the automatic verification of the slide puzzle captcha.

3.2   Model Architecture

Resnet-Based Gap Recognition Model. The residual network was proposed by Kaiming He and Xiangyu Zhang in 2015. Inserting a residual block in the network can solve the degradation problem well. For the pre-processed captcha gap, the Resnet-18 model is established for predictive identification. The model includes convolutional layer, pooling layer, activation layer, input and output layer.

We select the Rectified Linear Unit (ReLU) as activation function, because it has a great propulsion effect on the convergence speed of the random gradient descent, and the calculation speed is high. The loss function selects smooth L1 loss, which is more robust. When the prediction frame is very different from the actual positioning, the gradient value is not too large. The first layer of the model is the input layer. This layer converts the previously saved sliding captcha image information into the input format required by the convolution layer.

The second layer of the model is the convolutional layer. After the input layer, the image information has been stored in a $224 \times 224 \times 3$ network, the next calculation is the most important step in the convolutional neural network, taking the fifth layer convolution of the model as an example, Layer 5 uses a 3×3 filter and 14×14 input for convolution calculation, the filter slides 2 units per length, that is, stride $= 2$, then the sliding window is 2×2. After the convolution operation, the offset parameter b is added, finally, the activation function f(x) is input.

The third layer of the model is the pooling layer. We use the max-pooling function to give the maximum value in the adjacent matrix region [19]. In this model, the pooling operation of the third layer uses the max-pooling function. The input matrix size is 112×112, and the step size is 2. The pooling operation is performed for each 2×2 sub-region, and the maximum number is selected. The value of the corresponding element of the output matrix.

Figure 1 is a model network structure diagram of the model.

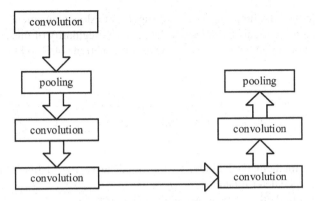

Fig. 1 Model structure diagram

Yolov3-Based Gap Recognition Model. The Yolov3 network uses the first 52-layer network of the Darknet-53 network except for the fully connected layer. Based on the Yolov2, multi-scale features are used for object detection. Multiple independent logistic classifiers are used to replace Softmax so that multiple tags can be supported. Object. Yolov3 used dropout and data augmentation in training to prevent overfitting. Abandoning dropout and starting to use K-means clustering to get the size of the a priori box.

3.3 Trajectory Generation Algorithm

Since the background of the major mainstream websites recognizes the user's sliding mouse trajectory, the sliding trajectory must be generated according to the human behavior trajectory. There are two methods to simulate the human behavior trajectory. The first one is to establish a database for brute force cracking. This requires a large number of drag samples establishing databases. When the gap position is identified, the offset distance is calculated, select a track with the same offset distance and perform analog drag. However, considering that this method needs to traverse all the offset distances, this method is obviously complicated and poor scalability when the horizontal offset distance is large; the second method is the curve fitting, we use the least-squares method to simulate the human drag trajectory. By observing and analyzing the whole process of human dragging the slider, the behavior of dragging the slider is divided into three steps. The basic fitting steps of the least-squares method are as follows:

1) First, we determine the mathematical model of the fitted curve. Since we don't know whether the parameters are linear, polynomial, exponential or complex, we may want to perform segmentation analysis by observing the distribution of the fitted points. The segmentation obtained by observing is: the sliding distance of the first segment is 0, and the corresponding time is from 0 to 350 ms; The second segment is the stage from the start of dragging to rapid sliding, experiencing acceleration and then deceleration. The corresponding time is from 350 ms to 1200 ms, and its regularity

is similar to the tanh function. The third stage is the slow adjustment stage, humans need to match the specific position of the gap. The regularity of this stage is slight. We fit all sample points by the three regression equations of Eq. (1).

$$y = ax + b, \ y = me^{nx}, \ p(x) = \sum_{k=0}^{n} c_k x^k \tag{1}$$

2) Convert the mathematical model of the fitted curve into a linear model of the parameters to be determined.
3) Write the contradiction equations and the law equations.
4) Solving the equations of the equation, obtaining the undetermined coefficients of the fitted curve, and obtaining the fitted curve.
5) Calculate the sum of squared errors of the fitted curve.

The step of segmentation fitting:

1) Fit all sample points according to the three functions in Eq. (1) and select the function with the smallest variance.
2) Calculate the error between the fitted value and the actual value according to the function selected in step 1), and calculate the absolute value S of the error.
3) Compare the fitting point error and the error mean S. If the absolute value of the error of three consecutive points is greater than the mean S, then segment 7) from the point where the first error is greater than the mean; otherwise, without segmentation, Execute 5).
4) Repeat the above steps from the segmentation point to the last measured point re-fitting.
5) Fit the sample points according to the segmentation and variance function obtained in the above steps

The two major conditions for determining the optimal empirical function are:

1) The difference between the measured point where the error is positive and the measured point where the error is negative is less than the set adaptive parameter.
2) The function with the smallest variance is the optimal fit function.

3.4 Browser Automation Implementation

The slide puzzle captcha automatic response system identifies the location of the gap in the browser and then calculate the offset position to fit the sliding trajectory, we use the Flask web framework and the application programming interface of TencentAPI to directly feedback the recognition result. The system will send a verification request to the Tencent server, and drive the mouse to drag the slider to achieve automatically responding. After the driver page is opened, when the button click operation is obtained, try to switch to the iframe frame. After the switch succeeds, detecting whether there is a slider. If exists a slider, the sliding distance of the slider is calculated, then least squares curve fitting function used according to the calculated slider offset to obtain the sliding track. Lastly, try to obtain the control of the slider, sends a verification request to the Tencent server, submits the verified user IP address, and the captcha client verifies the callback: ticket and random strings.

4   Experiments

4.1   Data Set Acquisition and Preprocessing

In the initial stage, we need to train the convolutional neural network to ensure that we have enough features to reduce the model error. For a large number of slide puzzle captchas, it can not be automatically generated like the library "captcha" in Python, just like generating a textual captcha. Therefore, we collect slide puzzle captcha images from many websites such as Tik Tok, Bilibili, Jingdong, NetEase shield, and Geetest, A total of 1000 images, of which 500 are used as training sets and 500 are used as test sets. Here, there are two ways to collect dataset images:

1) Use Beautiful Soup in conjunction with regular expressions to extract image links.
2) Take a screen shot of the visible area through selenium, then locate the position and size of the picture element, and then use the Image in the PIL module to crop.

We choose the first method for one reason: The second method is to set the size of the browser window, and when the captcha is captured, the resolutions of different displays are different. We use data augmentation (rotation angle, adjust saturation, adjust exposure, adjust hue) to extend the data set. The captured data set is shown in Fig. 2 and Fig. 3.

Fig. 2. Training sets with different shapes   **Fig. 3.** Test sets with different shapes

In general, there are four methods to grayscale color images: component method, maximum method, average method, weighted average method. After the grayscale is completed, the picture RGB information is converted into a binary file for permanent storage. We use two-channel components as a grayscale image method.

Normalization is an indispensable step in image and processing, because for most machine learning algorithms and optimization algorithms, scaling feature values to the same interval can result in better performance models. We only normalize the size of the image, which can be easily done using the resize function in Python. Since the library "captcha" in Python cannot be used to automatically generate the slide puzzle captcha, the system must manually mark the captcha. We use the LabelImg software to mark the location of the gap.

In the whole preprocessing, it mainly includes grayscale processing, normalization processing, format transfer of picture information, etc. The functions and parameters involved are set as shown in Table 1.

Table 1. Preprocessing involves functions or parameters

Function or parameter	Function
Normalize	Normalized processing
Gray	Grayscale processing
Convert	Gap position information format conversion
Split	Image split
pickle_dump	Serialization
channel	RGB channel value
mean	Pixel average
std	Standard Deviation
id_to_data_values	Image pixel information to be serialized
id_to_size_values	Image size information to be serialized
id_to_box_values	Gap location information to be serialized
protocol	Serialization mode
resize	Change image size

4.2 Resnet-18-Based Gap Recognition Model

Model Parameter Configuration. The parameter values and functions involved in the gap recognition training and testing based on the Resnet-18 model are shown in Table 2. The parameters of the five convolutional layers are listed in Table 3.

Model Effect Test. In order to avoid over-fitting, we set the learning rate to 50% attenuation every 50 rounds, and performs dropout processing, Dropout was proposed by Hinton in 2012, which can effectively mitigate the occurrence of over-fitting. To a certain extent, the effect of regularization is achieved. The training parameters of the Resnet-18 model are shown in Table 4.

Table 2. Resnet-18 model training and testing involves functions or parameters

Function or parameter	Function	Value
my_metric	Evaluation index dictionary	–
smooth_l1_loss	Loss function	–
batch_pics	Batch training	
lr_sch	Learning rate	0.001 (initial)
Conv2D	Convolution of 2D input	–
filter_size	Filter size	3, 7
num_filters	Number of filters	64, 128, 256, 512
batch_size	Number of training per batch	16
epoch	Number of iterations	200
mean	Pixel average	–
std	Pixel standard deviation	–
dropout_rate	Dropout retention	0.5

Table 3. Resnet-18 model convolution layer parameter configuration

Layer	Output size	Filter size	Filters number	Stride
Conv 1	112×112	7×7	64	2
Conv 2	56×56	3×3	64	2
Conv 3	28×28	3×3	128	2
Conv 4	14×14	3×3	256	2
Conv 5	7×7	3×3	512	2

Table 4. Resnet-18 model training parameters

Loss function	Learning rate	Attenuation interval	Total number of training
Smooth l1	0.001	50	200

It is analyzed from Fig. 4 that in the performance of the test set, the number of successes of the model increases with the number of training times is increasing, and finally reaches saturation. The final success rate is about 88% (Fig. 5).

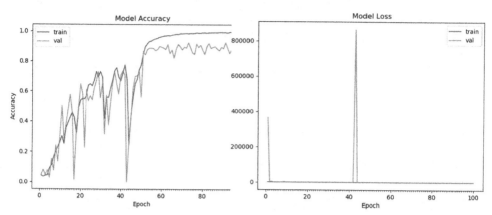

Fig. 4. The number of iterations and the success rate

Fig. 5. The number of iterations and the loss

4.3 Yolov3-Based Gap Recognition Model

Model Parameter Configuration. The parameter values and functions involved in the training and testing of the gap recognition model based on the Yolov3 model are shown in Table 5.

Table 5. Yolov3 model training and testing involves functions or parameters

Function or parameter	Function	Value
learning_rate	Learning rate	0.001
batch_size	Number of training per batch	16
filter_size	Filter size	1, 3
num_filters	Number of filters	32, 64, 128, 256, 512, 1024
epoch	Number of iterations	200
yolo_loss	Loss function	–
grid	Offset	–
pad	Padding	1
decay	Weight decay	0.0005
batch_normalize	Batch normalize	1

The parameter configuration of the convolution layer is shown in Table 6.

Model Effect Test. The basic network used by Yolov3 is Darknet-53, which simply replaces Softmax with multiple logistic classifiers, while Darknet-53 also uses Resnet's shortcut method. At the same time, we set weight decay, also known as L2 regularization, The idea of L2 regularization is to add an extra term to the loss function. The training parameters of the gap recognition model based on Yolov3 are shown in Table 7.

Table 6. Yolov3 model convolutional layer parameter configuration

Layer	Output size	Filter size	Filters number	Stride
Conv 1	256 × 256	3 × 3	32	1
Conv 2	128 × 128	3 × 3	64	2
Conv 3	–	1 × 1	32	1
Conv 4	–	3 × 3	64	1
Conv 5	64 × 64	3 × 3	128	2
Conv 6, 8	–	1 × 1	64	1
Conv 7, 9	–	3 × 3	128	1
Conv 10	32 × 32	3 × 3	256	2
Conv 11, 13, 15, 17, 19, 21, 23, 25	–	1 × 1	128	1
Conv 12, 14, 16, 18, 20, 22, 24, 26	–	3 × 3	256	1
Conv 27	16 × 16	3 × 3	512	2
Conv 28, 30, 32, 34, 36, 38, 40, 42	–	1 × 1	256	1
Conv 29, 31, 33, 35, 37, 39, 41, 43	–	3 × 3	512	1
Conv 44	8 × 8	3 × 3	1024	2
Conv 45, 47, 49, 51	–	1 × 1	512	1
Conv 46, 48, 50, 52	–	3 × 3	1024	1

Table 7. Yolov3 model training parameters

Loss function	Learning rate	Attenuation interval	Total number of training
yolo_loss	0.001	50	200

The success rate of the test set is 90%, exceeding the Resnet-18 model, it can be seen that although the network layer of Darknet-53 is more complex than Resnet-18, the training accuracy and effect are better than the Resnet-18 model. This phenomenon may be caused by the different composition of the network structure. Figure 6 shows the effect of the gap recognition.

Comparison. The comparison of the gap recognition model based on Resnet-18 and the gap recognition model based on Yolov3 is shown in Table 8.

4.4 Least-Squares Fitting Sliding Trajectory

In order to analyze the effect of the automatic response system, the relationship between the number of training times and the number of successful driving times is shown in Table 9 and Table 10 with 200 drag tests.

Fig. 6. Effect of gap recognition

Table 8. Comparison of test results

Model	Test set accuracy
Resnet-18	0.8821
Yolov3	0.8996

Table 9. Resnet-18 model drag success times and training times

Number of training	15	50	100	150	200
Number of success	35	111	143	153	152

Table 10. Yolov3 model drag success times and training times

Number of training	15	50	100	150	200
Number of success	35	115	146	155	150

From the data analysis, when the number of training before 100, the number of success increases with the number of training. However, after the number of training reaches 100, the number of success does not increase significantly. Even after 200 times, it is completely saturated and can't learn any new features. It is worth mentioning that, unlike the verification of the model in previous work, the drag success rate will be interfered by the platform. Fig. 7 shows the effect of the drag when it is successful.

5 Discussion

1) Nowadays, in order to improve security, many mainstream platforms have set up artificial obstacles to interfere with the verification process. For example, when the TencentAPI is called, the control of the slider may be released in the background, as

拖动下方滑块完成拼图

Fig. 7. Drag and drop effect diagram

shown in Fig. 8, the automatic response system fails, or when the number of attempts is too large, other ways of verification will occur, which is beyond the scope of this paper.

拖动下方滑块完成拼图

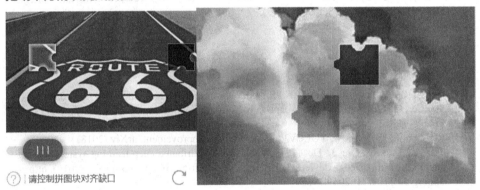

Fig. 8. Effect of losing control of the slider   **Fig. 9.** Schematic diagram of interference gap

2) Tencent established a database by collecting the dragging process of large quantities of real humans. The curve fitting method used in this paper lead to similar sliding trajectories, and the simulation level is not high enough. When the slide operation is performed in large quantities, it is easy to intercepted by Tencent.

3) The model cannot achieve high accuracy because the data set is not large enough. For the interference gap in one picture (the dark color is the real identification gap and the light color is the interference gap), as shown in Fig. 9, it is still outside the scope of this paper.

6 Conclusion

Slide puzzle captcha has become a major defense method for major mainstream platforms to resist hacker attacks, as a kind of DCG Captcha [16], side puzzle captcha has a good experience for users compared to character captcha. We attempt to find the design flaws of slide puzzle captcha on major platforms from the perspective of crackers, hoping to provide reference for designers and make a contribution to network security.

We use object detection model based on Resnet-18 and object detection model based on Yolov3 to identify the location of the gap. In the model training phase, by collecting slide puzzle captcha images as a data set, expanding the data set by data augmentation, and training model after graying and normalization, the test effect of the model is: The success rate of the object detection model based on Resnet-18 can reach about 88% in the step of identifying the gap position. The object detection model based on Yolov3 is better, reach the success rate of about 90%. Due to the interference mechanism of each platform, we simulate the human sliding trajectory by curve fitting with least squares method, the success rate is about 75%.

Acknowledgment. This work was supported in part by the Guangdong Province Key Research and Development Plan (Grant No. 2019B010137004), the National Key research and Development Plan (Grant No. 2018YFB0803504), the National Natural Science Foundation of China (Grant No. U1636215, 61572492, 61902083, 61976064), and Guangdong Province Universities and Colleges Pearl River Scholar Funded Scheme (2019).

References

1. Byrne, R.M.J., Johnson-Laird, P.N.: Spatial reasoning. J. Mem. Lang. **28**(5), 564–575 (1989)
2. Stauffer, C., Grimson, W.E.L.: Adaptive background mixture models for real-time tracking. Proc. CVPR **2**, 246–252 (1999)
3. Redmon, J., Farhadi, A.: YOLOv3: an incremental improvement. arXiv (2018)
4. Tian, Z., Luo, C., Qiu, J., Du, X., Guizani, M.: A distributed deep learning system for web attack detection on edge devices. IEEE Trans. Ind. Inform. **16**(3), 1963–1971 (2019). https://doi.org/10.1109/TII.2019.2938778
5. Tian, Z., et al.: Real time lateral movement detection based on evidence reasoning network for edge computing environment. IEEE Trans. Ind. Inform. **15**(7), 4285–4294 (2019)
6. Schuldt, C., Laptev, I., Caputo, B.: Recognizing human actions: a local SVM approach. In: Proceedings of the 17th International Conference on Pattern Recognition, 2004. ICPR 2004. IEEE (2004)
7. Girshick, R., Donahue, J., Darrell, T., Malik, J.: Rich feature hierarchies for accurate object detection and semantic segmentation. In: CVPR (2014)
8. Sermanet, P., Eigen, D., Zhang, X., Mathieu, M., Fergus, R., LeCun, Y.: OverFeat: integrated recognition, localization and detection using convolutional networks. In: ICLR (2014)
9. Girshick, R.: Fast R-CNN arXiv:1504.08083 (2015)
10. Szegedy, C., et al.: Going deeper with convolutions. In: CVPR (2015)
11. Redmon, J., Divvala, S., Girshick, R., Farhadi, A.: You only look once: unified, real-time object detection. In: CVPR (2016)
12. Liu, W., Anguelov, D., Erhan, D., Szegedy, C., Reed, S.: SSD: single shot multibox detector (2015)

13. Redmon, J., Farhadi, A.: YOLO9000: better, faster, stronger. CVPR **1**(2), 8 (2017)
14. Krizhevsky, A., Sutskever, I., Hinton, G.: ImageNet classification with deep convolutional neural networks. In: NIPS, Curran Associates Inc. (2012)
15. He, K., Zhang, X., Ren, S., Sun, J.: Spatial pyramid pooling in deep convolutional networks for visual recognition. In: ECCV (2014)
16. Hidalgo, J.M.G., Alvarez, G.: CAPTCHAs: an artificial intelligence application to web security. In: Advances in Computers, vol. 83 (2011)

Random Shilling Attacks Against Latent Factor Model for Recommender System: An Experimental Study

Mingrui Peng[1], Mohan Li[1(✉)], and Quanlong Guan[2]

[1] Cyberspace Institute of Advanced Technology, Guangzhou University, Guangzhou 510006, China
{2111906070,limohan}@gzhu.edu.cn
[2] Jinan University, Guangzhou 510006, China

Abstract. The recommender systems provide personalized recommendation by mining and leveraging the relationships between different users and items. Latent factor model (LMF) is one of the state-of-art methodologies for implementing modern recommender systems. Features can be extracted by decomposing the user-item rating matrix in latent space and be used to generate the recommendations. Unconstrained matrix decomposition and singular value decomposition are two typical latent factor models and are proved to be accurate in many applications. However, LFM-based recommender systems are inherently susceptible to shilling attacks which trying to inject fake ratings to change the recommendation results. In this paper, we study the impact of random shilling attack on unconstrained matrix decomposition and singular value decomposition. The attacks are launched on two real-life datasets. The robustness of the two methods are analyzed and some suggestions for improving robustness are provided.

Keywords: Recommender system · Latent Factor Model · Shilling attacks

1 Introduction

With the development of information technology and the Internet, people have stepped into an era of "information overload" [1]. It is difficult for users to look for the necessary information from the massive data. Recommender system is an effective tool to solve the problem by automatically analyzing user preferences and predicting the behaviors for personalized services [2].

The rating matrix is sparse in many scenarios because the item set is large and each user only scores a small number of items. Some traditional recommender algorithms, such as neighbor-based methods [3], perform poorly when rating matrix is sparse. However, Latent Factor Model (LFM) [4] is good at dealing with matrix sparsity and cold boot [5], thus is widely used in recommender system. LFM can be implemented based on different matrix decomposition methods, such as unconstrained matrix decomposition (UMF), singular value decomposition (SVD) and non-negative matrix factorization (UMF), etc. The principle of LMF is to transform the characteristics of users and items

© Springer Nature Singapore Pte Ltd. 2020
X. Sun et al. (Eds.): ICAIS 2020, CCIS 1254, pp. 154–165, 2020.
https://doi.org/10.1007/978-981-15-8101-4_15

into latent factor vectors from the user-item rating matrix [6]. The affinities of users and items can be computed based on the latent factor vectors, and recommendations can be generated according to the affinities.

However, LFM-based recommender systems are susceptible to shilling attacks because of the data sources of rating matrix may not be reliable and any user can rate any item [7]. Shilling attacks or profile injection attacks [8] interfere recommendation results by injecting a large number of fake ratings from malicious users into the user-item rating matrix. Random attacks [9] are a common type of shilling attacks. It can be divided into push attacks and nuke attacks according to the purposes. In this paper, we study the effects of random shilling attacks against two different types of matrix decomposition algorithms for recommender system. The contributions of this paper are as follows.

(1) We use RMSE to compare the accuracy of UMF and SVD algorithm on two different dataset.
(2) By injecting different proportions of random attack, we analyze and compare the vulnerability of the two types of algorithms.
(3) Based on the analysis, we give some suggestions on the robustness of LMF-based recommender systems.

The rest of this paper is organized as follows: we first introduce the development of recommender algorithms and discuss the classifications of shilling attacks in Sect. 2. The UMF, SVD, and the random shilling attacks are introduced in Sect. 3. Then in Sect. 4, we take three different sets of experiments to compare the accuracy and the robustness of two different algorithms. We inject different proportions of shilling attacks on two different data sets. Finally, conclusions are drawn in the Sect. 5.

2 Related Work

2.1 Recommender System

At present, the algorithms of recommender system mainly include collaborative filtering algorithms [2] and content-based recommender algorithms [12]. Since the Tapestry system of the Palo Alto Research Center introduced the concept of collaborative filtering for the first time in the 1990s, the research of recommender system become an independent discipline. From 1994 to 2006, the mainly research directions in the field of recommender system had focused on neighbor-based collaborative filtering recommender algorithms [10]. For example, Amazon.com used a neighbor-based recommender algorithm [11]. But it also some disadvantages. The sparseness of the data, cold boot, and malicious behavior can affect the recommendation result.

In recent years, the recommender system has developed in both academia and industry. Many companies have published their datasets for free source to hold a competition of recommender system. Meanwhile,many new and functional recommender algorithms have emerged in those competition. Especially, matrix decomposition algorithms started to attract people's attention from the Netflix competition [32].

Matrix decomposition is a training direction of current research on recommender system algorithms. It can transform the characteristics of users and items into features of latent factor, and then calculate the latent factor relationship between users and items. It also has high flexibility and accuracy [13]. The earliest matrix decomposition model uses SVD decomposition [14], but this method has two shortcomings. Firstly, it needs to fill missing values to rating matrix in advance; and the second is that the SVD decomposition was too complex to implement during this period. Until competition of the Netflix Prize in 2006, Simon Funk published his algorithm on the blog. He first initialized two low-rank matrices to represent user and item features, and then optimized the feature matrix by stochastic gradient descent [15] to make it closer to the original rating matrix. This algorithm perfectly solves the existing problem of traditional SVD. It is called the latent factor model [16].

2.2 Attack Against Recommender System

Nowadays there are more and more security issues, such as Blockchain [18], Internet of Vehicles [19], and Internet of Things [21]. We can learn some ideas from these attack and detection methods, such as a data-driven model [20], novel reputation frameworks [22], and lateral movement detection [17]. However common attack on recommender system is shilling attack. The shilling attack [31] can be divided into different categories according to different classification methods. For example, according to the purpose of attack, it can be divided into push attack and nuke attack. According to the required knowledge, it can be divided into low and high knowledge attacks. However, the most well-known classification method is simply to classify shilling attacks into random attack, love/hate attack, average attack, bandwagon attack, segment attack and so on [23].

Random attack selects fixed attack items and assigns them randomly. This attack does not need any required knowledge [24]; love/hate attack randomly selects attack items and assigns maximum or minimum values [25]. Compared to random attacks, the attack method is simple. It has lower cost. The average attack selects the fixed attack item and assigns the mean value of the global score [26]. This attack requires more knowledge of system. The bandwagon attack selects the item as the most popular item and assigns maximum score [27], this kind of attack will attract a lot of attention by using a small number of popular products. The injected fake users will establish similar relationships with a large number of users in this system, which can greatly affect results of the recommender system; Segment attack selects an item that is similar to the target item and assigns a maximum value [28], by utilize the characteristics of recommender system that recommend the item to the target user group that is interested in it. Therefore, It can recommend the forged target user to the potential users.

3 Overview of the Method

3.1 Latent Factor Model

In recommender system the rating behavior of users may be expressed as a user-item rating matrix R, where r_{ij} is a rating of the item j by the user i. Usually, users only score those items that they have used or purchased, and then the rating matrix R have a large number of missing values. The basic idea of the LFM [29] is to predict ratings from the result of matrix decomposition to complete the rating matrix. Considering that a user have different interests in different factors, we can divide the items into different categories. For a given category, the affinity of each item is determined, which helps a user to select specific items. In LFM algorithm, this category is called factor [30].

The detail of LMF is as follows. Suppose R is an m*n user-item rating matrix. The goal of LFM is looking for two low-dimensional matrices U: m * k and V: n * k. The parameter k represents the factor of item, and each column of U and V is called latent vector. The matrix U represents the k-dimensional latent vector of m users, and the matrix V represents the k-dimensional latent vector of n items. The multiplication of U and V can be approximated to the user-item rating matrix R completely. As shown in Eq. (1);

$$R_{m*n} \approx U_{m*k} V_{n*k}^T \tag{1}$$

The u_{is} in matrix represents the affinity of the user i for the latent factor s, the v_{js} represents the affinity of the item j for the latent factor s, and r_{ij} is the a rating from user i for item j. It can be expressed as Eq. (2);

$$r_{ij} \approx \sum_{s=1}^{k} u_{is} \cdot v_{js} = \sum_{s=1}^{k} (\text{Affinity of user i to concept s}) \times (\text{Affinity of item j to concept s})$$

$$\tag{2}$$

UMF and SVD are two commonly algorithms of matrix decomposition in recommender system.

Unconstrained Matrix Factorization (UFM) Unconstrained is a basic form of matrix decomposition. We can initialize two latent factor matrices U and V. The multiplication of U and V can approximate the user-item rating matrix R as close as possible. The definition of r_{ij} is the rating which is predicted to the item j for the user i [30], as shown in Eq. (3):

$$\hat{r}_{ij} = \sum_{s=1}^{k} u_{is} \cdot v_{js} \tag{3}$$

To prevent overfitting, the objective function is regularized as shown in Eq. (4):

$$J = \frac{1}{2} \sum_{(i,j) \in S} \left(r_{ij} - \sum_{s=1}^{k} u_{is} \cdot v_{js} \right)^2 + \frac{\lambda}{2} \sum_{i=1}^{m} \sum_{s=1}^{k} u_{is}^2 + \frac{\lambda}{2} \sum_{j=1}^{n} \sum_{s=1}^{k} v_{js}^2$$

$$\textit{subject to : No constraints on U and V} \tag{4}$$

The stochastic gradient descent method is used to minimize the loss function, as shown in Eq. (5)–(6). After calculating the error of the actual rating and the predicted rating for all given rating of the user-item rating matrix, it optimize the parameter u_{iq}, v_{jq} by iterating the partial derivative, as shown in Eq. (5)–(6):

$$\frac{\partial J}{\partial u_{iq}} = \sum_{j:(i,j)\in S} \left(r_{ij} - \sum_{s=1}^{k} u_{is} \cdot v_{js} \right)(-v_{jq}) + \lambda u_{iq}$$

$$\forall i \in \{1 \cdots m\}, q \in \{1 \cdots k\} \tag{5}$$

$$\frac{\partial J}{\partial v_{jq}} = \sum_{j:(i,j)\in S} \left(r_{ij} - \sum_{s=1}^{k} u_{is} \cdot v_{js} \right)(-v_{iq}) + \lambda v_{jq}$$

$$\forall i \in \{1 \cdots n\}, q \in \{1 \cdots k\} \tag{6}$$

u_{iq}, v_{jq} is updated as shown in Eq. (7)–(8):

$$u_{iq} \Leftarrow u_{iq} + \alpha \left(\sum_{j:(i,j)\in S} \left(r_{ij} - \sum_{s=1}^{k} u_{is} \cdot v_{js} \right) \right)(-v_{jq}) + \lambda u_{iq})\forall q \in \{1 \cdots k\} \tag{7}$$

$$v_{jq} \Leftarrow u_{jq} + \alpha \left(\sum_{j:(i,j)\in S} \left(r_{ij} - \sum_{s=1}^{k} u_{is} \cdot v_{js} \right)(-v_{iq}) + \lambda v_{jq})\forall q \in \{1 \cdots k\} \tag{8}$$

The iteration of parameters by the gradient descent will tend to a state of fitting. After this learning process, a new rating matrix can be obtained. Then, the most suitable recommendation can be given through the procedure of sorting and filtering operations.

Singular Value Decomposition (SVD). As shown in the formula (9), the user-item rating matrix R can be decomposed into a user factor matrix Q, a diagonal matrix Σ, and an item factor matrix P. The singular values in the diagonal matrix are arranged from large to small, and the sum of the singular values of the first 10% or even 1% occupies more than 90% of all singular values. Therefore, the scoring matrix can be approximated by the largest singular value and the corresponding left and right singular vectors, as shown in Eq. (9):

$$R_{m*n} = Q_{m*m} \Sigma_{m*n} P_{n*n}^{T} \approx Q_{m*k} \Sigma_{k*k} P_{k*n}^{T} \tag{9}$$

This paper compares the performance of UMF and SVD on two different datasets.

3.2   Random Shilling Attack

Recommender system is vulnerable to the shilling attack. Malicious users insert the fake ratings into rating matrix to interfering results of recommendation. Those attacks can be further subdivided into push attack and nuke attack. Push attack can increase the weight of recommended on the target item, and nuke attack can lower the ranking of the target item. Random shilling attack is a common type of shilling attack. It does not require too much required knowledge of this recommender system. And, it works by profile injection with random selection of users and items [23].

In this paper, we randomly select different proportions of random shilling attacks, and assign maximum and minimum values to the rating matrix. Then compare the result with two matrix decomposition algorithms on different two datasets. Finally, we conclude the robustness of the algorithm.

4 Analysis of Experiment

4.1 Experimental Setup

Experimental environment of the experiment is windows10 operating system, i7-8750H 2.20 GHz CPU, memory is 8 GB.

Dataset. In order to verify the experimental results, we use the following two data sets as experimental data:

1) MovieLens-1 M dataset. This dataset contains 1000,209 ratings for 6052 users on 3,952 movies. The range of the rating is 1 to 5 with the user preference increases from small to large.
2) Musical Instruments. This dataset is a collection of users who have scored their instruments on Amazon from May 1996 to July 2014. It contains 583933 ratings for 84,611 instruments by 10261 users. The range of the rating is 1 to 5.

Evaluation Criteria. The evaluation criteria for the recommended algorithms usually used average absolute error (MAE) and root mean square error (RMSE) [30]. The experiment of this paper selects RMSE as a criteria of evaluation. RMSE indicates the accuracy of prediction. The expression of RMSE is as Eq. (10);

$$RMSE = \sqrt{\frac{\sum\limits_{i,j \in T_{test}}^{n} \left(r_{ij} - \hat{r}_{ij} \right)^2}{n}} \tag{10}$$

$\hat{r}_{ij}$ represents the predicted rating from the user i to the item j, r_{ij} represents the actual rating of the item i by the user i, T_{test} represents the dataset of the test, and n represents the number of ratings in the test dataset.

Details Setting of LFM. After comparing the process of the UMF and SVD algorithms, we chose different configurations for the two algorithms in order to cover situations for a wider range. Specially, The SVD completes the rating matrix by selecting the first k singular values and the corresponding left and right singular vectors. However, UMF updates the parameters by iterating the parameters.

1) UMF configuration: the latent factor k is selected as 3, the iteration step length is set to 0.01, the regularization parameter is 0.4, and the number of iterations is 100.
2) SVD configuration: we select the parameter k = 90 as the optimal choice.

4.2 Analysis and Results of Experimental

In this work, we totally conduct three sets of comparative experiments: 1) Algorithm prediction accuracy experiment: we compare the accuracy of prediction in SVD and UMF on different datasets; 2) Robustness experiment of SVD algorithm: we inject 10%, 20%, 30% random shilling attacks to two different datasets respectively, and compare the robustness SVD algorithm; 3) Robustness experiment of UMF algorithm: we inject 10%, 20%, 30% random shilling attack into two datasets respectively Attack, and compare the robustness of UMF algorithm.

Accuracy Experiment of Two Algorithms. RMSE between the predicted rating and the given rating is used to compare the accuracy, as shown in Fig. 1, 2

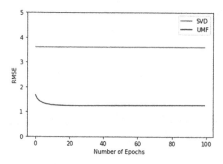

Fig. 1. RMSE on ml-1m   **Fig. 2.** RMSE on music_instrument

Figure 1 shows the RMSE between SVD and UMF on the ml-1 m dataset, and Fig. 2 shows the RMSE between SVD and UMF on the music_intrument dataset. As the results shown in the figure, it can be known that the RMSE of the UMF is always lower than the SVD. And after 100 iterations of matrix decomposition, RMSE gradually stabilizes. So we can infer that the accuracy of UMF is better than SVD.

The Robustness Experiment of SVD Algorithm. This experiment is mainly to research the robustness of the SVD algorithm by injecting 10%, 20%, and 30% random shilling attacks on the ml-1m and music_instrument dataset respectively. The results of RMSE are shown as follows; Table 1 is the result of RMSE by injecting push attack on two different dataset respectively and Table 2 is the result of RMSE by injecting nuke attack on two different dataset respectively.

Table 1. RMSE from push attack against SVD

Dataset	0%	10%	20%	30%
ml-1 m	3.83	3.91	4.08	4.16
music_instrument	4.29	2.56	1.53	1.12

Table 2. RMSE from nuke attack against SVD

Dataset	0%	10%	20%	30%
ml-1m	3.83	3.87	3.93	4.05
music_instrument	4.29	0.35	0.27	0.21

We can know from tables above, with the proportion of attacking profile increases on the ml-1m dataset, the RMSE increases. Comparatively, on the music_instrument dataset, the RMSE decreases on the contrary. The reasons for these results may that the music_instrument dataset is more sparse than the ml-1m dataset.

UMF Algorithm Robustness Experiment. According to the above experimental results, it can be concluded that SVD is vulnerable to random attacks. In this experiment, we analysis the robustness of UMF by injecting 10%, 20%, and 30% random attacks on two different datasets. As shown in Fig. 3, 4, 5 and 6:

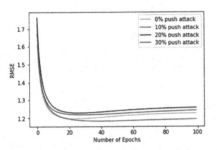

Fig. 3. Push attack against UMF on ml-1m

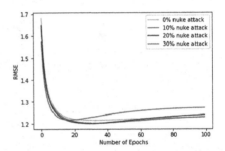

Fig. 4. Nuke attack against UMF on ml-1m

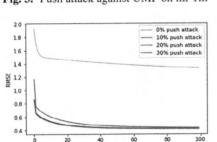

Fig. 5. Push attack against UMF on music_instrument

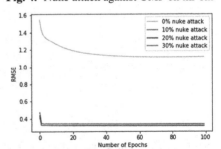

Fig. 6. Nuke attack against UMF on music_instrument

It can be seen from the result that random attack have less influence on the algorithm of UMF. The floating range of deviation is kept within 0.1 after multiple iterations. Obviously, the robustness of UMF is better than SVD, it can resistant different proportions of the random shilling attack. However, on music_instrment dataset the RMSE decreases on the contrary. It is considered that the dataset is too sparse to show expected results.

After filling with the maximum or minimum value, the prediction result becomes more accurate and the RMSE decrease contrarily.

By comparing the results of above three experiments, we can draw a comparison histogram. As shown in Fig. 7, 8, 9 and 10, in which different proportions of push attack and nuke attack are injected in two different datasets. The abscissa is the injection ratio and the ordinate is the deviation of RMSE between attack injection and normal case. Individually, Fig. 7 is the deviation of RMSE against different proportions of push attack which is injected into the ml-1 m dataset. Figure 8 is the deviation of RMSE against different ratios of nuke attack which is injected into the ml-1m dataset. Figure 9 is the deviation of RMSE on music_instrument against push attack, and Fig. 10 is the deviation of RMSE on music_instrument against nuke attack.

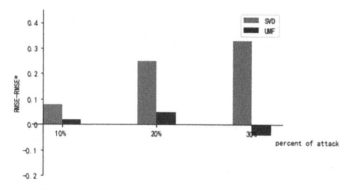

Fig. 7. Deviation of RMSE on ml-1m against push attack

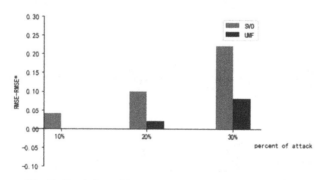

Fig. 8. Deviation of RMSE on ml-1m against nuke attack

It can be seen from the Experimental comparison chart that the UMF is more robust than the SVD algorithm. UMF can maximize the accuracy of prediction. However, for the problem of running times in two algorithms, the time for UMF to complete a recommendation far exceeds SVD, especially in the case of a large dataset. For example, the music_instrument dataset used in this experiment, it takes 240 s for UMF to complete a recommender result calculation, while SVD takes only 0.2 s.

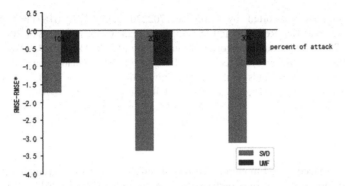

Fig. 9. Deviation of RMSE on music_instrument against push attack

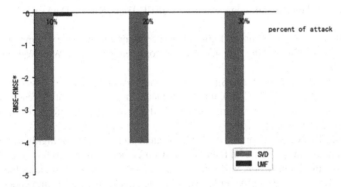

Fig. 10. Deviation of RMSE on music_instrument against nuke attack

5 Conclusions

Above all, three sets of comparison experiments were conducted on two different datasets by injecting different proportions of random shilling attacks on SVD and UMF recommender algorithm. Meanwhile we discuss the accuracy and the robustness of the two algorithms against different proportions of random shilling attacks according to the result of those experiments. From the results we can conclude, in terms of robustness against random shilling attacks, the UMF which using multiple iterations is better than SVD. And the accuracy of prediction is also higher than the SVD algorithm. However, because of multiple iterations it has to do, the cost of the running time is expensive especially when dealing with large-scale data. Therefore, in order to improve the robustness of the recommender algorithm, it may be a feasible idea to increase the number of iterations reasonably. However, increasing the numbers of iterations will increase the time cost. How to reduce the learning time of the model is still deserve further work. Finding an optimal solution between efficiency and accuracy, and providing more accurate and efficient recommender services for users is a direction that is worthy further research.

Acknowledgements. Supported by NSFC (61702220, 61702223, 61871140, U1636215, 61602210), National Key Research and Development Plan (Grant No. 2018YFB0803504), the Science and Technology Planning Project of Guangdong (2017A040405029, 2018KTSCX016, 2019A050510024), the Science and Technology Planning Project of Guangzhou (201902010041), the Fundamental Research Funds for the Central Universities (21617408, 21619404), Guangdong Province Universities and Colleges Pearl River Scholar Funded Scheme (2019).

References

1. Costa, H., Macedo, L.: Emotion-based recommender system for overcoming the problem of information overload. In: Corchado, J.M., et al. (eds.) PAAMS 2013. CCIS, vol. 365, pp. 178–189. Springer, Heidelberg (2013). https://doi.org/10.1007/978-3-642-38061-7_18
2. Adomavicius, G., Tuzhilin, A.: Toward the next generation of recommender systems: a survey of the state-of-the-art and possible extensions. IEEE Trans. Knowl. Data Eng. **17**(6), 734–774 (2005)
3. Sarwar, B., Karypis, G., Konstan, J.: Item-based collaborative filtering recommendation algorithms. In: Proceedings of the 10th international conference on World Wide Web, pp. 285–295. ACM (2001)
4. Kahaner, D., Moler, C.B., Nash, S.: Numerical methods and software (1989)
5. Wei, Z., Wang, J., Wei, F.: Combining latent factor model with location features for event-based group recommendation. In: Acm Sigkdd International Conference on Knowledge Discovery & Data Mining (2013)
6. Enatton, R., Roux, N.L., Bordes, A., et al.: A latent factor model for highly multi-relational data. In: Proceedings of the 25th International Conference on Neural Information Processing Systems North Miami Beach, vol. 2, no. 3, pp. 167–3175. Curran Associates Inc (2012)
7. Gunes, I., Kaleli, C., Bilge, A., Polat, H.: Shilling attacks against recommender systems: a comprehensive survey. Artif. Intell. Rev. **42**(4), 767–799 (2014)
8. Williams, C.A., Mobasher, B., Burke, R.: Defending recommender systems: detection of profile injection attacks. Serv. Oriented Comput. Appl. **1**(3), 157–170 (2007)
9. Burke, R., Mobasher, B., Williams, C., et al.: Detecting profile injection attacks in collaborative recommender systems (2006)
10. Bin, S., et al.: Collaborative filtering recommendation algorithm based on multi-relationship social network. Comput. Mater. Continua **60**(2), 659–674 (2019)
11. Linden, G., Smith, B., York, J.: Amazon.com recommendations: item-to-item collaborative filtering. IEEE Internet Comput. **7**(1), 76–80 (2003)
12. Pazzani, M.J., Billsus, D.: Content-based recommendation systems. In: Brusilovsky, P., Kobsa, A., Nejdl, W. (eds.) The Adaptive Web. LNCS, vol. 4321, pp. 325–341. Springer, Heidelberg (2007). https://doi.org/10.1007/978-3-540-72079-9_10
13. Koren, Y., Bell, R., Volinsky, C.: Matrix factorization techniques for recommender systems. Computer **42**(8), 30–37 (2009)
14. Billsns, D., Pazzani, M.J.: Learning collaborative information filters. In: CML, vol. 98, pp. 46–54 (1998)
15. Paras.: Stochastic Gradient Descent (2014)
16. Zhang, G., Liu, Y., Chen, J.: Latent factor model based on simple singular value decomposition for personalized comment recommendation. In: 2013 Fourth International Conference on Emerging Intelligent Data and Web Technologies. IEEE (2013)
17. Tian, Z., et al.: Real time lateral movement detection based on evidence reasoning network for edge computing environment. IEEE Trans. Industr. Inf. (2019). https://doi.org/10.1109/TII.2019.2907754

18. Tian, Z., Li, M., Qiu, M., Sun, Y., Su, S.: Block-DEF: a secure digital evidence system using blockchain. Inf. Sci. **491**, 151–165 (2019). https://doi.org/10.1016/j.ins.2019.04.011

19. Tian, Z., Gao, X., Su, S., Qiu, J., Du, X., Guizani, M.: Evaluating reputation management schemes of internet of vehicles based on evolutionary game theory. IEEE Trans. Veh. Technol. https://doi.org/10.1109/tvt.2019.2910217

20. Tian, Z., Su, S., Shi, W., Du, X., Guizani, M., Yu, X.: A data-driven model for future internet route decision modeling. Future Gener. Comput. Syst. **95**, 212–220 (2019)

21. Tan, Q., Gao, Y., Shi, J., Wang, X., Fang, B., Tian, Z.: Toward a comprehensive insight to the eclipse attacks of tor hidden services. IEEE Internet Things J. **6**(2), 1584–1593 (2019)

22. Tian, Z., Su, S., Yu, X., et al.: Vcash: a novel reputation framework for identifying denial of traffic service in internet of connected vehicles. IEEE Internet Things J. **7**(5), 3901–3909 (2019)

23. Lam, C., Yao, Q.: Large Precision Matrix Estimation for Time Series Data with Latent Factor Model (2009)

24. Gunes, I., Kaleli, C., Bilge, A., Polat, H.: Shilling attacks against recommender systems: a comprehensive survey. Artif. Intell. Rev. **42**(4), 767–799 (2012). https://doi.org/10.1007/s10 462-012-9364-9

25. Williams, C.A., Mobasher, B., Burke, R., Bhaumik, R.: Detecting profile injection attacks in collaborative filtering: a classification-based approach. In: Nasraoui, O., Spiliopoulou, M., Srivastava, J., Mobasher, B., Masand, B. (eds.) WebKDD 2006. LNCS (LNAI), vol. 4811, pp. 167–186. Springer, Heidelberg (2007). https://doi.org/10.1007/978-3-540-77485-3_10

26. Cheng, Z., Hurley, N.: [ACM Press the Third ACM Conference - New York, USA (2009.10.23–2009.10.25)] Proceedings of the Third ACM Conference on Recommender Systems - RecSys \"09 - Effective Diverse and Obfuscated Attacks on Model-Based Recommender Systems, p. 141

27. Cheng, Z., Hurley, N.: Robust collaborative recommendation by least trimmed squares matrix factorization. In: 22nd IEEE International Conference on Tools with Artificial Intelligence, ICTAI 2010, Arras, France, 27–29 October 2010, vol. 2. IEEE (2010)

28. Mobasher, B., Burke, R., Williams, C., Bhaumik, R.: Analysis and detection of segment-focused attacks against collaborative recommendation. In: Nasraoui, O., Zaïane, O., Spiliopoulou, M., Mobasher, B., Masand, B., Yu, P.S. (eds.) WebKDD 2005. LNCS (LNAI), vol. 4198, pp. 96–118. Springer, Heidelberg (2006). https://doi.org/10.1007/11891321_6

29. Aggarwal, C.C.: An Introduction to Recommender Systems. Springer, Heidelberg (2016). https://doi.org/10.1007/978-3-319-29659-3_1

30. Chai, T., Draxler, R.R.: Root mean square error (RMSE) or mean absolute error (MAE)? – arguments against avoiding RMSE in the literature. Geosci. Model Dev. **7**(3), 1247–1250 (2014)

31. Li, M., Sun, Y., Shen, S., Tian, Z., Wang, Y., Wang, X.: DPIF: a framework for distinguishing unintentional quality problems from potential shilling attacks. Comput. Mater. Continua **59**(1), 331–344 (2019)

32. Liu, G., Meng, K., Ding, J., Nees, J.P., Guo, H., Zhang, X.: An entity-association-based matrix factorization recommendation algorithm. Comput. Mater. Continua **58**(1), 101–120 (2019)

A General Framework of Smart Contract Vulnerability Mining Based on Control Flow Graph Matching

Shasha Du[1] and Huiwu Huang[2(✉)]

[1] Guangzhou University, Guangzhou, China
[2] Guangdong University of Technology, Guangzhou, China
393575614@qq.com

Abstract. A good smart contract can provide safe and reliable services to efficiently solve real-world problems. However, smart contracts written by developers create potential security vulnerabilities and can result in huge economic losses. Therein, detecting potential vulnerabilities in smart contracts plays an important role in maintaining the security of the blockchain. There are a series of schemes work on finding bugs in smart contracts, such as Oyente and ContractFuzzer, etc. However, existing solutions only address several types of security vulnerabilities on a single platform. In this paper, we propose a general framework to detect potential vulnerabilities of smart contracts. In order to abstract the execution logic of smart contracts, we need to convert them into control flow graphs. We use the Ullmann algorithm to discover vulnerabilities from these graphs. Also, we give a running example to illustrate how our framework can be used to detect the reentrancy problems written by solidity.

Keywords: Blockchain · Smart contract · Vulnerability mining

1 Introduction

A smart contract is a computer protocol intended to digitally facilitate, verify, or enforce the negotiation or performance of a contract. Smart transactions allow the performance of credible transactions without third parties. Smart contracts follow the "code is law" principle, and they cannot be modified once deployed. Because the contract does not have corresponding defense measures, the malicious user can attack the security breach of the contract.

At present, a variety of blockchain platforms have a large number of security vulnerabilities, some of which cause huge economic losses. The DAO event in Ethereum not only caused a loss of 3.6 million Ether but also led to the hard fork of Ethereum, which caused a great impact on the Ethereum platform.

In order to avoid serious damage to the security of smart contracts, developers need to do a lot of testing before releasing smart contracts. Many researchers

X. Sun et al. (Eds.): ICAIS 2020, CCIS 1254, pp. 166–175, 2020.
https://doi.org/10.1007/978-981-15-8101-4_16

have made a lot of efforts in detecting security problems in smart contracts. For example, Oyente, ContractFuzzer, etc. These tools use traditional vulnerability mining methods such as formal verification, fuzzy testing, and symbolic execution.

We summarize the current situation of smart contract security problems detecting: smart contracts generally have a large number of vulnerabilities and cause serious economic losses; the same type of security problems may exist in different blockchain platforms; existing tools only apply to some kinds of security problems, and only for one platform.

Our idea is to use control flow graph matching for smart contract vulnerability mining. We first convert the smart contract that needs to be tested into a control flow graph, and then further transfer the control flow graph into a digraph. Next, we use the Ullmann algorithm to verify the isomorphism of the graph. If a kind of vulnerability models can be isomorphic to the directed graph, then we assume that this type of vulnerability can be found in the smart contract.

Our framework perfectly satisfies the user who wants to test and verify their smart contracts, which is usually a requirement of smart contract developers. Our contribution in this paper includes 2 folds. First, we propose a smart contract analysis and verification framework based on the control flow graph matching and apply static code analysis techniques to the vulnerability detection of smart contracts. Second, for the same security problems that may exist on different platforms, our framework can be applied to smart contracts on different platforms and languages.

The rest of this paper is organized as follows. In Sect. 2, we introduce the backgrounds of vulnerability mining for blockchain platforms. In Sect. 3, we make the statement of our framework followed by a running example in Sect. 4. We finally conclude our paper in Sect. 5.

2   Backgrounds

2.1   Smart Contracts and Blockchain Platforms

A smart contract is a computer program that runs on a blockchain and is a digital version of a traditional contract. The Smart Contract sets out the terms of the contract, including some trigger conditions, which are executed once the conditions are met. Ethereum [9] is the first blockchain system to provide a complete smart contract development framework, providing application programming interfaces (APIs) to support the development of various blockchain applications.

Since then, more and more blockchain platforms start to use smart contracts for data management, transaction verification, and state processing. These platforms use different languages to write smart contracts. For example, Zen Protocol [8] is a new type of blockchain with a contracting language in F*. To ensure that smart contracts are safer and faster, EOS's [4] smart contracts are written in C++ and compiled into Web Assembly. The NEO smart contract can be used directly by almost any high-level programming language. The supported languages are C#, VB.Net, F#, Java, and Kotlin.

2.2 Security Problems in Smart Contracts

Because the high-level languages for writing smart contracts have Turing completeness, they can implement more complex logic, but it is also more likely to create security problems.

On June 17, 2016, The DAO [2] Smart Contract, which runs on the Ethereum public chain, was attacked. The hacker uses the recursive call in the contract to continuously transfer the money, causing the public funds raised by the contract to be continuously transferred to their sub-contracts. As a result, hackers used two accounts to repeatedly exploit Proposal to attack, thereby transferring 3.6 million Ether (worth 60 million dollar).

On July 3, 2019, DAppShield monitored hackers using random number attacks to launch a continuous attack on the EOS quiz game HiGold Game, which has realized profitability. Multiple EOS and Ethereum platform DApps were hacked because of random number generation vulnerabilities. Such as EOS Luckyos, EOS.Win, EosDice, Fomo3D [1] on Ethereum.

2.3 Existing Tools

Making use of traditional software vulnerability detection methods, many researchers have developed their own smart contract vulnerability detection tools.

Luu et al. developed a static analysis tool based on symbolic execution, Oyente [6], which can run directly on EVM bytecode without having to access high-level languages such as Solidity or Serpent. Oyente supports the detection of vulnerabilities such as transaction-ordering dependent, timestamp dependence, reentrancy vulnerability, and mishandled exceptions on Ethereum.

ContractFuzzer [5] is the first fuzzy test framework for smart contract security vulnerabilities based on the Ethereum, supporting gas exhaustion termination, exception handling confusion, reentrancy vulnerability, timestamp dependence, block number dependencies, dangerous delegatecall calls, and Ether Currency freeze.

Bhargavan [3] et al. proposed a smart contract analysis and validation framework that transforms smart contract source code and bytecode through Solidity and EVM tools to analyze and verify contract runtime security and functional correctness. At present, tools such as Coq [10], Isabelle/HOL, Why3 also implement the semantic representation of EVM and do some formal verification of smart contracts.

3   Framework

Our framework is divided into two parts. In the first part, we compile the smart contracts of different languages into bytecodes, decompile them into assembly code, and finally output the control flow graph. In the second part, the control flow graph is abstracted into a digraph, and we use the subgraph isomorphism algorithm to match them to the prevalent security problems model to find out whether it is vulnerable.

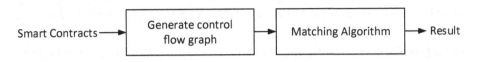

Fig. 1. The process of vulnerability mining.

3.1 Consturct the Control Flow Graph

When we need to detect smart contracts that have been posted on the blockchain, we can use the wallet's programming interface web3.eth.getCode() to get the bytecode of the contract. Smart contracts in bytecode form can be used directly to construct control flow graphs.

Compile the Source Code. If we want to detect the source code of a smart contract before publishing, compiling the source code into bytecode should be done at the beginning. The smart contract is always written by a high-level language with Turing completeness, and many complex trading functions are built in. In order to analyze it using a consistent approach, we first need to determine which kind of high-level language is used by the smart contract, and then use the compiler of the corresponding language to compile the source code into bytecode.

Generate Assembly Code. In this part, the smart contract in the form of bytecode and the compiled bytecode obtained in the previous step are decompiled to get assembly code for data stream analysis. The compiled bytecode of the smart contract is divided into three parts: deployment code, runtime code and auxdata. However, after the deployment, the real code is executed, so we only need to decompile the runtime code.

Dividing into Basic Blocks. The basic block should be divided into the following conditions: When the first instruction or statement of a program or subroutine is encountered, the current basic block is terminated, and the statement is treated as the first statement of a new block; When meeting a jump statement, a branch statement or a loop statement is encountered, the statement is used as the last statement of the current block, and the current block is ended; When you encounter other statements, add them directly to the current basic block.

Build the Edges Between Blocks. According to the jump command between the blocks and the division of the basic blocks, the set of edges between the basic blocks is obtained.

Generate Control Flow Graph. Construct a complete control flow graph based on the obtained basic block and the edge between the basic blocks

Model of Security Problems. In order to analyze the logical security problems in the smart contract, we also apply the above control flow graph construction method to model the existing prevalent smart contract security problems.

3.2 Matching Algorithm

The control flow graph consisting of two types of nodes, basic blocks and judgment nodes. In order to facilitate the search of the graph, we ignore the judgment node to convert the control flow graph into a directed connected graph. The idea of generating a directed connected graph is: when deleting a judgment node, two new edges are added, which are respectively pointed to the lower basic block of the judgment node by the upper basic block of the judgment node.

We compare the prevalent smart contract security problem models obtained in the previous section with the generated directed graph to detect whether there is a subgraph map, so that these models are isomorphic with the directed graph of the contract to be tested, so that we can check the security problems in the contract.

The graph isomorphism algorithm we use is the Ullmann algorithm [7] proposed by J. R. ULLMANN, which uses the means of enumeration to find the subgraph isomorphism. The purpose of this algorithm is to give a graph Q, and to find subgraphs in the graph G and Q isomorphism.

The Ullmann algorithm is defined as: for a given graph $G_\alpha = (V_\alpha, E_\alpha)$ and a given graph $G_\beta = (V_\beta, E_\beta)$, we need to find all subgraphs that are isomorphic to G_α in G_β. In the figure $G_\alpha = (V_\alpha, E_\alpha)$ and $G_\beta = (V_\beta, E_\beta)$, we recored the number of the node and sides as p_α, q_α ; where the adjacency matrix of $G_\alpha = (V_\alpha, E_\alpha)$ and $G_\beta = (V_\beta, E_\beta)$ are $A = [a_{ij}]$ and $B = [b_{ij}]$. After we define a mapping matrix M', which consists of $p_\alpha * p_\beta$ elements, each line can contain only one 1, and each column can contain at most one 1. We use this matrix M' to perform a series of row and column transformations on the matrix B to get our matrix C. Our matrix C is defined as follows:

$$C = [C_{ij}] = M'(M'B)^T \tag{1}$$

Where T is the transpose of the matrix.

If there is a homomorphic matrix of G_α in G_β, then the following formula must be satisfied:

$$(\forall i \forall j)\,(a_n = 1) \Rightarrow (c_n = 1) \quad 1 \leq i \leq p_\alpha, 1 \leq j \leq q_\alpha \tag{2}$$

Then M' points out a homogeneous mapping of $G_\alpha = (V_\alpha, E_\alpha)$ and $G_\beta = (V_\beta, E_\beta)$.

Assuming that one of the security problem models of the smart contract is G_α, the smart contract control flow graph to be detected can be abstracted as G_β. If M' constitutes a homogeneous mapping of G_β and G_α, then we believe that this type of security problem exists in the smart contract to be detected.

4   RunningExample

In order to describe the running process of our framework, in this section, we explain the steps of vulnerability mining in detail by taking the classic reentry vulnerability in The DAO of Ethereum as an example.

First, we get a source code with a reentrant vulnerability as shown in *(1) Victim Code*. The malicious smart contract invokes the function *withdraw()* to withdraw the money from the victim contract. The second line of the code checks whether the user's balance and the balance of the contract are greater than the amount to be fetched. The reentry vulnerability appears on line 5, and the *call.value()* function will call the user's *fallback()* function, and the malicious user calls the *withdraw()* function again in the *fallback()* function.

(1) Victim Code

```
1  function withdraw(address to, uint256 amount) {
2      require(balances[msg.sender] > amount);
3      require(this.balance > amount);
4
5      withdrawLog(to, amount);
6      to.call.value(amount)();
7      balances[msg.sender] -= amount;
8  }
```

As shown in *(1) Victim Code*, the user balance reduction on line 7 has not been executed yet, so the balance of the malicious contract still hasn't been updated from the first withdraw. Therefore, the malicious user can continuously recursively take it out. A lot of ethers that are not their own, until the gas is exhausted.

According to the process of our framework, we first construct the control flow graph of the smart contract in Fig. 2, and then abstract the control flow graph into a digraph as Fig. 3.

Next we need to combine the code to extract the verification matrix from the directed graph. The verification matrix of the reentry vulnerability has two columns, and the number of rows is determined according to the number of nodes of the directed graph. As shown by the matrix X, the directed graph has eight nodes, and the X matrix has eight rows, and each row represents a node in the directed graph. The column of the matrix represents the code logic that may have problems. The first column indicates whether there is a dangerous transfer money function *call.value()* in the address segment represented by the node.

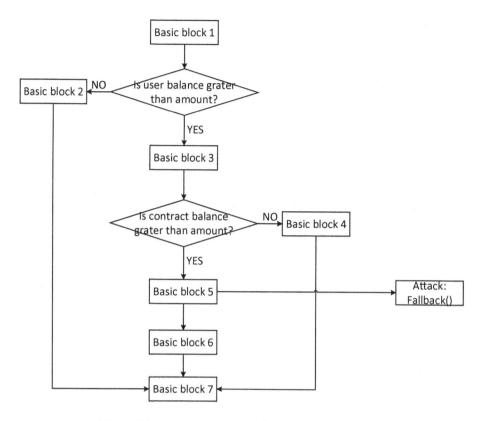

Fig. 2. The process of control flow graph generation.

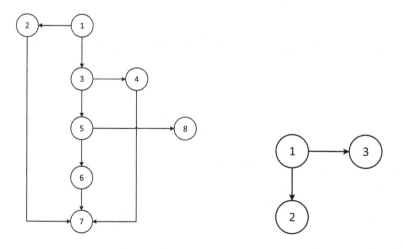

Fig. 3. Generated digraph.   **Fig. 4.** Reentrancy model diagram.

If it exists, the first column of the corresponding row of the node just fill in 1. Similarly, the second column of the X matrix represents the operation of the user balance reduction. We can see from the matrix X that there is a $call.value()$ function in the code segment corresponding to node 5, and there is an operation of reducing the user balance in the code segment corresponding to node 6.

$$X = \begin{pmatrix} 0\,0 \\ 0\,0 \\ 0\,0 \\ 0\,0 \\ 1\,0 \\ 0\,1 \\ 0\,0 \\ 0\,0 \end{pmatrix} \quad Y = \begin{pmatrix} 1\,0 \\ 0\,1 \\ 0\,0 \end{pmatrix} \tag{3}$$

Next, according to the Ullmann algorithm, we can get the adjacency matrix A corresponding to the directed graph transformed by the smart contract and the adjacency matrix B corresponding to the reentrant vulnerability model map. Where $A[i][j] = 1$ means that the vertex v_i has an edge with v_j, and $A[i][j] = 0$ means no border.

$$A = \begin{pmatrix} 0\,0\,0 \\ 1\,0\,0 \\ 1\,0\,0 \end{pmatrix} \quad B = \begin{pmatrix} 0\,1\,1\,0\,0\,0\,0\,0 \\ 0\,0\,0\,0\,0\,0\,1\,0 \\ 0\,0\,0\,1\,1\,0\,0\,0 \\ 0\,0\,0\,0\,0\,0\,1\,0 \\ 0\,0\,0\,0\,0\,1\,0\,1 \\ 0\,0\,0\,0\,0\,0\,1\,0 \\ 0\,0\,0\,0\,0\,0\,0\,0 \\ 0\,0\,0\,0\,0\,0\,0\,0 \end{pmatrix} \tag{4}$$

Next we construct a mapping matrix M' from A to B, $M'[i][j] = 1$ indicates the i vertex v_i in A corresponds to the j vertices in B, otherwise 0 means no correspondence. According to the matrices X and Y, we can find the correspondence of the matrice A and B. $X[5][1] = 1$, $Y[1][1] = 1$ indicates that the $call.value()$ function exists at this node. $X[6][2] = 1$, $Y[2][2] = 1$ indicates that there is a balance reduction operation at this node. Therefore, we correspond node 1 in Fig. 3 with node 2 in Fig. 4, and get $M'[1][5] = 1$; similarly, node 2 corresponds to node 6, and $M'[2][6] = 1$; In Fig. 4, only the remaining node 3 can be associated with node 8 in Fig. 3, resulting in $M'[3][8] = 1$. The remaining nodes that do not have a corresponding relationship are filled with 0, and finally get M'.

$$M' = \begin{pmatrix} 0\,0\,0\,0\,1\,0\,0\,0 \\ 0\,0\,0\,0\,0\,1\,0\,0 \\ 0\,0\,0\,0\,0\,0\,0\,1 \end{pmatrix} \tag{5}$$

Follow the formula $C = [C_{ij}] = M'(M'B)^T$, we can calculate the matrix C. The calculation process is as follows.

$$M'B = \begin{pmatrix} 0\,0\,0\,0\,0\,1\,0\,1 \\ 0\,0\,0\,0\,0\,0\,1\,0 \\ 0\,0\,0\,0\,0\,0\,0\,1 \end{pmatrix} \Rightarrow C = M'\,(M'B)^{\top} = \begin{pmatrix} 0\,0\,0 \\ 1\,0\,0 \\ 1\,0\,0 \end{pmatrix} \qquad (6)$$

Comparing matrices A, C, we can see that the place where 1 is in matrix A is also 1 in the matrix C, that satisfying the formula $\forall i \forall j : (A[i][j] = 1) \Rightarrow (C[i][j] = 1)$. So we can say that the mapping matrix we constructed M' is a homogeneous mapping. And Fig. 4 is the isomorphic subgraph of Fig. 3, from which we can conclude that there is a reentrant type of vulnerability in this detected smart contract. From the control flow graph, we can clearly see that if the malicious user calls the address of the basic block 1 again in the $fallback()$ function, the malicious user can continuously loop out a large number of ethers before the balance or gas is used up. So we can derive the exploit code (2) Attacker Code

(2) Attacker Code

```
1  function () payable {
2      if (msg.sender == victim) {
3          victim.call(
4              bytes4(
5                  keccak256(
6                      "withdraw(address,uint256)"
7                  )
8              ), this, msg.value);
9      }
```

5   Conclusion

The intelligent contract greatly expands the application scenario and practical significance of the blockchain, but frequent security incidents seriously hinder its development. This paper proposes a general framework of smart contract vulnerability detection, which is applicable to different blockchain platforms and can identify smart contracts in multiple programming languages. The subgraph isomorphic algorithm we used can solve the matching problem of control flow graph well. Next, we will try to build more vulnerability models and improve the isomorphic algorithms to improve the efficiency of vulnerability mining. Let our framework meet the ever-increasing vulnerability mining needs of smart contract size and complexity.

References

1. Fomo3D. https://exitscam.me/
2. The DAO smart contract. http://etherscan.io/address/0xbb9bc244d798123fde 783fcc1c72d3bb8c189413\#code
3. Bhargavan, K., et al.: Formal verification of smart contracts: short paper. In: Proceedings of the 2016 ACM Workshop on Programming Languages and Analysis for Security, pp. 91–96. ACM (2016)
4. Grigg, I.: Eos-an introduction. Whitepaper (2017). iang.org/papers/EOS_An_ Introduction.pdf (2017)
5. Jiang, B., Liu, Y., Chan, W.: Contractfuzzer: fuzzing smart contracts for vulnerability detection. In: Proceedings of the 33rd ACM/IEEE International Conference on Automated Software Engineering, pp. 259–269. ACM (2018)
6. Luu, L., Chu, D.H., Olickel, H., Saxena, P., Hobor, A.: Making smart contracts smarter. In: Proceedings of the 2016 ACM SIGSAC Conference on Computer and Communications Security, pp. 254–269. ACM (2016)
7. Ullmann, J.R.: An algorithm for subgraph isomorphism. J. ACM (JACM) **23**(1), 31–42 (1976)
8. Viglione, R., Versluis, R., Lippencott, J.: Zen white paper (2017)
9. Wood, G., et al.: Ethereum: a secure decentralised generalised transaction ledger. Ethereum Proj. Yellow Pap. **151**(2014), 1–32 (2014)
10. Yang, X., Yang, Z., Sun, H., Fang, Y., Liu, J., Song, J.: Formal verification for ethereum smart contract using COQ. World Acad. Sci. Eng. Technol. Int. J. Inf. Commun. Eng. **12**(6) (2018)

Placement and Routing Optimization Problem for Service Function Chain: State of Art and Future Opportunities

Weihan Chen[1,3], Xia Yin[1,3], Zhiliang Wang[2,3(✉)], Xingang Shi[1,3], and Jiangyuan Yao[4]

[1] Department of Computer Science and Technology, Tsinghua University, Beijing, China
[2] Institute for Network Sciences and Cyberspace, Tsinghua University, Beijing, China
wzl@cernet.edu.cn
[3] Beijing National Research Center for Information Science and Technology, Beijing, China
[4] School of Computer Science and Cyberspace Security, Hainan University, Haikou, Hainan, China

Abstract. Network Functions Virtualization (NFV) allows implantation of network functions to be independent of dedicated hardware devices. Any series of services can be represented by a service function chain which contains a set of virtualized network functions in a specified order. From the perspective of network performance optimization, the challenges of deploying service chain in network is twofold: 1) the location of placing virtualized network functions and resources allocation scheme; and 2) routing policy for traffic flow among different instances of network function. This article introduces service function chain related optimization problems, summarizes the optimization motivation and mainstream algorithm of virtualized network functions deployment and traffic routing. We hope it can help readers to learn about the current research progress and make further innovation in this field.

Keywords: Network function virtualization · Service function chain · Routing optimization

1 Introduction

Service Function Chain (SFC) [1] refers to connecting different network functions in specific sequence and providing corresponding service for users. The network functions in SFC are realized as different Virtualized Network Function (VNF). In actual network, SFC can be configured and adjusted according to different traffic demand. The configuration process involves two aspects: the placement of VNF and traffic steering among different VNFs. In terms of VNF placement, the network operators (or Internet

This work is supported by the Program of Hainan Association for Science and Technology Plans to Youth R & D Innovation (QCXM201910), the National Natural Science Foundation of China (61802092) and the National Key Research and Development Program of China under Grant No. 2018YFB1800401

© Springer Nature Singapore Pte Ltd. 2020
X. Sun et al. (Eds.): ICAIS 2020, CCIS 1254, pp. 176–188, 2020.
https://doi.org/10.1007/978-981-15-8101-4_17

Service Providers) need to select the location for VNF Instance (VNFI), which can run VNF and allocate the resource (CPU, memory, etc.) for each VNFI. And in terms of traffic steering (routing), the path used to transmit traffic through specific VNFs of SFC needs to be determined. Proper SFC configuration can be helpful for improving network performance and reducing operational cost.

In actual network environment, both users and network operators have their own performance requirements for network functions. For network operators, the requirements can be reducing VNF placement cost and improving resource utilization. And for common users, the requirements can be increasing network throughput and reducing traffic transmission delay. These performance requirements need to be satisfied by adopting appropriate SFC configuration (including VNF placement and traffic routing). However, different VNF placement and traffic routing schemes for SFC may affect network performance and operational cost. It is difficult to find optimal SFC configuration only depending on human experience. By modeling optimization problem for VNF placement and traffic routing and solving the problem, determining corresponding SFC configuration schemes and satisfying performance requirements can be easier.

During the modeling process, the placement and routing optimization problem can be considered independently or jointly. When treating VNF placement optimization problem independently, VNF deployment and operational cost is considered as the prior optimization objective, the cost may include minimizing placement cost (mentioned in [2]), minimizing traffic switching cost among different VNFs (mentioned in [3]), etc. And the constraints of placement problem mainly focus on resource capacity constraints, which can be host CPU core number, link capacity or other network resources. In contrast, the optimization objective of routing problem tends to prioritize routing cost. It aims to find a path with least cost. The cost has many choices (such as financial cost, delay, QoS requirement, etc. mentioned in [4]). Meanwhile, the main constraint of routing problem is that user traffic flow should pass through the services provided by the SFC in the specified order.

On the other hand, in order to achieve better network performance, the VNF placement problem and traffic routing problem can be considered jointly. The optimization objective can be the combination of placement and routing optimization objectives. The constraints are also similar with the VNF placement optimization problem constraints plus routing constraints. However, optimizing VNF placement and routing jointly may cause some conflict. Because lower placement cost means less VNFIs are deployed, which results in higher routing cost (some traffic may be routed to longer path in order to achieve necessary network functions). On the contrary, to realize lower routing cost, more VNFIs need to be deployed, which causes placement cost increasing. Hence, finding a trade-off solution for joint optimization problem is necessary.

Currently, there is a great deal of research focuses on placement and routing optimization problem for SFC [2–11]. They use different methods to model the optimization problem and develop corresponding algorithms to solve the problem efficiently. In this survey, we mainly focus on summarizing existing research about VNF placement and traffic routing optimization problem for SFC configuration. First, we introduce existing solutions of independent VNF placement problem and traffic routing problem, and then the joint optimization problem of placement and routing will be discussed. Each kind of optimization problem is presented in detail. In addition, we also discuss the future opportunities for placement and routing method of SFC.

2   Virtual Network Function Placement

2.1   Background

When a specific SFC is deployed, it first instantiates the required VNFs as VNFIs, and then places these VNFIs in proper location of the network. Different VNF placement schemes can affect the network performance and placement cost. For example, as shown in Fig. 1 (a), if only one VNFI for each VNF of SFC is placed in the network, the placement cost (approximatively the number of deployed VNFIs) is minimized, but the network performance is relatively low. SFC traffic throughput is equal to the available bottleneck bandwidth of path shown in Fig. 1 (a), which may not satisfy users' requirement. However, if the placement scheme as shown in Fig. 1 (b) is adopted, the network performance can be better (traffic throughput can be improved), but the placement cost also ascends. Hence, during the placement process, network operators usually hope to allocate minimized resources to each VNFI while satisfying the performance requirements.

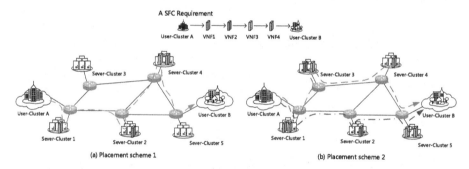

Fig. 1. VNF placement in actual network example

2.2   Existing Solutions

In the current optimization solutions of VNF placement, the actual network is usually considered as a graph which includes a set of nodes and edges. The nodes are the abstract of forwarding devices in the network. Some of the nodes can connect with the server-clusters, and VNF can be deployed in these clusters. Each server-cluster has its own physical resources, containing CPU, memory, storage, etc. These resources should be allocated to the VNF as requirements. The edges in the graph represent the links between different nodes, and edges also have physical resource, mainly referring to link capacity. According to user requirements and resource constraints, the optimization solutions need to deploy VNFIs which are required by specific SFC in the graph, and then realize expected optimization goal.

2.3 Optimization Objective

In general, the cost that physical devices use to run VNF is mainly considered. Ghaznavi et al. [2] and Luizelli et al. [3] propose to use minimizing operational cost as the optimization objective. Particularly, Ghaznavi et al. [2] aim to minimize the aggregate cost of allocating host and bandwidth resources. The host resources allocation cost is related to the resource demand for each VNF and the number of VNFIs running on host, and the bandwidth resources allocation cost is related to the volume of traffic on each link. Luizelli et al. [3] aim to minimize the virtual switching cost in physical devices, which is caused by software switching in order to steer traffic through VNFs of SFC.

2.4 Optimization Problem Formulation

Most optimization problems of VNF placement are modeled as Integer Programming problem [3] or Mixed Integer Programming (MIP) problem [2]. Besides the optimization objective mentioned above, the problems also include the related resources and user demand constraints such as physical device capacity constraint, location constraint, link capacity constraint, throughput constraint and so on. These constraints are the boundary of VNF placement optimization problem, and they help to find optimal solution under specified conditions.

2.5 Algorithm Form

Some VNF placement optimization problems are proved as NP-hard problem (such as in research [2]). That means it is difficult to realize fast solving for large-scale network. Therefore, some heuristic algorithms are proposed to realize fast solving. These heuristic algorithms include both classical algorithms (e.g. local search, greedy, etc.) and novel algorithms (e.g. bipartite graph matching [3], etc.). For example, Ghaznavi et al. [2] propose a local search heuristic solution called KARIZ. For a network topology (See Fig. 2 (a)), it assumes each type of VNF in the SFC (See Fig. 2 (b)) is deployed in a layer. Each layer contains a set of nodes in which the corresponding type of VNFIs can be installed (See Fig. 2 (c)). The traffic can be routed layer by layer. During this process, the optimal routing between two layers is found by solving the minimum cost flow problem, and then the number of VNFIs in each layer is computed according to the allocated throughput. The algorithm repeats this process until the traffic has reached the last layer. Finally, the optimal result will be found (See Fig. 2 (d)).

2.6 Summarization

Existing VNF placement solutions mainly aim to minimize deployment cost and improve network performance. They model the optimization problem with integer linear programming and use heuristic algorithms to realize fast solving. Although there is some gap in term of accuracy between the heuristic algorithms and direct solving method, heuristic algorithms have advantage in computational complexity when solving large-scale network optimization problem.

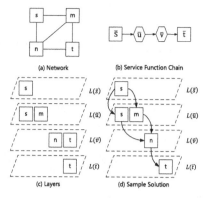

Fig. 2. Layers example of KARIZ [2]

3 Service Function Chain Routing for VNFs

3.1 Background

Besides VNF placement, traffic routing also needs to be considered. The process of routing traffic requires to determine the forwarding path that traverses each VNF of SFC in specified order and consider the related network characteristics (such as link load, link transmission delay, etc.). The network operators usually wish to compute forwarding path efficiently and the routing cost could be minimized. In practice, traditional shortest path algorithm (like Dijkstra's algorithm) can be helpful when computing forwarding path, but additional SFC constraints also need to be considered for satisfying user demands.

3.2 Existing Solutions

Similar to VNF placement optimization problem, SFC routing optimization problem also considers the actual network as a directed graph. The traffic should be transmitted from starting node to terminating node and pass through the VNFs of specified SFC. Meanwhile, the locations of these VNFs in the graph are assumed to be known in advance. The routing optimization solutions should calculate the shortest path with least cost and ensure the found paths are admissible.

3.3 Optimization Objective

The metric of SFC routing algorithm has many potential choices. It could be financial aspect (such as maintaining cost of forwarding devices, etc.) or network performance aspect (such as traffic propagation delay, user QoS demand, etc.). Existing optimization solutions usually aim to reduce the routing costs and improve the network performance like throughput [5]. For example, Dwaraki et al. [4] use delay as the only metric for link communication and VNF processing, and then minimize the delay cost when calculating forwarding paths. The reason is that delay is an important consideration in many networks, and it can also be used to represent dynamic loads on network links and on VNF processing nodes.

3.4 Algorithm Form

The SFC routing algorithms need to find a forwarding path that can transfer traffic from source to destination with least cost. Meanwhile, they also need to ensure the traffic can be processed by required network services. Dwaraki et al. [4] propose an Adaptive Service Routing (ASR) algorithm that transforms the original network graph into a "layered graph" and uses conventional shortest-path algorithms to calculate forwarding paths. And Sallam et al. [5] propose similar scheme which also constructs a new transformed graph and uses conventional shortest-path algorithms to compute SFC-constrained shortest path. The difference is that Sallam et al. [5] propose a pruning algorithm to simplify the constructed graph. It first constructs an initial graph (see Fig. 3 (a)) that contains original node (white node) and several copies (gray node), and the number of copies also depends on the length of SFC (in Fig. 3, the example SFC contains two VNFs). The copy node is reachable if the path from one node (can be either original node or copy node) to itself can satisfy partial SFC. Then, it removes the nodes only have outgoing edges (except source node) and the nodes only have incoming edges (except destination node). After that, the pruned graph can be obtained (see Fig. 3 (b)). This difference can help to reduce the computational time when using shortest path algorithm compared with ASR algorithm.

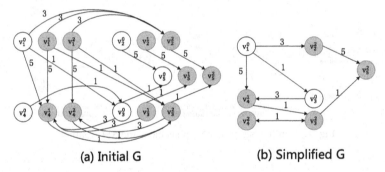

(a) Initial G   (b) Simplified G

Fig. 3. Initial and pruned graph for SFC-constrained shortest path algorithm [5]

3.5 Summarization

The major objectives of existing SFC routing solutions are routing traffic with least cost and meeting SFC demands. They usually transform the routing problem into shortest path problem with SFC constraints, and then use conventional shortest path algorithms to solve this problem. The metric used to select optimal path can be various, mainly depending on the choice of network operators. Meanwhile, the efficiency of computing SFC-constrained shortest path can also be guaranteed in large-scale network.

4 Joint Optimization of VNF Placement and SFC Routing

4.1 Background

When VNF placement and SFC routing optimization problems are considered jointly, there cloud be a conflict between these two problems. For example, as shown in Fig. 4 (a) and (b) (here we use the topology similar to [9]), there are three traffic requests T1 (from node 3 to 11), T2 (from node 11 to 1) and T3 (from node 10 to 5) demand SFC1 composed of VNF1, VNF2 and VNF3 (the order of VNFs is VNF1-VNF2-VNF3). In Fig. 4 (a), if there is only one instance of SFC1 in the network, traffic flow T2 and T3 have to be routed over longer path, which causes more routing cost. However, if we deploy two SFC1 instances in the network, as shown in Fig. 4 (b), the routing cost can be reduced due to using shorter forwarding paths. This example implies that optimizing VNF placement alone by instantiating fewer VNFIs may cause the traffic routing cost increasing. Whereas, if SFC routing optimization is considered preferentially, the additional VNF placement cost may be introduced, because more VNFIs are required to satisfy abundant traffic demand in today's network environment. Hence, joint optimization of VNF placement and SFC routing is necessary to find a trade-off optimal SFC deployment scheme.

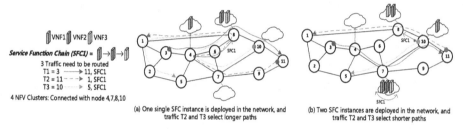

Fig. 4. Conflict between VNF placement and SFC routing

4.2 Existing Solutions

Joint optimization solutions should deploy required VNFs of SFC properly, which means the deployment scheme can achieve high resource utilization or minimize the resources that need to be allocated with VNFs. Meanwhile, user traffic flow should also be routed through specified VNFs with QoS requirements. Besides these tasks, some solutions also consider the migration of VNFIs in response to the variation of user demand or network situation. Next, we will introduce some existing joint optimization schemes for VNF placement and SFC routing.

4.3 Optimization Objective

The objective of VNF placement and SFC routing joint optimization can be diverse. Some joint optimization solutions usually combine the VNF placement and SFC routing optimization objectives together. For example, Addis et al. [6] propose using minimization of the maximum link utilization as network-level optimization objective, and minimization of allocated computing resources as VNFI-level optimization objective. And Zhang et al. [7] use maximizing the average resource utilization of each computing node and minimizing the average response latency of traffic scheduling as optimization objective. Since most existing optimization solutions belong to multi-objective optimization, they usually use weighted sum approach to represent the joint optimization objective.

On the other hand, some solutions do not explicitly represent the VNF placement and SFC routing optimization objectives mentioned above. For example, Gupta et al. [9] aim to minimize bandwidth consumption by instantiating proper number of VNFs and selecting shortest path for routing traffic. Similarly, Guo et al. [8] and Qu et al. [12] select maximizing resource utilization as the main optimization objective. In addition, considering reconstruction for variation of user demand or network situation, Tajiki et al. [10] takes minimization of energy consumption and reconfiguration cost into account as optimization objective. Meanwhile, Tajiki et al. [10] aim to minimize energy consumption by reducing the number of hops that the flow needs to traverse.

4.4 Optimization Problem Formulation

The type of optimization problem formulation mainly depends on the optimization objective. If the optimization objective is the combination of VNF placement and SFC routing optimization objectives, the joint optimization problem is usually modeled as Mixed Integer Linear Programming (MILP) problem [6, 7]. The reason is besides integer variables (like physical resources capacity), some SFC routing optimization solutions may involve real variables (like link delay).

By contrast, if the optimization objective does not involve real variables, the optimization solutions usually use ILP to model the optimization problem [9–11]. For example, Gupta et al. [9] aim to minimize bandwidth consumed. It precomputes the potential set of configurations for SFC and uses them as input for the ILP model. The ILP model can select the best configuration based on related constraints, and then compute the forwarding path for user traffic.

4.5 Algorithm Form

Since the joint optimization problems of VNF placement and SFC routing are basically NP-hard, most solutions propose corresponding heuristic algorithms to realize rapid solving. The details of each heuristic algorithm can be different according to the specific optimization problems. But the main idea of these heuristic algorithms is similar. They all rely on related network operational experience, leverage constraint relaxation, iteration and other methods to achieve the trade-off between optimality gap and computational complexity, and then find the result that is close to the optimal solution. However, the results solved by heuristic algorithm are usually near-optimal and the gap between near-optimal and optimal solutions cannot be estimated. Some typical examples of heuristic algorithms are presented as follows.

Heuristic algorithms usually obtain the near optimal solution through continuous iteration. For example, in Addis et al. research [6], there are two competitive optimization objectives: minimizing total virtualization cost (first objective) and minimizing maximum link utilization (second objective). Because this research prefers to improve user service quality, it first finds the best result according to the first objective, and then increases the value found in first objective step by step until the desired cost level of the second objective is found. Finally, the optimal VNF deployment and traffic routing policy can be determined. For maximization of resource utilization, Qu et al. [11] propose a bi-directional search methodology. It uses greedily search and shortest path routing to select the best physical machines that have enough computing resources to run VNFIs of the SFC. The algorithm executes both forward search (from source node of traffic) and backward search (from destination node of traffic). Backward search can help to improve the result found by the forward search. This method can avoid the algorithm trapping into local optimum.

Moreover, some existing solutions propose approximation algorithms to solve the joint optimization problem. For example, Zhang et al. [7] design a priority-driven weighted algorithm to find near optimal solution. The algorithm calculates the probability of placing VNF at a physical device by its reciprocal of RST (RST refers to remaining resource capacity of the physical device), and then places the VNF with the maximum probability for maximizing network resource utilization. Similarly, Guo et al. [8] propose a multiplicative weight update algorithm. It first formulates the dual of the original optimization problem, and then introduces dual variable for user traffic flow and weight variable for related physical resources. The algorithm will assign the SFC configuration for the adopted flow, and the weight variable will also be updated. The algorithm will be executed until all arrival flow is traversed. Unlike heuristic algorithm, approximation algorithm can guarantee the gap between the result solved by itself and optimum within bounds.

4.6 Summarization

VNF placement and SFC routing joint optimization solutions have the optimization objectives in both VNF-level (mainly consider deployment cost, resource usage, etc.) and routing-level (mainly consider link utilization, delay, etc.). Because of the conflict between these two levels, the optimization solutions need to balance the objectives of VNF-level and routing-level according to the requirements of network operators and users. Furthermore, in order to realize fast solving in large-scale network, these solutions propose different heuristic algorithms or approximation algorithms to exchange the accuracy of optimization results for lower computational complexity.

5 Comparison for Different Optimization Solutions

In this section, we will compare the different SFC placement and routing optimization solutions mentioned above. They are compared based on the optimization type, the objective of optimization problem, the formulation that used to model the optimization problem, algorithm type, algorithm complexity, algorithm strength and weakness. The details of the comparison are shown in Table 1.

Table 1. Comparison for different optimization solutions

Optimization type	Specific works	Optimization objective	Formulation Type	Algorithm Type	Strength	Weakness
VNF placement	KARIZ [2]	MIN deployment cost	MIP	Heuristic	Well optimize CPU cost during VNF placement, and time complexity is reasonable	The lower bound of algorithm cannot be guaranteed
	OCM [3]	MIN (switching) cost	N/A	Heuristic	Optimize internal switching CPU cost to improve network utilization	Time complexity of algorithm is affected by SFC length obviously
SFC routing	ASR [4]	MIN total routing delay	N/A	N/A	Use shortest path algorithms to simplify traffic routing optimization in layered graph	The large size of layered graph may affect algorithm run time
	SCSP [5]	MIN routing cost	N/A	N/A	Simplify the layered graph in [4], and improve algorithm efficiency	Ignore the VNF execute cost on network node
Joint optimization of VNF placement and SFC routing	VNF-PR [6]	MIN maximum link utilization and host cores number	MILP	Heuristic	Acceptable execution time for large scale optimization problem	No specific time complexity

(continued)

Table 1. (*continued*)

Optimization type	Specific works	Optimization objective	Formulation Type	Algorithm Type	Strength	Weakness
	BFDSU&RCKK [7]	MAX resource utilization and MIN average latency	MILP	Approximation (BFDSU) & Heuristic (RCKK)	Worst-case performance bound of algorithm (BFDSU) has been theoretically proved	Optimization effect of request scheduling is not obvious
	MWUA [8]	MAX overall resource utility	ILP	Approximation	Upper and lower bound of algorithm performance has been proved	Problem parameters is coarse-grained
	SPTG&CG-ILP [9]	MIN bandwidth consumed	ILP	Heuristic	Well optimize the bandwidth consumed in WAN scenario	Run time of CG-ILP is not acceptable in large scale network
	NSF [10]	MIN energy consumption	ILP	Heuristic	Novel solutions for energy-aware management of network traffic, low execution time	Optimality gap is evaluated by experiment, lack of theoretical proof
	REACH [11]	MAX network resources utility	ILP	Heuristic	Use bi-direction search to avoid local optima	Lack of evaluation for optimality gap

- N/A means the solution does not give out the type of optimization problem formulation or algorithm.
- MIN means minimize, MAX means maximize.

6 Future Research Prospects

At present, a lot of research has proposed corresponding solutions which optimize VNF deployment and traffic routing scheme for better performance. However, the user demands can usually be variable in real-time. If the SFC configurations cannot be adjusted to accommodate the variations, the network performance may decline (such as resources utilization decreasing, response latency increasing, etc.). Actually, most existing solutions don't consider this problem. Based on the real needs, SFC elastic scaling (or dynamic adjustment) is a good research direction. Two main kinds of elastic scaling approaches are shown as following.

6.1 Auto-Scaling Based on Threshold

Adel et al. [13] propose a dynamic auto-scaling algorithm called ElasticSFC to allocate or release VNF and bandwidth resource. The scaling decision is made depending on whether the CPU utilization of physical host or bandwidth consumption is higher than upper bound (or less than lower bound). However, scaling approaches based on threshold are reactive to adjust the SFC deployment scheme or routing policy, namely adjust SFC configurations after variations have happened (may have happened for a while). This may not be the best solution.

6.2 Auto-Scaling Based on Demand Prediction

Demand prediction can be used to determine the extent of scaling VNF instances dynamically and the forwarding paths of flow can also be adjusted according to the variants of VNFIs. Some online learning methods have been used in recent researches. For example, Fei et al. [12] propose an online-learning method called follow-the-regularized-leader (FTRL) for upcoming user flows prediction. It can directly predict the flow rates of SFC and help to determine the scaling strategy of VNFIs for minimizing deployment cost.

On the other hand, machine learning technology has attracted a lot of attention in the field of networking. It can be helpful in traffic classification, routing decisions, resource allocation [14] and so on. There are some solutions using deep learning technology in VNF selecting and chaining problem. Instead of traditional heuristic algorithms, they use deep learning techniques to solve optimization problems [15]. These methods can yield time efficiency and scalability benefit. Hence, combining machine learning technology with SFC placement and routing optimization problem can be another expected research direction in the future.

7 Conclusion

In this article, we first introduce VNF placement and SFC routing optimization problems independently. Then the joint optimization problem of VNF placement and SFC routing is introduced. For each kind of optimization problem, we describe the problem background, optimization objective, optimization problem formulation and algorithm form in details. Moreover, we also summarize and compare recent existing solutions, and then propose the future research prospects of SFC placement and routing problem.

References

1. Joel, H., Pignataro, C.: Service function chaining (SFC) architecture. RFC 7665 (2015)
2. Ghaznavi, M., Shahriar, N., Kamali, S.: Distributed service function chaining. IEEE J. Sel. Areas Commun. **35**(11), 2479–2489 (2017)
3. Luizelli, M.C., Raz, D., Sa'ar, Y.: Optimizing NFV chain deployment through minimizing the cost of virtual switching. In: IEEE INFOCOM 2018-IEEE Conference on Computer Communications, pp. 2150–2158. IEEE (2018)
4. Dwaraki, A., Wolf, T.: Adaptive service-chain routing for virtual network functions in software-defined networks. In: Proceedings of the 2016 Workshop on Hot Topics in Middleboxes and Network Function Virtualization, pp. 32–37. ACM (2016)
5. Sallam, G., Gupta, G.R., Li, B.: Shortest path and maximum flow problems under service function chaining constraints. In: IEEE INFOCOM 2018-IEEE Conference on Computer Communications, pp. 2132–2140. IEEE (2018)
6. Addis, B., Belabed, D., Bouet, M.: Virtual network functions placement and routing optimization. In: CloudNet, pp. 171–177 (2015)
7. Zhang, Q., Xiao, Y., Liu, F.: Joint optimization of chain placement and request scheduling for network function virtualization. In: 2017 IEEE 37th International Conference on Distributed Computing Systems (ICDCS), pp. 731–741. IEEE (2017)
8. Guo, L., Pang, J., Walid, A.: Joint placement and routing of network function chains in data centers. In: IEEE INFOCOM 2018-IEEE Conference on Computer Communications, pp. 612–620. IEEE (2018)
9. Gupta, A., Jaumard, B., Tornatore, M.: A scalable approach for service chain mapping with multiple SC instances in a wide-area network. IEEE J. Sel. Areas Commun. **36**(3), 529–541 (2018)
10. Tajiki, M.M., Salsano, S., Chiaraviglio, L.: Joint energy efficient and QoS-aware path allocation and VNF placement for service function chaining. IEEE Trans. Netw. Serv. Manag. **16**(1), 374–388 (2018)
11. Qu, L., Khabbaz, M., Assi, C.: Reliability-aware service chaining in carrier-grade softwarized networks. IEEE J. Sel. Areas Commun. **36**(3), 558–573 (2018)
12. Fei, X., Liu, F., Xu, H.: Adaptive VNF scaling and flow routing with proactive demand prediction. In: IEEE INFOCOM 2018-IEEE Conference on Computer Communications, pp. 86–494. IEEE (2018)
13. Toosi, A.N., Son, J., Chi, Q.: ElasticSFC: auto-scaling techniques for elastic service function chaining in network functions virtualization-based clouds. J. Syst. Softw. **152**, 108–119 (2019)
14. Zhang, J., Xie, N., Zhang, X., Yue, K., Li, W., Kumar, D.: Machine learning based resource allocation of cloud computing in auction. Comput. Mater. Contin. **56**(1), 123–135 (2018)
15. Pei, J., Hong, P., Li, D.: Virtual network function selection and chaining based on deep learning in SDN and NFV-enabled networks. In: IEEE International Conference on Communications Workshops (ICC Workshops), pp. 1–6. IEEE (2018)

DDoS Attack Detection Based on One-Class SVM in SDN

Jianming Zhao[1,2,3,4], Peng Zeng[1,2,3,4]($\boxtimes$), Wenli Shang[1,2,3,4], and Guoyu Tong[1,2,3,4]

[1] State Key Laboratory of Robotics, Shenyang Institute of Automation,
Chinese Academy of Sciences, Shenyang 110016, China
`{zhaojianming,zp,shangwl,tongguoyu}@sia.cn`
[2] Key Laboratory of Networked Control System, Shenyang Institute of Automation,
Chinese Academy of Sciences, Shenyang 110016, China
[3] Institutes for Robotics and Intelligent Manufacturing, Chinese Academy of Sciences,
Shenyang 110016, China
[4] University of Chinese Academy of Sciences, Beijing 100049, China

Abstract. Software Defined Networking (SDN) is a new type of network architecture, which provides an important way to implement automated network deployment and flexible management. However, security problems in SDN are also inevitable. DDoS attack belongs to one of the most serious attack types, which is fairly common for today's Internet. In SDN security fields, DDoS attack detection research has been received more and more attention. In this paper, a DDoS attack detection method based on one-class SVM in SDN is proposed, which provides a better detection accuracy. Furthermore, two new feature vectors, including middle value of flow table item's duration and protocol data traffic percentage, are extracted to integrate into the item of 11 feature vectors. Additionally, basing on selection and construction method of the 11 feature vectors, a DDoS attack behavior model is established by using one-class SVM algorithm, and the self-adaptation genetic algorithm is designed to optimize the corresponding parameters of the Gaussian kernel of one-class SVM. The experimental results in SDN show that, the proposed new feature vectors are shown to more better detection accuracy, and the proposed method is more feasible by comparing with the BP neural network and RBF neural network algorithms under the same 11 features vectors.

Keywords: DDoS attack detection · One-class SVM · SDN · Feature vector

1 Introduction

With the development of networking technology, the dynamic service demands for network resources can't be met under the existing network architecture, and the original network architecture has become a bottleneck for the development of various information systems. Due to the massive and heterogeneous characteristics of field devices, SDN (Software Defined Network) has attracted increasing attention by IOT (Internet of Things) researchers. SDN meets the requirements of the development architecture and dynamic deployment with layered views, and the revolutionary idea of SDN is being

© Springer Nature Singapore Pte Ltd. 2020
X. Sun et al. (Eds.): ICAIS 2020, CCIS 1254, pp. 189–200, 2020.
https://doi.org/10.1007/978-981-15-8101-4_18

widely studied and accepted [1]. However, the new network architecture needs to be fully considered on information security problems [2]. Moreover, DDoS (Distributed Denial of Service) attack is more and more frequent in recent years, and its attack methods are more and more diversified. In practice, the detection method for DDoS attack in traditional networks often requires professional hardware devices, and the detection efficiency and accuracy need to be improved with the continuous research due to the lack of global views. However, SDN can provide a new way for solving DDoS problems, and has attracted extensive attentions to launch a large scale of surveys and researches [3].

Aiming at detecting DDoS attacks in SDN, this paper firstly introduces basic SDN architecture, DDoS attack type and traditional DDoS attack detection methods. Then, two new feature vectors, including middle value of flow table item's duration and protocol data traffic percentage, are extracted to integrate into the item of 11 feature vectors. Finally, a DDoS attack detection model based on 11 feature vectors is presented by using one-class SVM (Support Vector Machine), and the self-adaptation genetic algorithm is designed to optimize the parameters of one-class SVM model. By the experimental analysis, the proposed feature vectors can contribute to more better detection accuracy, and the proposed algorithm is more efficient.

2 DDoS Attack Detection in SDN

2.1 Basic SDN Architecture

SDN is a new solution to the problem of traditional network architecture, and OpenFlow technology is core technology in basic SDN architecture. Furthermore, SDN designs the control plane and the forwarding plane to implement the forwarding strategy, and it can establish a dynamic strategy enforcement mechanism for the whole network [4]. By comparing with the traditional static route configuration, the dynamic transformation strategy is design to transform in SDN, and it separates the control rights and carries out the centralized management. Additionally, the control layer is clearly and correctly abstracted, and the openness of control rights makes transmission paths more intelligent [5].

The flow table item is an abstraction of the data forwarding function belonging to the SDN device. In traditional networks, the data forwarding function of switches and routers depends on the MAC (Media Access Control) address forwarding tables or IP (Internet Protocol) address routing tables which are saved in these devices, and it is similar to the flow table items used in SDN's switches. However, the flow table items of SDN also integrate network information at all levels, so that richer rules can be used for the data forwarding function. Now, the multi-flow table mechanism is supported, and it can be more efficient than one-flow table mechanism. Therefore, when the switch receives packets, it traverses all data in order. In the same flow table, packets are matched with all flow table items from top to bottom, and the flow table items with the same priority do not overlap. Additionally, the switch performs the corresponding operation on the packet according to the command of the flow table items. The main components of the flow table items are shown in Fig. 1.

Match Fields	Priority	Counters	Instructions	Timeouts	Cookie

Fig. 1. Main components of the flow table item.

2.2 DDoS Attack Detection

One of the major features is the use of OpenFlow table items for packet forwarding in SDN, and OpenFlow table items are more abundant and more flexible than traditional network forwarding tables. Y. Afek uses the "match" and "action" mechanisms of the data plane to implement anti-spoofing functions in the SDN network. Furthermore, this method can detect some spoofing attacks, such as SYN spoofing and DNS spoofing, and then process them by flow tables without any other devices and extra expansion. Because OpenFlow table items contain the information of their own matching packets, it is very suitable for the flow-based lightweight DDoS attack detection, which is less expensive than the fine-grained packet detection [6]. In a large network, W. Rui proposes a collecting method between controllers and switches, and they design a method of counting packets to insert into the OpenFlow tables. Additionally, this paper uses a lightweight DDoS attack detection model to detect anomalous DDoS behaviors and to reduce the flow collection overload [7]. Instead of detecting fine-grained packet information, a lightweight DDoS attack detection method is proposed by extracting the "6-tuple" feature vectors from the flow table items and using self-organizing map, and this method finds a balance of higher accuracy and lower system overhead for DDoS attack detection [8, 9]. D. Jankowski uses SOM algorithm to identify attacks based on the characteristics of the flow table, which can identify multiple DDoS attacks [10, 11].

In summary, the SDN's advantages central control and global view bring a new idea for DDoS attack detection, and many novel and effective detection methods have been proposed in many literatures. However, there are still some problems and shortcomings, such as more comprehensive feature vectors, practical application environment of detection method, and global perspective advantage of SDN.

3 DDoS Attack Detection Model

In order to propose a more efficient method about DDoS attack detection, we study three core points of the model process, including feature vectors collection, one-class SVM detection algorithm, and the optimization of model parameters based on self-adaptation genetic algorithm.

3.1 Feature Vector Collection

Through the existing literatures, we analyze three common kinds of DDoS attacks in SDN.

1. IP address spoofing. It is a common kind of DDoS attack, such as IP routing spoofing, and it randomly generates a large number of fake IP addresses to the target. If the target is weak, the authenticity of the attack source can't be analyzed for the received malicious requests, and the hidden purpose of the attacker can be achieved.
2. Slow connection attack. It belongs to a kind of application layer attack. When a HTTP slow connection attack occurs, the attacker will divide an HTTP packet into multiple parts and send them to the victim, and each part of those is small and relatively large in the interval time [12].
3. Flood attack. Its purpose is to block the victim's network bandwidth with large network traffic, and it uses a large number of requests to consume the victim's computing resources, for example SYN Flooding, UDP Flooding, HTTP Flooding, etc.

To detect the above attacks, we research on the flow table feature extraction method. Moreover, its basic idea is to extract the flow table items in the OpenFlow switch, and calculates and converts them into the feature vectors. By using the flow table items of the forwarding operation, they count the matching domain and information of the flow table items including Protocol, srcIP, dstIP, srcPort, dstPort and Count which represent the protocol class, source IP, destination IP, source port, destination port, count number in flow table items, respectively. Based on the above traditional 6 entries of flow table, this paper further analyzes other feature vectors commonly used to describe the DDoS attack behavior in SDN [13].

1. Flow packet statistics (FPS)
   When a DDoS attack occurs, the attackers will send a large number of data packets to the target. FPS is the statistics in time T, and the value will increase when a DDoS attack occurring.

$$\text{FPS} = \left(\sum_{i=1}^{N} PacketsNum_i \right) / T \tag{1}$$

2. Destinated host's flow table items rate (DFIR)
   When a DDoS attack occurs, the percentage of the flow table items including the affected host's destination address in total number of flow table items will increase.

$$\text{DFIR} = N_d / N \tag{2}$$

3. Single flow table proportion (SFP)
   Some normal flow table items are interactive, such as {$protocol_i$, $srcIP_i$, $dstIP_i$,} and {$protocol_i$, $dstIP_i$, $srcIP_i$,}, and this attack often makes many single items in a communication process, for example SYN Flooding.

$$\text{SFP} = N_s / N \tag{3}$$

The above three feature vectors can't fully describe the DDoS attack situation, and can't detect some special attacks. Therefore, we propose new feature vectors for the corresponding DDoS attack detection.

1. Middle value of flow table items' duration (FIDM)
   When an attack uses IP spoofing technology, the attacker will frequently change the forged IP address. The controller will issue the corresponding flow table items to the OpenFlow switch, and this will make no packet matching to those items in a short time. Therefore, it is important to check a large number of flow table items in the OpenFlow switch.

$$FIDM = \sum_{i=1, 2, \ldots N} T_i / N \tag{4}$$

2. The average value of protocol data traffic (PDTA)
   The attacker often uses the same protocol type to produce DDoS attacks. By calculating the average value of protocol data traffic, UDP Flooding, SYN Flooding, and HTTP Flooding can be effectively detected.

$$PDTA = \sum_{i=1, 2, \ldots N} \text{Count}_{protocol_i} / N \tag{5}$$

3.2 One-Class SVM Detection Algorithm

SVM detection algorithm is designed as a classifier, which can distinguish the normal and abnormal data. According to the complexity of the SDN's environment, the SVM's detection algorithm often collects the input feature vectors, and gets the detection algorithm of the network communication behavior. Additionally, the kernel function is one of the most important elements in the SVM algorithm, and it makes the non-linear mapping for the input data. However, the algorithm may consider the over-fitting problem, which makes the SVM detection not suitable for the application of network system.

One-class SVM is developed on the basis of traditional SVM, and is used to solve only one class of samples. In practice, the idea of SVM is to construct a generalized optimal classification surface, and the data points which belong to two categories of training data are exposed on both sides of this classification surface. Similarly, a one-class SVM assumes that the coordinate origin is an abnormal sample and constructs an optimal classification surface in the feature space to achieve the maximum margin between the targets and the coordinate origin [14].

This method uses the largest nonlinear margin algorithm to design detection algorithm, and the steps are listed as follows:

Step 1: through the data feature selection and construction methods, network traffic is extracted to meet the input characteristics of one-class SVM algorithm.

Step 2: this method selects the appropriate kernel function K (x, z) and the appropriate parameters of C to structure and solve the optimization problem:

$$\min_{\alpha} \frac{1}{2} \sum_{i=1}^{N} \sum_{j=1}^{N} \alpha_i \alpha_j y_i y_j K(x_i, x_j) - \sum_{i=1}^{N} \alpha_i \tag{6}$$

$$\sum_{i-1}^{N} \alpha_i y_i = 0$$

$$0 \leq \alpha_i \leq C \quad , \quad i = 1, 2, \ldots, N$$

Step 3: select the component $\alpha^* \left(0 \leq \alpha_j^* \leq C \right)$, and calculate b*

$$K(x_i, x_j) = \exp\left(-\frac{\|x1 - x2\|^2}{2\sigma^2} \right) \tag{7}$$

Step 4: the final decision function is computed as following:

$$f(x) = sign\left(\sum_{i-1}^{N} \alpha_i^* y_j K(x \cdot x_i) + b^* \right) \tag{8}$$

Step 5: the established decision function is used to classify and predict the test data set of communication behavior. If the accuracy is satisfying, the decision function of the detection algorithm is obtained. If the detection accuracy is not satisfying, the kernel function can be optimized and retrained to establish an more efficient detection classifier.

This paper combines the advantages of both the special nature of SDN network environment and the SVM algorithm, we mainly studied one-class SVM detection algorithm based on features. DDoS attack detection algorithm based on behavior patterns can reflect DDoS communication behaviors. The data of feature vector is the input of DDoS attack detection. Through the feature vector extraction method, the one-class SVM classifier is established. The process of detection algorithm is shown in Fig. 2.

3.3 Optimization of Model Parameters Based on Self-adaptation Genetic Algorithm

In this paper, Gaussian kernel function is used to perform the mapping, and the appropriate parameters of the Gaussian kernel function can not only improve the detection performance of DDoS attack detection, but also reduce the training time of DDoS attack detection model.

GA (Genetic Algorithm) is the solution of search problem in the process of simulating biological evolution, and it is based on the evolutionary methods such as genetic selection, variation, and reorganization in the biological world. Furthermore, it can solve various complex optimization problems, and achieve the optimal solution of the problems. Because traditional GA uses fixed selection, crossover, variation probability, individual selection based on the fitness function, which makes the process of genetic algorithm optimization is not strong to local search ability and the evolutionary speed is easily affected to slow down by individuals. In this paper, the adaptive GA algorithm is used to optimize the one-class SVM detection algorithm. The adaptive function of individuals is created by the baseline of detection rate.

$$f(g, c) = \frac{1}{\eta + \varepsilon} \tag{9}$$

Here, g and C of Gaussian kernel function are the optimization parameters, η is the actual detection rates, and ε is constant coefficient to avoid zero in the denominator.

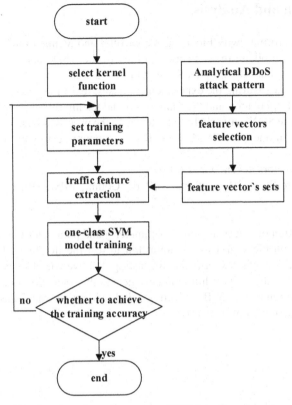

Fig. 2. Flow chart of one-class SVM detection algorithm

Adaptive GA algorithm dynamically adjusts the probability of intersection based on the individual fitness value, and the improved adaptive GA defines the similarity coefficient of the population and the adjustment formula for the probability of crossover and variation as follows:

$$\phi = \frac{EX + 1}{\sqrt{DX}} \tag{10}$$

$$p_c = \frac{1}{1 + e^{\frac{k_1}{\phi}}} - 0.1, \quad k_1 \in (0, +\infty) \tag{11}$$

$$p_m = \frac{k_2}{50\left(1 + e^{\frac{1}{\phi}}\right)}, \quad k_2 \in (0, +\infty) \tag{12}$$

The good similarity coefficient ϕ is based on the expected of EX and DX by calculating the fitness value, and the adaptive GA algorithm will give greater cross probability and smaller variation probability to poor individuals.

4 Evaluation and Analysis

The simulation is formed with FloodLight controller and Mininet tool, and the Flood-Light controller can obtain the network topology of the whole network. Additionally, the attack data is occurred with DDoS tool and the background traffic data is occurred with daily computers. During the experimental phases, real-time playback is carried out through the TCPReplay tool, and the training set and testing set for the detection model are injected into the SDN network. In order to verify the proposed DDoS attack detection algorithm based on one-class SVM, we collect 11 feature vectors by programing [15, 16].

The feature vectors are shown as follows:

{$protocol_i$, $srcIP_i$, $dstIP_i$, $srcPort_i$, $dstPort_i$, $Count_i$, FPS_i, $DFIR_i$, SFP_i, $FIDM_i$, $PDTA_i$}

1. For the selection of Gaussian kernel parameter g and parameter C, we optimize the model based on the adaptive GA algorithm to test the iterative wheel speed and detection rate. Through experiments for testing iterative wheel speed and detection rate, the optimization algorithm gradually gets higher detection rate with the optimization iteration in Fig. 3. By selecting suitable iterative wheel speed, it can have the effect to avoid the over-learning.

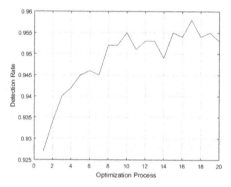

Fig. 3. Experiment for testing iterative wheel speed and detection rate

2. Figure 4 shows the results of the test data sample containing 9 feature vectors. After the parameter optimization, the accuracy rate of one-class SVM is 93.31%, and the GA optimization time is 23.69 s. Figure 5 shows the results of the test data sample containing 11 feature vectors. After the parameter optimization, the accuracy rate of one-class SVM is 95.16%, and the detection time and GA optimization time are 0.0588 s and 26.45 s, respectively. Therefore, the added feature vectors can improve the accuracy rate and the cost is accepted.

3. In order to further verify and compare the experimental results, we use the BP and RBF neural networks to test in the same 11 feature vectors [17]. It should be noted that the training data of one-class SVM cuts off the-1 class. But fewer training data

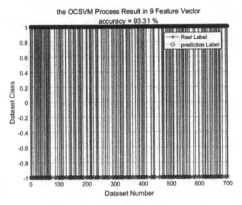

Fig. 4. Testing result with 9 feature vectors by one-class SVM

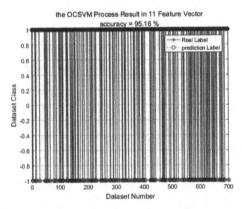

Fig. 5. Testing result with 11 feature vectors by one-class SVM

for one-class SVM can not affect the detection rate, and the accuracy rate of BP is 93.76%. By using the RBF neural network to test in the same 11 feature vectors, the accuracy rate is 94.47%. However, one-class SVM detection method takes longer than BP and RBF methods when optimizing the training model. But this cost of time only is occurred in the first step (Figs. 6, 7 and Table 1).

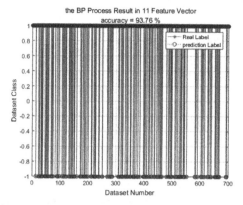

Fig. 6. Testing result with 11 feature vectors by BP algorithm

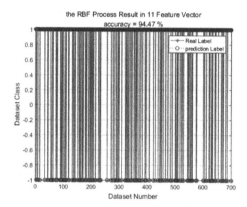

Fig. 7. Testing result with 11 feature vectors by RBF algorithm

Table 1. Accuracy rates of testing results

No.	Method	Accuracy rate
1	One-class SVM in 9 feature vector	93.31%
2	One-class SVM in 11 feature vector	95.16%
3	BP in 11 feature vector	93.76%
4	RBF in 11 feature vector	94.47%

5   Conclusions

In SDN's security fields, DDoS attack detection researches have recieved more and more attention. This paper proposes a DDoS attack detection method based on one-class SVM in SDN, and it can provide a better detection rate. Furthermore, we first design the collection of feature vectors, and two new feature vectors are presented, including middle value of flow table items' duration and the average value of protocol data traffic. Then, the feature vector's items are {$protocol_i$, $srcIP_i$, $dstIP_i$, $srcPort_i$, $dstPort_i$, $Count_i$, FPS_i, $DFIR_i$, SFP_i, $FIDM_i$, $PDTA_i$}. By using the largest nonlinear margin algorithm based on those feature vectors, we design a one-class SVM detection algorithm. In this algorithm, a DDoS attack behavior model is established, and the self-adaptation genetic algorithm is introduced to optimize the main parameters of one-class SVM model. The experiment results show that the proposed new feature vectors can provide the better detection rate. For the comparison and verification of experimental results, the BP neural network and RBF neural network algorithms are compared under the same 11 features vectors, and the proposed method is shown to be more efficient in the detection accuracy rate.

Acknowledgments. This work is supported by National Key R&D Program of China (Grant No. 2018YFB2004200), the National Natural Science Foundation of China (Grant No. 61773368), State Grid Science and Technology Project (Grant Project name: Security Protection Technology of Embedded Components and Control Units in Power System Terminal, No. 2019G—12. The authors are grateful to the anonymous referees for their insightful comments and suggestions.

References

1. Singh, S., Jha, R.K.: A survey on software defined networking: architecture for next generation network. J. Netw. Syst. Manag. **25**, 1–54 (2017)
2. Wan, M., Yao, J.Y., Jing, Y., Jin, X.: Event-based anomaly detection for non-public industrial communication protocols in SDN-based control systems, computers. Comput. Mater. Contin. **55**(3), 447–463 (2018)
3. Yan, Q., Yu, F.R., Gong, Q., et al.: Software-defined networking (SDN) and distributed denial of service (DDoS) attacks in cloud computing environments: a survey, some research issues, and challenges. IEEE Commun. Surv. Tutor. **18**(1), 602–622 (2016)
4. Hussein, A., Elhajj, I.H., Chehab, A., Kayssi, A.: SDN security plane: an architecture for resilient security services. In: IEEE International Conference on Cloud Engineering Workshop, pp. 54–59. IEEE, Berlin (2016)
5. Sahay, R., Blanc, G., Zhang, Z., et al.: ArOMA: an SDN based autonomic DDoS mitigation framework. Comput. Secur. **70**, 482–499 (2017)
6. Afek, Y., Bremler-Barr, A., Shafir, L.: Network anti-spoofing with SDN data plane. In: INFOCOM 2017 IEEE Conference on Computer Communications, pp. 1–9. IEEE, Atlanta (2017)
7. Rui, W., Jia, Z., Lei, J.: An entropy-based distributed DDoS detection mechanism in software-defined networking. In: IEEE Trustcom/BigDataSE/ISPA. IEEE, Helsinki (2015)
8. Braga, R., Mota, E., Passito, A.: Lightweight DDoS flooding attack detection using NOX/Open Flow. In: IEEE Local Computer Network Conference, pp. 408–415. IEEE, Denver (2010)
9. Binkui, L., Lei, Z., et al.: Security routing strategy based on switch level division in SDN. Appl. Res. Comput. **34**(2), 522–525 (2017)
10. Taejin, H., Sunghwan, K., Namwon, A.: Suspicious traffic sampling for intrusion detection in software-defined networks. Comput. Netw. **109**(2), 172–182 (2016)
11. Chen, J.R., Xu, R.M., Tang, X.Y., Victor, S., Cai, C.T.: An abnormal network flow feature sequence prediction approach for DDoS attacks detection in big data environment. Comput. Mater. Contin. **55**(1), 95–119 (2018)

12. Barbhuiya, F.A., Agarwal, M., Purwar, S., et al.: Application of stochastic discrete event system framework for detection of induced low rate TCP attack. ISA Trans. **58**, 474–492 (2015)
13. Da, J., Liangming, Z., Kun, Y.: A DDoS attack detection and mitigation with software-defined Internet of Things framework. IEEE Access **6**, 24694–24705 (2018)
14. Junrong, C., Wenli, S., Ming, W., et al.: Intrusion detection of industrial control based on semi-supervised clustering strategy. Inf. Control **46**(4), 462–468 (2017)
15. Rotsos, C., Sarrar, N., Uhlig, S., Sherwood, R., Moore, A.W.: OFLOPS: an open framework for OpenFlow switch evaluation. In: Taft, N., Ricciato, F. (eds.) PAM 2012. LNCS, vol. 7192, pp. 85–95. Springer, Heidelberg (2012). https://doi.org/10.1007/978-3-642-28537-0_9
16. Tang, X.Y., Zheng, Q.D., Cheng, J.R., Victor, S., Cao, R., Chen, M.Z.: A DDoS attack situation assessment method via optimized cloud model based on influence function. Comput. Mater. Contin. **60**(3), 1263–1281 (2019)
17. Dhirendranath, T., Punyaslok, G., Prabir, K.J., Sasanka, C., Harish, C.D.: Comparison of CFBP, FFBP, and RBF networks in the field of crack detection. Model. Simul. Eng. **2014**(2), 1–13 (2014)

Research on Remote Attestation Technology Based on Formal Software Behavior Measurement

Hanwei Qian$^{(\boxtimes)}$, Ming Yuan, and Lingling Xia

Jiangsu Police Institute, Nanjing 210013, China
qianhanwei@jspi.edu.cn

Abstract. The traditional static measurement method based on data integrity measurement can only prove that the software has not been tampered with, and cannot describe the software behavior status. Dynamic measurement can measure the software behavior in real time, but there is no doubt that it requires a lot of computing resources. In this paper, we propose static measurement architecture PMA, which using formal method to abstract and verify software behavior. In PMA, formal language abstracts software behavior, formal specification describes security policy, and software behavior measurement problem is transformed into formal proof. We also have implemented the corresponding code according to the PMA design principle. The experimental test verifies the feasibility of the PMA architecture.

Keywords: Software behavior measurement · Trusted computing · Proof-carrying code · Verification

1 Introduction

The main reason for the network security problem is that the computer does not establish an immune mechanism against malicious code attacks on the architecture. Trusted Computing establishes a specific set of integrity metrics to enable the computing platform to distinguish between trusted and untrusted code, thereby establishing effective prevention methods and measures for untrusted code. Remote Attestation proposed by TCG is one of the basic characteristics of trusted computing. Through the two sides of the network connection, mutual credibility is judged before the service is provided. Remote attestation is one of the most important security mechanisms for trusted computing to solve the trust between trusted computing platforms and trusted network nodes.

At present, there have been many achievements in research on remote attestation. TCG firstly proposed a configuration-based platform integrity proof. The specification proposes platform integrity architecture. Based on the Transitive trust model [1], hierarchical trust transfer from the BIOS to the operating system kernel is implemented. IMA [2] extends the chain of trust to the application. At the moment when the operating system loads the program into the memory, the program file is measured, and the measurement result is reported to the trusted computing chip TPM for processing. Inserting a metric

© Springer Nature Singapore Pte Ltd. 2020
X. Sun et al. (Eds.): ICAIS 2020, CCIS 1254, pp. 201–209, 2020.
https://doi.org/10.1007/978-981-15-8101-4_19

point in a system call creates a lot of redundancy. PRIMA [3] has improved the shortcomings of IMA redundancy and used a policy specification approach to reduce redundancy metrics. IMA and PRIMA are static measurement systems. The BIND [4] system sets the metric point by the programmer and inserts the hook function interface provided by BIND at the metric point, and measures the dynamics during the running of the program. LKIM [5] defines a series of variables that represent the state of the system. When these values change, they are re-measured and dynamic measures are implemented. The RAMT [6] system introduces the Integrity Measure Hash Tree (IMHT), and stores the integrity metric hash values of each module in the leaf nodes of the tree. Only the module to be verified needs to be sent to the root node path during verification. The hash value effectively protects the privacy of the entire platform. There are similar studies [7–9] on trusted models.

In general, remote attestation includes proof of platform identity and proof of platform integrity metrics. At present, the metric storage report machine of trusted computing is used for system integrity. In fact, the data integrity of the system can only indicate that the system has not been tampered with, and it does not indicate that there is no vulnerability or the system behavior conforms to the security policy. When the terminal is controlled by a hacker or the system itself has vulnerability, there is still a security threat. On the other hand, the static measurement system performs the trusted measurement when the terminal is started, but for the platform where the server and the industrial computer are not turned off for a long time, the system state and the startup time have already increased with the increase of the system running time. A major change has taken place and its credibility is gradually declining.

Aiming at the shortcomings of the integrity-based metrics in the current remote attestation mechanism, this paper uses the PCC [10] framework technology to draw on the abstraction and verification methods of software behavior in the formal method. This paper designs the PCC Measurement Architecture (PMA), proof of remote software. Its main feature is the measurement of the dynamic behavior of programs in computer systems. At any time, the software code in the running system is measured, and the TPM is used to protect the measurement architecture and sign the measurement results to improve the security of the entire system. Section 2 of this paper introduces software behavior measurement techniques, Sect. 3 describes PMA models and algorithms, implementation and testing, and Sect. 4 summarize the full text.

2 Software Behavior Measurement

2.1 Software Behavior Description

Most software systems are written in an imperative programming language such as C or Java. The existing formal tools and methods are not convenient for describing and verifying the behavior of these software. Therefore, it is necessary to abstract the software behaviors into formalized languages and become low-level abstract models. For example, expressions in C language can be variable expressions. Structure member expressions, etc., can be defined in theorem assistants such as coq or Isabelle, so that the syntax of the expression in the theorem assistant is more similar to the syntax of C or the Java language itself. The underlying abstract model can be further abstracted into a high-level abstract model. High-level abstract models are sufficiently expressive to more easily describe and verify high-level related security properties. The high-level definitions are more intuitive and clear (without exposing many unrelated underlying details), and high-level specification languages and high-level models are relatively simple, and it is easier to verify these properties at the top.

When defining the content of multiple different abstraction layers, it must be ensured that the behavior of each abstraction layer is (equivalent) consistent, that is, the behavior of different abstraction layers satisfies the refined relationship. Refined relationships define equivalence relationships between different abstract models or programs from an observable perspective. For example, a context refinement relationship means that A does not generate more behavior in any context, and the client does not observe the difference between A and B.

In fact, you can also use the top-down design to describe the software behavior, that is, define the high-level abstract language, and then generate the code that the software actually runs. For example, the COGENT [11] compiler generates C code, which is then compiled by some C compilers. The COGENT compiler also generates a formal specification in Isabelle/HOL [12] to accurately encode the semantics of the source COGENT program and provides a proof of perfection that this semantics has been correctly implemented by C code. This specification can be used to demonstrate higher level attributes about the COGENT program.

2.2 Software Behavior Verification

PCC which means Proof-carrying code is a framework for the mechanical verification of safety properties of machine-language programs, whose basic principle is that the credibility of executable code must be verifiable. The PCC verification framework generally includes machine model, security policy, program logic, program specification language, a proof representation language. A machine model is a formal description of the target machine that runs the program, including machine definition; machine state definitions, and operational semantics of machine instructions. A security policy is a formal description (definition) of software security, usually a description of the operational semantics of a machine or the state of a machine. Program logic is a Hoare-style logic system that includes logical kilometers and logic rules to reason the security of the verification program. The program specification language is used to describe user-specific program specifications. The proof representation language is used to encode the program security proof. Figure 1 depicts architecture of PCC.

When the code producer generates the executable code, it must produce proof that the executable code satisfies the security policy, and use the program logic rules to prove whether the program conforms to the security policy. Once the proof is complete, bind the executable code to the appropriate proof. Before executing the software of untrusted source, the host first determines whether the software can be safely executed according to whether the verification software has certain trusted attributes, thereby establishing a trust relationship between the host and the external software. In this process, the complete proof process is coded using the proof representation language. If the program or proof is illegally tampered with, the verification will fail and the host refuses to execute the code.

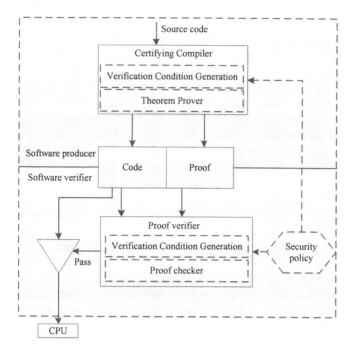

Fig. 1. PCC architecture

The PCC approach solves the problem of ensuring the security, reliability, and confidentiality of software by demonstrating checks without trusting the code provider. Strict security certifications ensure that the code does not violate any security policies that have been verified at runtime. The code party acceptor knows whether the executable code is safely executed by statically checking whether the security is correct. Such code acceptors no longer need to trust the provider of the PCC code. In fact, PCC expresses complete software code security in another abstraction, providing a new way to statically describe and measure the dynamic behavior of software. The correctness of the proof does not require manual inspection, which makes it possible to automate the inspection of security policies.

2.3 Security Policy Specification

In the PCC mechanism, the security policy is the core. The PCC allows the code verifier to define a security policy and then verify that the executable code conforms to the defined security policy. By defining a security policy, the code verifier accurately describes the behavioral attributes of the program and the conditions that must be met for safe operation. Security policies can not only define traditional security requirements such as memory security, pointer security, etc., but also define more abstract and more detailed security requirements. Security policies include the two main parts of security rules and interfaces. Security rules describe all legally secure operations of the program and the prerequisites that these operations should satisfy. The interface describes the calling convention between the code verifier and the external program, which is the precondition that the code verifier and the external program must satisfy before calling the other function. In a specific implementation, there may be multiple ways to represent security policies, such as first-order logic, type systems, modal logic, and the like.

In fact, the code producer and the code verifier negotiate the security policy and give the specification of the security code. The code producer translates the source code into annotated object code by issuing a proofing compiler and produces proof that the object code satisfies the security policy. After receiving the annotated object code and proof, the code verifier uses the same verification condition generator to perform symbol calculation on the object code, generate verification conditions, and check whether the additional proof is correct. Since the verification condition is for the target code, it is indeed the proof that the target code satisfies the security specification, thereby preventing the malicious code from spoofing the host by carrying a legal proof.

General security policies are expressed using pre-assertion and post-assertion. The Certifying compiler first proves that the assertions in the code are true, then generates the object file and attaches the proof to the code verifier.

3 PMA Model

3.1 PMA Architecture

In addition to using the traditional TPM platform configuration register (PCR) to describe the integrity status of the system, the PMA solution also increases the measurement and verification of software behavior. The issuer issues a metric certificate for a piece of software code to be executed. The attestor proves that the current software code does meet the security protocols and policies described in the metric certificate, thereby completing the purpose of remote proof platform behavior metrics.

The behavioral metrics include the code manufacturer, user platform, service provider, certificate issuing authority, and verification center.

The code manufacturer produces machine executable code and packages the corresponding abstract machine model of the code along with the rigorous proof that can be checked.

The user platform proves the certifier in the protocol, including the host and the trusted platform module. The TPM module built in the user platform mainly provides authenticity signature and hardware anti-record tampering service to ensure the authenticity of the system behavior measurement and report content.

Prove that the verifier (usually the service provider) submits proof of the security policy and verifies the software code and certification. The verifier verifies the authenticity and integrity of the platform system behavior by verifying the platform system behavior. This can be achieved by traditional signature mechanisms. Secondly, the system behavior results of the proof platform are analyzed to check whether they conflict with the certifier's security policy.

The certificate issuing authority is responsible for issuing and revoking the behavior measurement certificate. The verification center verifies that the behavior metric certificate has been revoked. PMA of the software behavior measurement based on the Trusted

Computing Platform is a metric certificate issued by the behavior measurement authority for various software codes. The metric certificate is jointly released with the software and hardware binding, and the platform certifier is based on the configured behavior metric. The certificate and TPM integrity metrics prove to the service provider that their currently running software behavior meets certain security attributes and has not been tampered with. Figure 2 depicts architecture of PMA.

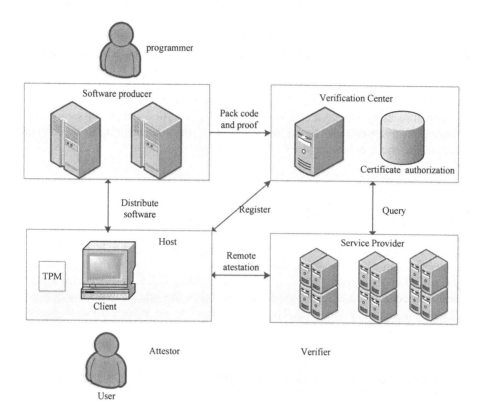

Fig. 2. PMA architecture

3.2 Measurement Algorithm

PMA includes the collaboration of multiple nodes of software producers, verification centers, service providers, and users. It has gone through five phases of production, release, start-up, verification, and running, which form a trusted software architecture.

Phase 1. Production phase. Programmers write trusted software code based on actual functional requirements and security policy requirements, and provide formal proof that the software code complies with the security policy. Software manufacturers generate PCC packages based on code and certification.

Phase 2. Release phase. The software manufacturer sets the relevant parameters of the verification center and sends the PCC package to the verification center. The certificate verification center issues a measurement certificate for each software.

Phase 3. Start-up phase. The user including the TPM and the host, downloads the trusted software PCC package and checks whether the PCC package complies with the security policy. Run the trusted software in the PCC package that complies with the security policy and register with the verification center. When the user's trusted software is running, a service request is initiated to the service provider. The service provider requires the user to provide remote proof.

Phase 4. Verify phase, the user calculates the platform software code and certification signature according to the service provider's certification request, and then performs remote certification to the service provider. The service provider verifies the TPM signature and the software behavior measurement signature. The verification center checks whether the software measurement certificate has been revoked and whether the certified software code is consistent with the software behavior certification commitment.

Phase 5. Running phase. The user runs trusted software. Service providers provide services to trusted software that complies with security policies.

The software behavior measurement and reporting process algorithms are the most critical part of the PMA verification phase throughout the run. When the attestor requests the service from the verifier, the verifier needs to perform the platform integrity verification on the attestor and query the verification center to perform the remote proof process of the interaction. The metric is responsible for recording the system behaviors related to the platform state trust during the actual loading and running of the system behavior, and expanding the related record results to the corresponding PCR in the TPM. The reporting process acts as a trusted remote attestation platform agent, responds to the verifier's request, and reports the relevant system behavior event records to the verifier.

During the PMA verification phase, users, service providers, and verification centers communicate to confirm that the behavior of trusted software runs in compliance with security policies. The complete verification algorithm flow is as follows..

Step 1. The user checks whether the certificate of the PCC package conforms to his own security policy, and lists the software that passes the security policy check as trusted software. When trusted software requires remote services, request authentication from the service provider.

Step 2. When the service provider verifies the identity of the user, it first generates a random number n, and sends the verification request and PCR number to the user.

Step 3. The user finds the corresponding request service program PCC package, and checks whether it is registered with the verification center. If it is not registered, register with the verification center.

Step 4. The user loads the identity certification key AIK, reads the root hash value hash 1 of the platform configuration storage data structure, performs a hash operation on the PCC package to generate hash 2, and concatenates the specified PCR, random number n, hash 1 and hash 2, and applies The TPM signs the generated value and finally generates a signature S.

Step 5. The user sends the trusted software PCC package, AIK signature, user PCR value and signature S to the service provider.

Step 6. The service provider initiates a query to the verification center to check whether the user is registered and obtains the user's public key. If the user is not registered, the service provider drops the connection.

Step 7. The service provider uses the user's public key to decrypt the encrypted data, and checks the random number n to verify the integrity and correctness of the AIK signature and PCR value.

Step 8. The service provider checks whether the certificate is valid based on the PCC certificate. The user checks whether the proof of the PCC packet conforms to his own security policy.

Step 9. Execute the service program in response to the user's service request.

3.3 Model Implementation and Verification

According to the principle of remote proof of software behavior measurement, it is further developed on the basis of Cube [13], which is developed by Beijing University of Technology, and some data verification module code is modified. Cube allows developers to implement the trusted software-based measurement mechanism, decision mechanism, control mechanism, and support mechanism as a component. It is integrated into a trusted software base through the Cube framework, and provides interconnection and interface conversion function support for collaboration between trusted software bases. The prototype system implements the measurement and certification of the software running on the terminal based on the trusted boot program and the trusted operating system measurement.

We implemented a proof of prototype system for software behavior measurement on the Ubuntu 16 platform. The TPM function was implemented by installing the TPM emulator [14], and Isabelle/HOL was installed to implement the system verification function. In the prototype system, the certificate issuing authority performs software behavior evaluation based on the executable file of the software vendor component and the data of the software abstraction certificate, and then issues a metric certificate. The TPM measures the software and then performs remote proofs following a certification protocol. In the actual test process, we selected a piece of code written in the Cogent language as the verification object. The test results show that the prototype system can verify the dynamic behavior of the software by static measurement.

4 Conclusions

This paper uses the abstraction and verification method of software behavior in the formal method, and designs a remote proof method based on the PCC Measurement Architecture (PMA), and implements it accordingly. Compared with the existing metric architectures, it changes the traditional metrics that simply use data integrity as the sole criterion. It is a static metric that implements traditional dynamic metrics to measure system behavior. The security policy is described by abstract protocol, which is very flexible and secure.

In the actual application process, the more powerful the specification language, the more nature of the description, it is difficult to be automatically proved. If part of the proof cannot be automatically generated, it is necessary to manually use the auxiliary tool to participate in the proof, such as the manual interaction given in Isabelle/HOL, in order to judge whether the behavior of the program conforms to the trusted strategy. At present, only simple strategies can be verified. Most of the theorem verification work requires manual participation. It cannot completely replace the traditional data integrity-based metrics. In the future, the automatic verification capability of the verification system should be further improved.

References

1. Li, T., Hu, A.: Efficient transitive trust model for mobile terminal. In: International ICST Conference on Communications and networking in China, pp. 233–238. IEEE (2012)
2. Sailer, R., Zhang, X., Jaeger, T., Van Doorn, L.: Design and implementation of a TCG-based integrity measurement architecture. In: Proceedings of USENIX Security Symposium, Lake Tahoe, California, USA, pp. 223–238. ACM Press, August 2004
3. Jaeger, T., Sailer, R., Shankar, U.: PRIMA: policy-reduced integrity measurement architecture. In: Proceedings of the Eleventh ACM Symposium on Access Control Models and Technologies, Lake Tahoe, California, USA, pp. 19–28 (2006)
4. Shi, E., Perrig, A., Van Doorn, L.: BIND: a fine-grained attestation service for secure distributed systems. In: Proceeding of the IEEE Symposium on Security and Privacy, Oakland, CA, USA, pp. 154–168. IEEE Press (2005)
5. Thober, M., Pendergrass, J.A., McDonell, C.D.: Improving coherency of runtime integrity measurement. In: Conference on Computer and Communications Security Proceedings of the 3rd ACM workshop on Scalable Trusted Computing, Alexandria, Virginia, USA, pp. 51–60 (2008)
6. Xu, Z.Y., He, Y.P., Deng, L.X.: Efficient remote attestation mechanism with privacy protection. J. Softw. **22**(02), 339–352 (2011)
7. Xie, X., Yuan, T., Zhou, X., Cheng, X.: Research on trust model in container-based cloud service. Comput. Mater. Contin. **56**(2), 273–283 (2018)
8. Alhussain, A., Kurdi, H., Altoaimy, L.: A neural network-based trust management system for edge devices in peer-to-peer networks. Comput. Mater. Contin. **59**(3), 805–816 (2019)
9. Li, D., et al.: Modelling the roles of cewebrity trust and platform trust in consumers' propensity of live-streaming: an extended TAM method. Comput. Mater. Contin. **55**(1), 137–150 (2018)
10. George, C.N.: Proof-carrying code. In: Conference Record of the 24th Symposium on Principles of Programming Languages, pp. 106–119. ACM Press, Paris (1997)
11. Cogent. https://github.com/NICTA/cogent
12. Isabelle/HOL. https://isabelle.in.tum.de/
13. Cube. https://github.com/biparadox/cube-1.3
14. Tpm-emulator. https://github.com/PeterHuewe/tpm-emulator

A Reversible Watermarking Scheme Based on Adaptive Block Sized Integer Transform

Qianwen Li[1], Xiang Wang[1(✉)], and Qingqi Pei[2]

[1] State Key Laboratory of Integrated Service Networks, Xidian University, Xi'an 710071, Shanxi, China
wangxiang@xidian.edu.cn
[2] Shanxi Key Laboratory of Blockchain and Security Computing, Xidian University, Xi'an 710071, Shanxi, China

Abstract. As the foundation of reversible watermarking technology, the integer transform technique, e.g. difference expansion (DE), has been widely studied. However, most integer transform schemes use the blocks of uniform size for embedding, resulting in that the embedding performance is not as good as the recently proposed histogram-shifting method. To solve this problem, this paper proposes a reversible watermarking scheme based on adaptive block sized integer transform. After predicting the texture complexity of different regions in the cover image, more watermarks are embedded in smooth regions by using larger sized blocks as the embedding units; in textured regions, the relatively smaller sized blocks are used as the embedding units, which decreases the amount of watermarks to reduce the distortion caused by embedding. Experimental results show that the proposed algorithm provides less image distortion compared with some existing reversible watermarking algorithms with the same embedded capacity (EC).

Keywords: Integer transform · Reversible watermarking · Double layer embedding · Adaptive

1 Introduction

Traditional watermarking techniques are inevitable to bring a degree of distortion to the cover image. In most cases, these distortions are not easily found by the image holder, but in the field of medical or military, such loss of image quality is not acceptable. This problem has not been solved until the reversible watermarking technology came present, which was first proposed by the United States researchers Honsinger et al. [1] in 1999. Compared with the traditional watermarking techniques, reversible watermarking technology not only can extract the embedded watermark information, but also recover the original cover image. Most recently proposed reversible watermarking algorithms can be divided into two categories: histogram shifting based [2–21] and integer transform based [22–27].

Histogram shifting technology exploits the correlation of pixels to calculate prediction error of pixels and forms the histogram. The watermarks are embedded by shifting

© Springer Nature Singapore Pte Ltd. 2020
X. Sun et al. (Eds.): ICAIS 2020, CCIS 1254, pp. 210–221, 2020.
https://doi.org/10.1007/978-981-15-8101-4_20

part of bins in histogram, and in order to avoid conflicts, other bins must be shifted to create embedded space. Ni et al. [2] proposed a histogram shifting algorithm firstly. The peak and zero points of the image histogram are found and the watermarks are embedded into the pixel points with the same grayscale values as the peak point by modifying the histogram. Li et al. [3] proposed a general framework to construct HS-based RDH, which can facilitate the design of RDH. Thodi et al. [4] proposed an expansion embedding algorithm called prediction-error expansion (PEE). This PEE algorithm model mainly includes two steps: prediction and histogram shifting. It can be seen from [5–9] that the performance of histogram shifting and data embedding closely relate to the prediction results. Sachnev et al. [10] and Li et al. [11] introduced sorting and adaptive embedding into PEE algorithm, and experiment results show that their algorithms are better than the RDH algorithms in the same period. Ou et al. [12] proposed a two-dimensional histogram shifting method to extend the conventional methods, which generates better performance. Based on Ou et al.'s method, Li et al. proposed a scheme in [13] to generate more elements in the histogram, which increases the total number of features (i.e., data carriers) and leads directly to the higher hiding capacity. Later on, Li et al. [14] proposed a method for data embedding by extending the maximum or minimum pixel value in a block named pixel value ordering (PVO). Inspired by histogram shifting algorithm, Tsai et al. [15] proposed a reversible data hiding method based on prediction and difference histogram.

The difference expansion (DE) algorithm proposed by Tian et al. [22] firstly. The DE algorithm groups pixels into pairs and the watermarks are embedded into the expansion error of pixel pairs. However, due to using two pixels to embed one bit watermark, the embedding capacity (EC) is limited to 0.5 bpp (bit per pixel). Alattar et al. [23] extended Tian et al.'s DE algorithm from pixel pair to pixel block to improve the embedding ability. This approach could embed several bits in one block in a single pass embedding. Weng et al. [27] proposed a integer transform scheme based on invariability of the sum of pixel pairs and PDA. A high compressibility of the location map is achieved in their approach. On the basis of these algorithms, Wang et al. [24] proposed a new integer transform method, which enables pre-calculate the embedding distortion of a given block. Experiment results show that Wang et al.'s method obtains a sufficient high embedding rate. However, in Alattar et al.'s and Wang et al.'s methods, the cover image is divided into the uniform sized blocks for embedding. Actually, for the regions of complex texture, the smaller sized blocks should be used because of the weak correlation in such area. Instead, in smooth areas, using the larger sized blocks can better exploit the high correlation among pixels. To this end, Weng et al. [26] used the correlation between the average of the block and the neighboring pixels around the block to predict the smoothness of the region. In Weng et al.'s method, although adaptive embedding is introduced, there are also some deficiencies, e.g., for a block with size $r \times c$, its $(r + c + 1)$ neighbours are used to estimate the texture feature of this block. However, the used predicted pixels are less and are all located at the lower right of the pixel block, the texture complexity of the predicted pixel block is not accurate.

To better accommodate the different texture region of the cover image, a reversible watermarking scheme based on adaptive block sized integer transform is proposed. In this algorithm, the embedding block size is decided according to its neighbouring blocks.

To ensure the decoder can acquire the same size of each block as the encoder, a two-pass embedding strategy is used.

The rest of the paper is organized as follows. In Sect. 2, Wang et al.'s integer-transform-based algorithm [24] is introduced and discussed briey. In Sect. 3, the proposed method is described in detail, including the embedding and extraction procedures. The experimental results compared with some other methods are reported in Sect. 4. Finally, we conclude our work in the last section.

2 The Related Methods

In this section, the integer transform based algorithm proposed by Wang et al. [23] is briefly presented. Several notations are firstly introduced. For an integer array of length $n, X = (x_1, \cdots, x_n)$, we define:

$$a(X) = \begin{cases} \lfloor \overline{X} \rfloor, \overline{X} - \lfloor \overline{X} \rfloor < 0.5 \\ \lceil \overline{X} \rceil, otherwise \end{cases} \quad (1)$$

where $a(X)$ is an integer-valued approximated to the average $\overline{X} = (1/n) \sum_{i=1}^{n} x_i$. The cover image is divided into n-sized non-overlapping pixel blocks, as shown in Fig. 1, where $B_{i,j}$ denotes a pixel block of the i-th row and j-th column.

Fig. 1. Non-overlapping pixel blocks

For an n-sized block, Wang et al.'s transform F can be presented as follows:

$$\begin{cases} x_1' = 2x_1 - 2f(a(X)) + w_1, \\ \cdots, \\ x_{n-1}' = 2x_{n-1} - 2f(a(X)) + w_{n-1}, \\ x_n' = 2x_n - a(X), \end{cases} \quad (2)$$

where $f(x) = \lceil x/2 \rceil$, x_i' represents the corresponding watermarked pixel value and $w \in \{1, 0\}$ is the watermark.

In the integer transform formulas, Wang et al. found an identical equation before and after embedding. To prevent the overflow/underflow, each watermarked pixel value should be contained in [0, 255]. We define:

$$I\&D = \{X \in A : 0 \le x_i - f(a(X)) \le 127(1 \le i \le n-1), 0 \le 2x_n - a(x) \le 255\} \quad (3)$$

where $A = \{X = (x_1, \cdots, x_n) \in B_{i,j} : 0 \le x_i \le 255\}$. With these definitions, we can prove that $F(x, w) \in A$, if $x \in D$. Therefore, if the values of a block belong to D, this block can be used to embed data by the integer transform.

For a given threshold $t > 0$, all blocks $X = B_{i,j} = (x_1, \cdots x_n)$ can be divided into 3 categories:

$$(1)E_t = \{X \in D : v(X) \le t\}; \quad (2)C_t = \{X \in A - E_t : v_h(X) \le t\};$$
$$(3)O_t = \{X \in A - E_t : v_h(X) > t\}. \tag{4}$$

where $v(X) = \sqrt{\sum_{i=1}^{n}(x_i - a(X))^2}$, $v_h(X) = \sqrt{\sum_{i=1}^{n}(\lfloor x_i/2 \rfloor - a(\lfloor X/2 \rfloor))^2}$. E_t is the set of embeddable blocks embedded by Eq. (2); C_t is the set of changeable blocks embedded by replacing their LSBs; the blocks belonging to set O_t stay unchanged to avoid large distortion caused by embedding. In addition, since $E_t \cup C_t$ and O_t can be separated by v_h and t, we only need a location map to mark the blocks in $E_t \cup C_t$ and the blocks in O_t don't need to be recorded. Such a location map usually occupies fewer payloads due to small size and effective compression.

Equation (2) indicates every $n - 1$ bits can be embedded into n pixels by Wang et al.'s method. For a n-sized block, the embedding distortion is calculated as follows:

$$\lambda = \sum_{i=1}^{n-1} (y_i - x_i)^2 + (y_n - x_n)^2$$
$$\approx \sum_{i=1}^{n-1} (x_i - 2f(a(X)))^2 + (x_n - a(X))^2$$
$$\approx \sum_{i=1}^{n} (x_i - a(X))^2. \tag{5}$$

When the cover image is divided into small-sized blocks, e.g., the block with 2×2 size, the embedding rate is $(n - 1)/n = 3/4 = 0.75$ bpp, resulting in low EC. However, because of the smaller size, the correlation of the pixels in a block is enhanced, and the prediction error $|x_i - a(X)|$ will be a small value, which means the distortion λ is small. On the contrary, if the cover image is divided into large-sized block with 8×8 size, the embedding rate is $(n (n - 1)/n = 63/64 \approx 0.98$ bpp, and the EC is higher. But the correlation of the pixels in the block is weakened, the prediction error $|x_i - a(X)|$ is larger, which means the distortion λ will be larger.

Obviously, it is better to use larger-sized blocks in the smooth region and use smaller-sized blocks in the area of complex texture. However, to ensure the reversibility, the embedded block size cannot be selected flexibly in Wang et al.'s algorithm, so the same sized blocks are used from beginning to ending. The experimental results show that when the block size is 4×4, the best effects will be obtained.

3 Proposed Method

In this section, we propose a new scheme to improve Wang et al.'s method, in which the size of embedding block can be flexibly selected according to the texture complexity of different regions in the cover image.

The last part of Sect. 2 mentions the adaptive selection strategy of block size theoretically. The following examples in this section show the distortion differences caused by different sized blocks in smooth and complex regions, which will illustrate the advantages of this method in a more intuitive way.

Figure 2 (a) shows an example of a smooth block: when using the original block 4×4 as an embedded unit, the embedding distortion λ caused by the mean value prediction could be calculated as:

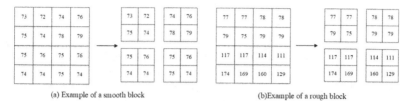

(a) Example of a smooth block   (b)Example of a rough block

Fig. 2. Example of different blocks

$$a(X) = 75, \ \lambda = \sum_{i=1}^{n} (x_i - a(X))^2 = 46. \tag{6}$$

As for using a small sized block 2×2, the embedding distortion λ could be calculated as:

$$\begin{cases} a_1(X) = 74, a_2(X) = 77, a_3(X) = 75, a_4(X) = 75, \\ \lambda_1 = 6, \lambda_2 = 10, \lambda_3 = 3, \lambda_4 = 2, \lambda = \lambda_1 + \lambda_2 + \lambda_3 + \lambda_4 = 21. \end{cases} \tag{7}$$

In a relatively smooth block, using a block of larger size as an embedded unit produces more distortion than using a block of smaller blocks, but the degree of distortion is light and the EC increases significantly.

Figure 2 (b) shows an example of a rough block: When using the original block 4×4 as an embedded unit, the embedding distortion λ could be calculated as:

$$a(X) = 107, \ \lambda = \sum_{i=1}^{n} (x_i - a(X))^2 = 18749. \tag{8}$$

As for using a small sized block 2×2, the embedding distortion λ could be calculated as:

$$\begin{cases} a_1(X) = 77, a_2(X) = 79, a_3(X) = 144, a_4(X) = 129, \\ \lambda_1 = 8, \lambda_2 = 2, \lambda_3 = 2983, \lambda_4 = 1510, \lambda = \lambda_1 + \lambda_2 + \lambda_3 + \lambda_4 = 4503. \end{cases} \tag{9}$$

It is obvious that, in a relatively rough block, using a smaller size block as an embedded unit causes much less distortion than using a larger sized block. Thus, we employ smaller-sized block as a unit with low embedded capacity in exchange for high image quality.

Besides, since the rhombus prediction proposed by Sachnev [10] is used as the prediction model in our algorithm (which will be introduced in next part), there is no need to mark the embedding block type with extra location map for reversibility, improving the embedding rate of effective information. Moreover, when a block is split into smaller blocks, it is worth noting about the problem of overflow/underflow.

The section is organized as follows: Sect. 3.1 gives the prediction pattern; Sect. 3.2 gives the adaptive selection of embedded block size which depend on the result of prediction pattern; Sect. 3.3 illustrates the details of embedding procedure and introduces the overflow and underflow processing; Sect. 3.4 provides an overview of the embedding process and the extraction process.

3.1 Prediction Pattern

Inspired by Sachnev et al.'s rhombus pattern prediction scheme [10], we improve Wang et al.'s prediction scheme by adaptively predicting the texture complexity of each block. The cover image is divided into $n_1 \times n_1$-sized non-overlapping pixel blocks (See Fig. 1). All blocks are divided into two parts (See Fig. 3): Shadow set $X = (x_1, \cdots, x_n)$ and Blank set $Y = (y_1, \cdots y_n)$, $n = n_1 \times n_1$. Shadow set and Blank set are interlaced and non-overlapping.

To guarantee the whole image is embedded, the double-pass embedding process has to be exploited. In the first-pass embedding, the textural information of blocks in the Shadow set is predicted by the correspondingly surrounding blocks in the Blank set, and then the embedding block size is determined adaptively. In the second-pass embedding, the blocks in Blank set are predicted in the same way.

The prediction formula is presented as Eq. (10). Using block $X_i = (x_1, \cdots x_n)$ as an example, in order to predict its complexity, we select four blocks $Y_i, Y_{i+1}, Y_{i-2}, Y_{i+2}$ surrounding it as predicters, calculating the average of their local variance Δv to represent the texture complexity of the context.

$$\Delta v = \frac{1}{4} \sum_{m=1}^{4} \sum_{k=1}^{n} ((y_{km} - \bar{Y}_m)^2/n), \tag{10}$$

where $\bar{Y} = (1/n) \sum_{i=1}^{n} y_i$ is the average of all the pixels in Y_i block. In the prediction scheme, we select four neighboring blocks around the predicted block to increase accuracy and consistency of the prediction results.

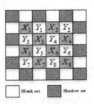

Fig. 3. Shadow set and Blank set

3.2 Selection of Embedded Block Size Adaptively

From Sect. 3.1, smaller local variance means the block is in the smooth area, and the corresponding region could be divided into larger-size blocks to embed more bits. Meanwhile, smaller-size blocks are more suitable for areas with complex textures. The average local variance Δv of all the blocks can be obtained after prediction. A threshold $T > 0$ is set to distinguish smooth regions and complex regions, and two sets E_1 and E_2 are defined to classify the blocks belonging to E_t:

$$E_1 = \{B_{i,j} \in B : \Delta v \leq T\}, E_2 = \{B_{i,j} \in B : \Delta v > T\}. \tag{11}$$

A block with $\Delta v \leq T$ is regarded as smooth block, belonging to E_1 set. Otherwise, it is regarded as rough block, belonging to E_2 set. For a rough block, the difference among pixels and the distortion will be larger than the smooth one. Thus, the blocks in E_2 set will be further divided into smaller blocks in embedding process.

3.3 Embedding Procedure

After adaptively selecting the block size, an example of embedding process is given in this section (See Fig. 4). To embed the middle block, the four blocks Y_1, Y_3, Y_4, Y_5 surrounding it are used for prediction. Thresholds are settled as $t = 50$ and $T = 200$.

According to the formula (4) and formula (10),

$$\begin{cases} a(X) = 119, v(X) = \sqrt{\sum_{i=1}^{n} (x_i - a(X))^2} \approx 14, \\ \bar{Y}_1 \approx 120, \bar{Y}_3 \approx 101, \bar{Y}_4 \approx 127, \bar{Y}_5 \approx 114, \Delta v \approx 391. \end{cases} \tag{12}$$

Since $v(X) < t$ and $\Delta v > T$, the block is classified into set E_2. After being further divided into small size 2×2 blocks, each small block is embedded data according to Eq. (2). According to Eq. (2) and Eq. (11), all blocks in Shadow set of the image are classified and embedded by the corresponding way. In addition, as long as there is only a small block overflow/underflow, the block is marked as an overflow/underflow block. The first-pass embedding is completed after the above procedure. The second-pass embedding scheme uses the modified pixels in the set of first-pass to calculate the predicted values. As the same way, the set in second-pass can be embedded in.

90	91	98	109	113	121	128	126	120	124	133	127
91	95	98	105	109	120	121	122	122	125	130	128
89	98	101	110	114	122	123	122	124	125	132	126
89	89	96	105	111	119	122	125	124	124	131	131
91	95	104	109	113	116	118	119	124	123	129	130
97	99	106	113	114	115	121	122	120	126	126	133
94	101	104	109	113	117	119	120	121	123	128	131
92	95	104	108	110	114	116	123	126	127	128	132
81	95	101	103	109	110	116	120	140	146	151	154
89	92	101	104	111	111	117	118	138	143	153	155
86	92	105	109	109	110	114	117	137	145	158	155
83	93	103	107	112	114	114	118	137	149	150	152

Fig. 4. Example to illustrate the embedding process

Reversibility can be met in the proposed method certainly. Double embedding method is introduced in embedding scheme and the two layers embedding processes are independent with each other, which means that blocks embedded in the first-pass will not affect the unembedded blocks and the second-pass embedding process will not influence the embedded blocks either. With the help of the threshold T and location map, the used embedded method in each block can be distinguished accurately. Then, the watermarks can be extracted and the initial image can be restored correctly.

Overflow/underflow problem in the embedding procedure cannot be avoided. Since the pixel value of the gray scale is from 0 to 255, some pixels will be out of the range after being modified in the embedding process. The overflow/underflow error may result in extracting information and restoring the original pixel value incorrectly. In order to avoid this kind of error, we calculate each watermarked pixel value in embedding unit and find the blocks with no overflow/underflow error. When a large block is divided into smaller blocks, if any smaller one occurs overflow/underflow error, the large block will be marked as an overflow/underflow block.

3.4 Procedure of Embedding and Extraction

The embedding and extraction procedure are described as follows. Noticed that, each layer, namely Shadow set and Blank set, is embedded with half of watermarks. For the Shadow set embedding as an example, the proposed dynamic block data embedding procedure will be firstly introduced.

Step 1: The cover image I is divided into no-overlapping blocks.
Step 2: In order to prevent overflowing, the value of pixels in each Shadow block is calculated by Eq. (2) and the blocks belonging to D are found. Setting threshold $t > 0$ and the Shadow blocks are divided into 3 types E_t, C_t and O_t as Eq. (4).
Step 3: Establish the location map L. For the blocks belonging to E_t are marked as 1 in L, and the blocks belonging to C_t are marked as 0. The blocks belonging to O_t do not need to be marked in L, because it can be distinguished by threshold $t > 0$.
Step 4: Using the 4 neighboring Blank blocks, the Δv of Shadow block is calculated by Eq. (10). Setting $T > 0$, Shadow blocks in E_t set will be divide into two E_1 and E_2 according Eq. (11).
Step 5: Watermarks w will be embed in the classified Shadow blocks as follows, where w combines original watermarks and LSB_S of some first-line pixels.

- The blocks in E_1 set are embedded by Eq. (2) directly. And the blocks in E_2 set are further divided into $(n_1/n_2)^2$ small blocks with size $n_2 \times n_2$ and for each small block, Eq. (2) is also used to embed data.
- For blocks in C_t set with $\Delta v \leq T$ data is embedded by replacing the pixels LSB_S. Otherwise, The blocks in C_t are further divided into $(n_1/n_2)^2$ small blocks with size $n_2 \times n_2$, and data is embedded by replacing the pixels LSB_S.
- In addition, the original LSB_S of pixels in blocks belonging to C_t set are recorded in a sequence C_{LBS}, watermarks and C_{LBS} are embedded into the remaining embeddable blocks.

Step 6: Noting that the blocks in E_2 set should be classified as an overflow/underflow blocks and be marked as 0 in L, if any small block in the blocks overflows/underflows after being calculated again by Eq. (2). Losslessly compress the location map, and append a unique end-of-stream (EOS) symbol to the compressed location map to identify its end. The resulting sequence is denoted as L'. Using LSB replacement, the auxiliary information (i.e. the threshold t and T, the length of watermarks l_w and compressed location map L') is embedded into LSB_S of some first-line pixels.

Step 7: After the Shadow set embedding is completed, the pixels of the Blank set are predicted with the embedded pixels. The same method is used to complete the watermark embedding, and finally the embedded watermark image I' is obtained.

Extraction scheme is the inverse of embedding scheme. In embedding procedure, the Shadow set is embedded in firstly, and then the Blank set, so when the extraction, the Blank set is extracted from firstly, then the Shadow set.

4 Experiment Results

In this section, using the six standard 512×512 sized gray-scale images: Airplane, Lena, Baboon, Barbara and Peppers, the performance of the proposed method is evaluated by experiments.

In first experiment, the influence of the size of block on algorithm performance will be discussed. Here, mainly two sized blocks are used: 8×8 size for the basic block and 4×4 size for the basic block. For smooth blocks we use the basic block size as the embedding unit; for complex blocks, basic block will be further divided into four smaller blocks as embedding unit. Figure 5 shows the performance. From the figure, we see that the proposed method with 4×4 basic size performs better. It is due to the correlation of the adjacent pixels between 4×4-sized block is better than the 8×8-sized block, which makes the prediction on the blocks of complex texture more accurate and the distortion caused by the embedding process is also less. Accordingly, we simply take 4×4-sized blocks in the following experiments.

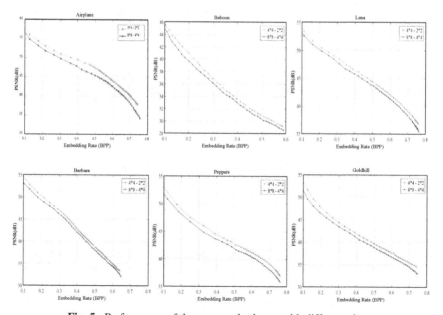

Fig. 5. Performance of the proposed scheme with different sizes.

Then, our scheme is compared with the three seminal methods of Wang et al. [23], Peng et al. [24] and Weng et al. [25]. In addition, since Wang et al.'s method with $n = 4 \times 4$ performs best, we take 4×4-sized blocks to test Wang et al.'s method. The comparison of the 4 algorithms on each image is shown in Fig. 6. It can be seen our method performs best, especially on the simpler texture image. On the image with more complex texture, the advantage of our algorithm is not very obvious. It is because the prediction scheme used in our embedding process is more accurate in the smooth region of image and the accuracy of the prediction results in complex region will be decreased. In addition, it also can be seen from the experimental results that when the embedding capacity is around 0.5 bpp, the embedding effect is better than that with other embedding capacity.

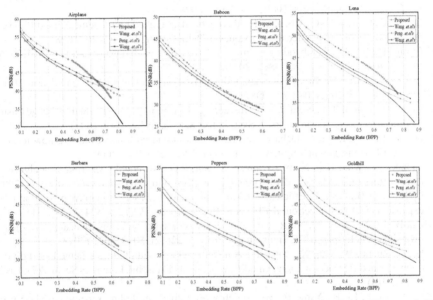

Fig. 6. Performance comparison between Wang et al. [23], Peng et al. [24] and Weng et al. [25] and the proposed approach.

5 Conclusion

In this paper, an adaptive reversible digital watermarking algorithm based on integer transform is proposed. The algorithm makes use of the characteristics of the image itself and combines the embedding scheme with the texture complexity features of the image, realizing a reversible digital watermarking scheme based on the flexible and adaptive selection of embedding unit size and embedding mode. The introduction of the double layer embedded method improves the PSNR of marked image, too. Experimental results show that the proposed method outperforms many other reversible watermarking schemes.

Acknowledgements. This work was supported by the Key Basic Research Plan in Shaanxi Province (Grant No. 2017ZDXM-GY-014).

References

1. Honsinger, C.W., Jones, P.W., Rabbani, M., Stoffel, J.C.: Lossless recovery of an original image containing embedded data, U.S Patent 6,278,791, 21 August 2001
2. Ni, Z., Shi, Y.Q., Ansari, N., Su, W.: Reversible data hiding. IEEE Trans. Circuits Syst. Video Technol. **16**(3), 354–362 (2006)
3. Li, X., Li, B., Yang, B., Zeng, T.: General framework to histogram-shifting-based reversible data hiding. IEEE Trans. Image Process. **22**(6), 2181–2191 (2013)
4. Thodi, D.M., Rodriguez, J.J.: Expansion embedding techniques for reversible watermarking. IEEE Trans. Image Process. **16**(3), 721–730 (2007)
5. Chang, C.-C., Lin, C.-C., Chen, Y.-H.: Reversible data-embedding scheme using differences between original and predicted pixel values. IET Inf. Secur. **2**(2), 35–46 (2008)
6. Coltuc, D.: Improved embedding for prediction-based reversible watermarking. IEEE Trans. Inf. Forensics Secur. **6**(3), 873–882 (2011)
7. Fallahpour, M.: Reversible image data hiding based on gradient adjusted prediction. IEICE Electron. Exp. **5**(20), 870–876 (2008)
8. Hong, W., Chen, T.S., Shiu, C.-W.: Reversible data hiding for high quality images using modification of prediction errors. J. Syst. Softw. **82**(11), 1833–1842 (2009)
9. Hu, Y., Lee, H.K., Li, J.: Debased reversible data hiding with improved overflow location map. IEEE Trans. Circuits Syst. Video Technol. **19**(2), 250–260 (2009)
10. Sachnev, V., Kim, H.J., Nam, J., Suresh, S., Shi, Y.Q.: Reversible watermarking algorithm using sorting and prediction. IEEE Trans. Circuits Syst. Video Technol. **19**(7), 989–999 (2009)
11. Li, X., Yang, B., Zeng, T.: Efficient reversible watermarking based on adaptive prediction-error expansion and pixel selection. IEEE Trans. Image Process. **20**(12), 3524–3533 (2011)
12. Ou, B., Li, X., Zhao, Y., Ni, R., Shi, Y.Q.: Pairwise prediction-error expansion for efficient reversible data hiding. IEEE Trans. Image Process. **22**(12), 5010–5021 (2013)
13. Li, X., Zhang, W., Gui, X., Yang, B.: A novel reversible data hiding scheme based on two dimensional difference-histogram modification. IEEE Trans. Inf. Forensics Secur. **8**(7), 1091–1100 (2013)
14. Li, X., Li, J., Li, B., Yang, B.: High-fidelity reversible data hiding scheme based on pixel value ordering and prediction-error expansion. Sig. Process. **93**(1), 198–205 (2013)
15. Tsai, P., Hu, Y.C., Yeh, H.-L.: Reversible image hiding scheme using predictive coding and histogram shifting. Sig. Process. **89**(6), 1129–1143 (2009)
16. Li, X., Zhang, W., Gui, X., Yang, B.: Efficient reversible data hiding based on multiple histograms modification. IEEE Trans. Inf. Forensics Secur. **10**(9), 2016–2027 (2015)
17. Weng, S., Zhang, G., Pan, J.S., Zhou, Z.: Optimal pvo-based reversible data hiding. J. Vis. Commun. Image Represent. **48**, 317–328 (2017)
18. Weng, S., Pan, J.S., Li, L.: Reversible data hiding based on an adaptive pixel embedding strategy and two-layer embedding. Inf. Sci. **369**, 144–159 (2016)
19. Weng, S., Liu, Y., Pan, J.S., Cai, N.: Reversible data hiding based on flexible block partition and adaptive block-modification strategy. J. Vis. Commun. Image Represent. **41**, 185–199 (2016)
20. Rad, R.M., Wong, K., Guo, J.M.: Reversible data hiding by adaptive group modification on histogram of prediction errors. Sig. Process. **125**, 315–328 (2016)
21. Yang, D., Yin, Z., Zhang, X.: Improved lossless data hiding for JPEG images based on Histogram modification. Comput. Mater. Continua **55**(3), 495–507 (2018)

22. Tian, J.: Reversible data embedding using a difference expansion. IEEE Trans. Circuits Syst. Video Technol. **13**(8), 890–896 (2003)
23. Alattar, A.M.: Reversible watermark using the difference expansion of a generalized integer transform. IEEE Trans. Image Process. **13**(8), 1147–1156 (2004)
24. Wang, C., Li, X., Yang, B.: High capacity reversible image watermarking based on integer transform, pp. 217–220 (2010)
25. Peng, F., Li, X., Yang, B.: Adaptive reversible data hiding scheme based on integer transform. Sig. Process. **92**(1), 54–62 (2012)
26. Weng, S., Pan, J.S.: Integer transform based reversible watermarking incorporating block selection. J. Vis. Commun. Image Represent. **35**, 25–35 (2016)
27. Weng, S., Zhao, Y., Pan, J.S., Ni, R.: Reversible watermarking based on invariability and adjustment on pixel pairs. IEEE Sig. Process. Lett. **15**(20), 721–724 (2008)

Design of Robot Routing Controller Based on OpenWrt

Hemin Ye[1] and Jiansheng Peng[1,2(✉)]

[1] School of Electronic Engineering, Guangxi Normal University,
Guilin 541004, Guangxi, China
sheng120410@163.com
[2] School of Physics and Mechanical and Electronic Engineering, Hechi University,
Yizhou 546300, Guangxi, China

Abstract. Based on the method that most robots use app to control data collection and the router and development board combined to control the robot, there are problems of long development cycle, large power consumption and high cost. We propose the design of a routing controller based on OpenWrt. The controller uses LuCI as the configuration page for control data acquisition, the designed control software processes and sends control commands, and the router directly controls the robot. The results show that the power consumption and cost of the robot are significantly reduced, and the development cycle is shortened by 5 days. In addition, the routing controller is suitable for multi-robot control in the state of the Internet of Things.

Keywords: Robot · OpenWrt · Routing controller · LuCI

1 Introduction

In recent years, industrial robots [1] and service robots [2] have developed rapidly, and sales have increased year by year [3]. For robot manufacturers, production cost and robot performance are two issues they need to consider. So how to ensure the high performance of the robot and reduce the cost? Considering that the core part of the robot is the controller of the robot, it determines the performance of the robot.

At present, most robots with remote control functions [4] modify the data through the mobile phone app [5], then interact with the router, and then the router transmits data to another control board to implement the robot control. In other words, manufacturers need to purchase routers and control boards at the same time when producing such robots, which lead to increasing production costs and increased energy consumption of robots. In addition, the data must pass through the router and then to the control board. This process delay will increase. As a result, the robot executes commands more slowly.

In response to the above problems, we designed a routing controller [7] based on OpenWrt [6]. The routing controller contains configuration pages and control software. Users can use the configuration page to modify the data to control the robot. The control software is responsible for reading the configuration data, processing the configuration

© Springer Nature Singapore Pte Ltd. 2020
X. Sun et al. (Eds.): ICAIS 2020, CCIS 1254, pp. 222–233, 2020.
https://doi.org/10.1007/978-981-15-8101-4_21

data, and finally sending commands to the robot. The system realizes rapid control of the robot through the cooperation of the configuration page and the control software. So we don't need to configure data through the app.

The robot in this article is a single robot based on the Internet of Things framework. The designed routing controller is suitable for multi-robot control in the state of the Internet of Things, and has the advantages of simple structure, low energy consumption and low cost. The configuration page for the routing controller is designed based on the LuCI framework. We just need to add the robot configuration page to the original framework. Therefore, it is less difficult to develop than an app, and the development cycle is shorter.

2 Overall Design of Routing Controller

The routing controller contains the LuCI configuration page and control software, as shown in Fig. 1. The LuCI configuration page is integrated into the routing controller system and initially has only the simple functionality of the routing configuration. In order to control the robot, we will add a page to configure the robot data on the basis of the original page to achieve interaction with the user. The control software is a set of programs designed and developed by us for controlling the robot. This software is installed on the system of the routing controller [8] and can interact with the LuCI configuration page for data. After the control software processes the read data, it will send control commands to the robot to control the robot's movement.

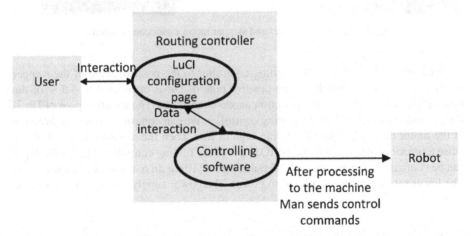

Fig. 1. Routing controller overall design.

3 Routing Controller and Stepper Motor Circuit Connection Design

The circuit connection between the routing controller and the stepper motor [9] is shown in Fig. 2. The first group of ports of the stepper motor is a pulse terminal, which is used to receive pulse signals, and drives the stepper motor according to the frequency of the pulse signal. The higher the frequency, the faster the rotation speed, and the lower the frequency, the slower the rotation speed. The second port Dir of the first group is used to control the direction of rotation of the stepper motor. Because the electrodes are positive and negative. So we can use the common positive or negative connection. Controlling direction is achieved by pulling up or down.

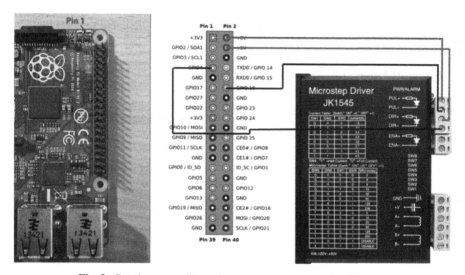

Fig. 2. Routing controller and stepper motor connection diagram.

We connect the +5 V of the routing controller to the positive stage of the stepper motor pulse terminal. Similarly, the positive pole of Dir is connected to +5 V of the routing controller, which is the common anode connection. The negative pole of Dir is then connected to GPIO4 of the routing controller. We can control the rotation direction of the motor by pulling the GPIO4 pin high or low. Then the negative terminal of the pulse terminal is connected to the GPIO18 pin of the routing controller. The GPIO18 pin can be configured to generate a PWM pulse signal [10] to drive the stepper motor. Spin. The lower set of ports is connected to power. The power supply is normally connected to +24 V.

4   Routing Controller Design

4.1   Routing Controller Routing Function Implementation

Our routing controller is implemented by installing the OpenWrt system on the hardware platform Raspberry Pi 3 B+ [11]. The Raspberry Pi is a microcomputer motherboard based on the ARM architecture [12], which is only the size of a card. The Raspberry Pi has the basic functions of the PC [13], such as: playing games, playing videos, making spreadsheets, and word processing. The raspberry PI 3B+ is equipped with

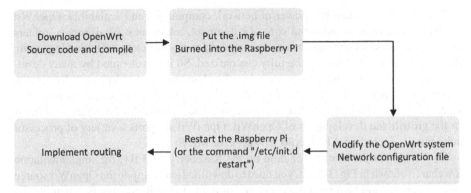

Fig. 3. Flow chart of routing function implementation.

a BCM2837(B0) from Boardcom Corporation, an integrated quad-core ARM corcor-a53 (ARMv8) 64-bit 1.4 GHz CPU, a maximum processing speed of 1.4 GHz, a gigabit Ethernet port (through the USB2.0 channel, the maximum throughput of 300 Mbps), four USB2.0 ports, 40 GPIO pins, support 2.4 GHz and 5 GHZ dual-frequency wi-fi, and support 802.11b/g/n/ac wireless protocol. Among them, 40 GPIO pins can be used for some extended functions of the system. For example, this article controls the robot through these 40 pins.

```
config interface 'loopback'
        option ifname 'lo'
        option proto 'static'
        option ipaddr '127.0.0.1'
        option netmask '255.0.0.0'

config globals 'globals'
        option ula_prefix 'fd11:2553:319d::/48'

config interface 'lan'
        option type 'bridge'
        option ifname 'eth0'
        option proto 'static'
        option ipaddr '192.168.1.1'
        option netmask '255.255.255.0'
        option ip6assign '60'
```

```
config interface 'loopback'
        option ifname 'lo'
        option proto 'static'
        option ipaddr '127.0.0.1'
        option netmask '255.0.0.0'

config globals 'globals'
        option ula_prefix 'fd11:2553:319d::/48'

config interface 'lan'
        option type 'bridge'
        option proto 'static'
        option ipaddr '192.168.1.1'
        option netmask '255.255.255.0'
        option ip6assign '60'
        option ip6hint '0'

config interface 'wan'
        option ifname 'eth0'
        option proto 'dhcp'
```

Fig. 4. Comparison file before and after modification of configuration file.

The OpenWrt system has powerful network components and scalability. OpenWrt system is often used in industrial control equipment, telephones, small robots, routers and other devices. Its package management provides a completely writable file system. This demonstrates its ability to be fully customized. So it is welcomed by many developers. In addition, the OpenWrt system has the characteristics of low cost, low power consumption, and small size. The OpenWrt system source code is open source. The community of the OpenWrt system is very active, which provides favorable conditions for the growth and development of OpenWrt. OpenWrt supports a variety of processor architectures, including ARM, X86, PowerPC or MIPS.

To implement the routing function on the Raspberry Pi 3 B+, the implementation flowchart is shown in Fig. 3. First, you need to download and compile the OpenWrt source code on ubuntu, and then burn the generated .img file to the Raspberry Pi. Then, access the OpenWrt system of the routing controller through the SSH protocol in the Xshell software. The next step is to modify the network configuration file in the "/etc./config" directory of the OpenWrt system. Figure 4 is a comparison of the configuration file before and after modification. The left is the file before the modification, and the right is the modified file. Finally, we run the "/etc./init.d restart" command to make the configuration just take effect.

4.2 Routing Controller Control Software Design

The relationship between the control software and each module is shown in Fig. 5. The user connects to the routing controller [21] through WiFi, and the configuration information can be modified on the configuration page of the routing controller. The modified configuration information is stored in the configuration file. The control software reads the configuration file information by calling the UCI library [14]. After processing, the control software calls the GPIO library [15] to control the stepper motor of the robot.

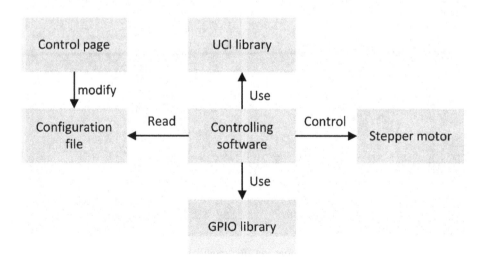

Fig. 5. The relationship between the control software and each module.

Control Software Installation. The control software installation process is shown in Fig. 6. First, we create the gpio_execute folder in the "pakage/feeds/packages" path of the OpenWrt source code. This folder contains the "src" directory and the "Makefile" file. There is a "main.c" file and a "Makefile" file in the "src" directory. The "Makefile" file is used to compile the "main.c" file. The main function of the "main.c" file is to read parameters from the "UCI" configuration file and configure "GPIO". To read the "UCI" configuration file, the "UCI" library must be referenced in "main.c". This "UCI" library is originally available in the OpenWrt system. It does not require us to add it to the system. It can be called directly. The next step is to compile the control software separately. Finally, we upload the "ipk" file generated after compilation to the routing controller [22] and install it.

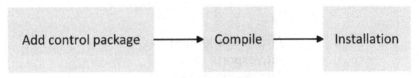

Fig. 6. Control software installation process.

Add GPIO Library. Our control software needs to call "GPIO". However, the Open-Wrt system does not have a library function that can call "GPIO". "wiringPi" is a library function written for Raspberry Pi to control "GPIO". "wiringPi" is open source code implemented in C. We can download the code online. If we don't use this library. We need to modify "GPIO" in the kernel. However, the Raspberry Pi does not have a corresponding manual describing these "GPIO" registers. So it is more difficult to write this driver yourself.

The process of adding the "GPIO" library to the Raspberry Pi is shown in Fig. 7. First, download the "GPIO" library source code from the Internet. Then, create a new "GPIO" library folder in the "package/libs/" directory of the OpenWrt source code. We create a new "src" folder in the new "GPIO" folder and copy the ".c" and ".h" files of the "GPIO" library function to the "src" directory. Next, we created a "Makefile" file in the

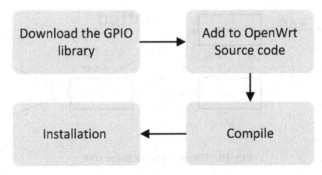

Fig. 7. Add GPIO library flow chart.

same directory of the "src" folder. The function of the "Makefile" file code is to compile the files in the "src" directory into ".so" dynamic library files. Finally, we compile and install the compiled "ipk" file on the routing controller.

4.3 Routing Controller Configuration Page Design

The routing controller operating system has a web configuration page like "LuCI", and the original "LuCI" page has some functions for setting routes [20]. Since our controller needs a page to interact with the user. Using this page, the user can set the corresponding value to control the motor rotation status. Now we choose to design such a page based on "LuCI".

/etc/network/interfaces
/etc/exports
/etc/dnsmasq.conf
/etc/samba/samba.conf

Fig. 8. Configuration files in different directories.

Fig. 9. Configuration flow chart using UCI.

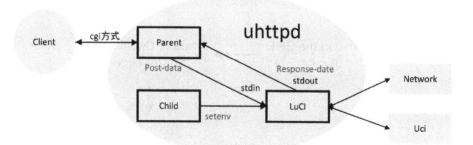

Fig. 10. Uhttpd working framework.

LuCI's UCI. "LuCI" is a collective name for "Lua" scripting language and "UCI" (Unified Configuration Interface). "LuCI" is also developed by the combination of "Lua" scripting language and "UCI". The Lua language includes only a streamlined core and the most basic libraries. Therefore, Lua is small and fast to start, making it suitable for embedding in our programs. "UCI" is a unified interface for OpenWrt system configuration. The third-party software of the OpenWrt system has its own configuration file and the storage location is different, as shown in Fig. 8. The syntax of these configuration files is also different. If you want to modify these configuration files, you must go to their respective directories. Therefore, this process is very tedious. The "UCI" of the OpenWrt system was born to solve the problem of unified configuration. After having the "UCI" unified configuration interface, the process of modifying the configuration file through the "UCI" configuration interface is shown in Fig. 9. We can directly modify the corresponding configuration files in the "/etc./config" directory. Then, we execute the "/etc./init.d" script to complete the configuration. In this way, we no longer have to find the configuration files of third-party software, and we don't need to write different syntax.

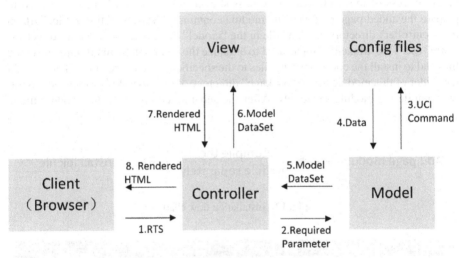

Fig. 11. MVC working principle diagram.

Web Server. "LuCI" uses the "C/S" architecture [16], and its web server "uhttpd" [17] is more streamlined. We use "uhttpd" to implement web page configuration. Figure 10 is the working framework of "uhttpd". For "request" processing, "uhttpd" uses the "cgi" processing method [18]. In the "cgi" mode, the "uhttpd" server will "fork" a child process. This child process uses "execl" to replace "LuCI" process space and uses "setenv" environment variables to pass some fixed format data (such as "PATH_INFO") to "LuCI". Other non-fixed format data ("post-data") is written by the parent process to "Stdin" of "LuCI" through "w_pipe" (write channel). "LuCI" writes the data on "stdout" when the data returns. At this point, the "r_pipe" (read channel) of the parent process reads the data.

MVC Architecture. "LuCI" adopts the "MVC" three-tier architecture [19]. "M" refers to the model, "V" refers to the view, and "C" refers to the controller. The working principle of the "MVC" three-tier architecture is shown in Fig. 11.

The working principle of MVC: 1. First, the client (browser) sends a request to the controller; 2. After receiving the request from the client, the controller sends the requested parameter set to the model; 3. The model identifies the corresponding parameters, and then the model reads, rewrites, or deletes the configuration file through the UCI interface; 4. The model gets the corresponding data from the configuration file (this step only exists when reading the configuration file); 5. The model returns the data set to the controller. These data sets include information read to the configuration file and identification information; 6. The controller sends the information returned from the model to the view, and then the view encapsulates and renders this information. At this time, we will use the prepared "html", "css", "js" and other files; 7. The view sends the rendered file to the controller; 8. Finally, the controller returns the rendered file to the client. After these steps, a dynamic page is presented to the user.

Design and Installation of Routing Controller Configuration Page. The   installation process of the configuration page is shown in Fig. 12. First, First, we need to prepare the added page module. The module contains a "Makefile" file, a ".lua" file in the "controller" directory, a ".lua" file in the "model" directory, and a "view" directory. ".htm" file. The "Makefile" file is used to organize the compilation and linking of source files and to install the corresponding files to the specified system directory. Then, we add the folder of this module to the "package" directory of the OpenWrt source code. Next, we compile the module separately. After the separate compilation, the module file is

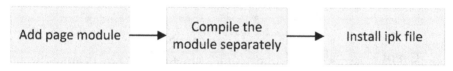

Fig. 12. Installation flow chart.

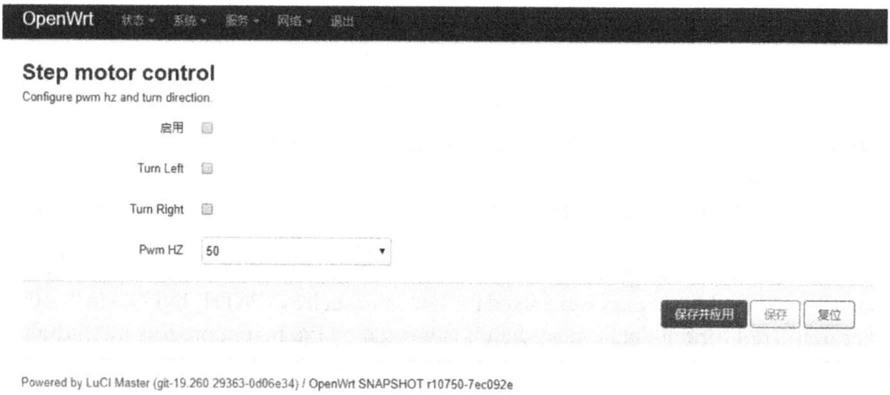

Step motor control
Configure pwm hz and turn direction.

启用 ☐

Turn Left ☐

Turn Right ☐

Pwm HZ   50 ▾

保存并应用   保存   复位

Powered by LuCI Master (git-19.260 29363-0d06e34) / OpenWrt SNAPSHOT r10750-7ec092e

Fig. 13. Configuration page schematic.

generated. This "ipk" file is equivalent to an installation package. Finally, we uploaded the ipk file to the Raspberry Pi system and installed it.

Our configuration page has four function keys as shown in Fig. 13. These function keys are: whether to enable stepper motor control (radio box), turn left (radio box), turn right (radio box), PWM frequency adjustment (drop-down box), and apply button. It must be noted that one of the "turn left" or "turn right" is selected, and the other cannot be selected. If neither of these radio boxes is checked, the robot will advance. The configuration page program flowchart is shown in Fig. 14.

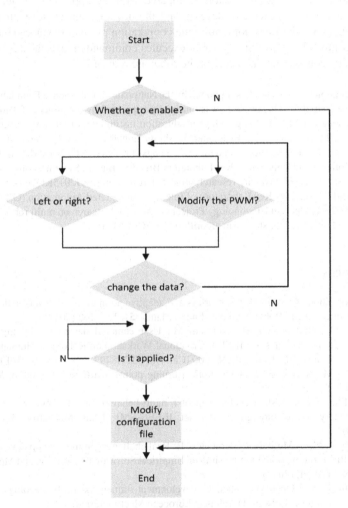

Fig. 14. Configuration page program flow chart.

5 Conclusion

The robot routing controller based on OpenWrt designed in this paper is suitable for multi-robot control in the state of the Internet of Things. Users modify configuration information on the configuration page. The control software reads the configuration information and sends control instructions to the robot's stepper motor after processing by the control software. After testing, the routing controller has realized the function of controlling the robot well. In addition, the configuration page we designed can replace the app to complete data collection. Compared with the app, the configuration page we designed is less difficult to develop and the development cycle is shorter. Since our routing controller does not require the cooperation of other development boards to directly control the robot. So our robot executes commands much faster. At the same time, energy consumption and cost of the robot are reduced.

Acknowledgement. This work is supported by the National Natural Science Foundation of China (Grant No. 61640305). This research was financially supported by the project of Thousands outstanding young teachers' training in higher education institutions of Guangxi, The Young and Middle-aged Teachers Research Fundamental Ability Enhancement of Guangxi University (ID: 2019KY0621), Natural Science Foundation of Guangxi Province (NO. 2018GXNSFAA281164). Guangxi Colleges and Universities Key Laboratory Breeding Base of System Control and Information Processing, Hechi University research project start-up funds (XJ2015KQ004), Supported by Colleges and Universities Key Laboratory of Intelligent Integrated Automation (GXZDSY2016-04), Hechi City Science and Technology Project (1694-3-2), Research on multi robot cooperative system based on artificial fish swarm algorithm (2017CFC811).

References

1. Yao, B., Zhou, Z., Wang, L.: Sensorless and adaptive admittance control of industrial robot in physical human. Robot. Comput.-Integr. Manuf. **51**, 158–168 (2018)
2. Green, A., Huttenrauch, H., Norman, M.: User centered design for intelligent service robots. In: Proceedings 9th IEEE International Workshop on Robot and Human Interactive Communication. IEEE RO-MAN 2000 (Cat. No. 00TH8499), pp. 161–166. IEEE (2000)
3. Hagele, M.: Robots conquer the world [turning point]. IEEE Robot. Autom. Mag. **23**(1), 118–120 (2016)
4. Luo, R.C., Chen, T.M.: Development of a multi-behavior based mobile robot for remote supervisory control through the Internet. IEEE/ASME Trans. Mechatron. **5**(4), 376–385 (2000)
5. Joorabchi, M.E., Mesbah, A., Kruchten, P.: Real challenges in mobile app development. In: ACM/IEEE International Symposium on Empirical Software Engineering and Measurement, pp. 15–24. IEEE (2013)
6. Fainelli, F.: The OpenWrt embedded development framework. In: Proceedings of the Free and Open Source Software Developers European Meeting (2008)
7. Ataslar, B., Iftar, A.: Decentralized routing controller design using overlapping decompositions. Int. J. Control **72**(13), 1175–1192 (1999)
8. Erzberger, H., McNally, D., Foster, M., Chiu, D., Stassart, P.: Direct-to tool for en route controllers. In: Bianco, L., Dell'Olmo, P., Odoni, A.R. (eds.) New Concepts and Methods in Air Traffic Management. Transportation Analysis, pp. 179–198. Springer, Heidelberg (2001). https://doi.org/10.1007/978-3-662-04632-6_11

9. Hakim, C.A., Hakim, S.: Surgically-implantable stepping motor, U.S. Patent 4,615,691[P], 7 October 1986
10. Kikuchi, H.: DC converter which has switching control unit to select PWM signal or PFM signal, U.S. Patent 8,035,365[P], 11 October 2011
11. Kumar, K.K.: Smart traffic system using raspberry pi by applying dynamic color changer algorithm. In: 2017 IEEE International Conference on Smart Technologies and Management for Computing, Communication, Controls, Energy and Materials (ICSTM). IEEE (2017)
12. Jaggar, D.: ARM architecture and systems. IEEE Micro 17(4), 9–11 (1997)
13. Lin, C.A.: Exploring personal computer adoption dynamics. J. Broadcast. Electron. Media 42(1), 95–112 (1998)
14. Fainelli, F.: The OpenWrt embedded development framework. In: Proceedings of the Free and Open Source Software Developers European Meeting, p. 106 (2008)
15. Henderson, G.: Wiring pi GPIO interface library for the raspberry pi. Internet (2013)
16. Steiert, H.P.: Towards a component-based n-Tier C/S-architecture. In: Foundations of Software Engineering: Proceedings of the Third International Workshop on Software Architecture, vol. 1, no. 05, pp. 137–140 (1998)
17. Banerjee, S., Liu, P., Patro, A.: ParaDrop: An Edge Computing Platform in Home Gateways. Fog for 5G and IoT, p. 13. Wiley, Hoboken (2017)
18. Boutell, T.: CGI programming in C & Perl. Addison-Wesley Professional, Boston (1996)
19. Sarker, I.H., Apu, K.: MVC architecture driven design and implementation of JAVA framework for developing desktop application. Int. J. Hybrid Inf. Technol. 7(5), 317–322 (2014)
20. Janarthanan, A., Kumar, D.: Localization based EComputers. In: Materials and Continua, Volutionary Routing (LOBER) for Efficient Aggregation in Wireless Multimedia Sensor Networks, Computers, Materials and Continua, vol. 60, no. 3, pp. 895–912 (2019)
21. Sun, Z., et al.: Designing and optimization of fuzzy sliding mode controller for nonlinear systems. Comput. Mater. Contin. 61(1), 119–128 (2019)
22. Shen, C., Chen, Y., Chen, B., Xie, J.: A compensation controller based on a nonlinear wavelet neural network for continuous material processing operations. Comput. Mater. Contin. 61(1), 379–397 (2019)

Cubic Convolutional Neural Network for Hyperspectral Image Classification

Le Sun[1,2(✉)] and Xiangbo Song[2]

[1] Jiangsu Engineering Center of Network Monitoring,
Nanjing University of Information Science and Technology, Nanjing 210044, China
sunlecncom@nuist.edu.cn
[2] School of Computer and Software,
Nanjing University of Information Science and Technology, Nanjing 210044, China
xiangbosong@nuist.edu.cn

Abstract. In recent years, the framework of convolutional neural network based on deep learning (DL) has made good progress in the field of hyperspectral image (HSI) classification. In order to improve the classification accuracy and reduce the time complexity of the model, we proposed an end-to-end cubic convolution neural network (C-CNN) framework for the classification of HSI. C-CNN uses one-dimensional convolution and principal component analysis (PCA) operation respectively to reduce the dimension of the original HSI, and merges the processed data. Then through convolving the data cube from the spatial domain and the spatial-spectral domain respectively, deep features of HSI are obtained. Batch normalization and dropout layers are used to prevent overfitting. The proposed C-CNN framework can achieve the optimal results within 80 epochs. Experimental results with widely used hyperspectral image datasets show that the proposed method surpasses the existing state-of-the-art methods based on DL.

Keywords: Hyperspectral image · Cubic convolutional neural network · Deep learning

1 Introduction

With the development of spectral imaging technique and the increasing demand, hyperspectral image classification as one of the most important research directions in the field of hyperspectral image research has received more and more attention [1,2]. Since the deep neural network has achieved great success in natural images, many scholars have tried to apply the deep learning(DL) to the classification of hyperspectral images and achieved better classification performance than most conventional classification methods [3,4]. Because convolutional neural network (CNN) directly extract the features of two-dimensional data without losing the spatial information, the most widely used network structure in the field of image and video is still based on CNN [5].

© Springer Nature Singapore Pte Ltd. 2020
X. Sun et al. (Eds.): ICAIS 2020, CCIS 1254, pp. 234–245, 2020.
https://doi.org/10.1007/978-981-15-8101-4_22

HSI is a three-dimensional data cube with rich spatial and spectral information [6]. Therefore, extracting both spatial and spectral information is more widely used in some methods based on DL. In [7,8], a spectral-spatial HSI classifier is proposed with a regularization technique for the HSI spectral–spatial classification to further improve the classification accuracy. Mei *et al.* [9] construct a five-layer CNN which has both supervised and unsupervised modes, it can learn sensor-specific spatial-spectral features for classification. Gong *et al.* [10,11] propose a multiscale convolution with determinantal point process (DPP) priors, which encourage the learned factors to repulse from one another. And it can be imposed over these factors to diversify them. In [12], a supervised learning method is proposed which extract features which exhibit spatial-spectral information of diverse regions and merge a diverse set of discriminative appearance factors to classify the HSI.

The existing methods can provide a good scheme for HSI classification, however there are two sides of problems that should be taken into attention [13]. Firstly, the dimensionality reduction processing of hyperspectral images has important influence on the classification results. Using effective dimensionality reduction method to extract spectral dimension information plays a particularly significant role for HSI classification [14–16]. Secondly, multi-scale and multi-layer make the framework based on CNN more and more complex, and the extracted features are more and more difficult to explain [17].

To overcome the two problem and further improve the performance of HSI classification, C-CNN is proposed in this paper. Our framework firstly uses one-dimensional convolution and PCA to effectively reduce the dimension of hyperspectral data, and fully excavates the information of spectral dimension. Different from the three-dimensional convolution, we carry out two-dimensional convolution on the hyperspectral data after dimensionality reduction from the spatial domain and the spatial-spectral domain respectively. By integrating the results of convolution, our framework achieves a brilliant classification performance. The contributions made in this paper are mainly divided into the following three aspects.

- We propose an effective dimensionality reduction method for hyperspectral data, which can fully extract favorable spectral information and eliminate redundant spectral information.
- For the spectral and spatial information, we make full use of the advantages of CNN to extract deeper features by convolution in spatial domain and spatial-spectral domain respectively.
- Our network can guarantee excellent performance with faster convergence speed and lower time complexity.

The remaining part of this paper is organized as follows: The proposed cubic convolutional neural network is presented in Sect. 2. Section 3 presents the experiment and result analysis. And conclusions are drawn in Sect. 4.

2   Cubic Convolutional Neural Network

In this paper, we propose a cnn-based network model named cubic convolutional neural network. C-CNN convolved hyperspectral images from different dimensions, and input the convoluted results into the full connection layer for classification. The following is an introduction to the C-CNN network model.

In this section, we'll explain the specifics of C-CNN, elaborate on how to build our architecture, and how to extract deep features with C-CNN network. CNN has two main characteristics: the connection between different layers of neurons is not fully connected, the weights of convolution operations are shared [18]. CNN makes full use of the local features contained in the data by means of local perception, shared weights and pooling. A traditional CNN is composed of several convolution layers, pooling layers and full connection layers [19]. In order to solve the classification problem of hyperspectral images, C-CNN is proposed.

2.1   Dimension Reduction

Dimensionality reduction preserves the most vital features of high-dimensional data, and removes noise and unimportant features, so as to improve the speed of data processing. It is well known that the dimensionality reduction of data is particularly important for the classification of hyperspectral images [20]. In our network, PCA and one-dimensional convolution are used to reduce the spectral dimension of hyperspectral data.

A kernel of size $1 * 1 * d$ also can reduce the dimension of hyperspectral data. Although the convolution kernel is a 3D kernel, the $1 * 1 * d$ convolution kernel is actually a one-dimensional convolution. Compared with PCA, one-dimensional convolution reduces dimension by integrating information through convolution operation. The principal components extracted by PCA have no information between channels, while the operation of one-dimensional convolution can extract information between channels by means of linear summation. Through the above two dimensionality reduction operations, we can effectively reduce the dimensionality of hyperspectral data to facilitate the classification of hyperspectral images.

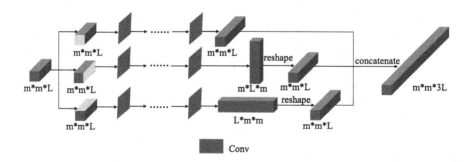

Fig. 1. Structure of cubic convolution.

2.2 Cubic Convolution

In this paper, a new cubic convolution method is proposed. For a cube data, we carry out two-dimensional convolution on three unique planes respectively and cascade the convolution results. The cube data $m * m * L$ is the input of network where L is the number of channels. As shown in Fig. 1, firstly, we convolve the cube data in the spatial domain, and the convolution kernel size is $r * r * 1$. The plane of m * m is named convolution plane. Secondly, we convolve the cube data in spectral-spatial domain where one dimension of the plane of convolution is the spectral dimension and another dimension is the spatial dimension. In this case, we can view the data as a data cube of size $m * L * m$ where m is the number of channels, and the convolution plane is $m * L$. Thirdly, we convolve the cube data in spectral-spatial domain and the convolution plane is on the side of convolution plane in second step.

Cubic convolution realizes the real 3D convolution by convolving the cube data from different convolution plane. The convolution operation on spatial domain extract spatial information. And the convolution operation on spectral-spatial domain extract the information within spectral dimension and spatial dimension [21]. In this way, the deep feature can be extracted for HSI classification.

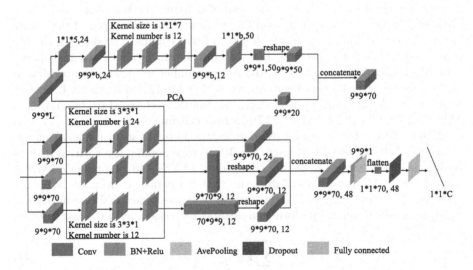

Fig. 2. Structure of cubic convolutional neural network.

2.3 Cubic Convolution Neural Network

For an original input $m * m * L$ hyperspectral data block which center pixel is to be classified, m is selected as 9 and L is the number of HSI channels. Details of the C-CNN network are shown in Fig. 2.

As shown in Fig. 2, BN and Relu layers are used before the convolution and pooling layers to improve the performance of the network. Our network used two dimensionality reduction methods to extract spectral dimension features from the original input image block, one-dimensional convolution and PCA operation respectively. In one-dimensional convolution, we first use a convolution layer which kernel size is $1 * 1 * 5$ and kernel number is 24 to convolve the input data. Padding is "valid" and stride is 2. Through the first convolution layer, we obtain $n = 24$ $9 * 9 * b$ feature maps of size $9 * 9 * b$. For the next three convolution layers, we all set the size of kernel to be $1 * 1 * 7$ and the number of kernels to be 12. Padding is "same" and stride is 1. And we get $n = 12$ feature maps which size is $9 * 9 * b$. Next, through the a convolution layer which kernel size is $1 * 1 * b$ and kernel number is 50, we obtain n $= 50$ feature maps which size is $9 * 9 * 1$. we use the reshape operation to change the feature maps with size $9 * 9 * 1,50$ to which with size $9 * 9 * 50$. Through the one-dimensional convolution, the 50 dimensions feature maps are obtained. Then, we merge the feature maps generated by one-dimensional convolution and PCA operation. We set the image channel as 20 after PCA, and we obtain the 70-dimensional feature maps finally.

Next, we handle the dimensionality reduction feature maps with using cubic convolution. The feature maps are convolved from different convolution plane, the front, the side and the top. The front side of the image block is the spatial domain. For the convolution layers of spatial domain, the kernel size is $3 * 3 * 1$, the kernel number is 24, and the padding is "same", so the output of the convolution layers in spatial domain is $9 * 9 * 70,24$ feature maps. The side and the top plane is spectral-spatial domain. For the convolution layers of spectral-spatial domain, the kernel size is $3 * 3 * 1$, the kernel number is 12, and the padding is "same", so the outputs of convolution layers $9 * 70 * 9$, 12 and $70 * 9 * 9$, 12 respectively. Through the reshape method, feature maps are changed to the same size, $9 * 9 * 70,24$, $9 * 9 * 70,12$ and $9 * 9 * 70,12$ respectively.

A new data cube is formed by merging the above feature maps which the size is $9 * 9 * 70$, 48. Finally, through the 3D average pooling layer with a $9 * 9 * 1$ pooling size, the feature maps are changed to $1 * 1 * 70,48$. A prediction vector with size $1 * 1 * C$ is produced after the flatten operation, dropout layer and fully-connected layer, where C is the number of classes. Since HSI classification is multiple classification, we performed a softmax regression, with the loss function

$$\Gamma_{\mathrm{s}} = -\sum_{i=1}^{n} \log \frac{e^{w_{y_i}^T x_i + b_{y_i}}}{\sum\limits_{j=1}^{m} e^{w_j^T x_i + b_j}} \tag{1}$$

where n denotes the size of batch, m denotes the number of classes to be classified, x_i is the i-th feature vector which belong to the y_i-th category, and b_j denotes the j-th weights and bias respectively.

3   Experiment and Result Analysis

In this section, we validate the performance of C-CNN on three hyperspectral datasets and compare with some state-of-the-art method of HSI classification.

3.1   Data Description

The datasets to be tested is selected as Indian Pines, Pavia University, and Salinas. The specific description of each dataset is as follows:

- Indian Pines is the earliest test data for hyperspectral image classification. The airborne visible/infrared imaging spectrometer sensor(AVIRIS) imaged a piece of Indian pine tree in Indiana, USA in 1992. The spatial resolution of the image obtained by the spectral imager is about 20 m. The wavelength range of AVIRIS imaging is 0.4–2.5 um, which is used for continuous imaging of ground objects in 220 successive bands. Since the [104–108], [150–163] and 220 bands cannot be reflected by water, the remaining 200 bands after the removal of these 20 bands are generally used for the research data. The ground truth contains 16 classes. The pseudocolor image and ground-truth classification map of the Indian Pine dataset is shown in Fig. 3.
- Pavia University data is a part of the hyperspectral data obtained by the German airborne Reflective Optics Spectrographic Imaging System (ROSIS) in 2003. The spectrometer continuously images 115 bands in a wavelength range of 0.43–0.86 um and 12 bands are eliminated due to noise. The size of the data is 610×340 and the spatial resolution is 1.3 m. The ground truth contains 9 classes. The pseudocolor image and ground-truth classification map of the Pavia University dataset is shown in Fig. 4.
- Salinas dataset is collected by AVIRIS from the Salinas valley in California, USA. The size of the image is 512×217 and its spatial resolution is 3.7 m. The image has 224 bands. Similarly, we used the remaining 204 bands after removing the [108–112], [154–167] and 224 band that cannot be reflected by water. The ground truth contains 16 classes. The pseudocolor image and ground-truth classification map of the Salinas dataset is shown in Fig. 5.

Fig. 3. Pseudocolor image and Ground-truth classification map of the Indian Pine dataset. (Color figure online)

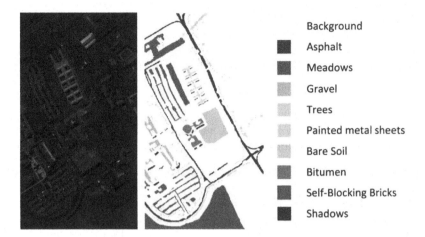

Fig. 4. Pseudocolor image and ground-truth classification map of the Pavia University dataset. (Color figure online)

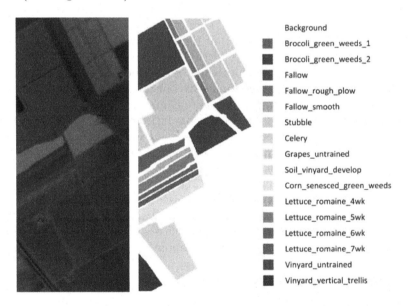

Fig. 5. Pseudocolor image and Ground-truth classification map of the Salinas dataset. (Color figure online)

3.2 Experiment Setting

In order to verify the performance of c-cnn, four cnn-based methods, 3-D Auto-CNN, SS-CNN, DPP-DML-MS-CNN and DR-CNN are selected and compare with our method. The indices representing the classification performance of these methods are overall accuracy (OA) and average accuracy (AA) [22]. In these methods, we only get the source code of DR-CNN. And other experiment results are obtained from their paper.

For the datasets, all the methods used 200 samples for each class of training and other samples are used to test the model. Since there are some classes which the number of samples is less than 200 in the Indian Pines dataset, only the first 8 categories with more samples were selected for training and testing, we selected 8 classes with large samples for training and testing. The number of training and testing samples of three datasets are list in Table 1, 2 and 3.

Table 1. The numbers of training and testing samples for the indian pines dataset.

♯	Class	Training	Test
1	Corn-notill	200	1228
2	Corn-mintill	200	630
3	Grass-pasture	200	283
4	Hay-windrowed	200	278
5	Soybean-notill	200	772
6	Soybean-mintill	200	2255
7	Soybean-clean	200	393
8	Woods	200	1065
-	Total	1600	6904

Table 2. The numbers of training and testing samples for the university of pavia dataset.

♯	Class	Training	Test
1	Asphalt	200	6431
2	Meadows	200	18449
3	Gravel	200	1899
4	Trees	200	2864
5	Sheets	200	1145
6	Baresoil	200	4829
7	Bitumen	200	1130
8	Bricks	200	3482
9	Shadows	200	747
-	Total	1800	40976

Table 3. The numbers of training and testing samples for the salinas dataset.

♯	Class	Training	Test
1	Broccoli green weeds 1	200	1809
2	Broccoli green weeds 2	200	3526
3	Fallow	200	1776
4	Fallow rough plow	200	1194
5	Fallow smooth	200	2478
6	Stubble	200	3759
7	Celery	200	3379
8	Grapes untrained	200	11071
9	Soil vineyard develop	200	6003
10	Corn senesced green weeds	200	3078
11	Lettuce romaines, 4 wk	200	868
12	Lettuce romaines, 5 wk	200	1727
13	Lettuce romaines, 6 wk	200	716
14	Lettuce romaines, 7 wk	200	70
15	Vinedyard untrained	200	7068
16	Vineyard vertical trellis	200	1607
-	Total	3200	50929

3.3   Classification Results of Hyperspectral Datasets

Table 4, 5 and 6 shows the comparison of experimental results between the proposed method and the existing method. For most classes, c-cnn results are better than the existing classification methods, and OA and AA are higher than the existing methods. Some classes may not have the highest accuracy, but they are closed to the best.

Table 4. Classification result with c-cnn on the indian pines dataset.

Class	3-D Auto-CNN	SS-CNN	DPP-MS-CNN	DR-CNN	C-CNN
1	88.28	96.28	99.03	98.20	98.31 ± 0.40
2	79.86	92.26	99.74	99.79	99.64 ± 0.21
3	71.13	99.3	100	100	**100 ± 0.00**
4	99.77	100	100	100	99.34 ± 0.25
5	91.74	92.84	99.61	99.78	99.42 ± 0.33
6	93.70	98.21	97.80	96.69	**99.95 + 0.01**
7	73.70	92.45	100	99.86	**100 ± 0.00**
8	98.20	98.98	100	99.99	99.26 ± 0.39
OA	89.01	96.63	99.08	98.54	**99.43 ± 0.14**
AA	87.05	96.29	99.52	99.29	**99.49 ± 0.40**

Figure 6 shows the accuracy and loss curves of training set and validation set on the Indian Pine, the Pavia University, and the Salinas dataset. From the

Table 5. Classification result with c-cnn on the university of pavia dataset.

Class	3-D Auto-CNN	SS-CNN	DPP-MS-CNN	DR-CNN	C-CNN
1	94.14	97.40	99.38	98.43	**99.97 ± 0.02**
2	92.78	99.40	99.59	99.45	**99.98 ± 0.01**
3	80.60	94.84	97.33	99.14	98.88 ± 0.05
4	83.42	99.16	99.31	99.50	**99.86 ± 0.10**
5	99.13	100	100	100	99.91 ± 0.05
6	95.62	98.70	99.99	100	99.96 ± 0.02
7	87.31	100	99.85	99.70	**100 ± 0.00**
8	98.39	94.57	99.02	99.55	**99.73 ± 0.14**
9	63.02	99.87	100	100	99.04 ± 0.26
OA	93.88	98.41	99.46	99.56	**99.88 ± 0.04**
AA	88.19	98.22	99.39	99.53	**99.70 ± 0.07**

Table 6. Classification result with c-cnn on the salinas dataset.

Class	3-D Auto-CNN	SS-CNN	DPP-MS-CNN	DR-CNN	C-CNN
1	94.15	100	100	100	**100 ± 0.00**
2	98.36	99.89	100	100	**100 ± 0.00**
3	93.59	99.89	100	99.98	98.68 ± 1.25
4	98.56	99.25	99.25	99.89	**100 ± 0.00**
5	98.61	99.39	99.44	99.83	**99.92 ± 0.03**
6	99.67	100	100	100	**100 ± 0.00**
7	97.96	99.82	99.87	99.96	**100 ± 0.00**
8	90.98	91.45	95.36	94.14	**99.68 ± 0.21**
9	99.74	99.95	100	99.99	99.93 ± 0.01
10	99.78	98.51	98.85	99.20	99.46 ± 0.23
11	79.51	99.31	99.77	99.99	96.89 ± 2.17
12	99.84	100	100	100	**100 ± 0.00**
13	90.86	99.72	99.86	100	**100 ± 0.00**
14	87.17	100	99.77	100	99.88 ± 0.10
15	97.40	96.24	90.50	95.52	95.42 ± 1.56
16	77.63	99.63	98.94	99.72	**100 ± 0.00**
OA	94.65	98.33	97.51	98.33	**99.12 ± 0.16**
AA	93.99	99.26	98.85	99.26	**99.37 ± 0.35**

Fig. 6 we can see our network converged rapidly within the first ten epochs, and basically ended up within the first 20 epochs. During the whole training process, loss and accuracy did not show severe shock which proves that the proposed network is excellent for feature extraction.

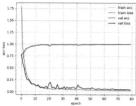 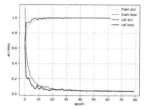 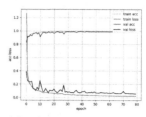

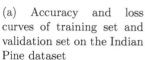

(a) Accuracy and loss curves of training set and validation set on the Indian Pine dataset

(b) Accuracy and loss curves of training set and validation set on the Pavia University dataset

(c) Accuracy and loss curves of training set and validation set on the Salinas datasets

Fig. 6. Accuracy and loss curves of training set and validation set on different datasets.

4   Conclusion

In this paper, a cubic convolutional neural network has been proposed for HSI classification. The proposed C-CNN model provides a distinctive way for hyperspectral image dimensionality reduction. And cubic convolution can obtain the abundant spatial and spectral features, which take full advantage of CNN. The experimental results show that the features extracted by c-cnn are effective and feasible.

References

1. Zhong, P., Gong, Z., Li, S., Schönlieb, C.-B.: Learning to diversify deep belief networks for hyperspectral image classification. IEEE Trans. Geosci. Remote Sens. **55**(6), 3516–3530 (2017)
2. Lee, H., Kwon, H.: Going deeper with contextual CNN for hyperspectral image classification. IEEE Trans. Image Process. **26**(10), 4843–4855 (2017)
3. Gu, Y., Liu, T., Jia, X., Benediktsson, J.A., Chanussot, J.: Nonlinear multiple kernel learning with multiple-structure-element extended morphological profiles for hyperspectral image classification. IEEE Trans. Geosci. Remote Sens. **54**(6), 3235–3247 (2016)
4. Wang, Q., Gu, Y., Tuia, D.: Discriminative multiple kernel learning for hyperspectral image classification. IEEE Trans. Geosci. Remote Sens. **54**(7), 3912–3927 (2016)
5. Pan, B., Shi, Z., Xu, X.: R-VCANet: a new deep-learning-based hyperspectral image classification method. IEEE J. Sel. Top. Appl. Earth Obs. Remote Sens. **10**(5), 1975–1986 (2017)
6. Yu, S., Jia, S., Xu, C.: Convolutional neural networks for hyperspectral image classification. Neurocomputing **219**, 88–98 (2017)
7. Gong, Z., Zhong, P., Yu, Y., Hu, W., Li, S.: A CNN with multiscale convolution and diversified metric for hyperspectral image classification. IEEE Trans. Geosci. Remote Sens. **57**(6), 3599–3618 (2019)
8. Xia, Z., Lu, L., Qiu, T., Shim, H., Chen, X., Jeon, B.: A privacy-preserving image retrieval based on AC-coefficients and color histograms in cloud environment. Comput. Mater. Continua. **58**(1), 27–44 (2019)

9. Mei, S., Ji, J., Hou, J., Li, X., Du, Q.: Learning sensor-specific spatial-spectral features of hyperspectral images via convolutional neural networks. IEEE Trans. Geosci. Remote Sens. **55**(8), 4520–4533 (2017)

10. Chen, Y., Zhu, K., Zhu, L., He, X., Ghamisi, P., Benediktsson, J.A.: Automatic design of convolutional neural network for hyperspectral image classification. IEEE Trans. Geosci. Remote Sens. **57**(9), 7048–7066 (2019)

11. Fu, P., Xu, Q., Zhang, J., Geng, L.: A noise-resistant superpixel segmentation algorithm for hyperspectral images. CMC-Comput. Mater. Continua. **59**(2), 509–515 (2019)

12. Zhang, M., Li, W., Du, Q.: Diverse region-based CNN for hyperspectral image classification. IEEE Trans. Image Process. **27**(6), 2623–2634 (2018)

13. Aptoula, E., Ozdemir, M.C., Yanikoglu, B.: Deep learning with attribute profiles for hyperspectral image classification. IEEE Geosci. Remote Sens. Lett. **13**(12), 1970–1974 (2016)

14. Makantasis, K., Karantzalos, K., Doulamis, A., Doulamis, N.: Deep supervised learning for hyperspectral data classification through convolutional neural networks. In: 2015 IEEE International Geoscience and Remote Sensing Symposium (IGARSS), pp. 4959–4962. IEEE (2015)

15. Wang, L., Zhang, J., Liu, P., Choo, K.-K.R., Huang, F.: Spectral-spatial multi-feature-based deep learning for hyperspectral remote sensing image classification. Soft Comput. **21**(1), 213–221 (2017)

16. He, Q., Yu, S., Xu, H., Liu, J., Huang, D., Liu, G., Xu, F., Du, Y.: A weighted threshold secret sharing scheme for remote sensing images based on chinese remainder theorem. CMC-Comput. Mater. Continua. **58**(2), 349–361 (2019)

17. Wang, Q., He, X., Li, X.: Locality and structure regularized low rank representation for hyperspectral image classification. IEEE Trans. Geosci. Remote Sens. **57**(2), 911–923 (2018)

18. Zhong, Z., Li, J., Luo, Z., Chapman, M.: Spectral-spatial residual network for hyperspectral image classification: a 3-D deep learning framework. IEEE Trans. Geosci. Remote Sens. **56**(2), 847–858 (2017)

19. He, L., Li, J., Liu, C., Li, S.: Recent advances on spectral-spatial hyperspectral image classification: an overview and new guidelines. IEEE Trans. Geosci. Remote Sens. **56**(3), 1579–1597 (2017)

20. Jiao, L., Liang, M., Chen, H., Yang, S., Liu, H., Cao, X.: Deep fully convolutional network-based spatial distribution prediction for hyperspectral image classification. IEEE Trans. Geosci. Remote Sens. **55**(10), 5585–5599 (2017)

21. Liu, T., Gu, Y., Jia, X., Benediktsson, J.A., Chanussot, J.: Class-specific sparse multiple kernel learning for spectral-spatial hyperspectral image classification. IEEE Trans. Geosci. Remote Sens. **54**(12), 7351–7365 (2016)

22. Gu, Y., Chanussot, J., Jia, X., Benediktsson, J.A.: Multiple kernel learning for hyperspectral image classification: a review. IEEE Trans. Geosci. Remote Sens. **55**(11), 6547–6565 (2017)

Malware Classifications Based on Static-Dynamic Features and Factorization Machines

Haixing Long[1(✉)], Zhangbin Li[1], and F. Jiang[2]

[1] Hunan University of Science and Technology, Xiangtan 411201, China
longhaixing@mail.hnust.edu.cn, lzb_xt@126.com
[2] Deakin University, Melbourne, Australia
Frank.Jiang@deakin.edu.au

Abstract. The malware uses morphological and polymorphic methods to evade detection, traditional malware recognition methods have gradually failed to cope with large and variable malware. To overcome drawbacks of static or dynamic analysis techniques, we merge the static and dynamic features as a new feature vector and form a feature matrix. In order to handle the effects of feature interactions we build a model for the interaction between tow feature vector in an efficient and effective manner, and apply Factorization Machine (FM) as the final classifier for malware classification because it can handle the feature sparsity effectively. The experimental results show that the method has a high accuracy for malware classification and a low false negative rate for malicious and benign dataset.

Keywords: Malware · Static analysis · Dynamic analysis · Factorization machines · Classification

1 Introduction

With the rapid development of the Internet, information software has an increasingly greater impact on people's lives and work. As the interests drive more and more malware, more and more hidden threats to normal software business, systems and networks Security issues are becoming increasingly important, and the detection and classification of malware is becoming more and more challenging. The malwares are continuously growing in volume (growing threat landscape), variety (innovative malicious methods) and velocity (fluidity of threats) [1], and the new generation cyber threats/attacks are becoming more targeted, persistent and unknown. According to recent reports by AV-TEST [2], approximately 112 million new pieces of malware are reported for the period from January 2019 to October 2019. The large number of malware makes the cost of sample research and malware detection higher, and the accuracy of malware classification is reduced. Research malware classification techniques can help the analysts to understand the risks and intensions associated with a malicious code sample. The insight so obtained can be used to react to new trends in malware development or take preventive measures to cope with the threats coming in future.

© Springer Nature Singapore Pte Ltd. 2020
X. Sun et al. (Eds.): ICAIS 2020, CCIS 1254, pp. 246–257, 2020.
https://doi.org/10.1007/978-981-15-8101-4_23

Malware analysis methods can usually be done in a static or dynamic way. Static analysis relies on analyzing static program source code or PE file to determine malicious, usually by extracting the static features of the software program for comparison. The advantages of static analysis are fast analysis speed and large processing capacity. Tian [3] and Islam [4] extracts printable strings information from the binary files of the malware. The problem with static analysis methods is that it is difficult to deal with obfuscation technology of malicious samples. Obfuscation technology will obscure and hide malicious codes, making it difficult to extract effective static features in the obfuscation code as expected. Dynamic analysis is to run the program in a controlled environment to monitor and analyze the dynamic behavior of samples. Dynamic behavior is typically analyzed using methods that monitor the API call. Galal [5] extracted the API sequence according to the function data dependency, saved it into the behavior space according to different action meanings and trained the classifier. Monitoring network traffic is also an effective means of dynamic detection, There are also many researches on network traffic detection. Liu [6] and Wang [7] Prevent malicious attacks by detecting abnormal traffic. Tan [8] proposed the self-organizing feature map neural network based on K-means clustering (KSOM) algorithms to improve the efficiency of network intrusion detection. Dynamic analysis solves the problem of malware paking and obfuscation to some extent, but it is obviously quite time consuming and resource consuming, and many malware behaviors are triggered only under certain conditions, such as specific time or operation, which makes it difficult to detect running malware in a simulated environment.

With the development of malware anti-detection technology, the defects of a single analytical method are obvious, and a lot of hybrid analysis methods combining static and dynamic have been proposed. Islam [9] combine static string feature vectors with dynamic API names and parameter feature vectors as integrated feature vectors for analysis. Shijo [10] also used printable strings information as static feature, and dynamic feature use N-grams to extract API call sequences. Although both static and dynamic analysis are used in both the above research, in essence, various features were considered independently, and then weights were allocated in the algorithm, without taking into account the combination of interaction between features.

To overcome drawbacks of static or dynamic analysis techniques, we proposed a classification method combining static and dynamic analysis. Firstly, we introduces the significance of classification of malware, the analysis of previous achievements and defects, as well as the contribution of this study, then presents the construction of classification model, analyses the static feature extraction and dynamic feature extraction of malicious software samples, as well as the combination of dynamic and static features, constructs the feature interactions model of double feature vectors and the corresponding factor decomposition machine, and finally carries out simulation experiments with data sets and compares the results.

2 Model Overview

Our malware classification model consists of three parts: Static analysis, Dynamic analysis, and Classification – all shown below in Fig. 1. By the Sect. 3 and Sect. 4, we will have detailed introduction for each part. Static analysis part is done by extraction the Printable Strings Information (PSI) features. Dynamic analysis part uses N-grams to extract the system-call substring as a dynamic feature. In the training classification part, FM can only deal with binary classification. In order to handle multi-classification tasks, it trains a classifier by using two kinds of samples one by one, trains multiple factorization machines, and finally establishes an integrated classifier by voting.

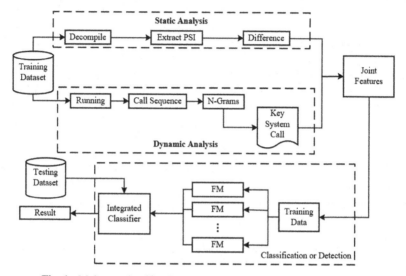

Fig. 1. Malware classification model based on factorization machine

3   Sample Processing and Features Extraction

3.1   Printable Strings Information

For any executable file, whether malicious or benign, its binary form contains a large amount of printable string information (PSI), which is a series of continuous sequences that can be represented by strings. For example, 'user32.dll', 'LoadLibraryA', appear as a continuous ASCII binary combination in a binary file, and generally end with '\0' (represented as '00000000' in binary form). According to the method of Tian [3], use the built-in strings extraction program in IDA Pro software to perform PSI extraction on the executable file, and specify an ASCII continuous string with a minimum length of 3. End. Strings smaller than 3 bytes are usually very common non-malicious strings. Ignoring them is more convenient for quick calculations. We extract the PSI according to the IDA Python program module of IDA Pro, and sort them statistically according to the frequency of PSI occurrence, thereby establishing a global list of malicious sample PSI.

After the global list of PSI features of the malware is obtained, the binary feature vector of the sample can be obtained by comparing the PSI in the global list with the

PSI appearing in each sample. The length of the feature vector is consistent with the length of the global list. The feature vector is represented as whether the PSI in the global list appears in the sample and recorded as 1 or 0. For example, Table 1 shows the PSI extracted from the three samples, and Table 2 shows the feature vector of the three samples.

Table 1. List of PSI extracted from Samples

	PSI
Sample A	'explorer.exe', 'urlmon.dll'
Sample B	'explorer.exe', 'user32.dll', 'LoadLibraryA'
Sample C	'user32.dll', 'ntdll.dll'

Table 2. Static feature vector

	'explorer.exe'	'user32.dll'	'urlmon.dll'	'LoadLibraryA'	'ntdll.dll'
Sample A	1	0	1	0	0
Sample B	1	1	0	1	0
Sample C	0	1	0	0	1

3.2 Static Features Selection

Because of the widely used of code obfuscation techniques in malware, many obfuscation characters are inserted into the executable to confuse the classifier, resulting in an increase in the length of the PSI global list. Therefore, PSI features need to be extracted to remove the irrelevant redundant PSI features. We first compare the PSI list of malware in each category with the PSI list of benign software, removing the PSI that also appears in benign software. We then ranked the PSI in each class by frequency, and chose the PSI at the top of the list to denote the features of the malware in that category. In Sect. 5, we selected the first 1000 dimensions as the representative PSI of each category through experimental comparison.

3.3 Dynamic Features Extraction

Programs in the Windows user mode implement kernel mode functions by calling the Native API, and the Native API in Windows are packaging in ntdll.dll. Through the monitoring of ntdll.dll, you can get the Native API call record of the system kernel during the running of the user programs. We use the NtTrace tool to monitor the system calls in ntdll.dll, obtain the call records generated when the program runs, and extract the API name to save as API call sequence. Malicious behavior usually needs to be done by a set of system call API sequences, so it is not possible to use a single API to determine whether a behavior is malicious. We extract the call fragment of the sample call according to the N-grams as the behavioral characteristics of the program.

The basic idea of n-grams is to slide the contents of the text into a window with words size N, forming a sequence of word fragments of length N. Think of the API as a word, n-grams as per the API in the sequence of malware calls. We demonstrate the n-grams handling of API call records in Fig. 2, so that the resulting call fragments with API sequence are likely to be API call sequences of some malicious behavior. Then, all gram call fragments are saved into a global list, and the malicious behavior of the program is determined by checking whether the behavior of a call sequence appears in the sample. Each sample is compared with the global list to check which gram call fragments have occurred. If any, the corresponding position is denoted by 1; otherwise, it is denoted by 0, as shown in Table 3.

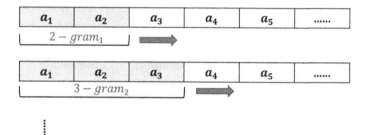

Fig. 2. API call sequence N-grams feature extraction process

Table 3. Dynamic feature vector (3-grams)

	$gram_1$	$gram_2$	...	$gram_k$
Sample A	1	0	...	0
Sample B	0	1	...	1
Sample C	1	1	...	0

3.4 Dynamic Features Selection

When N-grams are used to extract API fragments as dynamic features, the diversity of API combination will result in a large increase of feature dimensions, and there are also a lot of redundant and irrelevant API fragments, so the API fragments that are relatively important among them need to be extracted. Jang [12] based on previous researches on malicious behavior, developed an API system call dictionary that needs to be called when relevant malicious behaviors are carried out according to the behavioral characteristics of various types of malware. According to this dictionary, we extract the API fragments that contain the API system calls in the dictionary, so as to capture the before-and-after calls of key calls, examine the behavior operation call fragments related to these APIs, and remove the influence of irrelevant calls on the inferred program behavior.

3.5 Feature Joint

After screening the static PSI features, we selected the first 1000 dimensional features as the final static features according to the feature list of each category. The specific reasons are explained in part 5. In part 5, we also compared the classification performance under different N-grams and selected 3-grams as the final dynamic feature, with a dimension of 33962. After obtaining the static and dynamic features, we joint the static feature vectors and the dynamic feature vectors into the combined feature vectors. The combined feature vectors are also binary coded vectors. The combined feature vectors after joint are shown in Table 4. The j + k dimension joint feature is obtained after the joint of j-dimensional PSI static feature and k-dimensional n-grams dynamic feature.

Table 4. Joint feature vectors

	PSI_1	PSI_2	...	PSI_n	$3\text{-}gram_1$	...	$3\text{-}gram_n$
Sample A	1	1	...	0	1	...	1
Sample B	1	0	...	0	0	...	0
Sample C	0	0	...	1	1	...	1

4 Factorization Machines

Factorization Machine (FM) can be regarded as an improvement of linear regression or two-dimensional multinomial SVM. In machine learning, prediction is the estimate of a function: $y : \mathbb{R}^n \rightarrow T$. This function maps the n-length feature vector $x \in \mathbb{R}^n$ to a target domain T. In traditional linear regression or two-dimensional multinomial SVM, the general functions used are:

$$y(x) = w_0 + \sum_{i=1}^{n} w_i x_i + \sum_{i=1}^{n} \sum_{j=i+1}^{n} \langle V_i, V_j \rangle x_i x_j \tag{1}$$

Where w_0 and $w_i(i = 1, 2, \ldots, n)$ is the trainable parameters. But the first-order function does not take into account the feature $x_i(i = 1, 2, \ldots, n)$, only a single feature is considered separately. Therefore, when considering the relationship between features, the second-order function can be written as:

$$y(x) = w_0 + \sum_{i=1}^{n} w_i x_i + \sum_{i=1}^{n} \sum_{j=i+1}^{n} w_{ij} x_i x_j \tag{2}$$

Where w_{ij} represents the weight of the combination of x_i and x_j, so that the interaction between the two features can be taken into account. However, in this paper, due to the sparsity of features, there will be a large number of cross-terms $x_i x_j = 0$, so it is impossible to train and learn the weight parameter w_{ij}, thus seriously affecting the accuracy and stability of classification.

FM introduces the method of matrix factorization, and decomposes the matrix of cross-item parameter w_{ij}. FM introduces a secondary vector $V_i = (v_{i,1}, v_{i,2}, \ldots, v_{i,k})$ for each feature x_i, and estimates the w_{ij} using the dot product of the vector $\langle V_i, V_j \rangle$:

$$y(x) = w_0 + \sum_{i=1}^{n} w_i x_i + \sum_{i=1}^{n} \sum_{j=i+1}^{n} \langle V_i, V_j \rangle x_i x_j \qquad (3)$$

Where V_i denotes the implicit vector of the i-th feature, and $\langle \cdot, \cdot \rangle$ denotes the dot product of two vectors of k length:

$$\langle V_i, V_j \rangle = \sum_{f=1}^{k} v_{i,f} \cdot v_{j,f} \qquad (4)$$

Where the length k is hyperparameter, and the size of k defines the dimension of the matrix factorization.

Because of the need for classification task, the output $\hat{y}$ using Sigmoid function $\sigma(x)$:

$$\sigma(x) = \frac{1}{1 + e^{-x}} \qquad (5)$$

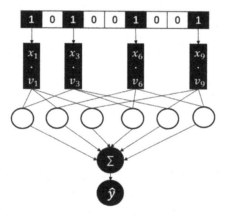

Fig. 3. The architecture of FM model

As shown in Fig. 3, the feature vector of sample A uses FM when each feature with a value of 1 learns a vector v_i, the hollow circle indicates the vector dot product operation, and the result of summation requires the Sigmoid transformation to obtain the second classification result.

5 Experiment

5.1 Data Set and Environment

The dataset [17] are from VirusShare [15] and MalwareBlackList [16]. As shown in the Table 5, the dataset contains 3,615 samples of different kinds of malware, 70% of which are randomly selected from the dataset as the training set and the remaining 30% as the testset. In order to test the performance of our model in detecting malware, another 153 installed benign software were selected for testing. Specific experimental methods and platforms are as follows:

(a) In the process of dynamic features, we used Vmware ESXi software to build the virtual environment. The experimental system was 32-bit Windows 7 Professional with 4G memory. The system call was captured using NtTrace (retrieved from http://www.how zatt.demon.co.uk/NtTrace/) combined with a python script, and each malicious sample was run on the system for 30 s in order to catch enough malicious behavior.
(b) Static features: IDA Pro 7.0 was used to decompile the malicious samples, and IDA Pro's IDAPython plug-in was used to write scripts to batch the samples.
(c) The experiments were implemented using Python 3.6 and were performed on a personal computer with a CPU of i5-6400 with 8G memory. The division of the training set and the baseline machine learning algorithm are completed using Sklearn, and FM is implemented using libFM.

Table 5. Tagged malware dataset

Class	Family	Quantity
Adware	FakeInstaller	435
	ScreenSaver	1211
	SideTab	174
Trojan	Llac	352
	Pakes	176
	Regrun	214
Worm	Mydoom	646
	Mytob	358
	Zwr	49

5.2 Evaluation

For the supervisory learning classification algorithm, the evaluation indicators used in this paper are accuracy rate (ACC), false positive rate (FPR), false negative rate (FNR), ROC curve and DET curve. They can all be described using these indicators: True Positive (TP), False Positive (FP), True Negative (TN), False Negative (FN):

- **ACC:** (TP-TN)/ (TP-FN-TN-FP)
- **FPR:** FP/(FP-TN)
- **FNR:** FN/ (FN-TN)
- **AUC:** Area enclosed by the coordinate axis under the ROC curve.

5.3 Experiments and Results

To evaluate the effectiveness of the FM method, several baseline machine learning methods were selected for comparison, such as **Support Vector Machine (SVM)**, **Random Forest (RF)** and the three probability models of **Naïve Bayesian (NB)**.

Effect of Parameters in Classification. In order to select the appropriate number of strings and the size of N in N-Grams, we respectively compare the classification effects of different number of strings and different size of N. As shown in Fig. 4, the accuracy of the FM is better than SVM when the number of PSI is greater than 500, reaching a maximum of 0.9208, which also exceeds other classification methods. We finally chose to use 1000-dimensional static features for feature combination to achieve the highest accuracy in each method.

Figure 5 shows the influence of different sizes of N in N-grams on classification in the selection of dynamic features. It can be seen that FM, SVM, RF and NB based on gaussian kernel all show high classification ACC after 3-grams, and FM, SVM and RF also perform well in 2-grams. In the case that the difference is several times of the feature dimension and the classification accuracy is similar, we choose to use the 3-grams with the final feature dimension of 48464 as the dynamic feature for the subsequent feature combination.

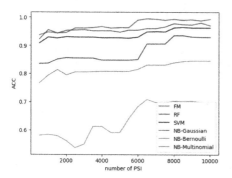
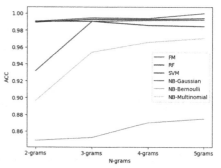

Fig. 4. ACC of different strings number   **Fig. 5.** ACC of different N in N-grams

Comparing Baseline Methods in Classification. After selecting the appropriate parameters, the static features and dynamic features are combined into joint features. We evaluated the effect of FM in the experiment, as shown the Table 6, by comparing the use of static features, dynamic features and joint features of ACC, it can be seen that the ACC of most classifiers is improved after the features are combined. In different features, FM achieved the highest classification ACC, in addition, the ACC of SVM and RF was very close to FM.

Effect of Parameters in Detection. In malware detection experiments, in order to accurately compare the performance of each classifier with different parameters, FPR and FNR are often used to evaluate the detection effect, because compared with the ACC of classification, it is more important not to miss malware and misreport benign software as malware. The lower the FPR and FNR are, the better the classifier is.

Table 6. The classification ACC of malware

	Static	Dynamic	Combined
SVM	0.9132	0.9941	0.9964
RF	0.9016	0.9929	0.9917
NB-Gaussian	0.8669	0.9911	0.9929
NB-Bernoulli	0.631	0.8528	0.864
NB-Multinomial	0.8692	0.954	0.9723
FM	0.9208	0.9947	1

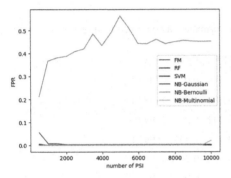

Fig. 6. FPR for different numbers of PSI

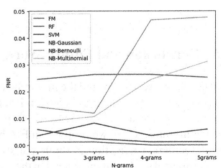

Fig. 7. FNR for different numbers of PSI

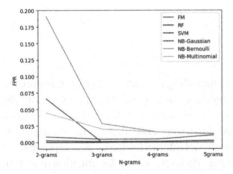

Fig. 8. FPR for different N in N-grams

Fig. 9. FNR for different N in N-grams

In the detection experiment, the adjustment and classification of parameters are the same. As shown in Fig. 6, in the case of static features, except for the NB method of Bernoulli model, the classification performance of all methods is very accurate and stable, with FPR value keeping below 0.06. In the FNR report, shown in Fig. 7, the FNR rate of each method is stable below 0.0015. Therefore considering sufficient training features and training time, we use 3000 quantity of PSI features for feature joint.

In dynamic features, as shown in Fig. 8 and Fig. 9, the three model of NB have relatively poor FPR performance under 2-grams. In FNR, the performance of each classifier is relatively stable, all of which are below 0.05, while the FNR values of SVM, RF and FM all remain below 0.01, showing very excellent performance without too much fluctuation. Therefore, 3-grams in both FPR and FNR were selected for feature joint.

Comparing Baseline Methods in Detection. After combining static and dynamic features, we evaluated the FPR, FNR, and AUC scores of the FM method and compared them with other baseline methods. Table 7 shows the comparison of FPR and FNR of various classifiers. In the final joint vector, FM achieved a minimum value of 0.0 in both FPR and FNR, and compared with the use of static and dynamic features, FM performed better after the joint features.

Table 7. Malware detection performance in combined features

	FPR	FNR	AUC
SVM	0.04	0.0	0.9833
RF	0.004	0.001	0.9870
NB-Gaussian	0.002	0.0	0.9750
NB-Bernoulli	0.0	0.447	0.9974
NB-Multinomial	0.0	0.29	0.9772
FM	0.0	0.0	1.0

6 Conclusion and Future Work

In this paper, we discovered the importance of including interactions between features to detect patterns of malicious behavior. Printable string information is extracted from the static binary file, and the behavior API fragment is extracted from the dynamic call record using n-grams. Then, we propose an FM-based malware classification model to handle both vector representation and high sparsity of model interaction items. A comprehensive experimental study was conducted in the malware data set and the classification of benign software to show the effectiveness of our system in the task of malware classification and malware family identification. Experiments show that the FM-based classifier achieves the highest accuracy and AUC in the classification of malware, surpassing other common machine learning classifiers, indicating that the cross learning among features makes the judgment of malicious program behavior more accurate.

We use FM to learn PSI features of malware samples and malicious behavior API fragments to classify malware. Although the classification results show very high performance, the data set used in the training and learning stage determines the classification results to some extent. That said, some data set collection efforts are needed in the face of the latest malware.

Acknowledgments. This work is supported by Natural Science Foundation of China (NSFC), under grant number 61300220 and 61370227, and by Natural Science Foundation of Hunan Province of China, under grant number 2017JJ2100.

References

1. Addressing big data security challenges: the right tools for smart protection (2012). http://www.trendmicro.com/cloud-content/us/pdfs/business/white-papers/wp_addressing-big-data-security-challenges.pdf
2. AV-TEST: The independent IT-security institute (2019). https://www.av-test.org/en/statistics/malware/
3. Tian, R., Batten, L., Islam, R., Versteeg, S.: An automated classification system based on the strings of trojan and virus families. In: 4th International Conference on Malicious and Unwanted Software (MALWARE), pp. 23–30. IEEE (2009)
4. Islam, R., Tian, R., Batten, L., Versteeg, S.: Classification of malware based on string and function feature selection. In: Second Cybercrime and Trustworthy Computing Workshop, pp. 9–17. IEEE (2010)
5. Galal, H.S., Mahdy, Y.B., Atiea, M.A.: Behavior-based features model for malware detection. J. Comput. Virol. Hacking Tech. **12**(2), 59–67 (2015). https://doi.org/10.1007/s11416-015-0244-0
6. Liu, J., Zeng, Y., Shi, J., Yang, Y., Wang, R., He, L.: MalDetect: a structure of encrypted malware traffic detection. Comput. Mater. Continua. **60**(2), 721–739 (2019)
7. Wang, Y., et al.: YATA: yet another proposal for traffic analysis and anomaly detection. Comput. Mater. Continua. **60**(3), 1171–1187 (2019)
8. Tan, L., Li, C., Xia, J., Cao, J.: Application of self-organizing feature map neural network based on K-means clustering in network intrusion detection. Comput. Mater. Continua **61**(1), 275–288 (2019)
9. Islam, R., Tian, R., Batten, L.M., Versteeg, S.: Classification of malware based on integrated static and dynamic features. J. Netw. Comput. Appl. **36**(2), 646–656 (2013)
10. Shijo, P.V., Salim, A.: Integrated static and dynamic analysis for malware detection. Procedia Comput. Sci. **46**, 804–811 (2015)
11. Juan, Y., Zhuang, Y., Chin, W.-S., Lin, C.-J.: Field-aware factorization machines for CTR prediction. In: Proceedings of the 10th ACM Conference on Recommender Systems, pp. 43–50. ACM (2016)
12. Jang, J.W., Woo, J., Mohaisen, A., Yun, J., Kim, H.K.: Mal-netminer: malware classification approach based on social network analysis of system call graph. Math. Prob. Eng. (2015)
13. Rendle, S.: Factorization machines. In: IEEE International Conference on Data Mining, pp. 995–1000, IEEE (2010)
14. Rendle, S.: Factorization machines with libfm. ACM Trans. Intell. Syst. Technol. (TIST). **3**(3), 1–22 (2012)
15. VirusShare. https://virusshare.com/
16. MalwareBlackList. http://malwareblacklist.com/
17. Hacking and Countermeasure Research Lab. http://ocslab.hksecurity.net/mal_netminer/download-malnet-miner/

A Review of Human Face Detection in Complex Environment

Long Chen[1], Yuling Liu[1(✉)], and Guojiang Xin[2]

[1] College of Computer Science and Electronic Engineering, Hunan University,
Changsha 410082, China
yuling_liu@126.com
[2] School of Informatics, Hunan University of Chinese Medicine, Changsha 410208, China

Abstract. Facial recognition technology has always been a challenging field in computer vision and pattern recognition. At present, facial recognition technology has been widely used in daily life. Much research has been done on facial recognition systems. However, we still need to continuously enhance and improve the facial recognition system in practical applications such as insufficient lighting and incomplete facial images. The main purpose of this article is to introduce the latest advances in face detection methods based on complex backgrounds, including feature-based, knowledge-based and appearance-based method.

Keywords: Face detection · Skin color segmentation · LBP algorithm · Adaboost algorithm

1 Introduction

Face image contains rich information, from which we can estimate identity, age, gender, race and etc. It is obvious to say that face recognition is superior to any other biometric measurements. For example, obtaining human face image is non-intrusive in nature. It is easily available and most importantly, facial images play an important role in our social interactions [1]. In the past decade, the face recognition had developed rapidly in many fields [2]. With the rapid development of HMI (human-machine interface) devices and social platforms, automatic face detection and face attribute recognition algorithms become more and more complete [3]. The research on face recognition began in the 1960s and has been greatly developed and improved in the past few decades, especially in recent years. Face recognition actually includes a series of related technologies for constructing a face recognition system, such as face image acquisition, face location, face recognition preprocessing, identity confirmation, identity search and etc. [4–6]. Face recognition plays a vital role in user authentication, which is essential for many user-based systems [7]. Face recognition systems face various types of face spoofing attacks, such as print attacks, replay attacks, and 3D mask attacks [8]. Due to the diversity of facial expressions, poses, and lighting, face detection has been a challenging field in computer vision and pattern recognition [9, 10]. In addition, face and facial expression recognition are very

© Springer Nature Singapore Pte Ltd. 2020
X. Sun et al. (Eds.): ICAIS 2020, CCIS 1254, pp. 258–266, 2020.
https://doi.org/10.1007/978-981-15-8101-4_24

essential in many areas, such as access management, human-computer communication, production control, e-learning, fatigue driving recognition and emotional robot [11].

Although face recognition technology has achieved great success, it is still challenging to recognize human face in unconstrained environments [12]. In order to successfully recognize faces, we need to perform three steps: face detection, face feature extraction, and face recognition [11, 13]. The purpose of this article is to summarize the previous literature on methods for face detection based on complex backgrounds.

2 Related Work

In 2001, Paul Viola and Michael Jones proposed a face detection method based on the AdaBoost algorithm, which can effectively detect faces in time. However, when the background of the image is very complicated, the false detection rate of this method is particularly high. Since 2006, the exploding deep learning explosion has brought a strong boost to the research of target detection. The general object detection and the detection tasks of various specific types of targets have been developed by leaps and bounds [14]. At the end of 2013, deep learning set fire to the target detection task. This fire is R-CNN, where R corresponds to Region, which means that CNN takes image regions as input. This work eventually developed into a series, which also inspired and derived a lot of follow-up work. Greatly promoted the development of the field of computer vision [15, 16].

Early face detection algorithms were performed on the assumption that a positive face had been obtained under normal lighting conditions. However, with the development of actual system requirements, the research under this assumption can no longer meet the needs. First, human faces have different face shapes, skin tones, and expressions. Furthermore, glasses, hair, jewelry and so on can cause the face to be blocked. Different imaging angles and conditions will also have a great impact on face detection. Face detection based on these influencing factors is called face detection under complex conditions.

Next section will introduce several common face detection methods based on complex conditions and compare their performance.

3 Face Detection Methods in Complex Environment

Generally, face detection is divided into four categories including feature-based, knowledge-based, template-based and appearance-based methods [19]. However, template-based methods require some assumptions to be made in advance. For example, the face must be viewed from the front without obstructions. This feature makes template-based method unsuitable for face detection under complex conditions. Therefore, we will detail the remaining methods that can implement face detection in complex backgrounds.

3.1 Feature-Based Methods

Faces have many features that can be distinguished from faces and many other objects. This method depends on the mining of facial features that have not undergone any changes in the image (such as occlusion, lighting, pose, etc.). There are some features that can be used to detect face(s) including skin colour, nose, ears, eyes, mouth, and etc. Furthermore, some studies have proved that colour of skin is an excellent feature for detecting faces among other objects. Due to different people have different skin colour and it is clearer when the race of people is also a metric of evaluation. However, the performance of skin segmentation is often affected by lighting conditions. In order to eliminate this adverse effect, it is necessary to compensate the illuminance of the image before using the skin segmentation algorithm. A skin detector usually converts a given pixel into an appropriate color space and then uses a skin classifier to mark whether the pixel is a skin pixel or a non-skin pixel. The skin testing process can be divided into two phases: the training phase and the testing phase. Training the skin detector involves three basic steps [20]:

Step 1: A database of skin plaques collected from different images. Such databases often contain patches of skin color from different populations under different lighting conditions.
Step 2: Choose the suitable color space.
Step 3: Learn the parameters of the skin classifier. Set a reasonable threshold for skin color segmentation.

The color space is converted from RGB to YCgCr after illumination compensation, so we can divide the image into skin and non-skin areas in this space. Threshold segmentation is the simplest method and has better computational performance than Gaussian skin color models. We treat pixels as skins if the following conditions are met:

$$\begin{cases} Y > 80 \\ 100 < Cg < 130 \\ 135 < Cr < 175 \end{cases} \tag{1}$$

The result of the threshold segmentation is a binary image, where white represents the skin area and black represents the non-skin area. Then we use a median filter to eliminate the noise. The median filter eliminates noise and reduces edge attenuation. The skin color segmentation effect is more obvious and effective after the light compensation.

One of the challenges for feature extraction methods is feature restoration. This can be happened when the algorithm attempts to retrieve features that are invisible due to large variations, for example, head pose when we are matching a profile image with a frontal image. Compared with other methods, feature-based methods have some advantages. Such as rotation independence, proportional independence and their execution time are so fast. Feature based methods contains facial features, skin color, texture, and multiple features. In this category of face detection methods, skin color segmentation is the most widely used method.

3.2 Knowledge-Based Methods

There is another method called the knowledge-based method. In the method some simple rules are defined for detecting faces from image and the rules also can be extended to detect faces from complicated background. Rules can be facial features. For example: two ears, a nose, a mouth and other facial features. First extract facial features in the input image according to the defined rules. Face candidates are then identified. It is worth noticeable that this method uses the position and distance between the selected features. The challenging problem in this approach is how to translate human knowledge into rules that can be applied to all faces with different conditions.

For decades, computer vision community has been studying facial features. Recognized facial expressions are reconstructed by RPCA (Robust Principal Component Analysis). The fiducials are detected and executed to remove facial expression features and geometric features represented using Gabor wavelets. The feature vector space is minimized by PCA (Principal Component Analysis) and LDA (Linear Discriminant Analysis) [1]. However, Gabor wavelet cannot improve the positioning accuracy. PCA enhancement technology combined with FFFT (Fast Fourier Transform of Face) is used in facial expression recognition algorithm [21]. Face recognition method based on face geometric features. The algorithm is represented by MIT's Brunelli group and Poggio group [22].

Among various knowledge-based face detection technologies, the LBP (Local Binary Mode) algorithm is a typical robust algorithm [22]. The local binary model LBP is an operator that describing the local texture features of an image. It has the advantages of simple calculation and strong separability. It can display some subtle features of the image, such as bright points, dark points, flat areas, edge points and corner points. The LBP algorithm selects a pixel, compares the gray level of the pixel with the gray level of the neighboring pixel, sets the bits of the neighboring pixels greater than the reference pixel value to 1, and sets the other bits to zero. The features generated in this way can effectively reflect the distribution characteristics of pixels and their neighboring pixels. Because it is less sensitive to changes in light intensity than the reference pixel. By selecting different neighborhood ranges and the number of different sampling points as parameters, different goals can be adapted. The following formula shows the LBP algorithm:

$$LBP_{N,R}(x_c, y_c) = \sum_{p=0}^{N-1} S(g_p + g_c) \times 2^p \tag{2}$$

$$S(x) = \begin{cases} 1, x \geq 0 \\ 0, x < 0 \end{cases} \tag{3}$$

The g_p is the center pixel, and the g_c is the neighborhood pixel. $S(x)$ is a step response function. Features extracted in this way are not sensitive to light. For the sample of the ORL face database, the resolution of the feature vector of the processed LBP image is $110 * 90$. There are many redundancies in the 9,900-dimensional feature vector and PCA to reduce redundancy in size [4]. Principal component analysis is a covariance matrix that extracts feature vectors. Since the covariance matrix feature vectors are orthogonal to each other, the redundancy is low. A feature vector with a large eigenvalue has a strong information carrying capacity. The sample points on the feature vector have the largest variance and the strongest discrimination ability. This allows smaller-sized features to carry a lot of information. The PCA is as follows.

$$Y = I \times (X - \overline{X})$$ (4)

I is the feature vector of the covariance matrix, X is the original feature vector, and Y is the feature vector after PCA. A feature vector with a larger feature value can be selected to represent the compressed image. The LBP algorithm eliminates the interference information that affects the recognition accuracy through block weighting. In addition, the reduction in feature size greatly reduces the computational cost of matching and classification.

3.3 Appearance-Based Methods

The appearance-based approach is another type of face detection method that requires the creation of a classifier by using statistical learning between huge instances. The Adaboost algorithm is a typical method based on learning, which will be described in detail in this article. The Haar-Like feature is a piece of information about the local appearance of the encoding object [23]. The images are classified according to these feature values instead of using pixels directly. Since the feature value provides information about the image, the entire image can be used for calculation [24]. The four main steps of the algorithm are as follows:

Step 1: Haar function selection. Since all faces have similar properties. For example, the eye area is darker than the nose area. These attributes are compared by using the Haar function.
Step 2: Creating an integral image. An integral image is formed by computing a rectangle adjacent to a rectangle existing at (x, y) as a single image representation.
Step 3: Adaboost training. In Adaboost learning algorithm, it is used to build the classifier to be trained. This algorithm helps to find smaller key visual features from a large number of potential features.
Step 4: Cascading classifier. The process of combining classifiers to quickly discard background windows so that more calculations can be performed on areas like faces.

Haar-Like Feature. The basic idea behind Haar-Like functions is to use machine learning. The cascade function is trained by many positive and negative images. After upgrading its classifier, it can be used to locate objects in different images (positive and negative images are those images respectively included face and faceless). In addition, the classifier uses positive and negative images to train its classifier. Therefore, the classifier can detect objects in it by extracting features in other images. The Haar eigenvalue can be calculated by the following formula:

$$Feature = \sum ie\{I, N\}wi.RecSum(x, y, w, h)$$ (5)

Where $RecSum(x, y, w, h)$ is the sum of the intensities of any given upright or rotating rectangle enclosed in the detection window x, y, w, h are used for the coordinates, dimensions and rotation of the rectangle respectively. The Haar wavelet is represented as a box classifier for extracting facial features by using integral images.

Integral Map. To calculate each feature, you need the total number of pixels under the white and black rectangles. To solve this problem, the researchers applied integral images. It simplifies the calculation of the total number of pixels. The sum of the pixels of any matrix region in the image can be obtained by a simple operation as shown in Fig. 1.

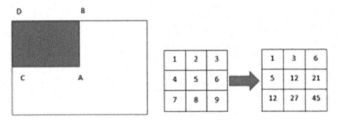

Fig. 1. Finding the sum of the shaded rectangular area

For example, assuming that A, B, C, and D are the values of the integral image at the corner of the rectangle, the sum of the original image values within the rectangle can be calculated according to the following equation. For any integer, only the size of the rectangle is added.

$$A - B - C + D = \sum (Pixels\ in\ White\ area)\ or\ \sum (Pixels\ in\ Black\ area) \quad (6)$$

In summary, the integral image is the sum of the pixel values of the input image which is mainly used to improve the speed of the operation of the cassette filter.

Adaboost Cascade Classifier. AdaBoost (Adaptive Boost) includes some weak classifiers to create multi-level efficient cascade classifiers. In other words, there are some weak classifiers and strong classifiers, where the weak classifier first checks each individual window and if they pass the detection of weak classifier, they will continue to be detected by the stronger classifier and the algorithm continues to execute this scheme until the pixel value ends. The advantage of this method is that the non-face window will be rejected early, then the execution time will be reduced and the accuracy will be improved.

3.4 Skin Segmentation and Adaboost Algorithm

In the previous chapters, we introduced several major categories of facial recognition methods, and introduced a more typical method for each major category. However, these methods have limitations. For example, skin color segmentation will produce false positives under complex background conditions, and some backgrounds will be marked as human faces. Especially in complex environments, the detection results are not satisfactory [25]. Compared with the LBP algorithm, the Adaboost algorithm has less computation and time. In the case of occlusion, the effect is good. However, in the complex background of multiple faces, the detection effect needs to be improved. Based on the above situation, some scholars have proposed a face detection method based on skin color segmentation and Adaboost algorithm [26]. Figure 2 illustrates the method that combines skin segmentation and Adaboost algorithm as face classifier.

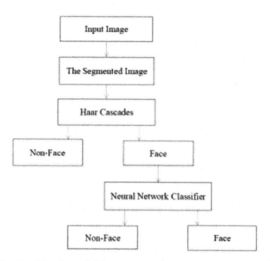

Fig. 2. Combination of skin segmentation and Adaboost algorithm

The combination of skin color segmentation and Adaboost algorithm can effectively improve the false detection rate of multi-face detection. Finally, we compare the performance of some algorithms discussed in this paper, shown in the following Table 1.

Table 1. Comparisons of different algorithms

Detection Method	Total face	Hits	False positive	HR (%)	FDR (%)
Skin color	300	278	28	92.6	9.15
LBP	300	275	18	91.6	5.80
Adaboost	300	270	19	90.0	6.25
Adaboost & skin color	300	281	16	93.6	5.36

The experimental results show that the combination of skin color segmentation and Adaboost algorithm is better than the single Adaboost algorithm and others. The HR (hit rate) increased and the FDR (false detection rate) decreased significantly.

4 Conclusions

Face detection is still an active research area now. Furthermore, over the last few years, many algorithms have made great progress, which can deal with complex situations well. However, the performance of current face detection algorithms in complex environments is not superior, and there is still a long way to go reach the effect of human eye detection. Lately, many methods and algorithms have been developed for each step of object classification on images and video sequences. Most of these methods are the fusion of multiple algorithms to improve the face hit rate. In the future, with the rapid development of the field of deep learning, face detection algorithms are expected to achieve further development. In this paper, the current face detection technologies are comprehensively reviewed, and the skin segmentation and Adaboost algorithm are combined in a complete system to effectively reduce the rate of missed detection and improve hit rate in complex backgrounds with multiple faces.

References

1. Mishra, R, Subban, R.: Face detection for video summary using enhancement-based fusion strategy under varying illumination conditions. In: 2014 International Conference on Science Engineering and Management Research (ICSEMR), pp. 1–8. IEEE (2014)
2. Akbulut, Y, Şengür, A, Budak, Ü, et al.: Deep learning based face liveness detection in videos. In: 2017 International Artificial Intelligence and Data Processing Symposium (IDAP), pp. 1–4. IEEE (2017)
3. Tathe, S.V., Narote, A.S., Narote, S.P.: Face detection and recognition in videos. In: 2016 IEEE Annual India Conference (INDICON), pp. 1–6. IEEE (2016)
4. Qu, X., Wei, T., Peng, C., et al.: A fast face recognition system based on deep learning. In: 2018 11th International Symposium on Computational Intelligence and Design (ISCID), vol. 1, pp. 289–292. IEEE (2018)
5. Xia, H., Zhang, L., Wu, X., Ke, F., Zhang, Q.: Improvement and implementation of adaboost human eye location method, vol. 38, no. 05, pp. 111–114 (2017)
6. Kang, Y., Liu, F., Yang, C., et al.: Color image steganalysis based on residuals of channel differences. Comput. Mater. Continua $59(1)$, 315–329 (2019)
7. Zhou, H., Mian, A., Wei, L., et al.: Recent advances on singlemodal and multimodal face recognition: a survey. IEEE Trans. Hum. Mach. Syst. $44(6)$, 701–716 (2014)
8. Pang, L., Ming, Y., Chao, L.: F-DR Net: face detection and recognition in one net. In: 2018 14th IEEE International Conference on Signal Processing (ICSP), pp. 332–337. IEEE (2018)
9. Cuimei, L., Zhiliang, Q., Nan, J., et al.: Human face detection algorithm via Haar cascade classifier combined with three additional classifiers. In: 2017 13th IEEE International Conference on Electronic Measurement & Instruments (ICEMI), pp. 483–487. IEEE (2017)
10. Zhang, D., Ding, D., Li, J., Liu, Q.: PCA based extracting feature using Fast Fourier transform for facial expression recognition. In: Yang, G.-C., Ao, S.-I., Huang, X., Castillo, O. (eds.) Transactions on Engineering Technologies, pp. 413–424. Springer, Dordrecht (2015). https://doi.org/10.1007/978-94-017-9588-3_31
11. Kang, Y., Liu, F., Yang, C., Luo, X., Zhang, T.: Color image steganalysis based on residuals of channel differences. Comput. Mater. Continua (CMC) $59(1)$, 315–329 (2019)
12. Yuan, C., Wu, Q., Wu, C., et al.: Expression recognition algorithm based on the relative relationship of the facial landmarks. In: 2017 10th International Congress on Image and Signal Processing, BioMedical Engineering and Informatics (CISP-BMEI), pp. 1–5. IEEE (2017)

13. Liu, C.: The development trend of evaluating face-recognition technology. In: 2014 International Conference on Mechatronics and Control (ICMC), pp. 1540–1544. IEEE (2014)
14. Dhamija, J., Choudhury, T., Kumar, P., et al.: An advancement towards efficient face recognition using live video feed: "for the future". In: 2017 3rd International Conference on Computational Intelligence and Networks (CINE), pp. 53–56. IEEE (2017)
15. Liu, Z., Xiang, B., Song, Y., Lu, H., Liu, Q.: An improved unsupervised image segmentation method based on multi-objective particle swarm optimization clustering algorithm. Comput. Mater. Continua (CMC) **58**(2), 451–461 (2019)
16. Shanmugavadivu, P., Kumar, A.: Rapid face detection and annotation with loosely face geometry. In: 2016 2nd International Conference on Contemporary Computing and Informatics (IC3I), pp. 594–597. IEEE (2016)
17. Zhang, K., Zhang, Z., Li, Z., Qiao, Y.: Joint face detection and alignment using multitask cascaded convolutional networks. IEEE Sig. Process. Lett. **23**(10), 1499–1503 (2016)
18. Huang, Q., Xiong, Y., Lin, D.: Unifying identification and context learning for person recognition. In: Proceedings of the IEEE Conference on Computer Vision and Pattern Recognition, pp. 2217–2225 (2018)
19. Sharifara, A., Rahim, M.S.M., Anisi, Y.: A general review of human face detection including a study of neural networks and haar feature-based cascade classifier in face detection. In: 2014 International Symposium on Biometrics and Security Technologies (ISBAST), pp. 73–78. IEEE (2014)
20. Gudadhe, S.R.: Selection & detection of skin and skin color background under complex background. In: 2018 International Conference on Research in Intelligent and Computing in Engineering (RICE), pp. 1–3. IEEE (2018)
21. Benedict, S.R., Kumar, J.S.: Geometric shaped facial feature extraction for face recognition. In: 2016 IEEE International Conference on Advances in Computer Applications (ICACA), pp. 275–278. IEEE (2016)
22. Gao, T., Lei, X., Hu, W.: Face recognition based on SIFT and LBP algorithm for decision level information fusion. In: 2017 13th International Conference on Natural Computation, Fuzzy Systems and Knowledge Discovery (ICNC-FSKD), pp. 2242–2246. IEEE (2017)
23. Lee, H.W., Peng, F.F., Lee, X.Y., et al.: Research on face detection under different lighting. In: 2018 IEEE International Conference on Applied System Invention (ICASI), pp. 1145–1148. IEEE (2018)
24. Patel, K., Han, H., Jain, A.K.: Secure face unlock: spoof detection on smartphones. IEEE Trans. Inf. Forensics Secur. **11**(10), 2268–2283 (2016)
25. Sannikov, K.A., Bashlikov, A.A., Druki, A.A.: Two-level algorithm of facial expressions classification on complex background. In: 2017 International Siberian Conference on Control and Communications (SIBCON), pp. 1–5. IEEE (2017)
26. Liu, H., Shen, X., Ren, H.: FDAR-Net: joint convolutional neural networks for face detection and attribute recognition. In: 2016 9th International Symposium on Computational Intelligence and Design (ISCID), vol. 2, pp. 184–187. IEEE (2016)

Protein Secondary Structure Prediction Using CNN and Random Forest

Ying Xu and Jinyong Cheng[✉]

School of Computer Science and Technology, Qilu University of Technology (Shandong Academy of Sciences), Jinan 250353, China
cjy@qlu.edu.cn

Abstract. Protein structure prediction is an important problem in computational biology. Protein secondary structure prediction is the basis of protein three-dimensional structure prediction. In order to find an efficient algorithm for protein secondary structure prediction, this paper predicted the secondary structure of protein based on the depth learning algorithm and random forest algorithm. This method improves the model structure of convolutional neural networks (CNN). The Rectified Linear Units (ReLU) activation layer is added after each convolution layer to solve the gradient disappearance problem. In order to preserve the important features of the original data to the maximum extent, the feature data is used as the input of the Random Forest (RF) classifier to classify and predict the protein secondary structure. Compared with the traditional convolution neural network method, this method improves the prediction accuracy. Experiments show that the prediction accuracy of the ensemble learner composed of convolution neural network (CNN) and Random Forest (RF) model is higher than that of the traditional convolution neural network model the 25PDB data set. Therefore, the combination of deep learning algorithm and random forest model can improve the prediction accuracy of protein secondary structure better.

Keywords: Protein secondary structure · CNN · Softmax · Random forest

1 Introduction

Protein is a molecule that dominates the life activities of living organisms. It plays an important role in the life activities of organisms. It plays an important role, such as the growth and reproduction of organisms and the process of genetics, which require the differentiation of cells help. Therefore, protein structure prediction is critical for the study of protein function and drug design. The spatial structure of the protein can be obtained experimentally, such as X-ray or nuclear magnetic resonance. However, with the rapid growth of protein sequence data, experimental methods cannot meet the actual needs. The experimental results show that the spatial structure of the protein depends on the primary structure of the protein. In fact, it is difficult to predict the spatial structure of a protein directly from a primary structure, and thus a secondary structure has been proposed. Since the prediction of protein secondary structure is the basis for obtaining

© Springer Nature Singapore Pte Ltd. 2020
X. Sun et al. (Eds.): ICAIS 2020, CCIS 1254, pp. 267–277, 2020.
https://doi.org/10.1007/978-981-15-8101-4_25

the spatial structure of proteins, the prediction method of protein secondary structure based on intelligent machine calculation has been developed rapidly [1].

Many machine learning methods and statistical methods are used for protein secondary structure prediction [3]. How to extract features from amino acid sequences and how to design classifiers is the key to improving the predictive performance of protein secondary structure. The accuracy of the method of extracting statistical features from the amino acid sequence of a protein is relatively low, usually no higher than 65% [6]. The PSIBLAST based position-specific scoring matrix (PSSM) reflects information on sequence evolution, amino acid conservation, and mutation. By combining PSSM data with machine learning, protein secondary structure predictions have made even greater breakthroughs. Support vector machine (SVM) [8], neural network (NN) [10] can improve the prediction accuracy to more than 70%. In recent years, artificial intelligence technologies including deep learning, reinforcement learning [7] and migration learning have been rapidly developed and widely used [14]. Deep learning methods have been successfully applied to image recognition and natural language processing. In recent years, deep learning methods have been used to predict the secondary structure of proteins [15, 16].

In this paper, a classification model based on the combination of CNN and random forest (RF) has greatly improved the accuracy of prediction. First, a CNN model was designed with six convolution layers, four pooling layers and four ReLU activation layers. Extract features from the Flatten layer and inputs them into a random forest (RF) classifier to obtain a probability output. The verification experiment was carried out on the 25PDB dataset, and the Q3 accuracy obtained by the CNN-RF model reached 79.39%.

2 Feature Extraction Based on Convolution Neural Network

2.1 Protein Dataset

The protein dataset used primarily in the experiments in this paper is the 25PDB dataset. The 25PDB dataset is a dataset containing 1,673 non-homologous protein samples selected by Hobohm and Sander, which includes 443 all α proteins, 443 all β proteins and 441 $\alpha+\beta$ proteins, and 346 α/β protein, and the 25PDB are selected with low sequence similarity of no more than 25%.

The classical protein secondary structure classification uses the 8-state classification, which includes: H (α-helix), E (β-strand), S (bend), C (test), B (β-bridge), G (310-helix), I (π-helix) and T (Turn). However, in actual experiments and work, in order to make protein secondary structure prediction more convenient, we classify the classic 8-state structure into three states, which are H, C, and E, respectively. The corresponding explanations are spiral, Curled and folded.

Sliding window technology is used in the sampling of protein amino acid sequences in most prediction programs. The main operation of the sliding window is to first select the appropriate size of the window according to the experimental needs and then recombine the data according to the fixed window size. Sliding window technology works well in protein secondary structure mainly because of the sequence of amino acid residues in the protein sequence. The size of the sliding window is generally chosen to be odd

[47]. When the size of the sliding window is determined, the current amino acid residue is at the center of the window, and the surrounding amino acid disability sequence is surrounded by adjacent amino acid residues. When the base is not enough to supplement the size of the sliding window, we use the zero vectors to complement it. Take the amino acid in the protein secondary structure as an example. For the input of one amino acid, there are 20 amino acid residues. When we take 13 as the sliding window to process the amino acid sequence, we can get a 260 for the first sliding. In the first swipe, we get a 260-dimensional (13×20) amino acid sequence. Figure 1 shows the PSSM matrix for amino acids processed through a sliding window.

S	L	S	S	S	E	L	T	E	L	K	Y	L
1	-5	-1	0	0	-5	-3	3	3	-4	-2	-6	-4
-1	-6	-1	0	0	-3	-5	-1	-1	-6	-1	-7	-4
3	-7	0	0	0	1	-6	-1	1	-7	-4	-7	-4
2	-7	3	2	4	6	-6	0	1	-7	-5	-5	-7
-1	-2	-2	-4	-5	-7	-4	-3	-1	-5	1	-7	-1
1	-6	-2	-1	1	0	-5	0	-1	-5	-3	-4	-4
3	-6	0	2	4	6	-5	3	1	-6	-3	-5	-5
0	-7	2	-1	-1	-4	-6	-2	-2	-7	-6	-7	-7
1	-6	-2	-2	-1	-4	-6	-1	-1	-6	-5	1	-6
-5	0	-2	-4	-5	-7	0	-4	-3	0	1	-3	-1
-5	6	-4	-4	-4	-7	5	-2	-3	6	-4	-1	6
0	-6	-1	2	0	-2	-5	0	-1	-6	7	-7	-6
-2	3	-3	-3	-3	-6	1	-2	-2	5	-2	-4	1
-5	-1	-5	-4	-5	-7	-1	-4	-5	-1	-3	9	1
-3	-7	-3	-2	-2	-5	-5	-3	-3	-6	-5	-8	-6
1	-6	3	3	2	-4	-5	2	3	-4	-4	-4	-6
-2	-5	3	1	-1	-4	1	1	-1	-4	-3	-6	-5
-5	-5	-5	-5	-5	-7	-5	-5	-5	-5	-7	-3	-5
-2	-5	-4	-4	-3	-3	-4	-4	-4	-4	-5	0	-3
-4	-1	0	-2	-4	-6	4	-2	-3	0	-3	-4	-2

Fig. 1. Process the PSSM matrix of amino acids through a sliding window.

2.2 Protein Dataset Feature Extraction Based on Convolutional Neural Network (CNN)

Recently, the network structure unique to convolutional neural network has extracted the most important features of data, which can be combined with multi-layer convolution and down-sampling, which not only retains the important features of the original data but also realizes the data dimensionality reduction processing, thus playing a good role in classifying the untrained input data. Due to these advantages, CNN is widely used in different research fields, such as image segmentation [18] semantic relationship classification [19], etc.

In this paper, deep convolutional neural networks are used to extract amino acid sequence features based on the PSSM matrix. Figure 2 shows the architecture of a convolutional neural network. Among them, the first three layers of convolution and maximum pooling are used to extract features. The fully connected layer and the Softmax layer are used to output three types of protein secondary structures.

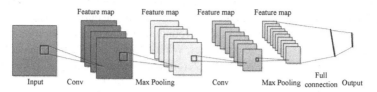

Fig. 2. The architecture of a convolutional neural network.

In the classical convolutional neural network model [25], there are convolutional layers, pooling layers, and fully connected layers, and then the output data is classified as input to the classifier. Since the full connection layer loses some feature location information, we do not use the fully connected layer, directly extract the features after the sixth convolution, and input the extracted features into a random forest (RF) classifier for classification. In order to improve the gradient dissipation of neural network, we added the ReLU activation layer after each convolutional layer. The network structure of this paper is the input layer, two convolutional kernel size of 7×7 and two convolutional kernel size of 5×5 convolutional layer, two convolutional kernel size of 3×3 convolutional layer, three pooling window of 2×2 pooling layer and Softmax layer for classification. The proposed architecture has 128 filters of 7×7 size and 1×1 steps in the first convolutional layer. The next layer is a 2×2 max pooling layer with a step size of 2. The second convolutional layer has 500 filters of size 5×5 and 1×1 steps. The next layer is a 2×2 max pooling layer with a step size of 2. The third convolutional layer has 100 filters of size 3×3 and 1×1 steps. Then, after a fully connected layer with 1 unit is a Softmax classifier.

To improve the gradient dissipation problem of the neural network, we added the ReLU activation layer after each convolutional layer. The network structure of this paper includes an input layer, a convolution layer, a pooling layer, a ReLU active layer, and a fully connected layer. The general convolutional neural network classifies and predicts the extracted features after full connection. This experiment extracts the features of the sixth layer of the convolutional layer and inputs them into the random forest classifier for training and prediction.

The Convolution Layer. The convolutional layer is a structural layer unique to convolutional neural networks for effectively extracting features of input data. It mainly uses the characteristics of local receptive fields and weight sharing on the convolutional layer. Separately, the local receptive field refers to that some data on the current convolutional layer is connected to the neurons of the local data of the previous layer, not all the neurons of the previous layer. Weight sharing means that the weight values used in the current network layer are all equal. The advantage of this is that it can reduce the use of parameters and make the convolution kernel effectively extract features.

The input data is the preprocessed protein data with the size of (13, 20). The convolution kernel of 5×5 is convoluted from the upper left corner of the data with the input size of (13, 20) in steps of 1, from left to right, from top to bottom to get the output. If not padding, the output size is $(13 - 5 + 1) \times (20 - 5 + 1)$.

For ease of programming, the model uses padding of 0 pairs of data to make the output size and input size the same. When the same convolution kernel is convoluted in motion, its weight is unchanged. Its weight is shared for the data. This feature of the convolutional neural network reduces the number of parameters and greatly improves the training speed 128 convolution kernels convolve data in the same way, and each convolution kernel automatically extracts features. In the image domain, different convolution kernels automatically extract image edge information, shading information, contours, etc. In theory, the model can automatically extract 128 features.

Assuming that the width of the convolution kernel is fw and the height is fh, the two-dimensional convolution equation is:

$$y_{n,m} = A \begin{bmatrix} x_{n,m} & x_{n+1,m} & \cdots & x_{n+fw,m} \\ x_{n\cdot m+1} & x_{n+1\cdot m+1} & \cdots & x_{n+fw,m+1} \\ \cdots & & & \\ x_{n,m+fh} & x_{n+1,m+fh} & \cdots & x_{n+fw,m+fh} \end{bmatrix} \tag{1}$$

The model uses ReLU as the activation function. The activation function is a non-linear mapping of the output of the convolution layer. The convolution neural network uses a linear model for convolution operation, such as assigning a weight to each input pixel when processing image problems. In the actual problem processing, the data we get will also have linear and indivisible data, so we need to use the activation function to deal with the nonlinear problem. Our commonly used activation functions include the sigmoid function and tanh function, as well as the now popular activation function— ReLU function. This activation function solves the problem of the disappearance of the gradient in the activation function mentioned above. The expression of the ReLU function is as follows:

$$F(x) = \max(0, x) \tag{2}$$

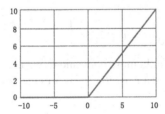

Fig. 3. Schematic diagram of ReLU function

The graph of the ReLU function is shown in Fig. 3 below. As can be seen from Fig. 3, when the input data is less than 0, the output result is 0, so the number of neurons with a value of 0 will increase, and the sparsely of the data will increase, so that it can be extracted. The more important feature of the input data reduces the amount of computation; when the input data is greater than 0, the output data exhibits growth of the function once, and the value of the gradient is 1, thus solving the problem of gradient disappearance.

At present, the ReLU activation function has become the mainstream neural network activation function. The total convolutional input and output equation is:

$$Y = relu(\sigma(WB + b)) \tag{3}$$

The Max-pooling Layer. The pooling layer is a dimensionality reduction process for extracting features extracted from the convolutional layer. It has the advantage that the dimension of the featured image can be made smaller while keeping the number of feature maps unchanged, so that the data after the convolutional layer is output can be made. At the same time, important feature information is saved, which can reduce the calculation complexity of the model and increase the calculation speed. Other pooling strategies include median and average pooling. The literature [20] has verified that the maximum pooling effect is better than other strategies.

In this study, the largest pooling layer creates a region with a pool size of 2×2. That is, the height and width (pool size) of the rectangle are both two and return the maximum value of four elements in each area. The step or span is also 2×2 in the vertical and horizontal direction of the feature map, so the merged areas do not overlap. In this model, the input data size is (13, 20), the data size obtained after one pooling is (7, 10), and the data size obtained by the last pooling is (4, 5). It can be seen that the pooling layer greatly reduces the dimension of the data. Correspondingly reduces the training parameters and improves the training speed.

The Softmax Layer. The Softmax layer uses Softmax activation to address the classification of the three classes of protein structures. In the multi-classification problem, we use Softmax regression, where $y(i)$ can take k ($k > 2$) values, and the corresponding m takes k.

For a given input x, the probability value $p = (y = j \mid x)$ is estimated for each category j. That is, the probability of its occurrence is estimated for each classification result. So, for $y = k$ ($k > 2$), the function of the regression model is as follows:

$$h_\theta(x^{(i)}) = \begin{bmatrix} p(y^{(i)} = 1 | x^{(i)}; \theta) \\ p(y^{(i)} = 2 | x^{(i)}; \theta) \\ \vdots \\ p(y^{(i)} = k | x^{(i)}; \theta) \end{bmatrix} = \frac{1}{\sum_{j=1}^{k} e^{\theta_j^T x^{(i)}}} \begin{bmatrix} \theta_1^T x^{(i)} \\ \theta_2^T x^{(i)} \\ \vdots \\ \theta_k^T x^{(i)} \end{bmatrix} \tag{4}$$

In order to make the formula more convenient, we use θ to represent all the model parameters. In Softmax regression, $\theta_1, \theta_2 \ldots \theta_k$ is arranged in rows to form a matrix θ, as shown below:

$$\theta = \begin{bmatrix} -\theta_1^T - \\ -\theta_2^T - \\ \vdots \\ -\theta_k^T - \end{bmatrix} \tag{5}$$

The loss function corresponding to Softmax regression is as follows:

$$J(\theta) = -\frac{1}{m} \left[\sum_{i=1}^{m} \sum_{j=1}^{k} 1\{y^{(i)} = j\} \log \frac{e^{\theta_j^T x^{(i)}}}{\sum_{l=1}^{k} e^{\theta_j^T x^{(i)}}} \right] \tag{6}$$

In the above formula, $1\{y^{(i)} = j\}$ represents an illustrative function. It can be deduced from the above that for a given input data x, the probability value $p = (y = j \mid x)$ estimated for each category j is as follows:

$$P(y^{(i)} = j | x^{(i)}; \theta) = \frac{e^{\theta_j^T x(i)}}{\sum_{l=1}^{k} e^{\theta_j^T x(i)}} \tag{7}$$

Random Forest Classifier. Random forest [24] is a statistical learning theory. It uses the bootstrap resampling method to extract multiple samples from the original sample, model the decision tree for each bootstrap sample, and then combine the predictions of multiple decision trees and forecast results. The specific steps are as follows:

Firstly, k self-help sample sets are generated from the original training data, and each self-help sample set is the entire training data of each classification tree.

Secondly, each self-help sample set grows into a single classification tree. At each node of the tree, m features are randomly selected from m features ($m \ll M$), and one feature is selected from this m feature for branch growth according to the principle of minimum node purity. This classification tree is fully grown to minimize the purity of each node and does not perform the usual pruning operations.

Finally, the new data is predicted based on the generated multiple tree classifiers and the classification results are determined by the number of votes of each tree classifier. A self-help sample set is generated every sampling. The remaining samples in the entire sample that are not in the self-help sample are called out-of-bag (OOB) data. The OOB data is used to predict the classification accuracy rate, and the prediction results of each time are summarized to obtain an OOB estimation of the error rate, which is used to evaluate the accuracy rate of the combined classifier.

3 Experiments and Results

3.1 Experiments

First, the corresponding PSSM matrix is generated by running the PSI-BLAST pro-gram to search the nr database. A sliding window of size 13 is slid along the protein sequence in the PSSM matrix to obtain 260-dimensional data.

The data is used as the input of the convolutional neural network, and the data is convoluted with 7×7, 5×5, 3×3 convolution kernels, and after six convolution operations, the convolutional neural network is extracted after the third convolution. As an input to the RF classifier, the extracted features are trained and predicted by RF, and the predicted results are the three states of the protein secondary structure: H, E, and C. Figure 4 shows the structure of CNN and RF classifier.

In this method, we repeatedly tested the selection of sliding windows in data processing and the selection of the size of the convolution kernel when extracting features from the convolutional neural network. When processing the PSSM matrix, we selected 9, 11, 13, 15, and 17 as the size of the sliding window, respectively, and obtained matrices with data dimensions of 180, 220, 260, 300, and 340 dimensions, respectively. Experiments show that when the sliding window size is 13, the prediction effect is the best. In the selection of the size of the convolution kernel, we use 2×2, 3×3, 4×4, and 5×5 as the size of the convolution kernel to conduct experiments. Finally, the convolutional layer

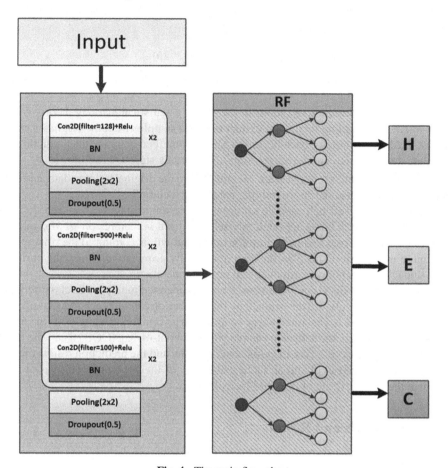

Fig. 4. The main flow chart

we set is 128 convolutional kernels of 7×7, 500 convolutional kernels of 5×5 and 100 convolutional kernels of 3×3.

After preprocessing the 25 PDB dataset, the traditional convolutional neural network and Softmax and the network structure of this paper were used to train and predict the data respectively, and the Q3 value of each set of data was obtained. Then, the average value was calculated to be the final predicted Q3 value of this method on the protein dataset.

3.2 Results

The method used in this paper to evaluate the effect of the algorithm is the Q3 method. Q3 is used for residues and is calculated by calculating the ratio of correctly predicted protein residues to the total number of residues in the secondary structure sequence of a known protein.

In this experiment, Q_H, Q_E, Q_C, Q3 [21] were used as the evaluation criteria for the prediction results. The values of Q_H, Q_E and Q_C can be obtained by the following equation:

$$Q_i = \frac{TP_i}{TP_i + FP_i} \quad i \in \{H, E, C\} \tag{8}$$

Where, TP_i represents the number of residues correctly predicted as the i state, and FP_i denotes the number of residues incorrectly predicted as the i state. Q3 could be obtained from the following equation:

$$Q_3 = \frac{TP_H + TP_E + TP_C}{T} \tag{9}$$

Where, T is the total number of residues. In order to verify the effectiveness of the method in this paper, we compared the method in this paper with some closely related protein classification methods. The comparison results are shown in Table 1.

Through experimental comparison, the average accuracy of Q3 obtained by the CNN algorithm on the test set for protein secondary structure prediction on the 25PDB dataset is 79.09%. For the three states H, E and C of the secondary structure of the protein, the prediction accuracy on the test set was 83.64%, 70.81% and 79.84%. Separately, the prediction accuracy of class E state on the test set is relatively difficult, so the prediction accuracy of state C is lower than that of the other two states, but the prediction accuracy of state C is better than that of the other two states.

Table 1. Protein prediction rate table

Method	Q_H	Q_E	Q_C	Q3
Bayes [22]	0.737	0.576	0.808	0.734
CNN + Bayes [22]	0.784	0.656	0.812	0.769
CNN	0.8364	0.7081	0.7984	0.7909
CNN-RF	0.8213	0.6864	0.8254	0.7939

From the analysis in Table 1, for the CNN-RF model in this paper, the average ac-curacy of Q3 obtained on the test set when performing protein secondary structure prediction on the 25 PDB dataset is 79.39%. For the three states H, E and C of the secondary structure of the protein, the prediction accuracy on the test set was 82.13%, 68.64% and 82.54%. The test results are higher than those of CNN + Bayes [22] structure and Bayes [22] structure. Separately, the prediction of the E-class state on the test set is more difficult, so the correct rate of prediction is lower than the other two types of states, but the prediction accuracy of state C is better than the other two states predict the correct rate.

Through experimental comparison, the prediction effect of the proposed CNN-RF method is superior to the CNN method and the other two methods. In this method, the ReLU activation layer is added to the convolutional neural network, and the features extracted by the sixth layer of convolution are directly used as the input of the RF classifier, which preserves the important original features of the data to the greatest extent, simplifying the calculation and solved the problem of gradient disappearance. Therefore, the accuracy of prediction is improved, and a better prediction effect is achieved.

4 Conclusions

As we have demonstrated, the CNN-RF method proposed in this paper adds a ReLU activation layer to the convolutional neural network. The features extracted by the sixth layer of convolution are directly used as the input of the RF classifier, which retains the important original features of the data to the greatest extent, simplifies the calculation and solves the gradient disappearance problem. The CNN-RF method can be useful for protein classification. This enables good performance to be achieved across data sets using only a small amount of labeled data.

Acknowledgments. This work is supported by National Natural Science Foundation of China (Grant No. 61375013), and Natural Science Foundation of Shandong Province (ZR2013FM020), China.

References

1. Davern, M.J., Kauffman, R.J.: Discovering potential and realizing value from information technology investments. J. Manage. Inf. Syst. **16**(4), 121–143 (2000)
2. Marlow, H., Tosches, M.A., Tomer, R.: Larval body patterning and apical organs are conserved in animal evolution. BMC Biol. **12**(1), 141–163 (2014)
3. Dao, D., Fraser, A.N., Hung, J.: Analysis and classification of large biological image sets. Bioinformatics **32**(20), 3210–3212 (2016)
4. Vorontsov, K., Potapenko, A.: Additive regularization of topic models. Mach. Learn. **103**, 303–323 (2014). https://doi.org/10.1007/s10994-014-5476-6
5. Cao, R., Bhattacharya, D., Adhikari, B.: Large-scale model quality assessment for improving protein tertiary structure prediction. Bioinformatics **31**(12), 116–123 (2015)
6. Zheng, L., Li, H., Wu, N.: Protein secondary structure prediction based on Deep Learning. DEStech Trans. Eng. Technol. Res. **12**(1), 141–163 (2017)
7. Shen, D., Wu, G., Suk, H.I.: Deep learning in medical image analysis. Annu. Rev. Biomed. Eng. **19**, 221–248 (2017)
8. Islam, M.N., Iqbal, S., Katebi, A.R.: A balanced secondary structure predictor. J. Theor. Biol. **389**, 60–71 (2016)
9. Zheng, L., Li, H., Wu, N.: Protein secondary structure prediction based on Deep Learning. DEStech Trans. Eng. Technol. Res. **865**, 303–323 (2017)
10. Tan, Y.T., Rosdi, B.A.: FPGA-based hardware accelerator for the prediction of protein secondary class via fuzzy K-nearest neighbors with Lempel-Ziv complexity based distance measure. Neurocomputing **148**, 409–419 (2015)
11. Wang, S., Peng, J., Ma, J.: Protein secondary structure prediction using deep convolutional neural fields. Sci. Rep. **6**, 18962 (2016)
12. Jiang, M., Wei, Z., Zhang, S.: Protein drug binding site prediction based on faster R-CNN. J. Mol. Graph. Model. **93**, 107454 (2019)

13. White, C., Ismail, H.D., Saigon, H.: CNN-BLPred: a convolutional neural network based predictor for β-lactamases (BL) and their classes. BMC Bioinform. **18**(16), 577 (2017)
14. Lafferty, J., McCallum, A., Pereira, F.C.: Conditional random fields: probabilistic models for segmenting and labeling sequence data **3**(2), 282–289 (2001)
15. Masetic, Z., Subasi, A.: Congestive heart failure detection using random forest classifier. Comput. Meth. Program. Biomed. **130**, 54–64 (2016)
16. Meng, R., Rice, S.G., Wang, J.: A fusion steganographic algorithm based on faster R-CNN. Comput. Mater. Continua **55**, 001–016 (2018)
17. Heinonen, J., Kipelainen, T., Martio, O.: Nonlinear Potential Theory of Degenerate Elliptic Equations, vol. 20, no. 1, pp. 75–80. Courier Dover Publications (2018)
18. Xu, J., Luo, X., Wang, G.: A deep convolutional neural network for segmenting and classifying epithelial and stromal regions in histopathological images. Neurocomputing **191**, 214–223 (2016)
19. Mursalin, M., Zhang, Y., Chen, Y.: Automated epileptic seizure detection using improved correlation-based feature selection with random forest classifier. Neurocomputing **241**, 204–214 (2017)
20. Masetic, Z., Subasi, A.: Congestive heart failure detection using random forest classifier. Comput. Meth. Programs Biomed. **130**, 54–64 (2016)
21. Pal, M.: Random forest classifier for remote sensing classification. Int. J. Remote Sens. **26**(1), 217–222 (2005)
22. Liu, Y., Chen, Y., Cheng, J.: Feature extraction of protein secondary structure using 2D convolutional neural network. In: 9th International Congress on Image and Signal Processing, BioMedical Engineering and Informatics (CISP-BMEI), pp. 1771–1775 (2016)
23. Pavey, T.G., Gilson, N.D., Gomersall, S.R.: Field evaluation of a random forest activity classifier for wrist-worn accelerometer data. J. Sci. Med. Sport **20**(1), 75–80 (2017)
24. Alabdulkarim, A., Al-Rodhaan, M., Tian, Y.: A privacy-preserving algorithm for clinical decision-support systems using random forest. Comput. Mater. Continua **58**, 585–601 (2019)
25. Xu, F., Zhang, X., Xin, Z.: Investigation on the Chinese text sentiment analysis based on convolutional neural networks in deep learning. Comput. Mater. Continua **58**, 697–709 (2019)

Classification of ECG Signals Based on LSTM and CNN

Ping Zhang, Jinyong Cheng[✉], and Yunxiang Zhao

School of Computer Science and Technology, Qilu University of Technology (Shandong Academy of Sciences), Jinan 250353, China
cjy@qlu.edu.cn

Abstract. The study on cardiovascular disease has always been a popular medical topic around the world. For the entire humanity, the study on arrhythmia has deep and significant meaning. This paper suggest a deep learning method which is based on LSTM (long short-term memory) and CNN (convolutional neural network), in order to identify ECG. Firstly, we reduce ECG signal noise and the processed ECG signal will be directly sent into the input layer of the network structure. Then, we use the network structure based on LSTM and CNN, fully extracting the features and dependency relationship in ECG signal. At last, five types tasks of ECG will be realized through the softmax classifier. Based on both under intra-patient paradigm and under inter-patient paradigm, we verified the results by using MIT-BIH arrhythmia dataset. The accuracy of the proposed algorithm is 88.38% under inter-patient paradigm and 99.08% under intra-patient paradigm. Through the comparison of several experiments, it is shown that the method proposed will have better effects with strong clinical value and practical significance by combining LSTM and CNN.

Keywords: LSTM · CNN · ECG classification

1 Introduction

In today's society, the main cause of death for most people worldwide is cardiovascular diseases, cancer and other non-communicable diseases. According to the World Health Organization report, it is estimated that by 2030, the number of deaths due to cardiovascular disease will reach 23 million. Cardiovascular disease is the first killer that poses a serious threat to human physical and mental health. Arrhythmia is one of the common diseases. Early detection of latent heart disease in the body can effectively prevent the emergence of heart disease. Electrocardiogram (ECG) is a key basis for cardiologists to judge heart disease. ECG signals have periodicity, and ECG signals are composed of P waves, QRS complexes, and T waves [1]. Compared with other medical methods, ECG has obvious advantages: fast, non-invasive, accurate and simple, and has been widely used in the detection of heart diseases [2].

The traditional ECG analysis relies on the analysis and observation of the naked eye of an expert to obtain the final result. In the process of collecting ECG signals, they are

© Springer Nature Singapore Pte Ltd. 2020
X. Sun et al. (Eds.): ICAIS 2020, CCIS 1254, pp. 278–289, 2020.
https://doi.org/10.1007/978-981-15-8101-4_26

very susceptible to different types of interference, and the ECG signals of patients at different periods are quite different. If it depends on the detection of human eyes, it may lead to misjudgment. The slow speed of manual ECG identification can easily cause delays in the patient's condition and the best time to miss treatment. The emergence of computer-based ECG automatic analysis and recognition technology solves the above problems. The ECG recognition process is divided into ECG signal pre-processing, feature extraction, and ECG signal recognition using a classifier. With the development of science and technology, pattern recognition methods are applied to ECG recognition, such as support vector machine [3], random forest [4], naive Bayes [5], and so on. The traditional method first needs to extract the information through the feature extraction method, and then send it to the classifier. In other words, if the effect of feature extraction is not good, it will eventually have a negative impact on the classification results.

Deep learning was first proposed by Hinton et al. In 2006 [6]. In recent years, deep learning has achieved remarkable results in many fields, such as speech recognition [7], image recognition [8, 9], and natural language processing [10]. At the same time, deep learning is also widely used in the recognition of ECG signals. Compared with traditional methods, deep learning methods have obvious differences. Deep learning algorithms have the skills to learn features automatically, eliminating the need for manual feature extraction of signals. Deep learning has a strong nonlinear fitting ability, which can fully mine the useful information and the correlation between ECG signals. Using deep learning can achieve good results in the classification and recognition of ECG signals.

Kiranyaz et al. [11] proposed an adaptive algorithm based on 1-D convolutional neural networks (CNNs), which combine feature extraction and classification of two main modules of ECG signal classification into a learning body. Fan et al. [12] proposed a multi-scale fusion ECG recognition method based on deep convolutional neural network (MS-CNN), which screened atrial fibrillation records in single-lead short electrocardiogram (ECG). Hannun et al. [13] designed a deep neural network (DNN) to classify 91232 records of 53549 patients into 10 kinds of arrhythmias, sinus rhythm and noise, with an accuracy of 83.7%. The accuracy of arrhythmia judgment is significantly higher than that of human cardiologists. Acharya et al. [14] designed a 9-layer deep neural network that uses data augmentation technology to solve the imbalance of ECG data and automatically recognizes five types of heartbeats in ECG signals. Oh et al. [15] proposed a structure combining convolutional neural network and long short term memory. The system has a good classification effect in dealing with variable length ECG data.

Most of the papers based on the MIT-BIH dataset divide the data set within the patient, that is, the experimental training set and the test set are from the same individual. This classification method has high accuracy, but lacks clinical application value. Under the intra-patient and inter-patient paradigms, experiments were performed using the algorithm proposed in this paper. The method proposed in this paper can guarantee the generalization ability of the algorithm to a certain extent, and has great clinical application value.

2 Related Work

2.1 Convolutional Neural Network

In recent years, Convolutional Neural Network (CNN) is one of the fastest growing networks in artificial neural networks. Convolutional neural network [16] is a deep feed-forward neural network. Its structure is composed of input layer, alternate convolution layer and pooling layer, full connection layer and output layer. Convolution layer is responsible for convolution operation and feature extraction. The most important of the convolutional layer are the two characteristics of local connection and weight sharing. The expression of the convolution process is:

$$V(i,j) = (X * W)(i,j) + b = \sum_{L-1}^{n-in} (X_L * W_L)(i,j) + b \tag{1}$$

where X is the input matrix and X_L is the L-th input matrix. W is convolution kernel matrix. b is biased. V (i, j) is the output matrix after convolution.

The pooling layer is also called down sampling, which is responsible for dimension reduction of features and data compression after convolution of the upper layer. Pooling can reduce overfitting and improve the fault tolerance of the model. The features of convolutional layer and pooling layer alternately extract input data layer by layer. Convolutional neural networks usually end with one or several fully connected layers. Figure 1 shows the structure of convolutional neural network.

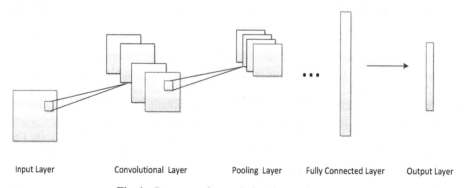

Input Layer   Convolutional Layer   Pooling Layer   Fully Connected Layer   Output Layer

Fig. 1. Structure of convolutional neural network

2.2 Long Short-Term Memory

Long Short-Term Memory (LSTM) is a special type of recurrent neural network [17]. It solves the problem of long-term dependencies of traditional RNNs. LSTM can well capture the front-to-back dependence of ECG signals, and has great advantages in the time series processing of ECG data.

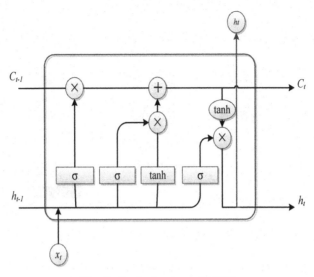

Fig. 2. Basic structure of LSTM

LSTM network is a chain loop network structure. An LSTM unit consists of an input gate, an output gate, and a forget gate. These three control doors protect and control the unit status. The basic unit of LSTM is shown in Fig. 2.

X_t represents the input of the current sequence. C_{t-1} indicates the state at the previous moment. h_{t-1} represents the output vector at the previous moment, and h_t can be obtained by operation. h_t indicates the output of the current state and updates the state to get C_t. The forgetting gate controls the degree of forgetting, that is, determines how much information of C_{t-1} can be transmitted to the current time C_t. The tanh function in the input gate creates a new cell state. The sigmoid function determines which values to update. The output gate obtains the output h_t corresponding to the current state according to the new state of C_t.

3 Methods

The network structure designed in this paper is composed of input layer, 13-layer one-dimensional convolutional layer, 7-layer pooling layer, 1-layer LSTM, 13-layer Batch Normalization, 4-layer Dense layer, and softmax classifier. The network structure designed in this paper is shown in Fig. 3. Firstly, convolution operation is carried out with convolution kernel number of 128 and convolution kernel size of 25. Use the Relu activation function after convolution. Following the convolution layer is the BN layer. Two layers of convolution and one layer of pooling. Dropout is 0.5 to avoid overfitting. Similar to the above structure, the convolution kernels are respectively 64 and 32, and the size of the convolution kernel is 16 for feature extraction on the data. Then, the data enters the LSTM layer. The above description uses convolution pooling and LSTM to extract ECG features. Finally, connect the four dense layers and complete the five classification tasks of the ECG signal through the softmax classifier.

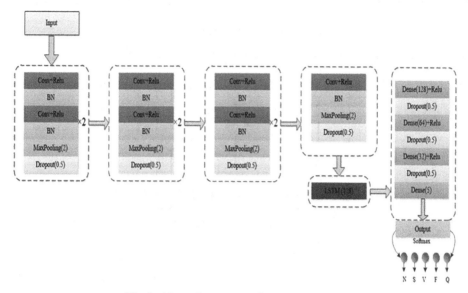

Fig. 3. Network structure of LSTM and CNN

3.1 Convolutional Layer and Pooling Layer

The main function of the convolution layer is to extract features and feature maps through the convolution kernel. The characteristics of local receptive field and weight sharing are used to effectively extract the input information. In this paper, 13 convolutional layers are constructed. After many experiments, appropriate parameters are selected. Finally, the number of convolution kernels is selected to be 128, 64, 32, and the convolution kernel sizes are 25 and 16, to perform deep feature extraction on ECG data. The main function of the pooling layer is to reduce the dimensions of features to improve model performance. The more commonly used pooling methods are the two methods of max-pooling and average-pooling. Through experiments, the max-pooling is used in the final model.

3.2 LSTM Layer

ECG data is periodic data. Feature extraction can be performed on ECG signals through convolution pooling, but it is difficult to extract the dependencies between ECG signals. The LSTM network structure can extract the time series characteristic waveform of ECG signal. Therefore, the combination of CNN and LSTM network structure can give full play to each other's advantages to the greatest extent. The data extracted from the convolution pool is sent to the LSTM layer.

3.3 Batch Normalization

Batch normalization (BN) can deal with the problem of gradient disappearance and gradient explosion well. We add Batch Normalization after the convolutional layer of each layer, which can effectively solve the problem of gradient disappearance and gradient explosion. At the same time, it can speed up training and improve performance.

3.4 ReLu Activation Function

In terms of calculation speed, ReLu activation function is fast. Just confirm that the input is greater than 0. In terms of convergence speed, the ReLu activation function is much faster than the sigmoid activation function and the tanh activation function. In the network structure, we use the ReLu activation function to replace the commonly used activation function, which improves the training speed of the network and accelerates the convergence speed of the network. The formula of the ReLu function is:

$$f(x) = \max(0, x) \tag{2}$$

3.5 Adam Optimizer

In choosing the optimizer, we chose to use the Adam optimizer. The use of the Adam optimizer can make convergence fast. Adam uses the first and second moment estimates of the gradient to dynamically adjust the learning rate of each parameter. Adam's algorithm formula is:

$$
\begin{aligned}
m_j &= \beta_1 m_{j-1} + (1 - \beta_1) g_j \\
v_j &= \beta_2 v_{j-1} + (1 - \beta_2) g_j^2 \\
\hat{m}_j &= \frac{m_j}{1 - \beta_1^j} \\
\hat{v}_j &= \frac{v_j}{1 - \beta_2^j}
\end{aligned}
\tag{3}
$$

where m_j is a first-order moment estimation of the gradient, v_j is a second-order moment estimation of the gradient. β_1 is the exponential decay rate, and the default value is 0.9. β_2 is the exponential decay rate, and the default value is 0.999. $\hat{m}_j$ is the correction for m_j, $\hat{v}_j$ is the correction for v_j.

The gradient update specification is:

$$\theta_{j+1} = \theta_j - \frac{\alpha}{\sqrt{\hat{v}_j} + \varepsilon} \hat{m}_j \tag{4}$$

3.6 Dropout

The concept of Dropout was first proposed by Hinton et al. In 2012 during the model training process, overfitting is easy to occur. The use of dropout can well prevent the occurrence of overfitting. Through multiple experiments, when the dropout is 0.5, the experimental effect is the best.

3.7 Cross Entropy Loss Function

In terms of loss function, we choose to use cross entropy loss function. The role of cross entropy is to judge the similarity between the real output and the expected output. The multi-class mathematical expression of cross entropy is:

$$L = - \sum_{c=1}^{N} y_c \log(p_c) \tag{5}$$

3.8 Softmax

The traditional binary classification problem uses a logistic regression model. Softmax is a derivative of logistic. In this paper, we choose the softmax classifier to solve the five classification tasks of ECG.

$$h_\theta(x^{(i)}) = \begin{bmatrix} p(y^{(i)} = 1|x^{(i)}; \theta) \\ p(y^{(i)} = 2|x^{(i)}; \theta) \\ \vdots \\ p(y^{(i)} = k|x^{(i)}); \theta) \end{bmatrix} = \frac{1}{\sum_{j=1}^{k} e^{\theta_j^T x^{(i)}}} \begin{bmatrix} e^{\theta_1^T x^{(i)}} \\ e^{\theta_2^T x^{(i)}} \\ \vdots \\ e^{\theta_k^T x(i)} \end{bmatrix} \tag{6}$$

In the above formula, $\theta_1, \theta_2 \ldots \theta_k$ are the parameters of the model.

4 Experiments and Results

4.1 Dataset

We use MIT-BIH database to verify and compare the classification effect of the model. The MIT-BIH database is the most commonly used dataset for ECG classification research, and it is also one of the three major ECG databases recognized internationally today. The data set contains 48 ECG data, a 2-lead ECG signal with a length of 30 min, and a sampling frequency of 360 Hz [18]. The classification of categories follows the standards set by the Association for the Advancement of Medical Instrumentation (AAMI) and is divided into five categories, as shown in Table 1.

According to the AAMI standard, the four records 102, 104, 107 and 217 are removed. According to the method proposed by De Chazal [19], 44 records are divided into two data sets DS1 and DS2, each data set contains 22 records, and the division method is shown in Table 2. This method of division divides the training set and test set from different individuals, fully considering individual differences, and has strong practical significance.

The ECG signal was sliced directly, with a segment length of 5 s and no QRS waveform detection was performed [20]. In the experiment, DS1 is the training set and DS2 is the test set. There were 27003 training data and 7942 test data. The data dimension is 1280. There are three main types of noise in ECG signals: power frequency interference, EMG interference, and baseline drift. For these three kinds of noise interference,

Table 1. Classification of categories follows the AAMI standard.

Category	Class
N	Normal beat Right and left bundle branch block beat Atrial escape beat Nodal (junctional) escape beat
S	Atrial premature beat Aberrated atrial premature beat Nodal (junctional) premature beat Supraventricular premature beat
V	Premature ventricular contraction Ventricular escape beat
F	Fusion of ventricular and normal beat
Q	Paced beat Fusion of paced and normal beat Unclassifiable beat

Table 2. Divided dataset proposed by De Chazal

Dataset	Records
DS1	101, 106, 108, 109, 112, 114, 115, 116, 118, 119, 122, 124, 201, 203, 205, 207, 208, 209, 215, 220, 223, 230
DS2	100, 103, 105, 111, 113, 117, 121, 123, 200, 202, 210, 212, 213, 214, 219, 221, 222, 228, 231, 232, 233, 234

wavelet transform can handle it well. For ECG data, the multi-resolution characteristics of wavelet transform can perform multi-scale transformation on local details, and to a large extent, the non-stationary characteristics of signals can be well processed. The formula of wavelet transform is as follows:

$$WT(a, \tau) = \frac{1}{\sqrt{a}} \int_{-\infty}^{\infty} f(t) * \psi(\frac{t - \tau}{a}) dt \tag{7}$$

where a is the scale factor, its role is to control the expansion and contraction of the wavelet function, τ is the translation amount, control the translation of the wavelet function.

In order to reduce the noise of the ECG signal, we perform wavelet removal of noise on the ECG data. We use wavelet to remove noise from ECG data. Using db6 wavelet base, the ECG data after noise reduction is obtained, as shown in Fig. 4.

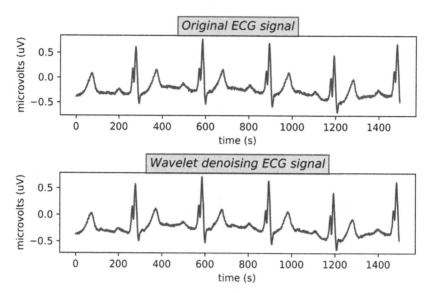

Fig. 4. Comparison of wavelet denoising effect

4.2 Results

In this paper, accuracy, sensitivity and specificity are used to evaluate the performance of the model. The formula is as follows:

$$accuracy = \frac{TP + TN}{TP + TN + FP + FN} \tag{8}$$

$$sensitivity = \frac{TP}{TP + FN} \tag{9}$$

$$specificity = \frac{TN}{TN + FP} \tag{10}$$

where TP is True Positive, FP is False Positive, TN is True Negative, FP is False Positive, and FN is False Negative.

Under intra-patient paradigm, the accuracy of classification of ECG signals using a model combining LSTM and CNN reached 99.08%. The accuracy, sensitivity, and specificity of the categories are shown in Table 3.

The accuracy, sensitivity and specificity of N category are 98.82%, 99.05% and 99.68%. The accuracy, sensitivity and specificity of V category are 98.06%, 99.51% and 99.49%. The accuracy, sensitivity and specificity of S category are 99.44%, 98.81% and 99.85%. The accuracy, sensitivity, and specificity of F category are 99.38%, 98.55%, and 99.83%. The accuracy, sensitivity, and specificity of Q category are 100%, 99.76%, and 100%.

Under inter-patient paradigm, the accuracy of classification of ECG signals using a model combining LSTM and CNN reached 88.38%. Confusion matrix is usually used to measure the accuracy of a classifier. The confusion matrix is shown in Fig. 5.

Table 3. Experimental results under intra-patient paradigm

Category	Accuracy	Sensitivity	Specificity
N	98.82%	99.05%	99.68%
V	98.06%	99.51%	99.49%
S	99.44%	98.81%	99.85%
F	99.38%	98.55%	99.83%
Q	100%	99.76%	100%

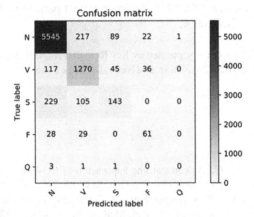

Fig. 5. Confusion matrix

Table 4. Experimental comparison results

Method	PCA+SVM	LSTM	CNN	LSTM+CNN
Accuracy	50.96%	76.73%	80.04%	88.38%

In order to evaluate the algorithm in this paper, the recognition methods based on SVM, LSTM, and CNN are implemented respectively. The experimental comparison results are shown in Table 4. Due to the large data dimensions; the SVM algorithm calculation requirements in machine learning are relatively large. We use PCA dimensionality reduction to extract features, finally reduce the dimensions to 30 dimensions, and send the data to SVM for classification. The accuracy of using the SVM classifier to classify ECG data into 5 categories is 50.96%. Before using machine learning algorithms to classify ECG data, performing dimension reduction on the data will lose some useful information and cause the results to be too low. The accuracy of using the traditional LSTM structure to classify the data into 5 categories is 76.73%. The accuracy of five classifications of ECG data using traditional CNN structure is 80.04%. Using the network structure of LSTM and CNN proposed in this paper to classify ECG data, the accuracy rate is 88.38%. Using a network structure that combines LSTM and CNN can fully extract ECG data and capture the association between signals, which is better than using CNN or LSTM alone.

5 Conclusion

In this paper, an ECG classification model based on LSTM and CNN is proposed. After denoising by wavelet transform, the data is directly sent to the input layer. Using the network structure of the phase structure of LSTM and convolutional neural network to extract features and dependencies in ECG signals, a very good result was achieved. The accuracy of the algorithm is 88.38% under inter-patient paradigm. The accuracy under intra-patient paradigm is 99.08%.

Acknowledgments. This work is supported by Key Research and Development Project of Shandong Province (2019JZZY020124), China, and Natural Science Foundation of Shandong Province (23170807), China.

References

1. Sannino, G., De Pietro, G.: A deep learning approach for ECG-based heartbeat classification for arrhythmia detection. Future Gener. Comput. Syst. **86**, 446–455 (2018)
2. Luz, E.J.S., Schwartz, W.R., Cámara-Chávez, G., et al.: ECG-based heartbeat classification for arrhythmia detection: a survey. Comput. Methods Prog. Biomed. **127**, 144–164 (2016)
3. Varatharajan, R., Manogaran, G., Priyan, M.K.: A big data classification approach using LDA with an enhanced SVM method for ECG signals in cloud computing. Multimed. Tools Appl **77**(8), 10195–10215 (2018). https://doi.org/10.1007/s11042-017-5318-1
4. Li, T., Zhou, M.: ECG classification using wavelet packet entropy and random forests. Entropy **18**(8), 285 (2016)
5. Padmavathi, S., Ramanujam, E.: Naïve Bayes classifier for ECG abnormalities using multivariate maximal time series motif. Procedia Comput. Sci. **47**, 222–228 (2015)
6. LeCun, Y., Bengio, Y., Hinton, G.: Deep learning. Nature **521**(7553), 436–444 (2015)
7. Amodei, D., Ananthanarayanan, S., Anubhai, R., et al.: Deep speech 2: end-to-end speech recognition in English and Mandarin. In: International Conference on Machine Learning, pp. 173–182 (2016)
8. Wu, H., Liu, Q., Liu, X.: A review on deep learning approaches to image classification and object segmentation. Comput. Mater. Continua **60**(2), 575–597 (2019)
9. Wu, X., Luo, C., Zhang, Q., et al.: Text detection and recognition for natural scene images using deep convolutional neural networks. Comput. Mater. Continua **61**(1), 289–300 (2019)
10. Xu, F., Zhang, X., Xin, Z., et al.: Investigation on the Chinese text sentiment analysis based on convolutional neural networks in deep learning. Comput. Mater. Continua **58**(3), 697–709 (2019)
11. Kiranyaz, S., Ince, T., Gabbouj, M.: Real-time patient-specific ECG classification by 1-D convolutional neural networks. IEEE Trans. Biomed. Eng. **63**(3), 664–675 (2015)
12. Fan, X., Yao, Q., Cai, Y., et al.: Multiscaled fusion of deep convolutional neural networks for screening atrial fibrillation from single lead short ECG recordings. IEEE J. Biomed. Health Inform. **22**(6), 1744–1753 (2018)

13. Hannun, A.Y., Rajpurkar, P., Haghpanahi, M., et al.: Cardiologist-level arrhythmia detection and classification in ambulatory electrocardiograms using a deep neural network. Nat. Med. **25**(1), 65 (2019)
14. Acharya, U.R., Oh, S.L., Hagiwara, Y., et al.: A deep convolutional neural network model to classify heartbeats. Comput. Biol. Med. **89**, 389–396 (2017)
15. Oh, S.L., Ng, E.Y.K., San Tan, R., et al.: Automated diagnosis of arrhythmia using combination of CNN and LSTM techniques with variable length heart beats. Comput. Biol. Med. **102**, 278–287 (2018)
16. LeCun, Y., Bottou, L., Bengio, Y., et al.: Gradient-based learning applied to document recognition. Proc. IEEE **86**(11), 2278–2324 (1998)
17. Gers, F.A., Schmidhuber, J., Cummins, F.: Learning to forget: continual prediction with LSTM, pp. 850–855 (1999)
18. Moody, G.B., Mark, R.G.: The impact of the MIT-BIH arrhythmia database. IEEE Eng. Med. Biol. Mag. **20**(3), 45–50 (2001)
19. De Chazal, P., O'Dwyer, M., Reilly, R.B.: Automatic classification of heartbeats using ECG morphology and heartbeat interval features. IEEE Trans. Biomed. Eng. **51**(7), 1196–1206 (2004)
20. Liang, X.: Classification of arrhythmia using combination of CNN and LSTM techniques. Southwest University (2019)

A Gaussian Mixture Background Extraction Based Video Triggering Method for License Plate Recognition

Jian Li[1,2], Aitao Lou[1,2], Bin Ma[1(✉)], Chunpeng Wang[1,2], and Ningning Li[2]

[1] Qilu University (Shandong Academy of Sciences), Jinan 250300, China
sddxmb@126.com
[2] Shandong Network Security and Information Technology Center, Jinan 250100, China

Abstract. Aiming at the problem that the camera triggering method of the existing license plate recognition system depends on the sensor, an improved Gaussian mixed background modeling and dual threshold triggering method are proposed. Firstly, the Gaussian model is established in units of rows, the parameters of the Gaussian model are updated and the pixel values are updated by the double threshold setting to separate the moving objective from the background. Then, the foreground image is denoised by Gaussian filter, and the connected domain is formed by morphological combination. The contour feature and color feature of the connected domain are used to determine whether it is a vehicle and trigger license plate location. The experiment proves that the algorithm can successfully trigger the vehicle and locate the license plate area, the trigger success rate is 96%, and the license plate positioning success rate is 94%.

Keywords: Video trigger · License plate location · Mixed Gaussian model

1 Introduction

License plate recognition is an important application of computer vision and pattern recognition in the field of intelligent transportation. With the development of computer vision and pattern recognition technology, license plate recognition is widely used in practice. The main process of conventional license plate recognition is image acquisition, license plate location, character segmentation and character recognition. The current image acquisition process is usually that the camera receives the trigger signal and takes a picture of the vehicle. The trigger mechanism [1] is mainly divided into external trigger and video trigger; Common license plate location algorithms are mainly based on texture features [2], color features [3], edge information [4], transform domain analysis [5] and morphological processing [6]; The character segmentation algorithms mainly include: projection method [7], connected domain method and prior knowledge method; character recognition algorithms mainly include template matching method [8], neural network method [9–11] and feature extraction method.

At present, the research hotspots of license plate recognition technology mainly focus on license plate location, character segmentation and character recognition. There are

© Springer Nature Singapore Pte Ltd. 2020
X. Sun et al. (Eds.): ICAIS 2020, CCIS 1254, pp. 290–302, 2020.
https://doi.org/10.1007/978-981-15-8101-4_27

relatively few studies on the triggering mechanism of image acquisition. However, the performance of the trigger mechanism has a great impact on the image quality captured by the camera and will affect the subsequent positioning and recognition process results. Therefore, research on the trigger mechanism is necessary.

The trigger mechanism for license plate recognition is to solve the image acquisition process, which ensures that the camera captures a clear image of the vehicle accurately. The trigger mechanism is mainly divided into external trigger and video trigger. The trigger signal of the external trigger is derived from the sensor used by the license plate recognition system, such as the ground sense coil and the infrared radiation sensor. The most widely used one is the ground sense coil. When the vehicle passes, the sensor transmits a trigger signal to the camera or system, triggering the camera to take a picture. In the case that the sensor trigger signal is stable, a high capture rate and image quality can be ensured and an optimal recognition effect can be achieved. However, because of the external trigger requiring to use sensors, the working environment of the license plate recognition system is greatly limited, the sensor has problems such as aging and damage and needs regular maintenance and replacement. Video triggering is a new trigger mechanism that has emerged in recent years. It automatically analyzes the input video stream through the system or camera. It does not need to accept the external trigger signal and intercepts the image at the right time to complete the license plate recognition process. The disadvantage of video triggering is that the analysis of the input video stream requires a large amount of memory, which has certain requirements on the performance of the algorithm and the computing power of the processor. Video triggering is possible with increased computing power and algorithm optimization.

Meng [12] proposed a method based on background difference method and setting double threshold to automatically detect the projectile and receive the trigger signal in real time while receiving the image data signal of the line CCD camera. Firstly, the background difference is made to the video, a double threshold is set, one is a trigger threshold and the other is a change threshold. The trigger is triggered when the difference is greater than the trigger threshold. The pixel value is updated proportionally between the trigger threshold and the update threshold. Since the threshold is relatively fixed, this method is not suitable for situations where the background is complex and variable. Yu [13] sets a virtual induction coil area in the video image. By counting the range and quantity of gray scale changes in the virtual coil area, the threshold is set and the license plate recognition is triggered, which is applied to the maintenance shop of Automobile Sales Service shop 4S. By setting the virtual coil area and counting the range and quantity of gray scales, better results can be obtained under indoor conditions. However, this method cannot be effectively triggered when the illumination intensity is abrupt and the background is complex. Qian proposed a method based on Surendra background update and inter-frame difference to implement vehicle triggering. Firstly, the initial background is established by the mean method, and the adjacent two frames are inter-frame difference. The background image and the difference image are again differentiated. The morphological operation and the connected domain mark are used to judge the vehicle position and trigger the license plate recognition. Ding proposed a method based on three-frame difference and clustering to implement vehicle triggering.

Firstly, the three consecutive frames are subjected to two-two difference, the local similarity and the linear weighted image of the difference image are calculated and clustered, the two images after clustering are "and" operated, detect the position of the vehicle and trigger the license plate recognition. The inter-frame difference method is simple and effective, but when the moving objective is close to the background color, the inter-frame difference cannot get good results and the threshold of the inter-frame difference is difficult to adapt to the background change. Li [14] proposed a method based on Gaussian mixture modeling and inter-frame difference to judge the submunition and smoke state in the shooting range, and realize automatic triggering of high-speed camera. Firstly, the background is updated by adaptive Gaussian mixture model and the difference image is obtained by inter-frame difference. Threshold segmentation is performed by the maximum inter-class variance method (OTSU) and the contour and shape of the segmented image are judged to determine whether smoke exists or not. Gaussian mixture modeling can effectively separate the moving objective from the background and it can get good results with the OTSU algorithm. However, since Gaussian mixture modeling needs to establish K Gaussian distributions for each pixel value and update parameters, that will greatly increase the computational complexity, reduce the system running speed and cannot meet the real-time requirements.

Therefore, we propose a triggering method based on improved Gaussian mixture background modeling and setting double thresholds. Firstly, the Gaussian model is established in units of rows, the parameters of the Gaussian model are updated and the pixel values are updated by the double threshold setting to separate the moving objective from the background. Then, the foreground image is denoised by Gaussian filter, and the connected domain is formed by morphological combination. The contour feature and the color feature of the connected domain are used to determine whether it is a vehicle and trigger license plate recognition. After 50 bayonet video tests taken by the drone, the algorithm can successfully trigger the vehicle and locate the license plate area. The vehicle trigger success rate is 96%, and the license plate positioning success rate is 94%.

We will introduce the idea of Gaussian mixture background modeling algorithm in Sect. 2. The improved Gaussian mixed modeling algorithm is introduced in Sect. 3.1, the triggering algorithm is introduced in Sect. 3.2 and the positioning algorithm is introduced in Sect. 3.3. The experimental results and analysis will be described in Sect. 4.

2 Mixed Gaussian Background Modeling

Mixed Gaussian background modeling [15] was first proposed by Stauffer and Grimson, which models each pixel according to a Gaussian distribution and updates the model parameters by an online EM approximation method [16–19] based on regression filtering.

Stauffer and Grimson assume that the set of pixel values for (x_0, y_0) at time t is $\{X_1, X_2, \ldots, X_t\} = \{I(x_0, y_0, t) | 1 \leq i \leq t\}$, where I is the sequence of video frames. When the background and illumination conditions are relatively stable, the pixel values at the same position at different times are relatively unchanged, recorded as stable pixel values. Noise is generated during image sampling. Assuming that the noise is mainly independent Gaussian noise, the pixel values will fluctuate up and down based on the stable pixel values. Thus, the distribution for this pixel value can be described by a single

Gaussian distribution centered on the average pixel value. However, video sequences in natural scenes usually have changes in illumination conditions, objective motion, etc., so a single Gaussian model cannot describe the distribution of pixels at different time sequences. If a illumination change occurs in a static scene, the corresponding Gaussian model needs to update the illumination changes to the background in a short time; If a moving objective appears in a static scene, the motion of the moving objective is reflected on the image, which may be a repeated Gaussian distribution of different magnitudes. Complex changes [20–22] obviously cannot be described by a single Gaussian distribution, so a mixed Gaussian distribution is proposed.

Assuming that the pixel distribution for (x_0, y_0) at $0 - t$ can be modeled by a mixed Gaussian model, the probability distribution of the current pixel can be expressed as

$$P(X_t) = \sum_{i=1}^{K} \omega_{i,t} * \eta\left(X_t, \mu_{i,t}, \sum_{i,t}\right) \tag{1}$$

Where K is the number of Gaussian distributions, $\omega_{i,t}$ is the weight of the ith Gaussian distribution at time t, $\mu_{i,t}$ is the mean of the ith Gaussian model at time t, $\sum_{i,t}$ is the covariance matrix of the ith Gaussian model at time t, η is a Gaussian probability density function. Because of the computing power and real-time requirements, K usually takes 3–5.

Since there is a matrix inversion operation in the calculation process, in order to further simplify the calculation, it is assumed that the color image R, G and B channel pixel values are independent of each other. By sacrificing the correlation between channels and reducing the computational complexity, the covariance matrix is defined as

$$\sum_{k,t} = \sigma_k^2 I \tag{2}$$

Usually when solving a mixed Gaussian model, the EM algorithm is used to find the optimal solution. However, since there are K Gaussian models for each pixel to describe its distribution, the computational complexity caused by the traditional EM algorithm is unacceptable. Therefore, it is judged whether or not the Gaussian model is satisfied by comparing the new pixel value with the existing K Gaussian distribution. The matching threshold is typically set to 2.5 times the standard deviation of the Gaussian distribution.

If the K Gaussian distributions do not match the current pixel values successfully, then update the existing Gaussian distribution. Using the current pixel value as the mean of the new Gaussian model, the variance of the new Gaussian model is the initial Gaussian distribution variance and the weight is the lowest prior weight to replace the lowest priority probability distribution in the existing Gaussian distribution.

$$\omega_{k,t} = (1 - \alpha)\omega_{k,t-1} + \alpha(M_{k,t}) \tag{3}$$

Where α is the learning rate of the Gaussian model, which controls the learning speed of the Gaussian model. $M_{k,t}$ is 1 for the model with a successful match and 0 for the remaining models.

For models that fail to match, μ and σ remain the same. The parameters of the matching Gaussian distribution are updated to

$$\mu_t = (1 - \rho)\mu_{t-1} + \rho X_t \tag{4}$$

$$\sigma_t^2 = (1 - \rho)\sigma_{t-1}^2 + \rho(X_t - \mu_t)^T(X_t - \mu_t) \tag{5}$$

The second learning rate ρ is

$$\rho = \alpha\eta(X_t|\mu_k, \sigma_k) \tag{6}$$

The above is the update process of the Gaussian mixture model. As the Gaussian model parameters are updated, the model will better describe the distribution of pixel values. In order to better separate the moving objective from the background, we need to make sure which Gaussian model can better match the background. Therefore, all Gaussian models need to be prioritized, and the priority *rank* is set to

$$rank = \omega/\sigma \tag{7}$$

For Gaussian distributions that can better match the background, the weight is relatively high, and at the same time, the lower variance can be guaranteed, so the priority is higher; vice versa.

Use the first B Gaussian distributions as background matching models, which is

$$B = \arg\min_b\left(\sum_{k=1}^{b} \omega_k > T\right) \tag{8}$$

Where T is the ratio of the background to the entire image.

From the perspective of the image, the Gaussian distribution corresponding to the static background will always maintain a high priority and the moving objective always corresponds to a lower priority distribution, even cannot be successfully matched. As an objective changes from motion to stationary, it will gradually become part of the background, which does not destroy the existing Gaussian model corresponding to the static background. The static background will still maintain a high priority until it stops completely and becomes part of the background; If a stationary objective begins to move, its original higher Gaussian distribution priority will gradually decrease and be replaced by other Gaussian distributions that better match the background until it becomes a moving objective.

3 Method

3.1 Improved Gaussian Mixture Background Modeling

The mixed Gaussian model can robustly overcome the disturbances such as illumination changes and branching, but it needs to establish K Gaussian distributions for each pixel, and update the weight, mean and variance of each Gaussian model in real time, the computational complexity is higher. In order to reduce the computational complexity, we propose a block scheme for establishing a mixed Gaussian model in units of rows.

Assuming that the pixel value set of pixel (x_i, y_0) at time t is $\{X_0, X_1, \ldots, X_{width-1}\} = \{I_m(x_i, y_j, t) | 0 \leq i \leq width - 1, 0 \leq m \leq t, 0 \leq j \leq height - 1\}$, Where I is the sequence of video frames. Then the weighted mean of the j rows is

$$\mu_w = \sum_{i=0}^{width-1} w_i I(x_i, y_j, t) \tag{9}$$

Where μ_w is the weighted mean, w_i is the weight corresponding to $I(x_i, y_j, t)$ and w_i is defined as

$$w_i = \frac{p_i}{I_{width}} \tag{10}$$

Where p_i is the frequency at which a pixel value appears in the row, I_{width} is the width of the image row. When calculating the weights, we sort the rows first and then count the number of times each pixel appears. The probability distribution of the row can be described as

$$P(I_j) = \sum_{i=1}^{K} \omega_{i,t} * \eta\left(I_j, \mu_{w,i,t}, \sum_{i,t}\right) \tag{11}$$

Where $\omega_{i,t}$ is the weight of the ith Gaussian distribution at time t, $\mu_{w,i,t}$ is the weighted mean of the ith Gaussian model at time t, $\sum_{i,t}$ is the covariance matrix of the ith Gaussian at time t and η is the Gaussian probability density function.

To establish a mixed Gaussian model, The first parameters to be sure is the weight, mean and standard deviation corresponding to each Gaussian distribution. Usually, the mean of the block Gaussian model is the average of the pixel values within each block, which will weaken the difference in pixel distribution. If each block is large enough, the average cannot represent the distribution within the block, and the model created and updated cannot correctly describe the pixel distribution, and the background update is slower; If each block is small enough, the difference between the average and the pixel distribution is weakened, but the speed of the block cannot be increased by the block, and the meaning of the block no longer exists. In order to ensure the validity and speed of the model, we use the weighted average as the mean of the Gaussian model when modeling each row of pixels.

In the Gaussian mixture modeling process, in order to simplify the calculation, Chris Stauffer and W.E.L. Grimson assume that the channels are independent of each other and the complex matrix inversion becomes the summation operation of each channel. In actual image processing, in order to simplify the calculation, the color image is usually not directly processed, but the correlation calculation is performed on the grayscale image. After conversion to a grayscale image, the relationship between the channels is completely ignored and the covariance matrix does not exist. Formula (11) can be simplified to

$$P(I_j) = \sum_{i=1}^{K} \omega_{i,t} * \eta\left(I_j, \mu_{w,i,t}, \sigma_{w,i,t}^2\right) \tag{12}$$

Therefore, in the subsequent modeling and calculation, we are all discussing grayscale images.

The update algorithm of the Gaussian model parameters is basically the same as Chris Stauffer and W.E.L. Grimson.

The purpose of Gaussian mixture background modeling is to separate moving objective from the background, and foreground and background pixel value updates are also important. Although we have built a Gaussian model in rows, the final thing that needs to be updated is each pixel value in the row. Therefore, an update strategy for pixel values needs to be established.

When the weighted mean of the row to be measured satisfies the matching condition with a Gaussian model in the sequence, the pixel of the row is considered to be the background. The pixel value of this row should be updated to

$$I'(x_i, y_j, t) = \frac{\left(I(x_i, y_j, t) - I'\right)^2}{I(x_i, y_j, t)} + I(x_i, y_j, t) \tag{13}$$

$I'(x_i, y_j, t)$ is the new background pixel value and I' is the sum of the predicted values of the Gaussian model sequence, which is

$$I' = \sum_{i=0}^{K} \mu_{w,i,t} \sigma_{w,i,t} \tag{14}$$

For rows that do not match successfully, they will be considered foreground and further judged that their pixel values are updated to

$$I'(x_i, y_j, t) = \begin{cases} 0 & dif \leq \sigma_{w,i,t}[rank[0]] \\ I(x_i, y_j, t) \pm \mu_{w,i,t}[rank[0]] / I(x_i, y_j, t)dif & others \\ 255 & dif \geq D * \sigma_{w,i,t}[rank[0]] \end{cases} \tag{15}$$

$$dif = |I(x_i, y_j, t) - \mu_{w,i,t}[rank[0]]| \tag{16}$$

$\mu_{w,i,t}[rank[0]]$ is the mean value corresponding to the Gaussian model with the highest priority, $\sigma_{w,i,t}[rank[0]]$ is the standard deviation corresponding to the Gaussian model with the highest priority and dif is the absolute value of the difference between the pixel value and the mean value of the pixel to be tested.

3.2 Trigger Algorithm

After modeling with the improved Gaussian mixture background, the stationary background and moving the foreground target can be extracted and updated in real time. Through the Gaussian mixture background modeling and morphological combination, etc., the vehicle position is located and the license plate location is triggered according to its position. The process is shown in Fig. 1.

Since the separated moving target image tends to have a large amount of noise points and non-vehicle area interference. Therefore, it is necessary to eliminate noise in the

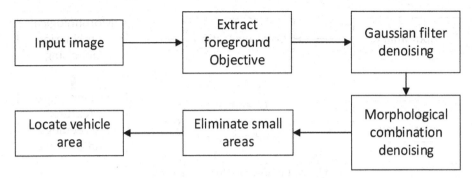

Fig. 1. Video trigger process

image. In the experiment, we used a Gaussian filter to eliminate noise. Gaussian filtering is a linear filtering that uses a distribution of two-dimensional Gaussian functions to smooth an image. The two-dimensional Gaussian function is rotationally symmetric, has the same degree of smoothness in all directions and does not change the edge orientation of the original image. The anchor pixels are not affected too much by pixels farther from the anchor point, ensuring the characteristics of the feature points and edges, and are not contaminated by high frequency signals during the filtering process.

Since the image completed by Gaussian filtering may still have small noise, morphological operations are used to eliminate small noise and connect small areas into connected domains. First, use the morphological closing operation of the 3 * 3 convolution kernel to eliminate the black noise point, and then use the 5 * 5 expansion operation twice to connect the small areas as much as possible. Through morphological operations, a certain number of connected domains are formed. In order to further reduce the interference, it is necessary to traverse all the connected domains to eliminate the area of less than 20 pixels.

Generally speaking, the vehicle has a large area in the connected domain, and there is a certain aspect ratio. Therefore, the position of the vehicle can be further judged using the area and the aspect ratio. According to the experimental measurement, the area and aspect ratio are as follows:

$$image / 20 \leq vehicle \leq image/5 \tag{17}$$

$$0.8 \leq ratio \leq 2.0 \tag{18}$$

After the above judgment, the vehicle position can be basically located. The license plate location is triggered by determining the position of the vehicle.

3.3 License Plate Recognition Algorithm

Conventional license plate images have obvious contrast, brightness and the features. Therefore, when locating the license plate, the color feature can be used to remove most of the non-license plate areas more quickly and obtain the license plate candidate area. The process is shown in Fig. 2.

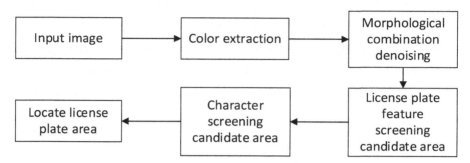

Fig. 2. License plate location process

Firstly, the RGB channel image is transferred to the HSV channel and the color matching is performed according to the threshold range of each channel corresponding to the license plate color in the HSV channel.

Because the relationship between pixel values and colors of each channel is not intuitive in the RGB model. The HSV model is more similar to the human perceived color and the pixel value is clearly related to the color. Therefore, the HSV model is more commonly used when matching colors. The approximate range of HSV models for license plate colors is shown in Table 1.

Table 1. License plate color corresponds to HSV model

	Blue	Yellow	White	Black
H(min)	100	26	0	0
H(max)	124	34	180	180
S(min)	43	43	0	0
S(max)	255	25	30	255
V(min)	46	46	221	0
V(max)	255	255	255	46

After the color matching is completed, a binary image is obtained and the area corresponding to the license plate color is extracted. Since there are noises, adhesions, separations, etc. in the target area, it is necessary to use morphological operations to connect small areas to form connected domains. According to experimental research, it is found that due to the relatively large spacing between the second character and the third character of the Chinese license plate, the license plate area may be disconnected in the horizontal direction and adhere to the car bumper, the middle net and other areas in the vertical direction. In order to obtain a more complete license plate candidate area and eliminate noise interference, we set the morphological combination with different size convolution kernels when performing morphological operations. The morphological combination steps are as follows:

Step 1: two erosion operations with a convolution kernel size of 5 * 3;
Step 2: two dilation operations with a convolution kernel size of 3 * 5;
Step 3: one erosion operations with a convolution kernel size of 5 * 3;

After the morphological combination process, the license plate candidate area does not break in the horizontal direction and does not stick in the vertical direction, forming an independent connected domain. To further eliminate noise, traversing the image contour, contours with square less than 20 pixels will be identified as noise, which are eliminated by modifying the pixel values.

The contour of the pre-processed image is detected, and the license plate candidate area is selected according to the shape feature of the license plate and the character and finally the license plate image is obtained.

Depending on the shape characteristics of the license plate, the area and aspect ratio of the contour are defined, which is

$$image \big/ 500 < plate < image \big/ 100 \qquad (19)$$

$$2.0 < whRatio < 4.0 \qquad (20)$$

Where *image* is the source image size, *plate* is the license plate candidate area size, and *whRatio* is the license plate outline aspect ratio. The standard Chinese license plate has an aspect ratio of approximately 3.14. Considering that the candidate area may contain non-license plate areas and shooting angles, it is necessary to increase the threshold range as much as possible. Since the shooting angle is not correct, the license plate area may have a certain angle of inclination, and an affine transformation is needed to correct, and the license plate candidate area is further selected.

There may be some license plate candidate areas that do not contain license plates and need to be further filtered using the area and aspect ratio characteristics of the license plate characters, which is

$$plate \big/ 70 < character < plate \big/ 5 \qquad (21)$$

$$0.5 < chwhRatio < 3.0 \qquad (22)$$

Where *character* is the size of the character area, *chwhRatio* is the aspect ratio of the license plate character. According to the Chinese license plate shape, the standard character area size is approximately $1\big/15$ of the entire license plate area and the aspect ratio of standard license plate characters is 0.5. Judging whether the candidate area contains the license plate by counting the number of sub-contours that match the area and aspect ratio of the license plate character. The number of sub-profiles is usually 2–8. After the above steps, the license plate can be basically successfully located.

4   Experiments

4.1 Virtual Loop Detector Design

In the experiment, we set two virtual coil areas, which are recorded as region1 and region2 in order from top to bottom, as shown in Fig. 3. Two virtual coil areas have the same width and height.

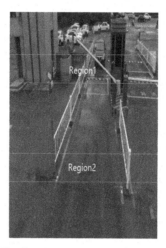

Fig. 3. Virtual loop detector design

Region1 monitors whether a vehicle has passed, once the vehicle is detected, the camera begins to take a series of images. Region2 judges whether the target is a vehicle again, stops taking images, extracts the clearest one and locates the license plate.

4.2   Experimental Results and Analysis

In the experiment, we used the DJI Phantom 3 Standard to shoot 50 videos at the traffic jam for testing. Experimental hardware parameters and camera parameters are as shown in Table 2.

Table 2. Experimental hardware parameters and camera parameters

Development language	C#
Third Party Library	Emgu CV
Operating environment	Intel(R) Core(TM) i7 – 6700 CPU @ 3.40 GHz, Windows 10
Drone camera parameters	12 million pixels
Video parameters	1080P (120 fps)

The comparison between our method and other trigger mechanisms is as shown in Table 3.

In the experiment, we did not compress the video. Through the method of video stream analysis, the response time and the accuracy of the trigger are close to the existing external sensor-dependent trigger mechanism. The experimental results prove that our method is effective and feasible. For the image captured by the trigger, using our license plate location method, the positioning accuracy is 94%.

Table 3. The comparison between our method and other trigger mechanisms

	Trigger success rate (%)	Response time (ms)
Ground sense coil	99.2	20
Infrared radiation sensor	98.4	35
Our method	96	50

5 Conclusion

Aiming at the problem that the camera triggering method of the existing license plate recognition system depends on the sensor, an improved Gaussian mixed background modeling and dual threshold triggering method are proposed. Firstly, the Gaussian model is established in units of rows, the parameters of the Gaussian model are updated and the pixel values are updated by the double threshold setting to separate the moving objective from the background. Then, the foreground image is denoised by Gaussian filter, and the connected domain is formed by morphological combination. The contour feature and color feature of the connected domain are used to determine whether it is a vehicle and trigger license plate location. The experiment proves that the algorithm can successfully trigger the vehicle and locate the license plate area, the trigger success rate is 96%, and the license plate positioning success rate is 94%.

References

1. Sun, F., Wang, G.: Triggering problems and application in license plate recognition technology. Northern Traffic (10) (2006)
2. Wan, Y., Xu, Q.Y., Huang, M.M.: On license plate location in complex background based on texture and color. Comput. Appl. Softw. (10), 259–262 (2013)
3. Li, W., Liang, D., Zhang, Q., et al.: A new method of vehicle license plate location based on edge color pair. Chin. J. Comput. (2), 204–208 (2004)
4. Li, L.Q., Peng, J.Y., Feng, X.Y.: New approach for precise license plate locating based on edge analysis and color statistics. Appl. Res. Comput. (1), 342–345 + 349 (2012)
5. Rajput, H., Som, T., Kar, S.: An automated vehicle license plate recognition system. Computer **48**(8), 56–61 (2015)
6. Wang, J., Huang, H., Qian, X., et al.: Sequence recognition of Chinese license plates. Neurocomputing **317**, 149–158 (2018)
7. Panchal, T., Patel, H., Panchal, A.: License plate detection using Harris corner and character segmentation by integrated approach from an image. Procedia Comput. Sci. **79**, 419–425 (2016)
8. Gao, C., Wang, F.L.: Algorithm of license plate recognition based on template matching and local HOG feature. Comput. Syst. Appl. **26**(1), 122–128 (2017)
9. Björklund, T., Fiandrotti, A., et al.: Robust license plate recognition using neural networks trained on synthetic images. Pattern Recogn. **93**, 134–146 (2019)
10. Geng Runhua, S., Tingting, M.X.: License plate recognition system based on BP neural network combined with template matching. J. Tsinghua Univ. (Sci. Technol.) **53**(09), 1221–1226 (2013)

11. Cheng, S.H., Gao, X., Zhou, B.: Vehicle recognition based on multi-feature extraction and SVM parameter optimization. Acta Metrologica Sin. (3), 348–352 (2018)
12. Meng, B., Cai, R., Tan, L.: Design of linear CCD precision target image triggering algorithm. Comput. Measur. Control (01), 251–255 (2019)
13. Yu, H., Ma, S., Wu, Y.: Research and Application in License Plate Recognition on Soft Trigger. Program. Controll. Fact. Autom. (12), 94–96 + 117 (2010)
14. Li, Y., Zhang, Z.: Research on automation trigger method for high speed photographic device based on image. J. Gun Launching Control (04), 26–29 (2010)
15. Stauffer, C, Grimson, W.E.L.: Adaptive background mixture models for real-time tracking. In: 1999 IEEE Computer Society Conference on Computer Vision and Pattern Recognition. IEEE (1999)
16. Ma, B., Shi, Y.-Q.: A reversible data hiding scheme based on code division multiplexing. IEEE Trans. Inf. Forensics Secur. **11**(9), 1914–1927 (2016)
17. Li, J., Ma, B., Wang, C.: Extraction of PRNU noise from partly decoded video. J. Vis. Commun. Image Represent. **57**, 183–191 (2018)
18. Wang, C., Wang, X., Xia, Z., Zhang, C.: Ternary radial harmonic Fourier moments based robust stereo image zero-watermarking algorithm. Inf. Sci. **470**, 109–120 (2019)
19. Wang, C., Wang, X., Xia, Z., Ma, B., Shi, Y.-Q.: Image description with polar harmonic fourier moments. IEEE Trans. Circ. Syst. Video Technol. (2019). https://doi.org/10.1109/TCSVT.2019.2960507
20. Sun, W., Hongji, D., Nie, S., He, X.: Traffic sign recognition method integrating multi-layer features and kernel extreme learning machine classifier. Comput. Mater. Continua **60**(1), 147–161 (2019)
21. Maamar, A., Benahmed, K.: A hybrid model for anomalies detection in AMI system combining k-means clustering and deep neural network. Comput. Mater. Continua **60**(1), 15–39 (2019)
22. Sun, M., Jiang, Y., Liu, Q., Liu, X.: An auto-calibration approach to robust and secure usage of accelerometers for human motion analysis in FES therapies. Comput. Mater. Continua **60**(1), 67–83 (2019)

Securing Graph Steganography over Social Networks via Interaction Remapping

Hanzhou Wu[1,2(✉)], Limengnan Zhou[3], Junchen Li[1,4], and Xinpeng Zhang[1,2,4]

[1] School of Communication and Information Engineering, Shanghai University,
Shanghai 200444, China
h.wu.phd@ieee.org
[2] Shanghai Institute for Advanced Communication and Data Science,
Shanghai 200444, China
[3] School of Electronic and Information Engineering, University of Electronic Science
and Technology of China, Zhongshan Institute, Zhongshan 528400, China
[4] School of Computer Science, Fudan University, Shanghai 200120, China

Abstract. The modern social networks are huge and complex, with lots of users and connections, and are well suited for steganography. Recently, Wu *et al.* introduce a novel steganographic approach through graph structure, which is represented by a series of sequential interactions over online social networking service (SNS). However, since the SNS is public to social users, according to the Kerckhoffs's principle, if an attacker masters the procedure to reconstruct the graph structure with interactions, the directly embedded data may be exposed. In order to address this problem, we put forward a new approach to remap the corresponding interactions of the vertices of the graph structure by a key, ensuring that even if the attacker reconstructs the graph structure perfectly, he cannot retrieve the directly embedded data. Compared with Wu *et al.*'s method, our method has a larger capacity for the same number of interactions, which has demonstrated the superiority and applicability.

Keywords: Steganography · Graph theory · Social networks · Security

1 Introduction

The modern digital communication is often associated with cryptography to protect the content. The resulting ciphertext can be transmitted over an insecure channel since the secret message is difficult to be decrypted without the key. However, cryptography leaves clear marks on the ciphertext for an eavesdropper to trace down, which may lead the attacker to interrupt the covert communication though he cannot access the original plaintext. As another way to secure communication, steganography [1,2], has the ability to even conceal the existence of the present communication, which has become an important security

© Springer Nature Singapore Pte Ltd. 2020
X. Sun et al. (Eds.): ICAIS 2020, CCIS 1254, pp. 303–312, 2020.
https://doi.org/10.1007/978-981-15-8101-4_28

technology nowadays. Steganography has its own place in modern information security. It is not intended to replace cryptography, but rather to supplement it.

Conventional steganographic arts [3–6], works by hiding a secret message into an innocent digital file, e.g., image, video and audio, by slightly modifying the noise-like component of the given digital file, without introducing noticeable artifacts. Generally, the given media used for steganography is called *cover*, and its modified version containing the additional message is called *stego*. It is true that, image based steganographic techniques are the most common use today. Audio based and video based techniques are also of increasing attention to researchers. It is pointed out that, the used cover actually could be arbitrary media file. Though many general steganographic algorithms can be applied to different cover objects, there should be unique treatment associated with each type of cover source since a different cover type always has its own statistical, perceptual and structural characteristics.

Recently, Wu *et al.* [7] introduce a graph-theoretic steganographic approach for social networks, which uses graph structure to conceal data. The secret data is first translated as an undirected graph, also called *message-graph*. Then the structure of the message-graph is concealed within a directed graph. The directed graph is represented by sequential user-interactions through a social networking service (SNS) platform. Wu *et al.*'s method is very innovative, and it is the first time to deeply combine behavior steganography [8] and graph theory into practical scenarios. However, the security of this approach needs to be enhanced. According to the Kerckhoffs's principle, if the attacker knows how to reconstruct the structure of the graph through social network interactions, the directly embedded data hidden in the graph would be obtained.

This motivates the authors in this paper to address this security problem by remapping the corresponding interactions of the vertices of the graph structure controlled by a secret key in this paper. It ensures that, even if the attacker reconstructs the graph structure perfectly, he cannot retrieve the directly embedded data. Moreover, compared with Wu *et al.*'s method, our method has a larger capacity for the same number of interactions, which shows the superiority.

The rest of this paper are organized as follows. We briefly review Wu *et al.*'s approach in Sect. 2. Then, in Sect. 3, we present the proposed approach. In Sect .4, we provide a toy example to illustrate our approach. We analyze the proposed work in Sect. 5. Finally, we conclude this paper in Sect. 6.

2   Prior Art Revisited

In this section, we review Wu *et al.*'s work [7], and point the security issue.

2.1   Framework of Wu *et al.*'s Method

In Wu *et al.*'s method, the first procedure is *Message-Graph Generation*. A graph $G(V, E)$, where $V = \{v_1, v_2, ..., v_n\}$ and $E = \{e_1, e_2, ..., e_m\}$ is utilized to carry a secret payload. Obviously, there are at most $2^{\binom{n}{2}}$ different undirected graphs with

n vertices, and each graph can represent a bitstream sized $\binom{n}{2}$. One can assume that the length of the secret message $\mathbf{m}$ is always $\binom{n}{2}$ since the steganographer can always append "0"s to the original bitstream so that its length is exactly equal to $\binom{n}{2}$. The key steps to generate a message-graph is shown as below:

1. Initialize $V_0 = \{v_1, v_2, ..., v_n\}$ and $E_0 = \varnothing$.
2. For every $m_z \in \mathbf{m}$:
   (a) if $m_z = 0$, do nothing.
   (b) if $m_z = 1$, update E_0 as $E_0 \cup \{(v_x, v_y)\}$, where $x = \min\{j | 1 \leqslant j \leqslant n - 1, \sum_{i=1}^{j}(n - i) \geqslant z\}$ and $y = x + z - \sum_{i=1}^{x-1}(n - i)$.
3. Construct the structure of undirected graph $G_0(V_0, E_0)$ based on V_0 and E_0.

In conclusion, every bit in bit-string is sequentially embedded as edges of the undirected graph $G_0(V_0, E_0)$, which is called message-graph. The edges of $G_0(V_0, E_0)$ correspond to "1"s in bitstream, and the edges of the complementary graph of $G_0(V_0, E_0)$ correspond to "0"s in bitstream. The second procedure is Message-Graph Embedding, namely, the message-graph $G_0(V_0, E_0)$ is embedded into a directed graph $G_1(V_1, E_1)$ for concealing. The key steps of embedding message-graph is shown as below:

1. Initialize $E_1 = \varnothing$.
2. For each $v_i \in V_0$ $(1 \leqslant i \leqslant n)$:
   (a) If $\exists j < i, (v_j, v_i) \in E_0$, then, $\forall j < i$, if $(v_j, v_i) \in E_0$, insert (v_i', v_j') to E_1.
   (b) If $\nexists j < i, (v_j, v_i) \in E_0$, insert (v_i', v_{n+1}') to E_1.

In brief, the edges in the directed graph $G_1(V_1, E_1)$ correspond to the edges in the undirected graph $G_0(V_0, E_0)$, and the direction is from the higher indexed vertex to the lower indexed vertex. If a vertex does not have any edges starting from it, an edge pointing to a specified vertex v_{n+1} would be added to the vertex. $G_0(V_0, E_0)$ is actually a subgraph of $G_1(V_1, E_1)$ if the directions are ignored. The structure of graph $G_1(V_1, E_1)$ would be represented by sequentially user interactions in a SNS platform, the users represent the vertices of the graph, and the interactions between users represent the edges between the vertices along with their indexes. The interactions would be produced orderly based on their indexes, which means a lower indexed interaction would be produced prior to a higher indexed interaction. The kind of interaction is not particular, it can be commenting, "liking" or any other chosen interactions.

The last procedure is Message-Graph Reconstruction. The precondition of the method is that both steganographer and receiver share a set U, which contains all vertices in $G_1(V_1, E_1)$. Notice that, V_1 can be a subset of U. Interactions in SNS platform are public and can be observed. Once the receiver has $G_1(V_1, E_1)$, $G_0(V_0, E_0)$ can be abstracted by ignoring directions and removing all the edges that linked to v_{n+1}'. More details are demonstrated in [7].

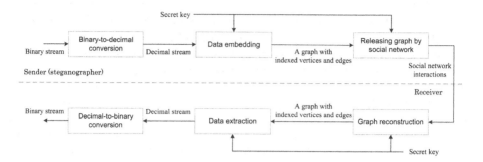

Fig. 1. Schematic diagram of proposed approach.

2.2 Security Concern

Wu *et al.*'s method has a capacity of $\binom{n}{2}$ bits when the size of vertex set V_0 is n, indicating an embedding rate of $0.5 \cdot (n-1)$ bits per vertex (bpv), which is superior in cover element utilization to traditional media based steganogrpahy [7]. However, there is a security concern of this method needing to take into consideration. Wu *et al.* construct $G_1(V_1, E_1)$ to conceal $G_0(V_0, E_0)$, and they also add redundant vertices and edges to distract potential attackers to enhance security. Both the steganographer and the receiver share the vertex set U and therefore the receiver does not retrieve the erroneous data [7]. Nevertheless, according to Kerckhoffs's principle, if an attacker masters the procedure to reconstruct the graph structure from users' interactions, the directly embedded data would be insecure. Since users and interactions are public, attackers can observe all social behaviors in SNS platform, we must consider avoiding the risk of leaking directly embedded data when under attack.

3 Proposed Method

At the beginning of this section, we illustrate the general steganographic framework, and then elucidate the key steps to embed data and extract data.

Figure 1 shows the schematic diagram of the proposed framework. Suppose that, the secret data is a binary stream, the steganographer should first convert the binary stream into a decimal stream. Then, according to the decimal stream and the secret key, the steganographer will produce a graph with indexed vertices and edges. It means that, each vertex and each edge will be associated with an index value, though such kind of information will not be apparently announced in the social network. Thereafter, the steganographer conveys the graph in social networks by producing a sequence of user interactions in a social network. At the receiver side, one can reconstruct the identical graph with indexed nodes and edges by observing the interactions in the social network with the shared secret key. The receiver will continue to extract the embedded information, i.e., a decimal stream, from the graph. Finally, the secret binary stream can be reconstructed. Compared to Wu's method, in our work, the indexes of vertices should be shared between the steganographer and the receiver, which ensures that, the indexes of edges will be always changing due to a key.

Suppose we can control $n + 2$ vertices, indexed from v_0 to v_{n+1}. The vertex set composed of v_1 to v_n is denoted by V. The edges whose both start point and end point are belonging to the vertex set V are denoted as the edge set E. The edge set E has m edges, and we design m to be an integer power of 2. We therefore describe the proposed data embedding procedure as follows:

1. Take a decimal random seed R ($1 \leqslant R \leqslant n$). There are m edges in E, and the indexes of edges are generated according to R, denoted as $\{e_1, e_2, ..., e_m\}$. Without the loss of generality, we assume that e_i has an index value of i.
2. Suppose the directly embedded data we want to transmit has $m \cdot \log_2 m$ bits, append '0's (or random bits) to the end of the data if the size is insufficient. Divide the secret data into m groups, denoted by $\{b_1, b_2, ..., b_m\}$. Each group therefore has $\log_2 m$ bits.
3. Convert $\{b_1, b_2, ..., b_m\}$ into decimal numbers, denoted as $D = \{d_1, d_2, ..., d_m\}$, where $0 \leqslant d_j \leqslant m - 1, \forall j \in [1, m]$.
4. A total of $m+1$ **F** operations, denoted by $\mathbf{F}(0), \mathbf{F}(1), ..., \mathbf{F}(m)$, will be orderly performed. The $\mathbf{F}(i)$ operation corresponds to one of the following cases.
   (a) If there is only one element d_j in D equal to i, the edge e_j is represented in the SNS platform.
   (b) If there is no element in D equal to i, then randomly choose a vertex in V and build an edge between it and v_0.
   (c) If there are $k \geqslant 2$ elements in D equal to i, denoted as $\{d_{j_1}, d_{j_2}, ..., d_{j_k}\}$, where $1 \leqslant j_1 < ... < j_k \leqslant m$, insert an edge between v_k and v_{n+1}, and then $\{d_{j_1}, ..., d_{j_k}\}$ are represented in the SNS platform by $\{e_{j_1}, ..., e_{j_k}\}$.
   (d) If i is equal to m, then insert an edge between v_R and v_0.

It is pointed that, during the data embedding, the directions of edges can be arbitrary. Moreover, the seed R has been self-embedded into the social network so that a receiver can auto-retrieve the secret data. $V \cup \{v_0, v_{n+1}\}$ including their indexes are shared between the steganographer and the receiver. Notice that, m is not pre-shared, since its value can be reconstructed by the receiver. The reason is, the receiver knows when to terminate the extraction procedure, which allows the receiver to determine m out by collecting the total number of embedded edges. The detailed data extraction procedure is described as follows.

1. Observe users and their social interactions, reconstruct the graph structure, and the sequence of interactions is determined by the time they occur.
2. A total of $m + 1$ **G** operations on interactions, denoted by $\mathbf{G}(i)$, $i \in [0, m]$, will be *orderly* performed. The $\mathbf{G}(i)$ operation is corresponding to one of the following cases.
   (a) If the edge belongs to E, then assign a value of i to the edge.
   (b) If the edge connects v_0, then skip to the next operation.
   (c) If the edge connects v_{n+1} and v_k, then assign i to the next k edges.
   (d) If $i = m$, and the edge connects $v_{R'}$ and v_0, then set $R = R'$.

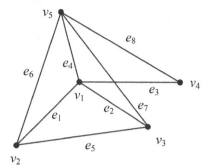

Fig. 2. An example of V, E and their index information.

Table 1. The bit-groups and their values.

Bit-group	b_1	b_2	b_3	b_4	b_5	b_6	b_7	b_8
Value	010	011	110	011	000	100	001	111

Table 2. The decimal values of the bit-groups.

Decimal number	d_1	d_2	d_3	d_4	d_5	d_6	d_7	d_8
Value	2	3	6	3	0	4	1	7

3. Generate the indexes of edges in E according to R.
4. According to the indexes of edges and their assigned values, we can get a string consisting of decimal numbers.
5. Convert each character of the decimal string into the corresponding binary number with a size of $\log_2 m$, and the direct embedded data can be obtained.

4 Example

In this section, we are to present a detailed example to interpret our method. We first formulate the problem of the example, then demonstrate the key steps of data embedding and data extraction for the example.

4.1 Description

Suppose that, the secret data we want to embed in a graph structure is "010, 011, 110, 011, 000, 100, 001, 111", which has a total of 24 bits. We are able to control 7 vertices, indexed from v_0 to v_6. We have $V = \{v_1, v_2, ..., v_5\}$. The edges which connect vertices in V are denoted by an edge set E. The size of E will be 8, i.e., $|E| = 8$, which is exactly equal to 2^3.

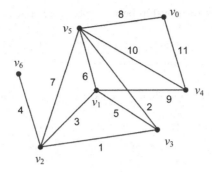

Fig. 3. The reconstructed graph structure from observations.

Table 3. The detailed information about **F** operations.

F operations	F(0)	F(1)	F(2)	F(3)		F(4)	F(5)	F(6)	F(7)	F(8)
Number	d_5	d_7	d_1	d_2, d_4		d_6	None	d_3	d_8	Seed
Edge	e_5	e_7	e_1	(v_2, v_6) e_2, e_4	e_6		(v_5, v_0)	e_3	e_8	(v_4, v_0)

Table 4. The detailed information about **G** operations.

G operations	G(0)	G(1)	G(2)	G(3)			G(4)	G(5)	G(6)	G(7)	G(8)
Edge	(v_2, v_3)	(v_3, v_5)	(v_1, v_2)	(v_2, v_6) (v_1, v_3)	(v_1, v_5)		(v_2, v_5)	(v_5, v_0)	(v_1, v_4)	(v_4, v_5)	(v_4, v_0)
Value	0	1	2	Skip,3,3			4	Skip	6	7	$R = 4$

4.2   Data Embedding

First of all, we take $R = 4$ as the random seed in this example to generate the indexes of edges. There are a total of 8 edges in E, denoted by $\{e_1, e_2, ..., e_8\}$. For convenience, the edges are indexed as shown in Fig. 2, e.g., $e_1 = (v_1, v_2)$, $e_7 = (v_3, v_5)$. Notice that, here, the edges have no directions.

Since the secret data has exactly $8 \cdot \log_2 8 = 24$ bits, there has no need to fill zeros in the end. We divide the secret data into 8 groups and index them by $\{b_1, b_2, ..., b_8\}$. Each group has 3 bits, which is shown in Table 1.

We convert each bit-group into a decimal number, which can be described as Table 2. In Table 2, the decimal numbers are represented by $D = \{d_1, d_2, ..., d_8\}$, where $0 \le d_i \le 7$ for all $1 \le i \le 8$. Thereafter, we *orderly* perform a total of 9 **F** operations, denoted by $\{\mathbf{F}_0, \mathbf{F}_1, ..., \mathbf{F}_8\}$. Each operation essentially is equivalent to adding new edges between vertices. The edges are released in the social network by user interactions. We detail the process below.

As there is only one element d_5 equal to 0, $\mathbf{F}(0)$ requires us to release $e_5 = (v_2, v_3)$ in the social network. As only $d_7 = 1$ and $d_1 = 2$, we release $e_7 = (v_3, v_5)$ and $e_1 = (v_1, v_2)$ orderly in the social network. For $\mathbf{F}(3)$, there are two elements equal to 3, we first release (v_2, v_6) to tell such side information to a decoder. Then, we orderly release $e_2 = (v_1, v_3)$ and $e_4 = (v_1, v_5)$. For **F4**, $e_6 = (v_2, v_5)$ is released. Since there has no element equal to 5, (v_5, v_0) is inserted for $\mathbf{F}(5)$.

Table 5. The mapping relationship between observed edges and original indexes.

Edge	(v_2, v_3)	(v_3, v_5)	(v_1, v_2)	(v_1, v_3)	(v_1, v_5)	(v_2, v_5)	(v_1, v_4)	(v_4, v_5)
Index	e_5	e_7	e_1	e_2	e_4	e_6	e_3	e_8

Table 6. Edges and their assigned values after arrangement.

Edge	(v_1, v_2)	(v_1, v_3)	(v_1, v_4)	(v_1, v_5)	(v_2, v_3)	(v_2, v_5)	(v_3, v_5)	(v_4, v_5)
Index	e_1	e_2	e_3	e_4	e_5	e_6	e_7	e_8
Value	2	3	6	3	0	4	1	7

Going on, $e_3 = (v_1, v_4)$ and $e_8 = (v_4, v_5)$ are corresponding to $\mathbf{F}(6)$ and $\mathbf{F}(7)$, respectively. Finally, (v_R, v_0) is released. Table 3 shows all the information.

4.3 Data Extraction

At the receiver side, the receiver observes the interactions between the users, and reconstructs the graph structure as shown in Fig. 3. In Fig. 3, the assigned value for each edge indicates its occurrence order, e.g., (v_2, v_3) means the first interaction happened in the social network. Thus, we can generate an edge-sequence according to the occurrence order.

Obviously, by removing those edges connecting v_0 or v_6, we can easily infer that $m = 8$. Then, a total of nine $\mathbf{G}$ operations on the edge-sequence can be performed, denoted by $\{\mathbf{G}(0), \mathbf{G}(1), ..., \mathbf{G}(8)\}$. For each operation, we will assign value(s) to edge(s) (if any). Table 4 shows the assignment information. For example, for $\mathbf{G}(3)$, (v_2, v_6) means that, the subsequent 2 edges will be associated with 3. For $\mathbf{G}(5)$, since the edge (v_5, v_0) connects v_0, therefore it will be skipped.

The receiver can obtain R since it is represented by the last social network interaction. The indexes of edges in E can be generated by R with a generator, which is only shared between the steganographer and the receiver. Therefore, the receiver has the ability to determine the indexes of the observed edges, which is shown in Table 5. By arranging the edges according to their indexes, along with their assignments, we can get Table 6, which allows us to recover the secret data (decimal) as "23630417". Obviously, the final bitstream is "010, 011, 110, 011, 000, 100, 001, 111".

5 Security and Capacity Analysis

In our method, one cannot obtain the directly embedded data unless he owns the vertex set, the edge set, the relationship between social network interactions and graph structure, and the indexes of edges. If an attacker notices the steganographic process through social network interactions, the graph structure may have a chance to be exposed to the attacker, because users and social network interactions are public and can be observed by anyone. However, the indexes of edges are unattainable to the attacker, even when the attacker is aware of the random seed. Because only the legal receiver has the generator to generate the indexes of edges through the random seed. Besides this, our method can also use Wu *et al.*'s idea of adding redundant user nodes and edges to increase security.

In case that an attacker uses exhaustive search, the order of magnitude he needs to search is the factorial of the number of edges. When the number of edges is large enough, the attacker is impossibly crack the directly embedded data in a short time. In addition, the receiver does not receive data directly and the attacker cannot identify the identity of the receiver from the transmission on the Internet, which improves the concealment of the receiver.

Compared with Wu *et al.*'s method, the capacity of our method is increased by multiples, depending on the number of available edges. In Wu *et al.*'s method, one interaction represents one bit, while in our method, one interaction represents $\log_2 m$ bits, and the capacity is $m \cdot \log_2 m$ bits.

6   Conclusion and Discussion

We propose a new method of transmitting secret data through the graph structure of social network interactions. The kind of interactions can be any kind of agreed social network behaviors. Compared with previous approach, we increase the capacity by utilizing the indexes of edges in graph structure without adding more interactions and the indexes of edges generated by generator according to a random seed ensure that even if the attacker extracts the graph structure from social network interactions, the directly embedded data would not be leaked.

From the perspective of traditional steganography, there are two directions could be investigated for future research. One is to increase the security of embedded data, and to propose steganographic method that make it difficult for the attackers to crack. The other is to improve the concealment of data transmission and reduce the risk of being perceived by attackers when the data is transmitted through social networks interactions. Wu *et al.* [9] proposed a model to minimize the risk of message delivering in social network, but there are more aspects to consider, such as structural risk, risk quantification, and so on. Besides, from the view of behavior steganography, there are numerous types of social behaviors could be used to conceal secret data, which can multiply the capacity if they are utilized sufficiently. When the steganographic method proposed in the paper is used, it is impossible for an attacker to obtain the directly embedded data. One direction that can be investigated for an attacker is to detect the existence of embedded data and cut off their interactions at the lowest cost. Perhaps, the community discovery algorithms [10,11], and this paper [12] would be helpful.

Acknowledgement. It was partly supported by the National Natural Science Foundation of China (NSFC) under grant Nos. 61902235, 61901096, U1636206, U1936214, 61525203. It was also partly supported by "Chen Guang" project under grant No. 19CG46, co-funded by the Shanghai Municipal Education Commission and Shanghai Education Development Foundation.

References

1. Simmons, G.: The prisoners' problem and the subliminal channel. In: Chaum, D. (eds.) Advances in Cryptology, pp. 51–67, Springer, Boston (1984). https://doi.org/10.1007/978-1-4684-4730-9_5
2. Fridrich, J.: Steganography in Digital Media: Principles, Algorithms, and Applications. Cambridge University Press, Cambridge (2009)
3. Holub, V., Fridrich, J.: Designing steganographic distortion using directional filters. In: IEEE Workshop on Information Forensics and Security, pp. 234–239 (2012)
4. Li, B., Wang, M., Huang, J., Li, X.: A new cost function for spatial image steganography. In: IEEE International Conference on Image Processing, pp. 4206–4210 (2014)
5. Luo, W., Huang, F., Huang, J.: Edge adaptive image steganography based on LSB matching revisited. IEEE Trans. Inf. Forensics Secur. 5(2), 201–214 (2010)
6. Pevný, T., Filler, T., Bas, P.: Using high-dimensional image models to perform highly undetectable steganography. In: Böhme, R., Fong, P.W.L., Safavi-Naini, R. (eds.) IH 2010. LNCS, vol. 6387, pp. 161–177. Springer, Heidelberg (2010). https://doi.org/10.1007/978-3-642-16435-4_13
7. Wu, H., Wang, W., Dong, J., Wang, H.: New graph-theoretic approach to social steganography. In: Proceedings of IS&T Electronic Imaging, Media Watermarking, Security and Forensics, pp. 539-1–539-7(7) (2019)
8. Zhang, X.: Behavior steganography in social network. In: Proceedings of Advances in Intelligent Information Hiding and Multimedia Signal Processing, pp. 21–23 (2017)
9. Wu, H., Wang, W., Dong, J., Wang, H.: A graph-theoretic model to steganography on social networks. arXiv Preprint arXiv:1712.03621.v5 (2017)
10. Newman, M.E.J.: Modularity and community structure in networks. Proc. Nat. Acad. Sci. 103(23), 8577–8582 (2006)
11. Newman, M.E.J., Girvan, M.: Finding and evaluating community structure in networks. Phys. Rev. E 69(2), 026113-1–026113-15 (2004)
12. Wu, H., Wang, W., Dong, J., Wang, H., Xiong, L.: The cut and dominating set problem in a steganographer network. arXiv Preprint arXiv:1802.09333 (2018)

MM-Stega: Multi-modal Steganography Based on Text-Image Matching

Yuting Hu[1], Haoyun Li[2], Jianni Song[2], and Yongfeng Huang[1(✉)]

[1] Department of Electronic Engineering and Beijing National Research Center
for Information Science and Technology,
Tsinghua University, Beijing 100084, China
yfhuang@mail.tsinghua.edu.cn
[2] Beijing University of Posts and Telecommunications, Beijing 100876, China

Abstract. This paper proposes a multi-modal steganography (MM-Stega) scheme based on text-image matching. Currently, most steganographic methods embed secret information into a cover by modifying its content. However, the distortion of the cover caused by the modification may be detected by steganalysis methods. Other steganographic methods hide secret information by generating covers, but the imperceptibility of this kind of steganographic methods is limited by the quality of the generated covers. Our method is different from these steganographic methods in two aspects. First, our method utilizes multi-modal covers, *i.e.*, texts and images, while most steganographic methods use single-modal covers. Second, our method embeds secret information in the relevance between the texts and images without modifying or generating a cover, thus our method has strong resistance to steganalysis. Our method is based on a text-image matching model which can measure the similarity between a text and an image. The text-image matching model utilizes a visual semantic embedding (VSE) model, which can project texts and images into a common subspace. After choosing a text from the text database randomly, several images relevant to the text are selected with the text-image matching model on the basis of the secret information that needs to be hidden. Experimental results and analysis prove that our method has adjustable hiding capacity and desirable security.

Keywords: Multi-modal steganography · Text-image matching ·
Visual semantic embedding · Steganography by cover selection ·
Coverless information hiding

1 Introduction

Steganography is a technique of embedding secret information imperceptibly into digital covers, such as images, texts and speeches [5, 10, 22]. Steganography can be

This research is supported by the National Key R&D Program (2018YFB0804103) and the National Natural Science Foundation of China (No. U1705261).

A few amazing views today. I'm warm weather-biased, and walking and riding was pleasant as heck!

Fig. 1. An example of tweets in Twitter. Text and images in a tweet are content-dependent.

roughly divided into three categories, *i.e.*, steganography by cover modification, steganography by cover synthesis and steganography by cover selection [7].

Steganography by cover modification embeds secret information by slightly modifying the content of the cover [12,18,28]. Since the content of the cover is modified during the embedding process, the stego (cover after embedding) is different from the original cover to some extent. Therefore, steganalysis methods may detect the steganography based on the modification traces [8,20].

The second category of steganography is to generate a cover in the light of the secret information. With the rapid development of natural language processing, it is possible to generate texts automatically based on recurrent neural networks [22]. However, the quality of the generated steganographic texts is considerably lower than the natural texts. It is easy for steganalysis methods to distinguish the generated stego texts from the natural texts [24,25].

Different from the above two kinds of steganography, steganography by cover selection embeds secret information by choosing natural covers from a constructed database. Hash functions are designed to transform a cover into a binary sequence by using the local features extracted from the cover [1,33]. After dividing the secret information into segments with the same length as the hash sequences, a series of covers are selected from the cover database by matching the secret information segments and the hash sequences. However, in these methods, the confidential messages contained by each cover are fixed, which increases the risk of leaking the secret information. Other method uses partial-duplicate image retrieval to transmit secret color image [31]. But this kind of methods are limited to transmit images only and the image recovered by the receiver is not the same as the original secret image. Besides, the covers (*i.e.* images or texts) transmitted by the existing steganographic methods may be content-independent while the contents in a post on the social networks such as Twitter[1] are likely to be relevant in semantics, as shown in Fig. 1. Therefore, these steganographic methods neglect the behavioral security and can be detected by side channel steganalysis [11,23].

In order to solve the issues mentioned above, we propose a multi-modal steganography scheme called MM-Stega. To the best of our knowledge, we are

---

[1] http://www.twitter.com/.

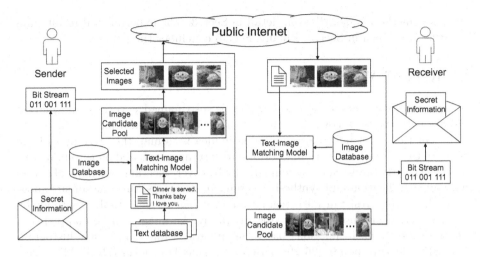

Fig. 2. The overall framework of the proposed multi-modal steganography.

the first to propose a steganographic method based on the relevance between two modalities. The overall framework of the proposed method is shown in Fig. 2. First the secret information is converted to a binary bit stream and divided into a number of segments. Then we trained our model with a large number of text-image pairs in the Twitter100k dataset [9]. The well-trained model can measure the similarity between a text and an image. A text database and an image database can be also constructed from the Twitter100k dataset. Given a text selected randomly from the text database, images in the image database are sorted according to the similarity between the image and the text. Then each image can represent a binary sequence on the basis of the sort index. The images of which the binary sequences are the same as the secret information segments are selected from the image database. Since the text and the selected images has semantic similarity, the combination of the text and the selected images can be transmitted to the receiver through social network without causing doubt.

Our method has three advantages over the previous steganographic methods. First, in contrast to steganography by modification and synthesis, our method utilizes natural covers. Thus, it can resist the detection of existing steganalysis methods. Meanwhile, different from the traditional steganography by cover selection which adopts only one modality of data, our method makes use of the relevance between two modalities of data, *e.g.*, texts and images. As a result, two more merits are attained. One is that the secret information contained by an image is not fixed, which brings about more security. Another is that the text and the images can be transmitted publicly on the Internet without arousing suspicion since the text and images are relevant in the semantic aspect.

The rest of this paper is organized as follows. Section 2 introduces related work about steganography by cover selection, and text-image matching. The proposed method is described in detail in Sect. 3. The experimental results and analysis are shown in Sect. 4. Finally, Sect. 5 concludes the paper.

2   Related Work

Steganography by cover selection, which is also named coverless information hiding, is to choose a cover (*e.g.* a text or an image) from a fixed database to represent the secret information. The basic idea is to map the attributes of the cover to the secret information according to certain rules based on the characteristics of the attributes. Since steganography by cover selection uses natural covers without modification and synthesis to transmit messages, this kind of steganography has strong resistance to steganalysis. Current steganographic methods by cover selection are mostly image steganography. An image can be mapped to a bit sequence by hash functions based on the gray value [33], HOGs histogram [34], SIFT feature points [26,29], Discrete Cosine Transform (DCT) [27], average pixel value [35] and so on. Since the hashing functions transform a cover to a certain bit sequence, the confidential messages contained by each cover is fixed. Thus these steganographic methods may leak the secret information. Visual words of images can also be used to hide text information by establishing a relational library between the visual words and text keywords [30]. The images which contain the sub-images with visual words related to the text information are used as stego-images for secret communication. Moreover, images can represent secret images with a set of appropriate partial duplicates of the given secret image [15,31]. However, these steganographic methods need to transmit several content-independent images, which neglect the behavioral security and may be detected by side channel steganalysis [11,23]. Besides coverless image steganography, there are also several text steganographic methods which are based on cover selection [2,32]. However, the hiding capacity of the method proposed in [2] is quite low and the method proposed in [32] will be unsuccessful probably.

Recently, visual semantic embedding (VSE) [6] is proposed for the task of text-image matching [21]. Text-image matching aims to find the images relevant to a given text. Since text and image are two different modalities, their similarity cannot be measured directly. The main idea of VSE is to map the two modalities into a common subspace and to embed the text and the image to vectors with the same dimension so that their similarity can be computed directly. This gives us some inspiration in steganography by cover selection. That is, secret information can be embedded in the relevance between the text and the image.

3   The Proposed Multi-modal Steganography

In this section, we will illustrate the proposed multi-modal steganography. The flow chart of our method for covert communication is represented in Fig. 3.

In our method, a text database and an image database are constructed by selecting a number of texts and images from the Twitter100k dataset [9], which is a large-scale text-image dataset. Then, a text-image matching model [6] is

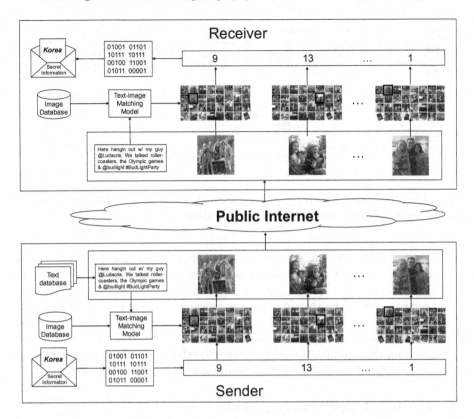

Fig. 3. The flow chart of the proposed multi-modal steganography for covert communication.

trained with the triplet rank loss on the Twitter100k dataset. Each text (image) in the text (image) database can be transformed to a vector with the text-image matching model. The similarity between the text and image can be computed by the dot product of their vectors.

To convey the secret information, the sender first converts the secret information into a binary sequence and divides it into n segments with the equal length k, where n and k are set according to the amount of the secret information and k is shared by the sender and receiver. Then each binary segment is transformed to a decimal number. In other words, the secret information is converted to n decimal numbers. After choosing a text randomly from the text database, all the images in the image database are sorted on the basis of the similarities between the images with the text. Then, n images can be selected according to the n decimal numbers. Each decimal number is regarded as the sort index of the image and the image selection is done without replacement. Then the combination of the text and the images is conveyed to the receiver.

The receiver shares the same text-image matching model and image database with the sender. After receiving a combination of one text and n images, all the

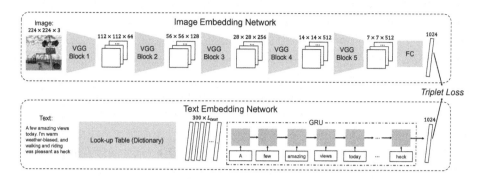

Fig. 4. The overall network structure of the text-image matching model, which consists of a text-embedding network and an image-embedding network.

images in the image database are sorted according to the similarities between the images and the text computed by the text-image matching model. The sort indexes of the received images can be obtained by matching them with the sorted images. Then, the sort indexes are converted into binary sequences and all the sequences are spliced together into a bit stream. Finally, the bit stream is converted to the secret information.

To sum up, the main parts of the proposed method are the text-image matching model, information hiding algorithm and information extraction algorithm.

3.1   The Text-Image Matching Model

We utilize a visual semantic embedding (VSE) model [6] as the text-image matching model in our method. The overall network structure of the text-image matching model is illustrated in Fig. 4, which contains a text-embedding network and an image-embedding network. The text and image embedding networks are used to project the two modalities into a common space, where the embeddings of the text and the image which share similar meanings are close to each other.

Text-Embedding Network. Recurrent neural network (RNN) has shown its efficiency in many machine learning tasks, especially when input and/or output are of variable length [4]. Each RNN has a recurrent hidden state whose activation at each time is dependent on the input at current time and the activations of the previous time. Thus, RNN can encode all the information of a sequence. Gated recurrent unit (GRU) [3] is a variant of RNN, which has an update gate and a reset gate. The update gate selects whether the hidden state is to be updated with a new hidden state and the reset gate decides whether the previous hidden state is ignored.

In the text-embedding network, a sentence is first converted into a sequence of 300-dim word vectors with a trainable look-up table. Then, a one-layer GRU is used to encode the sequence to a 1,024-dim vector, which is the output of the hidden state at the last time step. Finally, the text embedding u is normalized using its l_2 norm.

Image-Embedding Network. We adopt VGG19 [17] as the backbone of the image embedding network and the output dimension of the final fully connected (FC) layer is set to 1,024. The model pretrained on the ImageNet [16] is used for parameter initialization except for the final FC layer. The size of the input image is $224 \times 224 \times 3$ and the output of the image embedding network is a 1,024-dim vector. Then, the image embedding v is normalized with its l_2 norm.

Objective Function. With the text-embedding network and the image-embedding network, the similarity between the text c and the image i can be defined as an inner product of their embeddings.

$$s(i, c) = v \cdot u. \tag{1}$$

We use triplet loss to optimize the parameters of the model. Triplet loss is a common ranking loss used in the works of visual semantic embedding learning [14]. It is defined as follows:

$$l(i, c) = \max_{c'}[\alpha - s(i, c) + s(i, c')]_+ + \max_{i'}[\alpha - s(i, c) + s(i', c)]_+ \tag{2}$$

where $[x]_+ = max(x, 0)$, α is a margin, c' denotes the hardest negative text for the query image i and i' denotes the hardest negative image for the query text c. Here, the value of the margin α is set to 0.2.

3.2   Information Hiding Algorithm

There are four steps in the information hiding procedure, which will be introduced in detail as follows.

Text Selection. We choose a text randomly from the text database.

Image Ranking. For each image in the image database, we calculate the similarity between this image with the selected text based on the well-trained text-image matching model. All the images in the image database are sorted according to their similarities to the selected text.

Confidential Messages Preprocessing. We convert the confidential messages into a binary sequence. The binary sequence is divided into n segments with the equal length k. n is the number of the attached images to the selected text. k is the number of bits which are represented by an image. n and k are set according to the amount of the secret information, the size of the image database and the limitations of the data transmission platform. Then, each binary segment is transformed to a decimal number. Thus, the confidential messages are represented by n decimal numbers, $[i_1, i_2, ..., i_n]$. The maximum and the minimum of the decimal numbers are $2^k - 1$ and 0, respectively.

Image Selection. The n decimal numbers serve as the sort index of the image. To start with, we choose the $(i_1 + 1)$-th image in the sorted image database as the first image. Then this image is taken away from the sorted image database.

That is, the image selection is done without replacement so that no repeated images are chosen on the basis of the confidential messages. Afterwards, the rest $n-1$ images are chosen in this way.

After these four steps, we will get a text and n images which represent the confidential messages. Then the combination of the text and the images can be conveyed to the receiver.

3.3   Information Extraction Algorithm

The receiver shares the text-image matching model, the image database and k with the sender. After receiving the transmitted text and n images, three steps are operated to extract the confidential messages.

Image Ranking. For each image in the image database, the similarity between this image with the received text is calculated based on the shared text-image matching model. All the images in the image database are sorted according to their similarities to the received text.

Image Matching. By matching the received images with the sorted image database, n decimal numbers, *i.e.*, the sort indexes of the received images are obtained. It has to be noticed that the image should be taken away from the sorted image database after obtaining its sort index.

Confidential Messages Recovery. After subtracting 1 from all the n decimal numbers, each decimal number is converted to a binary sequence. Then, all the binary sequences are spliced together into a bit stream. Finally, the bit stream is converted to the confidential messages.

4   Experiments and Analysis

The performance of the proposed method can be evaluated from three aspects, *e.g.*, hiding capacity, text-image relevance and resistance to the steganalysis methods.

4.1   Hiding Capacity

The hiding capacity of the proposed method is proportional to the number of companied images with a text and the bits contained by each image. Assume each text is companied with n images and each image represents k-bit binary sequence, then the hiding capacity of the proposed method is $k \times n$ bits. The hiding capacity of the proposed method is adjustable. For n, the maximum number of images in one post is various on different website. For example, the maximum numbers are four and ten for Twitter[2] and Instagram[3], respectively.

---

[2] http://www.twitter.com/.

[3] http://instagram.com/.

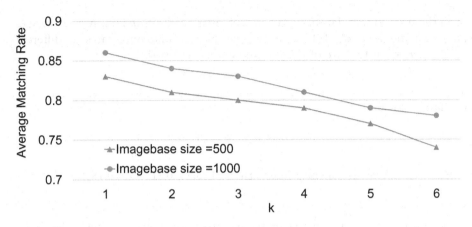

Fig. 5. The comparison of the average matching rates on different sizes of the image database.

And one post of Facebook[4] can contains more than fifty images. For k, k is limited by the size of the image database and the relevance between the text and the top 2^k most similar images, which will be discussed in detail in Sect. 4.2.

4.2 Text-Image Relevance

The imperceptibility of the proposed method depends on the relevance between the text and the companied images. The more relevant between the text and the images, the less suspicion will be aroused. In order to evaluate the relevance between the texts and images, we select 100 texts and 1,000 images from the Twitter100k dataset [9] to form a text database and an image database. All the texts and images are labeled by hand with several tags. Table 1 gives a summary of these tags.

Table 1. Tags of the texts and images in the constructed database.

people, male, female, groupphoto, bodypart, makeup, costume, clothes, shoe, scene, indoor, outdoor, food, vehicle, plane, car, ship, electronics animal, cat, dog, other_animal, greenplant, botany, flower

The relevance between a text and an image is measured by matching the tags. If a text and an image contain a common tag, the image is regarded as relevant to the text. Given a text, we define matching rate@K as the proportion of the relevant images in the top K similar images calculated by the text-image matching model. Average matching rate@K is the mean of the matching rate@K

---

[4] http://www.facebook.com/.

of all the texts in text database. When each image contains k bits, $K = 2^k$ images are in candidate pool. Table 2 shows the average matching rates at different values of k when the size of the image database is 1,000.

Table 2. The average matching rates at different values of k when the size of the image database is 1,000.

k	1	2	3	4	5	6
K	2	4	8	16	32	64
Average matching rate	0.86	0.84	0.83	0.81	0.79	0.78

We also calculate the average matching rate on the half of the image database. The experiment results are represented in Fig. 5. It can be found that the average matching rate decreases seriously when the size of the image database is reduced by half. Thus, the text-image relevance can also be further improved by enlarging the image database with the existing dataset such as the Twitter100k dataset [9]. As a result, the value of k can be set larger, which means each image is able to represent more secret information.

Some examples of the proposed method are given in Fig. 6. Each secret information is an English word of five characters, which can be transformed into 40-bit binary sequence. The values of n and k are set to 8 and 5, respectively. That is, each text is companied with 8 images and each image represents 5 bits.

Secret Information: *Japan*
The whole family did #cap10k in April. Proud of my boys! Fun morning. Love #ATX. #LifeIsGood #familyfitness #health

Secret Information: *Korea*
Here hangin out w/ my guy @Ludacris. We talked roller-coasters, the Olympic games & @budlight #BudLightParty

Fig. 6. Examples of the proposed multi-modal steganography. Each text is companied with 8 images and each image represents 5 bits.

4.3 Resistance to the Steganalysis Methods

An ideal steganographic method should have a good resistance to the steganalysis methods. However, existing steganalysis methods can successfully detect the steganography by modification [13, 19] and steganography by synthesis [24, 25]. In contrast to the previous steganography, the proposed multi-modal steganography embeds secret information without modifying or generating the cover. All the covers are natural and original. Meanwhile, the texts and images are relevant in semantics. Therefore, the secret information in the combination of the text and images cannot be detected by the existing steganalysis methods.

5   Conclusion

This paper proposes a novel multi-modal steganography (MM-Stega) scheme based on text-image matching. A visual semantic embedding (VSE) network is adopted as the text-image matching model. The secret information is hidden in the combination of a text and several relevant images. The required text database and the image database can be constructed from the existing Twitter100k dataset without much effort. The texts and images are not modified or generated in the information hiding process. Therefore, the proposed method can effectively resist the detection of the existing steganalysis methods.

References

1. Cao, Y., Zhou, Z., Sun, X., Gao, C.: Coverless information hiding based on the molecular structure images of material. Comput. Mater. Cont. **54**(2), 197–207 (2018)
2. Chen, X., Sun, H., Tobe, Y., Zhou, Z., Sun, X.: Coverless information hiding method based on the Chinese mathematical expression. In: Huang, Z., Sun, X., Luo, J., Wang, J. (eds.) ICCCS 2015. LNCS, vol. 9483, pp. 133–143. Springer, Cham (2015). https://doi.org/10.1007/978-3-319-27051-7_12
3. Cho, K., et al.: Learning phrase representations using RNN encoder-decoder for statistical machine translation. arXiv preprint arXiv:1406.1078 (2014)
4. Chung, J., Gulcehre, C., Cho, K., Bengio, Y.: Empirical evaluation of gated recurrent neural networks on sequence modeling. arXiv preprint arXiv:1412.3555 (2014)
5. Du, Y., Yin, Z., Zhang, X.: Improved lossless data hiding for JPEG images based on histogram modification. Comput. Mater. Cont. **55**(3), 495–507 (2018)
6. Faghri, F., Fleet, D.J., Kiros, J.R., Fidler, S.: VSE++: improving visual-semantic embeddings with hard negatives. arXiv preprint arXiv:1707.05612 (2017)
7. Fridrich, J.: Steganography in Digital Media: Principles, Algorithms, and Applications. Cambridge University Press, Cambridge (2009)
8. Fridrich, J., Kodovsky, J.: Rich models for steganalysis of digital images. IEEE Trans. Inf. Forensics Secur. **7**(3), 868–882 (2012)
9. Hu, Y., Zheng, L., Yang, Y., Huang, Y.: Twitter100k: a real-world dataset for weakly supervised cross-media retrieval. IEEE Trans. Multimedia **20**(4), 927–938 (2018)
10. Huang, Y., Liu, C., Tang, S., Bai, S.: Steganography integration into a low-bit rate speech codec. IEEE Trans. Inf. Forensics Secur. **7**(6), 1865–1875 (2012)
11. Li, L., Zhang, W., Chen, K., Zha, H., Yu, N.: Side channel steganalysis: when behavior is considered in steganographer detection. Multimedia Tools Appl. **78**(7), 8041–8055 (2019)

12. Li, X., Yang, B., Cheng, D., Zeng, T.: A generalization of LSB matching. IEEE Signal Process. Lett. **16**(2), 69–72 (2009)
13. Lie, W.N., Lin, G.S.: A feature-based classification technique for blind image steganalysis. IEEE Trans. Multimedia **7**(6), 1007–1020 (2005)
14. Liu, R., Zhao, Y., Wei, S., Zheng, L., Yang, Y.: Modality-invariant image-text embedding for image-sentence matching. ACM Trans. Multimedia Comput. Commun. Appl. **15**(1), 27 (2019)
15. Luo, Y., Qin, J., Xiang, X., Tan, Y., Liu, Q., Xiang, L.: Coverless real-time image information hiding based on image block matching and dense convolutional network. J. Real-Time Image Process. **17**(1), 1–11 (2019)
16. Russakovsky, O., et al.: ImageNet large scale visual recognition challenge. Int. J. Comput. Vis. **115**(3), 211–252 (2015)
17. Simonyan, K., Zisserman, A.: Very deep convolutional networks for large-scale image recognition. arXiv preprint arXiv:1409.1556 (2014)
18. Westfeld, A.: F5—a steganographic algorithm. In: Moskowitz, I.S. (ed.) IH 2001. LNCS, vol. 2137, pp. 289–302. Springer, Heidelberg (2001). https://doi.org/10.1007/3-540-45496-9_21
19. Wu, S., Zhong, S., Liu, Y.: Deep residual learning for image steganalysis. Multimedia Tools Appl. **77**(9), 10437–10453 (2018)
20. Xu, G., Wu, H., Shi, Y.: Structural design of convolutional neural networks for steganalysis. IEEE Signal Process. Lett. **23**(5), 708–712 (2016)
21. Yan, F., Mikolajczyk, K.: Deep correlation for matching images and text. In: IEEE Conference on Computer Vision and Pattern Recognition, pp. 3441–3450 (2015)
22. Yang, Z., Guo, X., Chen, Z., Huang, Y., Zhang, Y.: RNN-Stega: linguistic steganography based on recurrent neural networks. IEEE Trans. Inf. Forensics Secur. **14**(5), 1280–1295 (2018)
23. Yang, Z., Hu, Y., Huang, Y., Zhang, Y.: Behavioral security in covert communication systems. arXiv preprint arXiv:1910.09759 (2019)
24. Yang, Z., Huang, Y., Zhang, Y.: A fast and efficient text steganalysis method. IEEE Signal Process. Lett. **26**(4), 627–631 (2019)
25. Yang, Z., Wang, K., Li, J., Huang, Y., Zhang, Y.: TS-RNN: text steganalysis based on recurrent neural networks. IEEE Signal Process. Lett. **26**(12), 1743–1747 (2019). https://doi.org/10.1109/LSP.2019.2920452
26. Yuan, C., Xia, Z., Sun, X.: Coverless image steganography based on SIFT and BOF. J. Internet Technol. **18**(2), 435–442 (2017)
27. Zhang, X., Peng, F., Long, M.: Robust coverless image steganography based on DCT and IDA topic classification. IEEE Trans. Multimedia **20**(12), 3223–3238 (2018)
28. Zhang, Y., Ye, D., Gan, J., Li, Z., Cheng, Q.: An image steganography algorithm based on quantization index modulation resisting scaling attacks and statistical detection. Comput. Mater. Cont. **56**(1), 151–167 (2018)
29. Zheng, S., Wang, L., Ling, B., Hu, D.: Coverless information hiding based on robust image hashing. In: Huang, D.-S., Hussain, A., Han, K., Gromiha, M.M. (eds.) ICIC 2017. LNCS (LNAI), vol. 10363, pp. 536–547. Springer, Cham (2017). https://doi.org/10.1007/978-3-319-63315-2_47
30. Zhou, Z., Cao, Y., Sun, X.: Coverless information hiding based on bag-of-words model of image. J. Appl. Sci. **34**(5), 527–536 (2016)
31. Zhou, Z., Mu, Y., Wu, Q.J.: Coverless image steganography using partial-duplicate image retrieval. Soft. Comput. **23**(13), 4927–4938 (2019)

32. Zhou, Z., Mu, Y., Zhao, N., Wu, Q.M.J., Yang, C.-N.: Coverless information hiding method based on multi-keywords. In: Sun, X., Liu, A., Chao, H.-C., Bertino, E. (eds.) ICCCS 2016. LNCS, vol. 10039, pp. 39–47. Springer, Cham (2016). https://doi.org/10.1007/978-3-319-48671-0_4

33. Zhou, Z., Sun, H., Harit, R., Chen, X., Sun, X.: Coverless image steganography without embedding. In: Huang, Z., Sun, X., Luo, J., Wang, J. (eds.) ICCCS 2015. LNCS, vol. 9483, pp. 123–132. Springer, Cham (2015). https://doi.org/10.1007/978-3-319-27051-7_11

34. Zhou, Z., Wu, Q.J., Yang, C.N., Sun, X., Pan, Z.: Coverless image steganography using histograms of oriented gradients-based hashing algorithm. J. Internet Technol. 18(5), 1177–1184 (2017)

35. Zou, L., Sun, J., Gao, M., Wan, W., Gupta, B.B.: A novel coverless information hiding method based on the average pixel value of the sub-images. Multimedia Tools Appl. 78(7), 7965–7980 (2019)

Secure Outsourced Numerical Solution of Algebraic Equations

Ke Zeng, Peijia Zheng$^{(\boxtimes)}$ (ID), and Hongmei Liu

School of Data and Computer Science, Guangdong Key Laboratory of Information Security Technology, Sun Yat-Sen University, Guangzhou 510006, China
zengk8@mail2.sysu.edu.cn, {zhpj,isslhm}@mail.sysu.edu.cn

Abstract. Numerical methods are designed to provide numerical solutions of algebraic equations, because there are not analytical solutions for algebraic equations whose degrees are larger than four. In cloud computing, outsourcing numerical solutions to the cloud raises privacy issues due to the privacy sensitive coefficients. In this paper, we propose an effective privacy-preserving computation outsourcing protocol for the common numerical solutions of algebraic equations. We first present a protocol that can securely evaluate Newton iterative method with the preservation of the private coefficients, by relying on somewhat homomorphic encryption. We then provide two implementations of our protocol based on the two popular somewhat homomorphic encryption schemes, i.e., the Brakerski-Gentry-Vaikuntanathan (BGV) scheme and the CKKS scheme. We conduct experiments to compare the two implementations and analyze the security and effectiveness. The experimental results show that the proposed scheme is effective in practice, and the CKKS-based implementation is general better than the BGV-based implementation.

Keywords: Numerical solution · Newton iterative method · Fully homomorphic encryption · Signal processing in the encrypted domain · Cloud computing

1 Introduction

In the age of big data, enormous data are being generated exponentially in different areas, such as medical data, traffic data, business data, etc. To discovery meaningful information and make use of these data, various data analysis methods are developed, including numerical solution of algebraic equations, matrix factorization, data fitting, linear programming, etc. For example, solving characteristic equations is a necessary way to discovery the eigenvalues of matrices. Storing and processing these large-scale data are unaffordable tasks for a resource-limited data owner. Luckily, with the development of cloud computing, the data owner can outsource the data storage and processing tasks to the cloud. However, outsourcing the data storage and processing tasks will raise privacy issues. The cloud server may misuse data without asking the permission of the data owners. Therefore, it is necessary and meaningful to develop a secure outsourcing scheme for solving algebraic equations without revealing the private coefficient data to the cloud.

© Springer Nature Singapore Pte Ltd. 2020
X. Sun et al. (Eds.): ICAIS 2020, CCIS 1254, pp. 326–337, 2020.
https://doi.org/10.1007/978-981-15-8101-4_30

Signal processing in the encrypted domain (SPED) [1], can be used to help develop privacy-preserving applications in cloud computing. With SPED techniques, the cloud server can perform processing and analysis directly on encrypted data without learning the private information. There are already a considerable amount of researches in the field of SPED. Some frequently-used signal transforms have been realized in the encrypted domain, including encrypted domain discrete Fourier transform [2], discrete wavelet transform [3], number theoretic transform [4], and Walsh-Hadamard transform [5]. There are also many reports on developing practical privacy-preserving application, such as privacy-preserving content-aware search [6], encrypted image reversible data hiding [7], privacy-preserving image feature extraction [8], secure verifiable diversity ranking search [9], privacy-preserving matrix QR factorization [10], privacy-preserving video anomaly detection and localization [11].

Homomorphic encryption (HE) is a foundational tool in SPED. Specifically, HE can preserve some algebraic structures of the plaintext space after encryption. Based on HE, we can operate the plaintexts by means of manipulating the ciphertexts without performing decryption. We can classify existing HEs into different kinds. Partial homomorphic encryption (PHE) is a kind of HE that allows preserve one algebraic operation in the ciphertext space. Paillier encryption [12] is a famous partial HE, which is widely used to develop privacy-preserving applications. Recently, several somewhat homomorphic encryption (SWHE) schemes [13–15] are proposed to support both addition and multiplication in the ciphertext space. By using bootstrapping techniques [16], we can finally obtain fully homomorphic encryption (FHE) schemes that allow evaluations of any functions. However, the bootstrapping processes generally require high time and memory overheads, and thus, not so efficient in practice. As a compromise, SHWE is more much efficient, and also satisfies the requirements of some particular applications. Therefore, we adopt SWHE as our encryption method and design our privacy-preserving solutions.

Considering that solving algebraic equations is necessary in many applications, e.g., discovering eigenvalues of matrices by solving the characteristic equations, it is very likely that solving algebraic equations needs to be implemented in the encrypted domain. In this paper, we propose a privacy-preserving outsourced scheme that securely realizes numerical solutions of algebraic equations in the cloud without exposing the plaintext coefficients to the cloud. Specifically, we focus on the secure implementation of Newton iterative method, which is a popular numerical method to solve algebraic equations. The private coefficient data is encrypted and stored in the cloud server. We present a secure protocol allows the cloud server performs Newton iterative method and obtains the encrypted numerical solutions. We also conduct experiments to compare the performances of the proposed scheme under two different types of HEs, i.e., BGV and CKKS. We list two contributions of this paper as follows.

1. We have proposed a privacy-preserving protocol to perform Newton iterative method in the encrypted domain, by relying on SWHE.
2. We have conducted several experiments on the proposed protocol to compare the performances under two different HEs BGV and CKKS. The compassion results show that the CKKS-based implementation is generally better than the BGV-based implementation.

The rest of the paper is organized as follow. In Sect. 2, we introduce our security model, cryptographic tool, and Newton iterative method. Section 3 presents the proposed privacy-preserving protocol to implement Newton iterative method in the encrypted domain. We give our experimental results in Sect. 4. Section 5 concludes the paper.

2   Problem Statement

2.1   System Model

In Fig. 1, we sketch the proposed system model. Our model consists of three parties, the data owner, the cloud service provider (CSP), and the privacy service provider (PSP). The data owner has the coefficient data of the algebraic equation to be solved. These coefficient data is regarded as private sensitive.

The PSP generates the public encryption key *pk* and the private decryption key *sk*. The PSP sends both the public and private keys to the data owner, and delivers only the public key to the CSP. The data owner encrypts all the private coefficients and stores them in the CSP. The CSP executes a protocol with the assistance of the PSP, in order to find the solutions of the algebraic equation regarding to the encrypted coefficients. The encrypted solutions are then sent back to the data owner. The data owner will then decrypt these encrypted values with the secret decryption key to obtain the cleartext solutions.

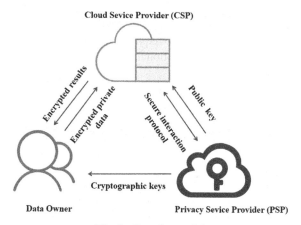

Fig. 1. Security model

2.2   Threat Model

Throughout this paper, we adopt the semi-honest security setting that is widely used in related works [17, 18]. The CSP and the PSP are assumed to follow the protocol honestly but try to learn the private information as much as possible from the encrypted inputs and exchanged messages. Besides, we also suppose that the CSP and the PSP are independent, namely there is no collusion between the CSP and the PSP. This is a reasonable assumption, because these service providers are unlikely to collude with each other for their own reputation and interests.

2.3 Cryptographic Tool: Somewhat Homomorphic Encryption

We employ somewhat homomorphic encryption (SHWE) as the data encryption method in our protocol. SWHE permits arbitrary homomorphic additions and a limited number of homomorphic multiplications on ciphertexts, without any interaction with other parties. Let us use $[[\cdot]]$ to denote the encryption operator. Then $[[\xi]]$ means an encryption value of a message ξ. For any two ciphertexts $[[\xi]]$ and $[[\eta]]$, we can homomorphically compute the sum and the product of their plaintexts as

$$[[\xi + \eta]] = [[\xi]] \oplus [[\eta]] \tag{1}$$

$$[[\xi\eta]] = [[\xi]] \otimes [[\eta]] \tag{2}$$

where $\oplus$ and $\otimes$ denote the homomorphic addition and multiplication, respectively. For convenience, we will use $[[\xi]]+[[\eta]]$ and $[[\xi]][[\eta]]$ to denote $[[\xi]]\oplus[[\eta]]$ and $[[\xi]]\otimes[[\eta]]$, respectively. We use two particular SWHE schemes in our experiments, i.e., the BGV scheme [19] and the CKKS scheme [20]. The BGV scheme is a leveled FHE without bootstrapping, whose hardness is based on learning with error (LWE) problems [21]. Different from the BGV scheme, the CKKS scheme supports approximate computation over encrypted data. We refer to [22, 23] for more details on the encryption/decryption algorithms, parameter settings, and security analyses of the two schemes.

2.4 Numerical Solution of Algebraic Equations

Given a algebraic equation of degree n

$$f(x) = a_0 + a_1x + a_2x^2 + \cdots + a_nx^n = 0 \tag{3}$$

where $x \in \mathbb{R}$ denotes the unknown number and $\{a_0, a_1, \ldots a_n\} \triangleq a$ are the coefficients. The process of solving the algebraic equation is to find a root $\bar{x}$ satisfying $f(\bar{x}) = 0$. The approaches to solve algebraic equation can be used in Spectrum analysis, Channel coding and decoding etc. There are many approaches to solving algebraic equations, such as Newton iterative method [24], secant method, etc. Among these approaches, Newton iterative method is one of the most famous methods to solve algebraic equations. Let us denote the derived function of $f(x)$ by $f'(x)$, which is given as

$$f'(x) = a_1 + 2a_2x + \cdots + na_nx^{n-1} \tag{4}$$

We show how to use Newton iterative method to solve algebraic equations in the following. Before the beginning of the iteration, we randomly choose an initial number $x_0 \in \mathbb{R}$, specify the minimum error ϵ_{min}, and determine the maximum iterations N_{max}.

1. Suppose that the current approximation is denoted by x_k.

2. Compute the function values of $f(x_k)$ and $f'(x_k)$. The tangent line ℓ to the curve $y = f(x)$ at $x = x_k$ is

$$y = f'(x_k)(x - x_k) + f(x_k) \tag{5}$$

The x-intercept of ℓ is set as the next approximation x_{k+1}, which is the root of $f'(x_k)(x - x_k) + f(x_k) = 0$. Specifically, we can have

$$x_{k+1} = x_k - \frac{f(x_k)}{f'(x_k)} \tag{6}$$

3. Compute the distance between x_k and x_{k+1}, i.e., $|x_k - x_{k+1}|$. If this distance is less than the predefined error ϵ_{min}, or the number of iteration is greater than N_{max}, then the iteration process ends and outputs x_{k+1} as the root of $f(x)$. Otherwise, go to Step 2 and continue the iteration process.

3   Privacy-Preserving Numerical Solution of Algebraic Equations

The BGV scheme and the CKKS scheme permit both homomorphic addition and multiplication, however, it is still inefficient to homomorphically evaluate more complex operations, such as comparison, division, etc. For efficiency consideration, we let the CSP complete the homomorphic division by running an interactive protocol with the PSP who has the decryption key.

3.1   Privacy-Preserving Newton Iterative Method

To implement Newton iterative method in the encrypted domain, we need to homomorphically implement the operations in the general term formula Eq. (6). Since Eq. (6) involves the division operation, we need to perform division in the encrypted domain. Specifically, the CSP will blind both the numerator and denominator, send them to the PSP. The PSP will decrypt them, perform division, and then send the encrypted quotient back to the CSP. By using this protocol, the CSP can succeed in solving algebraic equations in the encrypted domain. We provide the details of the privacy-preserving Newton iterative method in Algorithm 1. After obtaining the encrypted solution $[[\chi]]$, the CSP will send $[[\chi]]$ to the data owner. With the decryption key sk, the data owner can then decrypt $[[\chi]]$ and obtain the cleartext solution χ.

3.2   Security Analysis

We analyze the security of the proposed protocol against the semi-honest CSP or PSP. The CSP has encrypted coefficients $\{[[a_i]]\}_{i=0}^{n}$, the maximum iterations N_{max}, and the encrypted quotient sent from the PSP. The CSP has the encryption key pk and does not have the decryption key sk. Thus, the CSP cannot learn any information on the plaintext values from the stored ciphertexts and the intermediate data. The PSP has the encryption and the decryption keys. The PSP can obtain the quotient $\frac{f(x_k)}{f'(x_k)}$ during the decryption.

However, the PSP does not have the encrypted coefficients $\{[\![a_i]\!]\}_{i=0}^n$, so the PSP cannot learn the private sensitive coefficients $\{a_i\}_{i=0}^n$.

Algorithm 1 : Privacy-preserving Newton iterative method for solving algebraic equations

---

1: **Input of CSP**: Public encryption key pk, the maximum iterations N_{max}, and encrypted coefficients $\{[\![a_i]\!]\}_{i=0}^n$.

2: **Input of PSP**: Public encryption key pk and private decryption key sk.

3: **Output of CSP**: An encrypted solution $[\![\chi]\!]$ of the algebraic equation $a_0 + a_1 x + a_2 x^2 + \cdots + a_n x^n = 0$.

4: **CSP**:

5: Initialize the number of iterations $v \leftarrow 0$.

6: Initialize $\gamma \leftarrow [\![0]\!]$.

7: Randomly choose an initial integer $x_0 \in \mathbb{z}$, encrypt x_0, and set $[\![\chi]\!] \leftarrow [\![x_0]\!]$

8: If $v \geq N_{max}$, then end the iteration process and output $[\![\chi]\!]$. Otherwise, compute $[\![\chi]\!] = [\![\chi]\!] - \gamma$.

9: Homomorphically compute the function values $f(\chi)$ and $f'(\chi)$ in the encrypted domain with Horner's method, i.e.,

$$[\![f(\chi)]\!] = [\![a_0]\!] + [\![a_1]\!][\![\chi]\!] + [\![a_2]\!][\![\chi]\!]^2 + \cdots + [\![a_n]\!][\![\chi]\!]^n \tag{7}$$

$$[\![f'(\chi)]\!] = [\![a_1]\!] + [\![2]\!][\![a_2]\!][\![x]\!] + \cdots + [\![n]\!][\![a_n]\!][\![x]\!]^{n-1} \tag{8}$$

where $[\![\chi]\!]^n$ denotes the product of multiplying $[\![\chi]\!]$ n times.

10: Randomly choose an integer r, and then compute $[\![r]\!][\![f(\chi)]\!] = [\![rf(\chi)]\!]$ and $[\![r]\!][\![f'(\chi)]\!] = [\![rf'(\chi)]\!]$.

11: Send $[\![rf(\chi)]\!]$ and $[\![rf'(\chi)]\!]$ to the PSP.

12: **PSP**:

13: Decrypt the two received ciphertexts to obtain $rf(\chi)$ and $rf'(\chi)$.

14: Compute $\gamma \leftarrow \left[\!\left[\frac{rf(x_k)}{rf'(x_k)}\right]\!\right] = \left[\!\left[\frac{f(x_k)}{f'(x_k)}\right]\!\right]$.

15: Send γ to the CSP and goto Line 8.

---

4 Experimental Results

The CSP is deployed in a 64-bit Ubuntu 16.04 server with Intel Core i7-6950X CPUs @3.00 GHz and 64 GB memory. The PSP is deployed in a 64-bit Ubuntu 16.04 machine with Intel i5-3470U CPU @3.20 GHz and 8 GB memory. The data owner is simulated by a 64-bit Windows 8 PC with Intel i5-5350U CPU @1.80 GHz and 8 GB memory. The bandwidth of our local area network is 95 Mbps.

We provide two implementations of the proposed protocol by using two HE libraries HELib [25] and HEAAN [26], respectively. The parameter settings of HELib in our experiment is given as follows. The security parameter $\kappa = 80$, the plaintext base $p = 1021$, the Hensel lifting $\rho = 2$, the number of columns in key-switching matrix $\gamma = 2$, and the number of levels in the modulus chain $\Lambda = 20$. As for the parameters of HEAAN in our experiment, we have that the ciphertext modulus $\mathcal{E} = 2^{355}$, the scaling factor $\Pi = 2^{15}$, and the number of slots $\Theta = 2^{15}$.

4.1 The Implementation Based on HELib

HELib is a library implements the BGV scheme with the ciphertext packing technique and the Gentry-Halevi-Smart optimization. To process rational numbers with the BGV scheme, we need to choose a proper quantization factor to scale rational numbers to proper integers. We test the proposed method on three algebraic equations of degree four, i.e.,

$$2 + x + 3x^2 + 4x^3 - 2x^4 = 0, \qquad x_0 = -2.1 \qquad (9)$$

$$3 + 4x + 5x^2 - 4x^3 - 2x^4 = 0, \qquad x_0 = 6.6 \qquad (10)$$

$$3.2 + 4.3x - 6.7x^2 - 2.1x^3 + 1.1x^4 = 0, \qquad x_0 = -8.1 \qquad (11)$$

The quantization factor in our experiment is chosen as 100, and the maximum iteration number N_{max} is 8. In Table 1, we show the intermediate value x_ks at every stage by using the proposed secure Newton iterative protocol to solve the three algebraic equations in the encrypted domain.

Table 1. The value of x_k at every stage by using the HELib-based implementation of our privacy-preserving Newton iterative protocol for the three test equations. X denotes the solution obtained with the conventional Newton iterative method. $\epsilon = |X - \chi|$ is used to evaluate the distance between X and χ.

x_k	Equation		
	Equation (9)	Equation (10)	Equation (11)
x_0	−2.10	6.60	−8.10
x_1	−1.48	4.45	−5.98
x_2	−0.80	3.32	−4.50
x_3	−0.92	2.51	−3.44
x_4	−0.84	1.95	−2.70
x_5	−0.83	1.60	−2.23
x_6	−0.83	1.44	−1.99
x_7	−0.83	1.40	−1.92
x_8	−0.83	1.40	−1.91
χ	−0.83	1.40	−1.91
X	−0.830044	1.39045	−1.91764
ϵ	4.4×10^{-5}	0.00955	0.00764

We also provide the result X obtained with the conventional Newton iterative method, as well as the absolute difference between X and the result obtained with our method, i.e., $\epsilon = |X - \chi|$. From Table 1, we can see that all the ϵ s have the magnitude of 10 to the power of -3. Thus, the solutions obtained with the HELib-based implementation of our privacy-preserving Newton iterative method have enough precisions, compared with the solutions obtained with conventional methods.

4.2 The Implementation Based on HEAAN

HEAAN is a library implements the CKKS scheme, which has native support for approximate numbers and their arithmetic. We realize the proposed protocol by using HEAAN, and test it on Eqs. (9)–(11). The experimental results are shown in Table 2, from which we can see that all the ϵ s have the magnitude of 10 to the power of -4. Therefore, the solutions obtained with the HEAAN-based implementation of our privacy-preserving Newton iterative method are satisfactory precise.

Table 2. The value of x_k at every stage by using the HEAAN-based implementation of our privacy-preserving Newton iterative protocol for the three test equations. X denotes the solution obtained with the conventional Newton iterative method. $\epsilon = |X - \chi|$ is used to evaluate the distance between X and χ.

x_k	Equation		
	Equation (9)	Equation (10)	Equation (11)
x_0	−2.10	6.60	−8.10
x_1	−1.559	4.89585	−6.06454
x_2	−1.16977	3.6423	−4.57401
x_3	−0.934967	2.73646	−3.50438
x_4	−0.837616	2.10611	−2.76667
x_5	−0.828979	1.70279	−2.29757
x_6	−0.830017	1.4878	−2.04548
x_7	−0.829865	1.41039	−1.94711
x_8	−0.829865	1.39336	−1.92269
χ	−0.829865	1.39134	−1.911775
X	−0.830044	1.39045	−1.91764
ϵ	0.000179	0.00089	0.00011

4.3 Communication Overhead

In the experiments with the chosen parameter settings, the data size of a ciphertext in the HELib-based implementation is about 110 KB, and the data size of a ciphertext in the HEAAN-based implementation is nearly 70 KB. We also conduct experiment to study this relationship of communication overhead versus the degree of equation. The degree of the equation increases from two to five. We show the experimental result in Fig. 2, which shows that the HELib-based implementation requires more communication overhead than the HEAAN-based implementation for the algebraic equations of all degrees.

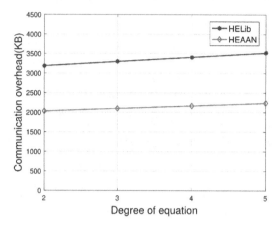

Fig. 2. Communication overhead comparison for the HELib-based and the HEAAN-based implementations.

4.4 Running Time

We compare the running times between the HELib-based implementation and the HEAAN-based implementation. Similarity, the degree of the algebraic equation varies from two to five. For each degree, we generate 20 equations, whose coefficients are random chosen within the interval $[-10, 10]$. The initial value x_0 is set as 10. We show the average running times of the two implementations for each degree in Fig. 3. When the degree is lower than three, the HELib-based implementation takes more time than the HEAAN-based implementation. However, as the degree increases, the running time of

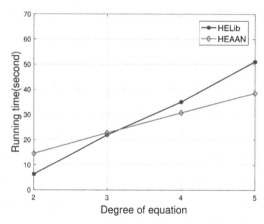

Fig. 3. Running time comparison for the HELib-based and the HEAAN-based implementations.

the HELib-based implementation becomes longer than that of the HEAAN-based implementation. This is because the HELib-based implementation needs to perform scaling
and quantization to obtain an integer version of x. As the degree increases, the absolute
value of the function value $f(x)$ is enlarged rapidly, which results in the rapid increase
of the practical running time simultaneously.

4.5 Precision

The accuracy of the solution obtained with Newton iterative method is related with the
coefficients of the equation. However, we can still study the trend of the accuracy by
calculating the mean value of the absolute differences ($\in$ s) between several equations.
Similarly, the degree of the test equation varies from two to five. For each degree, 20
equations are generated with random coefficients. The experimental results are shown
in Fig. 4. The average $\in$ of the HELib-based implementation is between 0.005 and 0.01.
As for the HEAAN-based implementation, the average $\in$ is less than 0.001. According
to our experimental results, therefore, the HEAAN-based implementation has a better
accuracy than the HELib-based implementation.

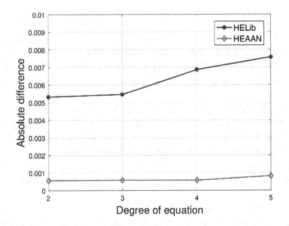

Fig. 4. Precision comparison for the HELib-based and the HEAAN-based implementations.

5   Conclusions

We have proposed a privacy-preserving protocol to securely outsource the computation
of Newton iterative method to the cloud, which is used to find numerical solutions of
algebraic equations in the encrypted domain. The proposed protocol relies on the homomorphic properties of SWHE. We have provided two implementations of the proposed
protocol by using the HELib and the HEAAN libraries. We have also conducted experiments to study the system performances, including communication overhead, running
time, and precision. With our privacy-preserving protocol, it is able to enrich the functionality of secure outsourced computation in cloud computing. In future, we will focus

on the following aspects of our works. 1) Beside Newton iterative method, we will consider the implementations of more different numerical methods for solving equations in the encrypted domain. 2) We will modify the proposed scheme to adopt to different application scenarios, such as secure outsourced computation with one cloud server, secure mobile cloud computing, etc.

Acknowledgements. This work was supported in part by the Guangdong Natural Science Foundation under Grant 2019A1515010746, in part by the Fundamental Research Funds for the Central Universities under Grant 19LGPY218, in part by the NSFC under Grant 61502547 and Grant 61672551, in part by Guangdong Science and Technology Plan Project under Grant 2013B090800009, in part by the Guangzhou Science and Technology Plan Project under Grant 2014Y2-00019 and Grant 201707010167.

References

1. Lagendijk, R.L., Erkin, Z., Barni, M.: Encrypted signal processing for privacy protection: conveying the utility of homomorphic encryption and multiparty computation. IEEE Sig. Process. Mag. **30**(1), 82–105 (2013)
2. Bianchi, T., Piva, A., Barni, M.: On the implementation of the discrete fourier transform in the encrypted domain. IEEE Trans. Inf. Forensics Secur. **4**(1), 86–97 (2009)
3. Zheng, P., Huang, J.: Discrete wavelet transform and data expansion reduction in homomorphic encrypted domain. IEEE Trans. Image Process. **22**(6), 2455–2468 (2013)
4. Pedrouzo-Ulloa, A., Troncoso-Pastoriza, J.R., Pérez-González, F.: Number throretic transforms for secure signal processing. IEEE Trans. Inf. Forensics Secur. **12**(5), 1125–1140 (2017)
5. Zheng, P., Huang, J.: Efficient encrypted images filtering and transform coding with walsh-hadamard transform and parallelization. IEEE Trans. Image Process. **27**(5), 2541–2556 (2018)
6. Fu, Z., Xia, L., Liu, Y., Tian, Z.: Privacy-preserving content-aware search based on two-level index. CMC-Comput. Mater. Continua **59**(2), 473–491 (2019)
7. Xiong, L., Shi, Y.: On the privacy-preserving outsourcing scheme of reversible data hiding over encrypted image data in cloud computing. Comput. Mater. Continua **55**(3), 523–539 (2018)
8. Wang, Q., Hu, S., Wang, J., Ren, K.: Secure surfing: privacy-preserving speeded-up robust feature extractor. In: 2016 IEEE 36th International Conference on Distributed Computing Systems (ICDCS), pp. 700–710. IEEE (2016)
9. Liu, Y., Peng, H., Wang, J.: Verifiable diversity ranking search over encrypted outsourced data. Comput. Mater. Continua **55**, 37–57 (2018)
10. Zhang, Y., Zheng, P., Luo, W.: Privacy-preserving outsourcing computation of qr decomposition in the encrypted domain. In: 2019 18th IEEE International Conference on Trust, Security and Privacy in Computing and Communications/13th IEEE International Conference on Big Data Science and Engineering (Trust-Com/BigDataSE), pp. 389–396. IEEE (2019)
11. Guo, J., Zheng, P., Huang, J.: Efficient privacy-preserving anomaly detection and localization in bitstream video. IEEE Trans. Circ. Syst. Video Technol. (2019)
12. Paillier, P.: Public-key cryptosystems based on composite degree residuosity classes. In: Stern, J. (ed.) EUROCRYPT 1999. LNCS, vol. 1592, pp. 223–238. Springer, Heidelberg (1999). https://doi.org/10.1007/3-540-48910-X_16
13. Brakerski, Z.: Fully homomorphic encryption without modulus switching from classical GapSVP. In: Safavi-Naini, R., Canetti, R. (eds.) CRYPTO 2012. LNCS, vol. 7417, pp. 868–886. Springer, Heidelberg (2012). https://doi.org/10.1007/978-3-642-32009-5_50

14. Lóopez-Alt, A., Tromer, E., Vaikuntanathan, V.: On-the-fly multiparty computation on the cloud via multikey fully homomorphic encryption. In: Proceedings of the Forty-Fourth Annual ACM Symposium on Theory of Computing, pp. 1219–1234. ACM (2012)
15. Brakerski, Z., Vaikuntanathan, V.: Efficient fully homomorphic encryption from (standard) LWE. SIAM J. Comput. **43**(2), 831–871 (2014)
16. Halevi, S., Shoup, V.: Bootstrapping for HElib. In: Oswald, E., Fischlin, M. (eds.) EURO-CRYPT 2015. LNCS, vol. 9056, pp. 641–670. Springer, Heidelberg (2015). https://doi.org/10.1007/978-3-662-46800-5_25
17. Elmehdwi, Y., Samanthula, B.K., Jiang, W.: Secure k-nearest neighbor query over encrypted data in outsourced environments. In: 2014 IEEE 30th International Conference on Data Engineering, pp. 664–675. IEEE (2014)
18. Araki, T., Furukawa, J., Lindell, Y., Nof, A., Ohara, K.: High-throughput semi-honest secure three-party computation with an honest majority. In: Proceedings of the 2016 ACM SIGSAC Conference on Computer and Communications Security, pp. 805–817. ACM (2016)
19. Brakerski, Z., Gentry, C., Vaikuntanathan, V.: (Leveled) fully homomorphic encryption without bootstrapping. ACM Trans. Comput. Theory (TOCT) **6**(3) (2014) Article no: 13
20. Cheon, J.H., Kim, A., Kim, M., Song, Y.: Homomorphic encryption for arithmetic of approximate numbers. In: Takagi, T., Peyrin, T. (eds.) ASIACRYPT 2017. LNCS, vol. 10624, pp. 409–437. Springer, Cham (2017). https://doi.org/10.1007/978-3-319-70694-8_15
21. Regev, O.: On lattices, learning with errors, random linear codes, and cryptography. J. ACM (JACM) **56**(6) (2009). Article no: 34
22. Halevi, S., Shoup, V.: Algorithms in HElib. In: Garay, J.A., Gennaro, R. (eds.) CRYPTO 2014. LNCS, vol. 8616, pp. 554–571. Springer, Heidelberg (2014). https://doi.org/10.1007/978-3-662-44371-2_31
23. Cheon, J.H., Kim, A., Kim, M., Song, Y.: Implementation of HEAAN (2016)
24. He, J.H.: Variational iteration method some recent results and new interpretations. J. Comput. Appl. Math. **207**(1), 3–17 (2007)
25. Halevi, S., Shoup, V.: HELib (2019). https://github.com.shaih/HELib
26. Cheon, J.H., Kim, A., Kim, M., Song, Y.: HEAAN (2019). https://github.com/snucrypto/HEAAN

A Novel Method for Enhanced Image Based Reversible Data Hiding

Junxiang Wang[⊠], Ying Zhang, Lin Huang, and Changlong Lu

School of Mechanical and Electronic Engineering, Jingdezhen Ceramic Institute, Jiangxi 333403, China
wjx851113851113@163.com

Abstract. Reversible data hiding (RDH) technology has been widely used due to its function on copyright protection and content integrity authentication. However, most conventional RDH schemes focus on its performance, i.e., embedding capacity and distortion, instead of its security. It means those RDH schemes could be easily inspect by most steganalysis methods, i.e., SPAM [44], to show some suspicious secret data hidden in it. Thus, the practicability of RDH is limited. In this paper, we creatively choose enhanced image as carrier to develop a secure RDH framework. On one hand, it is found that the statistical property of enhanced image is suit for reversible data hiding and thus achieve desired performance. On the other hand, enhanced image as carrier could provide more embedding space for security improvement. Thus, some security improvement skills from steganography field, such as multi-feature sorting, local clustering and so on, are introduced into above framework. Experimental results show the superiority of proposed scheme in the aspect of high performance and security level compared with other related algorithms.

Keywords: Reversible data hiding · Multi-feature sorting · Enhanced image · K-means clustering

1 Introduction

With the development of multimedia technology, the protection of intellectual property rights and the authentication of the data content are becoming more and more serious, and have attracted more and more attentions. As an effective technical mean, RDH algorithm [1] can embed secret data into the carrier in a visual imperceptibly way to protect the data. Recently, RDH technologies have play an important role in some sensitive scenarios with high data requirements, such as medical, military, judicial and so on.

At present, the dominant methods for RDH can be divided into: lossless compression (LC) [2, 3], difference expansion (DE) [4–6], histogram shifting (HS) [7–15] and their variants [16–18].

The first HS based RDH is originally proposed by *Ni et al.* [7], where the peak bin of the gray-scale histogram in the spatial domain is selected for data embedding. However, the embedding capacity of HS-based methods is often not satisfactory. To further improve

© Springer Nature Singapore Pte Ltd. 2020
X. Sun et al. (Eds.): ICAIS 2020, CCIS 1254, pp. 338–350, 2020.
https://doi.org/10.1007/978-981-15-8101-4_31

embedding performance, PEE is combined into HS-based RDH. Recently, *Wang et al.* [19] proposed a novel RDH general framework using multiple histograms modification (MH_RDH) which introduces much less image distortion, and thus it offers obviously improved image quality.

However, all the above HS based RDH methods are visually invisible, therefore, a series of RDH methods on image contrast enhancement are proposed, such as in [20–22]. Recently, *Wu et al.* [20] presented a novel RDH algorithm with image contrast enhancement. They deemed that the improvement of visual quality is more important than keeping the image PSNR high, it can lead to the image contrast enhancement while RDH is realized.

Recently, enhanced images are more and more widely used in our daily life, especially in the demonstration of photography copyright ownership aspects and so on. Therefore, we can directly assume that enhanced image as a carrier of data embedding may also achieve an unexpected effect.

The contributions of this paper mainly include the following two aspects: (1) Creatively take enhanced image as carrier for reversible data hiding and could achieve desired performance, i.e., large capacity and less distortion; (2) Develop some techniques, such as multi-feature sorting and local clustering, to improve the security of above reversible data hiding scheme.

The rest of this paper is organized as follows. Section 2 introduces some related works. Section 3 presents the details of the proposed RDH algorithm. Experiment results and analysis in Sect. 4, and Sect. 5 gives the conclusions.

2 Related Works

2.1 HS Based RDH and Its Characteristics

In this section, we briefly review the HS based RDH algorithm proposed by *Ni et al.* [7] and analyze its characteristics.

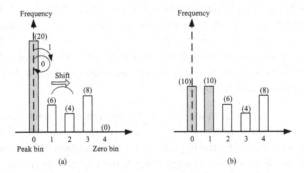

Fig. 1. Illustration of HS based RDH process. (a) The process of HS. (b) Result of HS.

The process is simply illustrated by Fig. 1(a) and the result is shown in Fig. 1(b). It selects a pair of peak bins and zero bin as side information and then shifts the bins between peak and zero bins by 1 towards zero bin to create vacant space nearby the peak bin. Finally, each pixel at peak bin is employed to embed 1bit secret message for RDH. Obviously, for the given payload, it can be seen from the Fig. 1 that the minimum distortion can be achieved when the zero bin is next to the peak bin.

2.2 Characteristics of Enhanced Images and Its Advantages for HS Based RDH

In this part, we focus on a typical image enhancement method in the image processing field, i.e., histogram equalization (HE) [23]. For a gray image, the method tends to build a mapping function between original gray value to the enhanced one and make the enhanced histogram distribution around a wider range and more even. The process of HE is shown in [23]. The process is simply illustrated in Fig. 2.

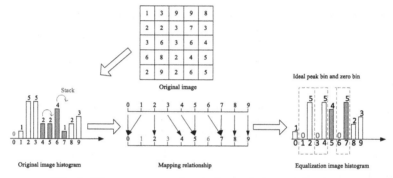

Fig. 2. Histogram comparison before and after equalization.

Characteristic 1. The adjacent low-frequency histogram columns are merged to reduce the difference of those low and high frequency bins. Consequently, the histogram becomes more uniform, which is defined as 'stack' phenomenon. The number of zero bin will increase by the 'stack' phenomenon. For example, for the Fig. 2, there is 1 zero bin in the original histogram, and 3 zero bins are obtained after the histogram equalization. At the same time, in order to achieve the wider distribution of the histogram, the histogram has the tendency of stretching towards both ends, it makes the histogram zeros more dispersed rather than concentrate on a continuous region, such as zero 1, 3 and 6 in the enhanced image histogram.

Characteristic 2. Different from the splitting phenomenon of RDH scheme associated with contrast enhancement process, only 'stack' phenomenon will occur in the HE process, which is guaranteed by the implementation mechanism of HE. Thus, the height of each bin in histogram will only change towards the increase direction.

According to the above analysis of the process and characteristics of HE, the number of zero bins is numerous and the ready-made peak bins can be selected nearby. Hence, if used the enhanced image after HE as the cover image, there will be no shifting distortion when the entire HS based RDH process is executed, which greatly reduces the distortion of the image. Therefore, the above characteristics make the enhanced image an excellent cover image in the RDH algorithm.

3 Proposed Scheme

Based on above mentioned characteristics for HE and HS based RDH, a security reversible embedding framework is proposed as follow. Firstly, a general framework is proposed. And then Some important measures, including 'global search for peak bins and zero bins', 'multi-feature sorting' and 'local K-means clustering', are detailed mentioned. Finally, a complete RDH process is provided.

3.1 General HS Based RDH Framework

The general framework for HS based RDH is shown in Fig. 3.

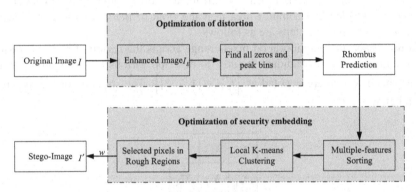

Fig. 3. Flowchart of the proposed method for reversible data hiding

The framework contains 5 key steps as follows:

(1) Construction of cover image: According to the above analysis of the advantages of HE in RDH, we use the enhanced image obtained from the original gray image after HE as cover image for embedding secret information in this paper.
(2) Global search for peak bins and zero bins: Find all zero bins Z_k in the cover image, in order to reduce distortion, we find the peak bins P_k next to all zero bins and the corresponding position of all peak bins in the image.
(3) Multi-feature sorting: In order to make the stego-image more difficult to be detected by the detector, multi-feature is used to construct a vector of measuring the pixel complexity, and then the pixels in the complex region are selected for subsequent embedding.
(4) Local K-means clustering: For the purpose of making the stego-image more security, we select pixels are closer to each other in space through clustering for priority embedding, when the complexity of pixels is relatively close.

(5) Histogram embedding: Apply HS based RDH scheme to embed secret information in the position of the final selected peak bin.

For the proposed framework, the first two steps, i.e., the construction of cover image and global search for peak bins and zero bins, the main purpose is to achieve the visual enhancement effect and avoid shifting distortion. Step 3 and step 4, i.e., the multiple-features sorting and use local K-means clustering, in order to improve the anti-detection of image, which is also the focus on this paper. In addition, for actual data embedding as shown in step 5, the conventional HS based RDH could be employed to ensure the reversibility of proposed algorithm.

3.2 Multi-feature Sorting

It is generally believed that conventional single feature sorting cannot accurately describe the texture characteristics of images and accurately locate complex regions. Therefore, this section presents the design idea of multi-feature sorting algorithm. This operation can effectively select the complex area near the front of the sorting to embed secret information. The specific steps are as follows.

In this paper, the neighborhood pixels range adopts the region of 3*3 is shown in Fig. 4, and using three candidate features to describe various texture features of the neighborhood, which are denoted as $\left\{f_i^j | j \in [1, 2, 3]\right\}$. The structure of the feature is shown below.

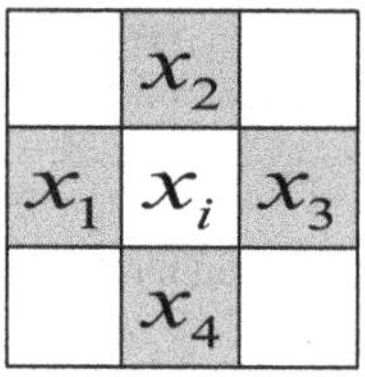

Fig. 4. Sketch map of neighborhood

(1) Variance of four neighboring pixel values. The feature value f_i^1 is defined as

$$f_i^1 = \frac{1}{4} \sum_{k=1}^{4} (x_k - \bar{x})^2, \quad k \in [1, 2, 3, 4] \tag{1}$$

where $\bar{x} = (x_1 + x_2 + x_3 + x_4)/4$ is the mean value of four neighboring pixels.

(2) Variance of the differences between four neighboring pixel values. The feature value f_i^2 is defined as

$$f_i^2 = \frac{1}{4} \sum_{k=1}^{4} (\Delta x_k - \Delta \bar{x})^2, \quad k \in [1, 2, 3, 4] \tag{2}$$

where $\Delta x_1 = |x_1 - x_2|$, $\Delta x_2 = |x_2 - x_3|$, $\Delta x_3 = |x_3 - x_4|$, $\Delta x_4 = |x_4 - x_1|$, and $\Delta \bar{x} = (\Delta x_1 + \Delta x_2 + \Delta x_3 + \Delta x_4)/4$ is the mean of those differences.

(3) HILL

In this paper, we define the HILL [24] feature of each pixel as a cost as one of our candidate features. The HILL feature is defined as follows.

$$f^3 = \frac{1}{\left| X \otimes H^{(1)} \right| \otimes L_1} \otimes L_2 \tag{3}$$

where $X = (x_1, x_2, \ldots, x_N)$ is the input image I_E, $f^3 = \left(f_1^3, f_2^3, \ldots, f_N^3 \right)$ are the corresponding output cost values, L_1 and L_2 are two low-pass filters, and $H^{(1)}$ is a high-pass filter.

Then, a comprehensive feature index is calculated through the above candidate features linear combination form, denoted as CM_i, so as to evaluate the texture characteristics of the pixel more accurately, as shown in Eq. (4).

$$CM_i = \sum_{j=1}^{3} w_j f_i^j \tag{4}$$

where i represents the i-th pixel x_i, and w_j represents the weight of f_i^j, the weight of the feature in this paper is obtained by fitting the prediction error.

3.3 Local K–Means Clustering

After our first principle, namely, *Complexity-First-Rule*, we adopted the second principle, i.e., *Clustering-Rule*, to cluster pixels with similar complexity, in order to make the pixels closer in space can be embedded preferentially. Local clustering process is shown in Fig. 5.

As shown in the Fig. 5, assuming that the length of secret data w is L, and the size of the obtained peak bins position *all_sort_peak_pos* after the first complexity sorting is $M \times N$, M represents the number of *all_sort_peak_pos* and N is 2, the steps of local clustering are shown below.

(1) Determining a percentage t value and intercept a section of length with the interval of $[L - floor(tL), L + floor(tL)]$ as *need_adjust_pos_martix* in the peak points position *all_sort_peak_pos* after sorting for *K-means* clustering. The corresponding pixels in the position interval $[1, L - (floor(tL) + 1)]$ as *not_adjust_pos_martix* are not adjusted.

(2) Using *K-means* clustering, selection of K is 3. As shown in Fig. 5, if the corresponding pixels from the selected location in space are divided into three categories, respectively *class1*, *class2*, *class3*, according to the each pixel complexity to calculate the average complexity of the corresponding class, namely *Cmean1*, *Cmean2*, *Cmean3*, then, according to the size of the average complexity of three kinds of pixels to sort, accordingly get *adjust_pos_martix*.

(3) Let the matrix after clustering with *not_adjust_pos_martix* joining together, so as to get the final sort peak point position *final_sort_peak_pos*, subsequent embedded process will directly on this position for embedding secret data.

On the basis of the *Complexity-First-Rule* sorting and the *Clutering-Rule*, it is obvious that we can infer that the location of the pixel to be modified is a complex area and the pixels are relatively close to each other in space. Therefore, the stego-image I' will be more secure and less easy to be detected.

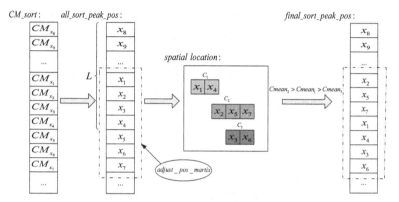

Fig. 5. Process of local *K-means* clustering

3.4 The Proposed RDH Process

Input enhanced image I_E as cover image and secret message w, the size of the secret message is L. The embedding and extraction process are as follows.

(1) The embedding process

Step1: Computing the grayscale histogram of I_E and denoting as $H = \{h_i \mid i = 0, 1, ..., 255\}$, where h_i is the histogram value of i-th bin.

Step2: Finding all zeros $Z_k = \{z_1, z_2, ..., z_k \mid k \in [1, 256]\}$ in the histogram H_i, and then searching for the peak bins next to the all zero bins as the initial peak point P_{init}, (P_{init}, Z_k) is obtained according to the following equation:

$$Z = \{Z_k \mid H(Z_k) = 0, Z_k \in [1, 256]\} \tag{5}$$

$$P_{init} = \begin{cases} Z_k - 1, & \text{if } H(Z_k - 1) \neq 0 \text{ and } H(Z_k + 1) = 0 \\ Z_k - 1, & \text{if } H(Z_k - 1) \neq 0 \text{ and } H(Z_k + 1) \neq 0 \text{ and } H(Z_k - 1) > H(Z_k + 1) \\ Z_k + 1, & \text{if } H(Z_k - 1) \neq 0 \text{ and } H(Z_k + 1) \neq 0 \text{ and } H(Z_k - 1) < H(Z_k + 1) \end{cases} \tag{6}$$

Step3: Determining the corresponding positions *all_peak_pos* of all peak points in the whole image I_E of 512×512, to perform rhombus prediction for the pixels at each peak position, then, to get prediction error.

Step4: Multiple features were used to calculate the complexity CM of each position pixel, and prediction error was used to fit the weight of each feature. Finally, a complexity vector was obtained, and the complexity was sorted from large to small to get the corresponding CM_sort and $all\_sort\_peak\_pos$.

Step5: According to the size L of embedded secret data w, local K-means clustering is carried out for the sorted peak position $all\_sort\_peak\_pos$ and the final peak position $final\_sort\_peak\_pos$ was obtained after adjusting the position.

Step6: Scanning the cover image in the sequential order, and embed the secret data using the following equation:

$$i' = \begin{cases} i, & \text{if } i = I(final\_sort\_peak\_pos(k)) \text{ and } w = 0 \\ i+1, & \text{if } i = I(final\_sort\_peak\_pos(k)) \text{ and } w = 1, \text{ where } w \in w_L \\ i, & \text{otherwise} \end{cases} \tag{7}$$

where k is the sequence number of final peak position $final\_sort\_peak\_pos$, i' denotes the pixel value of the stego-image I', L represents the length of secret data w.

(2) The extraction process

Step1: Scanning the stego-image I' in the same sequential order. Extract the secret data by using the following equation:

$$w = \begin{cases} 0, & \text{if } i' = I(final\_sort\_peak\_pos(k)) \\ 1, & \text{if } i' = I(final\_sort\_peak\_pos(k)) + 1 \end{cases} \tag{8}$$

Step2: Rescanning the stego-image I' after extracting all secret data bits. Restore the original image pixels according to the following equation:

$$i = \begin{cases} i', & \text{if } I(final\_sort\_peak\_pos(k)) \geq i' \\ i' - 1, & \text{if } I(final\_sort\_peak\_pos(k)) < i' \leq Z + 1 \end{cases} \tag{9}$$

4 Experimental Results

In this paper, our experiments are conducted on BOSSBase ver 1.01 [25] with 10000 gray-scale images of size 512×512. After histogram equalization, 10000 enhanced images were obtained, and subsequent work was carried out based on this. We use the typical steganalyzer with a 686-D SPAM feature [26] and an ensemble classifier [27]. 5000 images used for training and the rest 5000 images used for testing. We report the testing error, the security of the image is evaluated by the error rate, the higher error rate, the corresponding security is higher. In this paper, we mainly compare the security performance with Wang et al. [19] and Wu et al. [20], as well as a series of optimization experiments such as the following subsections. Note that in this paper, all experiments are implemented in MATLAB on the Intel(R) Core (TM) i3-4130 CPU @ 3.40 GHz and 4.00 GB of RAM.

4.1 The Comparisons with Other Analysis Methods

In this section, we selected the interaction of three features and clustering by selecting t = 2% for comparison with other algorithms. We mainly compared classification testing error rate under different capacities by using 10000 cover images and 10000 stego-images, we also make a comparative analysis of PSNR by using testing images *Lena* and *Baboon*.

(1) The comparison of classification testing error rate
   In this paper, we compared with *Wang et al.* [19] and *Wu et al.* [20] algorithm for testing error rates, respectively. Since the differences in algorithm design frame-work, *Wang et al.* [19] algorithm is more suitable for small capacity and medium capacity, we compared our scheme with *Wang et al.* [19] at embedded capacity 2000 bits, 8000 bits, 30000 bits and 50000 bits are shown in Table 1–2. In addition, consider that *Wu et al.* [20] scheme is suitable for larger capacity, we compared our scheme with *Wu et al.* [20] under 70000bits and 80000bits are shown in Table 3.

Table 1. The classification results compared with *Wang et al.* [19] under small capacity

Embedding capacity (bit)	Schemes	Error rate
2000	Proposed scheme	41.94%
	Wang et al. [19] scheme	9.51%
8000	Proposed scheme	30.34%
	Wang et al. [19] scheme	3.43%

Table 2. The classification results compared with *Wang et al.* [19] under medium capacity

Embedding capacity (bit)	Schemes	Error rate
30000	Proposed scheme	13.12%
	Wang et al. [19] scheme	1.07%
50000	Proposed scheme	6.68%
	Wang et al. [19] scheme	0.69%

As can be seen from Table 1, 2 and 3, the highest error rate of our proposed algorithm is 41.94% in small capacity and 13.12% in medium capacity, the highest error rate of *Wang et al.* [19] is 9.51% in small capacity and 1.07% in medium capacity, our proposed algorithm has a higher testing error rate than *Wang et al.* [19] algorithm in small capacity and medium capacity, so, our algorithm is more secure than *Wang et al.* [19] under small and medium capacity. In large capacity, the highest error rate of our proposed algorithm is 3.55%, the highest error rate of *Wu et al.*

Table 3. The classification results compared with *Wu et al.* [20] under large capacity

Embedding capacity (bit)	Schemes	Error rate
70000	Proposed scheme	3.55%
	Wu et al. [20] scheme	0.72%
80000	Proposed scheme	2.60%
	Wu et al. [20] scheme	0.76%

[20] is 0.76%, our algorithm has a higher testing error rate than *Wu et al.* [20] algorithm in large capacity. Since our algorithm chooses the complex region to embed secret data, when embedding secret data in complex region, the modified pixel is not easy to be found. While the algorithm of *Wang et al.* [19] and *Wu et al.* [20] choose the relatively smooth bins to embed, they pay more attention to distortion and embedding capacity. Obviously, the proposed algorithm will have certain superiority in confrontation detection.

(2) The comparison of peak signal noise rate (PSNR)

In this section, we describe the distortion of the image by testing the PSNR of the image. The higher PSNR, the smaller the distortion between the stego-image and the cover image, the quality of the image generated after embedding the information is higher. In the experiment, we adopt test images *Lena* and *Baboon*. Similarly, the comparison results with *Wang et al.* [19] in small capacity and medium capacity are shown in Table 4, and with *Wu et al.* [20] in large capacity is shown in Table 5.

Table 4. The PSNR comparison results with *Wang et al.* [19]

Image	Schemes	Embedding capacity (bit)			
		2000	8000	30000	50000
Lena	Proposed scheme	70.22 dB	65.69 dB	60.38 dB	58.27 dB
	Wang et al. [19] scheme	67.89 dB	61.96 dB	55.08 dB	51.73 dB
Baboon	Proposed scheme	70.01 dB	65.47 dB	60.30 dB	58.21 dB
	Wang et al. [19] scheme	63.80 dB	57.06 dB	47.76 dB	43.30 dB

According to the Table 4 and Table 5, for the test image *Lena*, our algorithm is compared with the algorithm of *Wang et al.* [19] and *Wu et al.* [20] for the PSNR, the maximum PSNR of our proposed method under small capacity and medium capacity are 70.22 dB and 60.38 dB, respectively, the maximum PSNR of *Wang et al.* [19] method under small capacity and medium capacity are 67.89 dB and 55.08 dB, respectively. The maximum PSNR of our proposed method under large capacity is 56.82 dB, the maximum PSNR of *Wu et al.* [20] method under large capacity is 47.92 dB, our method is much higher than *Wang et al.* [19] and *Wu et al.* [20]. Thus, it is well verified that the distortion of our algorithm is much

Table 5. The PSNR comparison results with *Wu et al.* [20]

Image	Schemes	Embedding capacity (bit)	
		70000	80000
Lena	Proposed scheme	56.82 dB	56.21 dB
	Wu et al. [20] scheme	47.92 dB	47.09 dB
Baboon	Proposed scheme	56.78 dB	56.21 dB
	Wu et al. [20] scheme	47.30 dB	48.28 dB

smaller than that of *Wang et al.* [19] and *Wu et al.* [20], namely our image quality has certain superiority. The main reason is that, in our algorithm framework, the peaks of the selected is located next to zero bins, this makes our algorithm without shifting distortion and we complex area is selected to embed secret information has been modified by the pixels are less likely to be found. Therefore, our algorithm does have certain superiority.

5   Conclusions

In this paper, based on the framework of the reversible embedding algorithm based on histogram shifting, three measures are proposed to improve the image security and visual quality. It mainly includes: 1. By using the high plasticity of the enhanced image, an algorithm of reversible information hiding on the enhanced image is proposed, which can directly reduce the shifting distortion of the image; 2. The sorting technology based on multi-feature, so as to select more complex areas for embedding information; 3. A set of local K-means clustering scheme for the sorted peak bins is presented, which can significantly improve the security performance of the algorithm. Experimental results show that the proposed algorithm has a great superiority in improving the security performance of reversible data hiding using grayscale image.

Acknowledgment. This work was supported by the National Natural Science Foundation of China under Grant 61762054, in part by the National Science Foundation for Distinguished Young Scholars of Jiangxi Province under Grant 20171BCB23072, in part by the National Science Foundation of Jiangxi Province under Grant 20151BAB217018, in part by the Major Program of Science and Technology Program of Jiangxi Provincial Education Department under Grant GJJ1707619. Many thanks to the anonymous reviewers for their insightful comments and valuable suggestions, which helped a lot to improve the paper quality.

References

1. Shi, Y., Li, X., Zhang, X., Wu, H.T., Ma, B.: Reversible data hiding: advances in the past two decades. IEEE Access **4**, 3210–3237 (2016)

2. Fridrich, J., Goljan, M., Du, R.: Invertible authentication. In: Proceedings of the SPIE Security and Watermarking of Multimedia Contents III, San Jose, CA, pp. 197–208 (2001)
3. Celik, M., Sharma, G., Tekalp, A., Saber, E.: Lossless generalized-LSB data embedding. IEEE Trans. Image Process. **14**(2), 253–266 (2005)
4. Tian, J.: Reversible watermarking using a difference expansion. IEEE Trans. Circ. Syst. Video Technol. **13**(8), 890–896 (2003)
5. Thodi, D.M., Rodriguez, J.: Expansion embedding techniques for reversible watermarking. IEEE Trans. Image Process. **16**(3), 721–730 (2007)
6. Fallahpour, M.: Reversible image data hiding based on gradient adjusted prediction. IEICE Electron. Express **5**(20), 870–876 (2008)
7. Ni, Z., Shi, Y., Ansari, N., Su, W.: Reversible data hiding. IEEE Trans. Circ. Syst. Video Technol. **16**(3), 354–362 (2006)
8. Sachnev, V., Kim, H., Nam, J., Suresh, S., Shi, Y.: Reversible watermarking algorithm using sorting and prediction. IEEE Trans. Circ. Syst. Video Technol. **19**(7), 989–999 (2009)
9. Hwang, H., Kim, H., Sachnev, V., Joo, S.: Reversible watermarking method using optimal histogram pair shifting based on prediction and sorting. KSII Trans. Internet Inf. Syst. **4**(4), 655–670 (2010)
10. Gao, X., An, L., Yuan, Y., Tao, D., Li, X.: Lossless data embedding using generalized statistical quantity histogram. IEEE Trans. Circ. Syst. Video Technol. **21**(8), 1061–1070 (2011)
11. Luo, L., Chen, Z., Chen, M., Zeng, X., Xiong, Z.: Reversible image watermarking using interpolation technique. IEEE Trans. Inf. Forensics Secur. **5**(1), 187–193 (2010)
12. Li, X., Li, B., Yang, B., Zeng, T.: General framework to histogram shifting-based reversible data hiding. IEEE Trans. Image Process. **22**(6), 2181–2191 (2013)
13. Qin, C., Chang, C., Huang, Y., Liao, L.: An inpainting-assisted reversible steganographic scheme using a histogram shifting mechanism. IEEE Trans. Circ. Syst. Video Technol. **23**(7), 1109–1118 (2013)
14. Peng, F., Li, X., Yang, B.: Improved PVO-based reversible data hiding. Digit. Sig. Process. **25**(2), 255–265 (2014)
15. Qu, X., Kim, H.: Pixel-based pixel value ordering predictor for high-fidelity reversible data hiding. Sig. Process. **111**(1), 249–260 (2015)
16. Xiao, D., Liang, J., Ma, Q., Xiang, Y., Zhang, Y.: High capacity data hiding in encrypted image based on compressive sensing for nonequivalent resources. Comput. Mater. Continua **58**(1), 1–13 (2019)
17. Xiao, X., Yang, Y., Li, R., Zhang, W.: A novel reversible data hiding scheme based on lesion extraction and with contrast enhancement for medical images. Comput. Mater. Continua **60**(1), 101–115 (2019)
18. Chen, Y., Yin, B., He, H., Yan, S., Chen, F., Tai, H.: Reversible data hiding in classification-scrambling encrypted-image based on iterative recovery. Comput. Mater. Continua **56**(2), 299–312 (2018)
19. Wang, J., Chen, X., Ni, J., Mao, N., Shi, Y.: Multiple histograms based reversible data hiding: framework and realization. IEEE Trans. Circ. Syst. Video Technol. **30**(8), 2313–2328 (2019)
20. Wu, H.-T., Tang, S., Huang, J., Shi, Y.-Q.: A novel reversible data hiding method with image contrast enhancement. Sig. Process. Image Commun. **62**, 64–73 (2018)
21. Celik, T.: Spatial entropy-based global and local image contrast enhancement. IEEE Trans. Image Process. **23**(12), 5298–5308 (2014)
22. Gu, K., Zhai, G., Yang, X., Zhang, W., Chen, C.W.: Automatic contrast enhancement technology with saliency preservation. IEEE Trans. Circ. Syst. Video Technol. **25**(9), 1480–1494 (2015)
23. Stark, J.A.: Adaptive image contrast enhancement using generalizations of histogram equalization. IEEE Trans. Image Process. **9**(5), 889–896 (2000)

24. Li, B., Wang, M., Huang, J., Li, X.: A new cost function for spatial image steganography. In: 2014 IEEE International Conference on Image Processing (ICIP), Paris, pp. 4206–4210 (2014)
25. Filler, T., Pevny, T., Bas, P.: BOSS (break our steganography system). http://www.agents.cz/boss. Accessed 20 Dec 2013
26. Pevný, T., Bas, P., Fridrich, J.: Steganalysis by subtractive pixel adjacency matrix. IEEE Trans. Inf. Forensics Security **5**(2), 215–224 (2010)
27. Kodovský, J., Fridrich, J., Holub, V.: Ensemble classifiers for steganalysis of digital media. IEEE Trans. Inf. Forensics Secur. **7**(2), 432–444 (2012)

A Novel Wireless Covert Channel
for MIMO System

Pengcheng Cao[1], Weiwei Liu[1]([✉]), Guangjie Liu[2], Jiangtao Zhai[2], Xiaopeng Ji[2], and Yuewei Dai[1,2]

[1] Nanjing University of Science and Technology, Nanjing 210094, China
lwwnjust5817@gmail.com
[2] Nanjing University of Information Science and Technology, Nanjing 210044, China

Abstract. Wireless covert channel by manipulating the distortions of signal in transmission is an important technique. The covert channels are undetectable by making artificial noise modulated from secret messages distribute as normal channel noise. Although the state-of-the-art work has excellent performance, the undetectability of the schemes for Multiple Input Multiple Output (MIMO) system is weak because the correlation of the raw signals received in all antennas. In this paper, a wireless covert channel for MIMO system is proposed to improve the undetectability. According to the distribution of normal channel noise, the secret messages are modulated into artificial noise in the data transmission of MIMO system. Meanwhile, in the channel state information (CSI) transmission, the CSI parameters are modified to reduce the correlation. Experimental results show that the undetectability of the proposed scheme is better than the existing MIMO schemes with the same reliability and transmission rate.

Keywords: Wireless covert channel · MIMO system · CSI modification · Undetectability · Reliability

1 Introduction

As a specific application of data hiding, covert channels are required to keep hidden secret data undetectable. With the rapid development of communication technologies, there is a noticeable tendency of the research on covert channels. The communication layer of covert channel is lowering, gradually from the network layer and data link layer to the physical layer. The most popular type of covert channels are network covert channels, which is established based on network traffic. Secret data is embedded by padding some bits into the packet headers [1] and manipulating the packet timing information [2–4] in network layer.

Supported by The National Natural Science Foundation of China (Grant No. 61602247, 61702235, U1836104, U1636117), Natural Science Foundation of Jiangsu Province (Grant No. BK20160840) and Fundamental Research Funds for the Central Universities (30918012204).

© Springer Nature Singapore Pte Ltd. 2020
X. Sun et al. (Eds.): ICAIS 2020, CCIS 1254, pp. 351–362, 2020.
https://doi.org/10.1007/978-981-15-8101-4_32

As the up-to-date covert channels, besides modifying some redundant fields of wireless communication protocols in data link layer [5,6], wireless covert channels conceal the very existence of secret data by modulating it into the delivered wireless signal in physical layer. Because of ubiquitous nature and localized transmission, wireless covert channels are difficult to detect their presence which has led to increasing attentions.

Some of the earlier implementation of wireless covert channels are introduced with the secret data embedded in the phase of STF, the frequency of CFO and Cyclic Prefix of Wi-Fi system [7]. The subcarriers in OFDM-based system which are reserved by communication protocols are also used to transmit the secret data [8]. The wireless covert channels can be established by covert relay in wireless relay networks [9]. These wireless covert channels are weak to the detection methods based on matching the fields of wireless communication protocols [10].

Due to the channel noise and fading in wireless communication, the distortion of the signal is found widely existed. So wireless covert channels with the secret data modulated into artificial noise can be established with negligible effect on the overt communication. The undetectability of this kind of wireless covert channels are improved with the signal with secret data mixed [11] or added [12] the random noise. In [11], the wireless covert channels established by mixing the random noise require sharing the mapping sequence to extract secret data at receiver. In [12], the wireless covert channels based on multiplex technique require extra power to add the random noise. The extra bandwidth and power have a notable influence on the performance of undetectability and reliability in the wireless covert channels. We have proposed a wireless covert channel based on constellation shaping modulation to improve the undetectability in previous work [13]. The distribution of artificial interference signal modulated from secret data is kept the same as that of normal artificial noise. Recently, the Multiple Input Multiple Output (MIMO) wireless communication has been rapidly developed. The wireless covert channels for MIMO system are rare. The wireless covert channel based on multiplex technique was extended to the MIMO system by choosing the best channel path for covert transmission [14]. The undetectability of the MIMO wireless covert scheme needs to be strengthened.

In this paper, a novel wireless covert channel for MIMO system is proposed to improve the undetectability. In the data transmission of MIMO system, according to the distribution characteristics of normal channel noise, the secret messages are modulated into artificial noise by model fitting modulation which makes the distribution of generated artificial noise the same as that of normal channel noise. In the channel state information (CSI) transmission of MIMO system which transmits CSI in implicit method, the channel effect parameters are modified to reduce the correlation of the raw signals received in all antennas of MIMO system. Compared with the existing MIMO schemes, both the undetectability and reliability of the proposed schemes are improved with the same transmission rate.

The rest of the paper is organized as follows. In the next section, some background including general model of MIMO wireless covert channel and performance metrics are introduced. In Sect. 3, some related works on wireless covert channel are summarized. In Sect. 4, we describe the proposed MIMO wireless covert channel scheme Sect. 5 gives the experimental results on undetectability and reliability. Finally, Sect. 6 concludes the whole paper.

2   Background

2.1   General Model of MIMO Wireless Covert Channel

Due to the channel impairments, the channel noise is ubiquitous existed in wireless communication. The wireless covert channels established by the modulating secret data into artificial noise become an important type of wireless covert channels. The generic model framework of MIMO wireless covert channel is shown in Fig. 1. It is presented that the covert transmission is attached to the overt transmission. The sender plays the roles of the overt sender and the covert sender. The receivers include the informed receivers and normal receivers. In what follows, the receivers refer to the informed receivers unless stated otherwise.

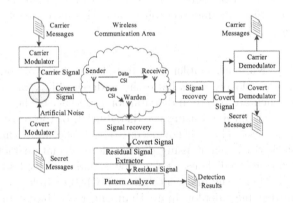

Fig. 1. Generic model of MIMO wireless covert channels.

At all antenna of the sender, the carrier and secret messages are modulated into carrier signal and artificial noise respectively. The composite signal generated by adding the artificial noise to carrier signal is transmitted from the sender to the receiver through MIMO wireless channel. At the receiver, the covert signals are recovered from the received raw signals by channel effect parameters in CSI which are also transmitted through MIMO wireless channel. In this paper, we assume that the transmission of CSI is active, which means the receiver transmits the pilot to the sender then the sender gives back the CSI. Then the carrier messages and secret messages can both be demodulated from the covert signal by carrier and covert demodulators respectively.

Due to the broadcast nature of wireless signal, some radio interception devices deployed by the potential wardens can also capture the raw signals and channel effect parameters in CSI. To find out the existence of secret messages, the residual covert signal and residual raw signal need to be extracted by removing the carrier signal from the received covert signal and raw signal respectively. Then the warden analyzes the characteristics of the residual covert signal and residual raw signal to obtain the detection results. In this study, we assume that the warden has partial knowledge over the distribution of channel noise in legitimate transmission by capturing massive normal channel noise and the dependence of the residual raw signal in different antennas.

2.2 Performance Metrics

Undetectability and reliability are the two main goals in the design of the wireless covert channels. The wireless covert channels which use artificial noise make no modifications in the other layers of the communication system. However, to the best of our knowledge, there is little specialized work concerning the detection of these wireless covert channels, especially in MIMO system. In [13], the KS test and regularity test for residual signal are employed as statistic-based tests which are developed from the detection for covert timing channels. In this paper, the statistic-based tests in undetectability and the measure of reliability are presented as follows.

Undetectability. Kullback-Leibler (KL) test [15, 16] and Kolmogorov-Smirnov (KS) test [17] are employed to evaluate the undetectability of MIMO wireless covert channels which are based on distribution differences. The KL divergences and KS distances are obtained using the distribution of the residual signal and reference channel noise. The warden needs to seek the approximate reference of channel noise or construct it using distribution estimation methods. Beside them, the correlation coefficients of the raw signals received in all antennas are employed to evaluate the undetectability of MIMO wireless covert channels further. The warden may deploy more than one radio interception device in specific area. Some of the radio interception devices may be deployed closer to the sender when compared with the receiver, which always means more moderate channel interference. Consequently, the undetectability of noise-based wireless covert channels should be benchmarked under noisy channel with a range of signal-to-noise ratio (SNR).

Reliability. The reliability of the MIMO wireless covert channel is measured in terms of the bit error rate (BER) of secret message bits for a given covert transmission rate under the common additive white Gaussian noise (AWGN) channel and flat fading channel. The covert transmission rate R is defined as the average number of secret message bits transmitted per subcarrier in a signal of wireless communication system.

3   Related Work

With the development of wireless communication [18–20], the covert channels applied in wireless environment are studied. To hide the transmission of the secret data, several kinds of wireless covert channels have been proposed. In [5,6], the secret messages are transmitted by modifying padding of frames, headers of the MAC, RLC and PDCP in the LTE systems. In [8], the subcarriers of specific frequency in OFDM-based system which are reserved in some communication protocols are used to transmit the secret data with little effect on the normal transmission. In [7], several wireless covert channels based on Wi-Fi communication protocol are introduced with the secret data embedded in the phase of STF PSK, the frequency of CFO FSK and Cyclic Prefix. In [9], the secret data are transmitted by covert relay on top of the cover data in wireless relay networks. These wireless covert channels can only be used in specific wireless communication system, and are very weak to field-matching methods.

Later, the secret messages are transmitted in the form of artificial noise. In [12], wireless covert channels based on multiplex technique (WCC-MT) is established. In these channels, the signal modulated from secret data and random noise are added in order to hide the generated artificial noise from detection. The power of the signal and the random noise must be lower than that of the carrier signal. And spread spectrum technique is applied in the secret data so that the artificial noise with low power has little influence on the transmission of carrier signal. The undetectability of this covert channel costs extra power of random noise. A wireless covert channel based on dirty constellation (WCC-DC) is proposed [11]. The signal modulated from secret message bits are mixed with random noise. So the mapping sequence is required to separate the secret signal and random noise. The undetectability of this covert channel costs extra bandwidth of shared mapping sequence. However, when the detector of adversary is near the sender, the regularity of residual signal may result in the poor resistance to some statistical tests [21]. Although these studies has been able to achieve improved performance in terms of undetectability, they are all implemented with extra requirement of bandwidth or power. A wireless covert channel based on constellation shaping modulation is proposed to improve the undetectability [13]. The secret data is directly modulated into the artificial noise which distribute like normal channel noise. In MIMO system, the wireless covert channel based on multiplex technique was extended by choosing the best channel path for covert transmission [14]. The undetectability of the MIMO wireless covert scheme needs to be strengthened.

4   Wireless Covert Channel for MIMO System

In this section, a wireless covert channel for MIMO System is proposed to strengthen the undetectability. The channel effect parameters are modified in the CSI transmission of MIMO system. The general framework of the proposed scheme is demonstrated in Fig. 2.

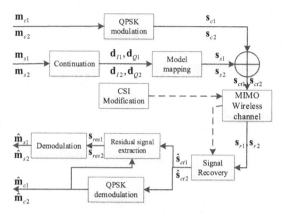

Fig. 2. Framework of proposed scheme.

Take the 2×2 MIMO system for example, it is assumed that the carrier signal s_{c1}, s_{c2} in different antennas are QPSK modulated from the carrier messages m_{c1}, m_{c2}. By model fitting modulation, the artificial noise s_{s1}, s_{s2} is modulated from the secret messages m_{s1}, m_{s2}. The covert signal s_{ct1}, s_{ct2} is also generated by adding artificial noise s_{s1}, s_{s2} to the carrier signal s_{c1}, s_{c2}. The channel effect parameters of CSI are modified at the same time. At the receiver, after the covert signal $\hat{s}_{ct1}, \hat{s}_{ct2}$ is recovered from raw signal s_{r1}, s_{r2}, the carrier messages $\hat{m}_{c1}, \hat{m}_{c2}$ are demodulated by QPSK. The secret messages $\hat{m}_{s1}, \hat{m}_{s2}$ can be demodulated from the residual recovered signal s_{res1}, s_{res2} which are extracted from $\hat{s}_{ct1}, \hat{s}_{ct2}$. The description of modulation, CSI modification and demodulation are detailed in the following subsections.

4.1 Modulation and CSI Modification

The modulation is employed to generate the artificial noise by secret messages. As shown in the framework, the secret message bits are converted into continuous variables with uniformly distribution on (0,1) in continuation. Then, according to the distribution of the normal channel noise, the components of the artificial noise in I and Q axes is generated from the continuous variables by model mapping. Meanwhile, the channel effect parameters in CSI are modified.

Take the modulation in antenna 1 for example, the secret messages are denoted by $m_{s1} = (m_{s1}[1], \ldots, m_{s1}[n])$. It is assumed that there are two secret message bits embedded in a subcarrier, so the element in m_{s1} can be further written as $m_{s1}[i] \in \{00, 01, 10, 11\}, i = 1, \ldots, n$. The secret message bits in I and Q axes are denoted by $m_{s1I} = (m_{s1I}[1], \ldots, m_{s1I}[n])$ and $m_{s1Q} = (m_{s1Q}[1], \ldots, m_{s1Q}[n])$ respectively in which the elements satisfy $m_{s1}[i] = (m_{s1I}[i], m_{s1Q}[i])$. The artificial noise s_{s1} are denoted by $x_{s1I} + j \cdot x_{s1Q}$. Here x_{sI}, x_{sQ} are components of the artificial noise in I and Q axes of the constellation at the sender satisfying $x_{s1I} = (x_{s1I}[1], \ldots, x_{s1I}[n])$, $x_{s1Q} = (x_{s1Q}[1], \ldots, x_{s1Q}[n])$.

Take I axis for example, the secret message bit $m_{s1I}[i]$ is first converted into a continuous variable by continuation. The function of continuation is defined as (1)

$$d_{I1}[i] = \left(\frac{m_{s1I}[i]}{2} + r\right) \bmod 1 \tag{1}$$

Where r is a random number with uniform distribution on $(0, 0.5)$. The continuation makes the continuous variables $\mathbf{d}_{I1}$ in I axis distribute uniformly on $U(0, 1)$.

In model mapping, the inverse cumulative distribution function (CDF) of the normal channel noise in I axis F_{sI}^{-1} is employed to take random continuous variables with uniform distribution on $(0, 1)$ as input and generate the I components of the artificial noise as output. The function of model mapping is defined as (2)

$$\mathbf{x}_{s1I} = F_{sI}^{-1}(\mathbf{d}_{I1}) \tag{2}$$

Equation (2) keeps the distribution of the generated I components the same as that of the normal channel noise. The continuation and model mapping encoder in Q axis work in the same way. The modulation in antenna 2 works in the same way.

At the same time, the channel effect parameters in CSI are modified. The actual matrix of channel effect parameters is denoted as (3)

$$\mathbf{H} = \begin{bmatrix} h_{11} & h_{12} \\ h_{21} & h_{22} \end{bmatrix} \tag{3}$$

Where the element h_{kl} means the effect parameter from the antenna k at sender to antenna l at receiver. Then the channel effect parameters are modified as (4)

$$\begin{cases} h_{k1}^* = h_{k1}(1 + \alpha_k) \\ h_{k2}^* = h_{k1}(1 - \alpha_k) \end{cases}, k = 1, 2 \tag{4}$$

Here α_k is the random parameter distributes the same as normal channel noise which is shared between the sender and receiver.

4.2 Signal Recovery and Demodulation

Before the corresponding demodulation, the receiver recover the matrix of channel effect parameters $\mathbf{H}$ from the received one $\mathbf{H}^*$ by the shared parameters. Then the covert signal is recovered from the raw signal, and the residual recovered signal is extracted from the recovered covert signal. At last, the secret message bits are demodulated from the residual recovered signal by the center value.

The residual signal is first extracted from the received covert signal. The received covert signal $\hat{\mathbf{s}}_{ct1}$ are denoted by $\hat{x}_{ct1I} + j \cdot \hat{x}_{ct1Q}$. The received cover message bits demodulated by QPSK is denoted by $\hat{\mathbf{m}}_{c1}$ which are re-modulated by QPSK to acquire the ideal carrier signal denoted by $\hat{\mathbf{s}}_{c1} = \hat{\mathbf{x}}_{c1I} + j \cdot \hat{\mathbf{x}}_{c1Q}$.

Here $\hat{x}_{c1I}[i], \hat{x}_{c1Q}[i] \in \{-1/\sqrt{2}, 1/\sqrt{2},\}$ are the ideal components of the carrier signal in I and Q axes by QPSK modulation. The residual signal $\mathbf{s}_{res1}$ is extracted by (5).

$$\mathbf{s}_{res1} = \hat{\mathbf{s}}_{ct1} - \hat{\mathbf{s}}_{c1} = (\hat{\mathbf{x}}_{ct1I} - \hat{\mathbf{x}}_{c1I}) + j \cdot (\hat{\mathbf{x}}_{ct1Q} - \hat{\mathbf{x}}_{c1Q}) \tag{5}$$

Take I axis for example, the secret message bits $\hat{\mathbf{m}}_{s1I}$ can be got by the center value $F_{sI}^{-1}(1/2)$ shared between the sender and receiver. The function of demodulation is defined as (6).

$$\hat{m}_{s1I}[i] = \begin{cases} 1, \hat{x}_{ct1I}[i] - \hat{x}_{c1I}[i] \geq F_{sI}^{-1}\left(\frac{1}{2}\right) \\ 0, \hat{x}_{ct1I}[i] - \hat{x}_{c1I}[i] < F_{sI}^{-1}\left(\frac{1}{2}\right) \end{cases} \tag{6}$$

The demodulation in Q axis works in the same way.

5   Experimental Results

In this section, the proposed wireless covert channel is benchmarked on undetectability and reliability. We compare the proposed scheme with two wireless covert channels for MIMO system. Wireless covert channels based on multiplex technique (WCC-MT) for MIMO system are earlier MIMO wireless covert channels. As the state-of-the-art scheme, wireless covert channel based on constellation shaping modulation (WCC-CSM) is directly applied in MIMO system.

5.1   Experimental Setup

Rayleigh flat fading channel is chosen for the simulation experiment on wireless communication system. The cover message bits and the secret message bits are both provide by a pseudo-random bits generator. The carrier signal to artificial interference signal ratio in proposed schemes is set to be $E_c/E_s = 13\,\mathrm{dB}$. All wireless covert channels are performed on more than 100000 symbols. The undetectability of the wireless covert channels is measured by the KL divergences and the KS distances of the I components, Q components and magnitudes of residual recovered signal and correlation coefficients of residual raw signal in different antennas. The KL divergences, the KS distances and the correlation coefficients are computed with 2000 components, and they are all presented with different SNRs. The reliability of the wireless covert channels is measured by BERs of secret message bits. In order to make a fair comparison, In WCC-MT for MIMO system, secret signal is generated by QPSK and the random noise is the AWGN. The powers of secret signal and random noise are set to be equal, and the carrier signal to artificial noise is set to be $13\,\mathrm{dB}$.

5.2   Undetectability

We compare the undetectability of proposed scheme with the existing MIMO methods. The KL divergences and the KS distances of I components, Q components, magnitudes and phases of residual recovered signal in proposed scheme are presented in Fig. 3, 4 and 5. The KL divergences and the KS distances of WCC-MT and WCC-CSM for MIMO system are presented for comparison. The covert transmission rate is set to $R = 0.2$ with the application of direct sequence spread spectrum codes. Each detection measure is obtained as an average over repeated experiments. In Fig. 3 and 4, with carrier signal to channel noise ratio E_c/N_0 increasing, the KL divergences and KS distances in proposed scheme and WCC-CSM keep steady, however the detection measures in WCC-MT increase obviously. In Fig. 5, with E_c/N_0 increasing, the correlation coefficients in proposed scheme keep close to 0, however the detection measures in WCC-MT and WCC-CSM increase obviously. In general, it shows that the undetectability of proposed schemes is better than that of existing methods with the same covert transmission rate.

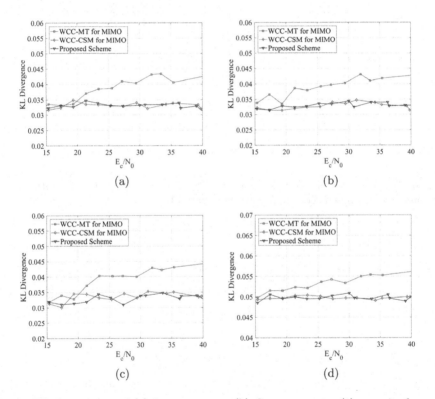

Fig. 3. KL divergences of (a) I components, (b) Q components, (c) magnitudes and (d) phases in proposed scheme and existing methods

5.3 Reliability

To test the reliability, we calculate the BERs of the secret message bits in proposed scheme in Rayleigh flat fading channel and compare them with the existing methods. The BERs in WCC-MT and WCC-CSM for MIMO system are

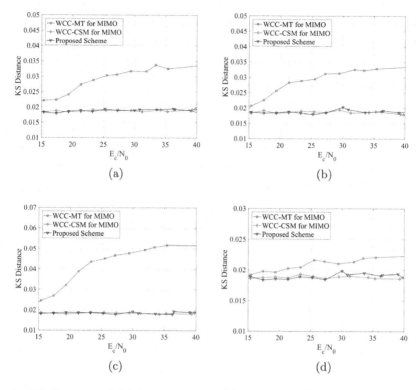

Fig. 4. KS distances of (a) I components, (b) Q components, (c) magnitudes and (d) phases in proposed scheme and existing methods

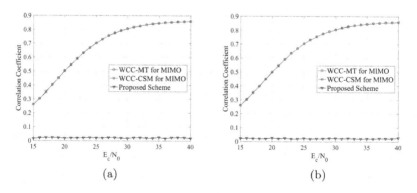

Fig. 5. Correlation coefficients of (a) I components and (b) Q components in proposed scheme and existing methods

presented for comparison. The direct sequence spread spectrum codes based on M-sequence are applied in the secret message bits to keep the covert transmission rate equal $R = 0.2$ in all schemes. The parameters of direct sequence spread spectrum codes applied in proposed scheme and WCC-CSM are set to be $m = 10$

which is $m = 5$ in WCC-MT. In Fig. 6, the BERs in proposed scheme are equal to those in WCC-CSM which are much lower than those in WCC-MT. In summary, it is proved that the proposed wireless covert channels are as reliable as the state-of-the-art method with equal covert transmission rate.

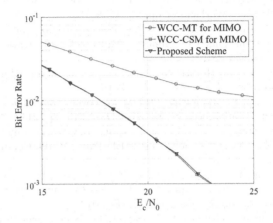

Fig. 6. BERs of proposed scheme and existing methods with equal transmission rate.

6   Conclusions

High degree of undetectability and reliability is the foundation for guaranteeing the success of MIMO wireless covert channels. In this paper, we modulate the secret messages into artificial noise by model fitting modulation in the data transmission of MIMO system, which makes the distribution of generated artificial noise the same as that of normal channel noise. The channel effect parameters are modified to reduce the correlation of the raw signals received in all antennas in CSI transmission of MIMO system. Compared with the existing MIMO schemes, the proposed schemes are more undetectable and reliable.

Even if the proposed scheme can achieve high undetectability and reliability, the reliability of wireless cover channel for MIMO system can be improved. We can employ the space-time codes into the MIMO schemes to improve the reliability and keep the undetectability in our future work.

References

1. Mileva, A., Panajotov, B.: Covert channels in TCP/IP protocol stack - extended version. Cent. Eur. J. Comp. Sci. 4(2), 45–66 (2014)
2. Gianvecchio, S., Wang, H., Wijesekera, D., Jajodia, S.: Model-based covert timing channels: automated modeling and evasion. In: Lippmann, R., Kirda, E., Trachtenberg, A. (eds.) RAID 2008. LNCS, vol. 5230, pp. 211–230. Springer, Heidelberg (2008). https://doi.org/10.1007/978-3-540-87403-4_12

3. Liu, G., Zhai, J., Dai, Y.: Network covert timing channel with distribution matching. Telecommun. Syst. **49**(2), 199–205 (2012)
4. Liu, W., Liu, G., Zhai, J., Dai, Y., Ghosal, D.: Designing analog fountain timing channels: undetectability, robustness, and model-adaptation. IEEE Trans. Inf. Forensics Secur. **11**(4), 677–690 (2017)
5. Grabska, I., Szczypiorski, K.: Steganography in long term evolution systems. In: Security and Privacy Workshops, pp. 92–99 (2014)
6. Szczypiorski, K., Mazurczyk, W.: Hiding data in OFDM symbols of IEEE 802.11 networks. In: International Conference on Multimedia Information Networking and Security, pp. 835–840 (2010)
7. Classen, J., Schulz, M., Hollick, M.: Practical covert channels for wifi systems. In: Communications and Network Security (2015)
8. Hijaz, Z., Frost, V.S.: Exploiting OFDM for covert communication. In: Military Communications Conference, 2010 - MILCOM 2010, pp. 2149–2155 (2010)
9. Hu, J., Yan, S., Zhou, X., Shu, F., Li, J., Wang, J.: Covert communication achieved by a greedy relay in wireless networks. IEEE Trans. Wirel. Commun. **17**(7), 4766–4779 (2018)
10. Rezaei, F., Hempel, M., Peng, D., Qian, Y., Sharif, H.: Analysis and evaluation of covert channels over LRE advanced. In: Wireless Communications and Networking Conference (WCNC), pp. 1903–1908. IEEE (2013)
11. Dutta, A., Saha, D., Grunwald, D., Sicker, D.: Secret agent radio: covert communication through dirty constellations. In: Kirchner, M., Ghosal, D. (eds.) IH 2012. LNCS, vol. 7692, pp. 160–175. Springer, Heidelberg (2013). https://doi.org/10.1007/978-3-642-36373-3_11
12. Kitano, T., Iwai, H., Sasaoka, H.: A wireless steganography technique by embedding ds-ss signal in digital mobile communication systems. Sci. Eng. Rev. Doshisha Univ. **52**, 127–134 (2011)
13. Cao, P., Liu, W., Liu, G., Ji, X., Zhai, J., Dai, Y.: A wireless covert channel based on constellation shaping modulation. Secur. Commun. Netw. **2018**, 1–15 (2018)
14. Hokai, K., Sasaoka, H., Iwai, H.: Wireless steganography using MIMO system. In: IEEE Fifth International Conference on Communications and Electronics (2014)
15. Cachin, C.: An information-theoretic model for steganography. Inf. Comput. **192**(1), 41–56 (2004)
16. Archibald, R., Ghosal, D.: A comparative analysis of detection metrics for covert timing channels. Comput. Secur. **45**(8), 284–292 (2014)
17. Cabuk, S., Brodley, C.E., Shields, C.: IP covert timing channels: design and detection. In: ACM Conference on Computer and Communications Security, CCS 2004, Washington, DC, USA, October, pp. 178–187 (2004)
18. Fang, W., Zhang, W., Zhao, Q., Ji, X., Chen, W., Assefa, B.: Comprehensive analysis of secure data aggregation scheme for industrial wireless sensor network. Comput. Mater. Continua **61**(2), 583–599 (2019)
19. Liu, Y., Yang, Z., Yan, X., Liu, G., Hu, B.: A novel multi-hop algorithm for wireless network with unevenly distributed nodes. Comput. Mater. Continua **58**(1), 79–100 (2019)
20. Wang, L., Liu, H., Liu, W., Jing, N., Adnan, A., Wu, C.: Leveraging logical anchor into topology optimization for indoor wireless fingerprinting. Comput. Mater. Continua **58**(2), 437–449 (2019)
21. Szczypiorski, K., Janicki, A., Wendzel, S.: "The good, the bad and the ugly": evaluation of wi-fi steganography. Comput. Sci. (2015)

Electronic Health Record Data Sharing Cryptographic Algorithm Based on Blockchain

Shufen Niu$^{(\boxtimes)}$ ⓘ, Wenting Li$^{(\boxtimes)}$ ⓘ, and Wenke Liu$^{(\boxtimes)}$ ⓘ

College of Computer Science and Engineering, Northwest Normal University,
Lanzhou, Gansu, China
sfniu76@nwnu.edu.cn, wenting_li201@163.com, 460228378@qq.com

Abstract. The data stored into the blockchain is immutable, which enhances the security of the data. In this work, we propose a blockchain-based scheme for electronic medical record data sharing that enables third-party data users to share patient's data without violating patient privacy. First, we propose a system model of the scheme. The scheme is constructed using a private blockchain and a consortium blockchain. The private blockchain stores the patient's diagnostic record (DR). The consortium blockchain stores secure indexes composed of keywords of DRs. Diagnostic records and keywords take the form of encrypted ciphertext information. Second, we use public encryption with keyword search (PEKS) technology to achieve a secure search of keywords on the consortium blockchain. In the decryption phase, we use proxy re-encryption (PRE) technology to enable third-party data users to securely access patient data. Finally, we evaluate the performance of the scheme through numerical simulation experiments.

Keywords: Electronic medical record · Blockchain · Keyword search · Proxy re-encryption

1 Introduction

The emergence of electronic medical records can effectively solve the current problems of patient diagnosis information storage, query, data sharing, medical errors, etc. [1]. The use of electronic medical records enables patients to have comprehensive diagnostic information and allows doctors to quickly and accurately understand the patient's past condition at the time of the visit and give new diagnostic results. The literature [2–7] provides a practical example of the application of electronic medical records. A blockchain is essentially a decentralized distributed storage system, which can provide platform support for the use of electronic medical records and generate permanent and irreversible modified records.

Supported by National Natural Science Foundation of China under Grants 61562077, 61662071, 61662069, 61772022.

In view of the advantages of blockchains in the application of electronic medical records, many scholars have proposed solutions for different problems in recent years. Yue et al. [8] proposed a blockchain-based data gateway architecture and used secure multi-party computing to enable third-party users to calculate stored data without infringing patient privacy. Xia et al. [9] proposed a data sharing framework based on the blockchain to solve access control problems related to sensitive information in the cloud. The scheme is based on a permissioned blockchain, which allows only the invited users to access and share patient data after verifying the identity and encrypting the key. Dias et al. [10] constructed an access control scheme based on the blockchain in an electronic healthcare environment. The scheme sets varying access rights between two different users. The solution is built on the consortium blockchain, in which the user's ownership is stored into the data transaction. Data managers can add, revoke, and change the privileges to users of restrict their access to data. Chen et al. [11] proposed a framework for sharing medical association data services based on the blockchain, with emphasis on an implementation scheme that does not depend on any untrusted third parties; the framework can achieve secure storage of patient data and privacy protection of patients. Zhang et al. [12] constructed a sharing protocol for security and privacy protection personal health information based on the blockchain and proposed a specific system model and scheme.

Unlike in the previously discussed schemes on the use of electronic medical records with the blockchain, patient privacy may be violated when third-party organizations or individuals other than hospitals or patients attempt to access patient data. In view of this situation, we propose a scheme for electronic medical record data sharing based on the blockchain that uses PRE technology to realize the access of third-party organizations or individuals to patient data.

By referring to the system model of documents [12], we use the private blockchain and the consortium blockchain to construct the scheme, in which each hospital has its own private blockchain, while many hospitals can establish a consortium blockchain. The patient's DR is encrypted and stored in the private blockchain of the hospital. The keyword of the diagnosis record is encrypted and stored into the consortium blockchain. A PEKS technology is used to realize the secure search of a patient's DR. When searching for patient data, we use proxy re-encryption to convert the searched ciphertext; in this manner, third-party data users can share patient data without violating patient privacy. The contribution of this article has the following threefold:

- On the basis of the blockchain, we propose a scheme electronic medical record data sharing to achieve secure access to patient data by third-party data users. The scheme is built on the private blockchain and the consortium blockchain. Each hospital has its own private blockchain and server, and each hospital also establishes a consortium blockchain with multiple hospitals. The patient's diagnostic record is stored into the hospital's private chain, and the security index of the diagnostic record's keywords is stored into the consortium blockchain.

- We use public encryption with keyword search technology based on the consortium blockchain to store the security index composed of the encrypted keywords into the consortium blockchain. When a patient, doctor, or data user needs to search for a keyword, the patient's own private key is used to generate a searching trapdoor and then sent to the consortium blockchain for data retrieval.
- We use proxy re-encryption technology to enable secure access to patient data by third-party data users. After searching for the original ciphertext of the patient's diagnostic record, the system administrator acts as an agent to re-encrypt the original ciphertext, and finally sends the converted ciphertext to a third-party data user, who decrypts the ciphertext with his or her own private key.

2 Preliminary

The Modified Decisional Bilinear Diffie-Hellman (mDBDH) Problem [13]. Let $e : G_1 \times G_1 \rightarrow G_2$ be a bilinear map. For all $a, b, c \in Z_q^*$, $Q \in G_2$. Given a tuple (g, g^a, g^b, g^c), determine $Q = e(g, g)^{ab/c}$. An algorithm A has advantage ε in solving mDBDH problem if:

$$|Pr[A(g, g^a, g^b, g^c, e(g, g)^{ab/c}) = 0] - Pr[A(g, g^a, g^b, g^c, Q)]| \geq \varepsilon$$

where the probability is over the random choices of $a, b, c \in Z_q^*$, the random choice $g \in G_1^*$ and the random bits of A.

Definition 1 (mDBDH assumption). We say that the ε-mDBDH assumption holds if no PPT algorithm has advantage at least ε in solving the mDBDH problem.

3 System Model

3.1 System Structure

In this system, suppose there are n hospitals that form a league. Each hospital has its own private blockchain and server. The patient's original ciphertext of its diagnostic record is stored into the hospital server, and the hash value is stored into the hospital private blockchain. The consortium blockchain stores the ciphertext of the diagnostic record keywords. The structure of the system is shown in Fig. 1. The four entities in the system are as follows:

System Manager. The system manager is in charge of the entire system, and every patient, doctor, and data user needs to register before entering the system. When a data user accesses the diagnostic record of a patient, the system manager plays the role of the proxy to generate the proxy re-encryption key and performs proxy re-encryption on the original DR ciphertext.

Patient. Patients need to register to the server of hospital before seeing doctor. After completing the registration, the hospital server gives the patient a token, which is equivalent to the patient's visit card, and the patient should keep the token secret. The patient presents the token when he or she sees the doctor, and the doctor generates a DR and keywords for the patient and encrypts them with the patient's public key.

Medical Service Providers (Hospital Servers and Doctors). Each hospital has a single server and several clients, and clients are operated by doctors. Doctors generate diagnostic records and new blocks for patients and broadcast new blocks to the hospital's private blockchain.

Data User. When third-party organizations or individuals (called data users) exist other than the hospitals and patients who need to access patients' data, obtaining searching trapdoors generated by patients is necessary to perform keywords searching in the consortium blockchain.

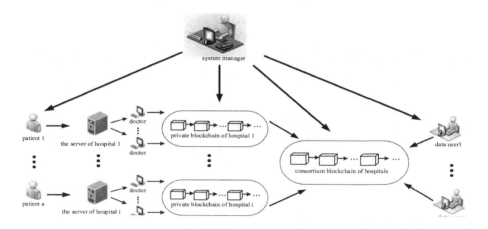

Fig. 1. System structure

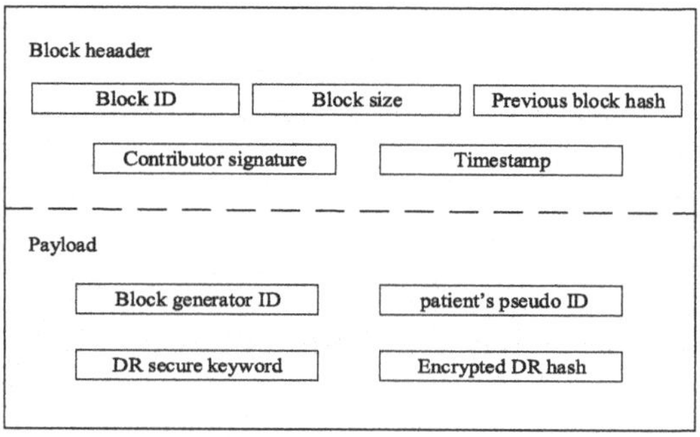

Fig. 2. Structure of a block in the private blockchain

3.2   Data Structure

The data structure of the private blockchain is shown in Fig. 2. The data structure of the consortium blockchain is shown in Fig. 3.

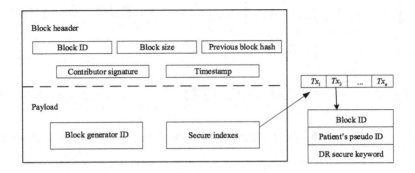

Fig. 3. Structure of a block in the consortium blockchain

4   Our Proposal

The proposed scheme can be divided into three phases: data generation, data storage, and data search.

Phase 1: System setup

- **Setup(λ):** Input security parameter λ, output system parameter $params = (q, G_1, G_2, g, e, h, H_1, H_2, H_3, H_4, H_5, H_6)$, where q is a large prime number, G_1 and G_2 are two cyclic groups of order q. e is a bilinear map, g is a generator of G_1, and set $h = e(g, g)$. Select hash functions: $H_1 : \{0,1\}^* \to Z_q^*$, $H_2 : \{0,1\}^* \to G_1$, $H_3 : \{0,1\}^* \to G_1$, $H_4 : \{0,1\}^\lambda \to G_2$, $H_5 : \{0,1\}^* \to Z_q^*$, $H_6 : \{0,1\}^* \to G_1$.
- **KeyGen($params$):** Patient randomly choose $x_a \in Z_q^*$ and compute $pk_a = g^{x_a}$ as public key, set $sk_a = x_a$ as private key. Doctor randomly choose $x_d \in Z_q^*$, compute $pk_d = g^{x_d}$, set $sk_d = x_d$ as private key. Data user randomly choose $x_u \in Z_q^*$, compute $pk_u = g^{x_u}$, set $sk_u = x_u$ as private key.
- **ReKeyGen(sk_a, sk_u):** Input the private keys of patient, data user (sk_a, sk_u), then generate a proxy re-encryption key $rk_{a \to u} = \frac{sk_u}{sk_a} mod\ q$ using the method in [14].

Phase 2: Data generation and storage
After patient a registers with hospital i, the hospital server randomly selects $\beta \in \{0,1\}^*$ as the registration basis for the patient, and the hospital server

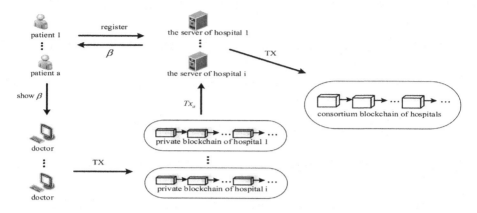

Fig. 4. Data generation and data storage

calculates $\mu = H_1(\beta)$ for the system storage. When the patient sees the doctor and presents β, the doctor produces diagnostic record $m \in \{0,1\}^*$, selects the keyword $w \in \{0,1\}^*$, and encrypts m, w with the patient's public key pk_a as follows:

- $Encrypt(pk_a, m, w)$: The doctor randomly chooses $r \in Z_q^*$, calculates $B = pk_a^r$, $C = e(g, H_2(\beta))^r \cdot m$, $t = e(g, H_3(w, \beta))^r$, $F = H_4(t)$. Calculate the vector $X = [X_1, X_2, ..., X_n]$, where $X_1 = g^{rH_1(w)}, ..., X_n = g^{rH_1^n(w)}$.
- Compute $r_0 = H_5(m, B)$, $A = g^{rH_1(w) + r_0(sk_d + H_1(w))}$, $Y = h^{r_0(sk_d + H_1(w))}$.

The encryption algorithm output is expressed as $C_a = (C_{a0}, C_{a1}, C_{a2})$, where $C_{a0} = (B, C)$, $C_{a1} = (B, F)$, and $C_{a2} = (A, X, Y)$. C_{a0} is ciphertext of the diagnostic record m, which is stored into the server of hospital i, and $hash(C_{a0})$ is calculated and uploaded to the private blockchain. C_{a1} is the ciphertext of keyword w. C_{a2} provides the basis for the proof of conformance on the consortium blockchain.

- Patient pseudo identity generation: The patient's real identity is denoted by RID_a. The doctor generates a pseudo identity for the patient and calculates $ID_a = RID_a \oplus H_1(\beta)$.

In providing proof of conformance on the private blockchain, the doctor produces proof $\eta = (\alpha, \beta')$ based on β and sk_d.

- Randomly choose $k \in Z_q^*$, compute $\alpha = g^{\frac{k + sk_d}{H_1(\beta)}}$, $\beta' = H_6(g^k) \oplus \beta$.

Then, the doctor formulates the transaction TX (Fig. 2) and broadcasts the transaction to the hospital's private blockchain. After receiving the new transaction, the verifier on the private blockchain verifies the new transaction.

- Extract ID_d, $\eta = (\alpha, \beta')$ from the block and search for μ in the system.
- Compute $\beta^* = H_6(\alpha^\mu \cdot pk_d^{-1}) \oplus \beta'$, check whether $H_1(\beta^*) = \mu$.

If the equation is true, then the new transaction is valid, and the verifier broadcasts a verification confirmation message. After receiving the $[\frac{2}{3}np]$ verification confirmation messages, the private blockchain receives the new transaction. Otherwise, the new block to is rejected and joins the private blockchain. np represents the number of nodes in the private blockchain.

Correctness

$$\beta^* = H_6(\alpha^\mu \cdot pk_d^{-1}) \oplus \beta') = H_6(g^{\frac{k+sk_d}{H_1(\beta)} \cdot H_1(\beta)} \cdot g^{-sk_d}) \oplus H_6(g^k) \oplus \beta$$
$$= H_6(g^k) \oplus H_6(g^k) \oplus \beta = \beta$$

Therefore, $H_1(\beta^*) = H_1(\beta) = \mu$.

In each private blockchain, the server extracts the block ID, patient pseudo identity, and secure keyword of each new block. Let $Tx_a = (ID_b, ID_a, C_{a1})$ $a \in \{1, 2, ..., l\}$. The server combines the secure indexes of all newly emerging 8 blocks, which are represented as new transactions in the format of Fig. 3. The server broadcasts the new transaction to the consortium blockchain by using ciphertext C_{a2} $a \in \{1, 2, ..., l\}$. After receiving the new transaction, the verifier on the consortium blockchain verifies that each secure index Tx_a $a \in \{1, 2, ..., l\}$ is as follows: checks whether $e(A, g) = e(X_1, g) \cdot Y$.

If the equation is true, then the new transaction is valid, and the verifier broadcasts a verification confirmation message. After receiving the $[\frac{2}{3}np]$ verification confirmation messages, the consortium blockchain receives the new transaction.

Correctness

$$e(A, g) = e(g^{rH_1(w)+r_0(sk_d+H_1(w))}, g) = e(g^{rH_1(w)}, g)e(g^{r_0(sk_d+H_1(w))}, g)$$
$$= e(X_1, g)e(g, g)^{r_0(sk_d+H_1(w))} = e(X_1, g) \cdot Y$$

Figure 4 shows the process of data generation and storage.

Phase 3: Data search and access
When doctor or data user wants to access a patient's historical data, the patient is required to use the private key to generate searching trapdoor T_w and pseudo identity ID_a', which had been previously generated for the patient.

- **Trapdoor**$(sk_a, w) : T_w = H_3(w, \beta)^{\frac{1}{sk_a}}$.
- **Test**: When the doctor or data user receives searching trapdoor T_w and pseudo identity ID_a', $Tx_a = (ID_b, ID_a', C_{a1})$ is extracted from the consortium blockchain. The doctor or data user checks whether $F = H_4(e(B, T_w))$. If this parameter holds, the server finds the private blockchain through ID_b to obtain C_{a0}.

Correctness

$$H_4(e(B, T_w)) = H_4(e(g^{sk_a \cdot r}, H_3(w, \beta)^{\frac{1}{sk_a}}))$$
$$= H_4(e(g, H_3(w, \beta))^r) = F$$

- **Decryption**

Case 1: When the patient shares data with the doctor, the server sends $C_{a0} = (B, C)$ to the patient, and $m = \dfrac{C}{e(B, H_2(\beta))^{\frac{1}{sk_a}}}$ is calculated.

Correctness

$$\frac{C}{e(B, H_2(\beta))^{\frac{1}{sk_a}}} = \frac{e(g, H_2(\beta))^r \cdot m}{e(g^{sk_a \cdot r}, H_2(\beta))^{\frac{1}{sk_a}}} = m$$

Case 2: When the data user shares data, the proxy (system administrator) runs the $ReKeyGen(sk_a, sk_u)$ algorithm to generate the proxy re-encryption key $rk_{a \to u}$ and re-encrypts the ciphertext with $rk_{a \to u}$ as follows:

- Compute $B' = B^{rk_{a \to u}}$, then the re-encrypted ciphertext is $C'_{a0} = (B', C)$. The proxy sends C'_{a0} to the data user, and the user calculates: $m = \dfrac{C}{e(B', H_2(\beta))^{\frac{1}{sk_u}}}$.

Correctness

$$B' = B^{rk_{a \to u}} = pk_a^{r \cdot \frac{sk_u}{sk_a}} = g^{sk_a \cdot \frac{sk_u}{sk_a} \cdot r} = g^{sk_u \cdot r} = pk_u^r$$
$$\frac{C}{e(B', H_2(\beta))^{\frac{1}{sk_u}}} = \frac{e(g, H_2(\beta))^r \cdot m}{e(g^{sk_u \cdot r}, H_2(\beta))^{\frac{1}{sk_u}}} = m$$

Figure 5 shows the process of data search.

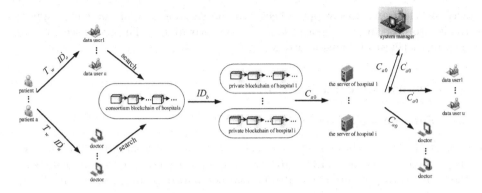

Fig. 5. Data search and access

5   Security Analysis

In this section, we will analyze how the proposed scheme can effectively meet the design goals presented in the previous section.

The Proposed Scheme Satisfies Data Security and Access Control. The basic features of the blockchain renders the data stored into the blockchain unchangeable, thus ensuring that the data cannot be modified unless attackers have 51% of the computing power of the entire network. The diagnostic record is encrypted using the patient's public key; in this manner, the data can only be decrypted with the patient's private key, thus further ensuring the confidentiality of the data. The ciphertext stored into the blockchain can only be obtained by authenticated visitors. Before the doctor or data user accesses the patient's historical data the searching trapdoor $T_w = H_3(w, \beta)^{\frac{1}{sk_a}}$ generated by the patient with the private key should be obtained, a scheme that is equivalent to authorizing the doctor or the user to search. Therefore, the patient can control his/her historical DR data to be accessed. As a trusted-third party, the system manager can control whether the data user is eligible for the re-encryption of the ciphertext. Therefore, the system manager can also control the access of patient's data.

The Proposed Scheme Satisfies Privacy Protection. The doctor generates pseudo identity $ID_a = RID_a \oplus H_1(\beta)$ for the patient. Eavesdroppers cannot obtain β, and the true identity of the patient cannot be guessed. The scheme achieves privacy protection through anonymity. As shown in Fig. 2, encrypted data are appended with the patient's pseudo identity, and the ciphertext contains random number r to ensure that the encryption results are different each time. Therefore, the eavesdroppers are not allowed to judge whether two or more DRs are from the same patient.

The Proposed Scheme Satisfies Secure Search. Only the patient can give the searching trapdoor generated by himself/herself with his/her private key and the previously obtained pseudo identity to the doctor or data user for data access. When an eavesdropper checks on the trapdoor, he or she cannot guess the keyword because it involves the patient's private key. Thus, this scheme can help resist keyword-guessing attacks.

6 Performance Evaluation

6.1 Functionality Comparison

This study has conducted a functional comparison with the literature on electronic medical records [5, 12, 15, 16] that have been proposed in recent years, and the results are presented in Table 1. The comparison found that both of two references [5, 16] are non-blockchain data storage platforms. The two previous studies [15, 16] cannot achieve the data search function. The above schemes do not have third-party data users that can safely share patient's data. The schemes in the literature in the table all satisfy the access control and privacy protection of the scheme, which are the basic attributes of the electronic medical record. A comparison with the above schemes shows that the scheme of this study has certain advantages in terms of functionality.

Table 1. Comparisons of functional properties

Functional properties	[5]	[12]	[25]	[26]	Ours
Blockchain-based	×	√	√	×	√
Access control	√	√	√	√	√
Privacy preservation	√	√	√	√	√
Secure search	√	√	×	×	√
Third-party data sharing	×	×	×	×	√

6.2 Computational Cost Analysis

Given that no similar scheme can be compared effectively with the computational cost of our proposed scheme, only computational cost is analyzed. P denotes bilinear pairing operation, M denotes multiplication operation, E represents exponentiation operation, and np denotes the number of nodes in the private or consortium blockchain. The results of the analysis are shown in Table 2.

Table 2. Computational overhead of proposed scheme

Phase	System setup	Data verification	Data search
Computational overhead	$2P + 12E + 10M$	PB: $4M \times [\frac{2}{3}np]$	Case 1: $2P + 5E + 2M$
		CB: $(P + 4M + 2E) \times [\frac{2}{3}np]$	Case 2: $2P + 6E + 5M$

Note: PB: private blockchain CB: Consortium blockchain

6.3   Numerical Simulation Experiment Results Analysis

A complete numerical simulation experiment is carried out on a Linux platform. The program is written in C by using the paring-based cryptography library [17]. The computations are run on PC with 2.9 GHz CPU frequency and 4 GB of RAM, using Linux operating system. In the numerical experiment, given that the scheme supports only a single keyword search, the basic field length of the single keyword is set to 1024 bits, such that the variable is set to $n \cdot 1024$, and n is a multiple of the single keyword length, which can also be understood as the number of keywords. We set n to 10, 20, 30, 40, and 50, and the experimental results take the average of 50 running results. The experimental results are shown in Table 3.

Table 3. Time cost (ms) of the scheme algorithms

Algorithms	Setup	Encrypt	Trapdoor	Test	DecCase1	DecCase2
n = 10	20	218	36	42	7	10
n = 20	21	412	72	83	8	11
n = 30	20	614	105	125	7	11
n = 40	20	825	145	167	7	11
n = 50	21	1021	172	212	7	11

From Table 3, variable n has no influence on the time generated by the system setup algorithm and the verification algorithm of the new block on the private blockchain. The encryption algorithm and the verification algorithm of the new block on the consortium blockchain are affected by the operation of multiple bilinear pairing operations, implying that the time cost is relatively large. In the data search phase, the time of the decryption algorithm in the two cases is hardly affected by the change in n. The trapdoor generation algorithm and the test algorithm involve a small proportion of the operation of the bilinear pairing, and most involve multiplication and exponentiation operation, indicating that the time cost is slower than the growth of the first two algorithms.

As shown in Fig. 6, the increase in keyword length has a relatively large impact on the time cost of the encryption algorithm, while the growths of the other three algorithms are relatively slow and less affected by the change of keyword length. In general, the time costs of the above four algorithms increase linearly, and they represent the increasing trend of the time cost of the whole scheme. The results show that with the increase of keyword length, the time cost will be controlled within a certain range.

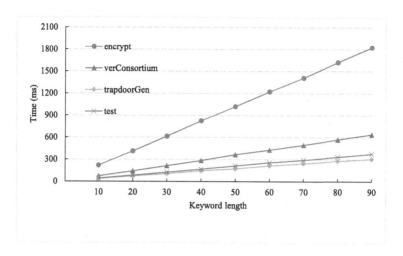

Fig. 6. Time cost analysis of the algorithm

7   Conclusions

We propose a scheme for blockchain-based electronic medical record data sharing for third-party data users. The scheme is based on the private blockchain and the consortium blockchain. The private blockchain stores the original ciphertext of the patient diagnostic record information, and the consortium blockchain stores a secure index composed of the keyword's ciphertext. The scheme achieves security goals for data security, access control and privacy protection.

References

1. Leventhal, J.C., Cummins, J.A., Schwartz, P.H., et al.: Designing a system for patients controlling providers' access to their eletronic: Health record: Organizational and tecchnical challenges. J. Gen. Intern. Med. **30**(1 Supplement), 17–24 (2005)
2. Abbas, A., Khan, S.U.: A review on the state-of-the-art privacy-preserving approaches in the e-health clouds. IEEE J. Biomed. Health Inform. **18**(2), 430–439 (2014)
3. Jiang, X., Liu, M., Yang, C., et al.: A blockchain-based authentication protocol for WLAN mesh security access. Comput. Mater. Cont. **58**(1), 45–59 (2019)
4. Song, R., Song, Y., Liu, Z., et al.: GaiaWorld: A novel blockchain system based on competitive PoS consensus mechanism. Comput. Mater. Cont. **60**(3), 973–987 (2019)
5. Yang, Y., Ma, M.: Conjunctive keyword search with designated tester and timing enabled proxy re-encryption function for e-health clouds. IEEE Trans. Inf. Forensics Secur. **11**, 746–759 (2015)
6. Zhang, L., Zhang, Y., Tang, S., et al.: Privacy protection for e-health systems by means of dynamic authentication and three-factor key agreement. IEEE Trans. Industr. Electron. **65**(3), 1 (2017)

7. Deng, Z., Ren, Y., Liu, Y., et al.: Blockchain-based trusted electronic records preservation in cloud storage. Comput. Mater. Cont. **58**(1), 135–151 (2019)
8. Yue, X., Wang, H., Jins, D., et al.: Healthcare data gateways: Found healthcare intelligence on blockchain with novel privacy risk control. J. Med. Syst. **40**(10), 218 (2016)
9. Xia, Q., Sifah, E., Smahi, A., Amofa, S., Zhang, X.: BBDS: Blockchain-based data sharing for electronic medical records in cloud environments. Information **8**(44), 1–16 (2017)
10. Dias, J.P., Reis, L., Ferreira, H.S., et al.: Blockchain for Access Control in e-Health Scenarios (2018)
11. Chen, Y., Ding, S., Xu, Z., et al.: Blockchain-based medical records secure storage and medical service framework. J. Med. Syst. **43**(1), 5 (2018)
12. Zhang, A., Lin, X.: Towards secure and privacy-preserving data sharing in e-health systems via consortium blockchain. J. Med. Syst. **42**(8), 1–18 (2018). https://doi.org/10.1007/s10916-018-0995-5
13. Shao, J., Cao, Z., Liang, X., et al.: Proxy re-encryption with keyword search. Inf. Sci. **180**(13), 2576–2587 (2010)
14. Canetti, R., Hohenberger, S.: Chosen-ciphertext secure proxy re-encryption. In: ACM CCS 2007. Full version: Cryptology ePrint Archieve: Report 2007/171 (2007)
15. Peterson, K., Deeduvanu, R., Kanjamala, P., Boles, K.: Ablockchain-based approach to health information exchange networks
16. Zhang, J., Xue, N., Huang, X.: A secure system for pervasive social network-based healthcare. IEEE Access **4**, 9239–9250 (2016)
17. The pairing-based cryptography library. http://crypto.stanford.edu/pbc/

A New Kind Linear Analysis of Invariant Bias of Midori-64 Related Keys

Hu Jun Ru[(⊠)]

PAP Engineering University, Xi'an, Shan Xi, China
hjrlxq@126.com

Abstract. Midori-64 is a 64-bit packet length, 128-bit key SPN (Substitution Permutation Network) structure lightweight block cipher. Using the method of related-keys technology and linear analysis, the key invariant deviation linear analysis of Midori-64 was carried out. According to the nature of the key expansion algorithm of Midori-64, a suitable input-output linear mask and key difference are selected to construct a 7-round related-keys invariant linear discriminator. Then, 11 rounds of Midori-64 algorithm are densely defined. Key recovery attack. The data complexity and time complexity of the attack are respectively $2^{62.99}$ and $2^{76.6}$. This paper is the linear analysis result of the first related key of the Midori algorithm.

Keywords: Block cipher · Related-keys · Midori algorithm · Linear mask

1 Preface

Linear analysis is an effective attack method proposed by Japanese scholar Matsui in 1993 for DES (Data Encryption Standard) password [1]. And in later analysis, linear analysis was extended and expanded, and representative ones were: multiple linear analysis [2], multidimensional linear analysis [3], and zero correlation linear analysis [4]. And in the development of linear analysis, it is worth noting that, inspired by the correlation key impossible differential analysis model, in ASIACRYPT2013, Bogdanov et al. proposed a linear analysis model of related key invariant deviation [5], this analysis model The proposal is a successful combination of linear analysis and related key attacks. And the literature [5] also uses this method to analyze LBlock and TWINE-128, and its analysis results are improved in the number of attack rounds compared to the best attack results of the current two algorithms. It can be seen that the analytical model has a good application prospect. At ASIACRYPT2015, Banik et al. proposed the SPN (Substitution Permutation Network) structure lightweight block cipher Midori [6], whose key length is 128 bits, and the packet length can be 64 bits and 128 bits, which are respectively recorded as Midori-64 and Midori-128. The number of iterations is 16 rounds and 20 rounds respectively. In this paper, the correlation key technique and linear analysis are combined to analyze the key invariant deviation linearity of Midori-64. Introduction to midori-64 algorithm.

© Springer Nature Singapore Pte Ltd. 2020
X. Sun et al. (Eds.): ICAIS 2020, CCIS 1254, pp. 376–384, 2020.
https://doi.org/10.1007/978-981-15-8101-4_34

2   Introduction to Midori-64 Algorithm

2.1   Algorithm Description

The Midori-64 algorithm uses an SPN structure with a master key length of 128 bits, a packet length of 64 bits, and an iteration round of 16 rounds. The round transformation is composed of four basic transformations, which are S box, replacement, column mixing, and round key addition. The XOR whitening key operation is added before the last round and after the last round, where the process of key whitening is named *WK* operation. And the last round was simplified, leaving only the S-box operation. The Midori-64 encryption process is shown in Fig. 1.

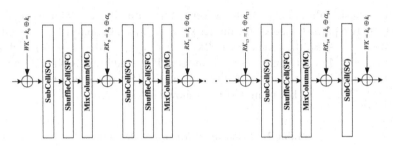

Fig. 1. Encryption process of Midori-64 algorithm

The 64-bit state in the encryption process is represented by a 4×4 state matrix, and each cell is 4 bits (nibble) in the following order.

S_0	S_4	S_8	S_{12}
S_1	S_5	S_9	S_{13}
S_2	S_6	S_{10}	S_{14}
S_3	S_7	S_{11}	S_{15}

S box (SC). See Table 1 for the 4 bit s box value used by Midori 64 algorithm.

Table 1. S-box mapping (in Hexadecimal)

x	0	1	2	3	4	5	6	7	8	9	A	B	C	D	E
$Sb_0[x]$	C	A	D	3	E	B	F	7	8	9	1	5	0	2	4

Replacement (SFC). The replacement order of 16 half byte states is

$$(S_0 S_1 S_2 S_3 S_4 S_5 S_6 S_7 S_8 S_9 S_{10} S_{11} S_{12} S_{13} S_{14} S_{15})$$
$$\leftarrow (S_0 S_{10} S_5 S_{15} S_{14} S_4 S_{11} S_1 S_9 S_3 S_{12} S_6 S_7 S_{13} S_2 S_8)$$

Column Mixing (MC). Matrix M acts on each column of the state matrix in the following way.

$$M = \begin{pmatrix} 0 & 1 & 1 & 1 \\ 1 & 0 & 1 & 1 \\ 1 & 1 & 0 & 1 \\ 1 & 1 & 1 & 0 \end{pmatrix} \qquad \begin{pmatrix} S_i \\ S_{i+1} \\ S_{i+2} \\ S_{i+3} \end{pmatrix} \leftarrow M \cdot \begin{pmatrix} S_i \\ S_{i+1} \\ S_{i+2} \\ S_{i+3} \end{pmatrix}$$

Key Plus (AK). XOR 64bit round key with 64bit status.

2.2 Key Extension Algorithm

The key expansion algorithm of Midori is very simple. Firstly, the 128bit master key k is divided into two parts: k_0 and k_1, the master key $k = k_0 \| k_1$. In midori-64, the whitening key is $WK = k_0 \oplus k_1$, the round key is $RK_i = k_{i \bmod 2} \oplus \alpha_i (0 \leq i \leq 14)$, and α_i is a round constant. Midori-64 has 16 rounds in total. If key addition is omitted in the last round, the round keys used in the first round and the 15th round will be $RK_0 \sim RK_{14}$ successively. The round key of midori-64 is shown in Table 2.

Table 2. Round key of Midori-64 algorithm

Wheel key	RK_0	RK_1	RK_2	RK_3	RK_4	RK_5	RK_6	RK_7
Formula	$k_0 \oplus \alpha_0$	$k_1 \oplus \alpha_1$	$k_0 \oplus \alpha_2$	$k_1 \oplus \alpha_3$	$k_0 \oplus \alpha_4$	$k_1 \oplus \alpha_5$	$k_0 \oplus \alpha_6$	$k_1 \oplus \alpha_7$
Wheel key	RK_8	RK_9	RK_{10}	RK_{11}	RK_{12}	RK_{13}	RK_{14}	
Formula	$k_0 \oplus \alpha_8$	$k_1 \oplus \alpha_9$	$k_0 \oplus \alpha_{10}$	$k_1 \oplus \alpha_{11}$	$k_0 \oplus \alpha_{12}$	$k_1 \oplus \alpha_{13}$	$k_0 \oplus \alpha_{14}$	

2.3 Attack Status of Midori-64

Since the introduction of the Midori algorithm, many scholars have used different analysis methods to analyze the security. The main attack results are as follows: [7] evaluates the ability of the Midori algorithm to resist fault attacks, and the results show that the algorithm must count down to 5 rounds. Added protection against fault attacks; the literature [8] proposed a 10-round impossible difference analysis for the Midori-64 algorithm using 6 rounds of impossible differential discriminators; the literature [9] is based on 6 rounds of discriminators, respectively for 10 The round and 11 rounds of Midori-64 algorithm carried out the intermediate encounter attack, and based on the 7-round discriminator, the 12-round Midori-64 algorithm was attacked by the middle; the document [10] carried out the Midori-64 under the weak key state. All-round analysis; literature [11] constructed a 9-round discriminator of Midori-64, and conducted 14 rounds of correlation key impossible differential analysis for Midori-64; this paper uses 7 rounds of correlation key invariant differential linear distinction The key recovery attack was carried out on 11 rounds of Midori-64.

3   A Key Invariant Diffractor for 7 Rounds of Midori-64

According to the properties of the key expansion algorithm of midori-64, 128bit master key k and k' is selected, and the master key difference is divided into $\Delta k = k \oplus k' = 00000000\delta000000000000000000000000$, where δ is the non-zero difference of 4bit, and 0 is the zero difference of 4bit. The difference of the K and K' of the extended keys is ΔK, and ΔrK_i is expressed as the difference of each round of. Select the input mask of the third round as $(a000000000000000)$, the output mask of the ninth round as $(0h0h000000000000)$, and a and h represent the non-0 mask of 4 bit length respectively. From Fig. 2, it can be concluded that the relationship between the difference of extended key $\Delta rK_i(3 \leq i \leq 9)$ and the linear mask $U_i(3 \leq i \leq 9)$ is as follows: $U_i \cdot \Delta rK_i = 0$, then the linear approximation $(a000000000000000) \rightarrow (0h0h000000000000)$ meets the requirements of the invariant deviation of related key. In Fig. 2, the setting "□" represents a 0 mask; $b, c_i, d_i, e_i, f_i, g_i(0 \leq i \leq 15)$ represents a non-0 mask; "?" represents a mask whose uncertainty is 0 or non-0.

4   11 Rounds of Key Recovery Attacks on Midori-64

By using the 7-round (round 3–9) related-keys invariant Deviation Linear differentiator constructed in Fig. 2, two rounds are extended to the encryption direction and the decryption direction respectively. Combined with the relationship between wheel keys and some and technologies, the key recovery attack is carried out on 11 rounds of midori-64. The influence of whitening key is not considered in the analysis process, as shown in Fig. 3. In Fig. 3, the status bytes involved in the encryption and decryption of the attack process are marked "*", and other irrelevant bytes are marked "□".

4.1   Attack Process

The command $x_1^j, x_{11}^j(0 \leq j \leq 15)$ indicates the initial state half byte during the attack, and I_i^j indicates the state half byte during the attack, and $RK_i^j(0 \leq i \leq 14, 0 \leq j \leq 15)$ represents the value of the $j + 1$ half byte of the round $i + 1$ key.

(1)   under the key k, N cipher text pairs (P, C) are collected, and under the key k', N cipher text pairs (P', C') are collected, and $k = k' \oplus \Delta$.

(2)   if $y_0 = x_1^{1,2,3,6,7,9,11,13,14}||x_{11}^{0,1,2,3,4,5,6,7,8,9,10,12,13,14}$ is selected, y_0 has a total of possible states of 2^{92}. A 16bit counter $N_0[y_0]$ is established for each state, and all of them are initialized to zero. Collect N cipher text pairs (P, C), calculate the logarithm of each state satisfied by these cipher text pairs, and add 1 to the corresponding counter $N_0[y_0]$. No more than 2^{64} cipher text pairs are divided into 2^{92} States, so the counter 16bit is enough.

(3)   if $y_1 = I_2^{5,10,15}||x_{11}^{0,1,2,3,4,6,7,12,13,14}||I_{10}^{6,11}$ is selected, y_1 has a total of 2^{60} states. A 16bit counter $N_1[y_1]$ is established for each state, and all of them are initialized to zero. Enumerate the 20bit round sub key $RK_0^{5,10,15}$ and $RK_{10}^{8,9}$. Because of $RK_0 = k_0 \oplus \alpha_0$, $RK_{10} = k_0 \oplus \alpha_{10}$, so $RK_{10} = RK_0 \oplus \alpha_0 \oplus \alpha_{10}$. Therefore, $RK_0^{5,10,15}$ can push out $RK_{10}^{5,10}$, calculate and update the state of $I_2^5 = RK_0^5 \oplus$

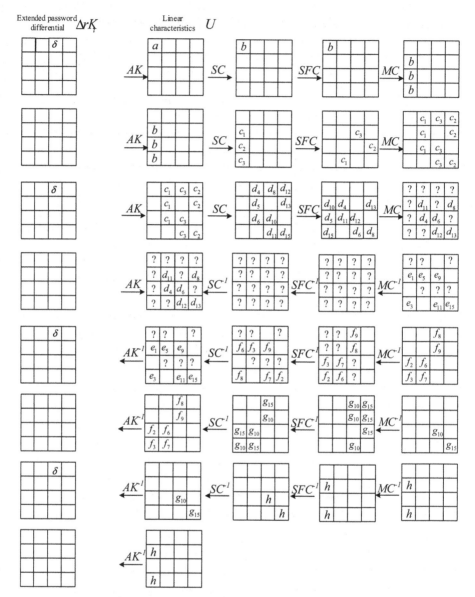

Fig. 2. 7-round distinguisher of Midori-64 algorithm

$[S_{14}(x_1^{14}) \oplus S_{11}(x_1^{11}) \oplus S_1(x_1^1)]$, $I_2^{10} = RK_0^{10} \oplus [S_9(x_1^9) \oplus S_3(x_1^3) \oplus S_6(x_1^6)]$, $I_2^{15} = RK_0^{15} \oplus [S_7(x_1^7) \oplus S_{13}(x_1^{13}) \oplus S_2(x_1^2)]$; $I_{10}^6 = S_6^{-1}[(x_{11}^8 \oplus RK_{10}^8) \oplus (x_{11}^9 \oplus RK_{10}^9) \oplus (x_{11}^{10} \oplus RK_{10}^{10})]I_{10}^{11} = (x_{11}^5 \oplus RK_{10}^5)$; then update the counter $N_1[y_1]+ = N_0[y_0]$. This step requires 11 rounds of $N \times 2^{20} \times 1/16 \times 1/11 \approx 2^{12.54}N$ encryption operations.

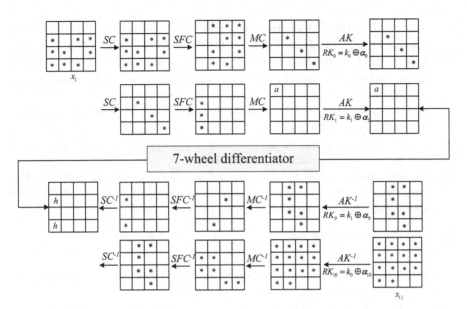

Fig. 3. Key-recovery attack on 11-round Midori-64 algorithm

(4) if $y_2 = I_2^{5,10,15}||x_{11}^{0,1,2,3,12,13,14}||I_{10}^{4,6,11}$ is selected, y_2 has 2^{52} states. A 16 bit counter $N_2[y_2]$ is established for each state, and all of them are initialized to zero. Exhaust the 12bit round sub key $RK_{10}^{4,6,7}$, calculate and update the state $I_{10}^{11} = S_{11}^{-1}[I_{10}^{11} \oplus (x_{11}^4 \oplus RK_{10}^4) \oplus (x_{11}^7 \oplus RK_{10}^7)]$; $I_{10}^4 = S_4^{-1}[(x_{11}^4 \oplus RK_{10}^4) \oplus (x_{11}^6 \oplus RK_{10}^6) \oplus (x_{11}^7 \oplus RK_{10}^7)]$, and then update the counter $N_2[y_2]+ = N_1[y_1]$. This step requires 11 rounds of $2^{60} \times 2^{12} \times 1/16 \times 1/11 = 2^{64.54}$ encryption operations.

(5) if $y_3 = I_2^{5,10,15}||x_{11}^{0,1,2,3}||I_{10}^{4,6,8,11}$ is selected, y_3 has 2^{44} states in total. A 16bit counter $N_3[y_3]$ is established for each state, and all of them are initialized to zero. Enumerate the 12 bit round sub key $RK_{10}^{11,12,13}$, calculate and update the status $I_{10}^8 = S_8^{-1}[(x_{11}^{12} \oplus RK_{10}^{12}) \oplus (x_{11}^{13} \oplus RK_{10}^{13}) \oplus (x_{11}^{14} \oplus RK_{10}^{14})]$, and then update the counter $N_3[y_3]+ = N_2[y_2]$. This step requires 11 rounds of $2^{52} \times 2^{12} \times 1/16 \times 1/11 \approx 2^{56.54}$ encryption.

(6) if $y_4 = I_2^{5,10,15}||I_{10}^{4,5,6,8,10,11}$ is selected, y_4 has 2^{36} states in total. A 16bit counter $N_4[y_4]$ is established for each state, and all of them are initialized to zero. Enumerate the 12 bit round sub key $RK_{10}^{0,1,2,3}$, calculate and update the status $I_{10}^5 = S_5^{-1}[(x_{11}^0 \oplus RK_{10}^0) \oplus (x_{11}^1 \oplus RK_{10}^1) \oplus (x_{11}^3 \oplus RK_{10}^3)]$; $I_{10}^{10} = S_{10}^{-1}[(x_{11}^0 \oplus RK_{10}^0) \oplus (x_{11}^2 \oplus RK_{10}^2) \oplus (x_{11}^3 \oplus RK_{10}^3)]$, and then update the counter $N_4[y_4]+ = N_3[y_3]$. This step requires 11 rounds of $2^{44} \times 2^{16} \times 1/16 \times 1/11 \approx 2^{52.54}$ encryption.

(7) if $y_5 = I_2^{5,10,15}||I_9^{1,3}$ is selected, y_5 has 2^{20} states in total. A 16bit counter $N_5[y_5]$ is established for each state, and all of them are initialized to zero. Enumerate the 12 bit round sub key $RK_9^{4,5,6,8,10,11}$, calculate and update the status $I_9^1 = S_1^{-1}[(I_{10}^4 \oplus RK_9^4) \oplus (I_{10}^5 \oplus RK_9^5) \oplus (I_{10}^6 \oplus RK_9^6)]I_9^3 = S_3^{-1}[(I_{10}^8 \oplus RK_9^8) \oplus (I_{10}^{10} \oplus$

$RK_9^{10}) \oplus (I_{10}^{11} \oplus RK_9^{11})]$, and then update the counter $N_5[y_5]+ = N_4[y_4]$. This step requires 11 rounds of $2^{36} \times 2^{24} \times 1/16 \times 1/11 \approx 2^{52.54}$ encryption.

(8) if $y_6 = I_3^0 || I_9^1$ is selected, y_6 has 2^8 states in total. A 16bit counter $N_6[y_6]$ is established for each state, and all of them are initialized to zero. Enumerate the 12 bit round sub key $RK_9^{4,5,6,8,10,11}$, calculate and update the status $I_3^0 = [S_{10}(I_2^{10}) \oplus S_5(I_2^5) \oplus S_{15}(I_2^{15})]; I_9^1 = I_9^1 \oplus I_9^3$, and then update the counter $N_6[y_6]+ = N_5[y_5]$. This step requires 11 rounds of $2^{20} \times 1/16 \times 1/11 \approx 2^{12.54}$ encryption.

(9) for the sub key k', using the same method, we can get the counter $N_6'[y_6']$, where y_6' is the value corresponding to the sub key k'.

(10) a 64 bit counter T_i and T_i' are set up and initialized to 0 respectively for the i linear approximation ($1 \leq i \leq \ell$). For the 2^8 values of y_6 and y_6', if the linear approximation is true, then $T_i+ = N_6[y_6]$, $T_i'+ = N_6'[y_6']$.

(11) calculate the statistical value $s = \sum_{i=1}^{\ell} \left[\left(\frac{T_i}{N} - \frac{1}{2} \right) - \left(\frac{T_i'}{N} - \frac{1}{2} \right) \right]^2$.

When N, n and ℓ are large enough, s obeys the normal distribution with expectation of $\mu_0 = \frac{\ell}{2N}$ and variance of $\sigma_0^2 = \frac{\ell}{2N^2}$ under the correct key guess:

$$s \sim \left(\frac{\ell}{2N}, \frac{\ell}{2N^2} \right)$$

Under the wrong key guess, s obeys the normal distribution with expectation of $\mu_1 = \frac{\ell}{2N} + \frac{\ell}{2^{n+1}}$ and variance of $\sigma_1^2 = \frac{\ell}{2N^2} + \frac{\ell}{2^{2n+1}} + \frac{\ell}{N2^n}$:

$$s \sim \left(\frac{\ell}{2N} + \frac{\ell}{2^{n+1}}, \frac{\ell}{2N^2} + \frac{\ell}{2^{2n+1}} + \frac{\ell}{N2^n} \right)$$

By using the nontrivial linear approximation of ℓ, we can distinguish the right key guess and the wrong key guess by the error probability α (the probability of the right key guess being the wrong key guess) and β (the probability of the wrong key guess being the right key guess). The number of known plaintexts needed is:

$$N = \frac{2^{n+0.5}}{\sqrt{\ell} - z_{1-\beta}\sqrt{2}} (z_{1-\alpha} + z_{1-\beta})$$

$z_{1-\alpha}$ and $z_{1-\beta}$ are quantiles of standard normal distribution, and the threshold value of judgment is $\tau = \mu_0 + \sigma_0 z_{1-\alpha} = \mu_1 - \sigma_0 z_{1-\beta}$.

If $s < \tau$, the guessed sub key is correct, otherwise it is wrong.

4.2 Complexity Analysis

In the above attack process, a total of 84 bit keys are guessed. If the two kinds of error probability are $\alpha = 2^{-2.7}$ and $\beta = 2^{-10}$, then $q_{1-\alpha} \approx 1$ and $q_{1-\beta} \approx 3.09$. Because $n = 64$ and $\ell = 2^8$ can get $N \approx 2^{62.99}$, we need $2^{62.99}$ cipher text pairs. The critical value is $\tau \approx 2^{-59.42}$. From step 2 to step 9, the computation complexity of the attack is $(2^{75.53} + 2^{64.54} + 2^{56.54} + 2^{52.54} + 2^{52.54} + 2^{12.54}) \times 2 \approx 2^{76.6}$ times 11 rounds of encryption. So the data complexity of completing 11 rounds of midori-64 attack is $2^{62.29}$, and the calculation complexity is $2^{76.6}$. The attack results show that the 11 rounds of midori-64 cipher algorithm is not immune to the linear analysis method of related-keys invariant bias. The main attack results of midori-64 algorithm are shown in Table 3. From Table 3, we can see that the related-keys invariant Deviation Linear Analysis of midori-64 is one more round than that of impossibility differential analysis, and it also has obvious advantages in time complexity compared with the intermediate encounter attack of 11 rounds.

Table 3. Comparison of results on cryptanalysis of Midori-64

Attack methods and Literature	Data complexity	Time complexity	Attack rounds
Impossible differential analysis [8]	$2^{62.4}$	$2^{80.81}$	10
Meet in the middle attack [9]	$2^{61.5}$	$2^{99.5}$	10
Meet in the middle attack [9]	2^{53}	2^{122}	11
Linear analysis of the invariant deviation of the related-keys in this paper	$2^{62.99}$	$2^{76.6}$	11
Meet in the middle attack [9]	$2^{55.5}$	$2^{125.5}$	12

5   A Subsection Sample

In this paper, the security of midori-64 is evaluated by using the linear analysis of related-keys invariant deviation. Firstly, seven rounds of related-keys invariant Deviation Linear differentiators are constructed by selecting appropriate linear mask and key difference, and then 11 rounds of midori-64 are attacked by key recovery. The result is one more attack round than that of midori-64 algorithm. The further research direction of the attack result is: the target algorithm has more than one pair of linear shells which meet the requirements of constructing the linear differentiator with constant key deviation. Combined with the properties of the key expansion algorithm of the given algorithm, finding the linear shells which can construct the differentiator with the longest number of rounds in these linear shells is the key technology to be further studied, which will effectively increase the attack Number of rounds.

References

1. Matsui, M.: Linear cryptanalysis method for DES cipher. In: Helleseth, T. (ed.) EUROCRYPT 1993. LNCS, vol. 765, pp. 386–397. Springer, Heidelberg (1994). https://doi.org/10.1007/3-540-48285-7_33
2. Kaliski, B.S., Robshaw, M.J.B.: Linear cryptanalysis using multiple approximations. In: Desmedt, Yvo G. (ed.) CRYPTO 1994. LNCS, vol. 839, pp. 26–39. Springer, Heidelberg (1994). https://doi.org/10.1007/3-540-48658-5_4

3. Hermelin, M., Cho, J.Y., Nyberg, K.: Multidimensional extension of Matsui's algorithm 2. In: Fast Software Encryption: 16th International Workshop, FSE 2009, vol. 5665, pp. 209–227 (2009)
4. Bogdanov, A., Rijmen, V.: Linear hulls with correlation zero and linear cryptanalysis of block ciphers. Designs Codes Crypt. **70**(3), 369–383 (2014)
5. Bogdanov, A., Boura, C., Rijmen, V., Wang, M., Wen, L., Zhao, J.: Key difference invariant bias in block ciphers. In: Sako, K., Sarkar, P. (eds.) ASIACRYPT 2013. LNCS, vol. 8269, pp. 357–376. Springer, Heidelberg (2013). https://doi.org/10.1007/978-3-642-42033-7_19
6. Banik, S., et al.: Midori: a block cipher for low energy. In: Iwata, T., Cheon, J.H. (eds.) ASIACRYPT 2015. LNCS, vol. 9453, pp. 411–436. Springer, Heidelberg (2015). https://doi.org/10.1007/978-3-662-48800-3_17
7. Wang, Y., et al.: Security evaluation of Midori algorithm against fault attack. Crypt. J. **4**(1), 58–78 (2017)
8. Chen, Z., Wang, X.: Impossible differential cryptanalysis of Midori. In: Mechatronics and Automation Engineering: Proceedings of the International Conference on Mechatronics and Automation Engineering (ICMAE2016), pp. 221–229. World Scientific (2017)
9. Lin, L., Wu, W.: Meet-in-the-middle attacks on reduced-round Midori64. IACR Trans. Symmetric Cryptol. **2017**(1), 215–239 (2017)
10. Guo, J., Jean, J., Nikolic, I., et al.: Invariant subspace attack against full Midori64. IACR Cryptol. ePrint Arch., 1189–1197 (2015)
11. Ren, Y., Zhang, W.: Impossible differential analysis of related key of Midori 64, 25 May 2017. http://www.arocmag.com/article/02-2018-05-001.html
12. Kaddi, M., Benahmed, K., Omari, M.: An energy-efficient protocol using an objective function & random search with jumps for WSN. Comput. Mater. Continua **58**(3), 603–624 (2019)
13. Wenjia, X., Xiang, S., Sachnev, V.: A cryptograph domain image retrieval method based on Paillier Homomorphic block encryption. Comput. Mater. Continua **055**(2), 285–295 (2018)
14. Amer, Y.A., Mahdy, A.M.S., Youssef, E.S.M.: Solving fractional integro-differential equations by using sumudu transform method and Hermite spectral collocation method. Comput. Mater. Continua **54**(2), 161–180 (2018)

A Formula Three Pixels Matching Steganography Algorithm

Min Long$^{(\boxtimes)}$, Sai Long, and Fenfang Li

College of Computer and Communication Engineering, Changsha University of Science and Technology, Changsha 410114, China
caslongm@aliyun.com

Abstract. TPM (three pixels matching) steganography adopted three pixels as an embedding unit, and extraction function was defined by minimizing the distortion of pixel value along with low pixel value difference distortion. Based on TPM, we proposed formula three pixels matching (FTPM) steganography in this paper. A formula is used to get the stego image pixel pair without searching the neighborhood set for the given image pixel pair and the embedded path selection of the secret information is implemented by the chessboard coverage algorithm. This method can embed digits in any notational system and protect the privacy of the embedded information. The experimental results and analysis show that the proposed method is flexible in the process of information hiding, and no extra storage space is required, while it also ensures the image quality.

Keywords: Data hiding · Steganography · TPM (Three pixels matching)

1 Introduction

Data steganography is a research to embed secret messages to the digital cover media, including image, video, audio, text, and so on. The digital cover media as the plaintext transmitted in public channel is less likely to arouse the interest of the third party and not easy to detect by hackers. There are two major factors to be considered when designing a steganography scheme. One is perceptual distortion caused by data hiding, the other is embedding capacity, which includes the maximum amount of secret messages that can be embedded into the cover media without any perceptual distortion. There is a trade-off between them. The higher the embedding capacity, the greater of the perceptual distortion. Generally, embedding efficiency is considered to a concurrent evaluation for embedding capacity and perceptual distortion.

LSB replacement [1] is the most famous steganography, which utilizes the characteristics that the human visual system is not sensitive to the variation of the least significant bits of a pixel. In LSB, the least significant bit is directly replaced by the secret bit, which causes some statistical information to be exposed. LSB matching (LSBM) [2] randomly increments or decrements the LSB of a pixel according to a pseudo-random number generator when the secret bit does not match the pixel' s LSB. LSBM revisited (LSBMR) [3] performs the operation by using a pair of pixels as a unit. Both LSBM and

© Springer Nature Singapore Pte Ltd. 2020
X. Sun et al. (Eds.): ICAIS 2020, CCIS 1254, pp. 385–396, 2020.
https://doi.org/10.1007/978-981-15-8101-4_35

LSBMR are undetectable with a chi-square attack, but they can still be detectable using stronger steganalytic attacks. In [4], an edge adaptive image steganography based on LSBMR (EALSBMR) was proposed, which can select the embedding regions according to the size of secret message and the difference between two consecutive pixels in the cover image. In [5], with the help of the error images, a steganographic scheme was proposed, where the target pixels were adaptively chosen based on a preprocessing phase. Kuo et al. [6] proposed a formula diamond encoding (FDEMD) data hide scheme, and it could conceal a digit in $(2k^2 + 2k + 1)$-ary system. It simplified the embedding procedure and embedded secret data without storing and calculating characteristic value matrix. Hong et al. [7] designed a new extraction function and neighborhood set of two pixels called adaptive pixel pair matching (APPM). It allowed embedding digits in arbitrary notational system and the distortion caused by embedment using APPM was minimized, therefore the resultant marked image quality could be well preserved [8]. Based on APPM, a formula adaptive pixel pair matching steganography algorithm was proposed [9], and the basic idea is to use the formula to get the stego image pixel pair without searching the neighborhood set for the given image pixel pair. In [10], three pixels were adopted as an embedding unit, and the extraction function was defined by minimizing the distortion of pixel value along with low pixel value difference distortion. Based on the above methods, a formula three pixel matching algorithm is proposed by constructing a formula to simply the embedding procedure. It can realize the data hiding in any notional system and does not need to calculate, store and query the modified neighborhood set table.

2 A Review of Three Pixels Matching (TPM)

In TPM, the extraction functions was designed to make the pixel value change as small as possible and the content of image can be preserved as much as possible. As regard to three pixels (x, y, z), the extraction function is given as follows.

$$f_{TPM}(x, y, z) = (r_B x + t_B y + z) \mod B \tag{1}$$

The coefficients (r_B, t_B) are obtained by solving optimization problems, and (r_B, t_B) are listed for $B \leq 64$ in [10]. When embedding secret information of B base with TPM method, the corresponding modified neighborhood Φ_B needs to be calculated. Figure 1 gives the modified neighborhood when $B = 23$ and the value in square lattice is $f(x, y, z)$. When the secret data is s $= 22$, $f(0, 0, -1) = 22$ as given in the dotted box, then the three pixel block is modified to $(0, 0, -1)$.

The TPM method extends the APPM method in reference [7], makes full use of the points in 3D space and takes into account the correlation between pixels, and realizes the embedding of secret information in arbitrary decimal of three pixels. However, this method has two disadvantages: (1) The modified neighborhood should be calculated for different B-ary. (2) It is necessary to query the modified neighborhood table when the pixel block is modified to embedding secret information.

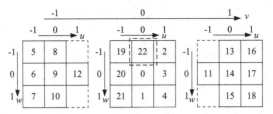

Fig. 1. $\Phi_{23}(0, 0, 0)$

3   The Proposed Formula Three Pixels Matching Method (FTPM)

In order to improve the flexibility of the method for different B-ary and avoid the query the modified neighborhood during the embedding process, this paper puts forward a formula three pixel matching embedding method to find the stego-pixel pair without querying a neighborhood set.

3.1   Checkerboard Coverage

In TPM, the image is firstly converted to a one-dimensional sequence, and then divided into non-overlapping blocks with three pixels in turn. To improve the privacy of the embedded information, the image is divided into blocks by checkerboard coverage method in this paper. As shown in Fig. 2, a box is randomly selected in the 4×4 Checkerboard, and the remaining areas of the checkerboard can be divided into several L-shape blocks. For a $N \times N$ Checkerboard, there is $(N^2 - 1)/3$ L-shape blocks. Due to the different positions of the randomly selected box, the coverage of the checkerboard is totally different. That is, the embedding path of the secret information is different, which will improve the privacy of the secret information.

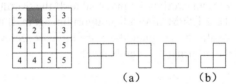

(a)   (b)

Fig. 2. Checkerboard coverage

3.2   Embedding Procedure

In combination with the checkerboard coverage algorithm, FTPM uses the extracted function coefficient table given in [10], and calculates the modification amount z of pixel pair (x, y) by the formula method to realize the hiding of secret data. Figure 3 shows the embedding process overview.

Firstly, use the key k to generate the position of the box in the checkerboard coverage, and divide the image into L-shape blocks by the checkerboard overlay algorithm.

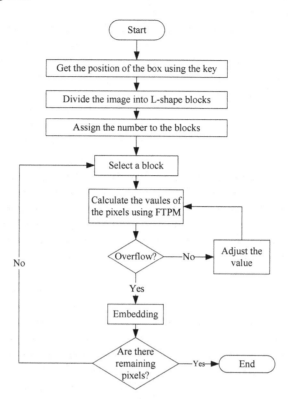

Fig. 3. The embedding process

Secondly, assign the number to all the blocks and select a L-shape block. Thirdly, use the FTPM embedding algorithm calculate the values of each pixel in the L-shape block, and check whether there is an overflow of pixel value. If the overflow occurs, adjust the original pixel value and use FTPM embedding algorithm again. If the overflow does not occur, modify the pixel value to complete the embedding of secret information. Repeat the third step until all the information is embedded.

Algorithm 1:

Input: The key sk, the coefficients (r_B, t_B), secret data S and range control parameter k.

Output: Stego pixel pair (x_i', y_i', z_i').

Prepare: Use the key sk to generate the special pixel points, and divide the image into non-overlapping L-type three-pixel blocks by the checkerboard coverage algorithm, then get the ith pixel block is (x_i, y_i, z_i).

Step 1: Set $f = (r_B x_i + t_B y_i + z_i) \bmod B$;

Step 2: Set $k = \left\lceil (\left\lceil \sqrt[3]{B} \right\rceil - 1)/2 \right\rceil$;

Step 3: Set $D = s - f$;

Step 4: If $D < 0$ then $D = D + B$;

Step 5: If $r_B > t_B$, then

$\qquad$ Set $Max = r_B$, $Mid = t_B$

$\qquad$ Else Set $Max = t_B$, $Mid = r_B$

Step 6: Set $next\_d = D \bmod Max$

Step 7: W $\left| t_{max} \right| < k$ hile $i = 1$ to 4 do

Set $d = next\_d$, $t_{max} = (D - d)/Max$

$\qquad$ If $\quad$ then

$\qquad\qquad$ If $d > 0$ then

$\qquad\qquad\qquad$ Set $next\_t_{min} = d \bmod Mid$

$\qquad\qquad$ Else

$\qquad\qquad\qquad$ Set $next\_t_{min} = -\left| d \right| \bmod Mid$

$\qquad\qquad$ End if

$\qquad\qquad$ While $i = 1$ to 2 do

$\qquad\qquad\qquad$ Set $t_{min} = next\_t_{min}$,

$\qquad\qquad\qquad\qquad$ $t_{mid} = (d - t_{min})/Mid$

$\qquad\qquad\qquad$ If $\left| t_{mid} \right| \le k$ & $\left| t_{mid} \right| \le k$

$\qquad\qquad\qquad\qquad$ If $r_B > t_B$ then

$\qquad\qquad\qquad\qquad\qquad$ Set $x_i' = x_i + t_{max}$,

$\qquad\qquad\qquad\qquad\qquad\qquad$ $y_i' = y_i + t_{mid}$,

$\qquad\qquad\qquad\qquad\qquad\qquad$ $z_i' = z_i + t_{min}$

$\qquad\qquad\qquad\qquad\qquad$ Return (x_1', x_2', x_3')

$\qquad\qquad\qquad\qquad$ Else

$$\text{Set } x_i' = x_i + t_{mid},$$
$$z_i' = z_i + t_{min}$$

Return (x_i', y_i', z_i')

End if

Else

Switch (i)

Case 1: If $next\_t_{min} \geq 0$, Then

$$next\_t_{min} = t_{min} - Mid$$

Else

$$next\_t_{min} = t_{min} + Mid$$

End if

Case 2: break;

End Switch

End if

End while

End if

Switch (i)

Case 1:

Set $next\_d = d - Max$

Case 2:

Set D=D-B,

$$next\_d = -(|D| \bmod Max)$$

Case 3:

Set $next\_d = d + Max$

Case 4: Print 'Error'

End Switch

End if

End While

Example 1: For a cover pixels pair (11,12,13), secret data $s = 8_{(27)}$ and we can get the coefficients $(r_{27}, t_{27}) = (9, 15)$ from the reference [10]. The stego image pixels pair $(x_i', y_i', z_i') = (11, 12, 13)$ is obtained by using Algorithm 1.

Step 1: calculate $f = (9 \times 11 + 15 \times 12 + 13) \bmod 27 = 22$;
Step 2: calculate $k = \left\lceil (\left\lceil \sqrt[3]{B} \right\rceil - 1)/2 \right\rceil = 1$;
Step 3: calculate $D = s - f = 8 - 22 = -14$. For $D < 0$, then $D = D + B = 7$;
Step 4: $r_{27} = 9 < t_{27} = 15$, then $Max = 15$, $Mid = 9$;
Step 5: $next\_d = D \bmod Max = 7$

ROUND 1: $d = 7, t_{max} = 0$

$$|t_{max}| \leq k, next\_t_{min} = d \bmod Mid = 7$$

Round 1: $t_{min} = 7, t_{mid} = 0$

$$|t_{min}| > k, next\_t_{min} = t_{min} - Mid = -2$$

Round 2: $t_{min} = -2, t_{mid} = 1$

$$|t_{min}| > k, \text{break}$$

ROUND 2: $d = -8, t_{max} = 1$

$$|t_{max}| \leq k, next\_t_{min} = d \bmod Mid = -8$$

Round 1: $t_{min} = -8, t_{mid} = 0$

$$|t_{min}| > k, next\_t_{min} = t_{min} - Mid = 1$$

Round 2: $t_{min} = 1, t_{mid} = -1$

$|t_{min}| \leq k \&\& |t_{mid}| \leq k$, then return $(10, 13, 14)$.

3.3 Extraction Procedure

Similar to the embedding algorithm, use the key k to generate the position of the box in the checkerboard coverage, and divide the image into L-shape blocks by the checkerboard overlay algorithm. Then, assign the number to all the blocks and select a L-shape block. Thereafter, calculate the extraction function value $s_i = (r_B x_i + t_B y_i + z_i) \bmod B$, and convert them to binary stream m. The detailed process is given as Fig. 4.

3.4 Solution to Overflow Problem

If an overflow or underflow problem occurs, that is, $(x', y', z') < 0$ or $(x', y', z') > 255$, a nearest (x'', y'', z'') should be found in the neighborhood of (x, y, z) such that $f(x'', y'', z'') = s_B$. This can be done by solving the optimization problem
　　Minimize: $(x - x'')^2 + (y - y'')^2 + (z - z'')^2$,
　　Subject to: $f(x'', y'', z'') = s_B, 0 \leq x'', y'', z'' \leq 255$.

4 Experimental Results and Analysis

4.1 Embedding Efficiency

Embedding efficiency (EE) is the ratio of the capacity or embedding rate (ER) to the expected number of changes per pixel or change rate (CR) as defined in [11], and it is considered as a reasonable measure for concurrent evaluation of the capacity and security of the embedding scheme.

$$EE = \frac{ER}{CR} \tag{1}$$

Figure 5 shows the comparison results of LSBM, LSBMR, EALSBMR, APPM, TPM and the proposed method. We can see that the EE of proposed method is higher than other methods. This is because the algorithm takes advantage of the local complexity and edge characteristics of the image, and can embeds more secret information.

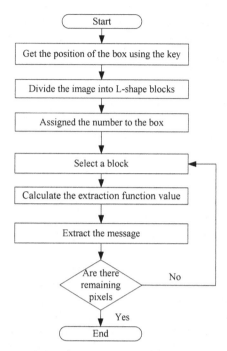

Fig. 4. Extraction procedure

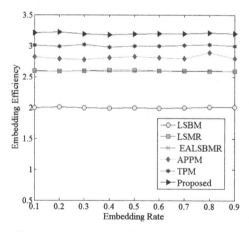

Fig. 5. Embedding efficiency of the algorithms

4.2 Image Quality

As message embedding, it will introduce the distortion in the image. Peak signal-to-noise ratio (PSNR) is usually used to measure the difference between the cover-image and the stego-image. The definition of PSNR is as (2), and is expressed in dB's.

$$PSNR = 10 \times \log_{10}\left(\frac{255^2}{MSE}\right) \tag{2}$$

where P is the peak signal value of the image, MSE is the averaged pixel-by pixel squared difference between the cover-image and stego-image, and it is defined as follows:

$$MSE = \frac{1}{M \times N} \sum_{i=0}^{M} \sum_{j=0}^{N} \left(p_{i,j} - p'_{i,j}\right)^2 \tag{3}$$

Here, the symbols $p_{i,j}$ and $p'_{i,j}$ represent the pixel values of the cover image and stego image in the position (i, j), respectively. M and N are the rows and columns of the cover image respectively. The experimental results in Table 1 show that the PSNR of the proposed algorithm is higher than LSBM, LSBMR, EALSBMR, APPM and TPM, and FATPM algorithm has little influence on image quality.

Table 1. PSNR of the algorithms

Embedding capacity (bpp)	PSNR (dB)					
	LSBM	LSBMR	EALSBMR	APPM	TPM	Proposed
0.5	52.41	52.87	52.83	53.16	53.33	53.67
1	52.20	52.21	52.20	52.39	52.51	52.91
1.5	49.82	50.04	50.02	50.17	50.23	50.31
2	46.23	46.43	46.41	46.85	46.96	47.22

4.3 Analysis of the Security

Anti-steganalysis is one of the most important criteria to measure the performance of a steganographic method. In this paper, two general steganalysis algorithms are used to evaluate the security of steganalysis algorithm. They are subtractive pixel adjacency matrix (SPAM) analysis algorithm based on gray image [12] and projection space rich model (PSRM) based steganalysis algorithm [13]. Experiments are carried out in two commonly used image databases, UCID [14] and NRCS [15]. The UCID database contains 1338 TIFF images and NRCS database contains 3148 TIFF images. Figure 6 shows receiver operating characteristic (ROC) curves of SPAM for LSBM, LSBMR, EALS-BMR, APPM, TPM and proposed method with embedding rate of 0.5bpp and 0.8bpp in NRCS. Figure 7 shows the comparison results in UCID. It can be seen from Figs. 6 and 7, the proposed method obtains excellent results. Figures 8 and 9 show the receiver operating characteristic (ROC) curves of PSRM for these methods in NRCS and UCID, respectively. PSRM based steganalysis also confirms the superior performance of the proposed method.

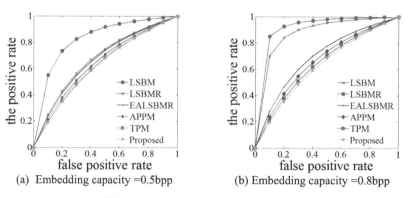

Fig. 6. ROC curves for SPAM in NRCS

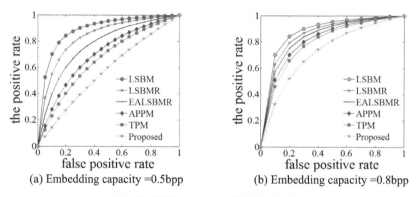

Fig. 7. ROC curves for SPAM in UCID

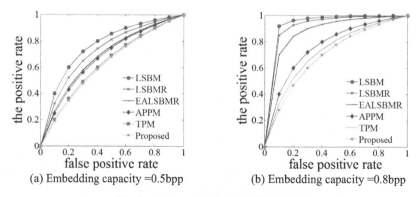

Fig. 8. ROC curves for PSRM in NRCS

In [16], a targeted steganalysis using B-spline fitting was proposed to detect the pulse distortion to the long exponential tail of the histogram of the absolute difference between the pixel pairs, and it attacked EALSBMR successfully. In this paper, we try to analysis

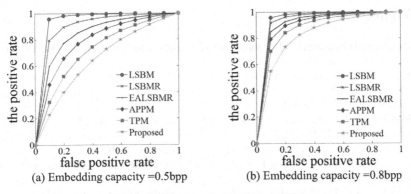

Fig. 9. ROC curves for PSRM in UCID

the proposed the method using this steganalysis. Figure 10 shows the comparison results between the proposed method and EALSBMR in NRCS and UCID. We can see that the targeted steganalysis using B-spline fitting fails to detect stego image by the proposed method with 0.5bpp and 0.8bpp embedding rates.

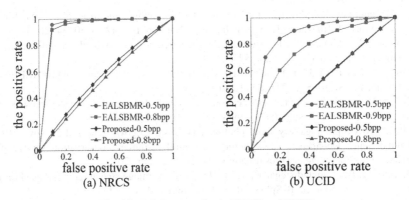

Fig. 10. ROC curves for in NRCS and UCID

5 Conclusion

This paper proposed a simple and convenient data embedding method based on TPM. Compared with the TPM method, it has the advantage of no needing to compute and store the neighborhood set. Compared with the FDEMD method, the secret data of any notional system is realized by the FTPM method, which makes the embedding notational system selection more flexible and protects the privacy of embedded information. The experimental results showed that FTPM method has high image quality and the strong anti-steganalysis ability.

References

1. Provos, N., Honeyman, P.: Hide and seek: an introduction to steganography. IEEE Secur. Priv. Mag. **1**(3), 32–44 (2003)
2. Ker, A.D.: Improved detection of LSB steganography in grayscale images. In: Fridrich, J. (ed.) IH 2004. LNCS, vol. 3200, pp. 97–115. Springer, Heidelberg (2004). https://doi.org/10.1007/978-3-540-30114-1_8
3. Mielikainen, J.: LSB matching revisited. IEEE Signal Process. Lett. **13**(5), 285–287 (2006)
4. Luo, W., Huang, F., Huang, J.: Edge adaptive image steganography based on LSB matching revisited. IEEE Trans. Inf. Forensics Secur. **5**(2), 201–214 (2010)
5. Afrakhteh, M., Lee, J.-A.: Adaptive least significant bit matching revisited with the help of error images. Secur. Commun. Netw. **8**, 510–515 (2015)
6. Kuo, W.C., Lai, P.Y., Wang, C.C., Wu, L.C.: A formula diamond encoding data hiding scheme. J. Inf. Hiding Multimedia Signal Process. **6**(6), 1167–1176 (2015)
7. Hong, W., Chen, T.S.: A novel data embedding method using adaptive pixel pair matching. IEEE Trans. Inf. Forensics Secur. **7**(1), 176–184 (2012)
8. Hong, W., Chen, M., Chen, T.S., Huang, C.-C.: An efficient authentication method for AMBTC compressed images using adaptive pixel pair matching. Multimedia Tools Appl. **77**(4), 4677–4695 (2017). https://doi.org/10.1007/s11042-017-4899-z
9. Long, M., Li, F.: A formula adaptive pixel pair matching steganography algorithm. Adv. Multimedia **2018**, 7682098 (2018)
10. Iu, J., Tang, G., Gao, Z., Shen, L.: Efficient steganography using triple pixels matching for large payload. J. Huazhong Univ. Sci. Technol. (Nat. Sci. Ed.) **42**(4), 50–54 (2014)
11. Omoomi, M., Samavi, S., Dumitrescu, S.: An efficient high payload ± 1 data embedding scheme. Multi-media Tools Appl. **54**(2), 201–218 (2011)
12. Pevný, T., Bas, P., Fridrich, J.: Steganalysis by subtractive pixel adjacency matrix. IEEE Trans. Inf. Forensics Secur. **5**(2), 215–224 (2010)
13. Holub, V., Fridrich, J.: Random Projections of residuals for digital image steganalysis. IEEE Trans. Inf. Forensics Secur. **8**(12), 1996–2006 (2013)
14. USDA: NRCS photo gallery. http://photogallery.nrcs.usda.gov/. Accessed 21 Nov 2019
15. United States Department of Agriculture: Natural resources conservation service photo gallery. http://photogallery.nrcs.usda.gov. Accessed 21 Nov 2019
16. Tan, S., Li, B.: Targeted steganalysis of edge adaptive image steganography based on LSB matching revisited using B-Spline fitting. IEEE Signal Process. Lett. **19**(6), 336–339 (2012)

Big Data and Cloud Computing

Design and Implementation of an Alarm Platform Based on Water Quality Big Data

Yan Xia[1], Jianjun Zhang[1(✉)], Weida Chen[2], Hua Wen[1], Guang Sun[3], and Haijun Lin[1]

[1] College of Engineering and Design, Hunan Normal University, Changsha 410081, China
2469692443@qq.com, jianjun998@vip.163.com, 2627902908@qq.com,
linhaijun801028@126.com
[2] Zhaoyin Network Technology (Shenzhen) Co., Ltd., Shenzhen 518057, China
526214479@qq.com
[3] Hunan Finance and Economics College, Changsha 410205, China
329804101@qq.com

Abstract. Water is one of the basic resources for human survival. Monitoring and protection of water pollution has been becoming a serious problem for humans. The water resource management departments at all levels have a large number of water quality testing data, but ignore the further exploration of the resource attributes and data values of water quality data. To this end, we designed and implemented a big data early warning platform for water quality monitoring based on the Internet of Things. Through the water quality monitoring sensors deployed in monitoring water fields, the collected indicator data has been transmitted in real time to the big data early warning platform deployed on Tencent Cloud through the 4G network. The monitoring water quality data will be processed and analyzed in real time according to the warning algorithm pre-set early, and the warning information could be pushed to the user in time to provide decision support for water conservation.

Keywords: Water quality monitoring · Early warning platform · Big data · Environmental protection

1 Introduction

In recent years, sudden water pollution incidents occur frequently in our country, which seriously threaten the safety of people's water use. Because there is no fixed way to discharge the sudden water pollution event, if not handled in time, it will seriously affect the safety of water supply. Automatic monitoring, identification of abnormal water quality indicators and pollution, rapid information release, to ensure the safety of water supply and water quality has become an urgent problem to be solved. In order to grasp the situation of water quality in time and ensure the safety of water supply, it is urgent to establish water monitoring and early warning system [1, 2].

The online water quality monitoring system is a comprehensive online automatic monitoring network consisting of modern sensor technology, computer application technology and communication network [3–6]. Most of the existing water quality monitoring

© Springer Nature Singapore Pte Ltd. 2020
X. Sun et al. (Eds.): ICAIS 2020, CCIS 1254, pp. 399–409, 2020.
https://doi.org/10.1007/978-981-15-8101-4_36

systems pay more attention to water quality data monitoring and collecting, but neglect the value of the collected data. Various water management departments have accumulated a large number of water quality index data, but they have neglected the resource attributes and data value of water quality data that they had obtained [7, 8]. Now we are in the era of big data, cloud computing, and artificial intelligence, it is possible to achieve the answers of these problems with big data tools, data mining methods, cloud computing analysis and other tools. There are some good examples. Weijie Chen et al. used the Internet of Things, cloud computing, and big data to build a big data platform for the garlic industry chain, which is used to solve problems such as the uncertainty of various planting ranges and yields, analysis of price fluctuation factors, and price prediction [9]. Sang Wook Han et al. designed and developed a cloud-based platform and air pollution information system using R language to measure fine dust in air pollution, export pollution information and protection reminders via smart phones [10].

For this reason, we designed and implemented a water quality monitoring data acquisition and processing platform, which can automatically collect water quality monitoring data, design and implement early warning processing based on water quality monitoring data, and push the warning information to the user automatically.

2 Platform Design

The water quality data monitoring and early warning platform we designed is mainly composed of three parts: a data sensing layer, a data transmission layer and an application layer. With some deployed water quality monitoring data sensors, the data sensing layer collects water quality data in the monitoring water areas, and process the data with a single-chip microcomputer. The data transmission layer uses a 4G module for transmission the collected water quality data. The application layer deployed on Tencent Cloud is used for data storage, data analysis, data visualization, related event early warning and early warning information push. The overall architecture of the platform is shown in Fig. 1. The data sensing layer is mainly responsible for the collection of water quality related indicators. We used sensors, such as solutes (TDS), pH (PH) and turbidity (TU), to collect commonly used indicator value, such as the solutes value, pH value and turbidity value, in monitoring water fields. These sensors are all plug-and-play models. The collected related index data is converted by the single-chip microcomputer to the data transmission layer, and then transmitted to the application layer on the cloud platform for processing with some 4G modules. Of course, we have only used some common water quality indicator sensors, but we can expand more sensors to collect the corresponding indicators as needed.

The data processing and analysis system was developed with the Admin LTE framework, the Layer jQuery pop-up plug-in, the blade template, and PHP. The data collected by multiple sensors is uploaded to the WEBAPI through the network, and will be stored in the HBase through the API for further analysis and processing. The data analysis module reads relevant data from the database for data cleaning, data purification, data visualization, early warning analysis and other processing operations. With the related APIs, Baidu Echart and Tencent Wechat related modules, the data processing and analysis system provides early warning, visualization and other related information services to the users. The data flow is shown in Fig. 2.

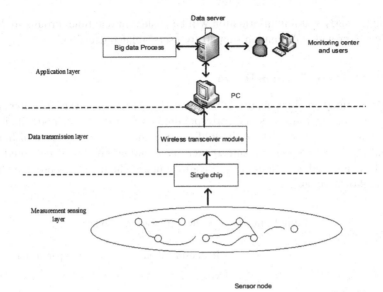

Fig. 1. Schematic diagram of the overall system

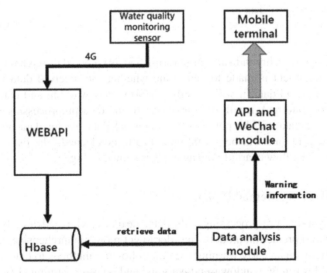

Fig. 2. System data flow diagram

3 Early Warning Module Design

Through the water quality indicator monitoring sensor, the relevant water quality indicator monitoring data can be collected, and transmitted in real time to the data processing and early warning platform deployed on Tencent Cloud through the 4G network. With the early warning module, the abnormal information or excessive data could be found in time, and the early warning information will be pushed in real time through tools such as WeChat to provide information support for users' related decisions.

3.1 Early Warning Program Design

The early warning module mainly performs early warning analysis of water quality monitoring data according to some corresponding early warning methods. Its input is the real-time water quality data of the Redis queue and the historical data of Influxdb. Its output is an early warning result. If there is an abnormal, it will be stored in the outlier_data table and written to the notification queue. The interfaces provided by this module is shown in Table 1.

Table 1. Interfaces of the early warning module

Interface	Request method	Request parameter
/admin/outlier/sse Get exception data list (Content-Type: text/event-stream)	GET	
/admin/outlier/delete Delete multiple abnormal data	POST	ids = [oid1, oid2,...]

After the water quality indicator monitoring data is received through the REST API, the cleaning judgment is made to determine whether the received data is valid data [11–16]. If it is valid data, it will directly perform early warning and data storage. If the warning is abnormal, it will be transferred to the data preprocessing step; if it is invalid data, the data will be put into the abnormal data list for data preprocessing, and the subsequent data will be put into the data to be cleaned. The list is waiting for preprocessing. The flow chart of data analysis is shown in Fig. 3.

3.2 Early Warning Method Design

After the analysis and pre-processing of the data, the data can be used directly to establish classification and prediction models. In order to get more comprehensive data implications, the system's data early warning uses the following methods to detect anomalies: fixed threshold warning, window trend warning, and quartile warning [17].

Fixed Threshold Warning. The fixed threshold warning uses the fixed specific value for early warning mainly based on the water quality standard value. When the collected data exceeds this specific value, the system will give an alarm message. According to the national project surface water environmental quality standard GB3838-2002 shown in the basic project standard, some data quality standards are intercepted as shown in Table 2 below. There are no direct indicators of conductivity and turbidity in China's surface water environmental quality standards. Conductivity indicators are expressed by surfactants, metal ions, salts, etc., and turbidity is reflected by suspended solids.

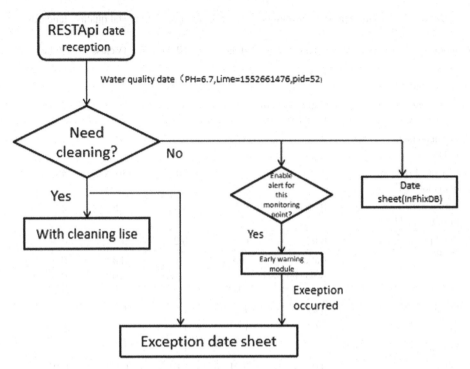

Fig. 3. Data analysis processing flow chart

According to the water quality standard given in Table 2, with Class III water as the standard (Class III water is suitable for concentrated drinking water), We selected a threshold value of 0.5 for data early warning, and give an alarm message when the data exceeds the standard value of 0.5. That is, if the standard value of a parameter is P, and there is a number A $\geq$ P + 0.5, the system will run the data alarm program. Of course, the threshold could be set according to the actual situation.

Sliding Window Trend Warning. The fixed threshold warning method judges whether the standard exceeds the standard by comparing the indicator monitoring value with a specific value, and then may give an early warning. This method can only give information on current monitoring indicators, but cannot predict the changing trend of the water quality indicators. If the set threshold is small, the alarm prompt will be frequently performed, but if the set threshold is too large, some over-standard monitoring data cannot be given an early warning. To this end, we have designed a trend warning method based on the time sliding window.

The trend warning based on the time sliding window is mainly based on the trend of the previous water quality monitoring data to judge whether the current data exceeds the trend range. We set the expected trend window (neighborhood) size based on the previous observation data to find the expectation (mean) of a monitoring indicator. If the currently monitored data exceeds this mean value, for a neighborhood, an early warning mechanism is initiated and an alarm message will be given. This method is mainly to

Table 2. Standard item standard limits for surface water environmental quality standards

Index		Iclass	IIclass	IIIclass	IVclass	Vclass
pH-(Dimensionless)		6~9				
Dissolved oxygen(DO)	≥	Saturation rate 90% (or 7.5)	6	5	3	2
Permanganate index	≤	2	4	6	10	15
Chemical oxygen demand(COD)	≤	15	15	20	30	40
Ammonia nitrogen(NH3-N)	≤	0.15	0.5	1	1.5	2
Total phosphorus (In P)	≤	0.02	0.1	0.2	0.3	0.4
		(lake, reservoir 0.01)	(lake, reservoir 0.025)	(lake, reservoir 0.05)	(lake, reservoir 0.1)	(lake, reservoir 0.2)
Copper	≤	0.01	1	1	1	1
Zinc	≤	0.05	1	1	2	2
Fluoride(In F)	≤	1	1	1	1.5	1.5
Selenium	≤	0.01	0.01	0.01	0.02	0.02
Arsenic	≤	0.05	0.05	0.05	0.1	0.1
Mercury	≤	0.00005	0.00005	0.0001	0.001	0.001
Cadmium	≤	0.001	0.005	0.005	0.005	0.01
Chromium (hexavalent)	≤	0.01	0.05	0.05	0.05	0.1
Lead (Pb)	≤	0.01	0.01	0.05	0.05	0.1

provide early warning for the stage of pollution in the water quality monitoring fields. it could take appropriate measures in time for decision-making, rather than take measures after the pollution has occurred and caused certain impact.

4 Testing and Analysis

4.1 Dataset Construction

In order to better test the platform and ensure the diversity, authenticity and reliability of the data, we designed the reptile program to climb the monitoring waters quality data of the national monitoring points in the recent period from the China Environmental Monitoring Station. The monitoring fields covered 165 monitoring water fields. Nearly 30,000 water quality monitoring data were collected to construct a water quality monitoring indicator data set for monitoring water diversity. The test data is shown in Table 3.

Table 3. Data of various indicators of national monitoring points

Monitoring substance	The amount of data	Numerical range
PH*	6661	6.16–9.98
DO	6320	0.17–19.6
COD$_{MN}$	6123	−0.1–25.6
NH$_3$-N	6485	0.01–19.5

4.2 Early Warning Testing and Analysis

For a monitoring point, we can set an early warning method for a monitoring point based on the fixed threshold warning and the time sliding window warning method mentioned above. Figure 4 shows the warning method setting interface in the platform. As can be seen from the Fig. 4, the "Taozi Lake" site has been set two warning methods for the fixed threshold and window trend, and the "Ji ling xi liang ko" site has been set for the quartile warning method. Multiple warning methods can be set for a monitoring site according as needed.

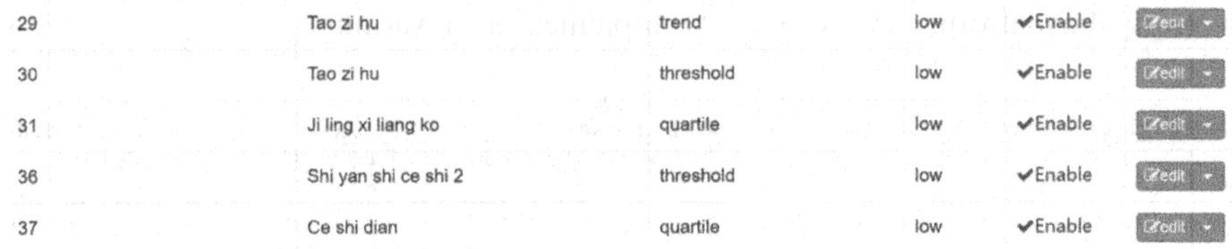

29	Tao zi hu	trend	low	✔Enable	edit ▾
30	Tao zi hu	threshold	low	✔Enable	edit ▾
31	Ji ling xi liang ko	quartile	low	✔Enable	edit ▾
36	Shi yan shi ce shi 2	threshold	low	✔Enable	edit ▾
37	Ce shi dian	quartile	low	✔Enable	edit ▾

Fig. 4. Warning method setting interface

Once some of the monitoring data in this monitoring point exceeds the set value, an early warning will be initiated and the data of these warnings will be displayed as an outlier. The results are shown in Fig. 5. You can export the exception data list in csv format or excel format by exporting csv and exporting excel. In Fig. 5, it can be seen that the platform gives information on the occurrence time and abnormality of water quality data anomalies at all monitoring points through early warning processing. As shown in Fig. 5, "长春南楼 (Changchun south tower)" monitoring sites had single or multiple monitoring water quality indicators exceeding the standards on July 30, August 6, September 3, and September 17, 2018. Among them, on September 3 2018, two of the monitoring indicators exceeded Cod and Nh3n standard value.

807	长春南楼	threshold	2018-09-17T00:00:00+08:00	nh3n>0.61
799	长春南楼	threshold	2018-09-03T00:00:00+08:00	cod>1.5,nh3n>1.74
793	长春南楼	threshold	2018-08-06T00:00:00+08:00	cod>2.9,nh3n>1.24
789	长春南楼	threshold	2018-07-30T00:00:00+08:00	cod>3.5,nh3n>0.99

Fig. 5. Warning information display interface

By looking at the 36th issue of the water quality automatic monitoring weekly report of the major watersheds in China's major river basins downloaded from China Environmental Monitoring Station, we found the original data of this time period. The original data is shown in Fig. 6. As shown in the last line in Fig. 6, the data monitored by this monitoring point during the period of 2018-09-03 showed that the permanganate index and ammonia nitrogen did exceed the standard. The previous section mentioned that the platform refers the Class III water as the standard, so the permanganate index CODMn standard is 6, and the ammonia nitrogen NH3-N standard is 1. It can be seen from Fig. 5 that the value of CODMn is 7.5 and the value of NH3-N is 2.74. So, the platform gives warning information: the permanganate index exceeded the standard value of 1.5, and the ammonia nitrogen exceeded the standard value of 1.74 during that period. In the national water quality monitoring report of key sections of major river basins, the water parameters of the monitoring site of Changchun South Building are CODMn = 7.5 and NH3-N = 2.74. The monitoring report also gives information on permanganate index and ammonia nitrogen exceeding the standard in the bottom of the last column. Therefore, the platform can successfully implement data warning.

Water quality status table of the 36th week of the key section of the major river basins in China

Ord-inal	River name	Point name	Sectional situation	Evaluation factor (unit: mg/L)				Water quality category		Main pollution indicator
				pH*	DO	COD Mn	NH3-N	This week	Last week	
1		Xilangkou, Jilin		7.09	8.76	5.7	0.08	III	III	
2		Songhuajiang-village, Changchun		6.45	9.36	-	0.09	I	II	
3	Songhua River	Songlin,Songyuan	Province boundary of Jilin and Heilongjiang	7.75	7.50	4.3	0.63	III	III	
4		Zhaoyuan		7.72	7.70	7.2	0.15	IV	IV	Permanganate index
5		Jiamusi River Island		6.92	6.51	5.9	0.45	III	IV	
6		Tongjiang	Before entering Heilongjiang	7.35	7.90	5.7	0.14	III	III	
7	Yin Ma River	Changchun South Tower	Before entering Songhua River	7.34	8.24	7.5	2.74	V	V	Permanganate index, ammonia nitrogen

Fig. 6. Changchun South Building 2018.9.3 time period data map

4.3 Early Warning Information Push

In order to transmit the warning information in time to the user, we used the Wechat-sender, a WeChat development tool from Tencent, to develop a WeChat test public account (of course, you can also apply for a non-test version of the public account). Wechat-sender is a toolkit based on Wxpy and tornado, and it can implement websites, crawlers, scripts, etc. Various other applications (such as logs, alarms, running results, etc.) could be sent to the WeChat. Using it, we can push the water quality early warning information of the monitoring waters to the relevant users.

In order to push the warning information to the users, the monitoring water site must be set as the warning information pushing site. The setting interface is shown in Fig. 7. As shown in Fig. 7, the "Hei he" monitoring site in the "Hei long jiang" water area had been set as the warning information pushing site, and there are two pushing forms: Wechat Pushing and Mailbox Pushing. Once a monitoring site is set as the warning information pushing site, the warning information will be sent to the users via the Wechat or the email when a warning occurs in the site.

Add a subscription monitoring point					
#	water Area	Monitoring points	WeChat push	Mailbox push	Operate
16	Shi yan xi tong	Shi yan shi ce shi1	Enabled	Enabled	✕Delete
17	Shi yan xi tong	Shi yan shi ce shi 2	Enabled	Enabled	✕Delete
31	Hei long jiang	Hei he	Enabled	Enabled	✕Delete
82	Bai ma he	Linyi waterlog bridge	Enabled	Enabled	✕Delete

Fig. 7. The warning pushing setting interface

In order to push the warning information to the users, we registered a test Wechat public number to connect the users. In order to get the warning information via the Wechat, a user needs to scan the QR code, which is shown in Fig. 8, to pay attention to the WeChat public number and connect the mobile terminal of the relevant personnel. Then the administrator will register the relevant users on the platform, so that the user can receive the abnormal situation of the water quality monitoring data in time and make corresponding treatment in time.

Fig. 8. WeChat test public number QR code

5 Summary

In order to mine the value of the water quality big data and protect the water resource, we designed and implemented an IoT-based water quality monitoring big data early warning platform. With some deployed water quality monitoring sensors, the collected indicator data is transmitted to the big data early warning platform deployed on Tencent Cloud in real time through the 4G network. By analyzing the monitoring data in real time with the waring algorithms, the platform will get the information on water quality indicators exceeding standards, and push the warning information to the users via the WeChat or the email. After deploying and testing, the platform has been working normally, and providing decision support for water resources protection.

In the next step, in order to detect more parameters, the water quality monitoring indicator database will be expanded by adding more water quality monitoring sensors. In order to achieve more accurate and comprehensive real-time monitoring data and timely warning information of water quality indicators exceeding standards, we will use more better data models or deep learning methods to fully exploit the resource value of water quality monitoring data. At the same time, in order to ensure the security and the integrity of the monitoring data during the transmission process, we will plan to use relevant encryption methods, such as the Dual-Chaining Watermark Scheme [18], to control data integrity and encrypt the monitoring data.

Acknowledgments. This work is supported by National Natural Science Foundation of China (61304208), Hunan Province Science and Technology Plan Project Fund (2012GK3120), Scientific Research Fund of Hunan Province Education Department (18C0003), Research project on teaching reform in colleges and universities of Hunan Province Education Department (20190147), Changsha City Science and Technology Plan Program (K1501013-11), Hunan Normal University University-Industry Cooperation. This work is implemented at the 2011 Collaborative Innovation Center for Development and Utilization of Finance and Economics Big Data Property, Universities of Hunan Province, Open project, grant number 20181901CRP04.

References

1. Zhang, Z., Cao, Q., Xie, T.: Design of water quality monitoring and warning system of drinking water source. Environ. Prot. Sci. **39**(1), 61–64 (2013)
2. Jiang, W., Huang, W.: Environmental monitoring and early warning system construction of centralized drinking water sources. Environ. Monit. Forewarning **2**(6), 5–7 (2010)
3. Gong, L., Hui, G., Hui, Z.: Development of Android platform based portable water quality detector. Chin. J. Environ. Eng. **10**(7), 3973–3976 (2016)
4. Hongsong, L., Jun, L.: New progress of study of water quality monitoring sensors. Transducer Microsyst. Technol. **31**(3), 11–14 (2012)
5. Chu, W., Yuanchao, Z., Da, L.: A biomimetic sensor for the detection of lead in water. Biosens. Bioelectron. **67**, 621–624 (2015)
6. Xiong, F.B., Zhu, W.Z., Lin, H.F.: Fiber-optic sensor based on evanescent wave absorbance around 2.7 μm for determining water content in polar organic solvents. Appl. Phys. B **115**(1), 129–135 (2014)
7. Bin, J.: Reuse of determination data sources: water quality testing in big data era. Water Purif. Technol. **36**(09), 1–3 (2017)
8. Yicheng, X.: Design and Implementation of Water Quality Monitoring Platform, pp. 17–27. Hunan Normal University (2017)
9. Weijie, C., Guo, F., Chao, Z.: Development and application of big data platform for garlic industry chain. Comput. Mater. Continua **58**(1), 229–248 (2017)
10. SangWook, H., Jung, Y.S., Dae-Young, K.: Development of cloud based air pollution information system using visualization. Comput. Mater. Continua **59**(3), 697–711 (2019)
11. Ningning, Z., Aizhang, G., Tao, S.: Research on data cleaning method based on SNM algorithm. In: 2017 IEEE 2nd Advanced Information Technology, Control Conference, pp. 2639–2643. Chongqing (2017)
12. Liangjun, Z., Lu, W., Liyun, T.: Python Data Analysis and Mining. Mechanical Industry Press, Beijing (2017)
13. Bloodgood, M., strauss, B.: Data cleaning for XML electronic dictionaries via statistical anomaly detection. In: the 2016 IEEE Tenth International Conference on Semantic Computing, pp. 79–86. Laguna Hills (2016)
14. Tang, N.: Big data cleaning. In: Chen, L., Jia, Y., Sellis, T., Liu, G. (eds.) APWeb 2014. LNCS, vol. 8709, pp. 13–24. Springer, Cham (2014). https://doi.org/10.1007/978-3-319-11116-2_2
15. Paul, A., Ganesan, V., Challa, J.S.: HADCLEAN: a hybrid approach to data cleaning in data warehouses. In: International Conference on Information Retrieval & Knowledge Management, pp. 136–142. Kuala Lumpur (2012)
16. De, S., Hu, Y., Chen, Y.: Bayeswipe: a multimodal system for data cleaning and consistent query answering on structured bigdata. In: 2014 IEEE International Conference on Big Data, pp. 15–24. Washington (2014)
17. Qu, L., Pan, L., Cao, D.: Study on fault early warning method of hydropower units based on vibration energy trend prediction and K-means clustering. Hydroelectric Power **45**(05), 102–106 (2015)
18. Baowei, W., Weiwen, K., Wei, L.: A dual-chaining watermark scheme for data integrity protection in internet of things. Comput. Mater. Continua **58**(3), 679–695 (2019)

Application of Random Forest Classifier in Loan Default Forecast

Huannan Zhang[1(✉)], Yilin Bi[1], Wangdong Jiang[1], Chuntian Luo[1], Shengjia Cao[1], Peng Guo[1,2], and Jianjun Zhang[3]

[1] Hunan University of Finance and Economics, Changsha 410205, China
1136345443@qq.com
[2] University Malaysia Sabah, Kota Kinabalu, Malaysia
[3] Hunan Normal University, Changsha, China

Abstract. Calculating the possible default risk of borrowers before issuing loans is the cornerstone of risk management of financial institutions and the basis of industry development. This study uses the idea of non-equilibrium data classification to statistically analyze the loan data provided by Kaggle, and then uses Sklearn-ensemble-Random Forest Classifier in Python to establish a random forest model for loan default forecast. The experimental results show that the random forest algorithm exceeds the decision tree and logistic regression classification algorithm in predicting performance on this data set. By using random forest algorithm to sort the importance of features, we can calculate the important characteristics that affect the default, and provide an important basis for the judgment of lending risk in the financial field.

Keywords: Risk management · Random forest algorithm · Loan default forecast · Big data analysis

1 Introduction

Loans are an important way for companies and individuals to solve the problem of capital operation. It is this demand that the bank's various loan businesses are targeting [1]. The good operation of this mechanism must prevent loan defaults and calculate the possible default risk of borrowers before issuing loans. It is the cornerstone of risk management of financial institutions and the basis of industry development [2].

Based on the idea of non-equilibrium data classification, this study statistically analyzes the loan data provided by Kaggle, and then uses Sklearn-ensemble-Random Forest Classifier in Python to establish a random forest model for loan default forecast. The experimental results show that the random forest algorithm exceeds the decision tree and logistic regression classification algorithm in predicting performance on this data set. By using random forest algorithm to sort the importance of features, we can calculate the important characteristics that affect the default, and provide an important basis for the judgment of lending risk in the financial field [3]. The first section of this paper mainly introduces unbalanced data classification and random forest algorithm; the second section mainly performs data preprocessing and data analysis. The third section

© Springer Nature Singapore Pte Ltd. 2020
X. Sun et al. (Eds.): ICAIS 2020, CCIS 1254, pp. 410–420, 2020.
https://doi.org/10.1007/978-981-15-8101-4_37

mainly constructs a random forest classification model for predicting loan defaults, and obtains the AUC value of the evaluation results of the model. By comparing the random forest algorithm with the decision tree and the logistic regression algorithm model, the conclusion that the random forest algorithm is better is obtained. Finally, by evaluating the importance of each feature, it is concluded which features have a greater impact on the outcome of the eventual default. The fourth section summarizes the full text.

2 Random Forest Classifier

2.1 Unbalanced Data Classification

Unbalanced data refers to one type (majority) of data far exceeds another type(minority), and is common in many fields such as network intrusion detection, financial fraud transaction detection, text classification, and the like. In many cases, we are only interested in the classification of a few classes [4]. The classification problem of dealing with unbalanced data can be solved by the penalty weight of positive and negative samples [5]. The idea is that in the process of algorithm implementation, different weights are assigned to the categories of different sample sizes in the classification. Generally, the small sample size has high weight and large sample. The quantity category has a low weight and is then calculated and modeled [6].

2.2 Introduction to Random Forest

Random forest belongs to the Bagging (short for Bootstrap AGgregation) method in integrated learning [7]. Random forests are made up of many decision trees, and there is no correlation between different decision trees. When we perform the classification task, the new input sample enters, and each decision tree in the forest is judged and classified separately. Each decision tree will get its own classification result, and which classification result of the decision tree Most, then random forest will use this result as the final result [8]. The process is shown in Fig. 1.

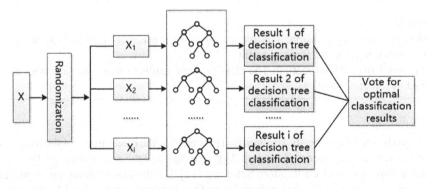

Fig. 1. Schematic diagram of random forest

2.3 Principles and Characteristics of Random Forest Algorithms

The Random Forest algorithm, which includes classification and regression problems, if there are N samples, there are N samples randomly selected (each time randomly selects one sample and then returns to continue selection). This selected N samples are used to train a decision tree as a sample at the root of the decision tree [9]. When each sample has M attributes, when each node of the decision tree needs to be split, m attributes are randomly selected from the M attributes, satisfying the condition $m << M$. Then use some strategy (such as information gain) from these m attributes to select 1 attribute as the split attribute of the node [10].

During the decision tree formation process, each node must be split according to the steps until it can no longer split. Note that no pruning is done during the formation of the entire decision tree [11]. Follow the steps to build a large number of decision trees, which constitutes a random forest. The algorithm steps are as follows (Table 1):

Table 1. Random forest algorithm

Random forest algorithm
Input：
T= Training set,
N_{tree}= The number of decision tree in forest,
M= Number of predictors in each sample,
M_{try}= The number of variables participating in the partition in each tree node,
$S_{sampsize}$= Size of Bootstrap samples
The process of Algorithmic：
for(i_{tree}=0;1 $<$ i_{tree}≤N_{tree}; i_{tree}++)
{
1.   Generate a Bootstrap data sample using the training set T, the size is $S_{sampsize}$
2.   Construct an untrimmed tree i_{tree} using the generated Bootstrap data. In the process of generating a tree i_{tree}, M_{try} variables are randomly selected from M and the best one is selected according to a certain standard (Gini value) for branching.
}
Output：
The problem of Regression: The average of the return values of all individual numbers is used as the forecast result.
The problem of Classification: The classification results of most decision trees are used as forecast results.

It can be seen from the above algorithm process that the randomness of the data space is implemented by Bagging (Bootstrap Aggregating), and the randomness of the feature space is implemented by a Random Subspace [12]. For the classification problem, each decision tree in the random forest classifies and predicts new samples, and then somehow aggregates the decision results of these trees to give the final classification results of the samples.

1. The introduction of two random factors in rows and columns in the data makes it difficult for random forests to fall into overfitting [13].
2. Random forests have good anti-noise ability [14].
3. When there are a large number of missing values in the data set, the random forest can effectively estimate and process the missing values [15].
4. Strong adaptability to the data set: can handle both discrete data and continuous data, the data set does not need to be standardized [16].
5. Can be ordered to the importance of variables, to facilitate the interpretation of variables [17]. There are two ways to calculate the importance of variables in random forests: one is based on the average drop accuracy of OOB (Out of Bag). That is, in the process of growing the decision tree, the OOB sample is first used to test and record the sample of the fault, and then the value of a column of the Bootstrap sample is randomly disordered, and the decision tree is used to predict and re-record. The number of wrong samples are recorded[18]. The number of two forecast errors divided by the total number of OOB samples is the error rate change of this decision tree. The average rate of error reduction is obtained by averaging the error rate changes of all trees in the random forest [19]. The other is based on the GINI drop method at the time of splitting. The random forest in the growth decision tree is splitting according to the decline of GINI impureness, and all the nodes in the forest that select a variable as a split variable are summarized. The amount of GINI dropped [20].

2.4   Random Forest Method for Unbalanced Data Classification

The random forest algorithm defaults to a weight of 1 for each class, which is to assume that the misclassification costs of all classes are equivalent. In scikit-learn, the random forest algorithm provides a class_weight parameter whose value can be a list or dict value, manually indicating the weight of different categories. If the parameter is "balanced", the random forest algorithm automatically adjusts the weight using the y value, and the various weights are inversely proportional to the class frequency in the input data.

The calculation formula is:

$$\frac{n_{samples}}{n_{classes} * np.bincount(y)} \tag{1}$$

"balanced_subsample" is similar to the "balanced" mode, which uses the number of samples in a sample with a return type instead of the total number of samples. Therefore, we can solve the problem of unbalanced data classification by this method.

3   Data Preprocessing and Data Analysis

The random forest is an algorithm based on the idea of integrated learning, which integrates multiple trees. Its basic unit is the decision tree, and these decision trees are independent of each other. The random forest contains the following ideas:

(1) Random selection of data samples
(2) Construction of decision tree
(3) Random selection of candidate features
(4) Forest forecast strategy

3.1 Data Set

The loan default data set used in this article is from the Kaggle data science competition platform. The data set is named "Give Me Some Credit". The data set contains 25000 samples, of which 150,000 samples are used as training sets and 100,000 samples are used as test sets.

The training set has a total of 150,000 borrowers' historical data, including 10026 default samples, accounting for 6.684% of the total sample, loan default rate of 6.684%, and 139,974 non-default samples, accounting for 93.316% of the total sample. It can be seen that the data set is a typical highly unbalanced data. The data set includes the borrower's age, income, family, etc. and the loan situation, a total of 11 variables, of which SeriousDlqin2yrs is the label tag, and the other 10 variables are predictive features. The following table lists the variable names and data types (Table 2):

3.2 Data Preprocessing

A preliminary exploration of the data reveals that there are missing values in the two variables, Monthly Income and Number of Dependents, which are 29731 and 3924 respectively.

The outliers include: The minimum value in the age variable is 0, which is an outlier.

Among the three variables NumberOfTime30-59DaysPastDueNotWorse, Number OfTime30-59DaysPastDueNotWorse, NumberOfTimes90DaysLate, there are a few values of 96,98, which may be abnormal values or a certain behavior code.

Data preprocessing: When we use the pandas library in Python to read data, set the na_values parameter in the function pd.read_csv() to list, and treat the 0 in the age variable and 96,98 in the three overdue variables as NaN. Value, then use the sklearn-preprocessing-Imputer library to replace all NaN in the dataset with the average of the corresponding columns.

3.3 Data Analysis

The experimental environment used in the experiment was Anaconda3+Python3.8. First, an exploratory analysis of the data is performed to analyze the distribution of the default rate on each independent variable, and a frequency distribution table as shown in Table 3

It can be seen from Table 3 that the population below 25 years old and the population aged 26–35 years have a default rate of more than 10%. As the age increases, the default rate decreases.

It can be seen from Table 4 that the number of real estate and mortgage loans of 99.47% of borrowers is less than 5, and the default rate of borrowers with more than 5 credits has increased significantly, and the default rate of borrowers exceeding 10 is over 20%.

It can be seen from Table 5 that the default rate of borrowers who have not exceeded 30–59 days is only about 4%. As the number of overdue increases, the default rate increases significantly. The other two variables, the frequency distribution table of the borrower's 60–89 days overdue and the borrower's overdue frequency of 90 and above

Table 2. Data set variables

Variable name	Description of variable	Genre
SeriousDlqin2yrs	Whether to default	Y/N
Revolving Utilization Of Unsecured Lines	The total amount of credit card and personal credit loan (excluding mortgages, installment payments like car loans, etc.) divided by the sum of credit lines	Percentage
Age	Borrower's age	Integer
NumberOfTime30-59DaysPastDueNotWorse	The number of times the borrower has overdue 30–59 days in the past two years	Integer
Debt Ratio	Monthly debt payments	Percentage
Monthly Income	Monthly income	Real number
Number Of Open Credit Lines And Loans	The number of Open loans and Lines of credit	Integer
NumberOfTimes90DaysLate	The number of times the borrower has overdue 90 days or more in the past two years	Integer
Number Real Estate Loans Or Lines	Number of mortgage and real estate loans including housing mortgage credit loans	Integer
NumberOfTime60-89DaysPastDueNotWorse	The number of times the borrower has overdue 60–89 days in the past two years	Integer
Number Of Dependents	Number of people (spouses, children, etc.) who need to be supported in the family, excluding themselves	Integer

also showed the same trend as Table 5. Therefore, it can be seen that the more times the borrower has overdue, the higher the default rate.

The "Give Me Some Cerdit" dataset has 10 variables, statistical analysis of each variable and the frequency distribution table shown above, except that the variable NumberOfOpenCreditLinesAndLoans (the number of open loans and credit loans) has no

Table 3. Frequency distribution table of variable age

Age	Number	Proportion	Number of defaulters	The percentage of default in this interval
<25	3028	2.02%	338	11.16%
26–35	18458	12.3%	2053	11.12%
36–45	29819	19.9%	2628	8.8%
46–55	36690	24.5%	2786	7.6%
56–65	33406	22.3%	1531	4.6%
>65	28599	19.1%	690	2.4%

Table 4. Frequency distribution table of the variable number real estate loans or lines

Number Real Estate Loans Or Lines	Number	Proportion	Number of defaulters	The percentage of default in this interval
<5	149207	99.47%	9884	6.6%
6–10	699	0.47%	121	17.3%
11–15	70	0.05%	16	22.8%
16–20	14	0.009%	3	21.4%
>20	10	0.007%	2	20%

Table 5. Frequency distribution table of the variable Number Of Time 30-59Days Past Due Not Worse

Number Of Time 30-59 Days Past Due Not Worse	Number	Proportion	Number of defaulters	The percentage of default in this interval
0	126018	84%	5041	4%
1	16032	10.7%	2409	15%
2	4598	3.1%	1219	26.5%
3	1754	1.2%	618	35.2%
4	747	0.5%	318	42.6%
5	342	0.23%	154	45%
6	140	0.09%	74	52.9%
≥7	104	0.07%	50	48.07%

significant correlation with the default rate. Other variables are related to whether the borrower ultimately defaults.

4 Modeling and Experimental Results

4.1 Random Forest Model

This experiment uses the sklearn-ensemble-Random Forest Classifier in Python to build a random forest model.

The parameter is set to:

N_estimators: The number of decision trees is set to 100.
Oob_score: Whether to use out-of-bag data, set to True,
Min_samples_split: When dividing nodes according to attributes, the number of samples per partition is set to 2,
Min_samples_leaf: The minimum number of samples with leaf nodes, set to 50,
N_jobs: Parallel number, set to −1 how many cores the computer CPU has, how many jobs are started
Class_weight: set to 'balanced_subsample', using y value to automatically adjust the weight, the various weights are inversely proportional to the category frequency in the input data.
Bootstrap: Whether to use the bootstrap sample sample, set to True.

4.2 Model Evaluation

The model evaluation index used in this experiment is the AUC (Area under the ROC curve) value. AUC is defined as the area under the ROC (Receiver Operating Characteristic) curve [21]. The horizontal axis of the ROC curve is False Positive Rate (FPR), the vertical axis is True Positive Rate (TPR), and since the ROC curve is generally above the line $y = x$, AUC The value ranges between 0.5 and 1 [22]. The AUC value is used as the evaluation criterion because many times the ROC curve does not clearly indicate which classifier works better, and as a numerical value, the classifier corresponding to the larger AUC is better.

The random forest model is compared with the logistic regression classification model and the decision tree classification model. The results are shown in the following table (Table 6).

Table 6. Comparison of random forests and other algorithms

Algorithms	AUC value
Random forest	0.86
Decision tree	0.80
Logistic regression	0.80

It can be seen from the table that the random forest algorithm has higher AUC values than the decision tree and the logistic regression algorithm, so the algorithm forecast performance of the random forest is better than the other two algorithms.

4.3 Feature Importance Metrics

This experiment uses the feature_ importance_ method of sklearn-ensemble-Random Forest Classifier to get the importance of each feature as shown in the following table (Table 7).

Table 7. Variable importance

Variables	feature_ importance
Revolving Utilization Of Unsecured Lines	0.3411
NumberOfTime30-59DaysPastDueNotWorse	0.1694
NumberOfTimes90DaysLate	0.1594
NumberOfTime60-89DaysPastDueNotWorse	0.0727
age	0.0677
Debt Ratio	0.0625
Monthly Income	0.0488
Number Of Open Credit Lines And Loans	0.0442
Number Real Estate Loans Or Lines	0.0223
Number Of Dependents	0.0117

As can be seen from the above table, the three characteristics of the borrower's total loan-to-credit ratio, the number of overdue 30–59 days in the past two years and the number of overdue over 90 days in the past two years are in the top three. There is a greater impact on whether the default is ultimately breached, so you can pay special attention to these characteristics of the borrower when processing the loan application.

5 Summary

This paper studies the random forest algorithm to predict loan defaults in the financial sector, using unbalanced data classification. In the process of constructing a single tree, randomly select some variables or features to participate in the tree node division, repeat multiple times and ensure the independence between the established trees. For the unbalanced data, the random forest method can be based on the parameter adjustment. The value automatically adjusts the weight to effectively solve the classification problem of unbalanced data. Experiments show that the random forest algorithm has better classification performance than the decision tree and logistic regression model, and has important reference significance for the loan default forecast problem in the financial field. In addition, by measuring the importance of each feature, in this experiment, the three characteristics of the borrower's age, debt ratio, and the number of real estate and mortgage loans can be greatly affected. It also has important reference significance for feature selection in other data mining.

This paper mainly studies the loan default forecast from the perspective of random forest algorithm, and adopts the parameter adjustment method to solve the data non-equilibrium problem in data processing. However, it still needs to be improved in data processing and model optimization. There are still many futures jobs. First, explore more and more efficient unbalanced data processing methods and optimize data in data processing. Secondly, in the algorithm selection, learning from other algorithm models, try to combine the optimization model to improve performance. Finally, in terms of rendering, try to use visualizations to present the results in a chart that is easier to understand.

Acknowledgments. This research work is implemented at the 2011 Collaborative Innovation Center for Development and Utilization of Finance and Economics Big Data Property, Universities of Hunan Province; Hunan Provincial Key Laboratory of Big Data Science and Technology, Finance and Economics; Key Laboratory of Information Technology and Security, Hunan Provincial Higher Education. This research is funded by the Open Foundation for the University Innovation Platform in the Hunan Province grant number 18K103; Open project, grant number 20181901CRP03, 20181901CRP04, 20181901CRP05; Hunan Provincial Education Science 13th Five-Year Plan (Grant No. XJK016BXX001), Social Science Foundation of Hunan Province (Grant No. 17YBA049).

References

1. Torvekar, N., Game, P.S.: Predictive analysis of credit score for credit card defaulters. Int. J. Recent Technol. Eng. **7**(1), 4 (2019)
2. Kurapati, N., Bhansali, P.K.: Predicting the credit defaulters using machine learning techniques. Int. J. Manag. Technol. Eng. **8**(11), 6 (2018)
3. Jinwang, W., Zhouyi, G.: Customer credit risk assessment of commercial banks based on unbalanced samples – a case study of bank A. Finan. Theory Pract. **07**, 51–57 (2018)
4. Zhao, J., Lu, H.: An over sampling random forest algorithm for unbalanced data classification. Comput. Appl. Softw. **36**(04), 255–261+316 (2019)
5. Wei, Z.: Research on stochastic forest algorithm based on unbalanced data (2017)
6. Dong, L., Wang, Y.: Adaptive random sampling algorithm based on maximum equilibrium degree. J. Northeast Univ. (Nat. Sci. Ed.) **39**(06), 792–796 (2018)
7. Alabdulkarim, A., Al-Rodhaan, M., Tian, Y., Al-Dhelaan, A.: A privacy-preserving algorithm for clinical decision-support systems using random forest. Comput. Mater. Continua **58**(3), 585–601 (2019)
8. Fang, K., Jianbin, W.: A review of random forest methods. Stat. Inf. Forum **26**(03), 32–38 (2011)
9. Shan, T., Zhang, M.: Risk analysis of P2P network loan default based on random forest. China Science and Technology Paper Online (2019)
10. Zhu, Y.: Credit bond default risk measurement based on KMV stochastic forest model (2019)
11. Ma, X., Sha, J., Wang, D.: Study on a forecast of P2P network loan default based on the machine learning LightGBM and XGboost algorithms according to different high dimensional data cleaning. Electron. Commer. Res. Appl. **31**, 24–39 (2018)
12. Li, W.: Research on P2P network loan default forecast model based on integrated classification algorithm (2019)

13. Yan, T., Wang, X.: Research on the early warning of P2P network loan default risk based on machine learning–evidence of loan transaction from 'auction loan'. Stat. Inf. Forum **33**(06), 69–76 (2018)
14. Ma, C., Zhao, H.: Research on the credit risk factors of P2P network loan subject based on random forest classification model. Jilin Univ. J. Soc. Sc. Ed. **59**(03), 39–48+231–232 (2019)
15. Dong, X.: Application of random forest in credit evaluation of P2P network borrowers (2019)
16. Zhou, L.: Research on loan default forecast based on unbalanced data classification (2013)
17. Li, L.: Research on enterprise credit risk evaluation based on stochastic forest algorithm (2012)
18. Qu, Y.: Stochastic forest forecast model of P2P network loan default (2018)
19. Xiaohong, Yu., Lou, W.: Credit risk evaluation, early warning and empirical research of P2P network loan based on random forest. Finan. Theory Pract. **02**, 53–58 (2016)
20. Cao, W., Li, C.: A comparative study of credit risk early warning model of P2P network lending in China based on Integrated Learning. Data Anal. Knowl. Discov. **2**(10), 65–76 (2018)
21. Zheng, J.: Research on credit evaluation of P2P borrowers based on stochastic forest model (2017)
22. Wang, S.: Comparative study on credit risk control of P2P network loan borrowers based on several common models (2019)

Research on Routing for Large-Scale Sensing in Wireless Sensor Networks

Mei Wu[1]($\boxtimes$), Pengfei Guo[2], and Ning Cao[3]

[1] School of Computer Science and Engineering, Wuhan Institute of Technology, Wuhan, China
wumei0604@hotmail.com
[2] Xiamen University Tan Kah Kee College, Zhangzhou, Fujian, China
[3] School of Internet of Things and Software Technology, Wuxi Vocational College of Science and Technology, Wuxi, China

Abstract. In a heterogeneous network, network nodes have different initial energies, even limited battery power, which determine that the network must work in an energy-saving manner. This paper aims to discuss models and algorithms to solve the limitations of low energy consumption, robustness, and scalability. Finally, it presents a design routing approach that provides information on a large temporal and spatial scale for wireless sensor networks.

Keywords: Large-scale · Routing · Optimization · Sensor networks

1 Introduction

Wireless sensor networks (WSNs) are applied across a diverse and large range of application domains. A sensor network is an infrastructure comprised of sensing, computing and communication elements. The network gives an administrator the ability to instrument, observe and react to events in a specified environment. The main object of wireless sensor networks (WSN) is to reliably detect and estimate event features from the collective information provided by sensor nodes.

A survey of routing technologies for wireless sensor networks has been established in recent years. There are several main branches of routing technologies: hierarchical clustering, evolutionary clustering, swarm clustering, flat routing, location-based routing, and QoS-based routing. Moreover, some protocols fit under more than one category.

This paper asks whether it is possible to introduce a universal strategy allowing the objectives of obtaining maximum network scale and minimum consumption of energy to be simultaneously achieved. Owing to dynamic process environments and the inherent limitation of various hardware and software resources, no single topology will always be best for any given application. A routing algorithm optimized for a specific topology may perform poorly on another type of topology [1].

This paper proposes one energy-efficient routing scheme that can scale to thousands of sensor nodes of multiple types. In addition, it introduces multiple topologies in the approach and consider a three-tier sensor architecture.

© Springer Nature Singapore Pte Ltd. 2020
X. Sun et al. (Eds.): ICAIS 2020, CCIS 1254, pp. 421–429, 2020.
https://doi.org/10.1007/978-981-15-8101-4_38

The rest of the paper is structured as follows. Section 2 presents related works. Section 3 describes current most common wireless network topologies. In Sect. 4, it presents system architecture on graph theory using clustering, and proposes an optimized routing algorithm for wireless networks based on clustering and hybrid topology. Section 5 shows the simulation results of optimized algorithm in improving network performance. Finally, Sect. 6 concludes the paper.

2 Related Works

In this Section, it reviews related work mainly in clustering algorithms and large-scale routing algorithms, both of which are in sensor networks. According to related criteria [2–4], the existing routing algorithms can be classified into different groups in wireless sensor networks. In a hierarchical network, TopDisc [5], which is based on minimum dominating set in graph theory, secures the fewest numbers of clusters in the whole network. However, it reduces the cost for the control and maintenance but does not consider the remaining energy of nodes and network robustness.

Both LEACH [6] and LEACH-C [7] are clustering hierarchy scheme based on a Voronoi diagram, and the latter dispersed the cluster heads throughout the network. To achieve a high degree of parallelism, the hierarchical PEGASIS [8] uses one chain-based binary aggregation way. The clustering algorithms [9–11] based on LEACH, randomly selects Cluster Head (CH) based on the idea of "wheel", which leads to unbalanced CH energy consumption in the whole network. In BEEC clustering algorithm [12], it introduced a competition mechanism in the final stage of CH selection, but it only considered one parameter the distance of node CH in the cluster construction stage, not the energy consumption of the whole WSN.

Literature [13] is an optimization algorithm based on LEACH. It considered the residual energy of nodes in cluster head election, which increases the probability of nodes with high residual energy being cluster heads. It lead to the cluster head of the adjacent base station exhausted prematurely compared to other cluster heads.

Literature [15] designs a routing protocol for a scenario where it is difficult to achieve time synchronization, location information and waking schedule shared. It Lets the data traffic from a sensor flows to its neighbors freely to save the energy utilized for routing path built. For a sensor, it does not share its waking schedule to its neighbors.

Literature [16] presents a new Energy-Efficient clustering protocol for WSNs using an Objective Function and Random Search with Jumps (EEOFRSJ) in order to reduce sensor energy consumption. First, the objective function is used to find an optimal cluster formation taking into account the ratio of the mean Euclidean distance of the nodes to their associated cluster heads (CH) and their residual energy. Then, it finds the best path to transmit data from the CHs nodes to the base station (BS) using a random search with jumps.

In literature [17], an asynchronous clustering and mobile data gathering based on timer mechanism (ACMDGTM) algorithm is proposed which would mitigate the problem of "hot spots" among sensors to enhance the lifetime of networks. The clustering process takes sensors' location and residual energy into consideration to elect suitable cluster heads. Furthermore, one mobile sink node is employed to access cluster heads in accordance with the data overflow time and moving time from cluster heads to itself.

3   Topology Structure Analysis

Network layer structure directly affects the upper layer routing protocols' performance. The current most common wireless network topologies are star, mesh and cluster-tree topology as shown in Fig. 1.

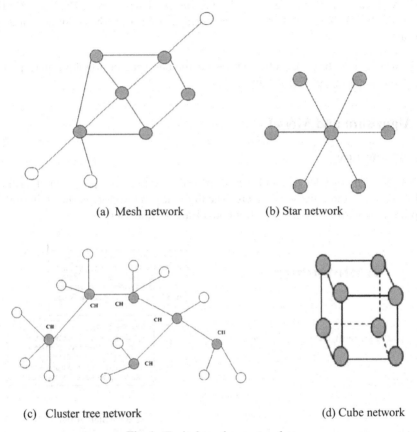

(a) Mesh network   (b) Star network

(c)   Cluster tree network   (d) Cube network

Fig. 1. Typical topology networks

Mesh Topology. Generally, there are multiple routing paths between two non-adjacent nodes. These networks are robust to failure of individual nodes and links as well. Compared to star topology, mesh topology has a longer range distance and decreases the data loss.

Star Topology. A star topology is a point-to-point architecture in which all nodes are considered peers and every sensor node has the equal role and function. The star topology has minimal overhead to maintain the infrastructure compared to other structures.

Cluster-Tree Topology. Cluster-tree topology blends the advantages of star topology and mesh topology. The cluster-head plays a more prominent role than other members in the network.

Regular Graph. A cubic graph is shown in Fig. 1(d), which is a classic structure of k-regular graph. A k-regular graph topology has regular degree in which all nodes are of degree k. Regular graph has a special robust feature, which is proposed by Nash Williams (1969) in [14]. This robust feature keeps average control overheads in networks as a constant.

However, a routing algorithm optimized for one specific topology may perform poorly on another type of topology.

4 Algorithm and Model

4.1 Architecture

In this paper, it considers a multi-sensor three-tier system, and proposed algorithm is build based on a three-tier architecture. The three-tier architecture is shown in Fig. 2. It is split into a Sensor Tier, a Relay Tier and a Base Station Tier.

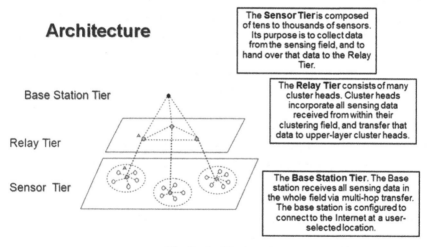

Fig. 2. Architecture

The Sensor Tier is composed of tens to thousands of sensors. Its purpose is to collect data from the sensing field, and to hand over that data to the Relay Tier.

The Relay Tier consists of many cluster heads. Cluster heads incorporate all sensing data received from within their clustering field, and transfer that data to upper-layer cluster heads. An example of the construction process for cluster heads in the first two levels of the hierarchy is shown in Fig. 2.

The Base Station Tier. The Base station receives all sensing data in the whole field via multi-hop transfer. The base station is configured to connect to the Internet at a user-selected location. Users can access the whole wireless monitoring system from off site.

The Sensor Tier is composed of a star topology network. The star topology has minimal overhead to maintain the infrastructure compared to mesh and other structures. Therefore, it is easy to maintain the underlying sensing network when a node fails by energy exhaustion or other reasons. We can use Regular Graph theory in computing the connectivity and distributing loading between the motes on networks. In this paper, we introduce a regular triangle structure in designing the Relay Tier structure to constitute a stable and high transmission reliability backbone tier.

4.2 Node Energy Dissipation Model and Algorithm

In this paper, it uses the same radio model presented by Heinzelman et al. in LEACH. The energy expended by the radio in transmitting a p-bit message over a distance d is given by:

$$E_{TX}(p, d) \begin{cases} p \cdot E_{elec} + p \cdot \varepsilon_{fs} \cdot d^2 \ if \ d \leq d_0 \\ p \cdot E_{elec} + p \cdot \varepsilon_{amp} \cdot d^4 \ if \ d > d_0 \end{cases} \tag{1}$$

The radio characteristics are set as follows:

$E_{elec} = 50nJ/bit$, ε_{fs} and ε_{amp} are power amplifier energy consumption coefficients in free space channel and multipath fading channel respectively. $\varepsilon_{fs} = 10pJ/(bit \cdot m^2)$. $\varepsilon_{amp} = 1.3 \times 10^{-3} pJ/(bit \cdot m^4)$. And initial energy of low sensor nodes is 0.5 J and initial energy of high-energy sensor nodes is 1 J.

The size of the aggregate message that a cluster head sends to the sink is 512 bits and the size of the route message that a sink sends to cluster-head nodes is 16 bits.

The election procedure for cluster-heads during network initial construction is as follows:

Step1. In the initial phase, we sort nodes in order of decreasing residual energy (EN), so we have a set of $EN = \{EN1, EN2,...ENn\}$, where n is the total number of sensor nodes.
Step2. Select the k nodes with highest residual energy from the set EN as CHs to get a set CHs (C), $C = \{CH1, CH2, ...CHk\}$. $k = n* \rho$, where ρ is the desired proportion of nodes which are cluster-head nodes.
Step3. Build a backup cluster- head set (B) for every CH. B belongs to {{EN}-{C}}.
Step4. When the residual energy of CH i is lower than the threshold (T), remove i from {C}, replace i by a newly elected CH.

Where k is expected numbers of cluster-heads and n is the total numbers of sensor nodes in the network.

5 Results

In this section, we focus on varying network size, keeping density and other parameters constant. We compare the performance of our protocol to LEACH in the heterogeneous environment use network lifetime term as the performance metric.

The scenario is considered in Figs. 3, 4, 5: a heterogeneous sensor network in a 100 × 100 m scenario. The total number of sensor in the network is 100. The proportion of cluster heads to 0.1 is given prior to initial network construction.

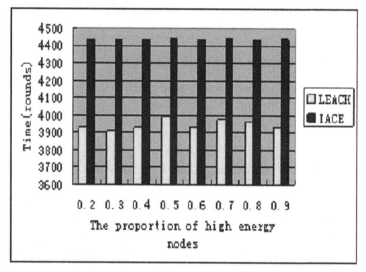

Fig. 3. Performance result for a 100 m*100 m heterogeneous network with initial energy 0.5 J per normal-nodes and 1 J per high-energy node. As the proportion of high-energy nodes increases step by step from 0.2 to 0.9, the network lifetime in IACE is longer than in LEACH where the number of nodes is kept constant. The number of nodes is 100. The proportion of head nodes among nodes is 0.1.

According Figs. 3, 4 and 5, the results show that in above cases, it performs very well in comparison with LEACH scheme. More nodes are still alive in network in IACE compared that of LEACH.

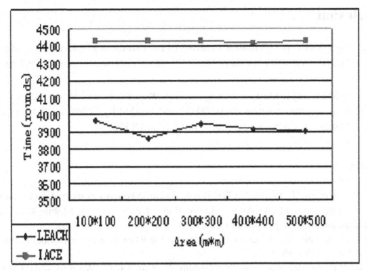

Fig. 4. The proportion of high-energy node is 0.3 (m = 0.3). Performance results for 100*100, 200*200, 300*300, 400*400 and 500*500 heterogeneous networks with initial energy 0.5 J per normal-node sand 1 J per high-energy node. The number of nodes is 100, 400, 900, 1600 and 2500 respectively. The proportion of head nodes among nodes is 0.1.

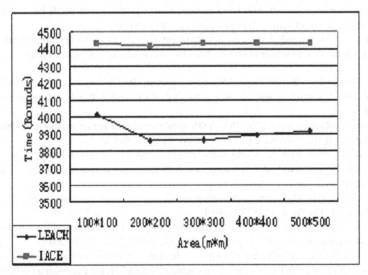

Fig. 5. The proportion of high-energy nodes is 0.2. Performance results for 100*100, 200*200, 300*300, 400*400 and 500*500 heterogeneous networks with initial energy 0.5 J per normal-node sand 1 J per high-energy node. The number of nodes is 100, 400, 900, 1600 and 2500 respectively. The proportion of head nodes among nodes is 0.1.

6 Conclusion

This paper analyzes the performance in terms of robustness and energy consumption and it is recommended especially for large-scale, dynamic, homogeneous and heterogeneous environments.

This research is supported by Scientific Research Project of Education Department of Hubei Province, grant number B2018049, and funded by Scientific Research Project of Wuhan Institute of Technology, grant number 18DQ42.

References

1. Xu, Y., Heidemann, J., Estrin, D.: Geography-informed energy conservation for ad hoc routing. In: Proceedings of the Annual International Conference on Mobile Computing and Networking, Mobicom, pp. 70–84 (2001)
2. Akkaya, K., Younis, M.: A survey of routing protocols in wireless sensor networks. Elsevier Ad Hoc Netw. J. **3**, 325–349 (2005)
3. Akyildiz, I.F., Su, W., Sankarasubramaniam, Y., Cayirci, E.: Wireless sensor networks: a survey. J. Comput. Netw. 393–422 (2002)
4. Li, X.F., Mao, Y.C., Yi, L.: A survey on topology control in wireless sensor networks. In: 10th International Conference on Control, Automation, Robotics and Vision, ICARCV, pp. 251–255 (2008)
5. Younis, O., Fahmy, S.: Distributed clustering in ad-hoc sensor networks: a hybrid, energy-efficient approach. In: Twenty-Third Annual Joint Conference of the IEEE Computer and Communications Societies, INFCOM, pp. 629–640 (2004)
6. Heinzelman, W., Chandrakasan, A., Balakrishnan, H.: Energy-efficient communication protocol for wireless microsensor networks. In: 33rd International Conference on System Sciences (HICSS) (2000)
7. Heinzelman, W., Chandrakasan, A., Balakrishnan, H.: An application-specific protocol architecture for wireless microsensor networks. IEEE Trans. Wirel. Commun. **1**, 660–670 (2002)
8. Lindsey, S., Raghavendra, C.S.: PEGASIS: power- efficient gathering in sensor information systems. In: IEEE Aerospace Conference, pp. 1125–1130 (2002)
9. Sirsikar, S., Wankhede, K.: Comparison of clustering algorithms to design new clustering approach. In: International Conference on Advances in Computing, Communication and Control (ICAC), pp. 147–154 (2015)
10. Liu, X.X.: A typical hierarchical routing protocols for wireless sensor network: a review. IEEE Sens. J. **15**(10), 5372–5383 (2015)
11. Emad, A., Lon, M.: New energy efficient multi-hop routing techniques for wireless sensor networks: static and dynamic techniques. Sensors **18**(6), 1863–1870 (2018)
12. Liu, J.J., Hu, Y.J.: A balanced and energy-efficient algorithm for heterogeneous wire-less sensor networks. In: IEEE Wireless Communications and Signal Processing (WCSP), Hefei, pp. 1–6 (2014)
13. Hou, H., Song, B., Zhou, W.Y.: Clustering routing optimization algorithm. Microelectr. Comput. Energy Effic. **32**(7), 121–124 (2015)
14. Crispin, N.W.: Valency Sequences which force graphs to have Hamiltonian Circuits, University of Waterloo Research Report, Waterloo, Ontario: University of Waterloo (1969)
15. Gao, D.M., Zhang, S., Zhang, F.Q., Fan, X.J., Zhang, J.C.: Maximum data generation rate routing protocol based on data flow controlling technology for rechargeablewireless sensor networks. Comput. Mater. Continua **59**(2), 649–667 (2019)

16. Mohammed, K., Khelifa, B., Mohammed, O.: An energy-efficient protocol using an objective function & random search with jumps for WSN. Comput. Mater. Continua **58**(3), 603–624 (2019)
17. Wang, J., Gao, Y., Liu, W., Wu, W.B., Lim, S.J.: An asynchronous clustering and mobile data gathering schema based on timer mechanism in wireless sensor networks. Comput. Mater. Continua **58**(3), 711–725 (2019)

A Research on the Detection of Fog Visibility

Xiaogang Zhang[1], Zhiping Guo[2(✉)], Xiaojun Li[1], and Pingping Yu[2]

[1] Hebei Earthquake Agency, Tangshan 050021, China
[2] School of Information Science and Engineering, Hebei University of Science and Technology, Shijiazhuang 050018, China
1299787528@qq.com

Abstract. The existing video visibility algorithm uses the apparent brightness of the target object from the image acquisition instead of the inherent brightness of the target object, which affects the accuracy of the visibility detection. Therefore, this paper designs a new visibility detection algorithm, which based on the digital camera response curve fitting. Experimental pictures are taken on the uniformity white diffuse surface with a fixed aperture, different exposure time. The average gray value of the pictures are calculated using the middle part of the experimental pictures. The double logarithmic curve is fitted of the pixel value of the image and exposure time. Then according to this curve, the value γ can be obtained, which is the conversion coefficient between the brightness and inherent brightness. The atmospheric extinction coefficient can be calculated by the inherent brightness, resulting in atmospheric visibility values. The algorithm chooses the pavement as a marker to solve the problem that the target is not easy to find on the road. The distance between the target point and the camera is calculated by the inherent lane mark line and the camera self-calibration method. Experimental results show that the proposed visibility detection algorithm has high accuracy and low cost. It is very suitable for the fog visibility monitoring on the high speed road.

Keywords: Visibility detection · Curve response fitting · Differential luminance algorithm · Surveillance video

1 Introduction

Atmospheric visibility is an important parameter to measure the visual air quality. It is not only one of the routine monitoring indicators of urban ambient air quality, but also one of the elements of road weather condition system. Especially in the traffic high-speed network, how to quickly and accurately grasp the weather conditions and help the high-speed management department to manage the high-speed road reasonably and effectively is an effective means to reduce traffic accidents in bad weather.

The traditional methods of atmospheric visibility monitoring are visual method and atmospheric transmission instrument method [1–3]. The method of visual inspection is used to determine the atmospheric visibility through the observation of human flesh and eyes, which is relatively poor in standardization and objectivity. The atmospheric transmission instrument calculates the atmospheric visibility by directly measuring the

© Springer Nature Singapore Pte Ltd. 2020
X. Sun et al. (Eds.): ICAIS 2020, CCIS 1254, pp. 430–440, 2020.
https://doi.org/10.1007/978-981-15-8101-4_39

atmospheric extinction coefficient between the two points. This method needs a long optical path (such as 300 m–2 km). The reliability of measurement is affected by the working stability of light source and photosensitive system, and the operation and maintenance cost is high in actual operation. In view of the above problems, some researchers at home and abroad began to study the visibility detection algorithm based on video image [4–7], which can make use of the existing digital monitoring resources, especially suitable for highway visibility detection system.

There are three kinds of algorithms for detecting daytime visibility based on digital images in China. The first one is the double brightness difference method [8–10] proposed by Lu Weitao and others from China University of science and technology, which has been proved to be effective and limited by a large number of experiments. This method takes pictures of two objects with different distances on the same straight line, and calculates the visibility according to the ratio of the brightness difference between the two objects corresponding to the sky background. It eliminates the influence of dark current and background astigmatism of digital camera system, and improves the measurement range and accuracy of DPVS (Digital camera visibility system). However, this method needs to know the ratio of the brightness difference between the two objects and the sky background, which can not be directly measured by digital camera, so it needs to be assumed, which causes the important error source of DPVS double brightness difference method to calculate the daytime meteorological visibility. The second one is that Professor Chen Qimei and Chen Zhaozheng of Nanjing University use the existing highway video monitoring system to apply wavelet transform [11], camera self calibration [12], PTZ algorithm [13] and other methods to visibility detection, and they have achieved some results, but the measurement distance of this method is limited, which is not effective when the visibility is high.

The third category is Visibility detection algorithm based on the prior theory of dark channel proposed [15] by Kaiming et al. [14]. This method first obtains the transmittance from the target to the camera point according to the prior knowledge of dark channel, and then further calculates the atmospheric extinction coefficient, so as to obtain the value of atmospheric visibility. The principle of the method is simple and the cost is low, but the calculation accuracy of transmissivity is high. The main algorithms of daytime visibility detection based on digital image abroad are as follows: kwontm et al. Put forward the method of using visual attributes of video image to measure visibility instead of indirect measurement of physical attributes of atmosphere and convert them into visibility, and solve the problem of spatial distance change in visibility by introducing the new concept of relative visibility (RV), but in quantifying human perception of RV and RV calculation The accuracy of the measurement still needs to be improved; nicolashautiere et al. Combined with Koschmieder's law, put forward the modeling method of fog and the visibility measurement method based on the known state, which can meet the requirements of real-time and stability, but because of the local variation of fog density, errors will be introduced to reduce the accuracy of the measurement results; miclearc et al. Developed the end-to-end laser emission and reception device By setting the appropriate image color space and filter, and putting forward the formula of braking distance under safe driving conditions, it can effectively give the driver early warning feedback information, but this method is easy to be interfered by the noise introduced from outside, which leads to the lack of robustness of the system.

Based on the high-speed road video monitoring system in Hebei Province, this paper proposes an improved method to improve the self brightness of the object and the sky background when the double brightness difference method is applied to the visibility detection of the high-speed road. By calculating the quantitative relationship between the exposure of the camera and the gray value of the pixel, and according to the gray value of the image, the self brightness value of the object and the sky can be obtained, so as to improve the double brightness The accuracy of visibility can be obtained by the method of degree difference, which can effectively reduce the error value in the calculation process and the measurement error value.

2 Visibility Detection Algorithm

2.1 Principle of Visibility Measurement

According to the theory of Koschmieder, the relationship between the self brightness L_0 and the apparent brightness of a fixed object L at a distance d from the observation position under the action of the atmospheric extinction coefficient k is as follows:

$$L(d) = L_0 e^{-kd} + L_f(1 - e^{-kd}) \tag{1}$$

Where, L_f is the sky background brightness.

According to the definition of CIE, only when the contrast between the target and the background is greater than 0.05 can the human eye distinguish it. At this time, the distance between the target and the observation point is defined as the current visibility value, and the calculation formula of the visibility value is:

$$V = -\frac{1}{k} \ln \frac{C_d}{C_0} = -\frac{1}{k} \ln 0.05 \approx \frac{3}{k} \tag{2}$$

Therefore, as long as the extinction coefficient k of the atmosphere is obtained, the visibility of the atmosphere can be obtained. From formula (1), it can be seen that the extinction coefficient k is related to the object's own brightness L_0, so how to get L_0 becomes the key to calculate the visibility.

2.2 Calculation Formula of Double Brightness Difference

$$V_d = \frac{3.912(R_2 - R_1)}{\ln[(G_{t1} - G_{g1})/(G_{t2} - G_{g2})]} \tag{3}$$

Among them, R_1, R_2 is the distance between the target and the camera, G_{T1} and G_{T2} are the apparent brightness 1 of the two target objects, and g_{G2} is the apparent brightness of the background sky of the two objects.

2.3 Pavement Background Generation

In order to eliminate the influence of vehicles on the road in the monitoring image, it is necessary to extract the background of the image. Common background extraction algorithms include frame difference method, average frame difference method and mixed Gaussian model method [16, 17]. Considering the time consumption and extraction effect, this paper uses the frame difference method to get the background image of traffic scene and update it in real time. The specific algorithm is as follows: for the scene in the video stream, randomly extract more than six frames of image, and subtract the two frames from each other. If the gray level of the corresponding region of the two frames of image changes little (less than a certain threshold T), then the region is considered as the background region. If the gray level of the corresponding region of the two frames of image changes greatly (more than a certain threshold T), then the region is considered as the target region, then the data in this region cannot Extract as background. The threshold T is obtained from experience and a large number of experimental data. Figure 1 shows the original image collected on the highway and the background image obtained by the frame difference method. The obtained color background image is converted to gray-scale image.

Fig. 1. Image of the pavement background

2.4 Camera Imaging Model

The camera imaging model is shown in Fig. 2, including three coordinate systems: pavement coordinate system (X_W, Y_W, Z_W), camera coordinate system (X_i, Y_i, Z_i), and imaging plane (U, V). The relationship between the three coordinate systems is shown in Eq. (4).

$$\begin{bmatrix} X_i \\ Y_i \\ Z_i \\ 1 \end{bmatrix} = \begin{bmatrix} 0 & 1 & 0 & 0 \\ -\sin\theta & 0 & \cos\theta & H\sin\theta \\ \cos\theta & 0 & \sin\theta & H\sin\theta \\ 0 & 0 & 0 & 1 \end{bmatrix} \begin{bmatrix} X_w \\ Y_w \\ Z_w \\ 1 \end{bmatrix}$$

$$U = \lambda\frac{X_i}{Z_i}, V = \lambda\frac{Y_i}{Z_i}, \tag{4}$$

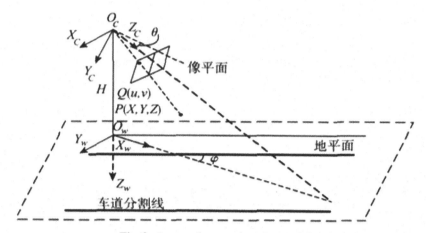

Fig. 2. Image of camera imaging model

Where λ is the zoom coefficient related to the camera focal length.

Thus, the mapping relationship between a point $(X_W, Y_W, 0)$ on the road surface and its point (U, V) on the image plane can be established, and the coordinates (X_W, Y_W) of any point on the road surface in the image plane can be inversely deduced, as follows:

$$\begin{cases} X_w = \frac{\varphi H \cos\theta - (v - v_0 H \sin\theta)}{(v - v_0)\cos\theta + \varphi\cos\theta} \\ Y_w = \frac{H(u - u_0)}{\varphi}\left[\frac{\varphi\cos\theta - (v - v_0\sin\theta\cos\theta)}{(v - v_0)\cos\theta^2 + \varphi\sin\theta}\right] \end{cases}, \tag{5}$$

The distance between this point on the image and the camera on the actual road surface can be obtained, as shown in formula (6):

$$D = \sqrt{X_w^2 + Y_w^2} \tag{6}$$

3 Visibility Detection Algorithm Based on Response Curve Fitting of Digital Camera

3.1 Digital Camera Response Curve Fitting

At present, most digital cameras are CCD or CMOS image sensors, which are composed of thousands of pixels. When photographing, each pixel will generate an electrical signal according to the amount of exposure it receives. The electrical signal is converted into an integer between 0 and 255 by the internal circuit of the camera, that is, the pixel value. Different exposure amounts correspond to different pixel values, which can be expressed by the following formula [18, 19]:

$$E = k \times PV^\gamma \tag{7}$$

Where k, k is the camera related constant, P is the pixel value, E is the exposure, and its value is:

$$E = H \times A \times T \tag{8}$$

Where, H is the irradiance of the incident light, A is the aperture area, and T is the exposure time. The incident irradiance is directly proportional to the incident light intensity I. According to the relationship between irradiance and radiation gray level given by Kolb:

$$H = I \frac{\pi}{4} \left(\frac{D}{f}\right)^2 \cos^4 \alpha \tag{9}$$

D is the aperture diameter, f is the focal length of the lens, α is the angle formed by the position of the pixel and the lens axis, combining formula (7)–(9), we can get:

$$I \times A \times T = k \times PV^\gamma \tag{10}$$

In order to obtain the value r, this paper adopts the following experimental method: set the shooting mode of the monitoring camera (select the model of the monitoring camera mainly used in Hebei Province: Yushi hic7621) to "manual" mode. Set the aperture to the minimum. Under good white illumination, a uniform white diffuse surface is found. At a distance of 0.5 m from the surface, the monitoring camera is used to take pictures of the surface under different exposure time settings. Then the obtained color image is transformed into gray image, and the average pixel value of the middle area of the image is read out. All the obtained images are processed as described above, and a scatter plot of the logarithm of the pixel value and the logarithm of the exposure time is drawn, that is, ln(pixel value) vsln (exposure time). The response curve of the digital camera is obtained by linear regression fitting of the scatter diagram [20–22] (Fig. 3).

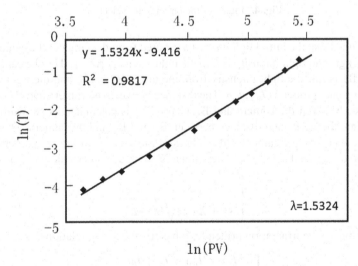

Fig. 3. Image of the digital camera response curve fit

3.2 Visibility Calculation

Yushi hic7621 can be controlled manually, so we control the camera manually at the monitoring end, adjust its aperture to the minimum (the same as the experimental mode), obtain the continuous frame of the captured image, and then use the background generation, image graying and other graphic processing operations to obtain the final visibility calculation image. As shown in Fig. 4, according to the definition of visibility, dark objects are selected as targets and sky as background. Because there is no fixed target on the highway, this paper chooses the dark road as the target, and uses the fixed Lane dividing line with known distance to measure the distance. In order to reduce the difference of Los elevation between the two groups of roads and the sky as much as possible, the algorithm in this paper uses the road at the far end of lane sign line as the target. For example, the endpoint of the sixth lane line in the image is selected as the target B1, the endpoint of the eighth lane line is selected as the target B2, and the upper area perpendicular to the target point is selected as the background W1, W2.

Fig. 4. Image of the target point selection

It is defined that the initial light intensity emitted from the target to the camera is I_{b0}, the sky background light intensity is I_{w0}, the light intensity received by the camera from the target B1 is I_{b1}, the light intensity from the target B2 is I_{b2}, and the light intensity from the sky background is I_{w1}, I_{w2}. The distance between the camera and B1 is x_1, and the distance between the camera and B2 ($X_1 + X_2$) is calculated as shown in Fig. 5. d_1 and d_2 are the horizontal distance between B1 and B2 and the camera. Their values can be calculated by the camera self calibration formula (6). If the height between the camera and the ground is known to be h, then X1 and X2 can be calculated as follows:

$$\begin{cases} X_1 = \sqrt{h^2 + d_1^2} \\ X_1 + X_2 = \sqrt{h^2 + d_2^2} \end{cases} \tag{11}$$

According to the irradiation principle, it has the following relations:

$$\begin{cases} I_{w1} = I_{w0} \times T_1 + I_{p1} \\ I_{w2} = I_{w0} \times T_{1+2} + I_{p1+2} \\ I_{w3} = I_{b0} \times T_1 + I_{p1} \\ I_{w4} = I_{b0} \times T_{1+2} + I_{p1+2} \end{cases} \tag{12}$$

Where, I_{p1} is the path light intensity from the atmospheric segment with length X_1, and T_1 is the transmittance of the atmospheric segment X_1. I_{p1+2} is the path light intensity from the atmospheric segment with length ($X_1 + X_2$), and T_{1+2} is the transmittance

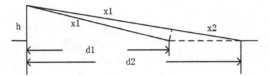

Fig. 5. Image of the calculation model for x and y

of the atmospheric segment $(X_1 + X_2)$, which is equal to the transmittance of the atmospheric segment X_1 times the transmittance of the atmospheric segment X_2 (this paper assumes that the atmosphere is uniform). From Lambert-beer law:

$$\begin{cases} T_2 = \exp(-x \times \sigma_{ext}) \\ T_2 = \frac{I_{w2}=I_{b2}}{I_{w1}=I_{b1}} \end{cases} \tag{13}$$

According to formula (3) and formula (12)–(13), the relationship between the visibility and the light intensity received by the camera from two targets and background is obtained:

$$V = \frac{3.912x_2}{\ln(\frac{I_{w1}-I_{b1}}{I_{w2}-I_{b2}})} \tag{14}$$

The average pixel values PV_{b1}, PV_{b2}, PV_W of the selected target region and background region in Fig. 4 were calculated. In this paper, a 5×20 sampling box was adopted for the target and a 10×60 sampling box was adopted for the sky region (the experiment showed that the size of the sampling box had little influence on the experimental results, but the sampling box could not be too large). With the same camera, the exposure time and aperture size of the target object are the same, and atmospheric visibility can be calculated according to Eq. (8) and (14):

$$V = \frac{3.912x_2}{\ln(\frac{PV_{w1}^{\gamma}-PV_{b1}^{\gamma}}{PV_{w2}^{\gamma}-PV_{b2}^{\gamma}})}, \tag{15}$$

Figure 6 is the video screenshot of different weather conditions of the k277 + 749 down section of Beijing kunshitai expressway. Table 1 shows the comparison between the visibility value calculated by the algorithm in this paper and the observed visibility value at that time. From the results, it can be seen that the error between the calculated results by the algorithm in this paper and the actual observation value is smaller, especially for fog days, the detection accuracy is higher. Table 2 is the average error comparison between the algorithm in this paper and the other two algorithms after calculating the visibility of multiple images in the same fog. It can be seen that the accuracy of the algorithm in this paper is higher than that of the other two algorithms. Therefore, the algorithm in this paper is very suitable for the detection of visibility in fog.

Fig. 6. Images of video in different weather conditions

Table 1. The ratio of observed visibility

	Actual observation value/m	Algorithm value of this paper/m	Accuracy rate/(%)
Scene 1	719	753	95.27
Scene 2	1284	1347	95.09
Scene 3	3476	3825	89.96
Scene 4	2664	2887	91.62

Table 2. Algorithm accuracy comparison table

	Wavelet algorithm	Contrast algorithm	Algorithm in this paper
average error/m	11.4259	15.0142	6.4175
Accuracy rate/(%)	88.17	85.03	92.57

4   Conclusion

In this paper, a visibility algorithm based on the fitting of the response curve of digital camera is proposed. The parameters of the monitoring camera are set. By photographing the diffuse reflection surface of the image and calculating the average gray value, the double logarithm curve of the average gray value of the image and the exposure time is fitted, thus the important parameter value γ of the mutual conversion between the apparent brightness and the fixed brightness is obtained, and the current visibility value is accurately calculated. This algorithm is compatible with the existing highway condition monitoring system in Hebei Province and can be accessed easily. Compared with the visibility meter, it has the following outstanding advantages: using the camera system widely laid on the highway, the detection cost is low, and the detection range is wide; by fitting the response curve of the digital camera, the inherent brightness is calculated according to the apparent brightness of the target, and the atmospheric extinction coefficient is calculated by the inherent brightness of the target, so as to further increase the detection accuracy of visibility.

Of course, the algorithm in this paper also has some shortcomings: the algorithm needs to test the monitoring camera to fit the corresponding curve of the camera, so it needs a large amount of work in the early stage, but this can be discussed with the monitoring camera manufacturer, and this part of the work can be transferred to the manufacturer to reduce the workload in the early stage.

Funding. This research was funded by Science and Technology Support Plan Project of Hebei Province, grant number 17210803D.

This research was funded by Science and Technology Support Plan Project of Hebei Province, grant number 19273703D.

This research was funded by Science and technology spark project of Hebei seismological bureau, grant number DZ20180402056.

This research was funded by education department of Hebei province, grant number QN2018095.

References

1. Yin, S., Luo, K., Mo, W.: Analysis of visibility data obtained by the artificial observation and the instrumental survey. Meteorol. Hydrol. Mar. Instrum. **9**(3), 66–69 (2009)
2. Xin, X., Cui, Y., Zhang, F.: Summary of present situation and development trend of visibility measurement technology. Metrol. Measur. Technol. **9**(3), 66–69 (2009)
3. Yin, S., Luo, K., Mo, W.: Analysis of visibility data obtained by the artificial observation and the instrumental survey. Meterorol. Hydrol. Mar. Instrum. **9**(3), 66–69 (2009)
4. Kwon, T.M.: Atmospheric visibility measurements using video cameras. Night Visibil. 303–312 (2004)
5. Hautiére, N., Tarel, J.P., Lavenant, J., et al.: Automatic fog detection and estimation of visibility distance through use of an onboard camera. Mach. Vis. Appl. **17**(1), 8–20 (2006). https://doi.org/10.1007/s00138-005-0011-1
6. Miclea, R.C., Silea, I.: Visibility detection in foggy environment. In: 2015 20th International Conference on Control Systems and Computer Science, Romania, pp. 959–964 (2015)
7. Zhou, Q., Chen, Z., Hen, Q.: Visibility detection system based on road monitoring camera. Electron. Measur. Technol. **32**(6), 72–76 (2009)
8. Lv, W., Tao, S., Liu, Y.: Measuring meteorological visibility based on digital photography-dual differential luminance method and experimental study. Chin. J. Atmos. Sci. **28**(4), 559–568 (2004)
9. Lv, W., Tao, S., Tan, Y., et al.: Error analyses of daytime meteorological visibility measurement using dual differential luminance algorithm. J. Appl. Meteorol. Sci. **16**(5), 619–628 (2005)

10. Chang, F., Chen, X., Xiao, M., et al.: Visibility algorithm design and implementation of digital camera visibility instrument. Microcomput. Appl. **32**(9), 35–41 (2013)
11. Chen, Z., Zhou, Q., Chen, Q.: Video visibility detection algorithm based on wavelet transformation. Chin. J. Sci. Instrum. **31**(1), 92–98 (2010)
12. Kou, Y., Kong, L.: Study on model and precision in spatial point detection based on different camera assignment. J. YanShan Univ. (04), 348–351 (2007)
13. Chen, Z.: PTZ visibility detection based on image luminance changing tendency. In: 2016 International Conference on Optoelectronics and Image Processing (ICOIP), Warsaw, pp. 15–19 (2016)
14. He, K., Sun, J., Tang, X.: Single image haze removal using dark channel prior. In: Computer Vision and Pattern Recognition, Miami, pp. 1956–1963 (2009)
15. Guo, S., Qi, W., Qi, Y.: Video visibility measurement method based on dark channel prior. Comput. Digit. Eng. **42**(4), 694–697 (2014)
16. Cheung, S.S., Kamath, C.: Robust techniques for background subtraction in urban traffic video. Proc. SPIE – Int. Soc. Opt. Eng. **5308**, 881–892 (2004)
17. Jiang, S., Wei, Z., Wang, S., et al.: A new algorithm for background extraction under video surveillance. In: 2011 International Conference on Intelligent Computing and Integrated Systems (ICISS 2011), Guilin, pp. 244–247 (2011)
18. Shu, N., Chen, X.: New method of recovering response curve in process of HDRI constructing. Comput. Eng. Des. **33**(3), 1032–1036 (2012)
19. Du, K.: Dual digital camera atmospheric visibility observation method: 102254315, pp. 10–22 (2014)
20. Deng, Z., Ren, Y., Liu, Y., Yin, X., Shen, Z., Kim, H.-J.: Blockchain-based trusted electronic records preservation in cloud storage. Comput. Mater. Continua **58**(1), 135–151 (2019)
21. Luo, M., Wang, K., Cai, Z., Liu, A., Li, Y., Cheang, C.F.: Using imbalanced triangle synthetic data for machine learning anomaly detection. Comput. Mater. Continua **58**(1), 15–26 (2019)
22. Xiao, D., Liang, J., Ma, Q., Xiang, Y., Zhang, Y.: High capacity data hiding in encrypted image based on compressive sensing for nonequivalent resources. Comput. Mater. Continua **58**(1), 1–13 (2019)

Design of a Big Data Platform for Water Quality Monitoring Based on IoT

Yifu Sheng[1], Jianjun Zhang[1(✉)], Weida Chen[2], Yicheng Xie[1], Guang Sun[3], and Haijun Lin[1]

[1] College of Engineering and Design, Hunan Normal University, Changsha 410081, China
535541992@qq.com, jianjun998@vip.163.com, 1431330481@qq.com,
linhaijun801028@126.com
[2] Zhaoyin Network Technology (Shenzhen) Co., Ltd., Shenzhen 518057, China
526214479@qq.com
[3] Hunan Finance and Economics College, Changsha 410205, China
329804101@qq.com

Abstract. Water is one of the basic resources for human survival. Water pollution monitoring and protection have been becoming a major problem for humanity. For water resource management departments at all levels, there are a large number of water quality testing data, but they neglect the potential exploration of the resource attributes and data values of water quality data. To this end, we designed and implemented a water quality monitoring big data platform based on the Internet of Things. Through the deployed water quality monitoring sensor, the collected indicator data is transmitted to the big data processing platform deployed on Tencent Cloud in real time with the 4G network. Then the collected monitoring data will be analyzed and processed in the platform, and the processing result will be visualized by Baidu ECharts. The testing results showed that the platform could provide decision support for water resource protection.

Keywords: Water · Quality monitoring · Influxdb · Big data · Water resources protection

1 Introduction

In recent years, sudden water pollution incidents have occurred all over the world, which seriously threaten people's water security. Since there are no fixed ways and means of discharge for sudden water pollution incidents, if this matter is not disposed in times, the water supply safety of tap water will be seriously affected. How to monitor the situation of water resources in real time and predict possible water pollution incidents have been becoming a challenge faced by everyone. In order to ensure the safety of water supply, it is extremely urgent to establish a water monitoring and early warning system [1, 2].

Now we are in an era of rapid development of science and technology. Networks and information processing technologies such as the Internet of Things, robots, big data, and cloud computing have been becoming increasingly mature. These techniques could

© Springer Nature Singapore Pte Ltd. 2020
X. Sun et al. (Eds.): ICAIS 2020, CCIS 1254, pp. 441–453, 2020.
https://doi.org/10.1007/978-981-15-8101-4_40

be widely used in industry, agriculture, commerce, environmental protection, natural language processing, and data security all aspects of people's lives. By using the Internet of Things, big data, cloud computing and other related technologies, Weijie Chen constructed a big data analysis and processing platform for the garlic industry chain to solve the uncertainties of planting scope and yield, price fluctuation analysis, prices forecasting and other issues. The proposed platform could provide information and decision support for the healthy development of the garlic industry [3]. With R language, smartphones and cloud computing related technologies, Song Wook Han developed an air pollution information platform based on cloud platforms. It could be used to process the measured fine dust information in the air and air pollution information. The pollution information and protection reminders will be pushed through smart phones [4]. By using big data analysis technology, Hangjun Zhou proposed an anti-fraud method that could be used for online e-commerce contracts in order to accommodate the large amount of contract data generated in e-commerce [5]. With the continuous development of cloud computing and big data technology, the use of cloud storage is more and more extensive, and a large amount of data is outsourced for public cloud servers, and the security problems that follow are gradually emerging. Yuling Liu proposed a verifiable diversity ranking search scheme over encrypted outsourced data. while preserving privacy in cloud computing, it also supports search results verification [6]. Zhangjie Fu proposed a Chinese multi-keyword fuzzy search scheme in a cloud environment, which realizes the fuzzy search of multiple Chinese keywords and protects the private key by using a pseudo-random function [7].

The online water quality monitoring system is a comprehensive online automatic monitoring network involving modern sensor technology, computer application technology and communication network [8–11]. By using IoT and big data related technologies, we designed and implemented a water quality monitoring big data acquisition and processing platform based on the Internet of Things. The platform realized the automatic collection of water quality monitoring data, data analysis, visualization, and early warning information push, and will provide information support for water resources protection.

2 Platform Design

With the rapid development of sensors and Internet of Things technologies, many water management departments had accumulated a large number of water quality indicators, but neglected the resource attributes and data values of water quality data obtained through testing. Now we are in the era of big data, the core value of big data needs to be rediscovered. With the tools of big data collection, mining, analysis and other tools, we could construct a big data platform to achieve scientific prediction and warning of the future situation, and then to make more scientific and intelligent decision-making.

2.1 System Architecture Design

The water quality monitoring big data platform we designed is mainly divided into three parts: data acquisition module, data transmission module and data analysis module. The framework of the system is shown in Fig. 1.

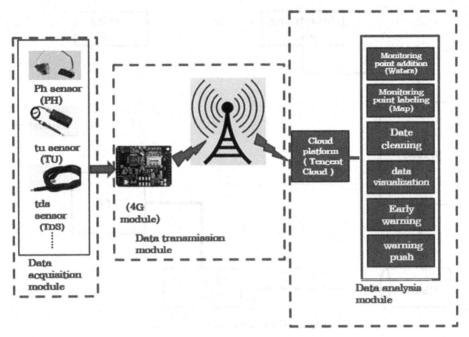

Fig. 1. The framework of the system

The data acquisition module is mainly responsible for the collection of water quality data of the monitoring water area. This work is mainly completed by deploying water quality index sensors such as PH sensors, TU sensors, and TDS sensors, etc. The main task of the data transmission module is to process the collected water quality index data through a SCM, and then use the 4G communication module to transmit these data to the data analysis and processing module deployed on the cloud platform. In order to analyze and process the water quality index data more conveniently and quickly, we deployed the data analysis module on the cloud platform and provided related information services such as visualization of analysis results and message push through corresponding APIs. This module mainly includes some sub-modules such as monitoring water management, monitoring point map marking, monitoring water quality index data cleaning, water quality index data analysis and visualization, water quality index exceeding standard warning, and early warning message pushing.

The data processing and analysis system is developed by using the Admin LTE framework, the Layer jQuery pop-up plug-in, the blade template, and PHP. The data collected by multiple sensors is uploaded to the WEBAPI through the network, and the data is stored in the HBase through the API for further analysis and processing. The data flow is shown in Fig. 2.

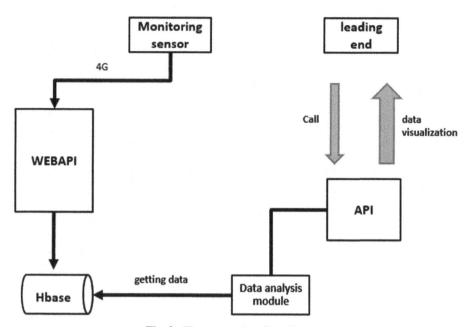

Fig. 2. The system data flow diagram

2.2   System Function Design

The data collected by the water quality monitoring sensor is transmitted to the big data platform deployed on Tencent Cloud through the mobile communication network using the 4G module. The big data platform mainly completes the processing of the collected monitoring index data, the visualization of the analysis results and the early warning processing. It mainly includes functional modules such as data analysis, data warning and system setting. The functional block diagram of the system is shown in Fig. 3.

The system setting module mainly performs functions such as user management, monitoring point management, monitoring point map labeling, and monitoring water area management. The user management module implements information management for platform administrators and platform users. The function of monitoring water area management and setting of monitoring points is to add, delete, and modify information such as monitoring water areas and monitoring point names and geographic coordinates. The Monitoring points map labeling module mainly implements map positioning and visualization of monitoring points.

The data analysis module mainly completes functions such as data viewing, data cleaning, and data visualization. Its main work is to clean the collected water quality index data of the monitoring water field, eliminate the illegal data, and realize the visualization of related data according to user needs. The data warning module mainly completes the setting of the early warning method, information push settings and other functions. When the water quality monitoring indicators of the relevant monitoring points exceed the standard, it will give early warning prompts and push the early warning information to the relevant users.

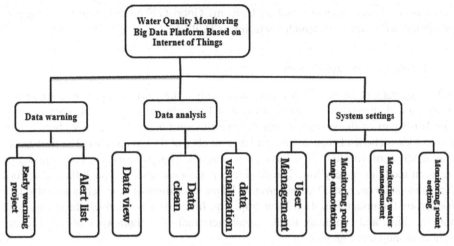

Fig. 3. The System function module diagram

3   System Function Implementation

3.1   Selection of Sensor Module and 4G Communication Module

The selection of monitoring sensors is very important for the collection of the water quality indexes. We chose three commonly used water quality monitoring sensors: PH, turbidity and TDS (total dissolved solids) for collection. Of course, more indicators monitoring sensors could be added according to actual needs. The selected indicator monitoring sensors are shown in Table 1.

Table 1. Sensor module selection

Index	Sensor module	Main parameter
PH	Guantuo turbidity PH sensor module	Measuring range: 0–14 PH Measurement accuracy: ±0.01 PH
TDS	DFRobot gravity	TDS measuring range: 0–1000 ppm TDS measuring range: ±10% F.S.
TU	Guantuo turbidity TU sensor module	Measuring range: 0–1000 NTU Working temperature: −20 °C–90 °C

In order to transmit the index data collected by sensors to the platform in time, we used 4G network to transmit information. The 4G module we selected is Gport-G43. It is a five-mode full Netcom 4G DTU, which supports mobile, Unicom 2G/3G/4G, and telecom 4G networks. The network supports a maximum downlink rate of 150Mbps and a maximum uplink rate of 50 Mbps. It can also work normally in remote areas lacking

3G and 4G network coverage (mobile, Unicom). Gport-G43 module connects serial port equipment to the internet, which conforms to TCP/IP.

3.2 Platform Software Design

After requirement analysis and preliminary design, the platform software system was designed with the Internet concept, Internet of Things technology, and big data analysis. The WEB part of the system adopts the mainstream Laravel framework abroad. This framework is chosen because it uses a large number of design patterns. The framework completely conforms to the five basic principles of design patterns. The coupling degree between modules is very low. The service container can easily expand the framework functions and write tests. The background UI adopts AdminLTE, which is a lightweight background template based on Bootstrap. The framework is relatively beautiful, with various skins, and can adapt to the mobile terminal. The framework of the software system is shown in Fig. 4.

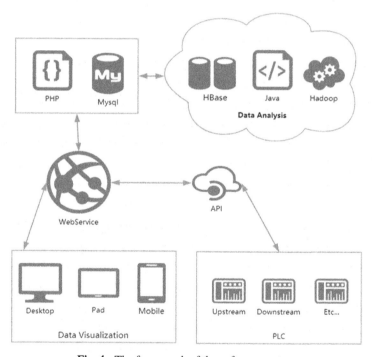

Fig. 4. The framework of the software system

In order to simplify the development process, we did not directly purchase the corresponding server hardware, but rented Tencent cloud space, deployed the entire system software platform on the Tencent cloud, and Tencent provided cloud computing resources to reduce the development costs and network security pressure. The development environment and programming language are: NET Framework 4.0, Microsoft Visual Studio

2017, JDK1.8, PHP7.2, Mysql5, Apache/Nginx, Apache Hadoop, InFluxDB. The collected water quality monitoring data are stored in Mysql database through API interface and WebService, and processed and analyzed in combination with tool frameworks such as HBase and InfluxDB commonly used in big data analysis. At the same time, Baidu's Echarts [12] was used to send the visualization results of monitoring data to terminals such as computers through Webservice.

3.3 Database Design

A complete water quality monitoring platform system should include at least three links: monitoring data collection, data analysis and data early warning. The water quality monitoring data collected by the monitoring platform are time-varying data with time series characteristics [13]. How to select an appropriate time series data engine is very important. With the rising and development of mobile internet, industrial internet, internet of things, and edge computing, time series data have shown explosive growth in the recent years. According to authoritative data published by DB-Engines, Fig. 5. shows the development trend of databases in the past two years. As shown in the Fig. 5, it can be found that among the development trends of various types of databases, the development trend of time series database is extremely strong. However, in the TOP 10 ranking of time series databases, semi-open source InfluxDB, as the benchmark of the new generation of time series databases, is far ahead in comprehensive scores. The ranking results are shown in Fig. 6. Therefore, InfluxDB is undoubtedly the first choice in application scenarios where time series data need to be stored. We chose InfluxDB as the time database in the platform.

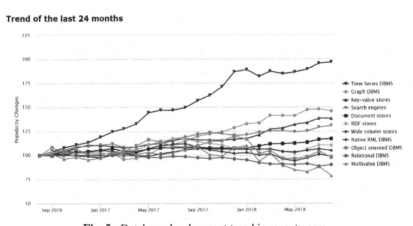

Fig. 5. Database development trend in recent years

Rank			DBMS	Database Model	Score		
Aug 2018	Jul 2018	Aug 2017			Aug 2018	Jul 2018	Aug 2017
1.	1.	1.	InfluxDB ➕	Time Series DBMS	11.57	-0.13	+3.47
2.	2.	⬆5.	Kdb+ ➕	Multi-model ℹ	3.51	+0.29	+1.85
3.	⬆4.	3.	Graphite	Time Series DBMS	2.60	+0.04	+0.30
4.	⬇3.	⬇2.	RRDtool	Time Series DBMS	2.47	-0.18	-0.59
5.	⬆6.	⬆7.	Prometheus	Time Series DBMS	1.52	+0.13	+0.92
6.	⬇5.	⬇4.	OpenTSDB	Time Series DBMS	1.42	-0.32	-0.49
7.	7.	⬇6.	Druid	Time Series DBMS	1.19	+0.01	+0.21
8.	8.	8.	KairosDB	Time Series DBMS	0.49	+0.04	-0.01
9.	9.	9.	eXtremeDB ➕	Multi-model ℹ	0.34	+0.01	-0.01
10.	10.	⬆11.	Riak TS	Time Series DBMS	0.30	+0.03	+0.05

Fig. 6. Time series database comprehensive score ranking

By analyzing the processed data structure and the range of values, and combining with the actual application requirements, we thought that the database of the software platform should mainly include data tables such as water_points, water_users, water_failed_jobs, water_early_warnnig_item, and the specific structure is shown in Fig. 7.

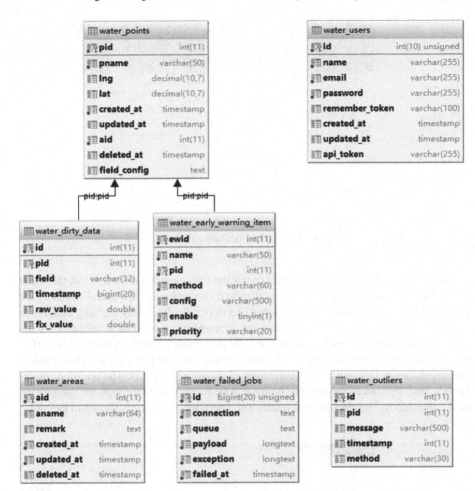

Fig. 7. The database structures

4   Module Function Implementation

The big data platform of the water quality monitoring data completes the functions of monitoring water fields' management, water quality monitoring data's cleaning, analysis and visualization, water quality index exceeding's waring, etc. The platform's software interface is shown in Fig. 8.

As shown in Fig. 8, this platform includes user management, data analysis, early warning processing, map labeling, monitoring area management, monitoring point management and other modules. We have monitored 148 waters fields and collected water quality index data from 222 monitoring points. Of course, monitoring waters could be added according to actual needs. After the sensors are deployed in the monitoring waters, a new monitoring point is added and water quality data can be collected at this new point. The data processing module is used to process the water quality index data collected

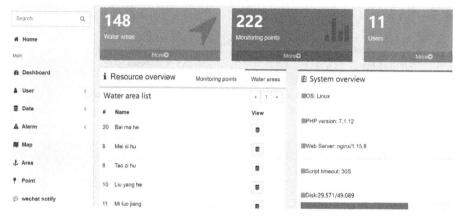

Fig. 8. The platform software's interface

by the sensors at each monitoring point. After the data cleaning is completed, the water quality index data of the monitoring is displayed according to the actual needs of the user. Early warning module allows users to set corresponding early warning conditions according to actual needs(You can also set different early warning conditions for the same monitoring point, such as different indicators values, different thresholds, different early warning algorithms, etc.). The map labeling module is mainly used to complete the map location labeling and visualization of monitoring points. The addition, modification and deletion of monitoring points can be implemented through the monitoring water area and monitoring point module. The operation interface is shown in Fig. 9.

Id	Monitoring point name		Water area	coordinate	operate
6	Analysis	Tao zi hu	Tao zi hu	112.9594570,28.1872240	Edit
8	Analysis	Liu yang he shang you	Liu yang he	112.9913180,28.2478550	Edit
9	Analysis	Liu yang he xia you	Liu yang he	113.6687710,28.1525220	Edit
10	Analysis	Mi luo jiang	Mi luo jiang	113.1839350,28.7947500	Edit
13	Analysis	Mei xi hu	Mei xi hu	112.9137490,28.2003300	Edit
15	Analysis	Ce shi shu iu	Ce shi shu iu	112.9137490,28.2003300	Edit

Fig. 9. Monitoring points' modifying interface

In order to enable users to view the water quality situation promptly, quickly and intuitively, the platform provide the function of viewing the monitoring water quality data. The design goal of this module is to display and export the water quality data of monitoring points, so that users can quickly understand the water quality data changing. The module's input is the RESTful architecture, which adds, deletes, checks, and changes the monitoring points' information, and its output is the HTTP state after execution and data in JSON format. The program flow is as follows: firstly, it use the middleware Auth to authenticate user permissions, secondly get the time range, thirdly use Thrift2 to establish a connection with the HBase database and traverse the data, then format the time format and convert the column names, and finally return the JSON result. The interface information is shown in Table 2.

Table 2. The interface's information of data viewing

Interface	Request method	Parameter
/admin/data/ajaxdata/{pid} Get water quality data, and pid shows ID of monitoring point	GET	stime: the star time etime: the end time The format is a millisecond timestamp
/v1/api/save/{pid}	GET/POST	Array: data [Time] (The format is a millisecond timestamp)

Since the data should be viewed in real time, data stored in the system must be collected by instruments and uploaded to the system in time. The water quality data were collected by multiple sensors, uploaded to WEBAPI through the network, and stored to HBase through API. In front-end display, the data analysis module directly takes out the data from the HBase for analysis, and then the front-end calls API to display [14, 15] as a line chart by calling Baidu's Chart plug-in. The results are shown in Fig. 10.

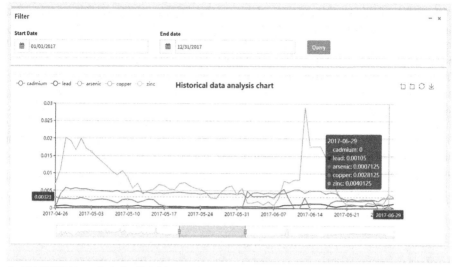

Fig. 10. Monitoring indicator data visualization

5 Conclusions

In order to make better use of water quality monitoring data and fully explore the application value of water quality monitoring data. We designed and implemented a water quality online monitoring platform based on the Internet of Things by using related technologies of the Internet of Things, Hadoop and related big data processing technologies. Relevant water quality index data, such as turbidity, PH, temperature and so on, are obtained in real time through sensors, wirelessly transmitted to an upper computer and then stored in an Hbase database of the platform for analyzing. The platform can be used to provide support for administration and decision-making. In the future, other types of sensors will be added to collect other index parameters of water in the monitoring water areas, and in order to provide real-time early warning and decision support, the alarm information pushing subsystem will be designed. At the same time, in order to ensure the security and integrity of the monitoring data during transmission, we will intend to use relevant encryption methods, such as the Dual-Chaining Watermark Scheme [16], to encrypt the monitoring data and to control data integrity.

Acknowledgments. This work is supported by National Natural Science Foundation of China (61304208), Hunan Province Science and Technology Plan Project Fund (2012GK3120), Scientific Research Fund of Hunan Province Education Department (18C0003), Changsha City Science and Technology Plan Program (K1501013-11), Hunan Normal University University-Industry Cooperation. This work is implemented at the 2011 Collaborative Innovation Center for Development and Utilization of Finance and Economics Big Data Property, Universities of Hunan Province, Open project, grant number 20181901CRP04.

References

1. Zhitao, Z., Qian, C., Tao, X.: Design of water quality monitoring and warming system of drinking water source. Environ. Protect. Sci. **39**(1), 61–64 (2013)
2. Wei, J., Wei, H.: Environmental monitoring and early warning system construction of centralized drinking water source. Environ. Monitor. Early Warn. **2**(6), 5–7 (2010)
3. Weijie, C., Guo, F., Chao, Z.: Development and application of big data platform for garlic industry chain. Comput. Mater. Continua **58**(1), 229–248 (2019)
4. SangWook, H., Jung, Y.S., Dae-Young, K.: Development of cloud based air pollution information system using visualization. Comput. Mater. Continua **59**(3), 697–711 (2019)
5. Hanigjun, Z., Guang, S., Sha, F.: A scalable approach for fraud detection in online e-commerce transactions with big data analytics. Comput. Mater. Continua **60**(1), 179–192 (2019)
6. Yuling, L., Hua, P., Jie, W.: Verifiable diversity ranking search over encrypted outsourced data. Comput. Mater. Continua **55**(1), 37–57 (2018)
7. Zhongjin, F., Jinwei, W., Baowei, W.: Fuzzy search for multiple chinese keywords in cloud environment. Comput. Mater. Continua **60**(1), 351–363 (2019)
8. Gong, L., Hui, G., Hui, Z.: Development of android platform based portable water quality detector. Chin. J. Environ. Eng. **10**(7), 3973–3976 (2016)
9. Hongsong, L., Jun, L.: New progress of study of water quality monitoring sensors. Transducer Microsyst. Technol. **31**(3), 11–14 (2012)
10. Xiong, F.B., Zhu, W.Z., Lin, H.F.: Fiber-optic sensor based on evanescent wave absorbance around 2.7 μm for determining water content in polar organic solvents. Appl. Phys. B **115**(1), 129–135 (2014). https://doi.org/10.1007/s00340-013-5583-2
11. Bin, J.: Reuse of determination data sources: water quality testing in big data era. Water Purif. Technol. **36**(09), 1–3 (2017)
12. Echarts and API using. https://blog.csdn.net/DekuiCaiNiao/article/details/71939147. Accessed 31 Aug 2019
13. Microkernel early warning engine architecture design based on time series data. https://www.cnblogs.com/liugh/p/9568701.html. Accessed 31 Aug 2019
14. Ying, H., Jian, L., Tingting, Z.: Research on monitoring communication system for sewage treatment process by android mobile based on client/server mode. Comput. Appl. Softw. **33**(12), 52–54 (2016)
15. Juan, C.: Analysis and application of data mining algorithm for internet of things based on hadoop. Comput. Age **06**, 29–31 (2018)
16. Baowei, W., Weiwen, K., Wei, L.: A dual-chaining watermark scheme for data integrity protection in internet of things. Comput. Mater. Continua **58**(3), 679–695 (2019)

Network Representation Learning Based Extended Matrix Factorization for Recommendation

Jinmao Xu, Daofu Gong$^{(\boxtimes)}$, Fenlin Liu, and Lei Tan

State Key Laboratory of Mathematical Engineering and Advanced Computing,
Zhengzhou 450001, China
gongdf@aliyun.com

Abstract. The growing heterogeneous data in the Internet effectively improves the performance of recommender systems (RS). The main problem faced by the traditional matrix factorization (MF) is how to fuse more heterogeneous information data in MF to improve the performance of RS. In view of this, this paper proposes an Extended Matrix Factorization (EMF) based on network representation learning. EMF integrates multiple types of data in Heterogeneous Information Network (HIN) to improve the accuracy of prediction rating. The nodes in HIN are first mapped to a low-dimensional representation vector by network representation learning (NRL). Then the representation vector is used as the input of the EMF, the parameters are optimized by the gradient descent, and finally the prediction model is obtained. The experiments on two real data sets show the effectiveness of the EMF. Compared with the baseline algorithms, the EMF model can obtain more accurate prediction rating.

Keywords: Matrix factorization · Network representation learning · Heterogeneous Information Network · Recommender systems

1 Introduction

In the era of big data, it has become an urgent requirement for people to obtain the content they are interested in from massive data information. Recommender system (RS) is an important tool for information retrieval. RS can help users quickly find the content they are interested in from the application platform of the Internet. RS can deal with information overload problem in the big data field.

Collaborative filtering (CF) is the state-of-the-art technology of RS. CF discovers the user's behavioral preferences through the user's historical behavior and predicts the user's rating of the product. Because of its good performance in rating prediction, the collaborative filtering algorithm represented by Matrix Factorization (MF) is widely used [1,2,22]. MF factors the user-item rating matrix to obtain the user latent feature matrix and item latent feature matrix respectively. The user's latent features reflect the user's preference on

© Springer Nature Singapore Pte Ltd. 2020
X. Sun et al. (Eds.): ICAIS 2020, CCIS 1254, pp. 454–465, 2020.
https://doi.org/10.1007/978-981-15-8101-4_41

each dimension of the latent features. The item's latent features represent the weight of the item's attribute on each dimension of the latent features. MF establishes the relationship between the user and the item through the latent feature, and then obtains the user's preference model.

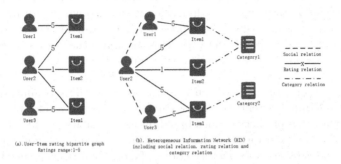

(a). User-Item rating bipartite graph
Ratings range:1~5

(b). Heterogeneous Information Network (HIN)
including social relation, rating relation and
category relation

Fig. 1. Example of Bipartite graph and HIN

In fact, as shown in Fig. 1(a), the user-item rating matrix can be seen as a bipartite graph. The rating prediction method based on CF predicts the missing value of the rating matrix based on the bipartite graph information [23]. On the one hand, the types of network data in the commercial platform are becoming more and more abundant, and it is impossible to model complete data information using only bipartite graphs. For example, the yelp platform includes not only user-item rating information, but also social information between users, category information of item (products) and so on. The large number of users and items leads to the sparsity of the user-item rating matrix, which cause the latent feature vector obtained by MF model cannot accurately characterize the features of users and items. This situation will affect the accuracy of rating prediction. Therefore, in the case of sparse rating data, we consider to use rich heterogeneous data information to improve the performance of the recommender system.

Sun et al. proposed using a Heterogeneous Information Network (HIN)[3], to model a network with different types of objects. A HIN example is given in Fig. 1(b). Unlike a homogeneous network, HIN can contain multiple types of nodes and multiple types of edges. The advantage of HIN is that it can fuse different types of objects and represent more complex interactions within a network. In real life, a lot of data information can be modeled as HIN, such as literature network, Twitter information network, e-commerce yelp, and the like. In recent years, a lot of work has been done on the problems in HIN. For example, how to measure node similarity in HIN [4], how to perform link prediction [5,14], and so on.

HIN can model multiple data sources information into heterogeneous network. At the same time, the network representation learning [12,15] (NRL) can map nodes in the network to low dimensional vector spaces. Deepwalk [6] generated a sequence of nodes using random walk on a homogeneous network, and then mapped each node to one vector space through skip-gram model. LINE [7] model defines the first-order and second-order similarity of nodes, which can get more differentiated node representation. Node2vec [8] added BFS (Breadth First Search) and DFS (Depth First Search) strategies for neighborhood search based on Deepwalk. Representation learning of information network is to map nodes or edges in the network into low-dimensional vectors, which can be applied to different data analysis tasks. The representation vector of the node maintains the structural features in the network. How to apply the node's representation vector to the recommender system's rating prediction task will be a challenging task.

In recent years, there has been a lot of work in the recommender system to utilize HIN model. SemRec [9] uses meta-path based model to assess user similarity and then predicts ratings based on user similarity. Zhao et al. defined the concept of meta-graph and then solved the problem of information fusion with the model of "matrix factorization+ factor factorization machine" [10]. Wang et al. believe that users (items) would have some common features in different meta-paths, and could learn a unified user (item) representation by integrating data from multiple meta-paths [11]. All the above methods use the meta-path to obtain the node sequence and then obtain the representation vector of nodes by NRL. Representation learning of information network is to map nodes or edges in the network into low-dimensional vectors, which can be applied to different data analysis tasks.

MF is a commonly used rating prediction algorithm, but the model has limitations. First, MF only factors a single matrix (such as a rating matrix, an adjacency matrix [10]). So it is difficult to process multiple data sources. How to integrate multiple data sources into MF is a problem worth studying. Second, MF is less explainable. The user and item latent feature matrix are optimized by the gradient descent algorithm, which has only mathematical meaning and cannot explain the specific meaning of the user and item latent feature matrix.

To address the two problems of MF, we propose an Extended Matrix Factorization (EMF) based on network representation learning. The contributions of this paper are as follows. First we try to integrate the multiple data sources information in EMF to improve the performance of RS, and explain in more detail how the user and item feature matrix are obtained in EMF. Second, EMF makes the user and item feature matrix have certain physical meanings.

2   The Proposed Approach

In this section, we propose an Extended Matrix Factorization (EMF) based on network representation learning. EMF can fuse multiple data sources information and improve the performance. First we introduce the framework.

2.1   Framework

In the traditional MF, MF only uses the rating matrix as the data source of the recommendation, and faces the problem of scarce data. When the user has no or only a small amount of rating behavior, the latent feature vector of the user (item) obtained by MF cannot accurately reflect the user preference and the item attribute. On the other hand, the user representation vector obtained from HIN contains the user's historical purchase record information, the user's social relationship information, and the like. These data greatly enrich the effective data source of the recommender system and provide more evidence for recommendation [16]. Therefore we consider the user (item) representation vector as the input to the MF.

It is our basic task to predict users' preferences based on the existing historical data. We believe that rich information (such as user's social relationship, item category information, etc.) contained in HIN is helpful for recommendations in cases where the rating data is scarce. Therefore, the main challenge of this task is how to design a recommendation model that can take advantage of the data information in HIN. The model finally obtains the user's predicted rating based on the fused data in HIN and the historical rating. Due to the good performance of the traditional MF in the rating prediction task [1], we propose an improved model of matrix factorization based on the user(item) representation vector to predict the user's rating. The specific process of the algorithm is as follows:

Step1. HIN construction: HIN is constructed by the user's social relationship, the user-item rating data, and the information of item's categories.

Step2. Feature extraction: The network representation learning algorithm extracts the user's feature vector matrix U and the item's feature vector matrix V from HIN.

Step3. Model training: The user's and item's features are taken as the input of the model, and the objective function is optimized by the gradient descent method to train the model.

Step4. Rating prediction: The user's ratings are predicted by the trained model.

We will introduce the specific steps in the algorithm in next section.

2.2   Motivation

The matrix factorization algorithm is a collaborative filtering model. MF considers the user's existing rating of the item as the user's historical behavior, and analyzes the user's preferences based on the user's historical rating of the item, thereby predicting the user's rating of the unpurchased item. The basic assumption is that the rating matrix is a low-rank matrix, indicating that the rows (columns) of the matrix are highly correlated.

As shown in Eq. 1, MF factors the rating matrix to two parts: user's latent feature matrix U and item's latent feature matrix V.

$$R \approx UV^T \tag{1}$$

where, $U \in R^{m \times k}$ and $V \in R^{n \times k}$ respectively represent user's and item's latent feature matrices, and each row represents a k-dimensional feature vector of a user and an item, $k \ll \min(m, n)$. In general, the latent feature vector of the item, $v_j \in V$ is interpreted as the distribution of an item's attributes on the k-dimensional vector; where $u_i \in U$ is the latent feature vector of a user, indicating the user's preference distribution of the k-dimensional attributes. The inner product of the latent features of the user and the item is used as the predicted rating. The rating prediction formula is as shown in Eq. 2.

$$\hat{r}_{ij} = u_i v_j{}^T \tag{2}$$

The loss function is shown in Eq. 3:

$$e_{ij} = \min_{u_i, v_j} \sum_{i,j} \left(r_{ij} - u_i v_j{}^T \right)^2 \tag{3}$$

where $r_{ij} \in R$ is the value that the user has rated(the observed rating), and $\hat{r} = u_i v_j{}^T$ is the predicted value of the rating. By minimizing the loss function, the error between the predicted value and the observed rating is minimized, and the latent feature vectors u_i and v_j are obtained.

It can be seen that the input data source of the MF is the rating matrix. The model optimizes the k-dimensional latent feature vectors u_i and v_j of users and items based on the existing historical rating data. If the rating matrix R is denser, the latent feature vectors u_i and v_j can reflect more accurate user's preferences and item's attributes. For example, if a user rates many items, the model can get accurate user's preference. Conversely, if a user does not rate any item, it is difficult to get the user's preference.

The bottleneck of MF is that the model can only use historical rating data as input to learn the feature of users and items. Therefore, based on the historical rating data, we can add more abundant additional information (such as user social information, item category information) to extract more accurate feature of users and products. As mentioned above, HIN can effectively fuse information. Therefore, we consider using HIN to model multiple data sources information to solve the problem of multiple data sources fusion in the recommender system.

2.3   Feature Extraction

In this section, HIN shown in Fig. 2 is first constructed using the user's social relationship, the user-item rating data and the item category data. Then we use the network representation learning algorithm to learn the representation vector U, V of the node in HIN, where the U and V matrix can be regarded as the feature matrix of the user and the item. HIN fuses multiple sources of data. After the nodes in HIN are vectorized by the NRL, the obtained feature vector of the node retains the structural information in HIN. Nodes are easy to calculate for various tasks after vectorization. For example, the probabilistic model can be used to predict the neighbor nodes of one node, and the similarity between the two nodes can be determined according to the cosine distance of the node representation vector.

Different from the homogeneous information network, the main challenge in HIN representation learning task is that there are different types of nodes and

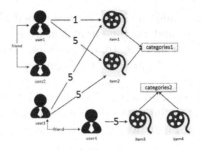

Fig. 2. An example of HIN

multiple semantic edges in HIN. Figure 2 shows an example of HIN. The nodes
are composed of three types of nodes: U (user), V (item), and C (category).

Shi et al. propose meta-path can represent the semantic relationship between
nodes in HIN [9]. The meta-path is defined as: $V_1 \xrightarrow{R_1} V_2 \xrightarrow{R_2} ... \xrightarrow{R_{m-1}} V_{n-1} \xrightarrow{R_m} V_n$,
where V represents the node, and R represents the relationship between
the nodes. We define the meta-path "UVU" to represent users who have
interactive behavior (purchase, comment, watch, etc.) on the same item.
In Fig. 2, the instance of meta-path "UVU" is $U_{user1}V_{item1}U_{user3}$, which
means user1 and user3 have viewed the same item1(movie1); If we define
the meta-path "$UVCVU$", one instance of the meta-path "$UVCVU$" is
$U_{user1}V_{item1}C_{categories1}V_{item2}U_{user4}$, which means user1 and user4 are interested
in the same category of items.

Dong et al. proposed that the most effective meta-path in most meta-path
based work is $UVCVU$[3,4,17,18]. So we chose "$UVCVU$" as the meta-path
used in our work. We use the meta-path based representation learning algorithm
to generate the feature matrix. First, random walk based on the meta-path is
performed on HIN to generate n sets of node sequences. Then, the node sequences
are vectorized by skip-gram algorithm, and the user feature vector matrix U
and the item feature vector matrix V are obtained. The feature vectors U, V
obtained by the network representation learning algorithm can maintain the
structural characteristics and semantic characteristics in HIN. At the same time,
the feature vector of the node can be applied to a variety of machine learning
tasks such as classification, clustering, link prediction, and more.

In the next section, we apply these feature vectors to the improved matrix
factorization model for rating prediction task.

2.4 Extended Matrix Factorization

In the previous section, the k-dimensional feature vectors of the user and the item
were obtained by performing representation learning on the nodes in HIN. We
need to consider how to apply the feature vectors to the rating prediction task.
MF factors the original rating matrix R into the user latent feature matrix U and
the item latent feature matrix V. The latent feature matrices U and V reflect the

characteristics of the user and the item. As mentioned above, due to the sparsity problem of the rating matrix, the latent feature matrices U and V cannot accurately describe the user and the item. Therefore, we consider extracting the features of users' and items' from HIN. HIN contains richer data information. User and item feature vectors u_i, v_j extracted from HIN provide more comprehensive description of users and items. Extended Matrix Factorization (EMF) uses feature vectors u_i, v_j as inputs to the improved matrix factorization model. In order to make a rating prediction, the formula is as follows:

$$R \approx UCV \tag{4}$$

where matrix R is a rating matrix, U and V respectively denote the user and item feature matrix. Here we introduce the concept of the connection matrix C.

In the original matrix factorization Eq. (1), the latent feature matrices U and V are first randomly initialized, and then the gradient descent function is used to optimize the objective function to obtain the latent feature matrix. In EMF, the feature matrices U and V are obtained from HIN through NRL. The feature matrix cannot be multiplied directly to obtain a rating matrix as in Eq. (2). Therefore, the connection matrix C is added here, and the connection matrix C is a square matrix of k rows and k columns, and the matrix includes k^2 parameters. The matrix C is used to fit the user feature matrix and the item feature matrix, so that the U, C, V three matrix products approximate the true rating matrix. Intuitively, we can think of the connection matrix C as a link between users and items. The connection matrix is trained by the existing data (observed rating) to find the relationship between the user features $u_i \in U$ and the item features $v_j \in V$, that is, the connection matrix C can reflect the relationship. The prediction rating we proposed is calculated as follows:

$$\hat{r}_{ij} = u_i C_{k \times k} v_j^T \tag{5}$$

It can be seen from Eq. (5). We multiply the features vector u_i of user i, the features v_j^T of item j, and the connection matrix $C_{k \times k}$ to predict the rating of user i for item j. We represent the predict rating as $\hat{r}_{ij} = u_i C_{k \times k} v_j^T$. We minimize the regularized root mean square error of the predicted rating $\hat{r}_{ij}$ and the observable rating r_{ij}, so that the predicted rating of the EMF model is constantly approaching the true rating. After this training process, we get the prediction model and obtain the connection matrix $C_{k \times k}$ through learning from the observed rating. The loss function is shown in Eq. (6):

$$\min_{C_{k \times k}} \sum_{(i,j) \in R_{train}} \left(r_{ij} - u_i C_{k \times k} v_j^T \right)^2 \tag{6}$$

where r_{ij} is the observed rating, $u_i C_{k \times k} v_j^T$ is the predict rating, u_i is the k-dimensional feature vector of user i, v_j is the k-dimensional feature vector of item j, $C_{k \times k}$ is the connection matrix and R_{train} is the training set of the rating matrix. After completing the training of the model, the prediction ratings of all the users are obtained, and the performance of the EMF model is evaluated in the test set.

3   Experimental Results

In this section, we verify the effectiveness of the EMF algorithm through experiments. This section will introduce the experimental evaluation metrics, experimental environment, baselines, experimental results and experimental analysis. We performed experiments on real data sets to verify the performance of the proposed method and compare it with existing methods.

3.1   Evaluation Metric

In order to verify the performance of the recommender system, we chose Root Mean Square Error (RMSE) and Mean Absolute Error (MAE) as the evaluation metrics. RMSE and MAE are commonly used to evaluate the prediction accuracy of model. RMSE and MAE are defined as follows:

$$RMSE = \sqrt{\frac{1}{|D_{test}|} \sum_{(i,j) \in D_{test}} \left(r_{i,j} - \hat{r}_{i,j}\right)^2} \tag{7}$$

$$MAE = \frac{1}{|D_{test}|} \sum_{(i,j) \in D_{test}} |r_{i,j} - \hat{r}_{i,j}| \tag{8}$$

3.2   Experimental Environment and Settings

This experiment was run in a python 3.5 environment and tested on a server. The server configuration is 2.10 GHz Intel Core E5-2620 CPU, 64 GB RAM, Windows 10 professional x64.

We validated the proposed EMF algorithm on the yelp. Yelp is an American review site where users can rate products and maintain a friend relationship between them. This data set is provided by the Yelp Dateset Challenge. The data we use includes the following three types:

Social Relationship Dataset: There are a total of 140,345 users' relationships for 17,066 users in the yelp dataset. Item category Dataset: There are 900 item categories in the yelp data set. One of these items may correspond to multiple categories. User-item Rating Dataset: A total of 37,000 users rated 200,000 of 22,500 items in the yelp dataset.

This experiment randomly divided the data set into a training set and a test set in a ratio of 8:2. Five experiments were repeated, and the average RMSE and MAE were taken as experimental results.

3.3   Baseline Models

We compare the following baselines with EMF:

RegSVD [19]: A standard matrix factorization model that uses only a rating matrix as the input data source. The performance of this model is highly dependent on the quality of the rating matrix. The richer the rating data, the more accurate the Regsvd prediction rating.

LLORMA [20]: A local matrix factorization method. After dividing the rating matrix into sub-matrices, the matrix factorization algorithm is performed on the sub-matrix.

SocReg [21]: Add user social information as a regular term to the matrix factorization model.

SemRec [9]: A recommendation algorithm based on meta-path for HIN. SemRec calculates the user's similarity based on the meta-path and predicts the rating based on the user similarity and the number of similar users.

EMF: The model proposed in this paper.

3.4   Experiment Analysis

Table 1 lists the experimental results of the baseline models and EMF models on the dataset of yelp.

Table 1. Performance of different methods with $K = 50$ on Yelp

Datasets	Metrics	Regsvd	LLORMA	SocReg	SemRec	EMF
Yelp	MAE	1.6277	1.3317	1.3311	1.1895	1.0284
	Improve	36.62%	22.77%	22.74%	13.54%	
	RMSE	1.9317	1.5385	1.5178	1.4662	1.3394
	Improve	30.66%	12.94%	11.75%	8.64%	

Regsvd and LLORMA are traditional matrix factorization algorithms that use only the rating matrix as input of the model without any additional data. Socreg uses the user's social relationship to improve the performance of the recommender system. The specific approach is to add social relationship as a regular term in the matrix factorization. This also proves that the additional social relationships can improve the performance of the recommender system when the users' rating data is sparse.

SemRec model performs better than Regsvd, LLORMA and SocReg. We think the main reason is that SemRec further fuses richer data. The user(item) representation vector obtained through the meta-path can well reflect user's feature, and this more efficient feature can improve recommender system performance. EMF also uses the meta-path based method to obtain user and item features. The user and item feature vectors are used as input of MF to fit the observable rating. The user and item feature vectors obtained through NRL fuse the information of multiple data sources in HIN, and the feature vector effectively extracts the semantic information in HIN. The user and item feature vectors are taken as the input of MF, by training the connection matrix C, the improved matrix factorization model can obtain better prediction results. The main reason why EMF has a better recommendation effect than SemRec is that

SemRec relies too much on the similarity of users, which leads to the deviation of rating prediction. Since MF has a good performance in rating prediction task, we combine the feature extraction method based on the meta-path with MF algorithm, and then propose the EMF model. The experimental results show that the performance of the EMF model on both MAE and RMSE is better than the comparison algorithm.

3.5 Analysis of Parameter k

In this section, we mainly discuss the effect of the parameter k on the performance of the model. In MF, the parameter k refers to the dimension of the latent feature vector; in the EMF model, it refers to the dimension of the connection matrix C. The dimension of latent feature vector k is closely related to the performance of MF. In general, the larger the value of k in the matrix factorization model, the more dimensions of latent feature vector in the model. It is generally believed that vectors with higher dimension can accurately describe the features of the object. On the contrary, if the value k is small, the vector with lower dimension may not accurately describe the object, which will reduce the performance of the model. We set up different k-value in the EMF model for experiments. The experimental results in the figure below show that the error of the prediction rating is very high when the value of k is small. In the yelp dataset, when k is set to 50, the model has the lowest RMSE and the model achieves the best performance. It is shown that the vector's dimension is sufficient to reflect the feature of the nodes in HIN, the performance of the recommender system tends to be stable.

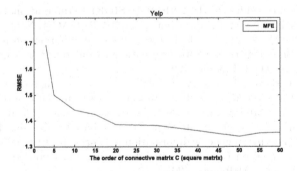

Fig. 3. The influence of parameter k on performance.

4   Conclusions

The matrix factorization algorithm obtains the user and item latent feature matrix by factoring the rating matrix. The inner product of two latent feature vectors is used as the prediction rating. The matrix factorization model predicts the user's rating by user's history rating. In view of the sparsity of rating matrix, additional information of users or items is added into the model to improve the performance of the recommender system. We propose EMF model, and EMF model implements rating prediction that fuses multiple data sources. At the same time, the EMF model uses the representation vectors of users and items learned from HIN as model inputs. From the perspective of HIN, it can be explained that the representation matrix of the user and the item can be regarded as the user and item features extracted from HIN, which enhances the explainability of the recommender system.

References

1. Koren, Y., Bell, R., Volinsky, C.: Matrix factorization techniques for recommender systems. Computer **42**(8), 30–37 (2009)
2. Liu, G., Meng, K., Ding, J., Nees, J.P., Guo, H., Zhang, X.: An entity-association-based matrix factorization recommendation algorithm. Comput. Mater. Cont. **58**(1), 101–120 (2019)
3. Sun, Y., Han, J.: Mining heterogeneous information networks: a structural analysis approach. In: Proceedings of ACM SIGKDD Explorations Newsletter, pp. 20–28. ACM, New York (2012)
4. Sun, Y., Han, J.: Pathsim: meta path-based top-k similarity search in heterogeneous information networks. In: Proceedings of the VLDB Endowment, pp. 992–1003. ACM, Washington (2011)
5. Cao, B., Kong, X.: Collective prediction of multiple types of links in heterogeneous information networks. In: Proceedings of the IEEE International Conference on Data Mining, pp. 50–59. IEEE, Shenzhen (2014)
6. Perozzi, B., Al-Rfou, R., Skiena, S.: Deepwalk: online learning of social representations. I:n: Proceedings of the 20th ACM SIGKDD International Conference on Knowledge Discovery and Data Mining, pp. 701–710. ACM, New York (2014)
7. Tang, J., Qu, M., Wang, M., et al.: Line: large-scale information network embedding. In: Proceedings of the 24th International Conference on World Wide Web, pp. 1067–1077. ACM, Florence (2015)
8. Grover, A., Leskovec, J.: node2vec: scalable feature learning for networks. In: Proceedings of the 22nd ACM SIGKDD International Conference on Knowledge Discovery and Data Mining, pp. 855–864. ACM, San Francisco (2016)
9. Shi, C., Zhang, Z., Luo, P., et al.: Semantic path based personalized recommendation on weighted heterogeneous information networks. In: Proceedings of the 24th ACM International on Conference on Information and Knowledge Management, pp. 453–462. ACM, Melbourne (2015)
10. Zhao, H., Yao, Q., Li, J., et al.: Meta-graph based recommendation fusion over heterogeneous information networks. In: Proceedings of the 23rd ACM SIGKDD International Conference on Knowledge Discovery and Data Mining, pp. 635–644. ACM, Halifax (2017)
11. Wang, Z., Liu, H., Du, Y., et al.: Unified embedding model over heterogeneous information network for personalized recommendation. In: Proceedings of the 28th International Joint Conference on Artificial Intelligence, pp. 3813–3819. AAAI, Macao (2019)

12. Qiu, J., Dong, Y., Ma, H., et al.: Network embedding as matrix factorization: unifying DeepWalk, LINE, PTE, and node2vec. In: Proceedings of the Eleventh ACM International Conference on Web Search and Data Mining, pp. 459–467. ACM, Marina Del Rey (2018)

13. Jiang, Z., Liu, H., Fu, B., et al.: Recommendation in heterogeneous information networks based on generalized random walk model and bayesian personalized ranking. In: Proceedings of the Eleventh ACM International Conference on Web Search and Data Mining, pp. 288–296. ACM, Marina Del Rey (2018)

14. Chen, H., Yin, H., Wang, W., et al.: PME: projected metric embedding on heterogeneous networks for link prediction. In: Proceedings of the 24th ACM SIGKDD International Conference on Knowledge Discovery and Data Mining, pp. 1177–1186. ACM, London (2018)

15. Cui, P., Wang, X., Pei, J., et al.: A survey on network embedding. IEEE Trans. Knowl. Data Eng. **31**(5), 833–852 (2018)

16. Ma, H., Zhou, D., Liu, C., et al.: Recommender systems with social regularization. In: Proceedings of the Fourth ACM International Conference on Web Search and Data Mining, pp. 287–296. ACM, Hong Kong (2011)

17. Dong, Y., Chawla, N.V., Swami, A.: metapath2vec: scalable representation learning for heterogeneous networks. In: Proceedings of the 23rd ACM SIGKDD International Conference on Knowledge Discovery and Data Mining, pp. 135–144. ACM, Halifax (2017)

18. Huang, Z., Zheng, Y., Cheng, R., et al.: Meta structure: computing relevance in large heterogeneous information networks. In: Proceedings of the 22nd ACM SIGKDD International Conference on Knowledge Discovery and Data Mining, pp. 1595–1604. ACM, San Francisco (2016)

19. Paterek, A.: Improving regularized singular value decomposition for collaborative filtering. In: Proceedings of KDD Cup and Workshop, pp. 5–8. ACM, San Jose (2007)

20. Lee, J., Kim, S., Lebanon, G., et al.: LLORMA: local low-rank matrix approximation. J. Mach. Learn. Res. **17**(1), 442–465 (2016)

21. Ma, H., Zhou, D., Liu, C., et al.: Recommender systems with social regularization. In: Proceedings of the Fourth ACM International Conference on Web Search and Data Mining, pp. 287–296. ACM, Hong Kong (2011)

22. Wang, G., Liu, M.: Dynamic trust model based on service recommendation in big data. Comput. Mater. Cont. **58**(3), 845–857 (2019)

23. Bin, S., et al.: Collaborative filtering recommendation algorithm based on multi-relationship social network. Comput. Mater. Cont. **60**(2), 659–674 (2019)

Forensic Technology for Source Camera Identification

Lan Chen[1]([✉]), Anran Li[1], and Lei Yu[2]

[1] School of Computer Science and Technology, University of Science and Technology of China,
Huangshan Road 443, Hefei 230026, Anhui, China
{roma2016,anranLi}@mail.ustc.edu.cn
[2] School of Medical Information Technology, Anhui University of Chinese Medicine,
Hefei 230012, Anhui, China
Fishstonehfut1006@163.com

Abstract. Source camera identification is a major branch of forensic source iden-tification. It's purpose is to determine which camera was used to capture the image of unknown provenance only by using the image itself. We study the recent devel-opments in the field of source camera identification and divide the techniques described in the literature into six categories: EXIF metadata, lens aberration, CFA and demosaicing, sensor imperfections, image statistical features and convo-lutional neural network. We describe in detail the general ideas of the approaches used in each category. We summarize the six techniques at the end of the article and point out the challenges for future forensic.

Keywords: Forensics · Source camera identification · Digit camera · Image

1 Introduction

The advancement of digital technology has brought high-performance and lowprice dig-ital imaging devices to people. With the popularity of digital cameras, tens of millions of digital pictures have been generated every day. Because of the ease of use and accessi-bility, digital cameras have been exploited by many wrongdoers to commit crimes, such as shooting child pornography for profiteering, infringing copyright by copying prints. Reliable identification of the camera captured a particular digital image is always a must in the court to determine the source of images presented as evidence. Source camera identification (SCI) technology in the field of multimedia forensics is specifically used to solve such kind of problems. This paper will describe in detail the various techniques of SCI proposed in the literature.

Although the standard stages inside a digital camera is general, various hardwares updates, different software algorithms and different combinations of the hardwares and the softwares in the internal process of digital cameras form different cameras. As is shown in Fig. 1, different cameras are macroscopically expressed as different imaging effects in the same scene under the same shooting conditions, which is resulted by the difference of internal components in different cameras.

© Springer Nature Singapore Pte Ltd. 2020
X. Sun et al. (Eds.): ICAIS 2020, CCIS 1254, pp. 466–477, 2020.
https://doi.org/10.1007/978-981-15-8101-4_42

(a) Agfa DC 504   (b) Agfa dc 830i   (c) Canon Ixus55

(d) Nikon CoolPixS710   (e) Samsung L74wid   (f) Samsung NV15

Fig. 1. Variations across images of the same scene, each one acquired with a different camera model.

The technology of SCI is based on the assumption that all kinds of hardwares and softwares involved in the internal processing of a camera will leave their own proprietary traces in the image, which are camera-specific and independent of the image content. The technology of SCI explores to capture and extract a variety of trace features in the image left by the hardwares such as lenses and sensors, the softwares such as exchangeable image file (EXIF) metadata as well as color filter array (CFA) and demosaicing, and the combination of multiple components in the acquisition pipeline.

The source camera identification is used mainly in two scenarios. In one scenario, it is to determine if the digital image of unknown provenance was shot with an certain instance/model/brand camera. In the other scenario, given some images and some certain instance/model/brand cameras, it is to determine which instance/model/brand camera took which image. The camera source identification is a process of assigning a digital image to a digital camera, and therefore, the problem of SCI is a typical classification problem.

The rest of the paper is structured as follows. Section 2 give an overview of the structure and processing stages of a typical digital camera. The first half of Sect. 3 describes in detail the various types of traditional SCI techniques and approaches in the literature, and the latter part of Sect. 3 focuses on the development of convolutional neural networks (CNN) technique used in the field of SCI. Section 4 concludes the paper about the state of the art and point out the challenges for future forensic.

2 The Imaging Pipeline of Digital Cameras

Figure 2 shows the stylized image acquisition pipeline. Light from a scene enters the camera through a lens, then passes through a set of filters before reaching the imaging sensor. An infrared filter blocks infrared radiation and only allows the visible part of the spectrum to pass. An anti-aliasing filter reduces aliasing which happens when the spacing between pixels of the sensor is not able to support finer spatial frequency of target objects. The imaging sensor is the core component of a camera that is an array of many very small addressable unit charge-coupled device (CCD) or complimentary metal-oxide semiconductor (CMOS) elements, each of which represents a pixel in an image. The sensor collects the photons and converts them into voltages, which are subsequently sampled to a digital signal in an analog-to-digital (A/D) converter. Each pixel of CCD or CMOS imaging sensors captures only intensity information from the light hitting it, so only a monochrome output can be produced by each pixel. In order to generate a color image, a CFA is used in front of the sensor. The CFA is a mosaic of color filters in which each element blocks out a certain portion of the spectrum and allows only one specific color to pass. The existence of CFA results in that each sensor pixel detects only the light intensity of one specific color. Most digital cameras use the CFA of one kind of four Green-Red-Green-Blue (GRGB) Bayer patterns. The output from the sensor with a Bayer filter is a mosaic of red, green and blue pixels of different intensities. In order to form the final color, the missing color is calculated using various interpolation algorithms to obtain all the basic three colors for each pixel. Then the post-processing such as gamma correction and white balance adjustment is performed on the image. Finally, the digital image is written to the camera memory device in a selected format such as JPEG compression.

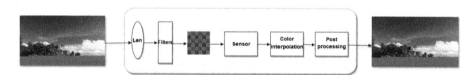

Fig. 2. Standard digital camera processing pipeline.

3 Techniques of Source Camera Identification

Each stage of the imaging process presents features unique to that stage on the image. For each imaging stage, the components of different brand/model cameras would left their own fingerprints on the image. Each technique uses unique fingerprints left by the components of certain stage(s) in cameras. The first five SCI techniques to be described below need to manually extract features, and the CNN approach of deep learning techniques can automatically extract features and classify.

3.1 EXIF Metadata

In the post-processing phase of imaging in a camera, digital cameras embs large amounts of metadata including image capture conditions in the EXIF header. Table 1 lists EXIF metadata extracted from an image. By checking the camera make and model tags in the EXIF metadata, the make and model of the camera captured the image are determined. However, EXIF metadata is not always reliable because EXIF metadata is most vulnerable to be tampered maliciously by third parties. But once it is proven that these information have not been modified, source identification based on EXIF metadata is a simple and effective method.

Table 1. Partial EXIF metadata extracted from a digital image

Camera make	Canon
Camera model	Canon power shot S410
Data/Time	2018:10:12 10:00:00
EXIF version	0220
Width × Height	2272 × 1704
X resolution (dpi)	180.0
Y resolution (dpi)	180.0
Flash used	Yes
Focal length	7.4 mm
CCD width	0.28 mm
Exposure time	0.06 s (1/160)

3.2 Lens Aberration

When the optical system projects scene to the sensor, lens distortion artifacts inevitably occurs in the digital image. Researchers have modeled some of the lens distortion artifacts and SCI technique estimates the model parameters of interest as a feature vector for SCI.

Radial Lens Distortion. Radial lens distortion is the geometrical aberration that makes straight edges in a scene appear curved edges in an image. Figure 3 shows two forms of barrel distortion and pincushion distortion.

F. Devernay et al. [12] use the polynomial model $r_u = r_d + k_1 r_d^3 + k_2 r_d^5$, r_u, r_d to express lens radial distortion of an image where r_u, r_d are the undistorted radius and distorted radius respectively, and k_1 and k_2 are the first order and second-order distortion parameters which can be estimated by minimizing the total error between curved and straight lines. Different lens of cameras have its own radial distortion characteristics. Choi et al. [10] measured the parameters (k_1, k_2) as a feature vector and obtain an accuracy of 91.53% with three different model cameras operated at fixed focal lengths. However, this technique has one major limitation when images from a specific camera are taken by zoom lens with different manual zooming.

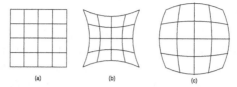

Fig. 3. Radial lens distortion: (a) An ideal rectangular grid, (b) barrel distortion and (c) pincushion distortion.

Chromatic Aberration. Chromatic aberration (CA) is a phenomenon where lights of different wavelengths could not converge at the same position on the focal plane. Such displacements are recognized as color fringes in images. CA is categorized as axial chromatic aberration and lateral chromatic aberration. Farid et al. [18] derived an expression for modeling the lateral chromatic aberration as follows,

$$x^{(w)} = \alpha^{(w)} \left(x^{(g)} - x_o^{(w)} \right) + x_o^{(w)} \tag{1}$$

$$y^{(w)} = \alpha^{(w)} \left(y^{(g)} - y_o^{(w)} \right) + y_o^{(w)}$$

where $(x^{(g)}, y^{(g)})$ is green channel coordinates, and $(x^{(w)}, y^{(w)})$ is red or blue color channel coordinates. The feature parameters (x_o, y_o, α) are determined based on maximizing the mutual information between the corrected R and B channels with the G channel.

Van et al. [27] used 6-dimensional feature vectors for distinguishing source cell phones and got a 92% identification accuracy by SVM. The advantage of the method is it does not impose any restriction. However, it is not enough for identifying source cameras of the same model. Yu et al. [30] obtained a stable enough chromatic aberration pattern to distinguish different copies of the same lens by using a white noise pattern and by the introduction of the lens focal distance.

3.3 CFA and Demosaicing

Most cameras pair a sensor with a CFA and then apply a demosaicing process to interpolate two missing colors with the color information of the neighbor raw pixels in order to obtain a full-color image.

Inter-pixel Correlations. CFA and demosaicing process produce unique interpixel correlations which have been modeled and measured for SCI. Brayman et al. [5] found both the size of interpolation kernel and the demosaicing algorithm vary from camera to camera. They used the Expectation Maximization (EM) algorithm to obtain two sets of classification features: one set is the weighting coefficients and the other is the frequency spectrum of probability maps for varying sizes of kernels. They considered the 5×5 neighborhoods over two model cameras for the SVM classifier and achieves the classification accuracy of 95.71%. This method is limited to images that are not heavily compressed as the compression artifacts suppress and remove the spatial correlation between the pixels.

Cao et al. [7] proposed a partial second-order derivative correlation model from the original model so as to depress the impact of image content on the estimation procedure and detect correlation in both the intra-channel and the cross-channel. Their experiments on SVM classifier achieved a 97.5% accuracy over a set of 14 different model cameras. The 250 most relevant features which were found with sequential floating forward selection are highly effective in distinguishing different post-processes images and are more sensitive to small scenery variations.

CFA Pattern. The CFA pattern itself is a model-specific feature used to narrow down the recognition range. Takamatsu et al. [25] found the noise variance of the pixels becomes smaller after the interpolation. The CFA pattern is determined by the means of applying the discrete Fourier transform to a 1D sequence of variances and measuring the ratio of the average variances of all interpolated pixels and observed pixels. Choi et al. [9] proposed an intermediate value counting algorithm to estimate the CFA pattern of the digital cameras from a single image. The authors considered the interpolated color sample values are not greater than the maximum of neighbor samples and are not less than the minimum of neighbor samples. For each channel, the intermediate values are counted based on the defined neighbor pattern. Finally, the Bayer pattern is estimated using the count information of the three channels. The experimental results show [9] is robust to cropping but a failure for JPEG compression.

3.4 Sensor Imperfections

The manufacturing process of sensors inevitably produce imperfections, such as defects in pixel arrays and the pixel nonuniformity (PNU), which leave proprietary camera/sensor fingerprints in the images.

Pixel Defects. Geradts et al. [14] find CCD sensor array sometimes contain defects which appear as white points in an image when shot in a black background. Due to each CCD sensor has distinct pattern of pixel defects, the CCD camera can be identified by counting white points in an image. However, this method has certain limitations. Firstly, the number of visible pixel defects of a camera differs in images and changes with the image content. Secondly, the number of visible pixel defects is affected greatly by the shooting temperature. Thirdly, many high quality CCD digital cameras use built-in mechanisms to compensate for the pixel defects so that the defects are not visible in the image.

Pattern Noise. The pattern noise is defined as any noise component that survives frame averaging, which is a deterministic component present in every image the sensor takes and thus can be used for SCI. PNU noise caused by different sensitivity of pixels to light is the main source of pattern noise.

[23] relies on this component noise and use correlation to establish the presence of a certain pattern in an image. The camera reference pattern P_C is obtained by averaging the noise residual of N images of the specified camera. The correlation ρ_C between the noise residual n of the test image p and the camera reference pattern P_C is examined

to decide the image attribution, as is shown in Eq. 2. The identification accuracy is satisfactory even for cameras of the same model, and is also good for identifying images that are subjected to JPEG compression, gamma correction, and resampling. However, the prediction is unsatisfactory when the test image is cropped or inconsistent with size of the images used in the camera reference pattern [28].

$$\rho c(p) = corr(n, P_c) = \frac{(n - \bar{n}) \cdot (P_c - \bar{P}_c)}{||n - \bar{n}|| \cdot ||P_c - \bar{P}_c||} \tag{2}$$

In the real world, investigators can not have a full access to all of the possible source cameras. Costa et al. [11] proposed an approach of SCI considering such an open set recognition scenario. As Different regions of an image contain different information about the source camera fingerprint [22], Costa considers nine regions of interest (ROI) of each image instead of only using the central region or the whole image as is done in [21, 23]. Camera fingerprint and the test image are represented by two kinds of a 36-dimensional feature vector respectively. They set up a SVM classier by the training set of positive examples and the available negative samples for solving the SCI problem. The result of the experiments shows the recognition accuracy of the proposed approach is statistically improved when compared with the methods of [23] and [21] and is also higher than other two methods when distinguishing cameras of the same model.

3.5 Image Statistical Features

Instead of paying attention to one component of image acquisition pipeline, the researchers calculate various kinds of statistics regardless of the original image content for SCI from a black-box perspective.

Color Features. Color features of images mainly rely on CFA, the demosaicing algorithm and the color processing. Kharrazi et al. [19] proposes the 12dimensional color feature vector which characterizes average pixel value, neighbor distribution center of mass, inter-channel correlation and RGB pairs energy ratio of an image. Gloe et al. [16] add six color features about white point correction to further extend this color feature set. The six color features represent the dependency between average pixel values of three color channels.

Image Quality Metrics. Image quality refers to visual appearance differences which depends on the joint action of optical systems, sensor properties and internal post-processing pipelines. Image quality metrics (IQM) is proposed in [2] to quantify the image quality. Kharrazi et al. [19] use 13 IQMs and categorize them into three classes based on the pixel difference, the correlation and the spectral distance. Kharrazi et al. compute these features as the average over three color channels. Celiktutan et al. [8] use the subset of the above feature sets and evaluate separately for each color channel to identify the source cellphone camera.

Wavelet Statistics. Wavelet decomposition is able to capture noise features across different spatial positions, scales and directions of an image [24]. Kharrazi et al. [19] implement the one-level wavelet decompositions of three color channels and obtain a

9-dimensional feature vector formed by the means for each of the 3 sub-bands. In [8], the decompositions are increased to three levels and the previous feature set are extended to 72 wavelet statistical features overall. Gloe et al. [15] forms a 27-dimensional variant that take mean, standard deviation and skewness into account from each of three one-level decomposition detail sub-bands to evaluate different image feature for SCI.

Binary Similarity Measures. Binary similarity measures (BSM) consider similarity to describe binarised neighborhood features across or in different bit planes of a digital image [1]. These features can be categorized into several types of measures according to differences between bit planes, histogram and entropy features, and Ojala histograms. Celiktutan et al. [8] take relations between color channels into account to add the BSM feature set. As the result, the selected measurements have amounted to 480 BSM features for SCI.

3.6 CNN of Deep Learning Technology

In recent years, CNN technology has been widely applied in the area of computer vision. CNN models have achieved good performance in image classification [29], image recognition [13] and image forgery detection [31]. However, a CNN model can also learn features that characterize images shot with different cameras directly from images and classify the images automatically.

Luca Baroffio et al. [3] firstly propose the use of CNN to solve the problem of SCI. They built and tested the CNN model based on two levels of identification granularity which are device-level and model-level respectively. The results of experiments show that the recognition precision for the model-granularity reaches 0.941 after voting election. However, the recognition precision for the device-granularity is only 0.298. It is obvious that the CNN model is not powerful enough for the feature learning for different devices of the same model, but it can easily learn artifact features left by different camera models.

Amel TUAMA et al. [26] use a layer of preprocessing consisted of a high pass filter before the CNN model. They use a denoising filter to obtain noise residuals for all the input images, which works as $N = I - F(I)$ where F is a denoising filter and I is an original image. Then the noise residuals are fed to the subsequent layers for advanced feature extraction and classification.

Their experiments result indicates that the preprocessing layer consisted of different denoising filters plays the important role in the overall identification accuracy. The filtering function of the wavelet filter has suppressed much camera model-related features generated in the acquisition pipeline of a camera which are the required features for the CNN model to learn for camera model classification.

Luca Bondi et al. [6] propose another idea in 2017 to treat CNN as a feature extractor. Specifically, a CNN model is used to capture artifacts in the images left by the processing pipelines of each camera model. Then, it works with a support vector machine (SVM) for classification. There are two advantages in using such a proposed approach. Firstly, highly abstract data representations of the images can be obtained. Secondly, the CNN can be trained only once to learn an image feature extraction methodology which generalizes well on other camera models not involved in model training.

Inspired by the fact proved in the area of manipulation detection that using nonlinear residuals can potentially improve the robustness of the algorithm to post-processing operations, [4] propose augmented convolutional feature maps (ACFM) which make the CNN model robust to resampling and recompression. In their algorithm, the nonlinear residual features extracted by a median filter are added to the feature maps produced by the constrained convolutional layer to create the ACFM. The set of ACFM is then fed to a sequence of regular conventional layers to further learn and classify. The experimental results show that learning the association between linear features and MFR features in the deeper layers of the network can significantly improve the robustness of CNN in real-world scenarios. The prediction residual features learned by the constrained convolutional layer outperform the general fixed linear residuals.

Artur Kuzin et al. [20] find another algorithm for SCI being robust to postprocessing operations. The authors choose DenseNet 161 [17] to construct highly abstract data representations and use radical data augmentations for the training images, which directly implements the CNN model being robust against gamma, resize and JPEG transformations. It is inferred from the experimental results that if the CNN model is to be robust to one or some transformations, it just needs to perform the same transformation/transformations in the image training set. The precondition for acquiring a promised identification rate is to have a sufficiently complex structure of a CNN network and a sufficient number of transformated images.

4 Conclusion and Future Challenges

In the article, we have classified SCI techniques into six categories and the general ideas of the approaches used in each category are given. We summarizes the techniques mentioned in the paper in Table 2. For the time being, the six kinds of SCI techniques mentioned have developed maturely in their respective fields, but the comprehensive application of multiple techniques is rarely documented in the literature. However, in view of the fact that image artifacts are not generated independently, it is necessary to explore more ways to combine different technologies to improve the identification accuracy in the future.

Table 2. Summary of techniques for SCI

Techniques	EXIF metadata	Lens aberration		CFA and demosaicing		Sensor imperfections		Statical features	Deep learning
Subcategory	EXIF metadata	Radial lens distortion	Chromatic aberration	Inter-pixel correlations	CFA pattern	Pixel defects	Pattern noise	Statical features	CNN
Reference no.	13	11	30	6	10	15	25	21	22
Image format	JPEG	JPEG	JPEG	–	Raw	–	TIFF	JPEG	JPEG
Classifier	–	SVM	SVM	SVM	Intermediate value counting	Defective pixel locations	Correlation	SVM	DenseNet
Detection granularity	Model	Model	Model	Model	Model	Model	Instance	Model	Model
Limitations	It is vulnerable to be tampered	It can not work when images are taken with different manual zooming	It suffers from cropped images	It can not work when images are heavily compressed	It is a failure for JPEG compression	It is affected by the image content, shooting temperature and built-in mechanisms	It can not work when geometry operations are performed on images	Identification accuracy decreases when images are recompressed	Transformation forms of test images must be consistent with that used during training

References

1. Avcibas, I., Kharrazi, M., Memon, N., Sankur, B.: Image steganalysis with binary similarity measures. EURASIP J. Appl. Sig. Process. **2005**, 27492757 (2005). https://doi.org/10.1155/ASP.2005.2749
2. Avcibas, I., Sankur, B., Sayood, K.: Statistical evaluation of image quality measures. J. Electron. Imaging **11**(2), 206–224 (2002)
3. Baroffio, L., Bondi, L., Bestagini, P., Tubaro, S.: Camera identification with deep convolutional networks. arXiv preprint arXiv:1603.01068 (2016)
4. Bayar, B., Stamm, M.C.: Augmented convolutional feature maps for robust CNN-based camera model identification. In: 2017 IEEE International Conference on Image Processing (ICIP), pp. 4098–4102. IEEE (2017)
5. Bayram, S., Sencar, H., Memon, N., Avcibas, I.: Source camera identification based on CFA interpolation. In: IEEE International Conference on Image Processing (2005)
6. Bondi, L., Baroffio, L., Güera, D., Bestagini, P., Delp, E.J., Tubaro, S.: First steps toward camera model identification with convolutional neural networks. IEEE Sig. Process. Lett. **24**(3), 259–263 (2016)
7. Cao, H., Kot, A.C.: Accurate detection of demosaicing regularity for digital image forensics. IEEE Trans. Inf. Forensics Secur. **4**(4), 899–910 (2009)
8. Celiktutan, O., Sankur, B., Avcibas, I.: Blind identification of source cell-phone model. IEEE Trans. Inf. Forensics Secur. **3**(3), 553–566 (2008)
9. Choi, C.H., Choi, J.H., Lee, H.K.: Cfa pattern identification of digital cameras using intermediate value counting. In: Proceedings of the Thirteenth ACM Multimedia Workshop on Multimedia and Security, pp. 21–26. ACM (2011)
10. Choi, K.S., Lam, E.Y., Wong, K.K.: Source camera identification using footprints from lens aberration. In: Digital Photography II, vol. 6069, pp. 172–179 (2006)
11. Costa, F.O., Eckmann, M., Scheirer, W.J., Rocha, A.: Open set source camera attribution. In: 2012 25th SIBGRAPI Conference on Graphics, Patterns and Images, pp. 71–78. IEEE (2012)
12. Devernay, F., Faugeras, O.D.: Automatic calibration and removal of distortion from scenes of structured environments. In: Investigative and Trial Image Processing, vol. 2567, pp. 62–72. International Society for Optics and Photonics (1995)
13. Fang, W., Zhang, F., Sheng, V.S., Ding, Y.: A method for improving CNN-based image recognition using DCGAN. CMC: Comput. Mater. Continua **57**(1), 167–178 (2018)
14. Geradts, Z.J., Bijhold, J., Kieft, M., Kurosawa, K., Kuroki, K., Saitoh, N.: Methods for identification of images acquired with digital cameras. In: Enabling Technologies for Law Enforcement and Security, vol. 4232, pp. 505–512. International Society for Optics and Photonics (2001)
15. Gloe, T.: Feature-based forensic camera model identification. In: Shi, Yun Q., Katzenbeisser, S. (eds.) Transactions on Data Hiding and Multimedia Security VIII. LNCS, vol. 7228, pp. 42–62. Springer, Heidelberg (2012). https://doi.org/10.1007/978-3-642-31971-6_3
16. Gloe, T., Borowka, K., Winkler, A.: Feature-based camera model identification works in practice. In: Katzenbeisser, S., Sadeghi, A.-R. (eds.) IH 2009. LNCS, vol. 5806, pp. 262–276. Springer, Heidelberg (2009). https://doi.org/10.1007/978-3-642-04431-1_19
17. Huang, G., Liu, Z., Van Der Maaten, L., Weinberger, K.Q.: Densely connected convolutional networks. In: Proceedings of the IEEE Conference on Computer Vision and pattern Recognition, pp. 4700–4708 (2017)
18. Johnson, M.K., Farid, H.: Exposing digital forgeries through chromatic aberration. In: Proceedings of the 8th Workshop on Multimedia and Security, pp. 48–55. ACM (2006)
19. Kharrazi, M., Sencar, H.T., Memon, N.: Blind source camera identification. In: 2004 International Conference on Image Processing, ICIP 2004, vol. 1, pp. 709–712. IEEE (2004)

20. Kuzin, A., Fattakhov, A., Kibardin, I., Iglovikov, V.I., Dautov, R.: Camera model identification using convolutional neural networks. In: 2018 IEEE International Conference on Big Data (Big Data), pp. 3107–3110. IEEE (2018)
21. Li, C.T.: Source camera identification using enhanced sensor pattern noise. IEEE Trans. Inf. Forensics Secur. **5**(2), 280–287 (2010)
22. Li, C.T., Satta, R.: On the location-dependent quality of the sensor pattern noise and its implication in multimedia forensics (2011)
23. Lukas, J., Fridrich, J., Goljan, M.: Digital camera identification from sensor pattern noise. IEEE Trans. Inf. Forensics Secur. **1**(2), 205–214 (2006)
24. Mallat, S.G.: A theory for multiresolution signal decomposition: the wavelet representation. IEEE Trans. Pattern Anal. Mach. Intell. **7**, 674–693 (1989)
25. Takamatsu, J., Matsushita, Y., Ogasawara, T., Ikeuchi, K.: Estimating demosaicing algorithms using image noise variance. In: 2010 IEEE Computer Society Conference on Computer Vision and Pattern Recognition, pp. 279–286. IEEE (2010)
26. Tuama, A., Comby, F., Chaumont, M.: Camera model identification with the use of deep convolutional neural networks. In: 2016 IEEE International workshop on information forensics and security (WIFS), pp. 1–6. IEEE (2016)
27. Van, L.T., Emmanuel, S., Kankanhalli, M.S.: Identifying source cell phone using chromatic aberration. In: IEEE International Conference on Multimedia Expo (2007)
28. Van Lanh, T., Chong, K.S., Emmanuel, S., Kankanhalli, M.S.: A survey on digital camera image forensic methods. In: 2007 IEEE International Conference on Multimedia and Expo, pp. 16–19. IEEE (2007)
29. Wu, H., Liu, Q., Liu, X.: A review on deep learning approaches to image classification and object segmentation. TSP **1**(1), 1–5 (2018)
30. Yu, J., Craver, S., Li, E.: Toward the identification of DSLR lenses by chromatic aberration. In: Media Watermarking, Security, and Forensics III, vol. 7880, p. 788010. International Society for Optics and Photonics (2011)
31. Zhang, J., Li, Y., Niu, S., Cao, Z., Wang, X.: Improved fully convolutional network for digital image region forgery detection (2019)

Interest Mining Model of Micro-blog Users by Using Multi-modal Semantics and Interest Decay Model

Dongbai Jia[1], Zhaowei Qu[1(⊠)], Xiaoru Wang[1], Fu Li[2], Luhan Zhang[1], and Kai Yang[1]

[1] Beijing Key Laboratory of Network System and Network Culture, Beijing University of Posts and Telecommunications, Beijing, China
{jdb_2017140889,zwqu,wxr,luhanzhang,kaiyang}@bupt.edu.cn
[2] Department of Electrical and Computer Engineering, Portland States University, Portland, OR 97207-0751, USA
lif@pdx.edu

Abstract. In order to meet the personalized needs of users and provide better recommendations, how to analyse the user interest accurately has become the focus of research currently. Due to the short content of micro-blog data, the sufficient semantic information it is difficult to get, which leads to the difficulty in accurately mining user interest. Traditional methods mainly use social relations to mine user interest, solving the problem of sparse data to a certain extent. But for users with single social relations, there is a cold start problem, which makes it unable to establish an effective user interest model. In addition, user interest will change over time which results in deviations when using traditional feature extraction methods. In order to solve the problems, we present an interest mining model of micro-blog users by using multi-modal semantics and interest decay model. It builds a connection among semantic relations in multidimensional features. It can solve the data-sparse problem, as well as the cold start problem. The fusion of multiple data semantic represents user interest features more comprehensively. To solve the problem of user interest migration, we propose an interest decay model to assist mining user interest better. In this paper, experiments are carried out on the dataset of 2, 938 user information extracted from micro-blog. The experimental results show that the method proposed in this paper significantly improves the accuracy of user interest mining compared with the existing methods.

Keywords: Interest decay model · Multi-modal data · Micro-blog user interest

Supported by the National Natural Science Foundation of China (No. 61672108, No. 61976025).

© Springer Nature Singapore Pte Ltd. 2020
X. Sun et al. (Eds.): ICAIS 2020, CCIS 1254, pp. 478–489, 2020.
https://doi.org/10.1007/978-981-15-8101-4_43

1 Introduction

In recent years, with the development of information networks, the Internet has entered the lives of people with rapid momentum. In the new era, the social needs of people have been more transferred to the Internet [1]. Because of the needs for social activities, micro-blog has achieved tremendous development in recent years, and the number of registered users of it is increased rapidly. At the end of 2018, the number of micro-blog users has exceeded 430 million, with nearly 30,000 entertainment stars and more than 400,000 KOLs [2]. The huge user communities, massive texts and image information are waiting to be extracted. It is also a vast invisible fortune for companies. The research on micro-blog user interest has a broad application prospect, attracting attention and researchers from all over the world. The current research on user interest mining is mainly divided into two aspects:

(1) Research on interest mining based on social relationships of users
The interest mining methods based on social relations of users are mainly carried out by building user relationship communities [3]. However, this kind of research method will leads to community overlap, which brings out the uncertainty of user interest identification. Meanwhile, since some micro-blog users don't even have social relationships, these algorithms also result in cold start, which greatly reduces the prediction accuracy of such users.
(2) Research on interest mining based on text information of users
The interest mining methods based on text information of users only consider the text [4–6] in the massive micro-blog data, ignoring the images and self-evaluation information of users. The classification results are not accurate, due to the neglect of such data information. As a result, the analysis results of interest mining are not accurate enough either.

To solve the problems in the existing algorithms, we propose an interest mining model of micro-blog users by using multi-modal semantics and interest decay model, without using social relationships. Instead, we use three types of data issued by micro-blog users, including images, blog texts, and tags. This model avoids the problem of inaccurate user identification caused by using single-dimensional data [7]. In this paper, we improve the accuracy of user interest recognition by using Multi-Layer Perceptron, which is adapted to analyze the relations among features and merge three types of data features organically. In addition, the existing methods do not take into account the phenomenon of user interest migration. In this paper, an interest decay model is proposed to calculate the retention of user interest quantitatively, through which the user interest mining model can be obtained more precisely.

2 Related Work

As early as in the 1970s, the initial prototype of the social platform was shown to the netizens in the form of BBS, but only with one-way news and messaging function. Since the birth of Web2.0, the social platform has been redefined and evolved till now and future continuously. Micro-blog was born in 2008, attracting a large number of people. Micro-blog has produced large-scale structured data of images and descriptions. Many scholars have studied the interest of micro-blog users, and found problems of data sparsity and user interest transformation in the research process.

Because most micro-blog texts are short texts with sparse features, many scholars try to use natural language processing to expand feature information. Yan Tao et al. used keyword co-occurrence or query word expansion technology to expand the dimensions of texts [8] to maximize the expansion of feature dimensions. S. Banerjee et al. expanded the text from the knowledge-based on Wikipedia and search engine to expand the feature dimensions [9]. Although these methods can expand the feature space of the text effectively, they are not good at solving the problem of data sparsity of short micro-blog texts. One reason is that too many waste words are imported, leading to only a little is useful. In order to solve the data sparsity problem, B. Sriram et al. took the difference between the features of micro-blog texts and ordinary texts [10] into account, and then selected multi-class features by adding metadata ones. Although this method solved the stated problem, it treated multivariate data as the same type. Jin Zeng et al. proposed to fuse the multi-modal data in micro-blog [11] to mine user interest better, but the fusion method was simple splicing of the feature without considering the correlations among different features. Therefore, based on previous studies, we propose a new feature fusion method. We use Multi-Layer Perceptron to train the importance of data features of different modalities and characterize multiple features organically. Finally, we mine the inner connections of the three kinds of modalities (user tags, texts, and images) to obtain user interest features in a more accurate way.

There is a problem of "information overload" in social platforms. Massive amounts of information are generated every day, and user interest also changes over time [12]. As a result, there are deviations in single feature extraction. Yongbin Qin et al. proposed a method of micro-blog user interest mining based on text clustering and interest decay [13]. They introduced a time factor by using the time-series LDA model to compress the microblog-theme matrix into a user-topic matrix. However, the factors defined artificially can only represent the trend of interest decay [14]. Therefore, by introducing the Ebbinghaus memory forgetting curve in psychology, we obtain the user interest decay curve by analyzing the frequencies of texts sent by microblog users. Then we regard the decay factor as inputs to one of the channels of Text-CNN and put related parameters from the deep learning models to the decay model of the user interest. As a result, we improve the accuracy of mining interest of users.

3   Methodology

This paper is to establish a user interest model to mining the interest of micro-blog users. Our algorithm has two subtasks. The first one is to obtain user interest multimodal features, and the second one is to design a function f to obtain the user interest. For the first subtask, we consider that the user interest multimodal features are constructed by the interest decay value, semantic features of micro-blog image, semantic features of blog texts, and user tags. To obtain the user interest multimodal features, first we fit the user interest decay curve by analyzing typical users' blog. Then we acquire three dimensions of user data and fuse the user interest value with the above features to obtain the user interest feature vector. The specific framework of the above task is shown in Fig. 1. For the second subtask, we define the user interest mining function $f(X_i) \rightarrow Y$. X_i represents the interest multimodal feature vector of the user i, $X_i = \{x_1, x_2, \cdots, x_n\}$, n represents the dimensions of feature vectors. Y represents the user interest category, $Y = \{y_1, y_2, \cdots, y_m\}$, m represents the types of user interest. Using the trained function f, the user interest feature vector can be used to obtain the user interest result. After the two subtasks, we can finally frame the user interest model.

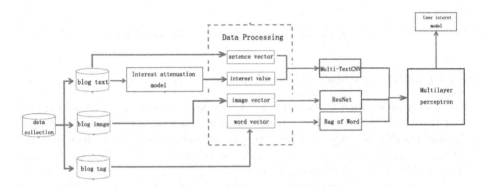

Fig. 1. The framework of the model.

3.1 Interest Decay Model

As shown in Fig. 1, we propose an interest decay model to calculate the interest value of the user. The memory forgetting curve proposed by H. Ebbinghaus describes the rules of the human brain for forgetting new things. The retention rate of memory is decreasing with the passage of time. The user's hobbies are also a form of memory. Therefore, the fresher micro-blog in the user's list, the more representative of the user's current interest. According to the memory forgetting curve, the user's current interest is slightly influenced by the blogs published in the past time, although it had been published many times. For each topic, we analyze the publish frequency of typical users, obtain the correlation between the frequency and the number of days. Through the fitting curve, we can find that the user interest value is gradually decreasing over time. Suppose t is the distance from the published time to current time, then the memory value of interest decay model is defined as $M(M_w = 1 - 0.42t^{0.3})$. The fitting curve is shown in Fig. 2:

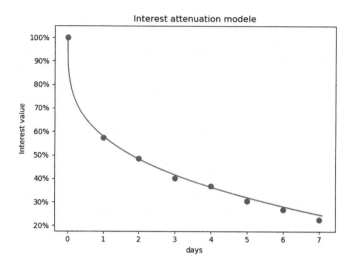

Fig. 2. Fitting curve of the interest decay model.

3.2   Data Processing

For a micro-blog user U_i, we crawled texts, images and tags of his blog. For blog text, $D = \{w_1, w_2, \cdots w_s\}$ is the set contains different words, s represents the number of words appear in the user U_i published blog texts. Since sentence vector can make better use of the syntactic information and semantic features of micro-blog text, we proposes $V(D_j) = V(w_1) + V(w_2) + \cdots + V(w_s)$ as the sentence vector of the published blog text j. To get the interest value of each blog text, we use the interest decay model to calcucate it, and get the memory value $M(D_i)$. $I = \{i_1, i_2, \cdots i_n\}$ is the set of images published in micro-blog, n represents the number of pictures. $T = \{t_1, t_2, \cdots t_q\}$ is the set of user tags.

This paper proposes a multi-TextCNN neural network model to train the micro-blog text. One channel is used to receive the user interest value, another channel is used to receive the sentence vector of the blog text. In this way, we can get the feature set of the blog text $B = \{b_1, b_2, \cdots b_o\}$, o is the number of features. For each picture i, we use the ResNet neural network to obtain the feature map $F = \{f_1, f_2, \cdots f_m\}$, m is the number of features. The features of the tags are constructed by the Bag-of-words model.

3.3   Fusion Based on Images, Blog Texts and Tags

The dimensions of the three feature vectors are different. If we simply splice the features, it will lose some information of the features, and affect the accuracy of the results. So it is necessary to fuse the three feature vectors in an effectively way. The traditional multimodal feature fusion methods are generally linear fusion. Such methods cannot obtain a good fusion effect, so we use Multi-Layer Perception to fuse multi-modal features. We simulate the cognitive process of the human brain, establish a multi-layer structure, and extract the features of the sample from the lower layer to the upper layer. It can be used to form joint feature representations of different types of data. Multi-Layer Perception can train the proportion of different features in the supervised learning model. We can gain the different gravity of these three kinds of features, then we fuse the three different features with the specific gravity as the user multi-modal features.

3.4   Design the Function F

We use the classifier softmax as the function f. f can divide the N dimensions user multi-modal features into the predicted categories $Y = \{y_1, y_2, \cdots y_{10}\}$. Then we define a counting function $Count(y_i)$ to record the probability of each category [15]. Sorting $Count(y_i)$ from high to low, we select the top 3 ranked categories as the user interest, therefore the user interest model is established.

4   Experiment

In this paper, an Interest Mining Model of Micro-blog Users by Using Multi-mode Semantics and Interest Decay Model is proposed. The algorithm has two major tasks: semantic feature representation based on interest decay model and fusion based on the multi-modal semantic feature. Through the establishment of the user interest decay model, we obtained a value that fully and accurately represents a user's current interest level. During the process of feature fusion, we ensured the acquisition of the relations among multi-modal features and generated the user interest model with large size of more precise features. This chapter will verify the performance of this model through the following three sets of experiments:

Experiment 1: Performance evaluation of the semantic feature extraction based on the user interest decay model.

Experiment 2: Performance evaluation of multi-feature semantic fusion algorithm.

Experiment 3: Cold start evaluation experiment based on multi-feature semantic fusion algorithm.

Experiment 4: Performance evaluation experiment of micro-blog user interest mining algorithm based on multimodal data semantics and interest decay model.

4.1   Experimental Data Collection and Processing

We crawled the user information of 10 key categories in Sina microblog which contains: fashion, film, music, animation, games, travel, sports, emotions, food and science. We obtained the ID numbers and URLs of 5700 users and extracted blog texts, user tags and shared images of users. Then we crawled 1648987 images, 214,896 blog texts and 3249 user tags as data sets from 2938 micro-blog users of 10 categories in total. Images, blog texts, and tags data are shown in Table 1:

Table 1. Micro-blog user's data.

Categories	Total	Text	Tag	Image
Fashion	305	20577	191	124325
Film	362	29532	353	233196
Music	268	19573	231	57306
Animation	275	18762	367	168763
Game	345	29726	414	238196
Travel	268	21325	159	105321
Sport	377	25783	485	109132
Emotion	269	15383	379	35766
Food	271	23642	393	211653
Science	198	10593	277	65329

4.2 Experiment 1: Performance Evaluation of the Semantic Feature Extraction Based on the User Interest Decay Model

The method in this section is fitting a user interest decay function curve to calculate the interest retention value of each blog at the moment by analyzing the texting frequencies of typical micro-blog users. Next, we put the interest values as the auxiliary parameters into one channel of the multi-channel text-cnn, and the word vectors of the micro-blog into the other. Finally, we performed the model training, completed the user blog feature extraction with the factor of the interest decay value, and obtained the user interest classification. Compared with the results of the common multi-channel Text-CNN algorithm [16] and the Twitter-LDA algorithm [17], the accuracy of our algorithm has improved greatly. The experimental results are shown in Table 2:

Table 2. Performance evaluation of the semantic feature extraction based on the user interest decay model

Algorithm	F1 rate	Accuracy rate	Recall rate
Multi Text-CNN	68.35%	73.63%	63.07%
Twitter-LDA	67.57%	68.33%	67.52%
Text-CNN based on interest decay	**72.12%**	**74.22%**	**70.02%**

From the above results, the algorithm in this paper is obviously the best among the three. Compared to the multi-channel Text-cnn-based algorithm which takes a random fix value as input. This algorithm generates corresponding user interest values for different blog texts and adaptively adjusts the interest weights to correctly simulate user interest. Compared with the Twitter-LDA algorithm, our algorithm can extract text features more comprehensively without worrying about the over-fitting problem, and also reduce the time complexity.

4.3 Experiment 2: Performance Evaluation of Multimodal Data Fused Algorithm

The method in this section is using the multi-channel Text-CNN model to deeply study the blog texts and obtaining the 64-dimensional feature vectors of all blog texts for each user. Then utilizing the word bag model [18] to classify user tags, and the residual network ResNet [19] to obtain users images with a 1000-dimension feature vector. Finally fusing these three features by using the Multi-Layer Perceptron to obtain user interest. Compared with the results of the simple ResNet image classification algorithm, the multi-channel text-cnn text classification algorithm, the word bag model label classification algorithm, and the SVM fusion algorithm based on three features, the accuracy of our algorithm is improved greatly. The results are shown in Table 3:

Table 3. Performance evaluation of multimodal data fused algorithm

Algorithm	F1 rate	Accurancy rate	Recall rate
ResNet	57.95%	56.38%	61.27%
Bag of words	60.67%	55.25%	72.09%
Multi Text-CNN	68.35%	73.63%	63.07%
Multimodal data fused (SVM)	73.51%	84.27%	63.72%
Multimodal data fused (MLP)	**78.38%**	**81.57%**	**77.82%**

From the above results, the algorithm in this paper is the most accurate one among these five algorithms. One reason for the inaccurate results of ResNet image classification algorithm is that the classifier is extremely terrible in emotions and science classification recognition. Because both types appear in text form, which leads to the inaccurate recognition of the images, resulting in a low recognition rate of the algorithm. The reason for the poor results of the word bag model is that it is difficult to distinguish the tags of animation and games. The two tags are close to each other, so the similarity in feature extraction leads to poor user interest mining accuracy. The multi-channel Text-CNN text classification algorithm is the most accurate algorithm for single-dimensional user interest mining. Compared to images and tags, the text is more likely to reflect the user's interest. But since it only involves one type of feature, the accuracy is not high enough either. The using of SVM fusion algorithm based on three features improved the accuracy by a large extent. However, due to the limitations of the SVM algorithm, it's unable to extract the correlations among features. Therefore, the feature fusion is only a simple weight addition, which makes the classification result less accurate. In this paper, we use the multi-layer perceptron to train relations among the three-dimensional features. By using the correlations to obtain the corresponding weights of relevant features, we make the user interest feature distribution more precise and achieve better user interest mining results.

4.4 Experiment 3: Cold Start Evaluation Experiment Based on Multimodal Data Fused Algorithm

The experiments in this section are based on cold-start users. The multi-modal data fusion model is compared with the model based on the micro-blog user interest mining algorithm TCID-MUIM and collaborative filtering algorithm [20]. The accuracy is improved by the Multimodal data fused algorithm. The experiments result proves that the multi-modal feature fusion method can extract more features and improve the accuracy to some extent. The experimental results in this paper are shown in the following Table 4:

Table 4. Cold start evaluation experiment based on multimodal data fused algorithm

Algorithm	F1 rate	Accurancy rate	Recall rate
TCID-MUIM	55.39%	50.74%	61.23%
Collaborative Filtering	50.66%	46.22%	55.87%
Multimodal data fused (MLP)	**62.71%**	**54.71%**	**69.72%**

The experiments results show that the proposed algorithm is more accurate than the collaborative filtering algorithm and TCID-MUIM. For cold-start users, it is difficult to obtain their social relationships. Due to this reason, we cannot conduct an effective analysis, so the F1 value of the collaborative filtering algorithm is low. TCID-MUIM algorithm has the same problem, it doesn't fuse the multimodal data. This causes the result that it can't solve the cold start. On the contrary, the algorithm of this paper can mine the user's information from multiple angles. We integrate it with user-owned tags and pictures and texts, thus improving the accuracy of the algorithm.

4.5 Experiment 4: Performance Evaluation Experiment of Micro-blog User Interest Mining Algorithm Based on Multimodal Data Semantics and Interest Decay Model

The method in this section is using the interest decay function to obtain the interest value of users at different times and then inputting the interest value into the feature extraction model as an auxiliary parameter. We obtain multi-dimensional user interest features and use the Multi-Layer Perceptron to fuse the features to obtain the user interests. The result in this section is compared with the three commonly used micro-blog user interest mining models. The accuracy of user category recognition of different interest models is obtained. The recognition accuracy of the micro-blog user interest mining algorithm TCID-MUIM is 78.22%, which is based on text clustering and interest decay. The accuracy of micro-blog user interest recognition based on SVM model fusion is 84.27%. The accuracy of micro-blog user interest recognition based on the fast-RNN model [21] is 78.35%. It turns out that the multi-layer perceptron which combines the interest decay model with multi-modal data features has the best accuracy of identifying the user interest categories. The comparison results of the four different models are shown in Table 5:

Table 5. Performance evaluation experiment of micro-blog user interest mining algorithm based on multimodal data semantics and interest decay model

Algorithm	F1 rate	Accurancy rate	Recall rate
TCID-MUIM	72.39%	78.22%	65.61%
Fast-RNN	74.63%	78.35%	70.53%
Multimodal data fused	73.51%	84.27%	63.72%
IDMFM	**78.97%**	**85.83%**	**79.23%**

The results show that the model proposed in this paper has an accuracy rate of 85.83%, a recall rate of 79.23%, and an F1 value of 78.97%, which proves a good classification effect when predicting the user interest category. Compared with the best user interest recognition models among the others, it improved the accuracy rate by 2%, the recall rate by 8%, and the F1 value by 3%. It is enough to show that the multi-modal data combined with the interest decay model has a better user interest recognition effect than the traditional models. The evaluation results generated by four different user interest models are as follows:

(1) Evaluation results of TCID-MUIM model: The analysis of identifying the training results by generating the confusion matrix, turns out that the classification effect of the category of science is the worst. It shows that science is a macro concept, the information sent by users under this category is relatively simple, and all of them are science-related blog texts. So, the interest migration degree is not significant over time. But the number of micro-blogs generated by such users is much less than other categories, which leads to the cold start phenomenon. Since the model specifies a time factor, the cold start problem cannot be well resolved. That's why the results in the category prediction are not very good.

(2) Evaluation results of the micro-blog user model based on multi-modal data: The F1 value of this algorithm is slightly better than the above model, but the categories of games and animations are not well recognized. One reason is that these two categories are similar to each other, which makes it easier to drive the interest between the two. That means the user may like animations for a while but soon change to games. Since the model is not designed to consider the drift of interest, it's difficult to accurately distinguish categories with a great change in interest accurately.

(3) Evaluation results of the ada-boost model based on Fast-RNN: Although the accuracy of this type is lower than the above model, the recall rate is greatly improved, resulting in a better F1 value. This model mainly relies on a strong classification model which consists of multiple weak classification models. So, the evaluation result on the F1 value is better than others, which means there is no case where the accuracy rate is high, but the recall rate is low. However since the weak models constructed by the model do not consider the problem of interest drift, the effect is slightly inferior to the model in this paper.

(4) Multi-modal data fusion model evaluation based on an interest decay model (IDMFM): Compared with the best single-mode data blog, each evaluation measure is increased by more than 5%, indicating that the addition of the interest decay model can more simulate the user interest drift accurately. Meanwhile, the Multi-Layer Perceptron can be used to mine the relations among various models, which makes the user interest mining effect even better.

5   Conclusion

This paper proposes an Interest Mining Model of Micro-blog Users by Using Multi-modal Semantics and Interest Decay Model to represent user interest and analyzes the data representations. In the experiment, we analyze three different modalities of 10 categories of micro-blog users. The experiment results indicate that the prediction effect of the user interest mining by fusing the multi-layer perceptron with the multi-modal features is better than simply splicing the features. The user interest mining model after adding the interest decay model can better express the user interest. The experiment results have proved the effectiveness and accuracy of this algorithm. What needs to be improved is that, although interest classifications have included the categories as much as possible, there are still many types remain to be covered. Besides, although the model has been fused with three different features for classification, there are still misjudgments for very similar user interest categories. In the future, more dimensional features can be incorporated without considering the time complexity, such as the browsing data of users, by which the accuracy of the model can be further improved.

References

1. Wen, K.: Survey of microblog and Chinese microblog information processing. J. Chin. Inf. Process. **26**(6), 27–37 (2012)
2. Efimova, L. et al.: Finding "the life between buildings": an approach for defining a weblog community. In: Internet Research 6.0: Internet Generations. Association of Internet Researchers (2005)
3. Cong, L., et al.: A collaborative filtering recommendation algorithm based on domain nearest neighbor. J. Comput. Res. Dev. **9**, 1532–1538 (2008)
4. Jing, P., et al.: A novel text clustering algorithm based on inner product space model of semantic. Chin. J. Comput. **8**, 1354–1363 (2007)
5. Yun, Q., et al.: User interest modeling approach based on short text of micro-blog. Comput. Eng. **40**(2), 275–279 (2014)
6. Juan, W., et al.: Research on emotional analysis of short text in microblog based on improved theme model. China Comput. Commun. **6**, 134–141 (2019)
7. Donghui, L., et al.: Research on data fusion of adaptive weighted multi-source sensor. Comput. Mater. Continua **61**(3), 1217–1231 (2019)
8. Man, Y.: Feature extension for short text categorization using frequent term sets. In: Aleskerov, F., et al. (eds.) ITQM, pp. 663–670. Elsevier (2014)
9. Banerjee, S., et al.: Clustering short texts using wikipedia. In: SIGIR 2007: Proceedings of the 30th Annual International ACM SIGIR Conference on Research and Development in Information Retrieval, pp. 787–788. ACM (2007)
10. Sriram, B. et al.: Short text classification in twitter to improve information filtering. In: Crestani, F., et al. (eds.) SIGIR, pp. 841–842. ACM (2010)
11. Zeng, J., et al.: Research on user interest recognition based on multi - mode data. Inf. Sci. **36**(1), 124–129 (2018)
12. Yu, W., et al.: Thinking and idea of network public opinion management in new media era. J. Dalian Marit. Univ. **17**(3), 53–58 (2018)
13. Qin, Y., et al.: Microblog user interest mining based on text clustering and interest decay. Appl. Res. Comput. **5**, 1–3 (2019)
14. Weijin, J., et al.: A new time-aware collaborative filtering intelligent recommendation system. Comput. Mater. Continua **61**(2), 849–859 (2019)
15. Hongbin, W., et al.: PMS-sorting: a new sorting algorithm based on similarity. Comput. Mater. Continua **59**(1), 229–237 (2019)
16. Jiang, M., et al.: Text extraction in video and Images. Comput. Sci. **44**(S2), 8–18 (2017)
17. Zhao, W.X., et al.: Comparing twitter and traditional media using topic models. In: Clough, P., et al. (eds.) ECIR 2011. LNCS, vol. 6611, pp. 338–349. Springer, Heidelberg (2011). https://doi.org/10.1007/978-3-642-20161-5_34
18. Wang, W., et al.: Sentiment analysis of micro-blog based on CNN and Tree-LSTM. Comput. Sci. **5**, 1371–1375 (2019)
19. He, K., et al.: Deep residual learning for image recognition. CoRR. abs/1512. 03385 (2015)
20. Qin, X., et al.: A personalized micro-blog recommendation algorithm based on collaborative filtering. Softw. Eng. **20**, 14–17 (2017)
21. Wan, S., Li, B., Zhang, A., Wang, K., Li, X.: Vertical and sequential sentiment analysis of micro-blog topic. In: Gan, G., Li, B., Li, X., Wang, S. (eds.) ADMA 2018. LNCS (LNAI), vol. 11323, pp. 353–363. Springer, Cham (2018). https://doi.org/10.1007/978-3-030-05090-0_30

A MOPSO Based Design Exploration Algorithm for Micro-processor with Elitist Learning Strategy

Niangao Liu[1(✉)] [iD] and Tian Zhi[2]

[1] School of Information Science and Technology,
University of Science and Technology of China, Hefei 230026, China
andygao@mail.ustc.edu.cn
[2] State Key Laboratory of Computer Architecture, ICT, CAS, Beijing, China

Abstract. As the continuous development of processor technology, the design space exploration (DSE) has a critical impact on overall performance. However, due to the lack of systematic way, DSE is usually time-consuming and unaccomplished, leaving much of the opportunity unexploited. In this paper, on the basis of particle swarm optimization (PSO), a multi-object optimization algorithm with elitist learning strategy (ELS) is proposed, with which we construct a prediction model for microprocessor design in the purpose of optimizing performance and efficiency. The proposed algorithm is compared with two other multi-object optimization algorithms by three metrics. The experiment conducted shows the proposed algorithm is more efficient and more effective.

Keywords: Design space exploration · Multi-objective particle swarm optimization · Elitist learning strategy · Prediction model

1 Introduction

Since the birth of computers, the architecture and performance of microprocessor has developed rapidly, which is in good agreement with the famous Moore's law in the past decades. However, in recent years, with the continuous development of integrated circuit technology and the increasing diversification of applications, the complexity of microprocessor is ever increasing [1–8]. After decades of rapid development of microprocessor, there are theoretical bottlenecks and problems in many aspects. If these problems are not solved, they will greatly affect the future of microprocessor.

When designing a microprocessor, we can obtain various design schemes to meet different performance, power and reliability constraints by the search and analysis of the design space, which is called design space exploration (DSE). With the continuous reduction of the feature size in integrated circuits and the increasing integration of chips, more and more factors need to be considered. This is a great challenge for microprocessor architects, because the size of design space grows exponentially with the number of relevant design parameters. It is very time-consuming to simulate the

© Springer Nature Singapore Pte Ltd. 2020
X. Sun et al. (Eds.): ICAIS 2020, CCIS 1254, pp. 490–502, 2020.
https://doi.org/10.1007/978-981-15-8101-4_44

behavior of microprocessor and evaluate each parameter, which is difficult to meet the research requirements of microprocessor design. In order to reduce the cost of simulation, various prediction model were proposed, such as linear regression prediction model [9], genetic algorithm model [10], neural network model [11], etc. At present, a lot of achievements have been made in the analysis and prediction models, but there are still some problems as:

1) The convergence speed of some optimization algorithms is slow, and the algorithms are easy to fall into local optima.
2) There are too many training parameters which lead to a high training cost in some prediction models.
3) The microprocessor design space exploration based on predictive model mainly focused on the construction of the model, while the research on searching the optimal solution set of prediction model was less.

PSO is a relatively new intelligent optimization algorithm, which has strong optimization ability and fast convergence speed [12]. PSO has been widely used in multimodal optimization problems [13–15]. Multi-objective particle swarm optimization (MOPSO) is proposed by Coello *et al.* [16]. The algorithm introduces external archive to store Pareto optimal set, and uses roulette method to select *gbest* from the archive. Through these improvements, PSO can be applied to multi-objective optimization. MOPSO has been successfully applied in solving multi-objective optimization problems. However, the standard MOPSO algorithm has some shortcomings, such as local optima and slow convergence speed.

In this paper, based on PSO, a multi-objective particle swarm optimization algorithm with ELS (ELSMOPSO) is proposed to optimize the prediction model of microprocessor parameter design. In the process of updating the archive, the mechanism of ELS is introduced, which enables particles getting rid of the local optima that may occur in the optimization process, avoiding premature convergence to the sub optimal solution, so as to improve the search ability of the algorithm.

2 Basic Concepts

2.1 DSE

With the increasing complexity of microprocessor design, especially the development of multi-core technology, there are more and more parameters related to microprocessor design, which makes the design space increase exponentially. The method of exhaustively simulating all design parameters to obtain the optimal set is obviously not allowed in nowadays. DSE, on the other hand, is the process of finding the optimal parameter design scheme set to meet the design requirements by using the existing resources in a reasonable time, so as to solve the problem of high experimental cost, as shown in Fig. 1. We can figure out from Fig. 1 that in order to improve the efficiency of design space exploration, there are mainly two methods:

1) Shortening the simulation time. The sampling technology we used can greatly reduce the execution time.
2) Using efficient multi-objective optimization algorithm.

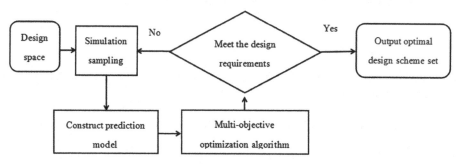

Fig. 1. DSE technique based on multi-objective optimization algorithm

2.2 PSO

PSO algorithm was invented by Kennedy and Eberhart in 1995 [12]. In a population of size N, the position of the i-th particle is denoted as $x_i = (x_{i1}, x_{i2}, \ldots, x_{iD})$. The historically best position is represented as $p_i = (p_{i1}, p_{i2}, \ldots, p_{iD})$. The best position it has found by the whole population is denoted as $p_g = (p_{g1}, p_{g2}, \ldots, p_{gD})$. The rate to change the position of the i-th particle is called velocity and is represented as $v_i = (v_{i1}, v_{i2}, \ldots, v_{iD})$. At each iteration step t, the i-th particle updates its d-th dimension of speed and position according to the formulas (1) and (2).

$$v_{id}(t) = \chi \left(v_{id}(t-1) + c_1 r_1 (p_{id} - x_{id}(t-1)) + c_2 r_2 (p_{gd} - x_{id}(t-1))\right), \quad (1)$$

$$x_{id}(t) = x_{id}(t-1) + v_{id}(t), \quad (2)$$

Where χ is the inertial factor, c_1 and c_2 are constants, usually 2.05. r_1 and r_2 are random numbers uniformly distributed in [0, 1]. The value of $\pm V_{MAX}$ is usually set to be the lower and upper bounds of the allowed search ranges as suggested in [17].

2.3 Multi-objective Optimization Problems

A maximization multi-objective optimization problem can be expressed as follows:

$$\begin{cases} \max \quad y = f(x) = (f_1(x), f_2(x), \ldots, f_m(x))^T; \\ s.t. \quad g_j(x) \leq 0 \, j = 1, 2, \ldots, p; \\ h_k(x) = 0 \, k = 1, 2, \ldots, q; \end{cases} \quad (3)$$

Where $x = \{x_1, x_2, \ldots x_D\} \in \Omega$ is the D-dimension decision space, $y = \{y_1, y_2, \ldots y_m\} \in \Lambda$ is the m-dimension objective function space, $g_j(x)$ is the inequality constraint function, and $h_k(x)$ is the equality constraint function. Several concepts of multi-objective optimization problems are defined as follows [18].

Definition 1 (Pareto domination): Given two vectors $u = \{u_1, u_2, \ldots, u_m\} \in \Lambda$ and $v = \{v_1, v_2, \ldots, v_m\} \in \Lambda$, we say that u dominates v (also write as $u \succ v$) if and only if: $\forall i \in \{1, 2, \ldots, m\} : u_i \geq v_i$, and $\exists j \in \{1, 2, \ldots m\} : u_j > v_j$.

Definition 2 (Pareto optimal): Given a vector $x' \in \Omega$, we say that x' is Pareto optimal if there is no $x'' \in \Omega$ s.t. $f(x'') \succ f(x')$.

Definition 3 (Pareto optimal set): Pareto optimal set is defined as:

$$P_s = \{x \in \Omega \mid \neg \exists x' \in \Omega, \ s.t. f(x') \succ f(x)\}.$$

Definition 4 (Pareto front): Pareto front is defined as:

$$P_f = \{y = f(x) \mid x \in P_s\}.$$

3   ELSMOPSO

In this section, we propose a MOPSO with ELS to avoid local optima and speed up the convergence progress.

3.1   Pbest and Gbest

In ELSMOPSO, a particle's flight is influenced by both the best position it has found (denoted as *pbest*) and the best position the whole population has found so far (denoted as *gbest*). Consequently, it is very important how choose them.

Each particle's *pbest* is selected according to the Pareto domination relationship between the current position of the particle and its *pbest*, which can be divided into three situations: 1) If the current position is dominated by its *pbest*, then its *pbest* is kept; 2) Otherwise, the current position replaces its *pbest*; 3) If neither of them is dominated by the other, then one of them will be randomly selected as its new *pbest*.

Each particle's *gbest* is to randomly select a particle from the archive, so as to realize information sharing and guide the particle to further search Pareto optimal.

3.2   Archive Update

A lot of Pareto optimal solutions will be found along the search process. ELSMOPSO uses an external archive (denoted as *REP*) to store the non-dominated solutions found at each iteration [16]. With the increase of algorithm iterations, more and more optimal solutions will be found. Therefore, the archive *REP* need to be updated at the end of every generation. The maximum capacity of the archive is denoted as N_{REP}. The archive update process is as follows:

- Step 1) A new set S is initialized to be empty. All the particles of the population and all the solutions in the old archive *REP* are added into the set S.

- Step 2) Execute the ELS on each particle in the archive *REP* and add all the new particles into the set *S*.
- Step 3) Perform the determine non-dominated solutions procedure (see Table 1) on the *S* to determine all the non-dominated solutions and stored them in the *REP*.
- Step 4) If *flag* == false, the duplicate particles in the archive *REP* will be deleted.
- Step 5) If $|REP| \geq N_{REP}$, calculate the crowding distance of the particles in *REP*, and arrange the optimal solution in descending order according to the crowding distance, keep the first N_{REP} optimal solution, delete the rest, and *flag* = true.

Table 1. The pseudo-code of determining Non-dominate solutions

Procedure Determine Non-dominated Solutions
1: begin
2: $REP = \{\}$;
3: for each solution i in the set S
4: f = true;
5: for each solution j in the set S
6:   if j dominates i
7:    f = false;
8:    break;
9:   end if
10: end for //j
11: if f == true
12:   Add solution i into set REP;
13: end if
14: end for //i
15:end

The ELS used in step 2 is first introduced into adaptive PSO by Zhan to solve the problem of falling into local optima in the process of single objective optimization [19]. In ELSMOPSO, the idea of Gaussian perturbation is introduced for all particles in the archive to avoid local optima and speed up the convergence progress. The pseudo code is shown in Table 2. Gaussian(0, 1) produces a random number, which satisfies the one-dimensional normal distribution with mean zero and standard deviation one.

In the process of perturbation, if $E_{id} = x_{max,d}$ and r is greater than 0, it will certainly cross the boundary after the perturbation is executed. In this case, the value of E_{id} is its upper bound $x_{max,d}$, that is, the local perturbation operation will be not effective. Therefore, in order to make the perturbation operation work, it is necessary to find a dimension whose value is not equal to its upper boundary as perturbation object again. In the same way, when $E_{id} = x_{max,d}$ and r is less than 0, it is also necessary to find another dimension whose value is not equal to its lower boundary as the perturbation object.

In step 4, *flag* is the identification of whether to de-duplicate particles in the archive, and the initial value is false before the start of ELSMOPSO iteration. In the process of ELSMOPSO iteration, the archive *REP* is the *gbest* of all particles. If there are multiple identical particles in the *REP*, they will be selected as *gbest* with higher probability than other particles, resulting in uneven distribution of Pareto optimal solution set. In order to make the Pareto optimal set distribution more uniform, it is necessary to de-duplicate particles in *REP* in the initial iteration. When the number of non-dominant solutions is greater than N_{REP}, the particles with small distance can be removed according to the crowding degree sort, so no need to de-duplicate particles in *REP* in the later stage.

Table 2. The pseudo-code of ELS

```
Procedure ELS
1: begin
2:   for each solution REP_i in the arcihve REP
3:       E_i = REP_i;
4:       r = Gaussian(0,1);
5:       d = rand(1,D);
6:       if r > 0
7:           while E_id == x_max,d
8:               d = rand(1,D);
9:           end while
10:      else
11:          while E_id == x_min,d
12:              d = rand(1,D);
13:          end while
14:      end if
15:      E_id = E_id + (X_max,d − X_min,d) * r;
16:      Keep the E_id within the range [ X_min,d , X_max,d ];
17:      Evaluate E_i ;
18:  end for
19:end
```

3.3 ELSMOPSO Main Algorithm

The algorithm of ELSMOPSO is the following.

1) Initialize the population P and their velocity, the size of P is N:

for $i = 1$ to N

Randomly initialize $P[i]$;
$pbest[i] = P[i]$;
Randomly initialize $V[i]$;

2) Evaluate all the particles in P.
3) All the particles that represent non-dominated solutions are stored in the external archive *REP*.
4) For each particle in P, randomly select a particle in the archive *REP* as its *gbest*, update its velocity and position with formula (1) and (2), evaluate the particle, and then update its *pbest* according to the principle introduced in Sect. 3.1.
5) Use the method described in Sect. 3.2 to update the archive *REP*.
6) If the maximum number of iterations is reached, stop the iteration and output the Pareto optimal set from the archive *REP*, otherwise go to step 4).

4 Prediction Model of Microprocessor Design

ELSMOPSO should have a good performance in solving the problem of microprocessor parameter design.

4.1 Simulation Framework and Benchmarks

At present, many kinds of multi-core simulators, such as GEMS, M5, GEM5 and SESC, have been developed in academic circles. Among them, gem5 is widely used. In this paper, we use GEM5 to model for performance and power. At the same time, we use seven benchmarks from SPEC2k (ammp, applu, equake, gcc, gzip, mesa, twolf) to evaluate the design space.

4.2 Configuration Sampling

In this paper, the sampling of microprocessor design configuration are fitted to obtain the objective functions, and then the prediction model is constructed. The design parameters we need to explore is shown in Table 3, which include 13 design parameters. These parameters can be combined into numerous different parameter configurations, and the performance of these configurations are comprehensively evaluated with seven benchmarks, which will further increase the number of simulations. For this design space, we randomly generate 4000 design configurations for regression model. This sampling configuration set is simulated with seven benchmarks, providing seven sets of observed responses, and then we can generate seven application-specific models. Because the methods of constructing these models are the same, we specify the ammp application-specific model as an example.

Table 3. Parameters within a group are varied together. A range $i::j::k$ denotes a set of possible values from i to k in steps of j.

Design parameters	Range	x_i	$|x_i|$	Design parameters	Range	x_i	$|x_i|$
depth	9::3:: 36	x_1	10	fix_lat	1::1::13	x_8	13
width	4,8,16	x_2	3	fpu_lat	2::1::24	x_9	23
gpr_phys	40::10::130	x_3	10	d2cache_lat	3::1::37	x_{10}	35
br_resv	6::1::15	x_4	10	l2cache_size	11::1::15	x_{11}	5
dmem_lat	34::1::307	x_5	274	icache_size	7::1::11	x_{12}	5
load_lat	1::1::19	x_6	19	dcache_size	6::1::10	x_{13}	5
br_lat	1::1::5	x_7	5				

Table 4 gives some basic information about the performance values and power values of the benchmark ammp on these sampling configurations. It can be seen from the table that the performance value is small, while the power value is large. In order to make the value of performance and power comparable, the data needs to be preprocessed. We carry out standard 0-1 transformation, and the values of performance and power will be transformed to [0, 1] interval.

Table 4. Basic information about the values of performance and power of benchmark ammp.

Name	Max	Min	Mean	Max/Min
Performance	1.574	0.1247	0.615	12.62
Power	224132.4	5238.7	35932.34	42.78
Power/Performance	142396.7	42010.4	58426.6	3.4

4.3 The Regression Model of Microprocessor Parameter Design

In the process of microprocessor design, it is a multi-objective optimization problem. In this paper, these parameters are predictors, the performance and power attribute values are observed responses, and then we formulate a regression model. Two sub objective functions of performance and power are obtained as follow:

$$f_i(x) = a_0 + \sum_{j=1}^{D} a_j x_j \quad i = 1, 2 \tag{4}$$

Where D is the dimension of the design space and a_j is the coefficient, and the regression model of microprocessor parameter design is constructed as follow:

$$\text{Maximize } F = (f_1(x), f_2(x)), \tag{5}$$

Then we can use the ELSMOPSO introduced in Sect. 3 to optimize the model.

5 Experimental Setup and Results

5.1 Performance Measures

In order to evaluate the prediction model of microprocessor parameter design based on ELSMOPSO, we use three algorithm performance metrics: maximum spread, spacing and coverage.

Maximum Spread (M-metric). The M-metric proposed by Deb [20]. It is defined as follows:

$$M = \sqrt{\sum_{k=1}^{m} \left(\max\{f_k^i\}_{i=1}^n - \min\{f_k^i\}_{i=1}^n \right)^2} \tag{6}$$

Where m is the dimension of the objective space. and n is the number of solutions of non-dominated solution set. The larger the M value is, the wider the range of solution set is.

Spacing (S-metric). Schott proposed a method to measure the distribution uniformity of non-dominated solution set [21]. S-metric is defined as

$$S = \sqrt{\frac{1}{n-1} \sum_{i=1}^{n} \left(d_i - \bar{d} \right)^2} \tag{7}$$

Where, $d_i = \min\limits_{1 \leq j \leq n, i \neq j} \sum\limits_{k=1}^{m} \left| f_k^i - f_k^j \right|, \bar{d} = \frac{1}{n} \sum\limits_{i=1}^{n} d_i$, n is the number of solutions of non-dominated solution set and m is the dimension of objective space. The more S value is, the more uniform the distribution of the solution set is.

Coverage (C-metric). The C-metric is proposed by Zizter [22]. It is define as

$$C(A, B) = \frac{|\{b \in B | \exists a \in A, s.t.a \succ b\}|}{|B|} \tag{8}$$

Where $| * |$ indicates the number of elements in the set $*$. When $C(A, B) < C(B, A)$, it means that solution set B is better than solution set A.

5.2 Experimental Setup

In order to verify the effectiveness of the algorithm and model, we select Nondominated Sorting Genetic Algorithm II (NSGA-II) and MOPSO to optimize the model, and compare with the experiment based on ELSMOPSO optimization. NSGA-II was proposed by DEB et al. [23], an improvement of NSGA, which is an excellent multi-objective evolutionary algorithm. The parameter settings of NSGA-II, MOPSO and ELSPSO are shown in Table 5.

For the prediction model in Sect. 4, NSGA-II, MOPSO and ELSMOPSO are used to optimize the model, which are run independently for 30 times, respectively recording the best value, worst value, average value and median value of the three algorithms for the three metrics.

Table 5. The parameters of NSGA-II, MOPSO and ELSMOPSO.

Algorithms	Parameters settings
NSGA-II	$N = 100$, $p_x = 0.9$, $p_m = 1/D$, $\eta_c = 20$, and $\eta_m = 20$
MOPSO	$N = 100$, $REP = 100$, $c_1 = c_2 = 2.05$, and $\chi = 0.729$
ELSMOPSO	$N = 50$, $REP = 100$, $c_1 = c_2 = 2.05$, and $\chi = 0.729$

5.3 Results and Analysis

Figure 2 shows the Pareto front obtained by random sampling of 30 experimental results of NSGA-II, MOPSO and ELSMOPSO. It can be seen from the figure that the Pareto optimal set obtained by ELSMOPSO is more uniform and spread than that obtained by NSGA-II and MOPSO.

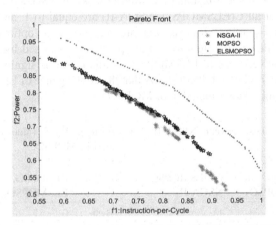

Fig. 2. Pareto fronts produced by NSGA-II, MOPSO and ELSMOPSO.

Table 6 is the statistical results of the M values of the three algorithms. The M mean value of ELSMOPSO is larger than that of NSGA-II and MOPSO, which shows that the algorithm can get a wider optimal set than NSGA-II and MOPSO.

Table 6. Distribution of M values.

M	NSGA-II	MOPSO	ELSMOPSO
Best	0.6779	0.5080	0.5635
Worst	0.2835	0.2122	0.5050
Mean	0.4817	0.3533	**0.5635**
Median	0.4939	0.3481	0.5635

Table 7 is the statistical results of the S of the three algorithms. The S mean value of ELSMOPSO is the smallest, which indicates that the distribution of the Pareto optimal set obtained by ELSMOPSO is the most uniform.

Table 7. Distribution of S values.

S	NSGA-II	MOPSO	ELSMOPSO
Best	7.5875e−05	1.3471e−04	1.9095e−04
Worst	4.2826e−04	6.9686e−04	3.0364e−04
Mean	2.6926e−04	3.3150e−04	**2.5004e−04**
Median	2.6835e−04	2.9548e−04	2.4505e−04

Table 8 is the statistical results of C-Metric between NSGA-II and ELSMOPSO. It can be seen that all C(ELSMOPSO, NSGA-II) are equal to 1, and all C(NSGA-II, ELSMOPSO) are equal to 0. It means that all solutions of the optimal set obtained by ELSMOPSO dominate all solutions of the optimal set obtained by NSGA-II, which shows that the convergence of ELSMOPSO on this model is significantly better than that of NSGA-II. Similarly, Table 9 shows that the convergence of ELSMOPSO on this model is significantly better than that of MOPSO.

Table 8. The C values between NSGA-II and ELSMOPSO.

C	C(NSGA-II, LSMOPSO)	C(ELSMOPSO, NSGA-II)
Best	0	1
Worst	0	1
Mean	0	**1**
Median	0	1

Table 9. The C values between MOPSO and ELSMOPSO.

C	C(MOPSO, ELSMOPSO)	C(ELSMOPS, MOPSO)
Best	0	1
Worst	0	1
Mean	0	**1**
Median	0	1

Based on the above analysis, the ELSMOPSO proposed in this paper is of good performance in the case of optimizing the prediction model of microprocessor parameter design, with good convergence speed and wide range of solution set distribution. Additionally, the obtained design scheme distribution is relatively uniform. The diversity of optimal solution set provides more solutions for architects.

6 Conclusion

The algorithm of PSO is simple and with less parameters to be adjusted, it's easy to implement in scientific research and engineering. That's why it has been paid great attention to and has been widely used in many fields. Aiming at the problem of micro-processor parameter design optimization, we derive the regression prediction model for performance and power by fitting the sampling of microprocessor parameter design. On the basis of PSO, we propose the ELSMOPSO algorithm with which we used to optimize the model. Our experiment shows that the convergence speed of ELSMOPSO is fast, and the Pareto optimal set is of good breadth and uniformity, which makes ELSMOPSO a sound and reasonable choice for architects.

References

1. Chen, Y., et al.: Dadiannao: a machine-learning supercomputer. In: IEEE/ACM International Symposium on Microarchitecture, pp. 609–622 (2015)
2. Du, Z., Fasthuber, R., Chen, T., Ienne, P., Temam, O.: Shidiannao: shifting vision processing closer to the sensor. In: ISCA'15 Proceedings of the 42nd Annual International Symposium on Computer Architecture (2015)
3. Liu, D., et al.: Pudiannao: a polyvalent machine learning accelerator. ACM SIGPLAN Notices 50, 369–381 (2015)
4. Zhang, S., et al.: Cambricon-x: an accelerator for sparse neural networks. In: IEEE/ACM International Symposium on Microarchitecture, pp. 1–12 (2016)
5. Liu, S., et al.: Cambricon: an instruction set architecture for neural networks. In: 2016 ACM/IEEE 43rd Annual International Symposium on Computer Architecture (ISCA) (2016)
6. Chen, T., et al.: Benchnn: on the broad potential application scope of hardware neural network accelerators. In: IISWC 2012, pp. 36–45 (2012)
7. Chen, T., et al.: Diannao: a small-footprint high-throughput accelerator for ubiquitous machine-learning. In: Proceedings of the 19th International Conference on Architectural Support for Programming Languages and Operating Systems, pp. 269–284. ACM (2014)
8. Du, Z., Lingamneni, A., Chen, Y., Palem, K.V., Temam, O., Wu, C.: Leveraging the error resilience of neural networks for designing highly energy efficient accelerators. IEEE Trans. Comput. Aided Des. Integr. Circuits Syst. 34(8), 1223–1235 (2015)
9. Joseph, P.J., Vaswani, K., Thazhuthaveetil, M.J.: Construction and use of linear regression models for processor performance analysis. In: The Twelfth International Symposium on High-Performance Computer Architecture (2006)
10. Cook, H., Skadron, K.: Predictive design space exploration using genetically programmed response surfaces. In: Proceedings of the 45th Design Automation Conference, DAC 2008, Anaheim, CA, USA, 8–13 June (2008)
11. Hamerly, G., Perelman, E., Lau, J., Calder, B., Sherwood, T.: Using machine learning to guide architecture simulation. J. Mach. Learn. Res. 7(3), 343–378 (2006)
12. Kennedy, J., Eberhart, R.: Particle swarm optimization. In: Proceedings of ICNN 1995 - International Conference on Neural Networks (1995)
13. Wang, J., Ju, C.W., Gao, Y., Sangaiah, A.K., Kim, G.J.: A PSO based energy efficient coverage control algorithm for wireless sensor networks. Comput. Mater. Continua 56, 433–446 (2018)
14. Mamoun, M.E., Mahmoud, Z., Kaddour, S.: SVM model selection using PSO for learning handwritten arabic characters. Comput. Mater. Continua 61, 995–1008 (2019)
15. Liu, Z., Xiang, B., Song, Y.Q., Lu, H., Liu, Q.F.: An improved unsupervised image segmentation method based on multi-objective particle swarm optimization clustering algorithm. Comput. Mater. Continua 58(2), 451–461 (2019)
16. Coello, C.A.C., Pulido, G.T., Lechuga, M.S.: Handling multiple objectives with particle swarm optimization. IEEE Trans. Evol. Comput. 8(3), 256–279 (2004)
17. Kennedy, J., Eberhart, R.: Swarm Intelligence. Morgan Kaufmann, San Fransisco (2001)

18. Reyes-Sierra, M., Coello, C.C.A.: Multi-objective particle swarm optimizers: a survey of the state-of-the-art. Int. J Comput. Intell. Res. **2**(3), 287–308 (2006)
19. Zhan, Z.H., Zhang, J., Li, Y., Chung, H.H.: Adaptive particle swarm optimization. IEEE Trans. Syst. Man Cybern. Part B Cybern. A Publ. IEEE Syst. Man Cybern. Soc. **39**(6), 1362–1381 (2010)
20. Deb, K.: Multi-Objective Optimisation Using Evolutionary Algorithms: An Introduction. Wiley, Hoboken (2001)
21. Schott, J.: Fault tolerant design using single and multicriteria genetic algorithm optimization, p. 203 (1995)
22. Zitzler, E., Thiele, L.: Multiobjective evolutionary algorithms: a comparative case study and the strength pareto approach. IEEE Trans. Evol. Comput. **3**, 257–271 (2000)
23. Deb, K., Pratap, A., Agarwal, S., Meyarivan, T.: A fast and elitist multiobjective genetic algorithm: NSGA-ii. IEEE Trans. Evol. Comput. **6**, 182–197 (2002)

A Watermarking Scheme Based on New Adaptive Parameter Strategy with Preserved PSNR

Wenbing Wang[1,2]([✉]), Fenlin Liu[1], and Daofu Gong[1]

[1] PLA Strategic Support Force Information Engineering University, Zhengzhou 450001, China
2007009@zzuli.edu.cn, liufenlin@vip.sina.com.cn
[2] Software Engineering College, Zhengzhou University of Light Industry, Zhengzhou 450000, China

Abstract. Robust watermarking is an effective way to protect an image copyright. This paper proposes a watermarking scheme with peak signal noise ratio (PSNR) guarantee. With the resistance of discrete wavelet transform (DWT) to image processing and singular value decomposition (SVD) to geometric attacks, the scheme embeds watermark based on difference quantization. The embedding strength of watermarks relies on the embedding parameters. Unlike other schemes that use fixed embedding parameters or obtain embedding parameters by multiple experiments, the proposed scheme is based on a new adaptive embedding parameter algorithm. The algorithm establishes the associations among the embedding parameters, and host images to determine the optimal embedding parameters. An experimental comparison with other similar schemes is given at the end of paper. The comparison indicates that the proposed scheme is superior to the previous schemes from the perspectives of imperceptibility and robustness, which are two requirements of a high-quality robust watermarking.

Keywords: Watermarking · Adaptive algorithm · Robustness

1 Introduction

The open network environment has promoted multimedia distribution and transmission; at the same time, the intellectual property protection of various content faces unprecedented challenges. Among all types of digital media protection methods, digital watermarks with characteristics such as invisibility and security have become increasingly attractive. Digital watermarking refers to the use of relevant ownership information called a watermark often hidden in images, videos, audio content, etc. and then extracted by detectors to identify content ownership.

Conventional image watermarking can be divided into two categories according to function: robust watermarking and fragile watermarking [1]; these approaches protect the image copyright and image content integrity, respectively. Robust watermarks refer to watermarks that can be explicitly extracted, even after being subjected to multiple attacks. Besides, modifications to covers will inevitably lead to degradation in the

X. Sun et al. (Eds.): ICAIS 2020, CCIS 1254, pp. 503–514, 2020.
https://doi.org/10.1007/978-981-15-8101-4_45

visual quality of watermarked images [2]. There are three essential requirements for robust watermarking: capacity, robustness, and invisibility. When the capacity is determined, to enhance robustness by strengthening the watermark, watermarking schemes usually sacrifice visual quality, and vice versa. It is the aim of a robust watermarking to maintain a trade-off among the capacity, visual quality, and robustness. According to the embedding domain, watermarking schemes can be divided into spatial domain schemes and frequency domain schemes. With the advantages of energy aggregation, multiple-resolution analysis, and time or frequency domain manifestation, the transform domain schemes provide stronger robustness and imperceptibility than the spatial domain schemes and are thus preferred [3]. Besides, hybrid schemes combining the advantages of the incorporated transforms can further improve the performance of watermarking and have become popular in recent years.

Because images are stored in real matrices, an increasing number of researchers have introduced matrix decomposition techniques from linear algebra into image watermarking schemes. The robust nature of singular value decomposition (SVD) has inspired researchers to apply it in robust watermarking. Among the watermarking schemes based on SVD, numerous methods that use grayscale images as watermarks have been proposed, with the advantage of a remarkably high capacity. Reference [4] combined DWT, Z-Transform, Arnold cat map, and SVD to achieve a semi-blind watermarking scheme. Reference [5] noted that in addition to the robustness of singular values, singular matrices are equally robust in SVD. Based on this conclusion, Reference [6] suggested that the first column in singular matrices is robust and presented the corresponding theoretical and experimental proof. The modification of one coefficient in singular matrices will influence fewer pixels than modifying a singular value. In [7], cover was segmented into non-overlapping blocks, SVD was applied to each block, and the watermark was embedded by modifying the relationships of the coefficients in the first column of the left singular matrix of the embedding blocks. The embedding blocks were selected by sorting the numbers of non-zero singular values in all the blocks. In [8], the embedding blocks selected by entropy were subjected to DCT-SVD transform before watermark embedding. The scheme in [9] used the ABC algorithm to select an embedding parameter and quality compensation parameters. The schemes in [10] and [11] modified the relationships among the coefficients in the first column of the singular matrix for color images. Reference [12] also focused on color images, but the watermark was encrypted by DNA encoding and coupled map lattice (CML) prior to inserting it into the right singular matrix.

In addition to embedding domain selection, embedding location determination, and embedding method design, the determination of embedding parameters is another focus of robust watermarking. Embedding parameters that regulate the embedding energy of watermarks balance the relationship between robustness and imperceptibility. Compared with fixed parameters, adaptive embedding parameters establish the linkage among parameters, watermarks, and host images. An increasing number of schemes have adopted artificial intelligence techniques, such as evolutionary algorithms and neural networks etc. to obtain adaptive embedding parameters. The scheme in [13] embedded watermark in QR decomposition domain and determined optimal embedding parameters by the firefly algorithm (FA). Unlike other schemes that used a single scaling factor, Reference [14] used a self-adaptive differential evolution (SADE) technique to generate a factor matrix of the same size as the watermark, considering the different components of cover. The embedding parameter selection methods in the above literature relied on experimental feedback mechanisms. The schemes in [15, 16], and [17] directly determined parameters based on the cover content, thereby eliminating repeated experiments and improving scheme efficiency. However, the embedding parameters were not adjusted through repeated experiments in them, and there is a high probability that the corresponding watermarked images may not reach the desired image quality. Reference [18] obtained the relationship between the embedding parameters and watermarked image quality, and when the preset quality was determined, the corresponding embedding parameters were obtained.

In summary, the main objective of this research is to design a robust block-based watermarking scheme based on the stability of the element relationships in the first column of the singular matrix with an adaptive embedding parameter strategy and PSNR guarantee. The proposed scheme first selects a given number of embedding blocks based on the watermark length and entropy. After applying DWT-SVD to each embedding block, the scheme embeds watermark by modifying the relationship between two elements in the first column of the left singular matrix. The embedding parameter is determined by the proposed adaptive embedding parameter strategy.

2   The Watermarking Scheme in DWT-SVD Domain

2.1   Embedding Process

This paper defines a host image as matrix $A \in R_{M \times N}$, M and N are even, an embedded watermark as $W = \{w_r | 1 \leq r \leq m\}$, $w_r \in \{0, 1\}$, m is the watermark length. The embedding steps are as follows:

Step 1: The host image is divided into 8×8 non overlapping blocks and sub blocks are denoted as $L = \{l_{i,j} | 1 \leq i \leq M/8, 1 \leq j \leq N/8\}$. Where $\lceil \rceil$ is the ceiling operator, and the number of sub blocks is $\lceil M/8 \rceil \times \lceil N/8 \rceil$.

Step 2: Calculate the entropy of $l_{i,j}$: $E_{i,j} = E_{i,j}^{visual} + E_{i,j}^{edge}$, where $E_{i,j}^{visual}$ and $E_{i,j}^{edge}$ are visual entropy and edge entropy of $l_{i,j}$ respectively. Sort $\hat{E}_{i,j}$ ascendingly and select the first m blocks as embedding blocks. The subscripts of embedding blocks are denoted as the sequence $S = \{s_r\}$, where $s_r \leq M/8 \times N/8$.

Step 3: Perform one-level Haar wavelet transform onto the host image A, the LL sub band is divided into 4×4 non-overlapping blocks. The embedding blocks are denoted as $B = \{b_{s_r} | s_r \in S\}$.

Step 4: Apply SVD to the embedding blocks, and denote the first column of left singular matrix as $\left[u_{1,1}^{s_r} u_{2,1}^{s_r} u_{3,1}^{s_r} u_{4,1}^{s_r} \right]^T$, the difference between $u_{2,1}^{s_r}$ and $u_{3,1}^{s_r}$ as $d_{s_r} = u_{2,1}^{s_r} - u_{3,1}^{s_r}$, and differences for all embedding blocks as $D = \{d_{s_r} | s_r \in S\}$.

Step 5: The embedding rules for embedding block b_{s_r} are as follows:

if $w_r = 1$ then

$$u_{2,1}^{s_r'} = \begin{cases} u_{2,1}^{s_r} + \frac{(t-d_{s_r})}{2}, & \text{if } d_{s_r} < t \\ u_{2,1}^{s_r}, & \text{otherwise} \end{cases} \tag{1}$$

$$u_{3,1}^{s_r'} = \begin{cases} u_{3,1}^{s_r} - \frac{(t-d_{s_r})}{2}, & \text{if } d_{s_r} < t \\ u_{3,1}^{s_r}, & \text{otherwise} \end{cases} \tag{2}$$

else

$$u_{2,1}^{s_r'} = \begin{cases} u_{2,1}^{s_r} - \frac{(t+d_{s_r})}{2}, & \text{if } d_{s_r} > -t \\ u_{2,1}^{s_r}, & \text{otherwise} \end{cases} \tag{3}$$

$$u_{3,1}^{s_r'} = \begin{cases} u_{3,1}^{s_r} + \frac{(t+d_{s_r})}{2}, & \text{if } d_{s_r} > -t \\ u_{3,1}^{s_r}, & \text{otherwise} \end{cases} \tag{4}$$

In (1) to (4), t is an adaptive embedding parameter obtained based on the preset PSNR, the selection strategy of t will be explained in the third section.

Step 6: Perform inverse SVD on b_{s_r} and inverse one-level Haar wavelet transform, The watermarked image A' is obtained.

2.2 Extraction Process

The corresponding extraction steps are as follows:

Step 1: Perform one-level Haar wavelet transform on the watermarked image A'^*. Partition LL sub band into 4x4 non-overlapping blocks and select the extracting blocks according to the embedding blocks obtained in the embedding process.

Step 2: Perform SVD on each extracting block and denote the first column in the left singular matrix as $\left[u_{1,1}^{s_r\,'*} \; u_{2,1}^{s_r\,'*} \; u_{3,1}^{s_r\,'*} \; u_{4,1}^{s_r\,'*} \right]^T$, the difference between $u_{2,1}^{s_r\,'*}$ and $u_{3,1}^{s_r\,'*}$ as $d_{s_r}'^* = u_{2,1}^{s_r\,'*} - u_{3,1}^{s_r\,'*}$.

Step 3: Extract a watermark bit from each extracting block. The extracting rules are as follows:

$$w_r^* = \begin{cases} 1, & fd_{s_r}'^* > 0 \\ 0, & \text{otherwise} \end{cases} \tag{5}$$

3 The Proposed Adaptive Embedding Parameter Strategy

In the embedding process described in the previous section, the balance between imperceptibility and robustness depends upon the embedding parameter t. A large t favors robustness while small t favors imperceptibility. On the basis of [18], this study utilizes the formula of PSNR to obtain the relationship among PSNR value, embedding parameters and covers, thereby computing the embedding parameter t according to the preset PSNR. This relationship ensure that the watermarked images achieve the preset quality level. Before introducing the determination method of t, this paper first gives two related propositions.

Proposition 1: for image A, LL, LH, HL and HH sub band coefficients in one-level Haar wavelet domain are denoted as $c_{i,j}^{LL}, c_{i,j}^{LH}, c_{i,j}^{HL}, c_{i,j}^{HH}, 1 \leq i \leq M/2, 1 \leq j \leq N/2$. The specifications of referred variables are detailed in Fig. 1. The low-frequency coefficients in the first level Haar wavelet domain have the same square error (SE) as the pixels of A:

$$\sum_{k=1}^{M} \sum_{l=1}^{N} (a_{k,l}' - a_{k,l})^2 = \sum_{i=1}^{M/2} \sum_{j=1}^{N/2} (c_{i,j}^{LL'} - c_{i,j}^{LL})^2 \tag{6}$$

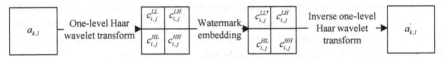

Fig. 1. The illustration of embedding process

Prove: When $c_{i,j}^{LL'} = c_{i,j}^{LL} + \Delta_{i,j}$, based on the relationship between the pixels of image reconstructed by inverse Haar wavelet transform and the coefficients of four sub bands at first level [19, 20], the following equations are obtained:

$$\begin{cases} a_{2i-1,2j-1}' - a_{2i-1,2j-1} = \frac{\Delta_{i,j}}{2} \\ a_{2i-1,2j}' - a_{2i-1,2j} = \frac{\Delta_{i,j}}{2} \\ a_{2i,2j-1}' - a_{2i,2j-1} = \frac{\Delta_{i,j}}{2} \\ a_{2i,2j}' - a_{2i,2j} = \frac{\Delta_{i,j}}{2} \end{cases}, 1 \leq i \leq \frac{M}{2}, 1 \leq j \leq \frac{N}{2} \tag{7}$$

$$\sum_{k=1}^{M} \sum_{l=1}^{N} (a_{k,l}' - a_{k,l})^2 = \sum_{i=1}^{M/2} \sum_{j=1}^{N/2} (\Delta_{i,j})^2 = \sum_{i=1}^{M/2} \sum_{j=1}^{N/2} (c_{i,j}^{LL'} - c_{i,j}^{LL})^2 \tag{8}$$

Proposition 1 is proved.

The proposition 1 shows that the low-frequency coefficients in one-level Haar wavelet domain have the same SE as the image pixels.

Proposition 2: for the proposed embedding process, given the specific cover and watermark, the relationship between the low-frequency coefficients in one-level Haar wavelet domain and modification of sub blocks satisfies the following equation:

$$\sum_{j=1}^{M/2} \sum_{i=1}^{N/2} (c_{i,j}^{LL'} - c_{i,j}^{LL})^2 = \sum_{s_r \in S_1} (x_{1,1}^{s_r})^2 \frac{(t - d_{s_r})^2}{2} + \sum_{s_r \in S_2} (x_{1,1}^{s_r})^2 \frac{(t + d_{s_r})^2}{2} \tag{9}$$

Where S_1 and S_2 are sub sequences of S, $x_{1,1}^{s_r}$ is the maximum singular value of b_{s_r}. The maximum singular values for all the embedding blocks are denoted as $X = \{x_{1,1}^{s_r} | s_r \in S\}$.

Prove: this paper denotes the modified b_{s_r} as b'_{s_r} and the SVD decomposition of b_{s_r} and b'_{s_r} are

$$b_{s_r} = \sum_{i=1}^{4} x_{i,i}^{s_r} \times U_i^{s_r} \times (V_i^{s_r})^T \tag{10}$$

$$b'_{s_r} = x_{1,1}^{s_r} \times \left(U_1^{s_r} + \Delta_{s_r}\right) \times (V_1^{s_r})^T + \sum_{i=2}^{4} x_{i,i}^{s_r} \times U_i^{s_r} \times (V_i^{s_r})^T \tag{11}$$

Where Δ_{s_r} is a disturbing vector for the first column of left singular matrix of b_{s_r}. Clearly, the modified embedding blocks can be divided to two categories: the embedding blocks with $d_{s_r} < t$ and $w_r = 1$ and that with $d_{s_r} > -t$ and $w_r = 0$. The subscripts of the two categories are denoted as sequence S_1 and S_2 which are sub sequences of S and do not overlapped. Δ_{s_r} corresponding to S_1 and S_2 is defined as

$$\Delta_{s_r} = \begin{cases} \left[0 \frac{(t-d_{s_r})}{2} - \frac{(t-d_{s_r})}{2} 0\right]^T , s_r \in S_1 \\ \left[0 - \frac{(t+d_{s_r})}{2} \frac{(t+d_{s_r})}{2} 0\right]^T , s_r \in S_2 \end{cases} \tag{12}$$

The difference between b_{s_r} and b'_{s_r} is

$$b'_{s_r} - b_{s_r} = x_{1,1}^{s_r} \times \Delta_{s_r} \times (V_1^{s_r})^T = x_{1,1}^{s_r} \times$$

$$x_{1,1}^{s_r} \times \begin{cases} \begin{bmatrix} 0 & 0 & \dots & 0 \\ \frac{(t-d_{s_r}) \times v_{1,1}^{s_r}}{2} & \frac{(t-d_{s_r}) \times v_{2,1}^{s_r}}{2} & \dots & \frac{(t-d_{s_r}) \times v_{4,1}^{s_r}}{2} \\ -\frac{(t-d_{s_r}) \times v_{1,1}^{s_r}}{2} & -\frac{(t-d_{s_r}) \times v_{2,1}^{s_r}}{2} & \dots & -\frac{(t-d_{s_r}) \times v_{4,1}^{s_r}}{2} \\ 0 & 0 & \dots & 0 \end{bmatrix} , s_r \in S_1 \\ \begin{bmatrix} 0 & 0 & \dots & 0 \\ -\frac{(t+d_{s_r}) \times v_{1,1}^{s_r}}{2} & -\frac{(t+d_{s_r}) \times v_{2,1}^{s_r}}{2} & \dots & -\frac{(t+d_{s_r}) \times v_{4,1}^{s_r}}{2} \\ \frac{(t+d_{s_r}) \times v_{1,1}^{s_r}}{2} & \frac{(t+d_{s_r}) \times v_{2,1}^{s_r}}{2} & \dots & \frac{(t+d_{s_r}) \times v_{4,1}^{s_r}}{2} \\ 0 & 0 & \dots & 0 \end{bmatrix} , s_r \in S_2 \end{cases} \tag{13}$$

The relationship between changes on the embedding blocks and SE of LL sub band coefficients is

$$\sum_{i=1}^{M/2} \sum_{j=1}^{N/2} (c_{i,j}^{LL'} - c_{i,j}^{LL})^2 = \sum_{s_r \in S_1} (x_{1,1}^{s_r})^2 \frac{(t-d_{s_r})^2}{2} + \sum_{s_r \in S_2} (x_{1,1}^{s_r})^2 \frac{(t+d_{s_r})^2}{2} \tag{14}$$

Proposition 2 is proved.

The first proposition indicates that there is an equivalence relation between SE of the image pixels and that of the low-frequency coefficients in one-level Haar wavelet domain. The second proposition show the relationship between SE of low-frequency coefficients and the modification of the embedding blocks. Based on the two propositions, this paper has

$$\sum_{k=1}^{M}\sum_{l=1}^{N}(a'_{k,l}-a_{k,l})^2 = \sum_{s_r\in S_1}(x_{1,1}^{s_r})^2\frac{(t-d_{s_r})^2}{2} + \sum_{s_r\in S_2}(x_{1,1}^{s_r})^2\frac{(t+d_{s_r})^2}{2}$$
(15)

The know formula of PSNR is

$$PSNR = 10\log_{10}\frac{MAX_A^2}{MSE}$$
(16)

$$MSE = \frac{1}{MN}\sum_{k=1}^{M}\sum_{l=1}^{N}(a'_{k,l}-a_{k,l})^2$$
(17)

Where MAX_A is the maximum pixel value of A. From (16) and (17), we get

$$\sum_{k=1}^{M}\sum_{l=1}^{N}(a'_{k,l}-a_{k,l})^2 = \frac{MAX_A^2\times M\times N}{10^{PSNR/10}}$$
(18)

Based on (15) and (18), the following equation is obtained.

$$\sum_{s_r\in S_1}(x_{1,1}^{s_r})^2\frac{(t-d_{s_r})^2}{2} + \sum_{s_r\in S_2}(x_{1,1}^{s_r})^2\frac{(t+d_{s_r})^2}{2}$$
$$= \frac{MAX_A^2\times M\times N}{10^{PSNR/10}}$$
(19)

The left part of (19) is related to the maximum singular value X, the difference D and the embedding parameter t. When the host image, watermark, and PSNR values are designated, the parameter t satisfying Eq. (19) can be obtained. The proposed determination method of the embedding parameter associates the PSNR formula with the watermarking based on the singular matrix robustness, thus the embedding parameter is directly related to the visual quality of watermarked image, and the scheme ensures that the visual quality reach the desired level.

4   Experimental Results

To evaluate the overall performance of the proposed scheme, this section compares the proposed scheme with [9, 21] and [22] based on imperceptibility and robustness. The experiments select eight standard tested images with size 512×512 as the covers, and one binary images of size 32×32 as the watermarks shown in Fig. 2. The upper and lower thresholds for the embedding parameter t are set to 1 and 0.01 respectively. PSNR (16) (17) is the measurement metrics of imperceptibility, and bit error rate (BER) (20) is the metrics for robustness.

$$ber = \frac{\sum_{r=1}^{m}(w_r^*\oplus w_r)}{m}$$
(20)

Where $\oplus$ is the bitwise logical XOR operator.

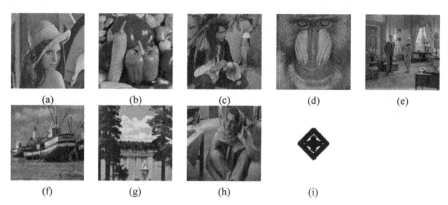

Fig. 2. (a) ~ (h)covers: Lena, Peppers, Man, Baboon, Couple, Fishingboat, Sailingboat, Barbara (i) The watermark W1 with size 32 × 32

4.1 Imperceptibility

Minimizing impact on covers is one of the goals of invisible watermarking schemes. Unlike other schemes that embedding parameters balance image quality against robustness, the proposed scheme uses preset PSNR value as a parameter to deduct the embedding parameter and achieves desired robustness. Figure 3 is the average of embedding parameter t and the mean value of obtained PSNR of ten test images when the preset PSNR is 30, 35, 40, 45, and 50 respectively. The curve of preset PSNR is substantially coincident with that of the obtained PSNR, which proves that this scheme can ensure that the watermarked image quality reaches preset values and the quality of watermarked images in the proposed scheme can meet requirements of applications from objective perspectives.

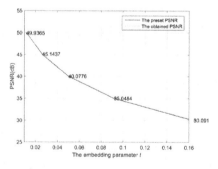

Fig. 3. The comparison between the preset PSNR and the obtained PSNR

4.2 Robustness

This study uses BER as metrics to measure robustness. The smaller the BER value, the higher the similarity between the extracted watermark and the original watermark. To verify the robustness of proposed scheme, this study selects 13 representative attacks, which include common image processing such as compression, filtering, noise, etc., as well as geometric attacks such as scaling and rotation. Table 1 shows the BER value of watermark W1 extracted from six attacked watermarked images. Among the 6 test images, Peppers and Man are weaker against median filtering and JPEG compression with low quality factor because the proposed scheme prefers embedding blocks with small entropy and Peppers and Man have relatively fewer smooth sections. In general, this scheme has preferable robustness against common attacks, especially histogram equalization, contrast enhancement, scaling down, and rotation.

Table 1. The BER value under various attacks

	Lena	Peppers	Man	Baboon	Couple	Boat
No attack	0	0	0	0	0	0
JPEG compression (QF = 20)	0.0020	0.1660	0.2197	0.0049	0.0381	0.1289
JPEG compression (QF = 70)	0	0.0068	0	0	0	0.0137
Gaussian filtering (sigma = 1.0)	0	0.0088	0.0313	0.0020	0.0068	0.0313
Median filtering (3 × 3)	0	0.0127	0.0166	0	0.0049	0.0166
Average filtering (3 × 3)	0	0.0078	0.0293	0.0020	0.0059	0.0283
Gaussian noise (v = 0.01)	0.0986	0.1221	0.1494	0.0781	0.0928	0.1113
Salt & pepper noise (v = 0.01)	0.0088	0.0293	0.0449	0.0098	0.0205	0.0186
Speckle noise (v = 0.01)	0.0107	0.0049	0	0.0059	0.0009	0.0039
Histogram equalization	0	0.0059	0.0020	0	0	0.0342
Contrast adjustment	0	0.0049	0.0137	0	0	0.0205
Cropping at center (25%)	0.0244	0.1631	0.1934	0.4072	0.1318	0.1387
Scaling(1->0.5->1)	0	0.0020	0.0137	0	0.0029	0.0176
Anti-clockwise rotation by 45°	0	0.0009	0.0020	0	0	0.0088

To evaluate performance, imperceptibility and robustness should be considered simultaneously. In this paper, the robustness of four schemes is compared under the premise that the PSNR values are about 41 dB. Table 2 show the comparisons among Ali et al. [9], Makbol et al. [22], Kang et al. [21] and the proposed scheme under 13 attacks with the preset PSNR set to 41 dB. Although the four schemes embed watermark by changing the relationship between two elements, two chosen elements in [21] are the maximum singular values of two matrices composed of middle frequency coefficients in DCT domain, with less similarities than the singular matrix entries. Therefore, Table 2 show that under most attacks especially noise attacks, Ali et al. [9], Makbol et al. [22] and the proposed scheme perform better than [21]. Although RIDWT transform utilized in [9] can resist continuous 90-degree rotation and row-column flipping, RIDWT includes pixel position exchange, which destroys the similarity of adjacent pixels in covers. This drawback results in the weak resistance to JPEG compression, median filtering, mean filtering, size reduction, and Gaussian filtering.

Table 2. The comparison of BER between the proposed method and the other schemes based on lena

	Kang *et al.* [21]	Ali *et al.* [9]	Makbol *et al.* [22]	The proposed scheme
PSNR	40.07	41.12	41.20	41.13
No attack	0	0	0	0
JPEG compression (QF = 20)	0.2070	0.3965	0.0137	**0.0020**
JPEG compression (QF = 70)	0.0205	0.0518	**0**	**0**
Gaussian filtering (sigma = 1.0)	0.0127	0.0313	**0**	**0**
Median filtering(3 × 3)	0.0049	0.4639	**0**	**0**
Average filtering (3 × 3)	0.0518	0.5049	**0**	**0**
Gaussian noise (m = 0, v = 0.01)	0.2529	**0.0869**	0.0977	0.0986
Salt & pepper noise (d = 0.01)	0.1650	0.0186	0.0137	**0.0088**
Speckle noise (v = 0.01)	0.1826	0.0137	0.0117	**0.0107**
Histogram equalization	0.0068	**0**	**0**	**0**
Contrast adjustment	0.0732	**0**	**0**	**0**
Cropping (25%)	0.0664	0.0322	0.0332	**0.0244**
Resizing (1-> 0.5-> 1)	0.0020	0.0176	**0**	**0**
Anti-clockwise rotation by 45°	–	**0**	**0**	**0**

5   Conclusion

In this paper, a difference-quantized watermarking scheme with a DWT-SVD embedding domain and singular matrix embedding location is proposed. The embedding parameters play a role in balancing imperceptibility and robustness. Unlike other schemes with fixed embedding parameters or parameters determined from trials, this study proposes a new adaptive embedding parameter strategy, which uses a preset PSNR to determine the embedding parameters and achieve adequate robustness. The stability of the relationships among singular matrix elements is utilized in the proposed scheme to further enhance the robustness. At the end of paper, the experimental results and a comparison with other schemes are given. The comparison shows that the proposed scheme is more practical than its counterparts in applications such as copyright protection.

References

1. Gong, D., Chen, Y., Lu, H., Li, Z., Han, Y.: Self-embedding image watermarking based on combined decision using pre-offset and post-offset blocks. Comput. Mater. Continua **57**(2), 243–260 (2018)
2. Kumar, C., Singh, A.K., Kumar, P.: A recent survey on image watermarking techniques and its application in e-governance. Multimed. Tools Appl. **77**(3), 3597–3622 (2017). https://doi.org/10.1007/s11042-017-5222-8
3. Liu, J., et al.: A robust zero-watermarking based on SIFT-DCT for medical images in the encrypted domain. Comput. Mater. Continua **61**(1), 363–378 (2019)
4. Jayashree, N., Bhuvaneswaran, R.S.: A robust image watermarking scheme using z-transform, discrete wavelet transform and bidiagonal singular value decomposition. Comput. Mater. Continua **58**(1), 263–285 (2019)
5. Chung, K.L., Yang, W.N., Huang, Y.H.: On SVD-based water-marking algorithm. Appl. Math. Comput. **188**, 54–57 (2007)
6. Fan, M.Q., Wang, H.X., Li, S.K.: Restudy on SVD-based watermarking scheme. Appl. Math. Comput. **203**, 926–930 (2008)
7. Chang, C.C., Tsai, P.: SVD-based digital image watermarking scheme. Pattern Recogn. Lett. **26**(10), 1577–1586 (2005)
8. Lai, C.C.: An improved SVD-based watermarking scheme using human visual characteristics. Opt. Commun. **284**(4), 938–944 (2011)
9. Ali, M., Ahn, C.W., Pant, M.: An image watermarking scheme in wavelet domain with optimized compensation of singular value decomposition via artificial bee colony. Inform. Sci. **301**, 44–60 (2015)
10. Su, Q., Niu, Y., Zhao, Y.: A dual color images watermarking scheme based on the optimized compensation of singular value decomposition. AEU-Int. J. Electron. C. **67**(8), 652–664 (2013)
11. Jia, S.: A novel blind color images watermarking based on SVD. Optik **125**(12), 2868–2874 (2014)
12. Wu, X., Kan, H.: A blind dual color images watermarking method via SVD and DNA sequences. In: Lin, D., Wang, X., Yung, M. (eds.) Inscrypt 2015. LNCS, vol. 9589, pp. 246–259. Springer, Cham (2016). https://doi.org/10.1007/978-3-319-38898-4_15
13. Guo, Y., Li, B.Z., Goel, N.: Optimized blind image watermarking method based on firefly algorithm in DWT-QR transform domain. IET Image Process. **11**(6), 406–415 (2017)
14. Hassan, V.M., Ali, A., Yasser, B.: Optimized watermarking technique using self-adaptive differential evolution based on redundant discrete wavelet transform and singular value decomposition. Expert Syst. Appl. **114**, 296–312 (2018)
15. Mohrekesh, M., Azizi, S., Shirani, S., Karimi, N., Samavi, S.: Hierarchical watermarking framework based on analysis of local complexity variations. Multimed. Tools Appl. **77**(23), 30865–30890 (2018). https://doi.org/10.1007/s11042-018-6129-8

16. Fazlali, H.R., Samavi, S., Karimi, N., Shirani, S.: Adaptive blind image watermarking using edge pixel concentration. Multimed. Tools Appl. **76**(2), 3105–3120 (2015). https://doi.org/10.1007/s11042-015-3200-6

17. Vaidya, P., PVSSR, C.M.: Adaptive, robust and blind digital watermarking using Bhattacharyya distance and bit manipulation. Multimed. Tools Appl. **77**(5), 5609–5635 (2018). https://doi.org/10.1007/s11042-017-4476-5

18. Huang, Y., Niu, B., Guan, H.: Enhancing image watermarking with adaptive embedding parameter and PSNR guarantee. IEEE Trans. Multimed. **21**(10), 5609–5635 (2019)

19. Bhardwaj, A., Ali, R.: Image compression using modified fast haar wavelet transform. World Appl. Sci. J. **7**(5), 647–653 (2009)

20. Porwik, P., Lisowska, A.: The haar-wavelet transform in digital image processing: its status and achievements. Mach. Graph. Vis. **13**, 79–98 (2004)

21. Kang, X.B., Zhao, F., Lin, G.F., Chen, Y.J.: A novel hybrid of DCT and SVD in DWT domain for robust and invisible blind image watermarking with optimal embedding strength. Multimed. Tools Appl. **77**(11), 13197–13224 (2017). https://doi.org/10.1007/s11042-017-4941-1

22. Makbol, N.M., Khoo, B.E., Rassem, T.H.: Block-based discrete wavelet transform-singular value decomposition image watermarking scheme using human visual system characteristics. IET Image Process. **10**(1), 34–52 (2016)

Mining Defects of Result-Sensitive Function Based on Information Entropy

Lin Chen[1,2], Chunfang Yang[1,2(✉)], Fenlin Liu[1,2], Daofu Gong[1,2], and ZhongXu Yin[1,2]

[1] Zhengzhou Science and Technology Institute, Zhengzhou 450001, China
chunfangyang@126.com
[2] State Key Laboratory of Mathematical Engineering and Advanced Computing, Zhengzhou 450001, China

Abstract. Result-sensitive function is a typical type of security-sensitive function. The misuse of result-sensitive functions often leads to a lot kinds of software defects. Existing defect detection methods based on code mining for result-sensitive functions usually require a gived security rule or an inferred security rule as input. Based on the principle of consistency, we propose a defect detection method based on information entropy. Firstly, the feature vector about usage of function is extracted from every function instance. Then, the information entropy is introduced to measure the abnormal degree of the feature vector. The function instances with high degree of abnormality is regarded as dangerous instances. Experiments show that the proposed method can effectively detect dangerous instances of security defects without a gived security rule.

Keywords: Code feature · Security-Sensitive function · Code mining · Software defect

1 Introduction

Robust and reliable software should be designed to handle multiple program failures. Even in the event of some underlying basic function failure, it need to fix the failure, try to restore normal program state or kill the program smoothly, instead of returning wrong execution result, crashing roughly, or showing other uncontrolled behaviors [1]. Usually, when a failure occurs, the failed function callee will get the failed information to the caller, and then the caller will handle the fault in a suitable way according to the failure information, so that the program remains in a security controllable state. However, if the developer does not handle the failure of the function execution, or does not implement the correct error handling, it may lead to a lot of software defects. A number kinds of vulnerabilty related to it are listed in the Common Weakness Enumeration (CWE) [13], such as "unchecked return value" numbered CWE-252 [14], "Lack of standardized error handling mechanism" numbered CWE-544 [15], etc., and thus formed many practical vulnerabilities, such as CVE-2019-8357 [16]], CVE-2019-14814 [17] and so on.

In order to detect the error handling defection, the researchers have proposed a number of static or dynamic defect detection methods [1–4], but most methods need to

© Springer Nature Singapore Pte Ltd. 2020
X. Sun et al. (Eds.): ICAIS 2020, CCIS 1254, pp. 515–523, 2020.
https://doi.org/10.1007/978-981-15-8101-4_46

use error handling rules as argorithom inputs. But mining security rules manually is very inefficient. When performing defect detection for a specific result-sensitive function, the code mining based defect detection methods [6–12] can automatically infer a specific security rule from the source code and then detect violations of the rule. However, due to the variety of implementations of the security usage specification, when multiple implementations are used in the source code project, the inferred rules may not be complete, resulting in a large number of false positives, or the inability to infer the security rules.

This paper believes that although the security usage specification of security-sensitive functions can be implemented in many ways, the number of instances with wrong usage is still smaller than the correct implementations. Based on this observation, this paper proposes a resul-sensitive function defect detection method based on the abnormal invocation behavior identification. Firstly, the proposed method extract behavioral features from every result-sensitive function instance. Then it try to find the dangerous instances with abnormal behavioral features. Under the premise that most function instances are in compliance with the security specifications, if the usage of a call instance is different from the usage behavior of most instances, then the invocation behavior of this function instance is an abnormal behavior. And the function instance is a dangerous instance with defection.

2   Result-Sensitive Function

Result-sensitive function is a typical security-sensitive function. The return value of the function show the execution of the function is success or failure. Figure 1 is a code block in the Linux kernel. The function `alloc_workqueue()` is a result-sensitive function.

```
1     fscache_object_max_active =
2             clamp_val(nr_cpus,
3                     fscache_object_max_active, WQ_UNBOUND_MAX_ACTIVE);
4
5     ret = -ENOMEM;
6     fscache_object_wq = alloc_workqueue("fscache_object", WQ_UNBOUND,
7                             fscache_object_max_active);
8     if (!fscache_object_wq)
9             goto error_object_wq;
10
11    fscache_op_max_active =
12            clamp_val(fscache_object_max_active / 2,
13                    fscache_op_max_active, WQ_UNBOUND_MAX_ACTIVE);
14
15    ret = -ENOMEM;
```

Fig. 1. A code block in the Linux kernel

The function `alloc_workqueue("fscache_object", WQ_UNBOUND, fscache_object_max_active)` in line 6 assigns the return value to the variable `facache_object_wq`, and line 8 checks the return value variable facache_object_wq, if the logical expression ! fscache_object_wq is true, it means that the function instance in line6 executed unsuccessfully, and the program needs processing for the failure of alloc_workqueue() specially; If the logic expression ! fscache_object_wq is false, it means that the function is executed successfully and the program can continue the subsequent business process. The function like alloc_workqueue is a typical result-sensitive function.

In order to describe the algorithm clearly, we first introduce some definitions that will be used later, where Definition 2 comes from [6].

Definition 1: Result-sensitive function: When a type of functions is executed, there are possibilities for success and failure due to different execution environments, and the success or failure state can be identified by the return value. Programs need to check the return value to judge the execution state of the function, and perform corresponding processing; if the function executed and failed, but the program processing the result incorrectly, it may lead to program defects. Such function is called result-sensitive function.

Definition 2: Nor-Error path/Error path: For a function instance of a result-sensitive function f, when f is executed successfully, the path from the check statement of the return value to the exit statement of the caller is called Nor-Error path; when f execution fails, the path from the check statement execution of the return value to the statement exiting the function body or ending the program run is called Error path.

According to the definition of the result-sensitive function, the behavior features of the function instance can be constructed from the following code forms: 1. Check on the return value; 2. The difference in the number of statements in the two different path branches; 3. The difference in the number of paths in the two different path branches; 4. The difference in the use of return value variables in different path branches. The first three features are used in [6], and the fourth feature is different from [6], which is a new observation of the characteristics of the use of result-sensitive functions.

Check on the Return Value

According to the definition and security features of the result-sensitive function, it can be analyzed that after the execution of such a function, the return value must be checked to determine the execution state of the function, in order to ensure the normal execution of the subsequent code. And the check of the return value must be performed before it is used, otherwise this check can not effectively reflect the real execution result of the function.

The Difference in the Number of Statements in the Two Different Path Branches

In the two branch paths after the check, the correct path completes the subsequent main function of the program, and the wrong path quickly exits the function body after completing the necessary cleanup work. The number of statements required for the correct path is often larger than the number of statements on the wrong path.

The Difference in the Number of Paths in the Two Different Path Branches

Since the correct path needs to complete the subsequent business functions, and the error path only needs to complete a single exit function, the correct path usually has a more complicated logical structure than the wrong path. Generally, the number of paths on the correct path is larger than the error. The number of paths on the path.

The Difference in the Use of Return Value Variables in Different Path Branches
There are two common modes for the function to pass the execution result to the external environment: one is to pass the execution result into the parameter and the other is to pass it out through the return value.

For the result-sensitive function that adopts the second data transfer mode, when the user uses the return value variable, in the correct path, the return value variable holds useful data, which is used in subsequent subsequent business functions, so there is The access operation to the return value variable; on the error path, the return value variable is only a sign of success or failure as a function, there is no useful data required to complete the business function, so it is generally not accessed operating.

The error value of the result-sensitive function often occurs in the following two situations: First, after the function is executed, the function execution is not determined according to the return value, which may cause the subsequent code to execute the code in the wrong running environment and cause the defect. Second, due to negligence, the error handling code is executed on the successful path of the result-sensitive function, and the business function code is executed on the failed path. According to the above analysis, the behavioral feature vector of the result-sensitive function is extracted from the following four aspects: the return value is checked before use, the difference in the number of statements in the path branch, the difference in the number of paths in the path branch, and the return value variable in different paths. Differences in usage in the branch. If the behavior feature vector of a call instance of the target function is significantly different from the behavior feature vector of other call instances, the invocation behavior of the call instance may be considered abnormal, and there may be a security flaw.

3   Mining Defects of Result-Sensitive Function

The dangerous instance detection method of the result-sensitive function proposed in this paper is shown in Fig. 2. The first is to use the behavior extraction process. The behavior of the result-sensitive function is defined in four aspects: the return value is checked before use, the difference in the number of statements in the path branch, the difference in the number of paths in the path branch, and the difference in the use of the return value variable in different path branches. Then, the abnormal behavior is judged. The information entropy is used to measure the abnormal degree of the behavior vector of each instance. The calling instance with high degree of abnormality is identified as a dangerous instance with possible defects.

3.1   Extract Usage Features

In order to extract the behavior vector of the function call instance, first define the behavior vector bv of the result-sensitive function as Eq. (1).

$$bv = \left(v(p_{check}), v(p_{stmt}), v(p_{path}), v(p_{used})\right) \tag{1}$$

and,

$$p_{check} = \left\{ ``\text{The return value was checked before using}"\right\}$$

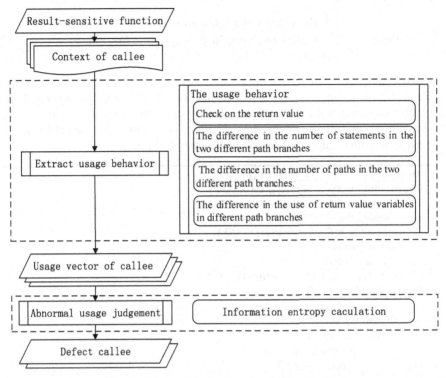

Fig. 2. Mining defects of result-sensitive function

$$p_{stmt} = \left\{ \begin{array}{c} \text{"The count of statements in Nor} - \text{Error path} \\ \text{is much more than it in the Error path"} \end{array} \right\}$$

$$p_{path} = \left\{ \begin{array}{c} \text{"The count of paths in Nor} - \text{Error path} \\ \text{is much more thant it in the Error path"} \end{array} \right\}$$

$$p_{used} = \left\{ \text{"The return value is used only in Nor} - \text{Error path"} \right\}$$

And their values are defined as Eq. (2):

$$v(p_{check}) = \left\{ \begin{array}{l} 1, \textit{Check before using the return value} \\ 0, \textit{others} \end{array} \right.$$

$$v(p_{stmt}) = \left\{ \begin{array}{l} 1, \text{"} \textit{the counts of statements in Nor} - \textit{Error path is} \\ \textit{much more than it in the Error path"} \\ 0, \textit{others} \end{array} \right.$$

$$v(p_{path}) = \left\{ \begin{array}{l} 1, \textit{the counts of paths in Nor} - \textit{Error path is} \\ \qquad \textit{much more than it in the Error path} \\ -1, \textit{the counts of paths in Error path is much} \\ \qquad \textit{more than it in the Nor} - \textit{Error path} \\ 0, \textit{others} \end{array} \right.$$

$$v(p_{used}) = \begin{cases} 1, \text{ the return variable is used only in Nor } - \text{ Error path} \\ -1, \text{ the return variable is used only in Error path} \\ 0, \text{ others} \end{cases} \quad (2)$$

For the path $path_1$, $path_2$, if the ratio between the number of statements of $path_1$ and the number of statements of $path_2$ is greater than the threshold λ_{stmt_obv}, the number of statements indicating $path_1$ is much larger tharn. $path_2$; If the ratio between the number of paths of $path_1$ and the number of paths of $path_2$ is greater than the threshold λ_{path_obv}, the number of paths indicating $path_1$ is much larger than $path_2$.

Algorithm 1. Extract the feature $v(p_{check})$

```
0:  procedure GetSecFeature(fᵢ, CFG, AST)
1:    if statement (fᵢ) is condition:
2:       return true
3:    returnVar = GetReturnVar(fᵢ,AST)
4:    if returnVar == NULL:
5:       return false
6:    pathSet = ExtractPath(returnVar, CFG)
7:    if pathSet == NULL
8:       return false
9:    for pᵢ ∈ pathSet do              /
10:       for statement in pᵢ
             if returnVar in statement:
11:             return false
12:    return true
```

For a result-sensitive function F, its instance set is $InsSet_F = \{f_1, f_2 \ldots f_n\}$. The specific steps of extracting the behavior vector of the function instance f_i are as follows.

Step 1: Use Algorithm 1 GetSecFeature() to get the value of $v(p_{check})$. If the return value is true, $v(p_{check}) = 1$, go to Step 2; if the return value is false, it means that the return value is not checked, so there is no correct path. And the wrong path, set $v(p_{check}) = 0$, $v(p_{stmt}) = 0$, $v(p_{path}) = 0$, $v(p_{used}) = 0$, exit.

Step 2: Get the number of statements on the two path branches, the number of paths, and the use of the return value variable.

Step 3: The path branch with a large number of statements is taken as the correct path, denoted as $rPath$, and $v(p_{stmt})$, $v(p_{path})$, $v(p_{used})$ are calculated according to Eq. (2).

The behavior vector for the instance f_i can be expressed as (3)

$$bv(f_i) = \left(v_{(f_i, p_{check})}, v_{(f_i, p_{stmt})}, v_{(f_i, p_{path})}, v_{(f_i, p_{used})} \right) \quad (3)$$

3.2 Abnormal Feature Judgment

After obtaining the behavior vectors of all the call instances of the result-sensitive function F, information entropy is introduced to calculate the degree of abnormality of each behavior vector.

The specific steps for calculating the entropy value of the jth component $v_{(f_i,p_j)}$ in the behavior vector of the calling instance f_i are:

Step 1: Construct the lexicon of the *j-th* component in the behavior vector $Word_{(p_j)}$, which consists of the *j-th* component of all call instances.

Step 2: The information entropy of the j-th behavioral class $v_{(f_i,p_j)}$ of the instance f_i is calculated using Eq. (4).

$$H(f_i, p_j) = -\frac{1}{\lg(N)} \times proj \times log_2(proj) \tag{4}$$

Among them, $proj$ is the frequency of $v_{(f_i,p_j)}$ appearing in the word bag $Word_{(p_j)}$.

Step 3: Calculate the information entropy of the instance f_i using Eq. (5)

$$H(f_i) = H(f_j, p_{check}) + H(f_j, p_{stmt}) + H(f_j, p_{path}) + H(f_j, p_{used}) \tag{5}$$

Finally, the larger the entropy value of the behavior vector, the greater the difference between the instance and the other instances of the function return value processing. The probability that the instance is a dangerous instance is greater.

4 Experiment and Analysis

This experiment verifies the defect detection algorithm of this paper. CVE-2019-16232 is a recently discovered vulnerability. The vulnerability is discovered in the code of drivers/net/wireless/marvell/libertas/if_sdio.c of Linux kernel version 5.2.14.

As   shown in Fig. 3, call `alloc_workqueue("libertas_sdio", WQ_MEM_RECLAIM, 0)` in line 2, and assign the return value to the variable `card->workqueue`. After the execution ends, the program does not check the function instance is successfully executed or not. Checking the return value `card->workqueue`, when `alloc_workqueue("libertas_sdio", WQ_MEM_RECLAIM, 0)` fails, it will cause a null pointer release error in subsequent code.

```
1      spin_lock_init(&card->lock);
2      card->workqueue = alloc_workqueue("libertas_sdio", WQ_MEM_RECLAIM, 0);
3      INIT_WORK(&card->packet_worker, if_sdio_host_to_card_worker);
4      init_waitqueue_head(&card->pwron_waitq);
5
6      /* Check if we support this card */
7      for (i = 0; i < ARRAY_SIZE(fw_table); i++) {
8                if (card->model == fw_table[i].model)
9                        break;
11     }
```

Fig. 3. Code block in CVE-2019-16232

As shown in Table 1. The table lists the extraction results of the behavior vectors of all 9 call instances of `alloc_workqueue()` in the source code repository.

Table 1. Features of alloc_workqueue()

Location of callee	Feature vector				Entropy
	P_{check}	P_{path}	P_{stmt}	P_{used}	
if_sdio.c: 1181	0	0	0	0	1.240
if_spi.c: 1157	1	1	1	0	0.606
main.c: 70	1	0	1	0	0.816
cfg80211.c: 3076	1	1	1	0	0.606
cfg80211.c: 3064	1	1	1	0	0.606
main.c: 1520	1	1	1	0	0.606
main.c: 1511	1	1	1	0	0.606
main.c: 1675	1	1	1	0	0.606
main.c: 1666	1	1	1	0	0.606

According to formulas (4) and (5), the entropy values of the feature vectors of the nine call instances can be calculated. The data in Table 1 shows that the instance position is if_sdio.c: 1181 The call instance of 1181 has the largest entropy value, which may be a call with a defect. Example. This test result is consistent with the actual situation in the CVE-2019-16232 report. Experiments show that this paper proposes that the result-sensitive function defect detection method is effective.

5 Summary

The result-sensitive function is a typical security-sensitive function, and misuse of such function could lead to many kinds of software defects. A defect detection method focused on the result-sensitive function was proposed based on identification the abnormal invocation behavior. The invocation behavior was expressed as a feature vector, which constitutes by four features, namely "The return value was checked before using", "The count of statements in Nor-Error path is much more than it in the Error path", "The count of paths in Nor-Error path is much more than it in the Error path", and "The return value is used only in Nor-Error path". And then the information entropy is used to measure the degree of abnormality of the behavior vector, and the instance with high degree of abnormality is identified as a dangerous instance with defect. Finally, the effectiveness of the method was verified by a experiment.

Acknowledgments. This study was supported in part by the National Natural Science Foundation of China (Nos. 61401512, 61602508, 61772549, U1636219, and U1736214), the National Key R&D Program of China (Nos. 2016YFB0801303 and 2016QY01W0105), the Key Technologies R&D Program of Henan Province (No. 162102210032), and the Key Science and Technology Research Project of Henan Province (No. 152102210005).

References

1. Marinescu, P.D., Candea, G.: Efficient testing of recovery code using fault injection. ACM Trans. Comput. Syst. **29**(4), 1–38 (2011)
2. Broadwell, P., Sastry, N., Traupman, J.: FIG: a prototype tool for online verification of recovery. In: Workshop on Self-Healing, Adaptive and Self-Managed Systems (2002)
3. Süßkraut, M., Fetzer, C.: Automatically finding and patching bad error handling. In: 6th European Dependable Computing Conference (EDCC), pp. 13–22. IEEE, Coimbra (2006)
4. Rubio-González, C., Gunawi, L.B., Arpaci-Dusseau, R., Arpaci-Dusseau, A.: Error propagation analysis for file systems. In: ACM SIGPLAN Conference on Programming Language Design and Implementation (PLDI), pp. 15–21. ACM, Dublin (2009)
5. Weimer, W., Necula, G.: Finding and preventing run-time error handling mistakes. ACM SIGPLAN Not. **39**(10), 419–431 (2004)
6. Yuan, K., Ray, B., Jana, S.: APEx: automated inference of error specifications for C APIs. In: The IEEE/ACM International Conference, pp. 472–482 (2016)
7. Jana, S., et al.: Automatically detecting error handling bugs using error specifications. In: 25th USENIX Security Symposium, pp. 345–362. USENIX Association, Austin (2016)
8. Weimer, W., Necula, G.C.: Mining temporal specifications for error detection. In: Halbwachs, N., Zuck, L.D. (eds.) TACAS 2005. LNCS, vol. 3440, pp. 461–476. Springer, Heidelberg (2005). https://doi.org/10.1007/978-3-540-31980-1_30
9. Acharya, M., Xie, T.: Mining API error-handling specifications from source code. In: Chechik, M., Wirsing, M. (eds.) FASE 2009. LNCS, vol. 5503, pp. 370–384. Springer, Heidelberg (2009). https://doi.org/10.1007/978-3-642-00593-0_25
10. Chen, L., Yang, C., Liu, F., Gong, D., Ding, S.: Automatic Mining of Security-Sensitive Functions from Source Code. Comput. Mater. Contin. **56**(2), 199–210 (2018)
11. Liang, B., Bian, P., Zhang, Y., Shi, W., You, W.: AntMiner: mining more bugs by reducing noise interference. In: IEEE/ACM, International Conference on Software Engineering, pp. 333–344. IEEE, Austin (2016)
12. Yun, I., Min, C., Si, X., Jang, Y., Kim, T., Naik, M.: APISan: sanitizing API usages through semantic cross-checking. In: USENIX Security Symposium, pp. 363–378. USENIX Association, Austin (2016)
13. Common weakness enumeration. https://cwe.mitre.org/. Accessed 21 Nov 2019
14. CWE-252: unchecked return value. https://cwe.mitre.org/data/definitions/252.html. Accessed 21 Nov 2019
15. CWE-544: Missing standardized error handling mechanism. https://cwe.mitre.org/data/definitions/544.html. Accessed 21 Nov 2019
16. CVE-2019-8357. https://cve.mitre.org/cgi-bin/cvename.cgi?name=CVE-2019-8357. Accessed 21 Nov 2019
17. CVE-2019-14814. https://cve.mitre.org/cgi-bin/cvename.cgi?name=CVE-2019-14814. Accessed 21 Nov 2019

Security Evaluation of Multi-dimensional Steganography Model Based on VoIP

Chuanpeng Guo$^{(\boxtimes)}$ (ID), Wei Yang, Liusheng Huang, Hao Zhan, and Yuqin Tan

School of Computer Science and Technology,
University of Science and Technology of China, Hefei 230026, China
guocp@mail.ustc.edu.cn

Abstract. Current research on information hiding technology is constantly developing towards the diversification of carriers and the complexity of algorithms. But research on how to effectively combine diverse carriers and steganography algorithms to construct high-security, large-capacity and high-robust parallel algorithms is not sufficient. To deal with this challenge, we present a multi-dimensional information hiding model in the presence of a steganayst and give a formal definition of the model. Furthermore, we define in detail behavioral constraints of each participant in the model, and clarify the capabilities and possible risks of each participant in multi-dimensional information hiding communication. Finally, based on information theory and attacker detection theory, the quantitative evaluation of the security of multidimensional information hiding model is given. All in all, the model clearly describes the principle of multi-dimensional information hiding. At the same time, it can provide a certain theoretical basis for designing a specific multi-dimensional algorithm.

Keywords: Network steganography · Steganalysis · Security evaluation

1 Indtroduction

As a useful supplement to traditional encryption technology, information hiding is to hide secret information into digital carriers, making it difficult for third parties to detect the existence of information. With the development of network communication technology, the combination of information hiding and network has given birth to an important branch – network steganography [8,16,30].

The development of network steganography has gone through the following stages. In the early days, the covert communication technology mainly based on computer-understandable network protocols was called network covert channel. Network covert storage channels (CSC), covert timing channels (CTC)

This work was supported by the National Natural Science Foundation of China (No. 61572456), and the Anhui Initiative in Quantum Information Technologies (No. AHY150300).

© Springer Nature Singapore Pte Ltd. 2020
X. Sun et al. (Eds.): ICAIS 2020, CCIS 1254, pp. 524–535, 2020.
https://doi.org/10.1007/978-981-15-8101-4_47

[1,19,22,26] have appeared successively. Subsequently, there appeared a network steganography of human-understandable multimedia data as an information carrier. Various steganographic algorithms based on compressed audio, video and various codecs have been proposed [15,28]. In recent years, network steganography has been further deepened and diversified in two directions.

Firstly, with the emergence of new technologies such as big data, cloud computing, and Internet of Things, the research focuses on how to use new carriers for steganography and steganalysis. Most studies [5,10,27] still focus on how to construct novel covert channels with good compromises in security, capacity, and robustness.

Secondly, network protocols are multi-carrier composite, so it is also an important direction to study how to use multiple steganographic algorithms to construct multi-dimensional covert channels with larger capacity and higher security. In 2010, Mazurczyk et al. [17] proposed a hybrid steganographic method LACK that combines covert storage channels and covert timing channels. In 2018, Xu et al. [29] proposed a hybrid covert channel for the LTE environment. The authors first improved the CTC, proposed a new convert timing channel, and then constructed a CSC to transmit synchronization signals at the MAC layer. Unlike traditional single-type carriers, VoIP is an interactive network streaming media that combines multiple carriers, including network protocols, audio, video, and text messaging. It has the inherent advantages to build multi-dimensional covert channels. Fraczek et al. [7] proposed the concept of multi-layer steganography based on VoIP streams. After years of research, Ker et al. [12,14] established the theory and safety evaluation basis of batch steganography.

Furthermore, the advancement of information hiding technology is inseparable from the breakthroughs in basic theories such as steganographic model, security assessment, and secure capacity calculations. To date, covert communication model based on information theory is arguably one of the most widely used models. In 1998, Zöllner et al. [31] first gave the definition of information entropy for steganographic security, which provided a way of thinking for the study of steganographic security. Cachin [2] defined an information-theoretic model for steganography with a passive adversary. In his opinion, steganographic analysis could be interpreted as a hypothesis testing problem and the security was defined by relative entropy. In addition to information theory based modeling and security analysis methods, Hopper et al. [9] defined a steganographic security based on computational complexity. Chandramouli et al. [3] recommended measuring security from the perspective of an attacker. They gave new definitons for steganography security and steganographic capacity. However, research on the multi-dimensional information hiding model is still insufficient.

This paper focuses on covert communication with multi-protocol carrier represented by VoIP. First, we present a multi-dimensional information hiding model in the presence of a steganayst. Then functions and behavior constraints of the participating parties in the model are introduced in detail. Finally, based on information theory and attacker-based security theory, a set of mathematical formulas that quantify the security of the new model is given.

In summary, this work makes the following contributions:

1. Combined with the characteristics of VoIP multi-protocol, a VoIP layered covert communication model with passive attacker is proposed and a formal definition is given. The characteristics and attributes of the layered model are studied.
2. We define the tasks of all participating parties in the model, and refine the behavioral constraints of senders, receivers and passive attackers in multi-dimensional covert communication.
3. From the perspective of attacker, we give quantitative indicators of the security of multi-dimensional information hiding models. Further mathematical reasoning supporting these indicators is given. Some results are given to guide the design of multi-dimensional convert communication.

The rest of the paper is organized as follows. Section 2 discusses related work on existing steganography model, security evaluation and multi-dimensional steganography. Section 3 provides some information on terminologies and notations used in the paper. Section 4 presents a VoIP-based covert communication model, followed by the formal definition of the model and behavioral constraints on the participants in the model. Section 5 details quantitative analysis of the security by mathematical reasoning. Finally, we conclude the paper and discuss future work in Sect. 6.

2   Related Work

In the field of information hiding, the most famous model is the prisoner model proposed by Simmons et al. [23] This model could well explain the principle of covert communication, but it was not enough to describe the entire covert communication system. Zöllner et al. [31] first gave the definition of information entropy for steganographic security, which provided a way of thinking for the study of steganographic security. However, due to the complexity of computing conditional entropy of the carriers, the proposed security definition cannot be used to guide the design of steganographic algorithm. Cachin [2] defined an information-theoretic model for steganography with a passive adversary. In his opinion, steganographic analysis can be interpreted as a hypothesis testing problem and the security was defined by relative entropy. His theoretical results have been widely used.

Moulin et al. [18] presented an information-theoretic analysis of information hiding. They formalized some notions, evaluated the hiding capacity and quantified the fundamental tradeoff between the achievable information-hiding rates and the allowed distortion levels for the information hider and the attacker. Based on Moulin's work, Wang et al. [25] further proposed how to build a perfectly secure steganography system. Sallee et al. [21] studied the maximum embedded capacity in a specific steganalysis algorithm and gave a way to get the maximum embedded capacity. Cox et al. [4] studied the steganographic security and security capacity when there is a correlation between secret information and the carrier, pointing out that the security capacity increases when the secret information and the carrier are independent of each other. Sullivan et al. [24] modeled the carrier using Markov chains and described steganographic security based on the divergence distance between the transition probability matrices before and after embedding.

Ker et al. [6,11,13] studied the square root law of steganographic capacity and give a formal proof of this law for imperfect stegosystems. In the follow-up work [12,14], they established the theory and safety evaluation basis of batch steganography. Sajedi et al. [20] presented an adaptive batch steganography (ABS) approach and an ensemble system using steganalyzer units, which can benefit from better classification performance than individual classifiers and more resilience to noise. Fraczek et al. [7] proposed the concept of multi-layer steganography based on VoIP streams. In their approach, the corresponding steganographic algorithm could be chosen to increase hidden capacity and concealment. The disadvantage is that the model was too complex and lacked universality. In addition to information theory based modeling and security analysis methods, Hopper et al. [9] defined a steganographic security based on computational complexity. Chandramouli et al. [3] recommended measuring security from the perspective of the attacker and solving security capacity. Then they gave new definitons for steganography security and steganographic capacity in the presence of a steganayst.

3   Terminologies and Notations

Streaming media refers to the form of audio, video, and multimedia files that are streamed over the network. Streaming is to divide a multimedia file into a group of data packets through a special compression method. Here each packet is represented by $p(k)$, k is the packet sequence number. Then a piece of streaming media containing N packets can be expressed as $P_N(k) = \bigcup_{k=0}^{N-1} p(k)$.

Hidden features are a set of carrier features suitable for information hiding extracted from a stream, denoted as symbol $\omega_i, 0 \leq i \leq L-1$, where L is the total number of hidden features extracted from a stream of long N. Such features include IP packets timing intervals, RTP and RTCP protocol fields, or speech encoder parameters, and so on. The L hidden features constitute a hidden feature set, which is denoted by the symbol $\Omega(P_N(k)) = (\omega_0, \omega_1, \ldots, \omega_{L-1})$. However, not all of the extracted L features can serve as carriers for information hiding. Due to the correlation between the carriers, the modification of one carrier by the steganography algorithm may affect the concealment of the other carrier. Only under the control of some hidden strategy, the hidden features are transformed by a certain mapping, and the resulting multi-dimensional information hiding can achieve more than the steganographic security and capacity of a single carrier. Here we select n mutually orthogonal features from the hidden feature set to form an n-dim hidden space, denoted as $C_n(P_N(k)) = \{c_i \mid i = 0, \ldots, n-1\}$. The hidden function refers to some transformation and inverse transformation of the carrier features C and the secret message M to obtain stego carriers S. Here,

F, G denotes the embedded function and the extraction function, respectively. The steganography process satisfies $G(F(C, M, K)) = M$, where K is the control key for steganography.

For multi-protocol carriers, many steganographic algorithms can be used in parallel to embed secret message. For some feature c_i in $n - dim$ hidden space, f_i (c_i) represents the hidden function corresponding to the feature c_i. Each hidden function and hidden feature can be a one-to-one relationship or a many-to-one relationship. Therefore, the hidden function vector corresponding to the $n - dim$ hidden space is defined as,

$$F(C_n(P(k))) = (f_1(c_1), f_2(c_2), \ldots, f_n(c_n)). \tag{1}$$

4   VoIP-Based Covert Communication Model

4.1   Model Framework and Formal Definition

There are three types of participants in this model: Alice, Bob, and Eve, which are covert sender, receiver and passive attacker, respectively. Alice and Bob intend to conduct covert communication through some kind of VoIP system. In the normal communication process between the two parties, Alice hides the secret information into the normal VoIP stream by some means of steganography. After receiving the synchronization information, Bob begins to extract secret message from the stego carriers and obtains the information after decryption. During the communication process, in addition to channel noise interference, there may be an attacker Eve, which is intended to detect whether there is secret information in the normal VoIP stream, or even destroy the communication process. The former is called passive attack and the latter is active attack. In this paper, we focus only on the most common forms of attack – passive attack (see Fig. 1).

Suppose Σ is a VoIP multi-dimensional information hiding model. Let $\Sigma = \langle C, M, K, S, Enc, Dec, Div, Com, F, G, \varphi, F_i \rangle$, where each symbol means the following,

$C : C(c_1, c_2, \ldots, c_n)$ represents a set of VoIP hidden features (see Sect. 3).

$M : M$ is set of secret message.

$K : K(K_e, K_s)$ is a set of encryption key K_e and steganographic control key K_s.

$S : S(s_1, s_2, \ldots, s_n)$ represents a set of composite stego carriers generated after steganography based on n hidden features.

$Enc : M' = Enc(M, k_e)$ represents the encryption function. Alice encrypts secret message before embedding it to ensure the information security. This process has no effect on the security of the covert communication system.

$Dec : M = Dec(M', k_e)$ represents the decryption function. Bob decrypt the original information after extracting the information.

$Div : Div(M') = (m'_1, m'_2, \ldots, m'_n)$ stands for secret message splitting function. The encrypted message is divided into n fragments. Each fragment corresponds to a steganographic algorithm and hidden feature.

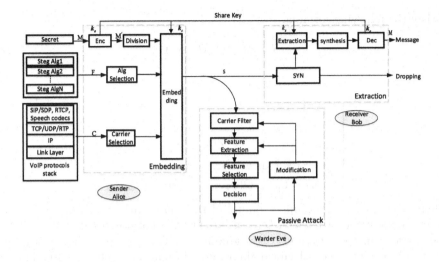

Fig. 1. VoIP-based covert communication model

$Com : M' = Com(m'_1, m'_2, \ldots, m'_K)$ represents secret message synthesis function. The extracted n fragments are combined into a complete secret message.

$F : F(f_1, f_2, \ldots, f_p)$ represents a set of embeddable functions, $F \subset \mathcal{F}$ (see Sect. 3).

$G : G(g_1, g_2, \ldots, g_L)$ represents a set of extraction functions. A fragment m'_i can be calculated by $m'_i = f_i(s'_i)$.

$\varphi(\bullet)$ denotes a multi-dimensional steganography control function, which effectively combines multiple steganography algorithms and carriers to obtain an algorithm with higher security and larger capacity.

$\Gamma_i : \Gamma_i(s_i) \to \{0, 1\}$ denotes decision function to decide whether steganography has occurred.

4.2 Behavioral Constraints on the Participating Parties

During the covert communication, the operations performed by Alice are as follows. Firstly, Alice encrypt secret message to prevent secret information that was successfully extracted from leaking. Next, Alice divides secret message into fragments according to the granularity of different hidden feature requirements. Alice has a relatively complete steganogrpahic algorithms and carrier library. She can choose different combinations of algorithms and carriers according to constraints of the network environment, security level of secret message, risk of attack, and the like. Finally, Alice should complete steganography under the premise of guaranteeing the quality of VoIP, and ensure that the carrier distortion caused by steganography is optimal. That is, VoIP stream is statistically indistinguishable before and after steganography. For Alice, all operations should satisfy the following formula,

$$S = \phi(F(C, M', K_s)) \tag{2}$$

s.t.

$$\begin{cases} G(S, K_s) = C, \\ I(M', S) \leq \varepsilon, \\ d_i(c_i, s_i) \leq D_i, c_i \subset C, s_i \subset S, \\ d(C, S) \leq \min(d_1, d_2, \ldots, d_n), \\ O(\phi_i) \leq \mathcal{C}_{max}, O(\phi_1, \phi_2, \ldots, \phi_L) \leq \mathcal{C}_{max}. \end{cases} \tag{3}$$

where, $\mathcal{C}_{max}$ denotes the upper bound of the computational complexity of the covert communication system, D_i is the upper bound of statistical distortion that the carrier can tolerate, and ε is a minimum value close to 0, indicating that even if stego carriers are obtained almost no information is achieved. In addition, the distortion caused by multi-dimensional steganography cannot exceed the minimum distortion caused by a single steganography.

Receiver Bob needs to extract secret message from the stego stream. Bob first needs to know when to start extracting secret information. Synchronization is also an urgent problem to be solved in covert communication. This paper does not do in-depth research. Bob performs $g(s_i) = m_i'$ to get each steganographic fragment. Then he continue to execute the synthesis function $Com(m_1', m_2', \ldots, m_K')$ to get the complete secret message M'. So Bob is constrained as $M' = Com(G(S))$.

The primary goal of passive attacker is to detect and identify covert communication. If a passive attacker obtains the original carrier, there will always be a way to discover the existence of covert communication by comparing the statistical structure of the original carriers and the stego carriers. In reality, the attacker does not have any information about steganographic algorithms and key except the suspect data to be detected and the detecting result indicators. Therefore, Eve needs to filter the data from the target traffic to get the hidden features, and then extract the classification features that can fully reflect the changes of the carrier before and after steganography. For a streaming media $P_N(k)$, assume that the attacker filters it to get N hidden features $(\omega_0, \omega_1, \ldots, \omega_{N-1})$. The attacker first makes a steganographic judgment for each hidden feature, and obtains N decisions $\Gamma_0(\omega_0), \Gamma_1(\omega_1), \ldots, \Gamma_{N-1}(\omega_{N-1})$. Using the idea of integrated classification [3], N decision results are further judged and the final decision Γ is given. Γ has false alarm rate α and missed alarm rate β, respectively defined as,

$$\begin{cases} \alpha \overset{def}{=} P(\Gamma = 0 \mid S = 1), \\ \beta \overset{def}{=} P(\Gamma = 1 \mid S = 0). \end{cases} \tag{4}$$

5   Security Measure and Analysis

It can be seen from the above that the detection result of steganalysis algorithm can measure the security of the steganographic algorithm. If the detection algorithm has high detection accuracy, the security of the steganography algorithm is low. Conversely, if the detection algorithm has low detection accuracy, it indicates that the steganography algorithm has high security and is difficult to detect. Of course, the security of the steganographic algorithms mentioned here is only relative. As the attacker masters the carrier knowledge, the capability of steganalysis is continuously improved, and the security of the steganographic algorithm is continuously reduced. Therefore, steganography and steganalysis is a game process. It is one-sided to discuss the security of the steganography algorithm.

As we know, steganalysis can be viewed as a two-class problem. Here the normal carriers are assigned to the negative category and the stego carriers in the positive category. Three statistical indicators are used to measure the classification efficacy of steganalysis, i.e. false positive rate (FPR), false negative rate (FNR), and accuracy (ACC). Figure 2 shows the confusion matrix for steganalysis.

		T=0 Y Predicted Class	T=1 N
Stego:S=0	P	Ture Positive (TP)	False Negative (FN) Type II Error
Normal:S=1	N	False Positive (FP) Type I Error	Ture Negative (TN)

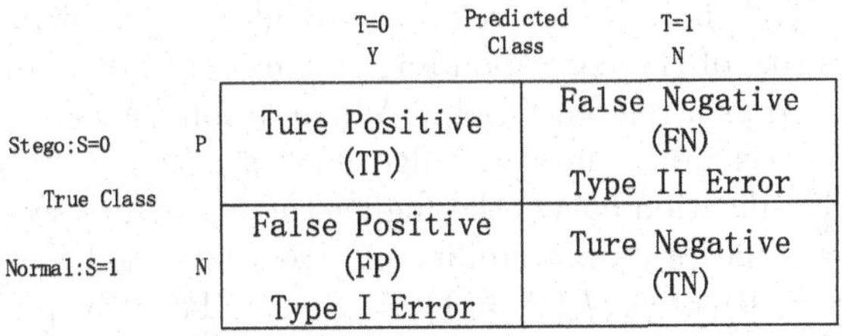

Fig. 2. The confusion matrix for steganalysis

As can be seen from Fig. 2, the attacker will inevitably make two mistakes. The cover carrier is mistaken as a stego carrier and is called type I error (false alarm rate α). The stego carrier is mistaken as a normal carrier and is called type II error (missing alarm rate β). The purpose of steganalysis is to increase the detection accuracy under the premise of the lowest false alarm rate and missed alarm rate. But if the two cannot be reduced at the same time, it is necessary to decide which indicator to give priority to according to the application requirements.

Moreover, when the proportion of positive and negative samples varies greatly, TPR and FPR can not reflect the detection effect of the classifier well. However, an ROC graph can depict relative tradeoffs between benefits (true positives) and costs (false positives). Figure 3 shows an ROC graph with Three classifiers labeled A through C. Point $A(0,0)$ in the figure is the ideal target point and the classification performance is best. A good classification model

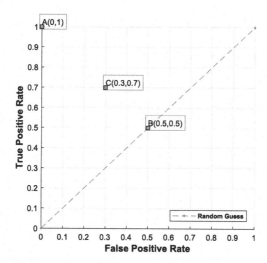

Fig. 3. A ROC graph showing three discrete classifiers

should be as close as possible to Point $A(0,0)$, away from the points (such as point $B(0.5, 0.5)$) in the main diagonal line. So we can use the distance of a classifier in the ROC chart from a reference point as a quantitative indicator to measure the security of the corresponding steganography algorithm. For example, point B is used as a reference point. When a point is closer to point B, the classification effect is worse, and the algorithm security is higher. Conversely, the better the classification effect, the higher the algorithm security.

Assuming that the prior probability of streaming media as a stego carrier is p_s, then $P(S = 0) = p_s, P(S = 1) = 1 - p_s$. For any point X, the joint probability distribution of the carrier S and the decision Γ can be calculated as follows,

$$P_X(S, \Gamma_X) = P(\Gamma_X \mid S)P(S) = \begin{bmatrix} (1-\alpha)p_S & \alpha p_S \\ (1-p_S)\beta & (1-\alpha)(1-p_S) \end{bmatrix} \tag{5}$$

For point B,

$$P_B(S, \Gamma_B) = \begin{bmatrix} 0.5p_S & 0.5p_S \\ 0.5(1-p_S) & 0.5(1-p_S) \end{bmatrix} \tag{6}$$

Then, the relative entropy of point X and point B is calculated as follows,

$$\begin{aligned} D(P_B&(S, \Gamma_B) \parallel P_X(S, \Gamma_X)) \\ &= \begin{bmatrix} 0.5p_S & 0.5p_S \\ 0.5(1-p_S) & 0.5(1-p_S) \end{bmatrix} \parallel \begin{bmatrix} (1-\alpha)p_S & \alpha p_S \\ (1-p_S)\beta & (1-\alpha)(1-p_S) \end{bmatrix} \\ &= -0.5p_S \log_2 \alpha(1-\alpha) - 0.5(1-p_S) \log_2 \beta(1-\beta) \end{aligned} \tag{7}$$

From the calculation results of relative entropy, the following conclusions can be drawn.

1. Since $0 < \alpha, \beta < 1, 0 < p_s < 1, D(P_B(S, \Gamma_B) \parallel P_X(S, \Gamma_X)) \geq 0$ can be obtained.

2. $\frac{\partial D(P_B(S,\Gamma_B)\parallel P_X(S,\Gamma_X))}{\partial p_r} = -0.5\log_2 \alpha(1-\alpha) - 0.5\log_2 \beta(1-\beta)$

   Suppose $\frac{\partial D(P_B(S,\Gamma_B)\parallel P_X(S,\Gamma_X))}{\partial p_r} \leq 0$, then

   $-0.5\log_2 \alpha(1-\alpha) - 0.5\log_2 \beta(1-\beta) \leq 0$,

   and,

   $\alpha + \beta \geq 1$

   In general, α and β of an effective detection algorithm are all in the range of $[0, 1]$, and both take relatively small values. So $\alpha + \beta \geq 1$ does not match the actual situation. The assumption is not true. So $D(P_B(S, \Gamma_B) \parallel P_X(S, \Gamma_X)) \geq 0$ is established. It can be seen that the more a priori knowledge the attacker has, the higher the detection ability and the worse the security of steganography algorithm.

3. The closer $D(P_B(S, \Gamma_B)\parallel P_X(S, \Gamma_X))$ is to 0, the closer the ROC curve is to the random guess line, indicating that the worse the detection effect, the higher the safety. Conversely, the farther away the ROC curve is from the random guess line, the better the detection effect and the lower the security.

6   Conclusion

In this paper, we present a multi-dimensional information hiding model in the presence of a steganayst and give a formal definition of the model. We clearly describes working principle of multi-dimensional information hiding model, and then analyze the behavior constraints of each participant in the model in detail. The proposed model can provide some theoretical guidance for designing related steganography algorithms and steganalysis algorithms. Finally, Based on information theory and attacker detection theory, a method for quantitative analysis of the security of multi-dimensional information hiding model is proposed.

In the future, we will continue to study security capacity and robustness in the multi-dimensional information hiding model. And under the guidance of the model, try to design a multi-dimensional information hiding algorithm.

References

1. Cabuk, S., Brodley, C.E., Shields, C.: IP covert timing channels: design and detection. In: Proceedings of the 11th ACM Conference on Computer and Communications Security, CCS 2004, Washington, DC, USA, 25–29 October 2004, pp. 178–187 (2004). https://doi.org/10.1145/1030083.1030108
2. Cachin, C.: An information-theoretic model for steganography. Inf. Comput. **192**(1), 41–56 (2004). https://doi.org/10.1016/j.ic.2004.02.003
3. Chandramouli, R., Memon, N.D.: Steganography capacity: a steganalysis perspective. In: Security and Watermarking of Multimedia Contents V, Santa Clara, CA, USA, 20 January 2003, pp. 173–177 (2003). https://doi.org/10.1117/12.479732

4. Cox, I.J., Kalker, T., Pakura, G., Scheel, M.: Information transmission and steganography. In: Barni, M., Cox, I., Kalker, T., Kim, H.-J. (eds.) IWDW 2005. LNCS, vol. 3710, pp. 15–29. Springer, Heidelberg (2005). https://doi.org/10.1007/11551492_2

5. El-Latif, A.A.A., Abd-El-Atty, B., Hossain, M.S., Elmougy, S., Ghoneim, A.: Secure quantum steganography protocol for fog cloud internet of things. IEEE Access **6**, 10332–10340 (2018). https://doi.org/10.1109/ACCESS.2018.2799879

6. Filler, T., Ker, A.D., Fridrich, J.J.: The square root law of steganographic capacity for Markov covers. In: Media Forensics and Security I, part of the IS&T-SPIE Electronic Imaging Symposium, San Jose, CA, USA, 19–21 January 2009, Proceedings, p. 725408 (2009). https://doi.org/10.1117/12.805911

7. Fraczek, W., Mazurczyk, W., Szczypiorski, K.: Multi-level steganography: improving hidden communication in networks. CoRR abs/1101.4789 (2011). http://arxiv.org/abs/1101.4789

8. Ghasemzadeh, H., Kayvanrad, M.H.: Comprehensive review of audio steganalysis methods. IET Sig. Process. **12**(6), 673–687 (2018). https://doi.org/10.1049/iet-spr.2016.0651

9. Hopper, N.J., von Ahn, L., Langford, J.: Provably secure steganography. IEEE Trans. Comput. **58**(5), 662–676 (2009). https://doi.org/10.1109/TC.2008.199

10. Hosam, O., Ahmad, M.H.: Hybrid design for cloud data security using combination of AES, ECC and LSB steganography. IJCSE **19**(2), 153–161 (2019). https://doi.org/10.1504/IJCSE.2018.10016054

11. Ker, A.D.: Batch steganography and pooled steganalysis. In: Camenisch, J.L., Collberg, C.S., Johnson, N.F., Sallee, P. (eds.) IH 2006. LNCS, vol. 4437, pp. 265–281. Springer, Heidelberg (2007). https://doi.org/10.1007/978-3-540-74124-4_18

12. Ker, A.D.: Batch steganography and the threshold game. In: Security, Steganography, and Watermarking of Multimedia Contents IX, San Jose, CA, USA, 28 January 2007, p. 650504 (2007). https://doi.org/10.1117/12.703334

13. Ker, A.D.: A capacity result for batch steganography. IEEE Sig. Process. Lett. **14**(8), 525–528 (2007). https://doi.org/10.1109/LSP.2006.891319

14. Ker, A.D., Pevný, T.: Batch steganography in the real world. In: Multimedia and Security Workshop, MM&Sec 2012, Coventry, United Kingdom, 6–7 September 2012, pp. 1–10 (2012). https://doi.org/10.1145/2361407.2361409

15. Liu, P., Li, S., Wang, H.: Steganography integrated into linear predictive coding for low bit-rate speech codec. Multimed. Tools Appl. **76**(2), 2837–2859 (2016). https://doi.org/10.1007/s11042-016-3257-x

16. Mazurczyk, W.: VoIP steganography and its detection–a survey. ACM Comput. Surv. (CSUR) **46**(2), 20 (2013)

17. Mazurczyk, W., Lubacz, J.: LACK - a VoIP steganographic method. Telecommun. Syst. **45**(2–3), 153–163 (2010). https://doi.org/10.1007/s11235-009-9245-y

18. Moulin, P., O'Sullivan, J.A.: Information-theoretic analysis of information hiding. IEEE Trans. Inf. Theory **49**(3), 563–593 (2003). https://doi.org/10.1109/TIT.2002.808134

19. Rowland, C.H.: Covert channels in the TCP/IP protocol suite. First Monday **2**(5) (1997). https://firstmonday.org/ojs/index.php/fm/article/view/528

20. Sajedi, H., Jamzad, M.: Adaptive batch steganography considering image embedding capacity. Opt. Eng. **48** (2009). https://doi.org/10.1117/1.3204231

21. Sallee, P.: Model-based methods for steganography and steganalysis. Int. J. Image Graph. **5**(1), 167–190 (2005). https://doi.org/10.1142/S0219467805001719

22. Shah, G., Molina, A.: Keyboards and covert channels. In: Proceedings of the 15th USENIX Security Symposium, Vancouver, BC, Canada, 31 July – 4 August (2006). https://www.usenix.org/conference/15th-usenix-security-symposium/keyboards-and-covert-channels

23. Simmons, G.J.: The prisoners' problem and the subliminal channel. In: Chaum, D. (ed.) Advances in Cryptology, pp. 51–67. Springer, Heidelberg (1983)

24. Sullivan, K., Madhow, U., Chandrasekaran, S., Manjunath, B.S.: Steganalysis for Markov cover data with applications to images. IEEE Trans. Inf. Forensics Secur. 1(2), 275–287 (2006). https://doi.org/10.1109/TIFS.2006.873595

25. Wang, Y., Moulin, P.: Perfectly secure steganography: capacity, error exponents, and code constructions. IEEE Trans. Inf. Theory 54(6), 2706–2722 (2008). https://doi.org/10.1109/TIT.2008.921684

26. Wendzel, S.: Novel approaches for network covert storage channels. Ph.D. thesis, FernUniversität in Hagen (2013). http://deposit.fernuni-hagen.de/2921/

27. Xiang, T., Hu, J., Sun, J.: Outsourcing chaotic selective image encryption to the cloud with steganography. Digit. Sig. Process. 43, 28–37 (2015). https://doi.org/10.1016/j.dsp.2015.05.006

28. Xiao, B., Huang, Y., Tang, S.: An approach to information hiding in low bit-rate speech stream, pp. 1–5. IEEE (2008)

29. Xu, G., Yang, W., Huang, L.: Hybrid covert channel in LTE-A: modeling and analysis. J. Netw. Comput. Appl. 111, 117–126 (2018). https://doi.org/10.1016/j.jnca.2018.02.001

30. Zielinska, E., Mazurczyk, W., Szczypiorski, K.: Trends in steganography. Commun. ACM 57(3), 86–95 (2014)

31. Zöllner, J., et al.: Modeling the security of steganographic systems. In: Aucsmith, D. (ed.) IH 1998. LNCS, vol. 1525, pp. 344–354. Springer, Heidelberg (1998). https://doi.org/10.1007/3-540-49380-8_24

Information Processing

A New Method for Measuring the Similarity of Vague Sets and Its Application in Fault Diagnosis

Yongzhi Liu[1,2(⊠)] and Dechang Pi[2]

[1] Alibaba Big Data School of Fuzhou Polytechnic, Fuzhou 350108, China
y_zliu@163.com
[2] College of Computer Science and Technology, Nanjing
University of Aeronautics and Astronautics, Nanjing 210016, China
nuaacs@126.com

Abstract. A new similarity measurement method of vague value is proposed which compare with the existing similarity measurement methods. The proposed method has good distinguishing degree and less computation steps and times which possess the basic properties and satisfying similarity measurement. By the data analysis of data membership degree investigate the pattern recognition to achieve the measuring. Moreover, comparison with the results of both methods has proved that proposed method is a more reasonable way to measure the similarity of Vague value, Finally, the method is proved to be effective in fault diagnosis.

Keywords: Vague value · Similarity · Fault diagnosis · Pattern recognition

1 Introduction

In general, people make decisions about certain things that often get the desired results based on incomplete, inaccurate or vague information, and inaccurate or vague information. The results will be almost the same when dealing with this information by using human thinking simulating with a computer. Fuzzy set theory plays an important role in intelligent systems such as fuzzy control, fuzzy expert systems and fuzzy decision support systems. In the literature, Zadeh proposed a fuzzy set [1]. Fuzzy set theory, the value of membership is determined by the closeness of membership, but the truth membership and false membership cannot be expressed at the same time. This indicates that fuzzy set theory is not the best tool for dealing with ambiguity.

To overcome the shortcomings of fuzzy set theory, Gau and Buehrer proposed a new Vague set theory in 1993 to deal with fuzzy information [2]. In the Vague set which each subject is given a certain degree of membership but the difference is that the degree of membership is a subinterval of [0, 1]. This subinterval not only provides evidence supporting x ∈ X but also provides evidence for x ∈ X. For example, 10 people were asked to vote on an even and the results for three cases were "support", "opposition" and "abstain". As a result, five people voted for the event which have

© Springer Nature Singapore Pte Ltd. 2020
X. Sun et al. (Eds.): ICAIS 2020, CCIS 1254, pp. 539–548, 2020.
https://doi.org/10.1007/978-981-15-8101-4_48

three opposed and two abstained that is impossible to process such fuzzy information with fuzzy sets. The concept of fuzzy sets enriches the way. people describe things and promotes the development of patterns recognition, machine learning and other fields. The similarity measure of fuzzy values is the basis of fuzzy research, and it is of great significance for the research of artificial intelligence such as knowledge representation and pattern recognition. The similarity measure of Vague values has attracted extensive attention from many scholars all over the world and the similarities have been studied by using different ways [3–10]. Chen [3, 4] proposed a method for Vague set similarity metrics. Hong et al. illustrate the irrationality of Chen's Vague set similarity measure with excellent examples, and propose a new Vague set similarity measure [5].

2 Vague Set

Definition 1: Let U be the universe of discourse,$\forall x \in U$, a vague set A in U is chartered by a truth-membership function $t_A(x)$ and false-membership function $f_A(x)$

$$t_A : U \rightarrow [0, 1] \ f_A : U \rightarrow [0, 1]$$

Where $0 \le t_A(x) + f_A(x) \le 1$.$t_A(x)$ is a true-membership function, the lower bound of membership degree expressing support $x \in A$.$f_A(x)$ is a false-membership function, the lower bound of membership degree expressing against $x \in A$. $u_A(x) = 1 - t_A(x) - f_A(x)$ is called vague degree. It describes the unknown degree of x relative to the vague set and is a measure of the unknown information of x relative to A.$0 \le u_A(x) \le 1$, The larger the $u_A(x)$ value, the more unknown information.

When U is continuous, a vague set A can be written as Eq. (1).

$$A = \int \left[t_A(x), 1 - f_A(x) \right] / x dx \ x \in U \tag{1}$$

When U is discrete, a vague set A can be written as Eq. (2)

$$A = \sum_{i=1}^{n} [t_A(x_i), 1 - f_A(x_i)]/x_i \ x_i \in U \tag{2}$$

For example, assume that U = [1–5]. Small is a vague set of U defined as Small = [0.5, 0.8]/1 + [0.7, 1]/2 + [0.3, 0.9]/3.

Definition 2: Let x be a vague value, $x = \left[t_A(x), 1 - f_A(x) \right]$, where $0 \le t_A(x) \le 1 - f_A(x) \le 1$, the vague value x can be divided into three parts: $t_A(x)$ is the truth-membership part,$f_A(x)$ is the false-membership part and $u_A(x) = 1 - t_A(x) - f_A(x)$ is the unknown part.

For example, if $\left[t_A(x), 1 - f_A(x) \right] = [0.6, 0.8]$, then we can see that $t_x = 0.6$; $1 - f_x = 0.8 \rightarrow f_x = 0.2 \ u_x = 1 - t_x - f_x = 1 - 0.6 - 0.2 = 0.2$. It can be interpreted as the degree that objects x belongs to vague set A is 0.6; the degree that objects x does not belong to vague set A is 0.2. If interpreted by ballot, it can be interpreted as 6 votes for support, 2 votes against and 2 abstentions.

3 Vague Operations and Relational Rules

Let $x = [t_x, 1 - f_x]$, $y = [t_y, 1 - f_y]$, $t_x, f_x, t_y, f_y \in [0, 1]$, $0 \le t_x + f_x \le 1$, $0 \le t_y + f_y \le 1$.

Vague value operations and relational rules are as Eq. (3) and (4).

$$x \wedge y = [\min(t_x, t_y), \min(1 - f_x, 1 - f_y)] \tag{3}$$

$$x \vee y = [\max(t_x, t_y), \max(1 - f_x, 1 - f_y)] \tag{4}$$

$$x \ge y \Leftrightarrow t_x \ge t_y \, \& f_x \ge f_y \tag{5}$$

$$\bar{x} = [f_x, 1 - t_x] \tag{6}$$

Let A and B be two vague sets on the U, such as Eq. (5) and (6).

$$A = \sum_{i=1}^{n} [t_A(x_i), 1 - f_A(x_i)]/x_i \tag{7}$$

$$B = \sum_{i=1}^{n} [t_B(x_i), 1 - f_B(x_i)]/x_i \tag{8}$$

Vague sets operations and relational rules are as Eqs. (5)–(8)

$$A \subseteq B \Leftrightarrow \forall x_i \in V, \, t_A(x_i) \le t_B(x_i) \, \& f_A(x_i) \ge f_B(x_i) \tag{9}$$

$$A = B \Leftrightarrow \forall x_i \in V, \, t_A(x_i) = t_B(x_i) \, \& f_A(x_i) = f_B(x_i) \tag{10}$$

$$A \cap B = \sum \{[t_A(x_i), 1 - f_A(x_i)] \wedge [t_B(x_i), 1 - f_B(x_i)]\}/x_i \tag{11}$$

$$A \cup B = \sum \{[t_A(x_i), 1 - f_A(x_i)] \vee [t_B(x_i), 1 - f_B(x_i)]\}/x_i \tag{12}$$

$$\bar{A} = \sum_{i=1}^{n} [f_A(x_i), t_A(x_i)]/x_i \tag{13}$$

4 Old Vague Similarity Measurement Method

In Ref. [3, 4], Chen defined a similarity measure Mc between the vague values x and y, denoted by Mc(x, y);

$$M_c = 1 - \frac{|S(x) - S(y)|}{2} = 1 - \frac{|(t_x - t_y) - (f_x - f_y)|}{2} \tag{14}$$

In Ref [5], Hong and Kim illustrate the problems of Mc and propose a modified method M_{hk}, denoted by $M_{hk}(x, y)$;

$$M_{hk}(x, y) = 1 - \frac{|t_x - t_y| + |f_x - f_y|}{2} \tag{15}$$

In Ref [6], Li Fan et al. illustrate the problems of Mc and propose a modified method M_{lf}, denoted by $M_{lf}(x, y)$;

$$M_{lf} = 1 - \frac{|S(x) - S(y)|}{4} - \frac{|t_x - t_y| + |f_x - f_y|}{4} \tag{16}$$

In Ref [7], Li Yanhong et al. proposed a similarity formula based on distance measure on the basis of M_{lf}, which is named M_{lyh}.

$$M_{lyh}(x, y) = 1 - \sqrt{\frac{(t_x - t_y)^2 + (f_x - f_y)^2}{2}} \tag{17}$$

In Ref [8], Yan Deqin et al. proposed a similarity formula based on distance measure on the basis of M_{lyh}, and the unknown parts is considered, which is named M_{lyh}.

$$M_{ydq}(x, y) = 1 - \sqrt{\frac{(t_x - t_y)^2 + (f_x - f_y)^2 + (\pi_x - \pi_y)^2}{2}} \tag{18}$$

Although M_{ydq} takes into account the unknown part, in the measurements of [0, 0], [0, 1] and [0, 1], [1, 1], the results are all zero, which is not reasonable. It is possible for the unknown part to vote in favour or against, so the unknown part can be divided into three parts, $t_x\pi_x, f_x\pi_x, .\pi_x\pi_x$. so Vage value is denoted

$$\left(t'_x, f'_x, \pi'_x\right) = (t_x + t_z\pi_x, f_x + f_x\pi_x, \pi_x + \pi_x\pi_x)$$

In Ref [9], Liu Huawen illustrate the problems of M_{ydq} and propose a modified method M_{lhw}, denoted by $M_{lwh}(x, y)$

$$M_{lwh}(x, y) = 1 - \frac{\left|\left(t'_x - f'_x\right) - \left(t'_y - f'_y\right)\right| + 2\left|\left(t'_x + f'_x\right) - \left(t'_y + f'_y\right)\right|}{4} \tag{19}$$

In Ref [10], Deng Weibin et al. illustrate the problems of M_{ydq} and propose a modified method M_{dwb}, denoted by $M_{dwb}(x, y)$

$M_{dwb}(x, y)$
$$= e^{-\left(\frac{(t_x - t_y)^2}{1 + t_x + t_y} + \frac{(f_x - f_y)^2}{1 + f_x + f_y} + (S(x) - S(y))^2 + (|t_x + \pi_x| - |t_y + \pi_y|)^2 + (|f_x + \pi_x| - |f_y + \pi_y|)^2\right)} \tag{20}$$

This method can solve the similarity problem of Vague very well and has a high degree of discrimination, but it does not give a good definition for some special values such as [0, 1] and the calculation is complex

5 Similar Properties of Vague Value

Let x and y be two vague values $x = [t_x, 1 - f_x]$, $y = [t_y, 1 - f_y]$, $0 \le t_x \le 1 - f_x \le 1$, and $0 \le t_y \le 1 - f_y \le 1$, defined a similarity measure $M(x, y)$ between the vagues x and y. $M(x, y)$ has the following properties

Property 1: $\forall x, y \in A, 0 \leq M(x, y) \leq 1$;

Property 2: $\forall x, y \in A, M(x, y) = M(y, x)$;

Property 3: $\forall x, y \in A, M(x, y) = 1$ if and only if $x = y$;

Property 4: $\forall x, y \in A, M(x, y) = 0$ if and only if $x = [0, 0], y = [1, 1]$ or $x = [1, 1], y = [0, 0]$;

Property 5: $\forall x \in A, y = [0, 1]$, the value of $M(x, y)$ can be any value in the $[0, 1]$ interval and is denoted as $\forall[0, 1]$.

Properties 1 to 4 are obvious and necessary for similarity measurement of vague values that the proof is omitted because it is easy to check. The Vague values of y in property 5 are special. $y = [0, 1]$, $t_y = 0$, $f_y = 0$, $u_y = 1$. It means that no one supports or opposes it. Their attitude is unknown and is meaningless to compare it with any vague value. Therefore, we stipulate that its $M(x, y)$ value is any value in the $[0, 1]$ interval.

6 New Similarity Measure for Vague Values

In order to better measure the similarity between vague values, this paper proposes a new measurement method based on the study of previous literatures. The following A is the vague sets, B is the vague sets.

Definition 3: $\forall x \in A, x = [t_x, 1 - f_x], u_x = 1 - t_x - f_x$, where, $t_{xu} = \frac{t_x}{t_x + f_x} \times u_x$, $f_{xu} = \frac{f_x}{t_x + f_x} \times u_x$;

Definition 4: $\forall x, y \in A, x = [t_x, 1 - f_x], y = [t_y, 1 - f_y], T = \min(t_x + t_{xu}, t_y + t_{yu}), F = \min(f_x + f_{xu}, f_y + f_{yu})$.

Definition 5: $\forall x, y \in A, x = [t_x, 1 - f_x], y = [t_y, 1 - f_y] M(x, y) = T + F$;

Definition 6: $A = \sum_{i=1}^{n} [t_A(x_i), 1 - f_A(x_i)]/x_i \ B = \sum_{i=1}^{n} [t_B(x_i), 1 - f_B(x_i)]x_i$
The similarity between A and B is defined as

$$S(A, B) = \frac{1}{n} \sum_{i=1}^{n} M(A(x_i), B(x_i)) \tag{21}$$

Theorem 1:
$$M(x, y) \in [0, 1]$$

Proof:

$$\because T = \min(t_x + t_{xu}, t_y + t_{yu})$$
$$F = \min(f_x + f_{xu}, f_y + f_{yu})$$
$$t_x + t_{xu} + f_x + f_{xu} = 1$$
$$t_y + t_{yu} + f_y + f_{yu} = 1$$
$$t_x \geq 0 \; t_{xu} \geq 0 \, f_x \geq 0 \; f_{xu} \geq 0$$
$$t_y \geq 0 \; t_{yu} \geq 0 \, f_y \geq 0 \; f_{yu} \geq 0$$
$$T + F = \min(t_x + t_{xu}, t_y + t_{yu}) + \min(f_x + f_{xu}, f_y + f_{yu})$$
$$\therefore 0 \leq T + F \leq 1$$
$$M(x, y) \in [0, 1] \; Q.E.D$$

Theorem 2: $M(x, y) = M(y, x)$

Proof:

$$\because M(x, y) = T + F$$
$$M(y, x) = T + F$$
$$\therefore M(x, y) = M(y, x) \; Q.E.D$$

Theorem 3: $M(x, y) = 1 \Leftrightarrow x = y$

Proof: ① $\because x = y$

$$M(x, y) = T + F \; T = \min(t_x + t_{xu}, t_y + t_{yu})$$
$$F = \min(f_x + f_{xu}, f_y + f_{yu})$$
$$f_x + f_{xu} = f_y + f_{yu}$$
$$t_x + t_{xu} = t_y + t_{yu}$$
$$t_x + t_{xu} + f_x + f_{xu} = 1$$
$$t_y + t_{yu} + f_y + f_{yu} = 1$$
$$\therefore M(x, y) = T + F = 1$$

② $\because M(x, y) = 1$

$$T + F = 1$$
$$\min(t_x + t_{xu}, t_y + t_{yu}) + \min(f_x + f_{xu}, f_y + f_{yu}) = 1$$
$$\text{But } T + F \leq 1$$
$$\therefore \text{if and only if } x = y \text{ then } T + F = 1$$
$$Q.E.D$$

So, The proposed Vague value similarity measure $M(x, y) = T + F$ satisfies properties 1 to 5 completely.

For example, Let x and y be two vague values, where $x = [0.4, 0.8]$ and $y = [0.3, 0.7]$, as shown in Table 1.

Table 1. Vague Similarity Computation Processes for x and y

x	t_x	f_x	u_x	t_{xu}	f_{xu}	$t_x + t_{xu}$	$f_x + f_{xu}$
[0.4,0.8]	0.4	0.2	0.4	0.267	0.133	0.667	0.333
y	t_y	f_y	u_y	t_{yu}	f_{yu}	$t_y + t_{yu}$	$f_y + f_{yu}$
[0.3,0.7]	0.3	0.3	0.4	0.2	0.2	0.5	0.5

Where, T = 0.5, F = 0.333, so the similarity of vague
values of x and y is M (x, y) = 0.833.

7   Data Analysis and Comparison

A set of experimental data shows that the similarity measurement method proposed in
this paper is simple, effective and highly discriminatory. as shown in Table 2.

Table 2. Comparison of different similarity methods

	1	2	3	4	5	6	7	8	9	10	11
x y	[0.4, 0.8] [0.3, 0.7]	[0.4, 0.8] [0.3, 0.8]	[0.4, 0.8] [0.3, 0.9]	[0.4, 0.8] [0.4, 0.7]	[0.4, 0.8] [0.4, 0.9]	[0.4, 0.8] [0.5, 0.7]	[0.4, 0.8] [0.5, 0.8]	[0.4, 0.8] [0.5, 0.9]	[0, 1] [1, 1]	[0, 1] [0.5, 0.5]	[1, 1] [0.5, 0.5]
$M_c^{[4]}$	0.9	0.95	1.0	0.95	0.95	1.0	0.95	0.9	0.5	1.0	0.5
$M_{hk}^{[5]}$	0.9	0.95	0.9	0.95	0.95	0.9	0.95	0.9	0.5	0.5	0.5
$M_{lf}^{[6]}$	0.9	0.95	0.95	0.95	0.95	0.95	0.95	0.9	0.5	0.75	0.5
$M_{lyh}^{[7]}$	0.9	0.929	0.9	0.929	0.929	0.9	0.929	0.9	0.29	0.5	0.5
$M_{ydq}^{[8]}$	0.9	0.9	0.827	0.9	0.9	0.827	0.9	0.9	0	0.134	0.5
$M_{lhw}^{[9]}$	0.93	0.923	0.89	0.928	0.912	0.93	0.937	0.93	0.25	0.5	0.75
$M_{dwb}^{[10]}$	0.93	0.974	0.967	0.974	0.972	0.969	0.975	0.929	0.08	0.434	0.171
M	0.833	0.933	0.917	0.904	0.867	0.958	0.953	0.834	∀[0, 1]	∀[0, 1]	0.5

we can see the data in Table 2 that M_c's formula is concise and M_c's measure of
similarity will produce inconsistency with facts, such as x = [0.4, 0.8], y = [0.3, 0.9] or
[0.5, 0.7], the value is 1, which is inconsistent with facts and contradicts with property
2. M_{hk}, M_{lf}, M_{lyh} have few reference factors, which leads to weak ability to distinguish
similarity.

Let y = [0.4, 0.7] or [0.4, 0.9], the values of M(x, y) are 0.95, same result. M_{ydq},
M_{lhw} considers the influence of unknown parts on support and opposition. The proposed

method improves the measurement ability of similarity, but it is still unsatisfactory, if it has the same value, but the x and y values are different. Base on the property 2. M_{dwb} considers the possible influencing factors and improves the discrimination of similarity, but the computation is complex and some similarity measures are inappropriate. Let x = [1], y = [0.5, 0.5], that is $t_x = 1, f_x = 0, u_x = 0, t_y = 0.5, f_y = 0.5$ and $u_y = 0$, M(x, y) = 0.5, but result is 0.171, which is unreasonable.

In addition, we propose a comparison of similarity with [0, 1], whose value is any value between [0, 1]. we also can see the data in Table 2 that the similarity measure value is distributed between [0,1], which also proves that our proposed property 5 is reasonable.

8 Application in Fault Diagnosis

The data of 7001AC bearing operation are collected, and the results are obtained by wavelet decomposition and normalization as shown in Table 3. Then, the similarity between the sample data and the tested data Vague is calculated by Definition 5, as shown in Table 4. Finally, the similarity between the sample data and the tested data Vague set is calculated by Definition 6. The results are shown in Table 5.

Table 3. Sample data and test data represented by Vague

	A1 (normal)	A2 (inner-race faults)	A3 (outer-race faults)	T1 (test data)	T2 (test data)
Ch(1)	(0.5112, 0.5563)	(0.1485, 0.1597)	(0.1479, 0.1536)	(0.5369, 0.5452)	(0.1424, 0.1528)
Ch(2)	(0.0542, 0.0742)	(0.1173,0.1292)	(0.099, 0.1029)	(0.0435, 0.054)	(0.1021, 0.12)
Ch(3)	(0.068, 0.0772)	(0.1504, 0.2022)	(0.1494, 0.1716)	(0.0543, 0.061)	(0.1779, 0.185)
Ch(4)	(0.0625, 0.0719)	(0.1185, 0.1465)	(0.138, 0.1539)	(0.05, 0.0623)	(0.1294, 0.138)
Ch(5)	(0.0685, 0.0737)	(0.0651, 0.0849)	(0.1185, 0.1375)	(0.0553, 0.066)	(0.0698, 0.0744)
Ch(6)	(0.0667, 0.0718)	(0.0862, 0.1063)	(0.0827, 0.1054)	(0.0561, 0.0659)	(0.0912, 0.1003)
Ch(7)	(0.0592, 0.0637)	(0.1365, 0.1372)	(0.1181, 0.1324)	(0.0502, 0.0628)	(0.129, 0.1412)
Ch(8)	(0.0522, 0.0568)	(0.0977, 0.1141)	(0.0902, 0.099)	(0.0453, 0.0521)	(0.1012, 0.1094)

The higher the similarity between the test sample and the sample data, the closer the test sample is to a certain type of fault. From Table 5, we can see that S(A1, T1) > S(A2,

Table 4. Vague similarity between test data and sample data

	M(A1, T1)	M(A2, T1)	M(A3, T1)	M(A1, T2)	M(A2, T2	M(A3, T2)
Ch(1)	0.99395	0.608788	0.607354	0.608553	0.993714	0.995149
Ch(2)	0.988655	0.925249	0.944574	0.951345	0.985248	0.995427
Ch(3)	0.986035	0.89605	0.901874	0.889459	0.979444	0.97362
Ch(4)	0.98753	0.928709	0.910393	0.932571	0.991391	0.990293
Ch(5)	0.98704	0.989483	0.935103	0.998735	0.996292	0.949327
Ch(6)	0.989613	0.968687	0.972034	0.975004	0.995931	0.992583
Ch(7)	0.991373	0.914245	0.931027	0.928874	0.993998	0.98922
Ch(8)	0.993169	0.946281	0.954609	0.950405	0.997292	0.988964

Table 5. Vague sets similarity between test data and sample data

	A1	A2	A3
S(A, T1)	0.989671	0.897187	0.894621
S(A, T2)	0.904368	0.991664	0.984323

T1) > S(A3, T1), The results show that the tested data T1 is closest to A1, indicating that it is normal. S(A2, T2) > S(A3, T2) > S(A1, T2),The results show that the measured data T2 and A2 are the closest, **which** indicating that the bearing inner ring fault.

The above similarity judgment is consistent with the result of clustering method [11], but simpler than clustering method. At the same time, the sequence of faults is given, which also provides a theoretical basis for fault diagnosis. Comparing with reference [12], there is no need to set parameters, which reduces human factors and improves reliability.

9 Conclusion

We have found some defects by studying the similarity measurement of vague value in the previous literature Base on this finding, We proposed a new similarity measurement method of vague value. Comparing with vague value [0, 1], which put forward the similarity measurement property 5. Through data analysis and comparison with the previous similarity measurement methods that can find that this method is effective. The method has the basic properties of good discrimination, low computational complexity and satisfying similarity measurement.

The result of this proposed method is the same as that of clustering method, which shows the rationality of this method, reduces the need of human factors, and improves the reliability. This method can also be applied to other equipment fault diagnosis. It is hoped that it will be widely used in future research work.

Acknowledgements. This paper was supported by start up fee for talent introduction and scientific research of Fuzhou Polytechnic (FZYRCQD201901).

References

1. Zadeh, L.A.: Fuzzy sets and their applications to cognitive and decision processes. In: Zadeh, L.A., et al. (eds.) pp. 1–39. Academic Press, New York (1975)
2. Gau, W.L., Buehrer, D.J.: Vague sets IEEE trans. Syst. Man Cybern. **23**, 610–614 (1993)
3. Chen, S.M.: Measures between vague sets. Fuzzy Sets Syst. **74**(2), 217–223 (1995)
4. Chen, S.M.: Similarity measure between vague sets and elements. IEEE Trans. Syst. Man Cybern. **27**(1), 153–158 (1997)
5. Hong, D.H., Kim, C.: A note on similarity measures between vague sets and between elements. Inf. Sci. **115**, 83–96 (1999)
6. Li, F., Xu, Z.: Measures of similiarity between vague sets. J. Softw. **12**(6), 922–927 (2001)
7. Li, Y., Chi, Z., Yan, D.: Similarity measures and entropy for vague sets. Comput. Sci. **29**(12), 129–132 (2002)
8. Yan, D., Chi, Z., Li, Y.: Measures of similarity between vague sets. Pattern Recogn. Artif. Intell. **17**(1), 22–26 (2004)
9. Huawen, L.: Basic of fuzzy pattern recognition-similarity measures. Pattern Recogn. Artif. Intell. **17**(2), 141–145 (2004)
10. Deng, W., Xu, C., Fan, Z.: Multi-criteria fuzzy decision making method based on similarity measures between vague sets. Syst. Eng. Theory Pract. **34**(4), 981–990 (2014)
11. Guoxing, Z., Zuoshi, L.: The method of fuzzy clustering for bearing fault diagnosis. J. Jiang Xi Univ. Sci. Technol. **27**(4), 15–17 (2006)
12. Chen, J., Jin, Y., Huang, G.: Fault diagnosis of rolling bearings based on similarity measures between vague sets. Bearing (5), 46–49 (2012)
13. Singh, P.K.: Concept learning using vague concept lattice. Neural Process. Lett. **48**, 31–52 (2018)
14. Liu, M., Zhang, X., Ge, S., Chen, X., Jianbin, W., Tian, M.: An application-oriented buffer management strategy in opportunistic networks. Comput. Mater. Contin. **60**(2), 559–574 (2019)
15. Yan, X., Song, W., Zhao, X., Wang, A.: Tibetan sentiment classification method based on semi-supervised recursive autoencoders. Comput. Mater. Contin. **60**(2), 707–719 (2019)
16. Kaur, K., Kaur, K.: Failure prediction, lead time estimation and health degree assessment for hard disk drives using voting based decision trees. Comput. Mater. Contin. **60**(3), 913–946 (2019)

Neural Network Based Deep Transfer Learning for Cross-Domain Dependency Parsing

Zhentao Xia, Likai Wang, Weiguang Qu$^{(\boxtimes)}$, Junsheng Zhou, and Yanhui Gu

Department of Computer Science and Technology, Nanjing Normal University, Nanjing, China
zt950607@foxmail.com, wlk_1181772577@foxmail.com,
wggu_nj@163.com, {zhoujs,gu}@njnu.edu.cn

Abstract. In recent years, dependency parsers perform well on the in-domain data, but perform poor on the out-of-domain. In this paper, we present a deep neural network for cross-domain dependency parsing. Our system is based on the stack-pointer networks (STACKPTR). Considering the importance of context, we utilize self-attention mechanism for the representation vectors to capture the meaning of words. In addition, to adapt three different domains, we utilize neural network based deep transfer learning which transfers the pre-trained partial network in the source domain to be a part of deep neural network in the three target domains (product comments, product blogs and web fiction) respectively. Results on the three target domains demonstrate that our model performs competitively.

Keywords: Cross-domain dependency parser · Stack-pointer network · Network-based deep transfer learning

1 Introduction

Dependency parsing is an important component in various natural language processing systems for semantic role labeling [1], relation extraction [2], and machine translation [3]. There are two dominant approaches to dependency parsing: graph-based algorithms [4] and transition-based algorithms [5].

With the surge of web data, cross-domain parsing has become the major challenge for applying syntactic analysis in realistic NLP systems. The goal of the Cross-domain Dependency Parsing is to predict the optimal dependency tree that can adapt different domains from source domain.

Existing studies on dependency parsing mainly focus on the in-domain setting, where both training and testing data are drawn from the same domain. How to build dependency parser that can learn across domains remains an under-addressed problem. In our work, we study cross-domain dependency parsing. Our system is based on the stack-pointer network dependency parser [6]. The model has a pointer network as its backbone, and is equipped with an internal stack to maintain the order of head words in tree structures. To capture the context of sentences, we obtain word representations by self-attention mechanism [7]. We model it as a domain adaptation problem, where we are given one

© Springer Nature Singapore Pte Ltd. 2020
X. Sun et al. (Eds.): ICAIS 2020, CCIS 1254, pp. 549–558, 2020.
https://doi.org/10.1007/978-981-15-8101-4_49

source domain and three target domains, and the core task is to adapt a dependency parser trained on the source domain to the target domain.

Nowadays, deep learning has achieved dominating situation in many research fields in recent years. It is important to find how to effectively transfer knowledge by deep neural network, which called deep transfer learning that defined as follows: *Given a transfer learning task defined by $<D_s, \tau_s, D_t, \tau_t, f_\tau(.)>$. It is a deep transfer learning task where $f_\tau(.)$ is a non-linear function that reflected a deep neural network.*

Inspired by the recent success of transfer learning in many natural language processing problems, we utilize neural network based deep transfer learning for cross-domain dependency parsing. It refers to the reuse the partial network that pre-trained in the source domain, including its network structures and connection parameters, transfer it to be a part of deep neural network which used in target domain [8].

The rest of this paper is organized as follows. Section 2 gives a description of our parser system, including the system framework and stack-pointer network with self-attention mechanism for dependency parsing. In Sect. 3, we describe neural network based deep transfer learning for domain adaptation. In Sect. 4, we list our experiments and discuss results.

2   Our Approach

The model architecture of our dependency parsing system, which uses STACKPTR parser [6] as its backbone. The structure of the system is shown in Fig. 1.

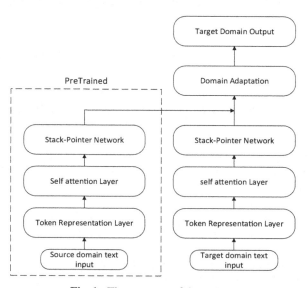

Fig. 1. The structure of the system

The system mainly contains four components: the token representation layer, the self attention layer, the stack-pointer network architecture for dependency parsing and the domain adaptation with deep transfer learning. We describe the four sub-modules in the following sections in details.

2.1 Token Representation

Let an input sentence is denoted as $S = \{w_1, w_2, \ldots, w_n\}$, where n is the number of words. The token representation has three parts:

Word-Level Embedding. We transform each word into vector representation by looking up pre-trained word embedding matrix $W_{word} \in R^{d_w \times |V|}$, where d_w is the dimension of the vectors and $|V|$ is the size of vocabulary.

Character-Level Embedding. To encode character-level information of a word into its character-level representation, we run a convolution neural network on the character sequence of w_i. Then the character-level embedding vector is concatenated with the word-level embedding vector for each word representation.

POS Embedding. To enrich word representation information, we also use POS embedding. Finally, the POS embedding vectors are concatenated with word embedding vectors as context information inputs $X = \{x_1, x_2, \ldots, x_n\}$ to feed into next layer.

2.2 Self Attention Layer

In order for the representation vectors to capture the meanings of words considering the context, we employ the self-attention, a special case of attention mechanism [7]. We adopt the multi-head attention formulation, one of the methods for implementing self-attention. Figure 2 illustrates the multi-head attention mechanism.

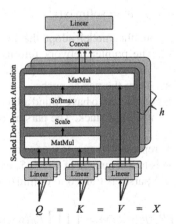

Fig. 2. The multi-head attention mechanism

Given a matrix of n vectors, query Q, key K and value V, The formulation of multi-head attention is defined by the follows:

$$\text{Attention}(Q, K, V) = \text{softmax}\left(\frac{QK^T}{\sqrt{d_w}}\right)V \tag{1}$$

$$\text{MultiHead}(Q, K, V) = W^M[head_1; \ldots, head_r] \tag{2}$$

$$head_i = \text{Attention}\left(W_i^Q Q, W_i^K K, W_i^V V\right) \tag{3}$$

Where [;] indicates row concatenation and r is the number of heads. The weights $W^M \in R^{d_w \times d_w}$, $W_i^Q \in R^{\frac{d_w}{r} \times d_w}$, $W_i^K \in R^{\frac{d_w}{r} \times d_w}$, $W_i^V \in R^{\frac{d_w}{r} \times d_w}$ are learnable parameters for linear transformation. As a result, the output of self attention layer is the sequence of representations whose include informative factors in the input sentence as model input.

2.3 Stack Pointer Network

Ma et al. [6] implement a new neural network architecture called stack-pointer networks (STACKPTR) for dependency parsing. STACKPTR parser has a pointer network as its backbone. This model is equipped with an internal stack to maintain the order of head words in tree structures.

The model firstly reads the whole sentence and encodes each word with BiLSTMs into the encoder hidden state e_i.

The decoder implements a top-down, depth-first transition system. At each time step t, the decoder receives the encoder hidden state e_i of the word w_i on top of the stack to generate a decoder hidden state d_t and computes the attention vector a^t using the following equation:

$$v_i^t = \text{score}(d_t, s_i) \tag{4}$$

$$a^t = \text{softmax}(v^t) \tag{5}$$

For attention score function, the model adopt the biaffine attention mechanism described in Dozat et al. [9]. The pointer network returns a position p according to the highest attention score in a^t and generate a new dependency arc $w_i \to w_p$ where w_p is considered as a child of w_i. Then the parser pushes w_p onto the stack. If the parser pointers w_i to itself, then w_i is considered to have found all its children. Finally the parser goes to the next step and pops w_i out of stack. The parsing process ends when only the root contains in the stack.

A dependency tree can be represented as a sequence of top-down paths $p_1, \ldots, p_k$, where each path p_i corresponds to a sequence of words $\$, w_{i,1}, w_{i,2}, \ldots, w_{i,li}$ from the root to a leaf. The STACKPTR parser is trained to optimize the probability:

$$P_\theta(y|x) = \prod_{i=1}^{k} P_\theta(p_i|p_{<i}, x) = \prod_{i=1}^{k}\prod_{j=1}^{l_i} P_\theta(w_{i,j}|w_{i,<j}, p_{<i}, x)$$

Where θ represents model parameters, $p_{<i}$ stands for previous paths already explored, $w_{i,j}$ denotes the jth word in path p_i and $w_{i,<j}$ represents all the previous words on p_i.

3 Domain Adaptation

From our study, insufficient target domain training data is an inescapable problem. Transfer learning relaxes the hypothesis that the training data must be independent, which motivates us to use transfer learning in our work. The model in target domain is not need to trained from scratch, which can reduce the demand of training data in the target domain and can learn enough knowledge from source domain.

In our work, the stack-pointer network is trained in source domain with training dataset. Second, we reuse the partial network that pre-trained in the source domain, including its network structure and connection parameters, transfer it to be a part of deep neural network which used in target domain. Finally, the transferred sub-network may be updated in fine-tune strategy. The overview of neural network based transfer learning is shown in Fig. 3.

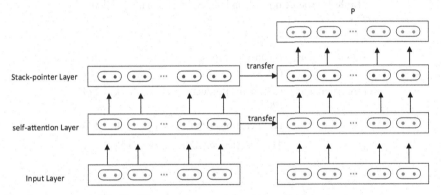

Fig. 3. The neural network based transfer learning

Concretely, we retain the parameters of encoder and decoder and abandon the parameters of the biaffine attention mechanism which trained in source domain. We re-train a new biaffine attention score and fine-tune the parameters of the whole network for each of the three target domains.

Besides, to avoid insufficient target domain dataset and can learn enough knowledge from source domain, we retain the self-attention parameters which trained in source domain and fine-tune for target domains since corpus of source domain is larger than three target domains. From our cognition, although target datasets are different areas, the understanding of semantic in Chinese is the same. Transfer learning can also help improve the network efficiently with limited amount of training data in target domains.

4 Experiments

4.1 Data and Evaluation Metrics

To meet the challenge of the lack of labeled data, Buchholz et al. [10] have manually annotated large-scale high-quality domain-aware datasets with a lot of effort in the past few years. They provide one source-domain and three target-domain datasets. Source domain data are selected from HLT-CDT and PennCTB treebanks (BC). For Target domains, data are selected from Taobao as comments products (PC), Taobao headlines as product blogs (PB) and web fiction "Zhuxian" (ZX) respectively. Table 1 shows distribution for the datasets.

Annotation Guideline. They references the HLT-CDT and UD annotation guidelines, and developed a detailed annotation guideline that aims to fully capture Chinese syntax and tries to guarantee inter-annotator consistency and facilitate model learning. The guideline includes 20 dependency labels. In order to reduce annotation cost, they adopt the active learning procedure based on partial annotation [11]. All training datasets are automatically complemented into high-quality full trees [12].

Table 1. Source domain and target domain data distribution

	Datasets	Train	Dev	Test
Source domain	Balanced Corpus (BC)	16.3k	1k	2k
Target domains	Comments Products (PC)	6.2k	1.3k	2.6k
	Product Blogs (PB)	5.1k	1.3k	2.6k
	The web fiction (ZX)	1.6k	0.5k	1.1k

Evaluation Metrics. We adopt the standard labeled attachment score (LAS, percent of words that receive correct heads and labels) and unlabeled attachment score (UAS, percent of words that receive correct heads) for evaluation.

4.2 Settings

We use the pre-trained weights of the publicly available Glove model [13] to initialize word embedding in our model, and use random initialization for POS embedding.

We employ Adam method to optimize our model. Following Ma et al. [6], we apply dropout training to mitigate overfitting. The hyper-parameters in our model are shown in following Table 2.

4.3 Result

Overall Results. In order to analyze our model, we compare with baseline model STACKPTR [6]. We conduct an ablation experiment on our model to examine the effectiveness of self-attention and transfer learning components. The overall results on test datasets are illustrated in Table 3.

Table 2. Hyper-parameters setting

Hyper-parameters	Description	Values
d_w	Size of word embedding	300
char_dim	Dimension of character embedding	50
pos_dim	Dimension of POS embedding	50
r	Number of heads	4
d_h	Number of hidden units in RNN	256
batch_size	Number of sentences in each batch	64
num_filters	Number of filters in CNN	50
learning_rate	Learning rate	0.001
decay_rate	Decay rate of learning rate	0.75
p_rnn	Dropout rate for RNN	0.5
p_in	Dropout rate for input embedding	0.5
p_out	Dropout rate for output layer	0.5

Table 3. The overall results on test datasets

Model	PC		PB		ZX	
	LAS	UAS	LAS	UAS	LAS	UAS
STACKPTR	61.1	67.9	69.8	74.8	74.6	78.8
STACKPTR + self attention	60.9	66.6	70.5	75.2	75.1	80.3
STACKPTR + transfer learning	61.9	68.2	70.7	75.1	75.4	80.0
STACKPTR + self attention + transfer learning	62.6	69.7	73.7	78.8	76.8	81.9

Loss Function. Figure 4 shows the loss curve of the model on three datasets. The model is learning a shared representation with better generalization, the losses of the model on three datasets converge much faster in first few epoch. But with more epochs, due to inductive bias, the converging speed for model keeps decreasing and start to be slow. But eventually all models on three datasets losses converged to optimal after 400 epochs.

LAS and UAS Scores. Figure 5 shows the LAS and UAS scores curve of our model on three datasets. On UAS and LAS, an interesting observation is that the model obtains competitive performance on ZX dataset, while performs slightly worse on PC dataset. Table 3 illustrates the performance of different variations of our model together with the results of baseline STACKPTR. Our model significantly outperforms the baseline.

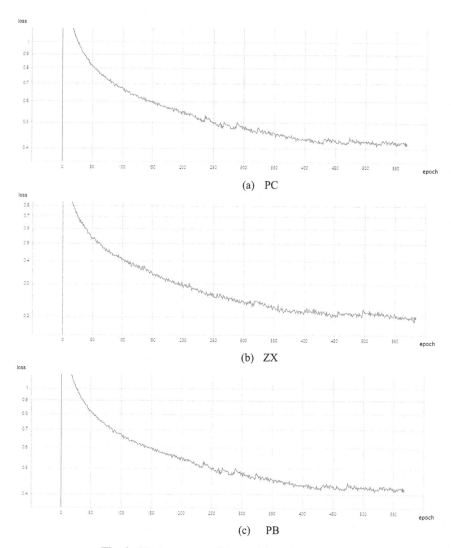

(a) PC

(b) ZX

(c) PB

Fig. 4. The loss curve of the model on three datasets

The results indicate that our model with self-attention mechanism and transfer learning can promote the performance in three different target domains. Recalling the model architecture, the self-attention model can obtain the interrelation between words in a sentence from different directions and get the sentence representation at different levels. Combining multiple single-head self-attention can improve the feature learning ability of the model, so that the model can better and more effectively extract the required feature representations from different perspectives. And transfer learning can also help improve the network efficiently with limited amount of training data in target domains.

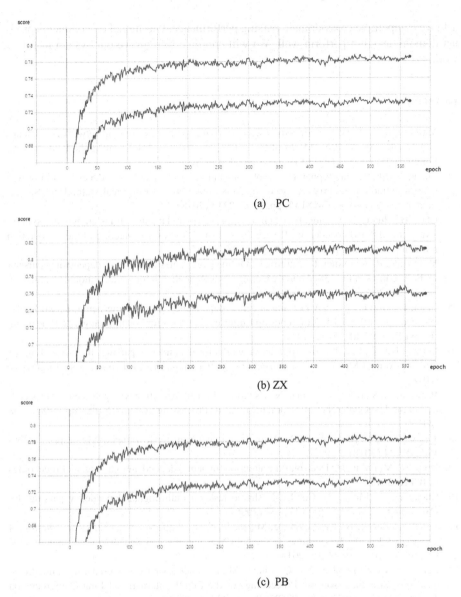

(a) PC

(b) ZX

(c) PB

Fig. 5. The UAS and LAS scores curve of the model on three datasets

5   Conclusions

In this paper, we present a deep neural network for cross-domain dependency parsing, which includes self-attention mechanism and neural network based deep transfer learning. The results suggested that using self-attention and transfer learning is a way to achieve competitive cross-domain parsing performance. Our model on comments product domain does not perform well. We will continue to improve our system in future work.

References

1. Marcheggiani, D., Titov, I.: Encoding sentences with graph convolutional networks for semantic role labeling. In: Proceedings of the 2017 Conference on Empirical Methods for Natural Language Processing (EMNLP), pp. 1506–1515 (2017)
2. Zhang, Y., Qi, P., Christopher, D.: Graph convolution over pruned dependency trees improves relation extraction. In: Proceedings of the 2018 Conference on Empirical Methods for Natural Language Processing (EMNLP), pp. 2205–2215 (2018)
3. Chen, H., Huang, S., Chiang, D., Chen, J.: Improved neural machine translation with a syntax-aware encoder and decoder. In: Proceedings of the 55th Annual Meeting of the Association for Computational Linguistics, pp. 1936–1945 (2017)
4. McDonald, R., Crammer, K., Pereira, F.: Online large-margin training of dependency parsers. In: Proceedings of the 43th Annual Meeting of the Association for Computational Linguistics, pp. 91–98 (2005)
5. Chen, D., Manning, C.: A fast and accurate dependency parser using neural networks. In: Proceedings of the 2014 Conference on Empirical Methods for Natural Language Processing (EMNLP), pp. 740–750 (2014)
6. Ma, X., Hu, Z., Liu, J.: Stack-pointer networks for dependency parsing. In: Proceedings of the 56th Annual Meeting of the Association for Computational Linguistics, pp. 1403–1414 (2018)
7. Vaswani, A., Shazeer, N., Parmar, N., Uszkoreit, J., et al.: Attention is all you need. In: Proceedings of the 31st Conference on Neural Information Processing Systems (NIPS), pp. 5998–6008 (2017)
8. Tan, C., Sun, F., Kong, T., et al.: A survey on deep transfer learning. arXiv preprint arXiv: 1808.01974 (2018)
9. Dozat, T., Manning, D.: Deep biaffine attention for neural dependency parsing. In: Proceedings of ICLR (2017)
10. Buchholz, S., Marsi, E.: CoNLL-X shared task on multilingual dependency parsing. In: Proceedings of CoNLL, pp. 149–164 (2006)
11. Jiang, X., Zhang, B., Li, Z., Zhang, M., Li, S., Si, L.: Supervised treebank conversion data and approaches. In: Proceedings of the 56th Meeting of the Association for Computational Linguistics, pp. 2706–2716 (2018)
12. Zhang, Y., Li, Z., Lang, J., Xia, Q., Zhang, M.: Dependency parsing with partial annotations: an empirical comparison. In: Proceedings of the Eighth International Joint Conference on Natural Language Processing (IJCNLP), pp. 49–58 (2017)
13. PenningTon, J., Socher, R., Manning, C.: Glove: global vectors for word representation. In: Proceedings of the 2014 Conference on Empirical Methods for Natural Language Processing (EMNLP), pp. 1532–1543 (2014)

Data Augmentation for Polarity Sentiment Analysis

Wenhuan Wang[1], Bohan Li[1,2,3(✉)], Ding Feng[1], Anman Zhang[1], and Shuo Wan[1]

[1] College of Computer Science and Technology,
Nanjing University of Aeronautics and Astronautics, Nanjing 211106, China
{wangwenhuan,bhli}@nuaa.edu.cn

[2] Key Laboratory of Safety-Critical Software, Ministry of Industry and Information Technology,
Nanjing 211106, China

[3] Collaborative Innovation Center of Novel Software Technology and Industrialization,
Nanjing, Jiangsu, China

Abstract. Twitter produces various colloquial tweets as an open communication platform. Previous research shows the frequency of negative sentences in spoken sentences is twice that of written texts. Negative items in negative sentences can shift the polarity of words with feelings, and leads to wrong classification. Therefore, negation processing is essential for the sentiment classification of tweets generated by Twitter. On the basis of considering the importance of negation which is often ignored in previous work, this paper firstly combines the technique of Conjunction Analysis (CA) with the technique of Punctuation Mark Identification (PMI) to detect the negation clue and its scope more accurately. In addition, We propose the OL-DAWE model. The model uses Data Augmentation (DA) approach to generate the opposed tweet according to the original tweet. The model extends learnable data and learns its polarity from both of positive and negative aspects of a tweet. In predicting the polarity of a tweet, the OL-DAWE model takes the positive (negative) degree of the original tweet into account, and also considers the negative (positive) degree of the opposed tweet. We conduct two experiments on two real-world data sets and analyze the experimental results from the perspectives of accuracy and robustness. We prove the effectiveness of our combined technology in negation processing and show that our OL-DAWE model in the polarity sentiment analysis of tweets is better than the baseline for its simplicity and high efficiency.

Keywords: Sentiment analysis · Data augmentation · Negation scope detection · Polarity shift

1 Introduction

Emerging of various social media and commercial websites has encouraged people to express their opinions on multiple platforms. New comments are generated every minute, and such massive amounts of data contribute to the generation of sentiment analysis (SA). SA is the computational analysis of the opinion, attitudes, emotions of speaker/writer

© Springer Nature Singapore Pte Ltd. 2020
X. Sun et al. (Eds.): ICAIS 2020, CCIS 1254, pp. 559–570, 2020.
https://doi.org/10.1007/978-981-15-8101-4_50

towards some topic and identification of non-trivial, subjective information from text repository [4]. The work on the positive or negative tendency of emotions is also called polarity sentiment analysis. For SA, many studies (such as [12, 18, 22, 23]) represent each word in the text as a continuous, low-dimensional and real-valued vector, also known as word embedding. However, a serious problem of Word Embedding is the polarity shift. Polarity shift refers to the reversal of text emotion due to some reasons. Negative items (i.e. negation cues) in the sentence is one of the most important causes of polarity shift. In [8, 11], the scope of a negation cue (a negative word or phrase) is assumed to be the negation cue to the end of the clause. This definition of negation scope ignores the complexity of language. For example, "The package of this eye shadow tray is not elegant but its colors match my heart", In this sentence, the scope of negation is from the negation cue "not" to its next word "elegant", but if the definition of [8] is followed, the positivity of "match" will be affected, and the word's polarity will be shifted. Therefore, it is necessary to detect negation cues in texts and fully determine their negation scope.

Since the frequency of negation in spoken sentences is twice as frequent as in written text [19] and tweets tend to be colloquial, it is necessary to measure the change of sentiment polarity in tweets brought about by negation. Most of the sentiment polarity analysis methods on tweets are deficient in two aspects: (i) ignoring the importance of negation cues and their scope; (ii) ignoring the emotional comparability between positive and negative tweets. We proposed an opposed learning model based on Data Augmentation (DA) and Word Embedding (OL-DAWE model) in this paper. The OL-DAWE model uses Word Embedding technology to learn the two opposing sides of a tweet obtained through DA and utilizes the polarity comparison between the original tweets and the opposed tweets to improve the prediction accuracy and robustness. To the best of our knowledge, this paper uses DA technology for the first time to apply opposed training and prediction to tweets polarity sentiment analysis. We focus on the negative sentences on Twitter, overcoming the difficulties of previous works which negated sentence processing, and ignored the complexity of negation cues and scope of negation. For the first time, a negation handling technology that combines Punctuation Mark Identification (PMI) technology with Conjunction Analysis (CA) technology is proposed.

The remainder of this paper is organized as follows. In the second section, we discuss the related work in negation cues and scope detection, Data Augmentation, and tweet sentiment analysis. In the third section, we propose three modules to illustrate our methods. The experimental description and analysis of the results are given in Section four. In the fifth section, we will give a summary of the work of this paper and describe our future development direction.

2 Related Work

2.1 Negation Control

A negative sentence containing one or more negation cues, where a negation cue can be a word (e.g. not), or a multi-word expression (e.g. by no means, no longer) inherently expressing negation. A negation cue is given in front of a positive word or phrase that will change the sentence polarity from positive to negative. In consideration of the negation distance, negation can be divided into local negation and long-distance negation. For example, "I do not like this eye shadow tray." is a local negation because the negation cue "not" acts directly on the sentiment carrying word "like" that follows it. Conversely, a long-distance negation like. "This eye shadow tray does not have beautiful colors, nice opaque and elegant box.", which implies that negation doesn't directly apply to sentiment carrying words.

The hypothesis of the negation scope in [8, 11] is the same as [17] that only the first punctuation after the negation cue is used as the sign of the end of negation. They all treat the negation distance as a simple problem and do not distinguish the length of the negation distance. [3] deems that the scope of negation to be negation cue's next 5 words. [20] supposes that the scope of a negation cue is several words of its right and expresses that the polarity of an emotional term can be flipped within the vicinity of negation. These negation scope definitions only consider local negation, while the texts they process all contain more or less long-distance negative sentences, which will affect the classification accuracy. Since long-distance negation is often associated with conjunctions, we propose a combination of PMI and CA to reduce the impact of negation on polarity shift.

2.2 Data Augmentation

Data Augmentation refers to a method of augmenting observation data to make it easier to analyze. The validation error must continue to decrease with the training error to build useful Deep Learning models. DA is a very powerful method to achieve this purpose. At present, DA is mostly applied for the field of image processing [6]. [21] covers the use of GAN image synthesis in medical imaging applications such as brain MRI synthesis and lung cancer diagnosis. [5] creates new instances by interpolating new points from existing instances via k-Nearest Neighbors.

In Natural Language Processing (NLP), the application of DA is very limited, on account of the difficulty to obtain universal data conversion rules that guarantee data quality and can be automatically applied to various fields. Currently, the common augmentation method is to replace synonyms selected from manual ontology [24] in NLP. In [13], DA is carried out through word similarity. In addition, different phoneme-font translation systems are adopted in [9]. For polarity sentiment analysis, however, the augmentation technology of synonym substitution does not consider the strong polarity comparison of emotional words, we first propose to use antonyms replacement to expand data sets with negation handling, using the original tweets data set to expand its opposed tweets data set. At the same time, we use these two data sets in training and prediction.

2.3 Sentiment Analysis

Research on opinion mining and sentiment analysis of tweets has grown considerably in the last decade [14, 25]. [7] demonstrates the usefulness of linguistic features and existing lexical resources used in micro-blogging to detect the sentiments of twitter messages. [15] uses a complex Bi-directional LSTM model to capture more context information. None of these approaches take into account the polar comparability of tweets and are less efficient due to their complex parameters and functions.

[2] designs a 2-step automatic sentiment analysis method for classifying tweets. They used a noisy training set to reduce the labeling effort in developing classifiers. [16] proposes an influence probability model for twitter sentiment analysis. If a username is found in the body of a tweet, it is influencing action and it contributes to influencing probability. [10] creates a twitter corpus by automatically collecting tweets using Twitter API and automatically annotating those using emoticons. However, the training set is also less efficient since it contains only tweets having emoticons. Considering the comparability of positive and negative polarity of sentiment, this paper analyzes two comparable data sets obtained by Data Augmentation technology in training and prediction. Due to the simplicity of the model and high efficiency, the preform is better than the above methods under certain conditions.

3   The OL-DAWE Model

In Sect. 3.1, we detail the process of data Augmentation (DA), the flow chart of which is shown in Fig. 1. Two comparable data sets will be trained and predicted in Sects. 3.2 and 3.3. In addition, the framework of our model is shown in Fig. 2.

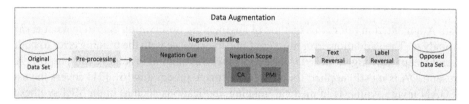

Fig. 1. The process of data augmentation

3.1   Data Augmentation and Negation Handling

Considering the positive and negative polarity of tweets' short text data set, this paper for the first time adopts the antonym replacement data augmentation technology in the short text sentiment analysis. Based on the antonym dictionary (e.g., WordNet [1]), it constructs the opposed data set of tweets in the original data set in the way of one-to-one by reversing the sentiment words of tweets. Note that the main difference between a tweet text and a traditional text (such as hotel reviews, film reviews, news articles) is that it contains multiple emojis that can express both positive and negative emotions. For example, :) and :-) both express positive emotions. We will replace positive emoticons with token EMO_POS and negative emoticons with token EMO_NEG. Specific measures to extend the data set are as follows:

Negation Handling. Negation handling in sentiment analysis includes two subtasks, namely negation cue, and scope detection. Negative cue detection is responsible for identifying negative words or phrases in sentences, such as no, not, rather than, etc. Negative scope detection is for defining the range involved in the negation cue.

Definition 1 (Negation Cue Detection). *Negation cue is a negative word or part of speech reflected in the sentence.*

This paper uses rule-based keyword matching technology to perform negation cue detection and replace it with token "Negation". For example, the negative cue "don't" in S1 of Table 1 is replaced by "Negation" in S2.

Deftnition 2 (Negation Scope Detection). *Negation scope detection technology study the range of language influences of negation cues in emotionally colored text.*

This paper proposes a combination of Conjunction Analysis (CA) and Punctuation Mark Identification (PMI) technology. PMI is sufficient to cope with local negation, while the combined technology is mainly beneficial to the processing of long-distance negation.

Table 1. Examples of negative sentences.

Example sentence	
S1	I don't like this eye shadow tray, another is beautiful. *EMO_NEG*
S2	I Negation like this eye shadow tray, another is beautiful
S3	This eye shadow tray doesn't [have beautiful colors, nice opaque and elegant box]
S4	I doesn't [think this eye shadow tray is elegant] but its colors suit me well

Punctuation Mark Identification (PMI). PMI technology defines the scope of negation is from "Negation" token to the first punctuation after it. For example, a simple local negation sentence S1 in 1, the first punctuation mark "," after the negation cue "not" is used to divide the two emotions of the speaker. But for long-distance negation, the punctuation mark sometimes fails to completely cover its negation scope, such as S3 in Table 1. The negation scope of S4 in Table 1 does not include items after "but". Therefore, we need to combine CA and PMI.

Conjunction Analysis (CA). Conjunctions complicate the scope of negation. Simply defining the negation scope based on the punctuation reduces the accuracy of the classification. Therefore, consider the conjunction in negative sentences is necessary. For example, in S4 in Table 1, the speaker does not like the exquisiteness of the eye shadow tray but likes the color of the eye shadow. The conjunction "but" lead to a confrontation between the two clauses. Considering the general situation, the conjunctions are divided into adversative conjunction and coordinating conjunction. Through the analysis of the data set, when a tweet is reversed, we deal with the negative sentence involving a conjunction word according to certain grammatical rules. The following is a brief description based on some examples in Table 1 and the underlined word is the negation cue. Besides, words in [] are in the scope of negation.

Text Reversal. If a tweet contains a negation token "Negation", the negation scope is first detected. All negation tokens are removed, the sentiment words in the negation scope are unchanged, and the sentiment words outside the negation scope are all reversed to their opposites. If the tweet contains the emoticon token "EMO_POS" (or "EMO_NEG"), it is inverted to "EMO_NEG" (or "EMO_POS"). Note that we are not looking for a full standard antonym word, because some words do not have antonyms, but instead, are replaced with words that express opposite feelings.

Label Reversal. For tweets in each training set, class labels are also reversed to their opposites (e.g., positive to negative, negative to positive) and added to the opposed data set. The final reversal result is as Table 2.

Table 2. The final reversal result.

Data set	Class	Tweet
Original	Negative	I *Negation* like this eye shadow tray, and it is *unpretty EMO_NEG*
Opposed	Positive	I like this eye shadow tray, and it is elegant *EMO_POS*

3.2 Training with Two Comparable Data Sets

In the training stage, the original tweets used for training are inverted to generate opposed tweets using DA technology. The training tweets are labeled as the original training data set and opposed training data set. The label of the opposed tweet is changed to the opposite of their corresponding original tweets. Training with two compared data sets (TTCDS) is performed with the combination of both original and opposed tweets. We will illustrate the effectiveness of TTCDS in solving the polarity shift problem through a sample of tweets.

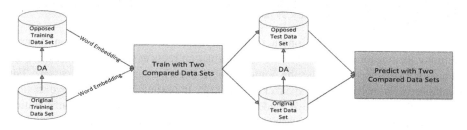

Fig. 2. The process of polarity sentiment analysis by OL-DAWE model

Original training sample. I don't like this eye shadow tray, and it is unpretty. Label: Negative.

Opposed training sample. I like this eye shadow tray, and it is elegant. Label: Positive.

In general, the word of "like" is considered to be a word with strong positive sentiment, but due to the negation cue "not", the polarity is shifted, and the word "like" is (incorrectly) associated with the negative label in the original training sample. Hence, its weight will be added by a negative score in maximum likelihood estimation. Therefore, the weight of "like" will be falsely updated. While in TTCDS, because of the removal of "Negation" token in the opposed tweet, "like" is (correctly) associated with the positive label, and its weight will be added by a positive score. Based on this, we can conclude that the learning errors caused by negation can be partly compensated in TTCDS.

3.3 Prediction with Two Comparable Data Sets

We first invert the test samples one-to-one into their opposed samples, forming the opposed test sample data set. And the two sample data sets are combined to make predictions. In the prediction process, we take emoticons into consideration. Predict with Two Data Sets (PTCDS) means that we consider two opposed tweets of x (original tweet) and x' (opposed tweet) to aid in predicting the class of the original sample x. Our main task is not to predict the class of x' in the opposed test data set, but to predict the class of x with the help of x'. As shown before, $p(\cdot|x)$ and $p(\cdot|x')$ represent the posterior probabilities of the original tweet x and the opposed tweet x', respectively. '$\cdot$' represents positive mark (+) or negative mark (−). Two sides of the tweet are considered in PTCDS. The positive or negative sentiment degree of a tweet is found using two components.

(i)   How much positive or negative is the tweet x, $p(+|x)$ or $p(-|x)$.
(ii) How much negative or positive is the opposed tweet x', $p(-|x')$ or $p(+|x')$.

The opposed tweets we created during the Data Augmentation phase might not be as good as the human-generated tweets. Since there is no accidental introduction to some noise data, and the requirement to maintain grammatical quality in tweets is lower than human languages. Therefore, we will use a trade off parameter in the PTCDS to leverage both original and opposed tweets. Assigning a relatively small weight to the opposite tweet can protect the model from being corrupted by combining low-quality tweets, that is, assigning a trade-off parameter $\alpha(0 < \alpha < 1)$ to the posterior probability $p(\cdot|x')$ of the opposed tweet. So, the prediction score of a weighted combination of two component predictions as follows:

$$\begin{cases} p(+|x, x') = (1 - \alpha) \cdot p(+|x) + \alpha \cdot p(-|x') \\ p(-|x, x') = (1 - \alpha) \cdot p(-|x) + \alpha \cdot p(+|x') \end{cases} \quad (1)$$

Experiments have shown that $p(\cdot|x')$ increases as α increases. We found that our experiments can perform well when α ranges between 0.5 to 0.7.

4 Experiments

In this section, we discuss the implementation of polarity sentiment analysis with Data Augmentation and conduct comparative experiments on different tweets data set.

4.1 Data Sets

Two data sets are scraped by twitter API i.e. Stanford data set (TSCDS) [9] and Sanders Twitter Sentiment Corpus data set (TSDS) [26]. Stanford data set contains 160,000 training tweets accompanied by 80,000 both positive and negative tweets. Whereas Sanders Twitter Sentiment data set contains 570 positive and 654 negative tweets.

4.2 Experimental Settings

In our experiment, tweets on each category in two data sets are randomly divided into five folds (with four as training data and one as test data). All of the following results are reported and analyzed with an averaged accuracy of five-fold cross validation. We implement the Naive Bayes Classifier based on a multinomial event model with Laplace smoothing and Support Vector Machines(SVMs) Classifier based on the LibSVM toolkit. The kernel function in the SVMs model is linear kernel, the penalty parameter is set to the default value, and the Platt's probability output is applied to approximate the posterior probability.

4.3 Evaluation

The performance of OL-DAWE model is compared with the existing methods (i) Simple Word-Embedding Model (SWEM) which has no additional parameters; (ii) Bidirectional LSTM (Bi-LSTM) model which uses a complex forward and backward recurrent neural networks to capture more contextual information; (iii) Simple OL-DAWE model(a comparative learning model based on Data Augmentation and Word Embedding, but without the combination of PMI and CWA).

The Effectiveness of the Combined Technology. Table 3 describes the performance evaluation of the OL-DAWE model with the combination of PMI and CA and the Simple OL-DAWE model with PMI technology only for the sentiment classifier with negation control. The performance of the classifier is improved by adding the combined technology into the negative tweets. The classifier (SVMs, Naıve Bayes, Logistic Regression) without CA for negation control can achieve approximate 80%–85% accuracy rate over twitter as shown in Table 3. Besides, the SVMs classifier achieve better performance over twitter data set and lead by approximate 1.5% in TSCDS and 4.5% in TSDS over other classifiers. The performance of the OL-DAWE model is significantly boost up after incorporating CA and PMI technique for sentiment analysis. In the OL-DAWE model, for incorporating CA and PMI, NB (89.69%, 90.65%), SVMs (90.06%, 90.00%), and LR (91.25%, 90.95%) significantly boost the performance by approximately 6.91%–8.16%, 7.96%–9.80% and 6.24%–8.27% respectively over two different Twitter data sets. Significant improvement gained with classifier over tweets data set results from the presence of a higher number of negative tweets i.e. approximate 50% and 53.43% in TSCDS and TSDS respectively. With different angles of evaluating, the performance of classifier over combined technology and uncombined technology. It is observed that classifiers give better performance with PMI and CA.

Table 3. Comparative analysis of simple OL-DAWE model and OL-DAWE model in accuracy.

Classifer	Technology	TSCDS	TSDS
NB	PMI	81.53%	83.74%
NB	PMI + CA	89.69%	90.65%
LR	PMI	82.10%	80.20%
LR	PMI + CA	90.06%	90.00%
SVMs	PMI	82.98%	84.71%
SVMs	PMI + CA	91.25%	90.95%

The Effectiveness of OL-DAWE Model. The OL-DAWE model is based on three classifiers, i.e., SVMs, Naïve Bayes, and Logistic Regression. Figure 3 shows that our model has a significant improvement over the baseline system in TSDCS and TSDS (increased 16.59% and 18.06% in the case of OL-DAWE model based on Naïve Bayes classifiers). This obvious improvement stems from the negation handling of tweets in our model. Since the tweet data set contains a large number of negative sentences, the polarity shift caused by it misleads the baseline model. In our model, the SVMs achieve the best results (the accuracy was improved by 1.56% compared to the Naïve Bayes classifier in TSCDS), which may because our negation processing further increases the interpretability of SVMs.

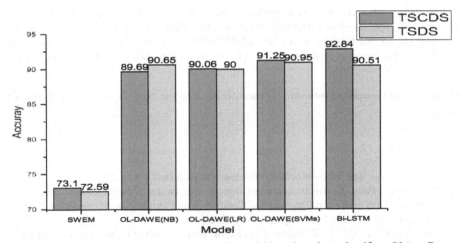

Fig. 3. The comparison between the OL-DAWE model based on three classifiers (Naïve Bayes, Logistic Regression and Support Vector Machines) and the baseline model and the most advanced model.

However, Fig. 3 also shows that in SA, the classifier using BiLSTM is about 1.59% more accurate than the OL-DAWE model in TSCDS. This finding is consistent with [11], where they hypothesize that the positional information of a word in text sequences may be beneficial to predict sentiment. This is reasonable since, for instance, the phrase "not really good" and "really not good" convey different levels of negative sentiment, while being different only by their word orderings. Surprisingly, on the TSDS, the classification accuracy of the OL-DAWE model based on the SVMs classifier and Naïve Bayes classifier is higher than that of the BiLSTM model (0.44% and 0.14%). The BiLSTM model requires a large number of compositional parameters, and the calculation is time-consuming with lower efficiency, while our model has fewer parameters and significantly improved computational efficiency. According to Occam's razor, simple models are preferred, if all else are the same. It shows that our model is better than the Bidirectional LSTM model when the data set is small.

5 Conclusion and Future Work

In this work, we first use the combination of Conjunction Analysis technology and Punctuation Mark Identification technology to detect negation cue and its scope. In addition, we propose a novel Data Augmentation approach, which creates opposed tweets that are sentiment-opposite to the original tweets one-to-one. The proposed OL-DAWE model makes use of the original and opposed tweets which gained by DA in pairs to train a sentiment classifier and make predictions. Experiments demonstrate that the OL-DAWE model is very effective for the polarity classification of tweets. In the future, we will study the sentiment analysis of Chinese short texts and create Chinese opposed data sets by using the Data Augmentation technology based on the antonym dictionary.

Acknowledgments. This work is supported in part by National Natural Science Foundation of China (61728204), Innovation Funding (NJ20160028, NT2018027, NT2018028, NS2018057), Aeronautical Science Foundation of China (2016551500), State Key Laboratory for smart grid protection and operation control Foundation, Association of Chinese Graduate Education (ACGE).

Declaration of Competing Interest.   The authors declared that there is no conflict of interest for this paper.

References

1. Wordnet homepage. https://wordnet.princeton.edu. Accessed 1 Nov 2019
2. Barbosa, L., Feng, J.: Robust sentiment detection on twitter from biased and noisy data. In: Proceedings of the 23rd International Conference on Computational Linguistics: Posters, pp. 36–44. Association for Computational Linguistics (2010)
3. Grefenstette, G., Qu, Y., Shanahan, J.G., Evans, D.A.: Coupling niche browsers and affect analysis for an opinion mining application. In: Proceedings of Recherche d'Information Assistée par Ordinateur (RIAO) (2004)
4. Haihong, E., Yingxi, H., Haipeng, P., Wen, Z., Siqi, X., Peiqing, N.: Theme and sentiment analysis model of public opinion dissemination based on generative adversarial network. Chaos, Solitons Fractals **121**, 160–167 (2019)
5. Han, H., Wang, W.-Y., Mao, B.-H.: Borderline-SMOTE: a new over-sampling method in imbalanced data sets learning. In: Huang, D.-S., Zhang, X.-P., Huang, G.-B. (eds.) ICIC 2005. LNCS, vol. 3644, pp. 878–887. Springer, Heidelberg (2005). https://doi.org/10.1007/11538059_91

6. He, M., Wang, H., Zhou, L., Wang, P., Ju, A.: Symmetric learning data augmentation model for underwater target noise data expansion (2018)
7. Kouloumpis, E., Wilson, T., Moore, J.: Twitter sentiment analysis: the good the bad and the omg! In: Fifth International AAAI Conference on Weblogs and Social Media (2011)
8. Li, S., Huang, C.R.: Sentiment classification considering negation and contrast transition. In: Proceedings of the 23rd Pacific Asia Conference on Language, Information and Computation, vol. 1, pp. 307–316 (2009)
9. Nicolai, G., Hauer, B., St Arnaud, A., Kondrak, G.: Morphological reinflection via discriminative string transduction. In: Proceedings of the 14th SIGMORPHON Workshop on Computational Research in Phonetics, Phonology, and Morphology, pp. 31–35 (2016)
10. Pak, A., Paroubek, P.: Twitter as a corpus for sentiment analysis and opinion mining. In: LREc, vol. 10, pp. 1320–1326 (2010)
11. Pang, B., Lee, L., Vaithyanathan, S.: Thumbs up?: sentiment classification using machine learning techniques. In: Proceedings of the ACL-02 Conference on Empirical Methods in Natural Language Processing, vol. 10, pp. 79–86. Association for Computational Linguistics (2002)
12. Wan, S., Li, B., Zhang, A., Wang, K., Li, X.: Vertical and sequential sentiment analysis of micro-blog topic. In: Gan, G., Li, B., Li, X., Wang, S. (eds.) ADMA 2018. LNCS (LNAI), vol. 11323, pp. 353–363. Springer, Cham (2018). https://doi.org/10.1007/978-3-030-05090-0_30
13. Wang, W.Y., Yang, D.: That's so annoying!!!: a lexical and frame-semantic embedding based data augmentation approach to automatic categorization of annoying behaviors using# pet-peeve tweets. In: Proceedings of the 2015 Conference on Empirical Methods in Natural Language Processing, pp. 2557–2563 (2015)
14. Wang, Y., Chen, W., Li, B., Boots, R.: Learning fine-grained patient similarity with dynamic bayesian network embedded RNNs. In: Li, G., Yang, J., Gama, J., Natwichai, J., Tong, Y. (eds.) DASFAA 2019. LNCS, vol. 11446, pp. 587–603. Springer, Cham (2019). https://doi.org/10.1007/978-3-030-18576-3_35
15. Williams, A., Nangia, N., Bowman, S.R.: A broad-coverage challenge corpus for sentence understanding through inference. arXiv preprint arXiv:1704.05426 (2017)
16. Wu, Y., Ren, F.: Learning sentimental influence in Twitter, June 2011. https://doi.org/10.1109/ICFCSA.2011.34
17. Xia, R., Wang, T., Hu, X., Li, S., Zong, C.: Dual training and dual prediction for polarity classification. In: Proceedings of the 51st Annual Meeting of the Association for Computational Linguistics (Volume 2: Short Papers), pp. 521–525 (2013)
18. Xu, F., Zhang, X., Xin, Z., Yang, A.: Investigation on the Chinese text sentiment analysis based on convolutional neural networks in deep learning. Comput. Mater. Contin **58**(3), 697–709 (2019)
19. Yaeger-Dror, M.: Negation in English speech and writing: a study in variation (1993)
20. Yang, K.: Widit in TREC 2008 blog track: leveraging multiple sources of opinion evidence, January 2008
21. Yi, X., Walia, E., Babyn, P.: Generative adversarial network in medical imaging: a review. Med. Image Anal. **58**, 101552 (2019)
22. Yue, L., Chen, W., Li, X., Zuo, W., Yin, M.: A survey of sentiment analysis in social media. Knowl. Inf. Syst. **60**, 617–663 (2018)
23. Zhang, A., Li, B., Wan, S., Wang, K.: Cyberbullying detection with BiRNN and attention mechanism. In: Zhai, X.B., Chen, B., Zhu, K. (eds.) MLICOM 2019. LNICST, vol. 294, pp. 623–635. Springer, Cham (2019). https://doi.org/10.1007/978-3-030-32388-2_52
24. Zhang, X., Zhao, J., LeCun, Y.: Character-level convolutional networks for text classification. In: Advances in Neural Information Processing Systems, pp. 649–657 (2015)

25. Zhang, Y., Wang, Q., Li, Y., Wu, X.: Sentiment classification based on piecewise pooling convolutional neural network. Comput. Mater. Contin. **56**(2), 285–297 (2018)
26. Ziegelmayer, D., Schrader, R.: Sentiment polarity classification using statistical data compression models. In: 2012 IEEE 12th International Conference on Data Mining Workshops, pp. 731–738. IEEE (2012)

Paper Recommend Based on LDA
and PageRank

Min Tao[1], Xinmin Yang[2], Gao Gu[1], and Bohan Li[1,3,4(✉)]

[1] College of Computer Science and Technology, Nanjing University of Aeronautics
and Astronautics, Nanjing 211106, China
{taomin,bhli}@nuaa.edu.cn
[2] 28th Research Institute of China Electronics Technology Group Corporation, Nanjing, China
[3] Key Laboratory of Safety-Critical Software, Ministry of Industry and Information Technology,
Nanjing 211106, China
[4] Collaborative Innovation Center of Novel Software Technology and Industrialization,
Nanjing, Jiangsu, China

Abstract. The explosive growth of the number of papers leads to the over-expansion of the paper information, resulting in the problem of information overload, causing a lot of trouble for researchers to find the papers they need. This paper implements a paper recommendation system based on LDA and PageRank. In this system, we recommend papers in the same field to researchers by modeling and analyzing paper data. Therefore, we can provide researchers with a quick and effective reference for related papers in the research field. In this paper, the probability distribution calculation and keywords extraction of paper topics and words are carried out according to the LDA of papers in the paper pool. At the same time, word2dec is used to represent the topic vector, doc2vec is used to represent the paper vector, and by calculating the system similarity between documents and topics, we get the top N papers that are most similar to the topic input by users. We use the PageRank algorithm to reorder the options in the reference network to get the final recommendation results. Under the experimental data set, the accuracy of system recommendation is more than 60%, which has high reliability and achieves the corresponding recommendation effect.

Keywords: LDA · PageRank · Recommender · System similarity

1 Instruction

The significant increasing number of publication, and the development of the Internet has greatly reduced the cost of obtaining paper information. However, it also brings great trouble to the researchers. The problem of information overload costs much on searching for the literature. This leads the concern on the research of paper recommendation system.

Now, the YouTube video recommendation system, Taobao commodity recommendation system, and other commercial recommendation systems have been a mature and practical application. However, compared with these commercial recommendation systems, due to the relatively small number of researchers and other reasons, the research

© Springer Nature Singapore Pte Ltd. 2020
X. Sun et al. (Eds.): ICAIS 2020, CCIS 1254, pp. 571–584, 2020.
https://doi.org/10.1007/978-981-15-8101-4_51

on paper recommendation is still not mature enough. With the advent of the big data era, the paper recommendation system has been concerned.

Wang Han [1] and others put forward a hybrid sorting learning collaborative filtering algorithm combining the LDA topic model and list sorting, which reflects the accuracy of sorting recommendation and alleviates the impact of data sparsity and has important reference value. Xu Jian [2] effectively improves the hit rate, ranking and effective hit rate of the scientific and technological paper system by combining collaborative filtering, content filtering, and PageRank algorithm. Xie Wei [3] and others designed a paper recommendation system based on the idea of the TextRank graph algorithm. In the actual use environment, the system was verified to have high accuracy and reliability, and effectively improved the recommendation efficiency of the paper review system. Liu Yaning [4] and others built a personalized citation recommendation model PCR model based on user preference and language model, which has achieved great performance improvement and has important reference significance. Li Bo-Han [5] and others propose An interaction-based method named GRIP (Group Recommender Based on Interactive Preference), which can use group activity history information and recommender post-rating feedback mechanism to generate interactive preference parameters. The results indicate the superiority of the GRIP recommender for multi-users regarding both validity and accuracy.

Weijin Jiang [6] and others improved collaborative filtering, introduced a fuzzy matrix of item attributes, and measured the relevance of items through fuzzy clustering. In the recommendation, considering the relevance of the items, the neighbor search is more accurate, and the accuracy and quality of the recommendation are improved. Aziguli Wulam [7] and others used a convolutional network to capture local features and used gradients to enhance the node leaf construction features of the decision tree. Use the leaf nodes of the tree to mine user behavior path features, and use the depth model to extract user abstract features. By combining machine learning and deep learning, a recommendation model with better test performance is implemented based on Kaggle competition. Mengwei Hou [8] and others considered the privacy issues in the recommendation system. During the recommendation process, two operations, namely, private neighbor selection and neighbor-based differential privacy recommendations, were adopted for privacy protection. Personalized recommendation privacy protection is considered later in this article. It has a certain reference value.

In previous studies, the problem of the paper recommendation system is defined as giving a researcher's research interest, looking for papers related to the interest [9]. However, the research interests given by researchers may lead to different interpretations and inaccurate descriptions. Therefore, this paper simplifies it to give a paper in the field that the researcher is studying, and calculates the system similarity according to the paper. We accomplish the task to recommend the paper to the researcher who interested in it.

The rest of this article is organized as follows. In the second part, we discussed the characteristics of the experimental data set and the related work of the experimental method in this paper. In the third part, we introduced the various models and algorithms used in this article. In the fourth part, we present the experimental process of this article, including improvements to PageRank. Then it is verified from the number of paper recommendations N and the number of selected topics, and compared with the traditional recommendation method. Finally, it summarizes the work of this paper and looks forward to the future development direction.

2 Related Works

In the subsect. 2.1, the characteristics of the data set are briefly introduced. Then, in the Subsect. 2.2, this paper briefly introduces the experimental research process.

2.1 Data Set Characteristics

In this paper, the ACL selection network paper is used as the data set, a total of 18718 papers. Considering the actual efficiency of keyword extraction and vector computing, the data set must be preprocessed.

Because the structure of the thesis is relatively fixed, the abstract of the thesis must contain the research content of the thesis, the theme of the thesis can be extracted from it. Besides, the title of the paper is a high-level summary of the content of the paper. So, the data set selects the title and summary of the more than 18000 papers as the original data set of the recommendation system.

For the convenience of research, each paper is stored in a separate TXT file, identified with a unique number, and all paper titles and abstracts are extracted and put into the paper pool.

2.2 Existing Methods

The key to the paper recommendation system is to identify the research topic of the paper. As a model that is easy to understand and has a strong ability to extract the main content of articles, LDA is widely used in text classification tasks. In this paper, LDA is used to extract the data set from the paper pool, to obtain the corresponding topic matrix.

For topic and document vector representation, this paper uses word2dec for topic vector representation and doc2vec for document vector representation.

Considering that word2vec can provide high-quality vocabulary vectors, this paper uses it to represent topic vectors. However, word2vec does not have an effective method to combine vocabulary vector into a high-quality document vector, so this paper uses doc2vec to represent the document vector.

Figure 1 is the research flow of this paper. Input a paper in the field, after subject extraction and vector representation, calculate the paper similarity [10], select the first n papers according to the calculation results, reorder them based on PageRank, and finally obtain the first n papers most related to the input documents.

3 Experiment Research

This section introduces, topic extraction and vector similarity calculation for the paper pool data, and finally, similarity calculation based on the vector cosine similarity algorithm [11]. According to the calculation results, select the top n paper, and reorder it

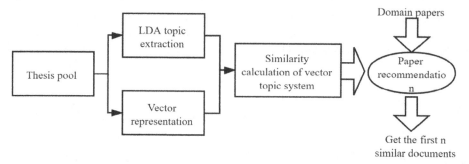

Fig. 1. Research flow

with the PageRank algorithm, to realize the recommendation of the paper, and finally summarize the experimental results.

(1) Latent Dirichlet Allocation

LDA model was proposed by BLEI et al. in 2003 [12], as an unsupervised machine learning method, it is used to identify the potential topic set $Z = \{ z_1, z_2, \ldots, z_n \}$, in the document set $D = \{ d_1, d_2, \ldots, d_n \}$. Since each word in LDA is considered as discrete data, the joint probability distribution of LDA is obtained by setting word set $W = \{ \omega_1, \omega_2, \ldots, \omega_n \}$, as follows:

$$\rho(\theta, z, \omega | \alpha, \beta) = \rho(\theta | \alpha) * \prod_{n-1}^{N} \rho(\omega_n | z_n, \beta) \tag{1}$$

θ and Z are implied variables, α β is obtained by EM algorithm, ω is an observation variable.

Figure 2 below is the graphical representation of the LDA model, and Table 1 is the symbol description:

The probability distribution calculation and keywords extraction of paper topics and words are carried out according to the LDA of papers in the paper pool.

(2) Word2vec

Word2vec [13] uses the context of words to map words to high-dimensional real space, thus simplifying the text content into the operation between vectors. By computing the word vector trained by Word2vec, the text semantic similarity can be obtained and the target of word clustering can be achieved. There are two models: Continuous Bag-of-Words model (CBOW) and Continuous Skip-gram Model (Skip-gram). As shown in Fig. 3, they are CBOW and Skip-gram model (W_t stands for the current central word). In this paper, the CBOW model is used to obtain word vectors.

(3) Doc2vec

In addition to adding a paragraph vector, Doc2vec [14] is equivalent to word2vec. Like word2vec, doc2vec has two models: distributed memory (DM) and distributed bag of

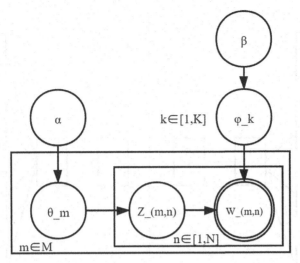

Fig. 2. Graphical representation of the LDA model

Table 1. Symbol description in the LDA model diagram representation

Symbol	Explain
$\vec{\alpha}$	Topic distribution super parameter
$\vec{\theta_m}$	Theme distribution of document m
$\vec{\varphi_k}$	Word distribution of theme K
K	Total number of subject words
M	Total number of documents
N_m	Total number of M documents
$Z_{m,n}$	Nth lexical topic in document m
$W_{m,n}$	Nth word in document m
$\vec{\beta}$	Super parameter of word term distribution

words (DBOW). As shown in Fig. 4 below are DM and DBOW models respectively. In this paper, the DM model is used for document vector representation.

(4) Page Rank

PageRank was proposed by page et al. in 1998 [14], which is a Google page ranking algorithm, used to identify the level of importance of the page [15]. The core idea is to use the link to the page as a vote for the page, and use the random walk to score the quality of the page.

In the paper recommendation, the citation relationship is an important recommendation basis. The paper is regarded as a node, the citation relationship is regarded as a

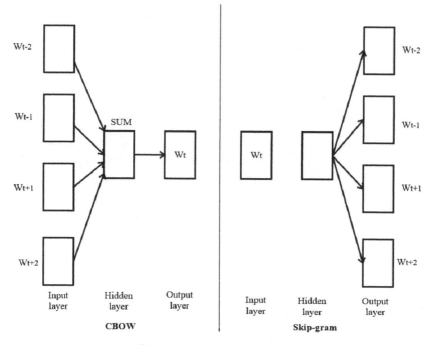

Fig. 3. Two models of word2vec

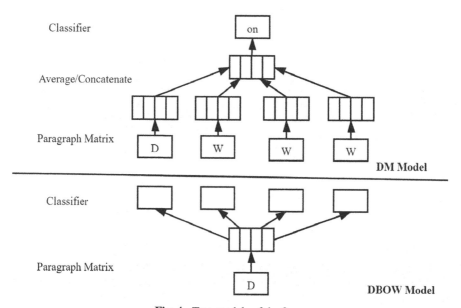

Fig. 4. Two models of doc2vec

directed edge, point to the cited paper. Thus, the citation network of the paper can be abstracted and simplified as a directed graph, as shown in Fig. 5 below, which represents a simple directed network.

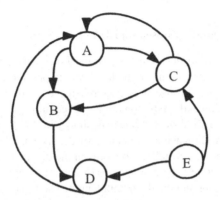

Fig. 5. Digraph G

In Fig. 5, each node distributes its PR value equally to other outgoing nodes. At the same time, each node collects the PR values of all incoming nodes to form its PageRank value. Take A as an example, the PR value of A is C evenly distributed to A and B, and D is separately distributed to A, while the PR value of A is equally distributed to B and C.

The PR value of the node A_i is denoted as $PR(A_i)$, the node A_i into the chain set is denoted as $I(A_i)$, and the in-degree of a node A_i is recorded as $N(A_i)$, then the basic idea of the PageRank algorithm can be expressed as (2):

$$PR(A_i) = \sum_{A_j \in I(A_i)} PR(A_j)/N(A_j) \tag{2}$$

To prevent grade sinking and grade infiltration [16], In the PageRank algorithm, the attenuation factor is introduced, which makes the probability of node staying at a certain point d $(0 < d < 1)$, while the rest PR values will still be evenly distributed to all pages. The modified PageRank algorithm is shown in (3):

$$PR(A_i) = d \cdot \sum_{A_j \in I(A_i)} \frac{PR(A_j)}{N(A_j)} + (1 - d)/N \tag{3}$$

To consider the influence of time factor, this paper adds time decay function based on PageRank and realizes the final recommendation effect by combining the LDA model, Word2vec and Doc2vec.

4 Our Solution

This experiment is divided into two modules. First, according to LDA, word2vec, and Doc2vec, we do word vector representation and similarity calculation. In the Subsect. 2.1, we introduce this part of the work in detail. According to the calculation results in Sect. 4.1, the paper set to be recommended is obtained, and then the PR value is calculated by adding the time decay function PageRank algorithm, and the paper to be recommended is reordered. This part of the work is introduced in the subsect. 2.1 in detail.

4.1 Paper Recommendation Based on LDA

As we all know, LDA has a strong ability to describe the global relationship of documents, while word2vec and doc2vec focus on the local way to predict words. In this paper, we combine these technologies and use more comprehensive vectors to represent documents, to achieve the recognition and prediction ability of recommendation task processing.

The experimental method of this paper is shown in Fig. 6, which projects theme and document into high-dimensional semantic space. As a single vector, the document vector is regarded as the "centroid" of all words in the document [17]. Considering the difference between different document lengths (number of words), the vector is normalized by dividing the vector and the document length. The topic vector is represented by a high-frequency word set, whose probability is the word distribution weight to express the contribution of words to the topic. By measuring the Euclidean distance between document topics, the document is represented by distance distribution.

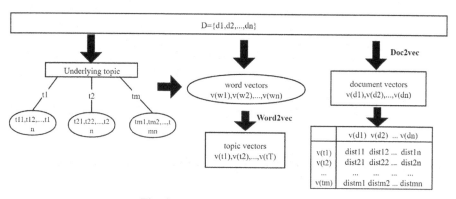

Fig. 6. Experimental flow and results

Set paper set $D = \{d_1, d_2, ..., d_n\}$, represented by word set $W = \{\omega_1, \omega_2, ..., \omega_T\}$. Through the LDA model, we can get the potential topic set $W = \{t_1, t_2, ..., t_m\}$, and the word probability set of each topic is $\{\theta_{i1}, \theta_{i2}, ..., \theta_{ik}\}$. Word2vec and doc2vec train each word in the vocabulary word set into a fixed-length vector $\{v(\omega_1), v(\omega_2), ..., v(\omega_N)\}$. To generate the corresponding topic vector, we extract the first n high-frequency words in the potential topic set and adjust the weight through (4) and (5) below.

$$\omega_i = \frac{\theta_i}{\sum_{n=1}^{h} \theta_n} \tag{4}$$

$$v_{\langle ti \rangle} = \sum_{n=1}^{h} \omega_{i_n} v(\omega_{in}) \tag{5}$$

The document vector $v(di)$ is calculated as (6), where C is the document length.

$$v(d_i) = \frac{\Sigma_{n=1}^{c} v(\omega_{i_n})}{c} \tag{6}$$

Thus, the Euclidean distance is used to obtain the distance distribution from the document to all topics in the semantic space. The calculation is as follows (7):

$$distance\big(v(d_i), v(t_j)\big) = \big|v(d_i) - v(t_j)\big| \tag{7}$$

The distance between the dissertation and each vector can be obtained through the topic distance distribution of the document vector, and the distance vector between the target dissertation and each topic can be obtained. The closer the topics are between the two papers, the more similar the topic distance distribution between the topics. Therefore, the topic distance vector can be obtained from the specific distance between each paper and the topic, and the similarity can be obtained by calculating the distance between the vectors.

In this paper, the vector cosine similarity algorithm [2, 11] is used for recommendation. Now, the vector of the target paper i is recorded as w_i, and the vector of any paper j to be recommended is recorded as w_j. Using the cosine similarity algorithm of vector, the similarity between the target paper and the paper to be recommended is recorded as $sim(i,j)$, which is expressed as (8):

$$sim(i, j) = \cos\big(\overrightarrow{w_i}, \overrightarrow{w_j}\big) = \frac{\overrightarrow{w_i} \cdot \overrightarrow{w_j}}{\big|\big|\overrightarrow{w_i}\big|\big|_2 \cdot \big|\big|\overrightarrow{w_j}\big|\big|_2} \tag{8}$$

The probability distribution of the LDA topic is closer to the specific document, and because more word vector information is involved, more other information is extracted. According to the similarity calculation results, the Top N paper list is obtained by sorting.

4.2 Paper Recommendation Based on PageRank

The traditional PageRank algorithm is used to identify the level of web pages, and the object-oriented are web links. However, there is a big difference between the citation network and the web page links. The publication time of the paper is usually an important factor in the recommendation of the paper. When the web page is labeled, the factor is not so important for the analysis of the network's importance. Therefore, based on the PageRank algorithm, the time decay function is added to avoid neglecting the publication time of the paper, resulting in the reduction of recommendation accuracy.

Through the previous similarity calculation, we get the recommended paper set $A = \{A_1, A_2, ..., A_n\}$, where the number of papers is n. Based on the citation network, the algorithm calculates the Page Rank value of the paper in a, which is recorded as $PR(A_i)$.

Considering that in the paper recommendation system, users are more willing to contact new papers, this paper adds a time decay function GD for the publication time of papers, which is defined as (9) (10):

$$GD = PR \cdot Age - Decay \tag{9}$$

To define the time decay, select the exponential function [18]:

$$Age - Decay = \exp(-\lambda \Delta t) \tag{10}$$

Where, $\Delta t = tr(recommendedyear) - tp(publishedyear)$, λ is the attenuation ratio. Therefore, the final PR calculation formula is as follows (11):

$$PR(A_i) = \left\{ d \cdot \sum_{A_j \in I(A_i)} \frac{PR(A_j)}{N(A_j)} + \frac{1-d}{N} \right\} \cdot \exp(-\lambda \Delta t) \tag{11}$$

The attenuation ratio λ in (9) indicates the influence degree of the time factor on the weight of the paper. In the experiment, 0.3 is selected, the initial PR value of the experiment is 1, and the attenuation factor is 0.75.

For n papers in the paper set A, the PageRank algorithm after adding time decay function is used for iterative calculation. The number of detection iterations is more than 5000, and the iteration is stopped. At this time, the calculation result is the final PR value of the paper.

Finally, rank the calculated PR values and output the Top N recommendation results.

5   Experimental

In this paper, according to the input paper title and abstract, through similarity calculation and PageRank calculation ranking, Top N papers are obtained for recommendation [3]. The recommended output examples are shown in Table 2 below. Top-N papers are selected by $sim\ (i, j)$, and then the output is reordered based on the PR value obtained by PageRank.

Table 2. Calculation results of N papers closest to a00-1034.txt when n = 10

Thesis ID(id)	File Name(file)	cosine similarity-sim(i, j)	PR value
2367	D08-1071.txt	0.6999453444340846	0.31333951
27	A00-1031.txt	0.6489357041982314	0.29633859
8985	P13-1028.txt	0.6374460721183068	0.28356865
7516	P07-1002.txt	0.6319530906583605	0.25012394
11089	Q13-1007.txt	0.6192361282879355	0.24985317
12205	W03-0303.txt	0.6037470473762523	0.21369972
14551	W09-1203.txt	0.5040372856440422	0.19357921
17675	W14-3312.txt	0.5732498332045749	0.16239670
11080	P99-1081.txt	0.5458519375387051	0.11399626
10896	P98-1119.txt	0.6101528705076721	0.11399626

Input: Papers conforming to the intended topic (txt file).

Output: list of Top-N similar papers (take a00-1034.txt, n = 10 as an example)

In this section, this article is based on the ACL conference proceedings as a data set, and thus the paper is recommended. This experiment aims at the accuracy of the recommendation results of the paper, and verifies from the number of recommended N and the number of selected topics, and analyzes the number of best-recommended papers and the number of selected topics. It also compares with traditional recommendation methods.

5.1 The Number of Topics

Because the number of LDA topics directly affects the vector dimension of the final generated paper, too little will lead to too much error in the calculation result, too much will cause overfitting. Therefore, this paper experimentally evaluates the recommended performance of this experimental method under the different number of topics.

As shown in Table 3, when 175–225 topics are selected, you can see that the Average 10 fold micro-F1 score of the recommendation result is at a high level, and the recommendation result is better.

Table 3. Average 10 fold micro-F1 score of our method under different number of topics

	Average 10 fold micro-F1 score (Standard deviation)				
	150 topics	175 topics	200 topics	225 topics	250 topics
Our method	0.764	0.773	0.781	0.789	0.772

5.2 The Number of N in Top-N

Because it is difficult to measure whether the subject meets the requirements, this paper calculates the accuracy based on the citation. If the recommended paper appears in the cited paper, it is considered as an effective recommended paper. Considering the actual query needs of readers, it is not appropriate to get too few results each time, so this paper adopts n = {6, 8, 10, 12, 14} for experiments. Each time, 100 papers are randomly selected from the paper pool as input sets, and their accuracy is tested under the conditions of n = 6, 8, 10, 12, 14. To ensure accuracy, the experiment is repeated three times. The accuracy of the recommended results is shown in Fig. 7:

5.3 Comparison with Traditional Recommendation Methods

Also, this paper compares the methods used in this paper with traditional LDA, TF-IDF, Word2vec based on the ACL conference paper data set. The comparison results are shown in Table 4. It can be seen that the TF-IDF prediction result is the best, but its running time is the longest, which is 2.7 times that of the method used in this experiment.

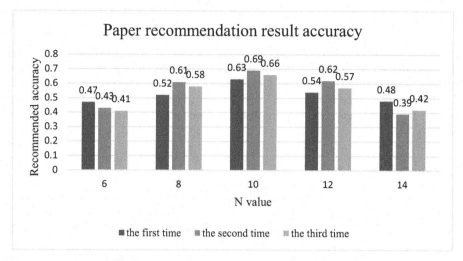

Fig. 7. Accuracy of paper recommendation results

Word2Vec has the shortest running time, but it has the fewest training features, and the final recommendation accuracy is also low. Although LDA takes less time than the method used in this paper, it has the lowest accuracy. Besides, TF-IDF and LDA do not consider text semantic information.

Table 4. Average 10 fold mircro-f1 score of different methods

	Average 10 Fold micro-F1 score
LDA	0.634(topic = 150)
TF-IDF	0.759
Word2vec	0.655
Our method	0.702(topic = 175)

Considering the three aspects of running time, prediction accuracy, and semantic information, Our method is better.

6   Conclusion

Based on keyword extraction and similarity calculation, this paper implements the paper recommendation system, which can provide convenience for researchers to consult literature and save time for paper searching. According to the similarity calculation results, the top n recommendation is carried out.

The following improvements will be considered in the future:

(1) There are some limitations in accuracy calculation based on paper citations. In the next step, we can consider the introduction of the crowdsourcing mechanism to achieve topic relevance calculation.
(2) Determine the dependence between citations in the citation network, to quantify the dependence between papers, and calculate the correlation with Katz [19] distance.
(3) Considering the influence factor [20] of the paper in the citation network, change the recommendation weight of the paper.

Acknowledgments. This work is supported in part by National Natural Science Foundation of China (61728204), Innovation Funding (NJ20160028, NT2018027, NT2018028, NS2018057), Aeronautical Science Foundation of China (2016551500), State Key Laboratory for smart grid protection and operation control Foundation, Association of Chinese Graduate Education (ACGE).

Declaration of Competing Interest.   The authors declared that there is no conflict of interest for this paper.

References

1. Wang, H., Xia, H.: Collaborative filtering recommendation algorithm mixing LDA model and list-wise model. Comput. Sci. **46**(09), 216–222 (2019)
2. Jian, X.: Scientific paper recommendation system based on PageRank. Electron. World **01**, 104–105 (2013)
3. Xie, W., Shen, Y., Ma, Y.: Recommendation system for paper reviewing based on graph computing. Appl. Res. Comput. **33**(03), 798–801 (2016)
4. Liu, Y., Yan, R., Yan, H.: Personalized citation recommendation based on user's preference and language model. J. Chinese Inf. Process. **30**(02), 128–135 (2016)
5. Li, B., et al.: GRIP: a group recommender based on interactive preference model. JCST **33**(5), 1039–1055 (2018)
6. Jiang, W., et al.: A new time-aware collaborative filtering intelligent recommendation system. Comput. Mater. Continua **61**(2), 849–859 (2019)
7. Wulam, A., Wang, Y., Zhang, D., Sang, J., Yang, A.: A recommendation system based on fusing boosting model and DNN model. Comput. Mater. Continua **60**(3), 1003–1013 (2019)
8. Hou, M., Wei, R., Wang, T., Cheng, Y., Qian, B.: Reliable medical recommendation based on privacy-preserving collaborative filtering. Comput. Mater. Continua **56**(1), 137–149 (2018)
9. Chumki, B., Haym, H., Cohen, W.W., et al.: Technical paper recommendation: a study in combining multiple information sources. J. Artif. Intell. Res. **14**, 231–252 (2001)
10. Lee, L.: Similarity-based Approaches to Natural Language Processing, TR-11-97. Harvard University, Cambridge (1997)
11. Salton, G.: Automatic Text Processing. Addison-Wesley, Boston (1988)
12. Qiu, Z., Wu, B., Wang, B., et al.: Gibbs collapsed sampling for latent Dirichlet allocation on spark. J. Mach. Learn. Res. **36**, 17–28 (2014)
13. Mikolov, T., Sutskever, I., Chen, K., et al.: Distributed representations of words and phrases and their compositionality. Adv. Neural. Inf. Process. Syst. **26**, 3111–3119 (2013)
14. Mahdizadeh, H., Biemans, H., Mulder, M.: Determining factors of the use of e-learning environments by university teachers. Comput. Educ. **51**(1), 142–154 (2008)

15. Brin, S., Page, L.: The anatomy of a large-scale hyper textual web search engine. Comput. Netw. ISDN Syst. **30**(1), 107–117 (1998)
16. Jin, J., Yuehao, X., Liu, Z.: Paper relational network mining based on PageRank. J. China Acad. Electron. Inf. Technol. **14**(09), 924–928 (2019)
17. Wang, Z., Ma, L., Zhang, Y.: A hybrid document feature extraction method using latent Dirichlet allocation and Word2Vec. In: 2016 IEEE First International Conference on Data Science in Cyberspace (DSC). IEEE Computer Society (2016)
18. Fanqi, M.: Personalized Query-Oriented Reference Paper Recommender System. Tianjin University (2014)
19. Liben-Nowell, D., Kleinberg, J.: The link-prediction problem for social networks. J. Am. Soc. Inf. Sci. Technol. **58**(7), 1019–1031 (2007)
20. Ekstrand, M., Kannan, P., Stemper, J., Butler, J., Konstan, J., Riedl, J.: Automatically building research reading lists. In: Proceedings of the Fourth ACM Conference on Recommender Systems, pp. 159–166 (2010)

An Improved Encoding Scheme for Distributed Video Coding Based on Wavelet Transform

Jian Zhang[✉], Jin Zhang, Xiaoyu Shi, and Huilong Yu

College of Communication Engineering, Nanjing Institute of Technology, Nanjing, China
zhangjian@njit.edu.cn

Abstract. Some improvement ideas have been made for distributed video coding scheme based on the wavelet transform domain. First, a simplified algorithm is introduced for integer wavelet transform coding to improve the computational efficiency of the encoding side. Secondly, in order to save the channel bandwidth, this paper proposed a direct filling method of the side information for the high-frequency part. At last, this article uses the idea of hierarchical transmission in traditional video coding for different transmission channel bandwidth. The simulation results show that the program greatly reduces the transmission bit rate with a good video transmission quality.

Keywords: Distributed Video Coding · Integer wavelet transform · Hierarchical transmission

1 Introduction

With the development of wireless broadband network, more and more mobile video terminals have been used in multimedia communications. Usually the processing capacity and power consumption of these terminal equipment are very limited, so the video encoder should be simple and easy to realize, and also have a good resistance to error performance and compression efficiency. Traditional video coding standards, such as MPEG and H.26x, have not been able to meet these requirements. In order to solve these problems, the domestic and foreign scholars have proposed a new Video compression method-Distributed Video Coding (DVC) [1, 2].

DVC is a new paradigm for video compression, with low encoding complexity and robustness to channel losses. It was proposed in 1970 s, based on nondestructive coding theory and lossy coding theory. A common approach to DVC theory is independent encoding followed by joint decoding with the side information (SI) [2]. In this way, the encoder leaver out a large amount of calculation, such as inverse transformation and quantification. It shifts computational complexity to the decoder to meet the requirements of the new application in this framework. Today, there are many DVC research groups in abroad, such as Bernd Girod's team at Stanford university, Kannan Ramchandran's group at the university of California, and European DISCOVER research group. These research institutions have put forward some low complexity video coding system [3, 5, 6]. There are several research achievements, such as DVC with feedback channel

© Springer Nature Singapore Pte Ltd. 2020
X. Sun et al. (Eds.): ICAIS 2020, CCIS 1254, pp. 585–595, 2020.
https://doi.org/10.1007/978-981-15-8101-4_52

of Bernd Girod and PRISM (Power-efficient Robust high-compression Syndrome-base Multimedia) of Ramchandran.

On this basis, the researchers put forward some new coding scheme [7, 11], Include Tagliasacchi proposed DVC based on WT, Adikari proposed DVC based on Recursive decoding, and Ramchandran proposed DISCUS Architecture. DVC Architecture is usually divided into two parts, key frame transmission and Wyner-Ziv frame transmission, so there are two transmission queue, key frame(K frame) and Wyner-Ziv frame(WZ frame). K frame usually adopts intraframe coding and decoding algorithm of the Traditional video, But WZ frame uses inside coding and inter decoding. WZ frame coding can be divided into Pixel-domain Wyner-Ziv Codec system (PDWZ) and Transform-domain Wyner-Ziv Codec system (TDWZ) [2]. Due to the lack of effective compression efficiency for PDWZ field, the present study direction is mainly in TDWZ field. At present, in TDWZ field, most popular technical architecture is Stanford's proposed Wyner-Ziv decoding scheme based on discrete cosine transform (DCT). However, these DCT based framework exist obvious shortage. In order to deal with convenience in practical application, the image normally is divided into 8*8 or 16*16 small pieces to separately process in DCT coding, which leads to "block effects". So, scholars put forward another kind of transform domain coding, based on wavelet transform, as shown in Fig. 1 [2]. Due to the flexibility of discrete wavelet transform (DWT) in non-stationary image signal, and the adaptability to visual characteristic ability of human, wavelet transform has become a mainstream technology of image compression.

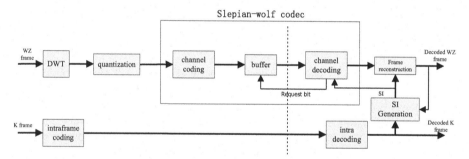

Fig. 1. WZ frame coding scheme based on DWT

Compared to DCT, DWT overcomes the "block effect", meanwhile both sides have the characteristics of energy concentration. In the traditional coding field, DWT is gradually replaced DCT, such as in the new generation of still image compression standard-JPEG2000. But DWT calculation is bigger, which limited its usage in DVC field [6, 10].

2 Simplified Integer Wavelet Transform Based on the Fast Algorithm

In recent years, in order to improve the efficiency of the wavelet transform, the scholars put forward many fast algorithm. The first generation wavelet transform with the aid of

Fourier transform, the calculation is complicated, and the range of application is limited. In 1994, Sweldens proposed the second generation wavelet transform theory based on division-forecast-update, and this theory made the wavelet transform can be calculated in the integer domain to avoid the quantization error in pretreatment. After that, Dewitte made the compression ratio increased by 10%, compared with the predictive coding and Haar wavelet, with single ascension and double ascension method. David. B. H. proposed a new method to compute integer wavelet transform (IWT) by binary coefficient, which avoids the multiplication to reduce the processing calculation, and make it easy for FPGA or DSP hardware realization. At present, popular WT fast algorithm include EZW, SPIHT SFQ, EPWIC, and EBCOT. In 2000s, the International Standard Organization (ISO) and the International Electro-technical Committee (IEC) jointly launched a new generation of still image compression standard-JPEG2000 based on discrete wavelet transform(DWT). Two types of ascension wavelet are used in the JPEG2000, one kind is reversible integer 5/3 wavelet transform, which is mainly used to realize lossless image compression and lossy image compression; Another is 9/7 wavelet transform, used for high quality lossy image compression [12, 16].

Compared to DWT, DCT have an advantage of a fast arithmetic speed. But DWT has potential advantages. For example, the PSNR value of DWT recovery image quality is 2 dB higher than DCT in the same code rate cases, and DWT avoids the DCT's "block effect". So, it is important to improve the computation efficiency of the DWT. In 2006, FuZhong and ZhuXiaoMing proposed a simplified wavelet fast algorithm on the basis of ascension algorithm in China university of science and technology, and the experimental results show that the new algorithm will raise the wavelet transform efficiency by 70% [14]. Ascension wavelet transform steps are divided into three steps, division, forecasting, update, as Fig. 2 shows.

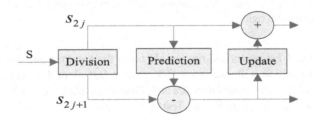

Fig. 2. Ascension wavelet transform diagram

Division: the original signal is decomposed into even signal s_{2j} and even signal s_{2j+1}.

Prediction: Keep even signal s_{2j} is changeless, predict odd signal s_{2j+1} through Interpolation method, d_j is the D-value between predictive value and the actual value, $d_j = s_{2j+1} - P(s_{2j})$, and P is the prediction operator.

Update: process uses d_j to update s_{2j}, in order to retain some characteristics of the original signal, such as remain the same of average value, this operation recorded as $a_j = s_{2j} + U(d_{2j})$, in which U as the update operator.

Take 5/3 Biorthogonal wavelet for example, Calculation formula of d_j and a_j as Shown below. Multiplication of Ascension coefficient (1/2 and 1/4) can be replaced by shift operation to reduce computation.

$$d_j = s_{2j+1} - \left[\frac{1}{2}(s_{2j} + s_{2j+1})\right] \tag{1}$$

$$a_j = s_{2j} + \left[\frac{1}{2}(d_{j-1} + d_j)\right] \tag{2}$$

In the traditional fast algorithm, first step is to make a one-dimensional DWT transform in row so there are Decomposition for high frequency and low frequency part in row, then the second step is to do one-dimensional DWT in column. Due to the low frequency part containing the most energy image, the importance of low frequency part is far higher than the high frequency part.

Considering the ability of encoder is limited in DVC, So the second one-dimensional IWT can be simplified, so they omit the high frequency part of the second operation. A picture of original image is treated as shown in Fig. 3. This makes WT calculation focus on high-efficiency low-frequency region, and ignore the high-frequency low-efficiency part.

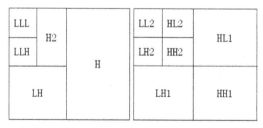

Fig. 3. Two layer wavelet transform subspace distribution (the simplified algorithm left, the traditional fast algorithm right)

As the Table 1 below shows, this article takes the foreman and coastguard video sequence to simulation with ascension 3/5 wavelet fast algorithm and the simplified algorithm proposed, in the same hardware and software environment. The result is that the latter is fast than the former by 57.4%. Test environment: ARM (model EBD9260, CPU 180 MHz), Linux (kernel version 2.6.19), video quality (QCIF, 176 * 144), processing frame number (300 frame).

3 High Frequency Part Filled with Side Information Method

In the Stanford scheme, which based on DCT or DWT video coding, encoder needs to generate hash code by down-sample and coarse quantization of each subblock in image, then calculate mean-square deviation of hash code between previous frame and current frame in the same position. If the mean-square deviation is less than the threshold value G, then decoder directly copy the same subblock from Previous frame in the same position. According to the calculation in this method, few can meet the requirements in low frequency part. But most in high frequency part can meet the requirements [15, 16].

Table 1. The efficiency contrast of the traditional fast algorithm and the simplified algorithm

	Traditional algorithm (millisecond/frame)	Simplified algorithm (millisecond/frame)	Efficiency compared
Foreman	26.69	16.95	+63.5%
Coastguard	33.35	18.31	+54.9%
Soccer	33.14	18.56	+56.0%
Hallmonitor	31.57	17.43	+55.2%

This paper holds that if two adjacent images is very close, such as foreman video sequence, whose PNSR of side information have close to 30 db by interpolation or extrapolation. Then, this method is useful. Because when PSNR is more than 30 dB, usually the human eye has been unable to distinguish two images [17, 18].

For example, this paper deals with image by using simplified IWT algorithm, secondly, gets the wavelet coefficient on the statistical analysis. As the Table 2 below shows, low frequency part of the image is very close to the original image in mean value and variance. Meanwhile, the low frequency part contains most of the energy of original image, high frequency part contains a small fraction (Table 3).

Table 2. Wavelet statistics of the Foreman video sequence

	Max	Min	Mean value	Variance	Energy
Original image	255	0	99.05	52.88	100%
LLL	250.75	−4.2	99.02	52.56	99.7%
LLH	34.25	−34.41	−0.45	2.92	0.04%
H2	35.48	−31.32	−0.74	1.09	0.07%
LH	20.11	−24.56	0.01	2.06	0.06%
H	17.24	−15.17	0.03	2.14	0.13%

According to the above analysis, the most information of the image stores in LLL subspace, which is the most important part of the transmission in DVC. Other subspace contain energy is very few, and the original image and SI have similar mean variance and energy in high frequency. LLL subspace is a bit different. In this conclusion, a new compression method is proposed in this paper-SI in high frequency fills the decoded image directly. But the low frequency subspace does not use this method because of its importance. This paper has taken 100 frames to do experiments, and got the same conclusion.

On the basis of the above analysis, this paper tries to quantitative analysis with the influence of the image quality in this method. Figure 4 is the result of first 100 frame in foreman and coastguard video sequence by the experiments. Figure 5 and Fig. 6 is the

Table 3. Wavelet statistics of the coastguard video sequence

	Max	Min	Mean value	Variance	Energy
SI image	255	0	92.05	47.88	100%
LLL	250.75	5.0	101.02	69.56	99.7%
LLH	30.25	−36.41	−0.72	2.11	0.04%
H2	37.34	−28.17	−0.53	1.23	0.08%
LH	22.04	−23.51	−0.01	2.17	0.06%
H	16.64	−14.20	0.05	2.10	0.12%

frame image of decoded video sequence. As can be seen from the graph, image PSNR is above 30 dB. This can meet the requirements of the human eye [13], and at the same time image decoding is superior in quality to the Stanford architecture [2].

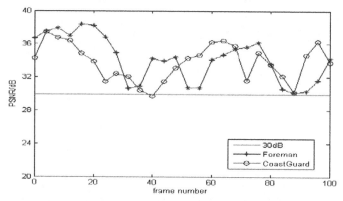

Fig. 4. Experimental results of foreman and coastguard (High frequency filled with side information)

Fig. 5. High frequency part filled with side information method-foreman (PSNR = 37.92) (left for the original image, and the middle for this paper decoding image, the right for Stamford scheme decoding image)

Fig. 6. High frequency part filled with side information method-coastguard (PSNR = 37.92) (left for the original image, and the middle for this paper decoding image, the right for Stamford scheme decoding image)

4 Embedded Coding Without Feedback

In the communication network, the bandwidth of the network is not stable, especially when the network congestion bandwidth declines. In order to solve the image and video transmission problems under the network environment, there appeared Scalability coding technology. Scalability is the ability to restore image or video through a part of compression bit stream. Scalability coding mainly includes the following three, SNR Scalability, Spatial Scalability, and Temporal Scalability, according to object. The first two kinds of methods can be used for image and video signal are applicable, but Temporal Scalability for video signal only. Encoder can also group different Scalability together for mixed Scalability coding. Scalability encoder can also divided into two kinds, hierarchical coding and Fine Granularity Scalability (FGS), according to Interval size. Hierarchical coding will is divided code flow into several layers, and its transmission or decoding only in stratified place. FCS can be cut off in any position, so its code rate is continuous variable. Meanwhile, FGS coding can also be called embedded coding because of embedded bit stream.

As shown in Fig. 1, DVC normally have feedback channel, because decoder can determine transmission code rate, according to the side information, and then encoder can make sure of amount of information, according to feedback code rate. But feedback channel is the most controversial part in DVC scheme, because it means not only a feedback channel needed, also requirement for real-time work with feedback channel delay. On the other hand, feedback channel simplifies the code rate control. Due to the excellent performance of WT, as well as the greatly improved wireless channel transmission environment, the author tried to cancel the feedback channel. The encoder control the rate according to the current signal intensity. Embedded coding can be accurate code rate control, which is suitable for multimedia communication network. The SI filled high frequence method, mentioned in the second part of this paper is fit for embedded codec. Encoder decides rate of code stream, according to real-time bandwidth, then use side information to fill the rest of the image. As the preparing work before transmission, first wavelet coding plane should be transformed into binary code flow plane, priority order of each subspace is LLL-LLH-H2-LH-H, As shown in Fig. 7.

The LLL subspace of the code flow accounts for 1/16 of the whole image, but contains 99.7% of the energy, so it has a highest priority of transmission. LLH and H2

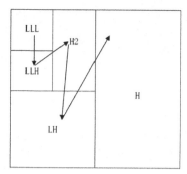

Fig. 7. Priority order of each subspace

subspace are similar to LH, the HL and HH module of the traditional wavelet transformation. LH and HL represent the horizontal and vertical direction of the high frequency part. HH represents a diagonal direction of the high frequency part. According to the discrimination ability of the human eye, HL and LH sensitivity is higher than HH high frequency part to the human eye. So here, the author design priority of LLH higher than H2, and in the same way, LH priority higher than H part. Secondly, in order to facilitate rate control, rate control method without feedback was adopt in this paper, and Turbo code used. as channel code. For the convenience of design process, two extra bytes have been joined in transmission code flow to identify transmitted bit number in the current channel bandwidth. According to the calculated results, only parts of the wavelet transform subspace need to be coded. Decoder cut off bit flow according to the first two bits.

This paper puts forward a simple calculation method, and suppose image transmission quality is QCIF176 * 144, code rate is 4/5 turbo code, video frame rate is 25 frame/s. So if all LLL, LLH, H2 subspace need to transmit, rate should be close to 300 KBPS. As the basis of the whole image, LLL part need 79 kbps. Therefore, the author thinks that when channel bandwidth is more than 79 kbps, it can meet the real-time transmission requirements.

5   The Analysis of Experimental Results

Turbo code and LDPC code are widely adopted in channel coding, both of them have inner robustness for transmission channel noise. However the algorithm and the practical application of Turbo code is more mature. So turbo is adopted in this experiment. First of all, when the channel bandwidth is very narrow, the only allowed transmission is the low-frequency LLL subspace, and the experimental results are as follows.

As the Fig. 8 shows, image is fuzzy, but can be identified. According to the research, when PSNR is more than 30 dB, which can accept [8, 9]. This is based on the identification of human ability to defined, because in this case the human eye is difficult to distinguish the difference between the two images. So in this transmission bandwidth, video image cannot completely meet the quality requirement. But that can meet the requirements of the real-time transmission. Whether transmission should first meet the quality requirements or real-time requirements, according to the practical situation to determine. The Figs. 9 and 10 below shows the comparison between and Stanford method [4] in different channel bandwidth. As can be seen from the graph, the new method can solve the DCT "block effect", at the same time the video output quality improves for 1–2 dB.

Fig. 8. Transmission quality in 80KBPS bandwidth (PSNR = 28.6 dB) (the left for the original image, and the middle for this paper decoding image, the right for Stamford scheme decoding image)

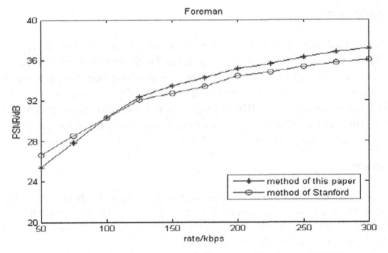

Fig. 9. RD performance contrast (foreman video images/QCIF)

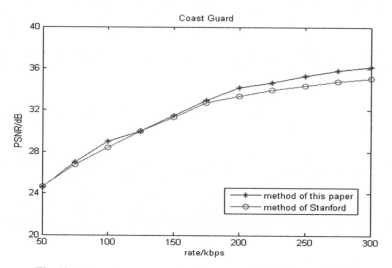

Fig. 10. RD performance contrast (coastguard video images/QCIF)

6   Conclusion

In this paper, some improvement ideas have been put forward for DVC scheme based on DWT, the experimental results show that, compared with Stanford university scheme, this scheme can provide better transmission quality in the more than 100 kbps transmission bandwidth cases. In recent years, scholars at home and abroad continuously put forward faster DWT algorithm. DWT will have greater room for development than DCT, so DVC based on DWT will also have more performance improvements in the future.

References

1. Fei, S., Juanjuan, Y.: Review of distributed video coding. In: IEEE 13th International Conference on Electronic Measurement & Instruments, pp. 315–320. IEEE (2017)
2. Dragotti, P.L., Gastpar, M.: Distributed source coding: theory, algorithms and applications. IEEE Trans. Circuits Syst. **19**, 230–244 (2011)
3. Vijayanagar, K.R., Kim, J., Lee, Y., et al.: Low complexity distributed video coding. J. Vis. Commun. Image Represent. **25**(2), 361–372 (2014)
4. Lu, H., Kong, X., Jiang, X., Chen, B.: Joint power allocation in wireless relay networks: the case of hybrid digital-analog transmission. Mob. Netw. Appl. **21**(6), 1013–1023 (2016)
5. Yu, L., Li, H., Li, W.: Wireless scalable video coding using a hybrid digital-analog scheme. IEEE Trans. Circuits Syst. Video Technol. **24**(2), 331–345 (2014)
6. Yang, W., Shang, W., Chen, J.: Anti-JPEG compression steganography based on the high tense region locating method. Comput. Mater. Contin. **59**(1), 199–214 (2019)
7. Yin, M., Gao, J., Shi, D., et al.: Band-level correlation noise modeling for Wyner-Ziv video coding with Gaussian mixture models. Circuits Syst. Signal Process. **34**(7), 2237–2254 (2015)
8. Sakomizu, K., Yamasaki, T., Nakagawa, S., et al.: A realtime system of distributed video coding. In: Proceedings of the International Conference on Picture Coding Symposium (PCS), pp. 538–541. IEEE (2010)

9. Jayashree, N., Bhuvaneswaran, R.S.: A robust image watermarking scheme using Z-transform, discrete wavelet transform bidiagonal singular value decomposition. Comput. Mater. Contin. **58**(1), 263–285 (2019)

10. Yu, L., Li, H., Li, W.: Wireless cooperative video coding using a hybrid digital analog scheme. IEEE Trans. Circuits Syst. Video Technol. **25**(3), 436–450 (2015)

11. Fan, X., Wu, F., Zhao, D., et al.: Distributed wireless visual communication with power distortion optimization. IEEE Trans. Circuits Syst. Video Technol. **23**(6), 1040–1053 (2013)

12. Deligiannis, N., Verbist, F., Slowack, J., et al.: Progressively refined Wyner-Ziv video coding for visual sensors. ACM Trans. Sensor Netw. **10**(2), 21–34 (2014)

13. Van, X.H., Ascenso, J., Pereira, F., Hoang, X.: HEVC backward compatible scalability: a low encoding complexity distributed video coding based approach. Signal Process. Image Commun. **33**, 51–70 (2015)

14. Li, Z., Meng, L., Shutong, X., Li, Z., Shi, Y., Liang, Y.: A HEVC video steganalysis algorithm based on PU partition modes. Comput. Mater. Contin. **59**(2), 563–574 (2019)

15. Cao, Y., Sun, L., Han, C., Guo, J.: Improved side information generation algorithm based on naive Bayesian theory for distributed video coding. IET Image Process. **12**(3), 354–360 (2018)

16. Zhenhua, T., Xiangyan, L., Tuanfa, T., et al.: Correlation noise modeling algorithm based on multiple probability distributions for distributed video coding. Acta Electron. Sinica **2**, 365–370 (2015)

17. Toto-Zarasoa, V., Roumy, A., Guillemot, C.: Source modeling for distributed video coding. IEEE Trans. Circ. Syst. Video Technol. **22**, 174–187 (2011)

18. Ye, F., Men, A., Xiao, H., Di, J., Yang, B.: Feedback-free distributed video coding using parallelized design. In: Picture Coding Symposium (PCS), pp. 217–220. IEEE (2012)

Image Processing Method of 3D Scattered Point Cloud

Hao Zhu[1,2]([⊠]), Baosheng Wang[2], and Kaiyun Xu[2]

[1] School of Communication,
Nanjing Institute of Technology, Nanjing 211167, China
zhuhao@njit.edu.cn
[2] Jiangsu Key Laboratory of Advanced Numerical Control Technology,
Nanjing 211167, China

Abstract. For 3D scattered point cloud, before surface reconstruction, preprocessing such as quantity reduction and surface denoising is needed. In this paper, a fast point cloud reduction algorithm based on farthest point sampling is proposed. The fast marching algorithm is used to expand the sampling area, and the farthest sampling condition is used to select the qualified sampling points. According to the characteristics of point cloud noise, a compound kMS point cloud denoising algorithm is designed based on k-d tree model and mean drift technology. Realize the fast and efficient denoising of point cloud data. The simulation results show that the algorithm proposed in this paper can effectively realize the function of point cloud reduction and denoising.

Keywords: Three dimensional point cloud · Point cloud simplification · Point cloud denoising

1   Introduction

In 3D model data extraction technology, the extraction results are usually described and saved in the form of scattered point cloud data. In the extraction process, due to many factors, the final point cloud data usually has some defects, so that these point cloud data are not suitable for surface reconstruction directly. Therefore, some preprocessing is needed before using 3D point cloud to model the surface. The common scattered point cloud mainly has the following two defects: first, the point cloud data is too large, there are a lot of redundant data. Secondly, there are some noise data in the point cloud, which makes the point cloud not smooth. In order to solve these two problems, this paper will discuss the simplification algorithm and denoising algorithm of scattered point cloud.

Supported by organization by Natural Science Foundation of Universities in Jiangsu Province (Grant No.: 16KJA460001), Creation Foundation Project of Nanjing Institute of Technology (Grant No.: ZKJ201611).

X. Sun et al. (Eds.): ICAIS 2020, CCIS 1254, pp. 596–606, 2020.
https://doi.org/10.1007/978-981-15-8101-4_53

2   Point Cloud Reduction Algorithm Based on Fast Moving Farthest Point

2.1   Farthest Point Sampling Technology

The basic idea of farthest point sampling is to take the target point as the starting point, search to the periphery continuously according to certain rules, and add the sampling points that meet the conditions set by the user into the current sampling area. Stop the search when the search threshold is exceeded. The farthest point sampling technology can be applied to image reconstruction, data clustering, pattern recognition and other fields. The feasibility of this technology is analyzed in reference [1].

Under the condition of isotropy, the information of point cloud can be represented by characteristic constant, second derivative and third derivative of random process. For sample point pairs (p_i, p_j) where $p_i = (x_i, y_i)$, $p_j = (x_j, y_j)$. The correlation of point pairs $E(p_i, p_j)$ is related to Euler distance d_{ij}. The correlation of point pairs is defined as follows:

$$E(p_i, p_j) = \sigma^2 e^{-\lambda d_{ij}} \tag{1}$$

where $d_{ij} = \sqrt{(x_i - x_j)^2 + (y_i - y_j)^2}$.

The most common application of the farthest point sampling method is point cloud densification. The farthest point search technology is combined with the extension technology of Voronoi diagram to search the farthest distance according to the known points. Shamos [2] shows that a new sampling point can be set up, which is located in the center of the circle formed by the farthest distance from the known point. Focusing on the new point and rebuilding Voronoi diagram, the point cloud can be densified. The essence of point cloud densification is to build new sampling points by using known sampling points, which is usually used for image inpainting.

Point cloud simplification can be realized by using the idea of point cloud densification in reverse. The basic idea is: take the current sampling point Sn as the center, set the distance o to search around according to the threshold value, after the farthest point is determined, the image characteristics within the search radius are relatively stable, so it can be simplified. Then select a sampling point Sn+1 as the center at the edge of the search radius, and continue to find the new farthest point until all the remaining sampling points are traversed.

2.2   Fast Marching Method

The fast marching algorithm provides a strategy of searching outward based on the target point. The research in [3] shows that the fast marching method is a fast and efficient algorithm for forward search. The algorithm uses a partial differential equation to describe the forward search process. For the convenience of description, take the two-dimensional point cloud search as an example, starting from the target point, search outward along the unit normal vector according to the velocity function $F(x)$, making the time to reach a peripheral point $T(x)$, the search path $C(p,t)$, where p is the given parametric variable. Then the process can be expressed by the following partial differential equation:

$$\frac{\partial C}{\partial t} = FN \tag{2}$$

The current velocity function $F(x)$ is only related to the current position. When its sign is constant, the gradient between it and the time function meets $|\Delta T|\, V = 1$. The above equation can be converted into Eikonal equation. Combined with the inverse difference, a set of stable solutions can be obtained by the following formula:

$$\left[\max\left(D_{ij}^{-x}T,0\right)^2 + \min\left(D_{ij}^{+x}T,0\right)^2 + \max\left(D_{ij}^{-y}T,0\right)^2 + \min\left(D_{ij}^{+y}T,0\right)^2\right] = \frac{1}{V} \tag{3}$$

Where D_{ij}^{-}, D_{ij}^{+} are forward and backward differences in x or y direction. Take the x direction as an example:

$$D_{ij}^{-x}T = \frac{T_{ij} - T_{i-1,j}}{h} \tag{4}$$

$$D_{ij}^{+x}T = \frac{T_{i+1,j} - T_{i,j}}{h} \tag{5}$$

Where h is the grid distance. From this, the arrival time T of each point can be obtained.

From the above analysis, we can see that the outer boundary of the search always moves from the smaller T to the larger T. The fast marching method uses the above ideas to search for the propagation boundary value T. The realization process is to build an active area around the propagation, and make the boundary expand continuously by searching outward, just like the process of water wave diffusion.

2.3 Fast Moving Farthest Point Sampling Algorithm

The fast-moving farthest sampling algorithm was first proposed by C. Moenning and N. A. Dodgson [4], which uses the fast-moving algorithm to continuously expand the sampling area, and uses the farthest sampling conditions to select the sampling points that meet the user constraints.

The basic idea of the farthest point sampling method is to continuously find the next sampling point in the unknown area, so as to complete the sampling of the whole target point cloud. Elder et al. Proved that selecting the next sampling point in the farthest point queue is to select the vertex satisfying the farthest point condition on the Voronoi diagram with boundary (BVD(s)) of the selected point clouds [5]. Therefore, the continuous expansion of Voronoi diagram is the precondition of the farthest point sampling. For the point cloud sampled from the farthest point, Voronoi diagram is calculated by calculating the weighted distance graph. This method comes from the improvement of M'emoli and Sapiros on the original fast-moving level set method, without any previous surface construction process.

The improved fast marching method is set in a closed hypersurface M in R_m, where the hypersurface has a zero level set distance function: $\Phi : R_m \rightarrow R, m \geq 3$. Ω_r is a collection of spheres whose radius is r and whose center is the point on the surface.

$$\Omega_r := \bigcup_{x \in M} B(x, y) = \{x \in R_m : |\varphi(x)| \leq r\} \tag{6}$$

For a smooth surface M and small enough r, Ω_r is a manifold with smooth boundary. In order to calculate the arrival time of the weighted distance graph of point set and the propagation in M at the speed $F(p)$. In Ω_r, Euclidean distance graph is used to estimate the natural distance in M. As shown in Eq. 12:

$$|\nabla_M T_M(p)| = F(p) \tag{7}$$

For $p \in M$, and the boundary condition $T_M(q) = 0$ can be approximately replaced by Eq. 8:

$$|\nabla T_{\Omega_r}(p)| = \tilde{F}(P) \tag{8}$$

Where $p \in \Omega_r$ and boundary condition $T_{\Omega_r}(q) = 0$. $\tilde{F}(P)$ is the extension of $F(p)$ from M to Ω_r.

The problem of calculating distance graph is transformed into calculating Euclidean distance graph with boundary. The improved fast marching method can achieve good computational simplification effect, and the complexity of the algorithm is $O(\log N)N$. N represents the number of meshes in Ω_r.

2.4   Point Cloud Reduction Steps

In order to simplify the scattered point cloud using the fast moving farthest point sampling algorithm, it is necessary to determine a large enough point cloud set $= \{p_1, p_2, ...p_{N_1}\}$. The size of the point cloud is larger than the thin cross section Ω_r. In the Ω_r, the initial point set $s \in p$ is selected to construct the initial BVD(S) and store it in a minimum heap. Propagates outward to each point in the initial point set. The specific method to realize the propagation process is to solve Eq. 8 under the condition of $\tilde{F}(P) = 1$, and store the results in the minimum heap data structure. This process is equivalent to calculating Euclidean distance graph from of given S and Ω_r.

Then, a maximum heap is built to store the cloud information of the target points to be selected. When inserting the points that meet the conditions into the minimum heap, the points are inserted into the data structure represented by the maximum heap according to the arrival time of Voronoi vertices, and the values in the maximum heap are adjusted continuously during the process of inserting the minimum heap. Among them, the vertices in BVD(s) are obtained by three or more propagation ripples (or two boundary regions) in the propagation process.

Next, extract the root node in the largest pile, which is the point to be output in the current mesh area. When the arrival time of the point is set to zero, it is inserted into the BVD(s) of the minimum heap, and the eliminated and generated Voronoi points are deleted and inserted from the maximum heap, respectively. The surface will propagate outward until the characteristic value of the mesh point is lower than the arrival time.

In the process of propagation, the root node is extracted from the maximum heap until it meets the constraints or reaches the extreme value given by the model. The constraints proposed by the user are represented by the distance p between the points. When the distance between the farthest points is greater than p, it is the reduced point.

The implementation of the above algorithm is divided into the following steps:

Step 1: find enough point clouds in Cartesian coordinates, so as to obtain cross-section band. According to the initial set of point clouds $S \in \Omega_r$, $n = |S| \geq 2$, the BVD(s) is calculated by using the improved fast marching method with the velocity function $\tilde{F}(p_i)$ as the standard. The arrival time of Voronoi vertices is stored in the maximum heap.

Step 2: extract the root node from the maximum heap to obtain S_{n+1}, and get a new set of points $S' = S \cup \{S_{n+1}\}$. According to the improved fast marching algorithm, a new surface is obtained and BVD(s) is calculated by propagating out of S_{n+1} domain.

Step 3: update the grid points in the minimum heap and adjust the arrival time. Insert the vertex of Voronoi element with boundary at S_{n+1} point, $BV(S_{n+1})$, into the maximum heap.

Step 4: continuously extract the root node from the maximum heap. If the point cloud cannot meet the conditions of user controlled point density P or the target model point cloud does not reach $N_2 < N_1$, cycle from step 2.

In this algorithm, the surface features can be preserved by increasing the weight. The weight is determined by the point set $p_i \in P$. Changing the size of $\tilde{F}(p_i)$ can affect the calculated BVD(s), and ultimately affect the sampling effect. In general, it is necessary to keep more information in the area with large curvature change and less information in the area with small curvature change. The above process can be realized by adding the curvature weight to the curvature change estimation of the local surface, further setting the value of $\tilde{F}(p_i)$, and finally making the point cloud focus on the area with large curvature change. The advantage of this method is that the calculated distance map itself reflects the weight information, so in the process of point cloud data filtering, only the point cloud needs to be simplified according to the density p standard set by the user.

3 KMS Compound Point Cloud Denoising Algorithm

3.1 Mean Shift Algorithm

Point cloud denoising technology is divided into two types according to the form of point cloud storage. For the ordered point cloud, because of the correlation between points, the filtering algorithm is usually constructed to smooth the point cloud data. Common filtering algorithms include Gaussian filtering, Wiener filtering, Kalman filtering, etc. For scattered point cloud, because there is no topological relationship between points, it is impossible to build filtering algorithm. The usual method is to establish the topological relationship between point clouds and then filter. The common feature of the above point cloud filtering is to smooth the point cloud data, so as to reduce the mutation of noise points. But at the same time of smoothing the noise, it is easy to lose the details of the target, making the edge of the target fuzzy. Therefore, the bilateral filtering method is proposed to improve the edge definition. In this section, considering the characteristics of the above filtering algorithm, a KMS composite point cloud denoising model based on mean shift algorithm and k-d tree is proposed. In the mean shift algorithm, the target points are shifted in the direction of the sample density iteratively, and the degree of each shift is called the mean shift. For the target point in space, the mean value of the offset is expressed in vector form. The offset mean vector is defined as follows:

$$M_h(x) = \frac{1}{k} \sum_{x_i \in S_h} (x_i - x) \tag{9}$$

Where S_h is a set of points, which is defined as follows:

$$S_h(x) = \left\{ y : (y - x)^T (y - x) \leq h^2 \right\} \tag{10}$$

It can be seen from Eq. 10 that S_h represents a sphere with radius h in n-dimensional space.

In Eq. 9, k represents that in the above S_h, there are k sample points x_i, and $(x_i - x)$ represents the offset of sample point x_i in the S_h region from the reference point x.

It can be seen that the offset mean vector $M_h(x)$ represents the average offset vector value of k sample points x_i in the S_h region relative to the reference point x. Considering that for the probability density function $f(x)$, its probability density gradient represents the direction where the probability density changes the most. It is not difficult to see that when k sample points are obtained from the same probability density function, these points will be distributed along the direction of probability density gradient. It can be seen that the direction of the offset mean vector is the same as that of the probability density gradient.

From Eq. 9, it can be seen that the value of $M_h(x)$ is only the average value of the distance between k sample points and reference points in the S_h region. According to the principle of statistics, the statistical characteristics near the reference point are related to the location of the sample points around it, and the closer the sample points have a greater impact on it. Based on the above analysis, Yizong Cheng proposed the definition of extended migration mean vector in reference [6], and added the definition of kernel function and weight on the basis of basic migration mean vector. The extended offset mean vector is defined as follows:

$$M_h(x) = \frac{\sum_{i=1}^{n} |H|^{-\frac{1}{2}} G(H^{-\frac{1}{2}}(x_i - x))w(x_i)(x_i - x)}{\sum_{i=1}^{n} |H|^{-\frac{1}{2}} G(H^{-\frac{1}{2}}(x_i - x))w(x_i)} \tag{11}$$

Where $w(x_i)$ is weight. $G(x)$ is unit kernel function. H is a $d \times d$ dimensional bandwidth matrix, usually defined as a diagonal matrix.

When H is defined as the proportional unit matrix $H = h^2 I$, Eq. 11 can be converted to Eq. 12

$$M_h(x) = \frac{\sum_{i=1}^{n} G(\frac{x_i - x}{h})w(x_i)(x_i - x)}{\sum_{i=1}^{n} G_H(\frac{x_i - x}{h})w(x_i)} \tag{12}$$

3.2 Smoothing Algorithm Based on Mean Shift

As mentioned above, the basic idea of mean shift algorithm is to make the target point drift along the direction of the probability density of the sample point until the threshold requirements are met. For the scattered point cloud, the number of noise is far less than the number of sample points, and the distribution density of sample points is far greater than the noise points. And the distribution density of sample points often reflects the local characteristics of the model. Therefore, the surface of the model can be smoothed by using the mean shift technique to shift each target point to the direction with high sample density. The principle of mean shift smoothing algorithm is shown in Fig. 1.

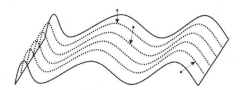

Fig. 1. Smoothing principle of mean shift.

The key of constructing the mean shift smoothing algorithm is to determine the drift direction of the target point. Literature [7] shows that the migration mean vector $M_h(x)$ is a normalized probability density gradient. The mean shift iterative formula can be derived from the gradient of probability density estimation of kernel function:

$$M_h(x) = \frac{\sum\limits_{i=1}^{n} G(\frac{x_i-x}{h})w(x_i)x_i}{\sum\limits_{i=1}^{n} G_H(\frac{x_i-x}{h})w(x_i)} - x = m_h(x) - x \qquad (13)$$

For a given datum point x, let the kernel function be $G(x)$, the weight be $w(x_i)$ and the iteration threshold be ε, then according to Eq. 13, the iteration steps of mean shift can be constructed as follows:

Step1: calculate $m_h(x)$.
Step2: assign $m_h(x)$ to x
Step3: judge $\|m_h(x) - x\|$. If the value is less than ε, it ends; otherwise, return to the first step to continue the iterative calculation.

3.3   KMS Composite Point Cloud Denoising

It can be seen from the above that the mean shift smoothing algorithm is to use iterative calculation to gradually drift the points that deviate from the target model back. This algorithm is suitable for the case that there are many noise points and the deviation from the target surface is not too far. This kind of noise often comes from the surface defects such as roughness and corrugation of the measured object, which is called system error. There is another kind of noise in point cloud data from system measurement channels, such as electrical noise, thermal noise, etc., which is called random error. This kind of random noise is less, but far away from the target surface. For this kind of noise, if the mean shift smoothing algorithm is used, it needs a lot of iterations before it can drift to the ideal position. This will lead to a sharp increase in the amount of computation, which will affect the calculation speed. For the above problems, this paper constructs a composite point cloud denoising model. Firstly, fast filtering algorithm is used to pre-denoise, and a small amount of random error is deleted. The residual point cloud is smoothed by means of mean shift smoothing algorithm, and finally approaches the target surface. For the scattered point cloud, before applying the filtering algorithm, it is necessary to establish the topological relationship between points. Literature [8] shows that the algorithms commonly used to establish the topological relationship of point cloud include octree, spatial cell, k-d tree and so on. In this paper, k-d tree method is used to establish point cloud topology. After the topological relationship of the point cloud is determined, the neighborhood of the target point can be established by using the spatial point backtracking method [9]. By calculating the average distance between the target point and the neighboring points, and comparing with the threshold value, we can distinguish whether the target point is noisy or not. The specific algorithm steps of KMS point cloud denoising model are as follows:

Step 1: use k-d tree algorithm to establish the topological relationship of scattered point cloud.

Step 2: establish the neighborhood of the target point by using the space point backtracking method.

Step 3: calculate the average distance between the target point and each point in the neighborhood (here referred to as the distance from point to neighborhood).

Step 4: calculate the distance from other points in the neighborhood to the neighborhood, and take the average value as the threshold value.

Step 5: compare the distance from the target point to the neighborhood and the size of the threshold value. If the threshold value is more than 2 times, it is considered as noise point deletion.

Step 6: go back to step 3 and continue to judge the next target point until you traverse all points in 3D space and continue to execute step 7.

Step 7: in the above neighborhood, select the target point to calculate the mean shift vector.

Step 8: substitute Eq. 2, 3 for iterative calculation.

Step 9: calculate $\|m_h(x) - x\|$. If it is less than the threshold value, end the iterative calculation and continue to execute step 10. Otherwise, return to step to continue the iterative calculation.

Step 10: go back to step 7 and continue to identify the next target point until the algorithm ends after traversing all points in 3D space.

4   Simulation Experiment

4.1   Experiment and Analysis of Point Cloud Reduction

In the experiment, the model point cloud data is simplified. In the experiment, different P values are set for the same model to verify whether different reduction effects can be obtained. Figure 2 shows the original point cloud, and Fig. 3 shows $P = 2$, which reduces the point cloud by 41%. In Fig. 4, $P = 3$, which reduces the point cloud by 60%. In Fig. 5, $P = 6$, reducing 90% of the point cloud.

In order to compare the calculation speed and memory utilization rate of the algorithm, this section uses the classical point cloud reduction algorithm such as iterative method, clustering, particle simulation and the algorithm in this paper to simplify the strawberry model. The goal of the reduction is to remove 90% of the data, and uses multiple reduction to get the average value of the calculation time and the maximum memory consumed. The experimental results are shown in Table 1. It can be seen that the algorithm proposed in this paper has obvious advantages in computing speed and memory consumption.

Fig. 2. Primitive point cloud   **Fig. 3.** Streamlining results when P1 = 1   **Fig. 4.** Streamlining results when P1 = 3   **Fig. 5.** Streamlining results when P1 = 6

Table 1. The comparison between our algorithm and several point cloud reduction algorithms.

	Algorithm in this paper	Iteration method	Clustering method	Particle simulation
Time to streamline (sec)	3.019	10.245	6.732	20.556
Memory consumed (kB)	4.16	10.34	7.93	8.19

4.2 Experiment and Analysis of Point Cloud Denoising

In this experiment, the classical Laplace denoising algorithm and the mean shift denoising algorithm proposed in this paper are used to denoise the different models of artificial added noise respectively. Through comparison, it is verified whether the mean shift denoising algorithm has the function of target detail recognition, and the speed of the two algorithms is compared. By denoising strawberry model point cloud, it takes 8.47 s to denoise with Laplace algorithm, and 5.15 s to denoise with the algorithm proposed in this paper. It can be seen that the improved mean shift algorithm proposed in this paper has some advantages in speed, at the same time, the algorithm can better identify the detailed characteristics of the target (Figs. 6, 7 and 8).

Fig. 6. Data before denoising

Fig. 7. Denoising results of Laplace algorithm

Fig. 8. Denoising results of the algorithm in this paper

5 Conclusion

This paper discusses the processing technology of discrete point cloud. Based on the existing research results, a fast marching method for image repair is introduced into the process of scattered point cloud reduction, and an improved fast marching farthest point algorithm is proposed. For the simplified point cloud, a KMS composite denoising algorithm is constructed, which can filter the scattered point cloud noise in two steps. After the above processing, the scattered point cloud data will be more suitable for the subsequent surface reconstruction.

References

1. Shaffer, E., Garl, M.: Efficient adaptive simplification of massive meshes. In: Proceedings of the IEEE 125 visualization, pp. 127–133. IEEE (2001)
2. Meonning, C., Dodgson, N.A.: Fast marching farthest point sampling for implicit surfaces and point clouds. Computer Laboratory Technical Report, pp. 565–572 (2003)
3. Sethian, J.A.: A fast marching level set method for monotonically advancing fronts. Proc. Nat. Acad. Sci. **93**(4), 1591–1599 (1996)
4. Carsten, M., Neil, A.: Fast marching farthest point sampling for implicit surfaces and point clouds. Computer Laboratory Technical Report, University of Cambridge, USA (2003)
5. Yuval, E., Michael, L.: The farthest point strategy for progressive image sampling. IEEE Trans. Image Process. **9**(4), 1305–1315 (1997)
6. Cheng, Y.: Mean shift, mode seeking and clustering. IEEE Trans. Pattern Anal. Mach. Intell. **17**(8), 790–799 (1995)
7. Hu, G., Peng, Q., Forrest, A.R.: Mean shift denoising of point-sampled surfaces. Vis. Comput. **22**, 147–157 (2006)
8. Pauly, M., Gross, M., Kobbelt, L.: Efficient simplification of point-sample surfaces. In: IEEE Processing Visualization, pp. 163–170 (2002)
9. Andrew, W.M.: An introductory tutorial on Kd-trees. Technical report, Computer Laboratory, University of Cambridge (1991)

Binocular Vision Detection and 3D Construction Based on Encoded Light

Hao Zhu[1,2(✉)], Mulan Wang[2], and Kaiyun Xu[2]

[1] School of Communication, Nanjing Institute of Technology,
Nanjing 211167, China
zhuhao@njit.edu.cn
[2] Jiangsu Key Laboratory of Advanced Numerical Control Technology,
Nanjing 211167, China

Abstract. A non-contact 3D data acquisition system based on fringe encoded light is analyzed. In this paper, the characteristics of encoding light structure based on space-time domain are studied, and the encoding combination with fringe boundary features is designed. This paper discusses the hierarchical reconstruction technology based on the three levels of projective radiation metric, which is better adapted to the measurement environment of inaccurate or uncalibrated camera parameters calibration, and more convenient to introduce the optimization algorithm. On the other hand, the affine coordinate system and the projective coordinate system are more widely used than the Euclidean coordinate system. The active binocular measurement system is constructed to collect the spatial information of 3D objects and store it in the form of point cloud.

Keywords: Encoded light · 3D construction · Binocular vision

1 Introduction

3D reconstruction based on machine vision refers to the process of reconstructing 3D information from single view or multi view images. Its main task is to acquire the two-dimensional image of the target by non-contact way based on the camera, grating, projector and computer, and then analyze and extract the spatial information to obtain the three-dimensional coordinate information of the target and store it in point cloud or other formats. There are two kinds of methods to obtain coordinate information of three-dimensional objects by machine vision technology: passive three-dimensional sensing and active three-dimensional sensing. The advantage of passive sensing method is that the hardware structure is relatively simple and easy to implement, but the corresponding point matching

Supported by organization by Natural Science Foundation of Universities in Jiangsu Province (Grant No.: 16KJA460001), Creation Foundation Project of Nanjing Institute of Technology (Grant No.: ZKJ201611).

algorithm is usually complex and the processing is long. On the other hand, the reflection of light on the measured object is larger in the passive sensing method. Based on the passive mode, the active three-dimensional sensing mode adds a structural light source to the target. Due to the depth change of the surface of the three-dimensional object in the direction of the projected light, the modulation of space or time will be produced to the projected structured light, forming distortion. The distortion of the two-dimensional image obtained from different angles is also different from each other. The three-dimensional data of the object can be extracted by demodulating the projection of the distortion. Relevant researches [1] shows that, using binocular vision technology can only reconstruct the target in projective space or affine space. Hartley [2] proposed that projective space, affine space and Euclidean space can use different transformation matrices to transform each other. Based on the above theory, this paper studies the hierarchical reconstruction technology composed of projective reconstruction, affine reconstruction and European reconstruction.

2   Mathematical Modeling of Vision Sensor

For a monocular vision system with only one projector and one camera, an equivalent camera can be virtual by rigid rotation and translation of the projector and camera [3]. But the precondition of the transformation is that the internal parameters of the projector and the camera are the same. In engineering practice, the above conditions are generally difficult to meet. Therefore, a binocular vision system consisting of one projector and two cameras is usually used for 3D detection. Generally speaking, the projector can be virtual as a pinhole image and the camera can be virtual as a linear camera, both of which meet the model described below. When the internal parameters of the two cameras are the same and the optical center is in the same horizontal plane, the height of the collected image is the same. The corresponding points can be determined by finding the feature points of the same height. Therefore, the binocular vision system can use two cameras of the same model, which are placed on a horizontal platform, and the projector is placed between the two cameras. The two cameras collect the projection image which is projected by the projector to the three-dimensional target at the same time (Fig. 1).

3   Coding Optical Technology

3.1   Principle of Encoded Light

In the active 3D measurement system, the projector projects light with certain characteristics to the target, and analyzes the spatial position of the corresponding points according to the pattern characteristics on the target. This kind of light with certain characteristics is called encoded light. Griffin et al. [4] studied the theory of encoded light, and proposed four features that encoded light needs

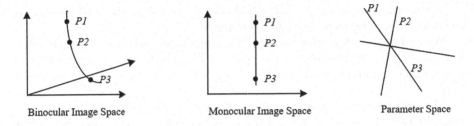

Fig. 1. Active binocular vision measurement system.

to meet: (1) The position of each point is determined by itself and four neighboring points around it. (2) The same code cannot correspond to more than two points. (3) All coding information is determined by a fixed base represented by symbols. (4) The size of coding matrix is required to reach the extreme value. After the above conditions are met, the corresponding relationship between the image feature points projected on the 3D object and the feature points on the projection template can be determined by decoding operation, so as to obtain the spatial position information of the data points.

According to the different coding forms, the common coding light can be divided into space-based coding and time-based coding. Space-based coding includes gray code grating coding, space phase coding, gray-scale coding and so on. In these models, the projection light encodes the spatial information with different stripe width, gray level and color information. Time-based coding refers to the acquisition of motion vectors in images at different times to obtain the shape information of objects, which is initially used to obtain the spatial position of moving objects. Because any measured surface can be regarded as the deformation of the reference plane over a period of time, the detection technology based on time coding is gradually applied to the field of 3D detection.

3.2   Coded Optical Design

In contrast, the advantage of space-based coding is that it is easy to extract features, the mathematical model is simple, and its disadvantage lies in its weak anti-interference ability to the outside world, especially not suitable for the information acquisition of moving objects. However, the anti-jamming ability based on time coding is strong, but how to determine the optical characteristics of coding is difficult to achieve. Based on the above characteristics, this section discusses a stripe encoded light model based on spatiotemporal coding.

Reference [3] studies how to design a coding structure to make it more suitable for the measurement of three-dimensional object space information. The basic characteristics of encoded optical structure are proposed:

For different sampling time, each pixel in the same position should form a feature vector; the same pixel is not associated with other pixels in at least one direction, to ensure that the coding structure has a certain degree of anti-interference.

For projection gray scale, only black and white colors are used to improve the calculation efficiency and anti-interference.

For an image with a given number of frames, there should be as much detection information as possible. When coding, the combination coding of current information should be used as much as possible to maximize the detection coding space.

For coding feature detection, fringe boundary feature is used as much as possible. On the one hand, for n stripes, there are 2n stripe boundaries, which can contain more information. On the other hand, the boundary information only has the jumping state but no width, which can avoid the stripe width corrosion and deformation caused by interference and is more in line with the ideal mathematical model.

Based on the above conditions, a coding combination with fringe boundary features can be designed, using '0' and '1' to represent the switching state of black-and-white stripes. The corresponding stripes in each frame constitute a binary coding state. With the change of time parameters, the change of projection pattern is represented by the switching of coding state. The principle of stripe coding is shown in Fig. 2.

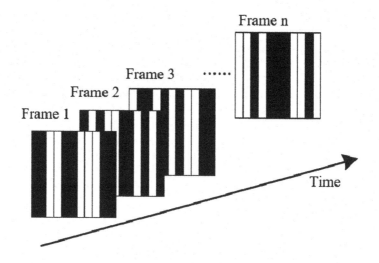

Fig. 2. Principle of stripe coding.

The above coding structure shall meet the following conditions:

Every coding stripe has at least one jump between the images. If there is no jump all the time, it is considered to be caused by the inherent texture of the object.

If the color of adjacent stripes is the same in a certain frame, the fringe boundary is considered invisible.

Stripe coding should be conducive to amplifying the error information in detection, so as to discover and discard the frame in time.

The jump structure in fringe coding should be distributed reasonably, which is convenient for the realization of projection and acquisition.

In reference [3], a comprehensive coding rule based on algebra, graph theory and Hadamard matrix is introduced.

The first step is to use graph theory to set the center core of coding, that is, the center stripe and the nearby coding.

The second step is to generate the initial coding matrix by Hadamard algorithm.

The third step is to make use of different columns in the commutative algebra commutative coding matrix to make the matrix meet the design requirements of stripe coding.

After the projection of the fringe on the three-dimensional measurement target is obtained, the pixels in the same position in the multi frame image are encoded according to the time sequence, the corresponding fringe boundary position and the jump situation are calculated, the projection data points are matched with the corresponding fringe coding points, and then the depth information of the three-dimensional object surface can be solved by the reconstruction model in the following paper.

4   3D Layered Reconstruction Technology

4.1   A Subsection Sample

The technology of three-dimensional layered reconstruction is gradually developed in the relevant theories put forward by Faugeras [1] and others in the 1990s. Different from the traditional 3D reconstruction technology, which directly establishes the 3D data structure of the target in the European coordinate system, the 3D hierarchical reconstruction establishes a reconstruction framework, which reconstructs the geometric model of the target step by step. The advantage of this technology is that it can better adapt to the measurement environment where the camera parameters are inaccurate or uncalibrated, and it is easier to introduce the optimization algorithm. Compared with the target Euclidean coordinate system of 3D reconstruction, affine coordinate system and projective coordinate system are more widely used. Therefore, Faugeras [1] divides hierarchical reconstruction technology into three steps: projective reconstruction, affine reconstruction and metric reconstruction.

The results show that there is a set of non singular transformations between the reconstructed projective matrices in the above three steps. When the transformation is affine transformation, affine reconstruction can be obtained, and when the transformation is Euclidean transformation, metric reconstruction can be formed.

4.2   Implementation of Projective Reconstruction

Set the corresponding point set in the two images as x_j and x_j'. Existence matrix F for any existence j:

$$x_j'Fx_j = 0 \tag{1}$$

This matrix is called the basic matrix between two images. Let (P_1, P_1') and (P_2, P_2') be two cameras, $(P_1, P_1', \{X_1\})$ and $(P_2, P_2', \{X_2\})$ are two reconstructions from x_j to x_j', then there is a non singular matrix

$$P_2 = P_1H, P_2' = P_1'H \tag{2}$$

And for each j:

$$X_{2j} = H^{-1}X_{1j} \tag{3}$$

Therefore, there are the following relationships:

$$P_2X_{2j} = P_2(H^{-1}X_{1j}) = P_1HH^{-1}X_{1j} = P_1X_{1j} = x_j \tag{4}$$

Equation 4 shows that both point $H^{-1}X_{1j}$ and point X_{2j} are mapped to the same point x_j, and all pass through the corresponding center line of the camera P_2. In the same way, it can be deduced that the above two points are also on the center line corresponding to the camera P_2'.

For multiple images, if the camera takes m images of n target points from the perspective m, where x_j' is the image point of the j' point under the i-th camera P^i, then for all the images, there are the following equations:

$$W = \begin{bmatrix} \lambda_1^1 x_1^1 & \cdots & \lambda_n^1 x_n^1 \\ \cdots & \cdots & \\ \lambda_1^m x_1^m & \cdots & \lambda_n^m x_n^m \end{bmatrix} = \begin{bmatrix} P^1 \\ P^2 \\ \cdots \\ P^m \end{bmatrix} \begin{bmatrix} X_1 & X_2 & X_n \end{bmatrix} = \tilde{P}\tilde{X} \tag{5}$$

Where W is the measurement matrix and λ_j^i is the projection depth.

Equation 5 shows that the measurement matrix W can be decomposed into a matrix $\tilde{P}$ representing camera motion and a matrix $\tilde{X}$ representing the shape of space objects. Therefore, as long as the photographing depth λ_j^i can be estimated by some method, three-dimensional space points can be calculated by Eq. 5.

Equation 1, as long as the corresponding image points are known, the camera matrix is not needed to solve F. In reference [5], an 8-point algorithm is provided, which can solve the above basic matrix linearly based on 8 matching points. 8-point algorithm is a commonly used method to solve the basic matrix. The disadvantage of the 8-point algorithm is that on the one hand, when the selection point changes, the difference of the basic matrix is large, on the other hand, the data calculation of the algorithm is large. Based on the above shortcomings, a basic matrix estimation.

The basic idea of Hough transform is to use the duality of point and line to map the curve in the space to a point in the parameter space, so as to transform the problem of detecting the shape of space into the problem of peak statistics. Considering that Hough transform can transform the collinear points in rectangular coordinate system into a group of curves intersecting at one point in parameter domain, and the spatial points encoded by the same fringe boundary are also mapped into a group of collinear points on monocular imaging surface, so we can first transform the fringe encoded feature points in binocular vision system into collinear points in monocular vision system, and then transform Hough into a group of curves. When there is no error in the conversion process, the above curves should intersect at one point. If there is an error, there will be multiple intersections for the above curve group. The above process is shown in Fig. 3.

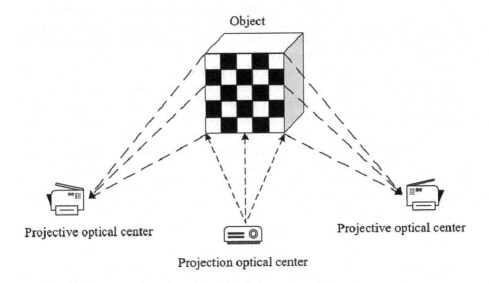

Fig. 3. Monocular imaging transformation and Hough transformation.

As shown in Fig. 3, after Hough transformation, if there are multiple intersections in the curve group, and the intersections are distributed in the circle with radius r, the radius is defined as Hough radius, which is recorded as R_{Hough}. In order to simplify the calculation, the maximum distance between two intersections can be taken as Hough radius.

According to the above definition, there is a correlation between Hough radius and basic matrix estimation. If the true value of the basic matrix is F and the estimated value is $\hat{F}$, there is the following relationship:

$$\lim_{F \to \hat{F}} R_{Hough} = 0 \qquad (6)$$

Therefore, Hough radius can be used as the evaluation function of the basic matrix. When the noise distribution of image acquisition is isotropic zero mean Gaussian distribution and independent distribution, the 8-point algorithm can be used as the initial value of L-M estimation, and the Hough radius as the L-M optimization factor, so as to solve the optimal solution in the sense of maximum likelihood.

$$\min_{p \in P} \sum R^p_{Hough} \tag{7}$$

After estimating the basic matrix F, a group of projection matrices can be constructed according to the geometric model of trigonometry.

4.3 Affine Reconstruction Design

According to the previous analysis, there is an affine transformation between affine reconstruction and Euclidean reconstruction, and the affine transformation remains unchanged at infinity. Therefore, if the coordinates of infinite plane in projective space can be determined, it can be transformed from projective reconstruction to affine reconstruction.

Figure 4 shows the establishment of an ideal binocular reconstruction model in affine space. C_1 and C_2 are two cameras with identical internal parameters in affine space. The optical axis and y axis of the two cameras are parallel and coincide with the x axis. P is the measured point. p_1 and p_2 are the projections of P on C_1 and C_2. L_1 and L_2 are the corresponding polar lines. Because L_1 and L_2 are parallel to each other, their poles e_1 and e_2 are at infinity. If the projective model can be transformed into the above model, then the infinite surface can be determined, thus the affine reconstruction can be completed.

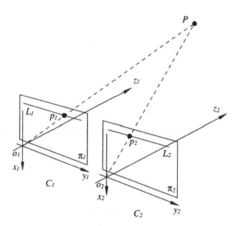

Fig. 4. An ideal binocular imaging model in affine space.

Since the poles e_1 of the camera C_1 are at infinity, it is advisable to set:

$$e_1 = \left[\, 1,\, 1,\, 0 \,\right]^T \tag{8}$$

According to the camera basic model, the basic matrix between C_1 and C_2 is

$$\bar{F}e_1 = 0 \tag{9}$$

Then

$$\bar{F} = \begin{bmatrix} 0 & 0 & 0 \\ 0 & 0 & -1 \\ 0 & 1 & 0 \end{bmatrix} \tag{10}$$

The binocular correction algorithm proposed by Charles [7] provides a non singular transformation, which can transform the basic matrix F obtained from projective reconstruction into the matrix v in Eq. 10, so the poles in the original image can be projected to the infinite position, thus completing the affine transformation.

4.4   European Reconstruction Design

In the model shown in Fig. 4, let the coordinate of P point in C_1 coordinate system be (x, y, z), the translation distance between C_1 and C_2 be d, then the coordinate of P point in C_2 coordinate system is $(x - d, y, z)$. According to the central projection principle of the camera, we can know:

$$\begin{cases} x_1 - x_0 = f_x \frac{x}{z} \\ y_1 - y_0 = f_y \frac{y}{z} \\ x_2 - x_0 = f_x \frac{x-d}{z} \\ y_2 - y_0 = f_y \frac{y_1}{z_1} \end{cases} \tag{11}$$

Where, x_0, y_0, f_x, f_y are the internal parameter of the camera, $(x_1, y_1), (x_2, y_2)$ are the coordinates of p_1, p_2.

It can be seen from Fig. 4 that there is only a translation relationship between the coordinate system C_1 and the world coordinate system, so the coordinate system C_1 can be set as the world coordinate system, which can be obtained from Eq. 11

$$\begin{cases} x = \frac{d(x_1-x_0)}{x_1-x_2} \\ y = \frac{df_x(y_1-y_0)}{f_y(y_1-y_2)} \\ z = \frac{df_x}{x_1-x_2} \end{cases} \tag{12}$$

It can be seen from Eq. 12 that when the camera internal parameters are determined, the three-dimensional coordinates of the space points P can be obtained from the coordinates of p_1, p_2 of P point in C_1 and C_2 coordinate systems.. The three-dimensional coordinates of all data points on the surface of the target can be obtained by traversing the image points in the two cameras and saved as a point cloud format.

5   Experiment and Analysis

The fringe encoded structured light shown in Fig. 5 is projected on the model to detect the 3D data of the model, and the results are represented by point cloud format. The test results of 3D data of the model are shown in Fig. 6. The left figure shows the measurement target and the right figure shows the measurement result. As shown in the figure, the number of three-dimensional points of the reversing lamp modelF is 27614. As can be seen from the figure, the 3D point cloud results can basically reflect the shape characteristics of the model.

First frame
Second frame
Third frame
Fourth frame

Fig. 5. Stripe encoded optical structure.

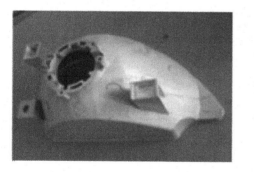

Fig. 6. Sampling experiment of reversing lamp model.

6   Conclusion

In this paper, the coding light detection technology based on machine vision is studied. The vision measurement technology based on encoded light technology is analyzed and discussed. This paper studies the construction of machine vision measurement system, and discusses the calibration technology of camera and projector. The mathematical model of active sensing binocular vision measurement system is obtained. This paper discusses the technology of structured light coding, analyzes the characteristics of structured light coding, and introduces the method of boundary stripe coding based on spatiotemporal coding. This paper analyzes the basic principle of three-dimensional layered technology, and realizes the measurement and description of the target three-dimensional point cloud model by using the layered method of projective reconstruction, affine reconstruction and metric reconstruction. The experimental results show that the proposed method is feasible.

References

1. Maybank, S.J., Faugeras, O.D.: A theory of self-calibration of a moving camera. Int. J. Comput. Vis. **8**(2), 123–151 (1992)
2. Hartley, R.I.: Euclidean reconstruction from uncalibrated views. In: Mundy, J.L., Zisserman, A., Forsyth, D. (eds.) AICV 1993. LNCS, vol. 825, pp. 235–256. Springer, Heidelberg (1994). https://doi.org/10.1007/3-540-58240-1_13
3. Ankang, Y.: 3D layered reconstruction technology based on structure encoded light. Southeast University, March 2009
4. Griffin, P., Narasimhan, L., Yee, S.: Generation of uniquely encoded light patterns for range data acquisition. Pattern Recogn. **25**(6), 609–616 (1992)
5. Luong, Q., Faugeras, O.: The fundamental matrix: theory, algorithms, and stability analysis. Int. J. Comput. Vis. **17**(1), 43–75 (1996)
6. Leavers, V.: Shape Detection in Computer Vision Using the Hough Transform. Springer, New York (1992). https://doi.org/10.1007/978-1-4471-1940-1
7. Loop, C., Zhang, Z.: Computing rectifying homographies for stereo vision. In: IEEE Computer Society Conference on Computer Vision and Pattern Recognition 1999, January 1999

Aerodynamic Modeling and Transient Performance Improvement of a Free Jet Altitude Test Facility

Feng Wu[1,2], Limin Gao[1], Xinyun Wu[3(✉)], Xudong Feng[4], Lintao Leng[4], and Yaoyu Li[3]

[1] School of Power and Energy, Northwestern Polytechnical University, Xi'an 710072, China
wufeng_my@qq.com
[2] The National Key Laboratory of Aerodynamic Design and Research, Xi'an 710129, China
[3] School of Information and Software Engineering,
University of Electronic Science and Technology of China,
Chengdu 610054, China
786465958@qq.com
[4] Key Laboratory of Science and Technology on Aero-Eigine Altitude Simulation,
AECC Sichuan Gas Turbine Establishment, Chengdu 610000, China

Abstract. An inlet-engine altitude test facility for flight condition simulation is modeled for the system dynamic performance improvement. The system model equations are solved with an improved Euler integral method. To simulate the interaction between the tested engine and the test bench accurately, a turbojet engine module is introduced in the system model. By modeling and simulation, a linear temperature compensation control algorithm based on the control error is validated for feasibility; controller parameters optimization for cabin static pressure stabilizing is also carried out. In this paper, some issues like temperature transient performance and engine operate impact restraint on cabin static pressure are discussed efficiently and economically. With the characteristics of high efficiency and economy, the modeling and simulation tools are suitable for the optimization of such systems.

Keywords: ATF · Aerodynamic modeling · Transient performance improvement

1 Nomenclature

The symbol name in the article is shown in Table 1.

© Springer Nature Singapore Pte Ltd. 2020
X. Sun et al. (Eds.): ICAIS 2020, CCIS 1254, pp. 618–630, 2020.
https://doi.org/10.1007/978-981-15-8101-4_55

Table 1. Nomenclature in article.

A = area	C_p = specific heat at constant pressure
C_V = specific heat at constant volume	C_t = response time factor
T = temperature	C = heat capacity
F = force	h = heat transfer factor
I = inertia	K_e = enhancement factor
K = specific heat ratio	Ma = Mach number
p = pressure	p_s = static pressure
Psch = test cabin pressure	Δp = pressure drop
PW = power	R = gas constant
t_s = simulation time step	T = time
V = volume	v = velocity
Wa = mass flow	α = flow coefficient
ρ = density	λ = Velocity factor
ω = rotate speed	ATF = altitude test facility

2 Introduction

In the development of aircraft, airframe inlet and engine compatibility evaluation is an important issue. It has great advantages to make the compatibility evaluation in ground altitude test facility (ATF), such as no risk of flight crash, much more measurement probes allowed and wider flight envelope can be simulated than that in a real flight platform.

To make the compatibility evaluation, both the inflow condition (including the inflow total pressure, total temperature, inflow Mach, attack angle, slip angle) and the engine exhaust environment pressure should be represented the same as that at flight condition. The ATF is designed to implement this function by utilizing the air supply and exhaust components (such as compressors, valves, pipes, chambers, air supply nozzles, coolers, heaters etc.) and the control system for the whole facility [1].

The transient performance of ATF and engine can interact on each other. For example, when the engine is accelerating, the intake plenum pressure will drop because more mass flow is aspirated into the engine. Therefore, the lower density of intake plenum will change the air-fuel ratio of the engine and change the transient performance. The ATF and the propulsion system is dynamic coupled. It is detrimental for the test evaluation and will provide incorrect test results of the engine performance. It's necessary to decrease the interaction between ATF and engine [2].

The traditional direct-connect altitude test facility only simulate the total pressure and total temperature for the engine inlet, this is obviously different from that discussed in this paper which can simulate flight Mach, flight attack angle and slip angle additionally. Some old experience from the direct connect facility need assessment for applicability [3].

The modeling and simulation has been proved to be a useful tool to research the transient performance of system like ATF [4].

3   Solution Method

In this paper, we use the lumped parameter method to describe the model behaviors. Such control volumes have properties with no spatial dependence [4]. All the model components are divided into three kinds: potential component, flux component and function. Some components are listed in Table 2.

Table 2.   Model component classification.

Potential component	Flux component	Functions
Such as:	Pneumatic valve	Controller
Pneumatic volume	Flow resistance	Ejector
Heat capacity	Air supply free jet nozzle	...
Inertia	Cooler	
...	Heat resistance	

The solver takes the following steps to calculate the whole system model. First, all the potential components listed in Table 1 are initialized, and Flux component states are calculated by formula (1), second, the potential component state derivative of time are calculated using formula (2), Third, potential component state is updated using integration formula (3) by improved Euler method. Then iteratively, the simulation is marching through formula (1–3).

$$F_s = f\left(\sum P\_s, Func, F\_p\right) \tag{1}$$

$$\frac{dP\_s}{dt} = f\left(\sum F\_s, Func, P\_p\right) \tag{2}$$

$$P\_s(t + \Delta t) = \int_t^{t+\Delta t} \frac{dP\_s}{dt} dt + P\_s(t) \tag{3}$$

P_p = potential component parameters, (such as volume size, mass, heat capacity…).
P_s = potential component states, (such as pressure, temperature, rotation speed…).
F_p = flux component parameters, (such as valve opening, pipe Roughness, resistance).
F_s = flux component states, (such as mass flow, heat flow, power output).
Func = functions, (define output/input relations).

An external engine model is introduced to represent the tested engine effect on facility by using a couple interface to transfer simulation data. In the facility and engine model interface, the facility model transfers the total pressure and total temperature to the engine model inlet, and the exhaust static pressure to the engine nozzle. Reversely the engine model transfers the intake mass flow, the total pressure and the total temperature after the low pressure turbine to the facility model to calculate the intake and exhaust performance.

4 Modeling Approach

In this paper, an object oriented modeling method is used to construct the model, which can provide better maintainability if physical equations of components need modification, and this technology also makes it easier to change the structure of the system model consisted of many components. Object oriented modeling method can make the physical description of the components independent form each other, and use the connection to transfer data between model components, similar to the physical connection in the real world.

The fidelity of the whole system depends on the descriptions of all components. This section will focus on the physical descriptions of the pneumatic components used in this paper.

4.1 Volume Modeling

In order to achieve the pressure and temperature change in pipes, chambers, cabin, an open system transient equation is introduced. Using Eq. (4), (5), the temperature gradient dT/dt and the pressure gradient dp/dt can be calculated. In Eq. (4), (5), subscript i represents different inflow or outflow ports connected with the volume. Q is the heat flow into or out of the system in heat source ways RT.

$$\frac{dT}{dt} = \frac{\sum_1^i (c_p T_i - c_V T) Wa_i + Q}{pV \times c_V} RT \tag{4}$$

$$\frac{dp}{dt} = \frac{\sum_1^i c_p T_i Wa_i}{V \times c_V} \tag{5}$$

When studying the temperature issue, the heat transfer between air flow and volume container (such as pipe and other metal structure container) cannot be ignored. The heat flow from air to steel can be calculated by Eq. (6) which will cause the steel temperature increase or decrease, the heat transfer coefficient h is simplified to a constant. The heat capacity Csteel is determined with steel mass and specified heat capacity as Eq. (7).

$$C_{steel} \frac{dT_{steel}}{dt} = Ah(T_{air} - T_{steel}) = -Q \tag{6}$$

$$C_{steel} = \rho_{steel} V c_{steel} \tag{7}$$

4.2 Air Valve Modeling

The air valve is used to control the mass flow passed which is interrelated with upstream pressure and the pressure ratio between upstream and downstream (Eq. (8)). The inlet air density is another influence factor, for a single valve the minimum flow area is determined by valve opening. α is the flow coefficient, generally a function of valve opening. In this paper, the minimum flow area is simplified to a liner function of opening and the flow coefficient is constant.

To meet the demands of huge airflow, the supply and exhaust valve should be very huge if just take one single valve in supply or exhaust leg. But the cost and weight will raise rapidly with the size increase. So several small valve parallel connection is a better choose. In the modeling, the valves in each parallel leg were simplified into one valve with a total area equal to the sum of the areas of the individual valves.

$$\mathrm{W}a = \alpha A_{min}\omega\sqrt{2p\rho}\,\psi \tag{8}$$

$$\psi = \begin{cases} \sqrt{\dfrac{k}{k+1}\left(\dfrac{2}{k+1}\right)^{\frac{2}{k-1}}} \; if \; critical \\ \sqrt{\dfrac{k}{k-1}\left(\left(\dfrac{p_{out}}{p_{int}}\right)^{\frac{2}{k}} - \left(\dfrac{p_{out}}{p_{int}}\right)^{\frac{k+1}{k}}\right)} \end{cases}$$

For the reasons of mechanic and hydraulic inertia, the valve action will lags behind the controller command which orders the valve to open or close. To represent this delay, a 1-order process with time delay is utilized.

4.3 Free-Jet Nozzle Modeling

The free-jet air supply nozzle in the facility is used to generate supersonic or subsonic flow which can sink into the airframe inlet inside. The mass flow swallowed from the intake plenum by the nozzle can be calculated from Eq. (9), (10) in uncritical or critical situation respectively.

$$Wa = \sqrt{\frac{k}{R}\left(\frac{2}{k+1}\right)^{\frac{k+1}{k-1}}}\frac{p_{tot}A_t}{\sqrt{T_{tot}}}\left(\frac{k+1}{2}\right)^{\frac{1}{k-1}}\lambda\left(1 - \frac{k-1}{k+1}\lambda^2\right)^{\frac{1}{k-1}} \tag{9}$$

$$Wa = \sqrt{\frac{k}{R}\left(\frac{2}{k+1}\right)^{\frac{k+1}{k-1}}}\frac{p_{tot}A_t}{\sqrt{T_{tot}}} if \; critical \tag{10}$$

The jet flow Mach number is another important attribute of free jet nozzle, which is identified as the simulated flight Mach number as the airframe inlet faces. Generally the airflow out from the nozzle will experience expansion or compression, only the area at the nozzle outlet is with uniform Mach number distribution, which is known as a diamond shape.

The uniform Mach number within the diamond area can be calculated by the algorithm (shown in Fig. 1) for different pressure ratio range. The pressure ratio range boundary PR1, PR2, PR3 can be acquired by Eq. (11), (12), (13). Obviously all the boundary is related to the ratio of nozzle throat area and outlet area. If the pressure ratio between nozzle inlet total pressure and exhaust static pressure is lower than PR3, the free jet nozzle will work at an uncritical status while the Ma all over the nozzle is less than 1.0.

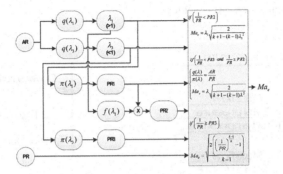

Fig. 1. Mach calculate algorithm.

$$q(\lambda) = \left(\frac{k+1}{2}\right)^{\frac{1}{k-1}} \lambda \left(1 - \frac{k-1}{k+1}\lambda^2\right)^{\frac{1}{k-1}} \tag{11}$$

$$\pi(\lambda) = \left(1 - \frac{k-1}{k+1}\lambda^2\right)^{\frac{k}{k-1}} \tag{12}$$

$$f(\lambda) = \frac{4k}{k+1}\left(\frac{\lambda^2}{k+1-(k-1)\lambda^2}\right) - \frac{k-1}{k+1} \tag{13}$$

4.4 Mixer Ejector Modeling

In the cabin, only a small part of airflow from the air supply nozzle will be sucked into the airframe inlet and into the engine. In this case, the spill flow of the rest with high speed will flow through the cabin and mix with the main flow escaped from engine nozzle in the gas collector, sometimes for cooling demand, some cold air from the atmosphere will mingle into the flows. Total pressure loss and heat exchange will occur during the mix process [5].

Therefore, the mass flow equation, momentum equation and energy equation is introduced to calculate the mixer outlet total pressure and temperature. For a given cabin static pressure, the mixer outlet total pressure is determined if other parameters keep constant. It should be noticed here that the mixer outlet pressure is affected by the exhaust system downstream, so the cabin static pressure, known as the simulated environment pressure, will be affected in the same way [6]. This model inputs and outputs are shown in Fig. 2.

In Eq. (14–17), some simplifications are made, no friction and no heat exchange between flow and mixer wall, mixer inlet static pressure is uniform, no pressure loss for the spill flow from air supply nozzle to mixer inlet. In the calculation, the mixed flow total temperature is obtain from Eq. (17), and then the mixed flow velocity can be calculated with Eq. (15), (16), finally the total pressure of mixed flow can be get from Eq. (14). After several iterations the correct cabin pressure corresponding to the existing exhaust downstream pressure is achieved.

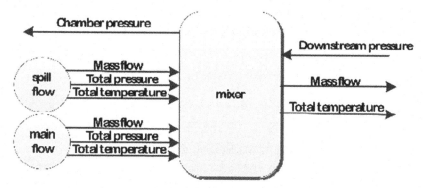

Fig. 2. Mixer model inputs and outputs.

Mass continuity

$$Wa_{main\,flow} + Wa_{spill\,flow} = Wa_{mix\,flow} \tag{14}$$

Momentum conservation

$$F_{A1} + F_{A2} + F_{A3} - F_{mix} - F_{wall\,fric} = (Wa \cdot v)_{mix} - (Wa \cdot v)_{main\,flow} - (Wa \cdot v)_{spill\,flow} \tag{15}$$

$$(Wa \cdot v) + pA = Wa\left(v + \frac{p}{\rho v}\right) = \frac{k+1}{2k}Wa \cdot \sqrt{\frac{2k}{k+1}RT^*} \cdot \left(\lambda + \frac{1}{\lambda}\right) \tag{16}$$

Energy conservation

$$\left(Wa \cdot cp \cdot T^*\right)_{main\,flow} + \left(Wa \cdot cp \cdot T^*\right)_{spill\,flow} = \left(Wa \cdot cp \cdot T^*\right)_{mixed\,flow} \tag{17}$$

4.5 Engine Modeling

The transient engine model is adopted from Gasturb [7, 8], the engine inlet pressure and temperature is coupled with the air supply nozzle outlet parameters, and the engine exhaust static pressure is coupled with the cabin static pressure. On the contrary, the engine calculated intake mass flow, exhaust pressure, exhaust temperature and total exhaust mass flow is transferred to the facility model. So the interaction between the facility and engine can be simulated in this way.

In the model, the volume effect of engine component is ignored. And power balance between turbine and compressor is list as Eq. (18). The control system is active which employ PID type controller as well [7]. Other detailed thermodynamic descriptions of the gas engine will not be discussed here.

$$PW_{compressor} = PW_{turbine} - \frac{dn}{dt} n I_{spool} \tag{18}$$

4.6 Other Components Modeling

Some other components used in the simulation such as Cooler, Controller are simplified and will be briefly introduced here. As a function of inlet temperature and mass flow, the cooler pressure drop is modeled with flow resistance which is fitted with test data. The heat transfer is not involved in the calculation and the cooler outlet temperature is set to a constant value. The controller used in this paper is a standard feedback circuit, firstly the difference between the target and the measured parameter is transformed to range − 1~1, then a standard PID function transformed the signal, after another transform block the signal is rectified to range 0~1 [9].

5 Transient Performance Improvement

In this paper, a free jet ATF system concept is presented in Fig. 3 and is modeled. The cold flow and hot flow is supplied into volume PA1, PA2, and valve VA1, VA2 handle the pressure control of PA1 and PA2. Valve VB1 and VB2 handle the mass flow control of that flow into the volume PI. The free jet nozzle inlet total pressure is control with valve VS1 and the test cabin static pressure is controlled by valve VC. The PC and PE represent the volume after the test cabin and volume before the exhaust pressure. Valve VE make the exhaust compressor working at suitable pressure ratio condition. With this model concept, the test transient operation and the corresponding requirement for both the facility configuration and control algorithm are evaluated to simulate the flight condition as accuracy as possible [10].

5.1 Transient Air Supply Temperature and Pressure

Transient pressure and temperature control is applied with valve VB1, VB2, VS1, of which VB1 handle the air supply hot leg, VB2 handle the cold leg, VS1 handle the pressure of chamber PI. The VB1 and VB2 control the hot/cold airflow ratio that supplied into the chamber PI, by changing the airflow ratio the temperature of PI is changed. The mass flow control target of VB1 and VB2 is calculated with the free jet air supply nozzle mass flow requirement. VS1 is a leak valve so the pressure of chamber PI can be hold constant or changed as expected while the inflow changing. The VB1 and VB2 valve is used to keep the supply pressure of each leg constant, so as to the mass flow control by VB1 and VB2 is only related to valve minimum flow area. This is a basic concept of air supply system.

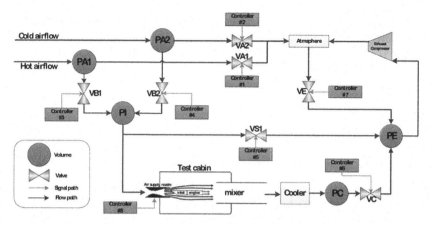

Fig. 3. Free jet test facility concept.

To control the intake plenum temperature, the former temperature control algorithm is to control the VB1 and VB2 mass flow following energy equation, Wa_{VC1}, Wa_{VC2} is the mass flow through valve VB1 and VB2, T_{VC2}, T_{VC2} is the supply air temperature of different leg. Wa_{ASN} is the needed air flow of air supply nozzle. For demand of intake plenum pressure control, the total supplied air flow from two legs $Wa_{VC1} + Wa_{VC2}$ must be more than the air supply nozzle needed, so a factor Kair (less than 1.0) is introduced to scale the mass flow ratio.

$$Wa_{VC1}T_{VC1} + Wa_{VC2}T_{VC2} = (Wa_{VC1} + Wa_{VC2})T_{target} \qquad (19)$$

$$Wa_{VC1} + Wa_{VC2} = Wa_{ASN}/Kair \qquad (20)$$

Because of heat transfer between steel structure(pipe, valve, plenum chamber) and air flow when their temperature is different, when the simulated temperature need a shift, the real temperature transient will slow than expected. To evaluate how worse this problem will be, a transient test process which represents flight acceleration from Mach 0.8 to 1.2 at altitude 11 km is simulated as shown in Fig. 4. The difference is big in temperature raise slope, for the model with heat transfer, obvious lag in temperature can be observed. The heat capacity of steel structure and heat transfer coefficient used here is in normal range by existing altitude facility [11].

To improve the transient performance of temperature control, a linear temperature target fixed method is used in the temperature algorithm, the basic concept is to change the temperature control target in Eq. (21) based on the existing temperature lag, shown in Fig. 5.

$$T_{target} = T_{expect} + K_{fix}(T_{expect} - T_{real}) \qquad (21)$$

Using the improved algorithm, the same simulation is carried on. As can be seen in Fig. 6, the temperature transient control error is reduced to 1°. Here the Kair is set as 4.0 which means four times of the temperature error is compensated into new fixed target.

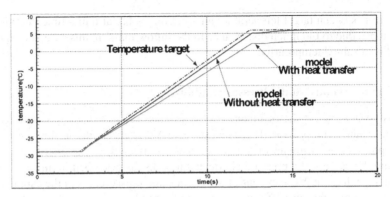

Fig. 4. Comparison between models with or without heat transfer

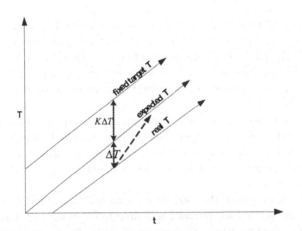

Fig. 5. Linear temperature target fixed method

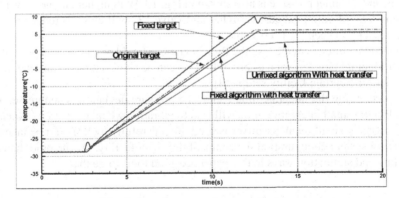

Fig. 6. Transient temperature performance

If the error between target temperature and real one is big at initial time, the vibration may happen due to too much disturbance to the inflow mass, in this case, the algorithm should be disabled temporarily.

5.2 Engine Exhaust Static Pressure Stabilizing

Exhaust system is consist of mixer, cooler, exhaust valve, exhaust pressure stabilize system, exhaust compressor. The exhaust valve VC controls the airflow go through, so the pressure downstream of the cooler will be affected, as the distribution spread upstream the cabin static pressure is affected too, just as described in mixer modeling. The final result is the VC can control the cabin static pressure. From the cabin to valve VC, the system transient performance is complicated because of mixer-cooler-volume feature is linked together that will inevitably bring in time delay in system dynamic response.

When the engine is operating (accelerate or decelerate) in the free jet altitude test [12], the engine mass flow, pressure and temperature leaving the turbine (p6 and T6) will change rapidly. The momentum and energy of engine exhaust flow and spill flow from the ASN will change accordingly, which will result in test cabin static pressure wave. And the exhaust control system should recover the pressure as soon as possible, and no oscillation occurs [13].

To evaluate how bad will the cabin static pressure diverge from the target, a facility simulation is carried out with engine model. The simulated altitude is 9 km. After the system is stable, the engine power level is pulled up and down, the main engine parameters in the acceleration and deceleration is shown in Fig. 7. The mass flow varies from 70 kg/s to 106 kg/s.

With higher power level, the total momentum and heat into the mixer will raise and as a result the cabin static pressure will drop to fill more spill flow into the cabin for balancing the ejection effect. The change of cabin static pressure (Psch) is shown in Fig. 10, and the deviation is about 5% with the configuration in use. The valve VC opening and VC inlet pressure is also shown in Fig. 10. With higher engine power level, the ram effect of entire exhaust is higher and valve VC will close to reduce the mass flow passed by to keep the Psch stable.

In the real altitude engine test, the Psch deviation should be as lower as possible and recover to initial target as soon as possible. This can be achieved by optimizing the PID controller for a certain facility setup [14].

By decreasing the integrate time factor, the pressure deviation is suppressed obviously. But too small integration time will lead to vibration when the $\Delta Psch / \Delta m$ is big, such as when a small diameter mixer is used. So a carefully look should be taken into the control system configuration for compatibility with facility. On the other hand, the modeling and simulation ways in this paper are good tools to do that.

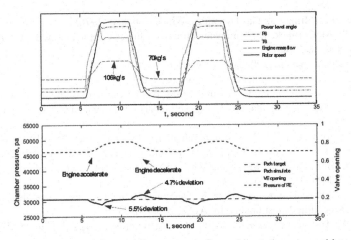

Fig. 7. Engine operation and the corresponding cabin static pressure history

6 Conclusion

With the modeling and simulation, more detailed information about the free jet altitude test facility can be get from the analysis. Some existing problem can be exposed, solutions can be evaluated before the real one is built. Even some concepts can be simulated with no harm. In this paper, some issues like temperature transient performance and engine operate impact restrain on cabin static pressure are discussed in an efficient and economical way. More transient performance improvement will be gained with further work in the near future.

There are also lots of test facility issues can be analyzed, this paper cannot cover all these issues, but it's shown as a useful tool to evaluate different concept designs. Not only for control system design and optimization, but also for facility component improvement.

Acknwledgement. Great thanks to the support of National Natural Science Foundation of China (51506108) and Aviation Science Fund (20141024002).

References

1. Li, X.Y., Zhu, Q.S., Zhu, M.Z., Wu, H., Wu, S.Y., Zhu, M.C.: The freezing Rènyi quantum discord. Sci. Rep. **9**(1), 1–10 (2019). https://doi.org/10.1038/s41598-019-51206-9
2. Bierkamp, J., Köcke, S., Staudacher, S., Fiola, R.: Influence of ATF dynamics and controls on jet engine performance. In: ASME Turbo Expo 2007, GT2007-27586 (2007)
3. Montgomery, P., Burdette, R., Klepper, J., Mihoan, A.: Evolution of a turbine engine test facility to meet the test need of future aircraft system. In: Proceeding of ASME TURBO EXPO GT-2002-30605 (2002)
4. Montgomery, P., Burdette, R., Krupp, B.: A real-time turbine engine facility model and simulation for test operation modernization and integration. In: Proceeding of ASME TURBO EXPO 2000-GT-0576. (2000)

5. Maurice, J., Hoffman, J.: Gas Dynamics. Wiley, Hoboken (1976)
6. Kebe, S., McCormick, D.: Parameter effects on mixer-ejector pumping performance. In: AIAA 88–0188 (1988)
7. Gasturb12 user manual. (2012). www.gasturb.de
8. Kurzke, J.: Gasturb computer deck. www.gasturb.de
9. Gold, B., Rader, C.: Digital Processing of Signals. McGraw-Hill Book Co., New York (1969)
10. Kurzke, J.: Transient simulations during preliminary conceptual engine design. ISABE 2011-1321. (2011)
11. Montgomery, P., Garrard, D.: Test and evaluation of hypersonic aeropropulsion systems along flight trajectories in a time-varying flight environment. In: AIAA-2005-3900 (2005)
12. Huffman, B.C., Lavelle, T.M., Owen, A.K.: An NPSS model of a proposed altitude test facility. In: AIAA 2011-312 (2011)
13. Takeshi, T., Masaharu, K., Nanahisa, S.: Dynamic characteristic tests of single spool turbojet engine using altitude test facility. In: AIAA-2007-5012 (2007)
14. Braig, W.: Transient aero engine testing at stuttgart altitude test facility. In: ISABE 99-7074. (1999)

Power Data Security Protection Mechanism Based on Blockchain

Xinyan Wang[1], Long Qin[1], Shaoyong Guo[2], Dong Li[1], Fang Yuan[1], BeiBei Zhu[1], and Keqin Zhang[2(✉)]

[1] State Grid Henan Electric Power Company Information Communication Company, Zhengzhou, Henan, China
[2] Beijing University of Posts and Telecommunications, Beijing, China
zhangkeqin@bupt.edu.cn

Abstract. In order to solve the problem of data leakage and data unavailability when power data is shared, this paper proposes a power data security protection mechanism based on Blockchain. Firstly, in the aspect of data protection model, a Blockchain-based data protection model architecture is proposed, including power company, system service interface, Blockchain and data storage platform. Secondly, in order to achieve data consistency and irreparable modification, this paper designs a smart contract system in the Blockchain module. In the aspect of data security storage, a storage mechanism combining Blockchain storage and distributed storage is adopted. Finally, in order to verify the power data security protection mechanism based on Blockchain, the detailed process of power data security protection mechanism is designed from three aspects: power company identity registration process, power data protection process and power data acquisition process.

Keywords: Power data · Data security · Data sharing · Blockchain

1 Introduction

With the rapid development and application of mobile Internet, big data, cloud computing and other technologies, the data access methods of power grid systems have become more and more. When these different access methods share power system data, it is easy to cause leakage and destruction of power data, which jeopardizes the security of the power grid [1, 2]. The power system is a key infrastructure related to the national economy and the people's livelihood, so power data security protection has attracted the attention of more and more research groups.

Currently, power data protection research includes four aspects: early prevention, standardized management, encryption mechanism, and application of new technologies. Early prevention: In order to discover the loopholes in the power network in advance, the literature [3] analyzed the possible risks of the power data network, and proposed a power network risk prediction model based on entropy weight-gray. The literature [4, 5] proposed measures to prevent attacks against possible attacks, and improved the anti-attack capability of power data networks. Standard management: In order to improve

© Springer Nature Singapore Pte Ltd. 2020
X. Sun et al. (Eds.): ICAIS 2020, CCIS 1254, pp. 631–639, 2020.
https://doi.org/10.1007/978-981-15-8101-4_56

the security of power data from the perspective of management, the literature [6] puts forward the data management and processing specifications for the operation experience of the power network monitoring system; Based on the characteristics of power data, the literature [7] establishes a data security management system from the three dimensions of people, systems and data, and improves the data security management capabilities. Encryption mechanism: In order to protect the privacy of power data and prevent data leakage, the literature [8] optimizes the protection model of power data based on quantum key theory; The literature [9] proposed a power data encryption mechanism based on USBKEY. Application of new technologies: The literature [10] adopts virtualization technology to effectively solve the problem of security protection of high-frequency data and low-frequency data. In [11], the blockchain technology application data is used to solve the single point of failure problem existing in the existing central data protection architecture system; The literature [12] applies deep learning techniques to solve the problem of power data complementation.

From the existing research, the safety of power data is becoming more and more important, and more achievements have been made. However, existing data sharing between data owners still does not guarantee the privacy, integrity, and availability of data, leading to data breaches. In order to solve this problem, this paper analyzes and utilizes the decentralization and data cannot be modified of blockchain technology, and proposes a power protection mechanism based on blockchain.

2   Blockchain-Based Data Protection Model

2.1   Architecture

In order to protect the key data of the power company and ensure the security of critical infrastructure, the blockchain-based data protection model architecture proposed in this paper is shown in Fig. 1.

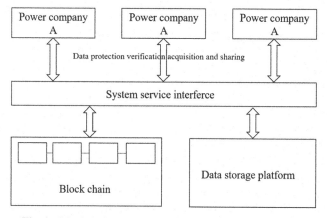

Fig. 1. Blockchain-based data protection model architecture

As shown in Fig. 1, the blockchain-based data protection model architecture proposed in this paper includes four aspects: power company, system service interface, blockchain, and data storage platform.

Power Company: As a production unit of power data, in the daily operation process, it is necessary to perform data interaction with a superior power company and a power company with business contacts. Therefore, power companies need the ability to protect, verify, acquire, and share data.

System Service Interface: It is mainly used to provide data protection functions for power companies. To facilitate access by various power companies, RESTful interfaces can be used to diversify access methods. Through the system service interface, the power company interacts with the blockchain node and the data storage platform to realize data security protection.

Block Chain Node: Considering the security of power data, this paper uses Ethereum's alliance chain technology to build blockchain. In terms of consensus algorithms, this paper uses the PoA algorithm. In order to ensure the security of data access, the identity management smart contract and data management smart contract are constructed to realize the registration and authentication of power user identity and the protection and sharing of power data. The security protection of the power data is realized by storing the hash value of the power data. In terms of data integrity, the Merkle tree is used to store data summary information.

Data Storage Platform: Distributed data storage technology can be used to achieve high reliability and redundant storage of power data. In order to ensure the security of the data, the power data is encrypted during the storage phase.

2.2 Smart Contract

Considering that smart contracts have good effects in data security and data flexible management, in order to achieve data consistency and irreparable modification, this paper designs intelligent contract system in blockchain module. The relationship of the intelligent contract system is shown in Fig. 2.

Fig. 2. Smart contract system diagram

In the smart contract system diagram, it mainly includes four types of contracts: data identity control contract, data identity basic information, data identity management contract, and data management contract. Among them, the data identity control contract as a unique identification contract for each power company, can be used for power company identity registration and identity management.

The basic information of data identity includes the data identity, the data identity number, and the corresponding public key information. Data identity management contracts include identity creation voting contracts and identity reset contracts, which are mainly used to create and improve data identity of power companies. In order to ensure the independence and security of data identity, after the creation of data identity, the identity reset contract can only reset the affiliated information and key information of data identity, and it is not allowed to reset the related information identifying the uniqueness of data identity. Data management contract includes data storage contract, data sharing contract and authority control contract. Among them, data storage contract is mainly used to store hash value of power data, including key information such as data source, data purpose, data creation time, data hash value, etc. Data sharing contract is mainly used to identify the sharing relationship between power companies, so as to realize data mutual access between different power companies, mainly including data identity, authorized data identity, authorization period and authority scope. Authority control contract is based on the relationship of power companies. It implements hierarchical authority control on power companies, so as to maximize the security of data.

3 Power Data Security Protection Mechanism

3.1 Power Company Identity Registration Process

In order to realize the security protection and sharing of power data, power companies first need to register in the blockchain. After receiving the registration request from the power company, the blockchain can only join the blockchain with the consent of N nodes. The specific value of n needs to be negotiated between power companies to achieve consistency. If the registration is successful, each power company can act as a blockchain node.

Step 1: generate a public-private key pair. Electric power company uses a ECDSA elliptic curve algorithm, according to the agreement of the blockchain, to generate the key pair ⟨public key, private key⟩ which is sent to the blockchain node, and the private key is kept in secret locally.

Step 2: send the public key and identity information. The power company packs the generated public key information, the name of the power company, qualification certification materials and other relevant information, calls the data communication service of the blockchain node through the system service interface, sends the packed data to all blockchain nodes, and entrusts the authoritative and familiar blockchain node Q to create an identity and create a voting contract.

Step 3: create a voting contract. The entrusted blockchain node Q creates a voting contract for power company a's identity and requests other blockchain nodes to vote.

Step 4: voting of blockchain nodes. All nodes of the blockchain alliance vote the registration request of power company A based on the attribute information and relevant qualification materials of power company A.

Step 5: create power company A's identity and related contracts. When the blockchain node Q receives the consent of N or more blockchain nodes, it applies for data identity control contract to create digital identity information and relevant contracts for power company A, and saves the relevant information of power company A.

Step 6: Registration succeeded. Power company a receives a successful registration return message.

The identity registration process of power company a joining the blockchain is shown in Fig. 3.

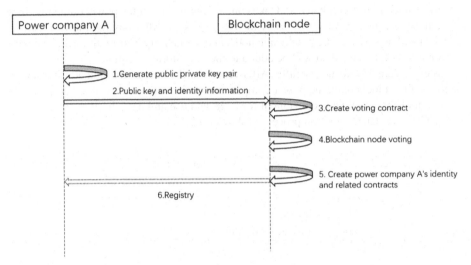

Fig. 3. Power company identity registration process

3.2 Power Data Protection Process

After the power company has successfully registered in the blockchain, the power data generated in its business process can be stored in the blockchain node and data storage platform. In terms of data security storage, a storage mechanism combining block chain storage and distributed storage is adopted, in which the block chain node stores the hash value of each power data, and the distributed storage node stores the encrypted original data. The mutual assistance of blockchain nodes and data storage platforms can effectively improve the security and reliability of power data, and provide data acquisition and sharing operations.

Step 1: generate the key and encrypt the data to be protected. In order to preserve the stored data, the power company first uses 3DES algorithm to generate random key Ki, and encrypts the data to be protected and its related accessories.

Step 2: store the encrypted attachment data. The information of power company identity, hash value of attachment data, attribute of attachment data and so on are packed with DA, and the data package DA-KI is obtained by encrypting the data with KI. Call data storage platform through system service interface, store DA and encrypted data package DA-KI in data storage platform.

Step 3: store power company identity, data summary and other relevant information. In order to ensure the security of power company identity, data summary, data number, data fingerprint and other key information in power data, these information are packed and signed. Call the blockchain node through the system service interface, and send the signed key data to the blockchain node.

Step 4: verify the identity and data. After receiving the data saving request, the blockchain node uses the data identity control contract to locate the data management contract of the power company, and takes out the public key of the power company from the authority control contract to verify the received data. After passing the verification, the data will be stored in the blockchain node, and the identity information and summary information of the new data will be added to the data storage contract.

Step 5: data added successfully. After receiving the successful data addition information of the blockchain, the power company saves the data number of the current data in the blockchain, which is convenient for later data use and data sharing.

The power data protection process is shown in Fig. 4.

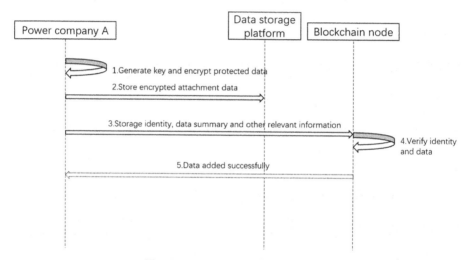

Fig. 4. Power data protection process

3.3 Power Data Acquisition Process

Access to power data includes the power company's access to its own data, and the power company's access to data from other power companies in the alliance blockchain. Among them, the data of other power companies that the power company obtains including three processes: the power company that owns the data adds other power companies that request data to the trust list of the blockchain, the power company requesting data applies to the blockchain for data, the power company requesting data requests for data attachment from the data storage platform. The power company's acquisition of its own data includes two processes of requesting data from the blockchain and requesting data attachments from the data storage platform.

Take Power Company B requesting for the data of power company A in the alliance blockchain as an example. Figure 5 shows the details of the acquisition process of the power data. The process for a power company to obtain its own data is similar to the latter two processes and will not be described in detail.

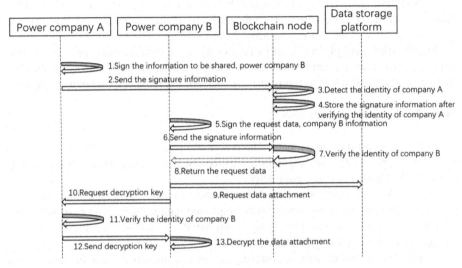

Fig. 5. Power data acquisition process

Phase 1: Increase the trust list of company B to the blockchain

Step 1: Sign the information to be shared, power company B, etc. In order to enable the power company B to access the shared data, the power company A first sorts out the number of the relevant data that needs to be shared with the power company B; after that, it signs the identity and data number of the power company B with its own private key.

Step 2: Send the signature information. Power company A calls the system service interface and sends the signature information to the data sharing contract module in the smart contract of the blockchain.

Step 3: Detect the identity of company A. The data sharing contract sends the information about the power company A to the authority control contract and requests it to verify the identity of the power company A.

Step 4: Store the signature information after verifying the identity of company A. After the data sharing contract verifies the identity of the power company A, it requests for data storage contract, and writes the identity of the power company B in the data number shared by the power company A to the power company B.

Phase 2: Obtain data

Step 5: Sign the request data, company B information, etc. When the power company B needs to obtain the data of the power company A, the power company B first uses its own private key to sign its own identity and the acquired data number.

Step 6: Send the signature information. The power company B calls the system service interface and sends the signature information to the data sharing contract module in the smart contract of the blockchain.

Step 7: Verify the identity of Company B. The data sharing contract sends the information about the power company B to the authority control contract and requests it to verify the identity of the power company B.

Step 8: After verifying the identity of company B, the system returns the request data. After the data sharing contract verifies the identity of the power company B, the data storage contract is invoked to return the data hash of the request to the power company B.

Phase 3: Obtain data attachments

Step 9: Request data attachment. The power company B calls the data storage platform through the system service interface to request the encrypted data attachment by using the data hash value as a parameter.

Step 10: Request decryption key. After obtaining the encrypted data attachment, the power company B sends its own identity, requested data number, data hash value and other information to the power company A through the system service interface to send an application for obtaining the decryption key.

Step 11: Verify the identity of company B. Power company A calls the data sharing contract through the system service interface to check the identity of data B and the authenticity of the requested data.

Step 12: Send decryption key. The power company A obtains the public key of the power company B from the data identity management contract after verifying the identity of the power company B, and encrypts the data decrypted key using B's public key.

Step 13: Decrypt the data attachment. The power company B decrypts the key sent by the power company A using its own private key, and then obtains the information of the data attachment.

4   Conclusion

By analyzing and utilizing the decentralization of blockchain technology and data non-tampering, this paper proposes a blockchain-based power data security protection mechanism, which better solves the problem of data leakage and data unavailability when sharing power data. In the aspect of mechanism verification, this paper designs the process of power data security protection mechanism from three aspects: power company identity registration process, power data protection process and power data acquisition process. The research results of this paper have achieved good results in solving the data preservation between the alliance power companies. However, the data sharing strategy only implements a one-to-one data sharing mechanism between power companies. The shared control program is also complex and inconvenient for efficient data sharing. In the next step, we will study how to effectively implement data sharing mechanisms among multiple power companies, so as to achieve efficient data sharing under the premise of ensuring power data security.

References

1. Kaikai, G., Wenshan, H., Kun, Z., et al.: Design and implementation of a hand-held device for power data acquisition and analysis based on mobile network. Power Syst. Prot. Control **46**(8), 110–116 (2018)
2. Li, T., Jingxiang, L., Xiaoguang, Z.: Design of power data acquisition system based on LPWAN. Electr. Technol. **19**(8), 95–100 (2018)
3. Wenjing, L., Meng, L., Ningzhe, X., et al.: Risk prediction of power data network based on entropy weight-gray model. J. Beijing Univ. Posts Telecommun. **41**(3), 39–45 (2018)
4. Ronghui, J.: Protection strategy of data injection attack in power dispatching automation system. Automation **5**, 37 (2018)
5. Qi, W., Wei, Y., Wei, T., et al.: Review of research on false data injection attacks for power information physics systems. Acta Automatica Sin. **45**(1), 72–83 (2019)
6. Xiwu, L., Guoping, C., Jiang, Y., et al.: Data specification and data processing of smart grid monitoring operation big data analysis system. Autom. Electr. Power Syst. **42**(19), 169–176 (2018)
7. Fan, Y., Qin, Z., Jie, L., et al.: Research on the construction of sichuan power data asset security management system of state grid. Electr. Power Inform. Commun. Technol. **16**(1), 90–95 (2018)
8. Zhiyu, C., Dejun, G., Dong, W., et al.: Optimal data protection model for power service based on quantum key. Autom. Electr. Power Syst. **42**(11), 113–121 (2018)
9. Wei, Y., Li, T., Wei, L., et al.: Research and implementation of network storage user data protection based on USBKEY. J. Netw. Inform. Secur. **4**(6), 62–69 (2018)
10. Zhuoqun, X., Lei, Z., Jing, W., et al.: A method of power user privacy protection based on virtual ring architecture. Inform. Netw. Secur. **18**(2), 48–53 (2018)
11. Ting, Y., Junjie, Z., Weixin, Z., et al.: Data blockchain generation algorithm for power information physical fusion system. Electr. Power Autom. Equipment **38**(10), 74–80 (2018)
12. Shouxiang, W., Haiwen, C., Zhixin, P., et al.: Reconstruction method of power system measurement missing data using improved generation-oriented network. Proc. CSEE **1**, 1–7 (2019)
13. Song, R., Song, Y., Liu, Z., et al.: Gaiaworld: a novel blockchain system based on competitive poS consensus mechanism. Comput. Mater. Continua **60**(3), 973–987 (2019)
14. Li, C., Gang, X., Chen, Y., et al.: A new anti-quantum proxy blind signature for blockchain-enabled internet of things. Comput. Mater. Continua **61**(2), 711–726 (2019)
15. Deng, Z., Ren, Y., Liu, Y., et al.: Blockchain-based trusted electronic records preservation in cloud storage. Comput. Mater. Continua **58**(1), 135–151 (2019)

A Decentralized Multi-agent Reinforcement Learning Approach for Resource Sharing and Allocation in Renewable Energy Powered Wireless Networks

Yu Gong[1(⊠)], Yifei Wei[1], Qiao Li[1], Lianping Zhang[2], and Xiaojun Wang[3]

[1] Beijing University of of Posts and Telecommunications,
Beijing, People's Republic of China
{gongyu428,weiyifei}bupt@edu.cn
[2] Alibaba Cloud Computing, Beijing, People's Republic of China
lianping.zlp@alibaba-inc.com
[3] Dublin City University, Dublin, Ireland
xiaojun.wang@dcu.edu.cn

Abstract. Energy efficiency (EE) and spectral efficiency (SE) are two key pillars of 5G NR. Energy harvesting and transfer as a promising way to EE introduces new challenges to the guarantee of both EE and SE due to its natural causality. In this paper we consider a multi-cell network in which the base stations (BSs) are powered by renewable energy and propose a resource sharing and allocation policy to simultaneously guarantee the EE and SE of the network. The goal of jointly optimizing EE and SE is formulated as a nonconvex optimization problem. A decentralized multi-agent reinforcement learning approach is proposed to solve the problem. Each BS interacts with other BSs, obtains the information of their energy budget and available bandwidth, and makes resource sharing and allocating decisions to maximize resource efficiency. Simulation results verify the convergence of our proposed learning algorithm. In comparison with other resource allocation schemes our proposed resource sharing and allocation approach can significantly improve the resource efficiency of the network.

Keywords: Wireless communication · Renewable energy · Reinforcement learning · Energy efficiency · Spectral efficiency

1 Introduction

After about a decade of research in energy efficient techniques for wireless communication systems driven by the environmental and economical concerns,

This work was supported by the National Natural Science Foundation of China (61871058) and Key Special Project in Intergovernmental International Scientific and Technological Innovation Cooperation of National Key Research and Development Program (2017YFE0118600).

energy efficiency (EE) has become a key performance metric in the design of wireless networks. Together with spectral efficiency (SE), which is a conventional performance metric in communication systems, EE and SE have become two key pillars of 5G NR and beyond. Energy harvesting and transfer, which reduces the consumption of traditional energy by harvesting renewable energy such as environmental or radio frequency energy, is a promising approach to EE [1]. However, renewable energy is dynamically changing in both time and spatial domains. This energy causality introduces new challenges into the guarantee of EE and SE in renewable energy powered wireless communication systems.

Intensive research has been conducted to investigate the EE-SE relationship and to try to simultaneously maximize EE and SE in traditional energy powered wireless communication systems. The fundamental tradeoff of EE and SE is presented in [2] where the authors demonstrate that rather than always coincide EE and SE may even conflict. When take the circuit power consumption into consideration SE will first increase and then decrease with the increasing EE. The authors of [3] prove that EE is strictly quasiconcave in SE in downlink OFDMA networks with QoS constraint. A resource allocation algorithm is then proposed to achieve the optimal EE-SE tradeoff (EST) based on their quasiconcave relationship. [4] investigates the effects of a particular type of noise in channels. [5,6] proposes the information can be embedded into the quantum carrier, and the receiver can decode the information to ensure the security of the information and provide guarantee for the effective allocation of resources. Further more, adopting this RE metric in optimal resource allocation algorithms, the amount of bandwidth can be significantly reduced by using a relatively small extra amount of power and vice versa, which means this RE metric can make the most of power and spectrum resources. EST in more specific scenarios, such as Massive MIMO systems [7], cognitive network [8], D2D multicast groups [9] and visible light communication systems [10], etc., have also been considered.

In renewable energy powered wireless systems, jointly guaranteeing EE and SE is more challenging due to the energy causality. A lot of effort has been taken to conquer the unstability of renewable energy sources and to optimize the network performance from different point of view. One of the seminal contributions on this topic is [11] in which the authors for the first time introduce the concept of energy cooperation. By transferring a portion of one energy harvesting node's energy to another energy harvesting node, the energy files can be reshaped and be adapted to maximize the network capacity. Energy cooperation between hybrid energy (renewable energy and traditional energy) powered base stations (BS) is proposed in [12] to minimize the traditional energy consumption. A mulch-terminal network with energy harvesting transmitter is considered in [13]. Joint transmit power control and energy transfer policies are proposed to maximize the total throughput of the network.

We note that there is only limited work on optimizing both EE and SE in renewable energy powered multi-cell wireless systems. In this paper we investigate resource sharing and allocation policy for renewable energy powered multi-cell wireless systems by exploiting both the energy and user diversities among

BSs to jointly guarantee EE and SE of the network. The main contribution of this paper is the decentralized reinforcement learning based resource cooperation approach proposed for multiple BSs, which is different from the energy and spectrum cooperation method proposed in [?] where the method can only be used in two BSs scenarios.

The rest of the paper is organized as follows. Section 2 describes the system model. Section 3 formulates the resource sharing and allocation problem. The proposed decentralized multi-agent reinforcement learning approach is presented in Sect. 4. Section 5 evaluates the proposed solution by analyzing the simulation results. Section 6 concludes this paper.

2   System Model

This section presents the system scenario, the energy and spectrum sharing model and the adopted EE, SE and RE definitions.

2.1   System Scenario

Consider a cellular network in which there are neighboring BSs powered by renewable energy. The set of BSs is denoted by $\mathcal{K}$ with $|\mathcal{K}| = K$ where $|\cdot|$ indicates the cardinality of a set. BSs operate on separate frequency bands using OFDMA air-interface. Each BS $k \in \mathcal{K}$ serves one user equipment (UE) denoted by U_k[1] and both the BS and UE work in single antenna mode. Each execution period (from tens of seconds to tens of minutes), the energy budget for BS k is $\overline{P}_k$ which is determined by the renewable energy generation rate. The total energy budget of K BSs is $\overline{P} = \sum_{k=1}^{K} \overline{P}_k$. BS k is assigned with bandwidth B_k which is divided into $N_k = B_k/B_{sub}$ subcarriers by the same sub-bandwidth B_{sub}. The total bandwidth for K BSs is $B = \sum_{k=1}^{K} B_k$ composed of $N = \sum_{k=1}^{K} N_k$ subcarriers. The set of total subcarriers for K BSs is denoted by $\mathcal{N}$ with $|\mathcal{N}| = N$. Assume perfect channel state information (CSI) is available at both the BS and UE. In practice, FDD system can obtain CSI through feedback from UE while TDD system via uplink pilot signal. Assigning one subcarrier to only one UE, the achievable data rate in the downlink transmission from BS k to U_k on subcarrier $n \in \mathcal{N}$ with AWGN is given by

$$r_k^n = B_{sub} \log_2(1 + \frac{p_k^n |H_k^n|^2}{B_{sub} N_0})   \tag{1}$$

where p_k^n and H_k^n are the transmit power and the channel impulse response which reflects the joint effects of path loss, shadowing, and multi-path fading from BS k to U_k on subcarrier n. N_0 is the spectral density of AWGN. $g_k^n = |H_k^n|^2/B_{sub} N_0$

---

[1] Note that although we set the system scenario as one BS serving one UE for the purpose of succinctness, our proposed algorithm can easily be extended to the scenarios of one BS serving multiple UEs.

is noted as the channel gain to noise ratio. The data rate of U_k and the total data rate of K UEs that can be achieved are separately given by

$$R_k = \sum_{n=1}^{N} \rho_k^n r_k^n \tag{2}$$

$$R = \sum_{k=1}^{K} R_k = \sum_{k=1}^{K} \sum_{n=1}^{N} \rho_k^n r_k^n \tag{3}$$

where $\rho_k^n \in \{0,1\}$ is the subcarrier assignment index with $\rho_k^n = 1$ or $\rho_k^n = 0$ meaning assigning subcarrier n to U_k or not. The bandwidth occupied by BS k and K BSs for transmission can be separately expressed as

$$B_k^T = \sum_{n=1}^{N} \rho_k^n B_{sub} \tag{4}$$

$$B^T = \sum_{k=1}^{K} \sum_{n=1}^{N} \rho_k^n B_{sub} \tag{5}$$

The total transmit power of BS k and K BSs are expressed respectively as follows

$$P_k^T = \sum_{n=1}^{N} \rho_k^n p_k^n \tag{6}$$

$$P^T = \sum_{k=1}^{K} P_k^T = \sum_{k=1}^{K} \sum_{n=1}^{N} \rho_k^n p_k^n \tag{7}$$

The entire energy consumption of BS k and K BSs are separately given by

$$P_k = P_k^T + P_k^C \tag{8}$$

$$P = P^T + P^C = \left(\sum_{k=1}^{K} \sum_{n=1}^{N} \rho_k^n p_k^n \right) + \left(\sum_{k=1}^{K} P_k^C \right) \tag{9}$$

where P_k^C is the constant circuit power consumption of BS k and P^C is the total circuit power consumed by K BSs during each execution period.

2.2 Energy and Spectrum Sharing Model

The amount of energy transferred from BS k to BS $k' \in \mathcal{K} \not\supseteq \{k\}$ is denoted by e_k with $e_k > 0$, $e_k < 0$ and $e_k = 0$ successively meaning that BS k has sufficient energy and supplies e_k amount energy to other BSs, BS k is deficient in energy and demands e_k amount energy from other BSs, and BS k does not share energy with other BSs. In practice, energy can be transferred through wireless

(wireless power transfer [11]) or wired (smart grid [12,13]) method. The constraint of energy consumption of BS k with energy sharing can be expressed as

$$P_k = P_k^T + P_k^C \leq \overline{P}_k - e_k \tag{10}$$

which can be rewritten as

$$P_k^T \leq \overline{P}_k - P_k^C - e_k \tag{11}$$

We can also describe the constraint on P_k^T with energy sharing from the perspective of the power consumption of other BS $k' \in \mathcal{K} \not\supseteq \{k\}$ as

$$P_k^T \leq \sum_{k=1}^{K} \overline{P}_k - \sum_{k=1}^{K} P_k^C - \sum_{k' \in \mathcal{K} \not\supseteq \{k\}} P_{k'}^T \tag{12}$$

Note that (11) and (12) have the same physical meaning despite the different form of descriptions from different perspectives.

The number of subcarriers released by BS k for BS $k' \in \mathcal{K} \not\supseteq \{k\}$ is denoted by m_k with $m_k > 0$, $m_k < 0$ and $m_k = 0$ successively meaning that BS k's m_k subcarriers can be occupied by other BSs, BS k occupies m_k subcarriers released by other BSs, and BS k does not share spectrum with other BSs. The bandwidth occupied by BS k for transmission with spectrum sharing is constrained by

$$B_k^T \leq (N_k - m_k) B_{sub} \tag{13}$$

From the perspective of the bandwidth occupation of other BS $k' \in \mathcal{K} \not\supseteq \{k\}$, (13) can also be described as

$$B_k^T \leq B - \sum_{k' \in \mathcal{K} \not\supseteq \{k\}} \sum_{n=1}^{N} \rho_k^n B_{sub} \tag{14}$$

2.3   Energy, Spectral and Resource Efficiency

Common definition of EE (bits/s/Joule) and SE (bits/s/Hz) for wireless communication systems can be separately expressed as follows

$$\eta^{EE} = \frac{R}{P} = \frac{\sum_{k=1}^{K} \sum_{n=1}^{N} \rho_k^n r_k^n}{\left(\sum_{k=1}^{K} \sum_{n=1}^{N} \rho_k^n p_k^n \right) + \left(\sum_{k=1}^{K} P_k^C \right)} \tag{15}$$

$$\eta^{SE} = \frac{R}{B^T} = \frac{\sum_{k=1}^{K} \sum_{n=1}^{N} \rho_k^n r_k^n}{\sum_{k=1}^{K} \sum_{n=1}^{N} \rho_k^n B_{sub}} \tag{16}$$

Resource efficiency (RE) is a unified performance metric that combines EE and SE. Adopting the RE metric (bits/Joule) investigated and proved in [?], RE can be expressed as

$$\eta^{RE} = \eta^{EE} + \gamma \eta^{SE} = \frac{R}{P} \left(1 + \gamma \frac{P/\overline{P}}{B^T/B} \right) \tag{17}$$

where γ is a weighted parameter that controls the balance of EE and SE. RE turns into EE when $\gamma = 0$ and turns into SE when $\gamma \to \infty$. The emphasis of RE smoothly changes from EE to SE when γ increases from 0 to ∞.

3   Problem Formulation

Our goal is to optimize RE by sharing energy and spectrum among BSs and allocating subcarrier and power to UEs. Using the RE metric (17), energy consumption constraint (11) and bandwidth occupation constraint (13) for BS k, the RE optimization problem is formulated as

$$\max_{\mathcal{P}, \varrho, \varepsilon, \mathcal{M}} \quad \eta^{RE}(\mathcal{P}, \varrho, \varepsilon, \mathcal{M})$$

$$\text{subject to} \quad C1 : \sum_{n=1}^{N} \rho_k^n p_k^n \leq \overline{P}_k - P_k^C - e_k, \forall k \in \mathcal{K}$$

$$C2 : \sum_{n=1}^{N} \rho_k^n B_{sub} \leq (N_k - m_k) B_{sub}, \forall k \in \mathcal{K}$$

$$C3 : p_k^n \geq 0, \forall k \in \mathcal{K}, \forall n \in \mathcal{N}$$

$$C4 : \sum_{k=1}^{K} \rho_k^n \leq 1, \forall n \in \mathcal{N} \tag{18}$$

where $\mathcal{P} = \{p_k^n\}$, $\varrho = \{\rho_k^n\}$, $\varepsilon = \{e_k\}$ and $\mathcal{M} = \{m_k\}$ is subsequently the feasible power control, subcarrier assignment, energy sharing and spectrum sharing policy. $C1$ limits the power consumption of each BS, $C2$ constrains the bandwidth occupation of each BS, $C3$ is the minimum requirement on transmit power of each UE, and $C4$ guarantees that each subcarrier is exclusively assigned to one UE. The solution for (18) is denoted by $\{\mathcal{P}^\star, \varrho^\star, \varepsilon^\star, \mathcal{M}^\star\}$ which is the optimal resource allocation and sharing policy that can maximize RE of the cellular network.

Set $\mathcal{M} = \mathbf{0}$ in (18), only energy sharing (ES) is implemented among BSs; similarly, set $\varepsilon = \mathbf{0}$, there is only spectrum sharing (SS). Set $\mathcal{M} = \varepsilon = \mathbf{0}$, there is no energy and spectrum sharing (NESS) among BSs and (18) turns into a conventional resource allocation problem without resource sharing. The above three cases can be considered as benchmarks for our proposed energy and spectrum sharing (ESS) resource allocation policy.

4   Proposed Solution

Problem (18) is a nonconvex optimization problem. This section provides a decentralized multi-agent learning approach based on reinforcement learning to solve (18).

4.1   Reinforcement Learning and Convergence

Reinforcement learning (RL) is a computational approach that approximates yet distinguishes the conventional optimal control approaches by the learning of the agent that directly interacts with its external environment and maximizes its long-term goals. A RL approach consists of three aspects: state, action and reward. Each interaction, the agent interacts with the environment, takes an action based on a decision policy, receives a reward as a feedback from the environment and updates its state. The task of RL is to maximize the long-term reward during a infinite number of interactions. In this paper, the RL agent uses the one-step Q-Learning algorithm [14] in which the learned decision policy is determined by the state-action value function Q, which estimates long-term discounted rewards for each state-action pair. Given state $X \in \mathcal{S}$ where $\mathcal{S}$ is the set of states and action $A \in \mathcal{A}$ where $\mathcal{A}$ is the set of actions, in each time step, the agent updates the state-action pair (X, A)'s Q value $Q(X, A)$ by choosing an action from $\mathcal{A}(X)$ which represents the set of actions that can be chosen in the given state X, receiving an immediate reward R and moving to the next state $Y \in \mathcal{S}$, based on the following rule:

$$Q(X, A) \longleftarrow Q(X, A) + \beta(R + \lambda V(Y) - Q(X, A)) \tag{19}$$

where λ $(0 \leq \lambda < 1)$ is a future value discount factor and β is the learning rate. $V(Y)$ is given by:

$$V(Y) = \max_{a \in \mathcal{A}(Y)} Q(Y, a) \tag{20}$$

This Q-learning algorithm will converge to an optimal decision policy if all state-action pairs continue to be updated [15, 16].

4.2 Proposed Decentralized Multi-agent Reinforcement Learning Approach

In the context of our system scenario, each execution period BS k $(\forall k \in \mathcal{K})$ needs to decide which subcarriers should be occupied and what amount the transmit power per subcarrier should be for its occupied subcarriers. Since N subcarriers are available in the network, we design that each BS has N RL agents with the nth agent deciding whether it should occupy subcarrier n and the level of transmit power on this subcarrier. This decision is made based on the decision knowledge (the occupied subcarriers and the corresponding transmit power on them) and the state information (the energy budget and available bandwidth) of other BSs, which can be achieved by interacting and exchanging information with other BSs in a cooperative way [17]. In practice, BSs can exchange information through X2 interface or by estimating UEs' measurements reports [18, 19].

Hence, at each time step, the action space of the N-agent of BS k, denoted by $\mathcal{A}_k = \{(\rho_k^1, \cdots, \rho_k^n, \cdots, \rho_k^N)\}$, is a set of binary vector with $\rho_k^n \in \{0, 1\}$ is the action space of the nth agent which determines to assign the nth subcarrier to BS k $(\rho_k^n = 1)$ or not $(\rho_k^n = 0)$. At time step t, the nth $(\forall n \in \mathcal{N})$ agent chooses ρ_k^n from $\{0, 1\}$ randomly and N agents reach a specific action for BS k, denoted by $A_k(t)$ $(A_k \in \mathcal{A}_k)$. The transmit power on each chosen subcarrier is assumed to be the same. The reward for taking action A_k is defined as

$$R = \begin{cases} 0, & \exists n \in \mathcal{N}, \rho_k^n = \rho_{k'}^n = 1 \\ \eta^{RE}, & \text{otherwise} \end{cases} \tag{21}$$

where $\rho_k^n = \rho_{k'}^n = 1$ indicates that two BSs occupy the same subcarrier and this leads to no reward, and η^{RE} is the RE achieved by all BSs' subcarrier choosing and power allocating decisions. For each action with a positive reward, the number of subcarriers occupied by BS k and K BSs are respectively given by

$$N_k^o = \sum_{n=1}^{N} \rho_k^n \tag{22}$$

$$N^o = \sum_{k=1}^{K} \sum_{n=1}^{N} \rho_k^n \tag{23}$$

Thus the transmit power on each occupied subcarrier is expressed as

$$p^o = \frac{\sum_{k=1}^{K} \overline{P}_k - \sum_{k=1}^{K} P_k^C}{\sum_{k=1}^{K} \sum_{n=1}^{N} \rho_k^n} \tag{24}$$

The state space $\mathcal{S}_k$ is defined as $\mathcal{S}_k = \{(S_E, S_B)\}$ where S_E and S_B are successively given by

$$S_E = \begin{cases} 1, & N_k^o \times p^o < \overline{P}_k - P_k^C, \text{ i.e. } e_k > 0 \\ 0, & N_k^o \times p^o = \overline{P}_k - P_k^C, \text{ i.e. } e_k = 0 \\ -1, & N_k^o \times p^o > \overline{P}_k - P_k^C, \text{ i.e. } e_k < 0 \end{cases} \tag{25}$$

$$S_B = \begin{cases} 1, & N_k^o \times B_{sub} < B_k, \text{ i.e. } m_k > 0 \\ 0, & N_k^o \times B_{sub} = B_k, \text{ i.e. } m_k = 0 \\ -1, & N_k^o \times B_{sub} > B_k, \text{ i.e. } m_k < 0 \end{cases} \tag{26}$$

where $1, 0, -1$ indicate that BS k takes e_k (m_k) energy (subcarriers) from other BSs, does not cooperate, gives e_k (m_k) energy (subcarriers) to other BSs. The state at time step t, denoted by $S_k(t)$ $(S_k \in \mathcal{S}_k)$, updates after taking action and does not affect the action that will be taken in the next time step $t + 1$.

The procedural form of the proposed decentralized multi-agent reinforcement learning algorithm is shown in Algorithm 1. The optimization behavior of Algorithm 1 over reward (21) is exploited by finding proper subcarrier assignments depending on the diversities of UEs' channel gain to noise ratio g_k^n. Algorithm 1 converges when Q value updates to the maximal value and this maximum keeps stable. The state and action corresponding to the convergence is the optimal resource allocating and sharing solution to (18).

5 Performance Evaluation

In this section, simulation results are presented to verify the performance of the proposed resource sharing and allocation algorithm. Five neighboring BSs are distributed in the cellular network. The bandwidth of each subcarrier is $B_{sub} = 15$ kHz. The ergodic Rayleigh fading with AWGN is adopted as the

---

Algorithm 1. The proposed decentralized multi-agent reinforcement learning algorithm

---

1: **Initialize** $Q(S_k, A_k) = 0, \forall S_k \in \mathcal{S}_k, A_k \in \mathcal{A}_k$
2: **repeat** (for each episode):
3:     Initialize S_k as $(S_E, S_B) = (0, 0)$
4:     **repeat** (for each time step t of this episode):
5:         Agent n ($\forall n \in \mathcal{N}$) determines $\rho_k^n = 0$ or $\rho_k^n = 1$ using greedy policy (20) and N agents reach an action $A_k(t)$;
6:         Take action $A_k(t)$, record the corresponding reward R calculated by (21), and update state to $S_k(t + 1)$;
7:         Update Q value:
8: $Q(S_k(t), A_k(t)) \longleftarrow Q(S_k(t), A_k(t)) + \beta(R + \lambda \max_{A_k \in \mathcal{A}_k} Q(S_k(t + 1), A_k) - Q(S_k(t), A_k(t)))$;
9:         $S_k(t) \longleftarrow S_k(t + 1)$.
10:     **until** S_k is terminal
11: **until** Convergence or Maximal number of iterations

---

channel model. The spectral density of AWGN is $N_0 = -112$ dBm. The average channel gain to noise ratio g_k^n is varied from 10 dB to 20 dB. All BSs have the same circuit power consumption $P_k^C = 1$ W. We set $\gamma = 1$ for the following simulations because [?] proved that both EE and SE are close to their maximal values when $\gamma = 1$. Learning rate in Algorithm 1 is $\beta = 0.5$ and the future value discount parameter is $\lambda = 0.9$. As described in Sect. 3, our proposed resource sharing and allocation algorithm with energy and spectrum sharing is denoted by ESS and the benchmark resource allocation schemes without or with only energy or spectrum sharing are respectively denoted by NESS, ES, SS.

First, we verify the convergence of the proposed algorithm. The maximal number of iterations is set to 20000. The renewable energy budget at each BS k is a value randomly generated between 1 W and 3 W. Figure 1 shows the convergence of the proposed multi-agent learning algorithm in terms of the average number of iterations needed for convergence with respect to the number of total subcarriers. As illustrated in Fig. ??, the average number of iterations increases with the increasing N from 5 to 25 (N_k from 1 to 5). This is because the action space $\{(\rho_k^1, \cdots, \rho_k^n, \cdots, \rho_k^N)\}$ exponentially increases with the increasing number of subcarriers N and it leads to an exponential growth of the number of iterations for the proposed algorithm to converge.

The comparison of optimal RE achieved by various resource sharing policies with increasing energy budget is shown in Fig. 1. Fix the total number of subcarriers as $N = 15$ ($N_k = 3$). The increasing energy budget at each BS is randomly generated from $[0.5, 1.5]$, $[1, 2]$, $[2, 3]$, $[3, 4]$, $[4, 5]$. Figure 1 illustrates that resource allocation with both energy and spectrum sharing can obtain higher RE than any other resource operation policies at all kinds of energy budget level. This is because a deficiency of one BS's energy budget can be complemented by other BSs's excessive energy budget or bandwidth by sharing policies. RE first increases and then decreases with the increasing energy budget for all kinds

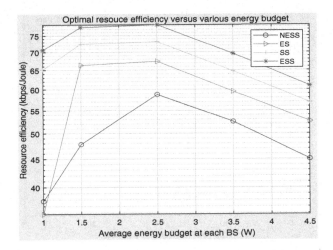

Fig. 1. Comparison of maximal RE achieved by other resource sharing policies with different level of energy budget.

of resource allocation policies with or without resource sharing policy. This is a result the definition of RE, according to (17) when transmit power reaches a specific value the growth rate of data rate produced by the increasing transmit power starts decreasing. In the context of our system scenario and the corresponding simulation parameters, the optimal amount of energy supply is around 2.5 W per BS and exceeding this line will drop the network performance in terms of RE.

The comparison of optimal RE achieved by various resource sharing policies with increasing number of total subcarries is plotted in Fig. 2. The energy budget of each BS is a value randomly generated from $[1, 3]$. Total number of subcarriers increases from 5 to 25 (N_k from 1 to 5). As shown in Fig. 2, the proposed resource sharing and allocating approach outperforms other resource allocation schemes in terms of RE at all level of the total number of subcarrier. This is because at each execution of the proposed learning approach, the agents try to find a better subcarrier assignment policy $(\rho_k^1, \cdots, \rho_k^n, \cdots, \rho_k^N)$ with the information of all BSs' average channel gain to noise ratio g_k^n ($\forall k \in \mathcal{K}, \forall n \in \mathcal{N}$) and the decision knowledge of other BSs to obtain a higher RE. After convergence or a maximal number of iterations, the best subcarrier assignment for a given g_k^n will be found to achieve the highest RE for the network.

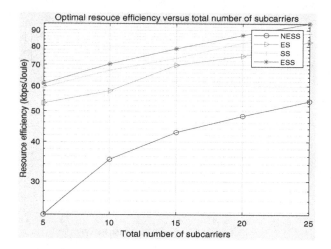

Fig. 2. Comparison of maximal RE achieved by other resource sharing policies with different number of subcarriers.

6   Conclusion

We propose a decentralized multi-agent reinforcement learning approach for resource sharing and allocating in renewable energy powered multi-cell networks to jointly maximize EE and SE. BSs interact with each other and obtain the information of the energy budget and available bandwidth of the network. Based on the information of other BSs each BS makes resource sharing and allocating decisions to share energy and spectrum with other BSs and to allocate subcarrier and power for itself with the goal of maximizing the RE of the network. Simulation results demonstrate the convergence and performance of our proposed learning algorithm. After a limited number of iterations the proposed learning algorithm converges to its optimal solution. Compared with resource allocation schemes with no resource sharing or only sharing energy or spectrum, our resource sharing and allocating approach can remarkably improve the RE of the network.

The proposed decentralized resource sharing approach can be extended to the scenario of energy harvesting heterogeneous cellular networks where the BSs can use the same subcarriers. Prudent power control method should be considered to alleviate the inter-cell interference. It is an interesting direction for our future work.

References

1. Buzzi, S., Chih-Lin, I., Klein, T.E., Poor, H.V., Yang, C., Zappone, A.: A survey of energy-efficient techniques for 5G networks and challenges ahead. IEEE J. Sel. Areas Commun. **34**(4), 697–709 (2016)

2. Chen, Y., Zhang, S., Xu, S., Li, G.Y.: Fundamental trade-offs on green wireless networks. IEEE Commun. Mag. **49**(6), 30–37 (2011)
3. Xiong, C., Li, G.Y., Zhang, S., Chen, Y., Xu, S.: Energy- and spectral-efficiency tradeoff in downlink OFDMA networks. IEEE Trans. Wirel. Commun. **10**(11), 3874–3886 (2011)
4. Qu, Z., Wu, S., Wang, M., Sun, L., Wang, X.: Effect of quantum noise on deterministic remote state preparation of an arbitrary two-particle state via various quantum entangled channels. Quantum Inf. Process. **16**(306), 1–25 (2017)
5. Qu, Z., Cheng, Z., Liu, W., Wang, X.: A novel quantum image steganography algorithm based on exploiting modification direction. Multimedia Tools Appl. **78**(7), 7981–8001 (2018). https://doi.org/10.1007/s11042-018-6476-5
6. Qu, Z., Li, Z., Xu, G., Wu, S., Wang, X.: Quantum image steganography protocol based on quantum image expansion and grover search algorithm. IEEE Access **7**, 50849–50857 (2019)
7. Liu, Z., Du, W., Sun, D.: Energy and spectral efficiency tradeoff for massive MIMO systems with transmit antenna selection. IEEE Trans. Veh. Technol. **66**(5), 4453–4457 (2017)
8. Zhang, W., Wang, C., Chen, D., Xiong, H.: Energy-spectral efficiency tradeoff in cognitive radio networks. IEEE Trans. Veh. Technol. **65**(4), 2208–2218 (2016)
9. Bhardwaj, A., Agnihotri, S.: Energy-and spectral-efficiency trade-off for D2D-multicasts in underlay cellular networks. IEEE Wirel. Commun. Lett. **7**(4), 546–549 (2018)
10. Li, E., Zhang, W., Sun, J., Wang, C. X., Ge, X.: Energy-spectral efficiency tradeoff of visible light communication systems. In: 2016 IEEE/CIC International Conference on Communications in China (ICCC), pp. 1–5. IEEE (2016)
11. Gurakan, B., Ozel, O., Yang, J., Ulukus, S.: Energy cooperation in energy harvesting communications. IEEE Trans. Commun. **61**(12), 4884–4898 (2013)
12. Chia, Y., Sun, S., Zhang, R.: Energy cooperation in cellular networks with renewable powered base stations. IEEE Trans. Wirel. Commun. **13**(12), 6996–7010 (2014)
13. Tutuncuoglu, K., Yener, A.: Energy harvesting networks with energy cooperation: procrastinating policies. IEEE Trans. Commun. **63**(11), 4525–4538 (2015)
14. Watkins, C.J.C.H.: Learning with delayed rewards. Ph.D. thesis, Cambridge University Psychology Department (1989)
15. Watkins, C.J.C.H., Dayan, P.: Q-learning. Mach. Learn. **8**(3), 279–292 (1992). https://doi.org/10.1007/BF00992698
16. Sutton, R.S., Barto, A.G.: Introduction to Reinforcement Learning, 2nd edn. MIT Press, Cambridge (2015)
17. Tan, M.: Multi-agent reinforcement learning: independent vs. cooperative agents. In: Proceedings of the ICML, pp. 330–337. Morgan Kaufmann (1993)
18. Bernardo, F., Agust, R., Prez-Romero, J., Sallent, O.: An application of reinforcement learning for efficient spectrum usage in next-generation mobile cellular networks. IEEE Trans. Syst. Man, Cybern. Part C (Appl. Rev.) **40**(4), 477–484 (2010)
19. Bernardo, F., Agust, R., Prez-Romero, J., Sallent, O.: Intercell interference management in OFDMA networks: a decentralized approach based onreinforcement learning. IEEE Trans. Syst. Man Cybern. Part C (Appl. Rev.) **41**(6), 968–976 (2011)

TFFV: Translator from EOS Smart Contracts to Formal Verification Language

ZeHui Yan[1], Weizhong Qian[1(✉)], Zheng Yang[1], Weiru Zeng[1], Xi Yang[1], and Ang Li[2]

[1] School of Information and Software Engineering, University of Electronic Science and Technology of China, Chengdu, China
qwz_617@163.com
[2] Chengdu Hucheng Online Technology Co., Ltd., Chengdu, China

Abstract. In order to realize the formal verification of EOS smart contract and improve the universal processing of input, this paper divides the lexical units based on EOS smart contract, and uses the binary list to store the contents of each node of abstract syntax tree, and finally proposes a language transformation method based on the abstract syntax tree. This method can transform EOS smart contract source code into functional equivalent formal verification language for custom grammar construction, and realize the customized translation process by adding symbol table. This paper uses this method to design and implement a translator (*TFFV*) for formal verification of EOS smart contract. The translated EOS smart contract code has the characteristics of clear structure, reproducible, strong capacity expansion and strong adaptability. At present, *TFFV* has been successfully applied in the formal verification system. Some experimental results are given at the end of the paper to further illustrate the efficiency and advantages of *TFFV*.

Keywords: EOS (Enterprise Operation System) smart contract · Translator · Abstract syntax tree · Formal verification

1 Introduction

With the continuous development of blockchain technology [1–5], many security issues corresponding to smart contracts have become increasingly prominent. The DAO smart contract deployed on the Ethereum was attacked in June 17, 2016 [6]. The Dimensional Security Lab monitored that the Ethereum Smart Contract AMR had a high-risk transaction in July 8, 2018 [7]. It is only by the end of 2018 that the vulnerability of hackers using smart contracts has caused losses of more than $630 million. It can be seen that ensuring the security and reliability of smart contracts is of great significance to the security of blockchain and transactions on blockchain. In recent years, High-order logic theorem proving (HOLTP) has been used to verify the security of Ethereum smart contracts [8]. Compared with traditional security testing, this technology can achieve complete verification without security test cases, greatly improving the efficiency of security verification. Yang Zheng's team [9] built a general, extensible and reusable formal memory framework [10], an extensible general formal intermediate programming

© Springer Nature Singapore Pte Ltd. 2020
X. Sun et al. (Eds.): ICAIS 2020, CCIS 1254, pp. 652–663, 2020.
https://doi.org/10.1007/978-981-15-8101-4_58

language Lolisa [11], and a corresponding formal verification interpreter [12] to realize the automatic modeling process of the target program.

However, the security verification based on HOLTP has the problem of inefficiently translating the code of smart contract into formal verification language, especially when the source code such as EOS smart contract is written by a complex high-level language. From the Solidity language to the JavaScript language translator design showed us a development direction [13], that is, the design of automated translator to convert the smart contract to other programming languages, but there is no related work to translate the EOS smart contract into the formal verification language.

For the first time, this paper proposes a translator framework for EOS smart contract, through which the C++ based EOS smart contract can be translated into formal verification language. The main contributions of this paper include:

For the first time, this paper proposes a translator framework for EOS smart contract, through which the C++ based EOS smart contract can be translated into formal verification language. The main contributions of this paper include:

- Lexical unit division based on EOS smart contract: We designed a unique lexical unit division method for EOS smart contract for the characteristics of C++ syntax secondary encapsulation, which can perfectly identify and match EOS smart contract, and it also facilitates the division of non-terminators and the construction of grammar for syntax analysis.
- Construction method of abstract syntax tree for code structure reconstruction: We use Flex and Bison [14] to design lexical analyzer and parser, so we can abstract all the syntax supported by the Bison specification into a syntax tree. Because we use a binary list to store each variable of the abstract syntax tree, we can realize the customization of the syntax structure and the reconstruction of the code structure.
- *Sugar* conversion method: We propose a customized translation method based on abstract syntax tree, which supports flexible translation of specified grammar. Moreover, the method has flexible interface and supports different design schemes to achieve translation actions, which makes the translation process more efficient and the coupling degree of modules lower. This method is compatible with symbol table, and can return corresponding symbol table according to the requirement of formal verification. It is extensible.

The rest of this paper is structured as follows. Section 2 introduces basic concepts to support the design of *TFFV*. Section 3 proposes a design scheme of the overall architecture through the analysis of the real problem, and expounds the division of the lexical unit, the construction of the abstract syntax tree and the design of the *Sugar* transformation. Section 4 introduces a simple case to illustrate the efficiency and correctness of *TFFV*. Finally, Sect. 5 puts forward the conclusion and future research direction.

2 Basic Concepts

The process of translating an EOS smart contract into a formal verification language consists of three steps: First, the lexical analyzer recognizes the morpheme of EOS smart contract and corresponds to the lexical unit. Secondly, the abstract syntax tree is constructed according to the non-terminator in the parser. Finally, *Sugar* conversion and symbol tables are set up in the code generator to support formal verification.

2.1 Basic Definition

Table 1 lists the basic definitions involved in this paper, including the establishment of abstract syntax tree, the design of *Sugar* conversion and symbol table. All of these will be encountered in the following sections, and the components of a particular state will be represented by the appropriate Greek characters for the state signature.

Table 1. Basic definition of *TFFV*

R	Regular expression	L	Hierarchy of abstract syntax tree
$L(R)$	Set of regular matching strings	L_s	The stratification of *Sugar*
U_R	Complete set of matching patterns	β	Entry function (*Sugar*)
T	Abstract syntax tree	s	Interface function (*Sugar*)
τ	Node of ABSTRACT syntax tree	S	Translation function (*Sugar*)
$f(\tau)$	Reduced function	γ	General translation set

2.2 Division and Correspondence of Morphemes and Lexical Units

In this lexical analyzer, in addition to the matching and recognition of various characters in C++, special character separation processing encapsulated in EOS smart contract is also carried out to facilitate the operation of specific grammar by the parser and code generator. R is used to describe the lexical unit tokens of the programming language. $L(R) \rightarrow tokens$ are implemented in a Flex-based lexer in the form of conversion rules. Some examples are shown in Table 2.

Table 2. Patterns and corresponding actions in transformation rules

Model	Action
MULTI_INDEX	{yylval.a = newast("MINDEX",0,yylineno); return MINDEX;}
SEND_INLINE_ACTION	{yylval.a = newast("SIA",0,yylineno); return SIA;}
EOSIO_ABI	{yylval.a = newast("EABI",0,yylineno); return EABI;}
EOSIO_API	{yylval.a = newast("EAPI",0,yylineno); return EAPI;}
EOSIO_DISPATCH	{yylval.a = newast("EDIS",0,yylineno); return EDIS;}

It is obvious that the pattern is an R, and the action code fragment contains the defined lexical unit token. All R have and only one token corresponding to it.

2.3   Hierarchical Design of Abstract Syntax Tree

In the hierarchical design of T, each τ consists of non-terminals and terminators. Multiple non-terminals and terminators are expressed as $f(\tau)$ by grammar induction. And multiple unambiguous $f(\tau)$ are described by a non-terminal. The rules defined are as follows.

$$F(\tau) = \bigcup_{i=1}^{n} f_i(\tau), f(\tau) \in \tau \tag{1}$$

Secondly, in order to facilitate the conversion of a specific grammatical structure, this paper divides T into five layers L in Table 3 except for α.

Table 3. Abstract syntax tree layered design

Definition layer	Covers various definition sentence grammars
Type layer	Covers grammars such as basic types, structures, and templates
Declaration layer	Covers grammars that declare grammars and formal parameter lists
Statement layer	Covers all statement grammars
Expression layer	Covers the expression grammar in all statements

Each layer in Table 3 is composed of several different $f(\tau)$, and there is an inclusion relationship between $F(\tau)$. We stipulate that $L_{def}, L_{type}, L_{dec}, L_{stmt}, L_{expr}$ represent the five layers in the Table, and the rules of its definition are as follows.

$$\exists F_p(\tau) \ni F_{p+q}(\tau) : L_{def} = \bigcup_{i=1}^{n} F_i(\tau), p \leq n \tag{2}$$

In the same way, we can define four layers, i.e. $L_{type}, L_{dec}, L_{stmt}, L_{expr}$. The final defined abstract syntax tree rules are as follows.

$$T = \alpha \cup L_{def} \cup L_{type} \cup L_{dec} \cup L_{stmt} \cup L_{expr} \tag{3}$$

2.4   *Sugar* and Symbol Table Design

Sugar is a language conversion method defined in this paper. This method can be flexibly located in T, which is convenient for custom translation. The motivation of this method is to solve the Coq formal verification method based on theorem proof for C++ language. In order to correspond with L, and to facilitate the flexible use of *Sugar* conversion method, this paper divides *Sugar* into four layers of L_s in Table 4.

In the process of research, we found that the formal verification based on theorem proving needs to simulate the running state of smart contract in memory [15], so we must clearly divide the scope of the contract and allocate the memory space reasonably. T_s is designed in *TFFV* to implement support functions. In order to facilitate formal verification of the execution of the interpreter, we designed the T_s in Table 5.

We specify $T_{s.var}, T_{s.func}, T_{s.scope}$ to represent the three tables. The design of T_s includes the definition of its operation and data structure. In $T_{s.var}$ and $T_{s.func}$ structures,

Table 4. *Sugar* layered design

Type layer	Mainly for structural translation
Statement layer	Covers the translation of Statement layer grammars in T
Expression layer	Covers the translation of Expression layer grammars in T
Custom function layer	Provide a flexible translation interface

Table 5. Symbol table design

Variable symbol table	Contains processing of variables, arrays, structures, and classes
Function symbol table	For function processing
Scope symbol table	Handling all scenarios involving scope

we define pointer *type* and *name* to describe the attributes of variables, where $T_{s.var_{name}}$ and $T_{s.func_{name}}$ are the specific names of variables, and $T_{s.var_{type}}$ distinguish different types of variables.

Finally, we define the index *num* in $T_{s.var}$ and $T_{s.func}$ to number variables in top-down order, and translate it into integer numbers of int type, which is convenient for formal verification of interpreter verification. $T_{s.var_{num}}$ and $T_{s.func_{num}}$ share the sort index.

3   The Specific Design of *TFFV*

3.1   Problem Analysis

TFFV mainly solves various problems of manual translation of native smart contract in the process of formal verification. Next, two examples are given to illustrate the characteristics of the two languages and the key points of translation. First, the problem of EOS morpheme matching is shown in Fig. 1.

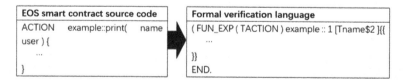

Fig. 1. Morpheme matching instance

In EOSIO [16], EOS officially encapsulates the syntax of C++ to facilitate the development. It requires that the translator can reasonably match all the morphemes in the EOS smart contract and convert them into tokens.

Secondly, Fig. 2 shows the problem of structural transformation and expression.

```
EOS smart contract source code
for(int i = 0; i < vt.size(); i++){
    if(vt[i].item == winItem[0]){
        return vt[i].num * rate;
    }
}
```

```
Formal verification language
( FOR(EVAR(Tint)8 ::= SINT 0 ; EVAR(Tint)8 < EVAR(TNULL)3 . size ( ) ;EVAR(Tint)8
(++) ){{
( IFN(EVAR(TNULL)3 [ EVAR(Tint)8 ] . item == Tstring:4[0 ]){{
RETURN EVAR(TNULL)3 [ EVAR(Tint)8 ] . num * EVAR(Tuint32_t)7 ;;
}} );;
}} );;
```

Fig. 2. Structural transformations and representations

Formal verification language is different from common high-level language or low-level machine language. In order to facilitate the low-level modeling and memory simulation of specific high-level language, formal verification language requires more stringent representation. For instance, taking the example in Fig. 2, each statement in the formal *statement* level needs to be marked with "()", and "END." needs to be added at the end of a verification code. The same ";" needs to take different forms in the formal language, such as ";" and ";" respectively represent the classification of the expression of the determination condition in the "for" *statement* and the link between the statement. In C++, declaring a variable and initializing it needs to be split into declaration statement and assignment statement in the formal language structure. In the formal language, in order to be able to easily divide different memory spaces for different scopes, the variables need to be converted to int integers.

The disadvantages of manual translation smart contract can be concluded as follows: first of all, manual translation is prone to errors, and once there is a slight error, formal verification fails. Secondly, the manual translation of smart contracts has a huge workload, and each time a new smart contract is encountered, it needs to be translated manually. Finally, once the smart contract language is updated, the perception of manual translation is weak. A reasonable design of a translator can perfectly solve the above problems, the following details the main design of *TFFV*.

3.2 Overall Architecture Design

We follow the traditional compiler design [17], and divide the interpreter of smart contract formal verification into three modules: Lexical analyzer, Parser and Code generator. The overall architecture is shown in Fig. 3.

The EOS smart contract source program is converted to tokens by Lexical analyzer, and then tokens are converted to T by the Parser, and T_s is generated. Finally, the Code generator traverses the entire T through the traversal function *EVAL* constructed by us. When τ is not empty, if β is not recognized, the conversion processing of the fixed format is directly performed; if β is recognized, it will be transferred to the *Sugar* and returned to the processing result. After this process, the EOS smart contract source code is translated into the expected formal verification language to support the implementation of the formal verification interpreter.

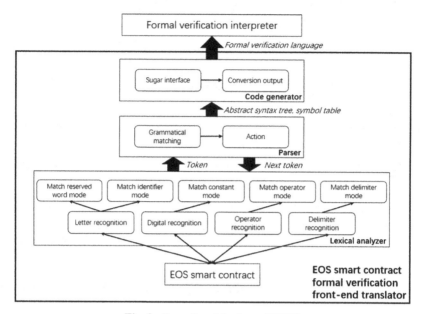

Fig. 3. Overall architecture of *TFFV*

3.3 Lexical Unit Division Based on EOS Smart Contract

We use the example in Fig. 1 to expand the lexical unit division of EOS smart contract. *ACTION* encapsulates the return type "void" of a function, and *name* encapsulates a structure type. For morpheme matching, *ACTION* and other types only need R recognition, and then the form of *ID* is saved for matching in T. However, specific morphemes such as EOSIO_ABI, SEND_INLINE_ACTION and so on need to be defined as shown in Table 2, specifically in the Lexical analyzer to facilitate morpheme matching and syntax analysis. Since Lex always selects the first listed pattern when the longest matching prefix matches multiple patterns [18], we always put special regular matching before general regular matching in design.

We specify that the common pattern such as *type* and *ID* that can match multiple strings is $\bar{R}$. For example, the pattern that can only match one string, such as EOSIO_ABI, is $R_n (n = 1, 2, 3 \ldots)$, assuming that the matched string is X. So, the algorithm can be obtained:

$$\exists X : \bar{R} \to X \wedge R_n \to X \Rightarrow U_R = \bigcup_{i=1}^{m} R_i \cup \bar{R}, m \geq n \tag{4}$$

We define the complete set of matching patterns as U_R. It can be seen that the key point of this algorithm is that if X can be matched not only by $\bar{R}$ but also by R_n, because we put R_n before $\bar{R}$, X will be matched according to the specific pattern R_n. For example, as shown in Fig. 1, many morphemes that are conducive to the subsequent establishment of T are matched in the way of R_n, which is not only conducive to the construction of T containing the EOSIO encapsulated morpheme, but also beneficial to the lexical supplement of source code library update. Assuming that the source code library of EOSIO has been updated, the newly encapsulated morpheme S_p is added, and the previously used morpheme S_q is deleted, the algorithm (4) can be improved as follows:

$$U_R = \left(\bigcup_{i=1}^{n} R_i - R_q \right) \cup R_p \cup \bar{R} \tag{5}$$

As in the above definition, we only need to rewrite the pattern R_p of the matching morpheme X before $\bar{R}$ and then delete the pattern R_q that matches another morpheme.

By dividing the lexical unit, it is convenient to add or delete patterns, and it is easy to get the tokens we need to construct T, which is convenient for the reconstruction of the code structure.

3.4 Construction Method of Abstract Syntax Tree for Code Structure Recurrence

The main problem solved by the construction of the T is the recurrence of the code structure, which is convenient for us to design β in T, and finally achieve flexible translation. So, in the design stage, we construct a unique structure τ, and use the way of linked list to organize and generate T. The specific definition of data structure of τ is shown in Table 6.

Table 6. Data structure definition of nodes in abstract syntax tree

τ_{tag}	A variable node's type	$\tau_{content}$	Semantic value
τ_{tag}	:= 1 Variable	τ_{type}	An expression node's type
	|2 Function	τ_{ivalue}	An integer constant node's value
	|3 Constant	τ_{fvalue}	A floating-point constant node's value
	|4 Array	τ_{sugar}	Identity of *Sugar* conversion
	|5 Structure	τ_{s_top}	Translation traversal stop tag
	|6 Class	τ_{s_change}	Change semantic value stop tag
τ_{line}	Line number information	τ_l	Left child
τ_{name}	Grammar name	τ_r	Right child

When T is constructed in the parser, τ_{line}, τ_{name}, $\tau_{content}$ in Table 6 are the main attributes of each τ. All operations in translation are based on obtaining the semantic value of the specified grammar name τ. τ_{tag}, τ_{type}, τ_{ivalue}, τ_{fvalue}, τ_{sugar} are auxiliary designs. The first three are to distinguish the types of tokens when constructing T grammar, while τ_{sugar} provides an entry for *Sugar* transformation method. The two fields τ_{s_top}, τ_{s_change} are not used in the construction of T, but in traversing T. τ_{s_top} indicates whether to continue to traverse the right child and τ_{s_change} indicates whether to change the semantic value. It is a design to improve the accuracy and efficiency of translation. Finally, τ_l, τ_r are designed to realize the abstract syntax tree construction mode of our adopted child-brother representation, as shown in Fig. 4.

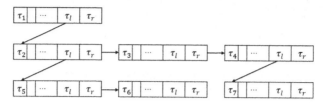

Fig. 4. Construction of child-brother representation

All the left children of τ point to the next level of grammar, which means that the τ pointed to is a non-terminal $F(\tau)$, and all τ in the same layer with the right children jointly describe a $f(\tau)$. Combined with the layered definition of T in 2.3, we can draw the following conclusion: Although the composition of grammar is uncertain, it is represented by variable length parameters, and The construction of T can be completed by constructing a function of the node of the grammar tree from bottom to top until the grammar α.

3.5 *Sugar* Conversion Method

We take the problem in Fig. 1 as an example to expand the design and necessity of *Sugar* conversion method and symbol table. The first is the "()" and ";" involved in Fig. 1, the main need to solve is the division of the *statement*. In Sect. 3.4, we specify τ_{sugar} as the identification of *Sugar* conversion, so we can get the following algorithm.

$$\exists \omega : \beta \in f_\omega(\tau) \rightarrow L_s \Rightarrow \forall \tau_{sugar}, \exists \omega : \tau_{sugar} \in f_\omega(\tau) \rightarrow \tau_{sugar} \in L_s \qquad (6)$$

For any β existing in T, there is a corresponding s in L_s. As mentioned in Sect. 3.2, we construct an *EVAL* function to traverse T. The definition of *EVAL* is as follows.

$$\tau \neq \emptyset \wedge \frac{\forall n : s_n \leftrightarrow S_n}{\exists s_n \in T} \wedge \exists p, q : s_p, \gamma \in S_q \wedge \tau \rightarrow \tau_l, \frac{\tau \rightarrow \tau_r}{!\tau_{s\_top}} \qquad (7)$$

It is not difficult to see from the structure display of the standard *EVAL* ergodic function defined by us that each s and S are one-to-one correspondence, so it shares the same hierarchical design. Where s may need to call γ, it may also need to call other s to handle nested translation actions. At the same time, when traversing τ, first traversing τ_l, Finally, stop traversing at the place marked by τ_{s_top}.

Through the above description, we can simply put the overall idea of the *Sugar* conversion method into the following rules.

$$\frac{L \rightarrow L_s, T_s}{T \rightarrow L \vdash \beta \rightarrow F(\tau) \vdash \beta \rightarrow f(\tau) \vdash \beta \rightarrow s \rightarrow S} \qquad (8)$$

As summarized previously, the main idea of the method is to locate the grammar that needs to be *Sugar* transformed from T, then define s in the ergodic function *EVAL* with β as the entry of grammar definition, and finally define our translation form in s, and realize the complete translation process by combining the corresponding L_s and T_s. For example, a piece of code C can be redefined and translated as follows.

$$C \stackrel{\text{def}}{=} f_C(\tau) = [C_0, \ldots, C_i] + + \ldots + +[C_j, \ldots, C_k] + + \ldots + +[C_m, \ldots, C_n] + + \ldots + +[C_y, \ldots, C_z]$$

$$= [C_0, \ldots, C_i] + + \ldots + +f_i(\tau) + + \ldots + +f_j(\tau) + + \ldots + +[C_y, \ldots, C_z]$$

$$\rhd \left(f_i(\tau) \stackrel{\text{def}}{=} [C_j, \ldots, C_k], f_j(\tau) \stackrel{\text{def}}{=} [C_m, \ldots, C_n] \right)$$

$$= [C_0, \ldots, C_i] + + \ldots + +f_i(\tau) + + \ldots + +F_k(\tau)$$

$$\rhd \left(f_i(\tau) \stackrel{\text{def}}{=} [C_j, \ldots, C_k], F_k(\tau) \stackrel{\text{def}}{=} [f_j(\tau), \ldots, f_k(\tau)] \right)$$

$$Translate(C) = Translate([C_0, \ldots, C_i] + + \ldots + +f_i(\tau) + + \ldots + +F_k(\tau))$$

Therefore, for $Translate([C_0, \ldots, C_z])$, in the end, it can be summed up as $Translate([F_0(\tau), \ldots F_Z(\tau)])$, which means that translating code from bottom to top, and also means that whether adding β to T or adding the operations related to T_s to T, the main foundation is the grammar analysis of T. Reasonable *Sugar* design is actually a thorough understanding of grammar.

4 Experiment

According to the above design, we have completed the implementation of a mature EOS smart contract formal translator. Next, we conduct translation processing on a complex smart contract and collect data to test the efficiency of *TFFV*. Due to the space limitation, only parts of the translation results of one EOS smart contract are shown.

Figure 5 is the formal verification language after translation. and *TFFV* also provide the symbol table for formal verification, which is shown in Fig. 6.

```
1   ( FUN_EXP ( Tvoid ) LuckyGame :: 1 [Taccount_name$2 ;Tstring$3 ]{{
2   require_auth( EVAR(Taccount_name)2 ) ;;
3   ( VAR(TNULL) 4  );;
4   ( VAR(Tuint32_t) 5  );;
5   EVAR(Tuint32_t)5 ::= parseInputSelected( EVAR(Tstring)3 , EVAR(Taccount_name)2 , EVAR(TNULL)4 ) ;;
6   eosio :: print ( "Game cost coins total:" , EVAR(Tuint32_t)5 , "\n" ) ;;
7   ( VAR(Tuint32_t) 6  );;
8   EVAR(Tuint32_t)6 ::= getRandNum( ) ;;
9   eosio :: print ( "Game rand:" , EVAR(Tuint32_t)6 , "\n" ) ;;
10  ( VAR(Tstring) 7  );;
11  ( VAR(Tuint32_t) 8  );;
12  EVAR(Tuint32_t)8 ::= getBonuse( EVAR(Tuint32_t)6 , EVAR(TNULL)4 , EVAR(Tstring)7 ) ;;
13  eosio_assert( EVAR(Tuint32_t)8 <= SINT 99 * winRate :: JOK , "Calculation bonus error." ) ;;
14  eosio :: print ( "Game item:" , EVAR(Tstring)7 , "total bonuses:" , EVAR(Tuint32_t)8 , "\n" ) ;;
15  ( IFE(SINT 0 == EVAR(Tuint32_t)8 ){{
16  eosio :: print ( "Not win! Good luck next time! \n" ) ;;
```

Fig. 5. Formal verification language after sample code translation

In all the test samples, the compiler can achieve 100% accuracy in translation. As long as the *TFFV* can recognize the lexical grammar, it can translate successfully according to the required pattern. Table 7 and Fig. 7 show the efficiency of *TFFV*.

The *Sugar* conversion method of *TFFV* allows nested operations, so the efficiency of translation depends on the complexity of the code with the increasing size of code. For a translation operation, if the call to *EVAL* is nested in the *Sugar* conversion module, the

```
1    变量符号表:
2    num:2,name:gamer,type:account_name
3    num:3,name:selected,type:string
4    num:4,name:v_selects,type:NULL
5    num:5,name:useCoin,type:uint32_t
6    num:6,name:randNum,type:uint32_t
7    num:7,name:winItem,type:string
8    num:8,name:bonuse,type:uint32_t
9    num:9,name:bonus,type:asset
10   num:10,name:memo,type:string
11   num:11,name:pos,type:
12   num:12,name:info,type:auto
13   num:14,name:gamer,type:account_name
```

Fig. 6. Part of the EOS smart contract translation symbol table

Table 7. Efficiency table of *TFFV* runs 100 times

Contract name	Code size (hundred lines)	Minimum execution time (ms)	Maximum execution time (ms)	Average execution time (ms)	Correct rate (100%)
test	0.42	2.034000	2.583000	2.383000	1
LuckyGame	1.25	3.317000	4.125000	3.625000	1
rps	1.80	7.834000	9.696000	8.696000	1
MultiBetting	3.06	6.916000	8.157000	7.157000	1

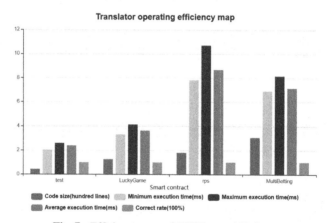

Fig. 7. Efficiency map of *TFFV* runs 100 times

time complexity of the translation will be greatly improved. It is not difficult to see from the above chart that *TFFV* runs stably, and the running time will not increase with the increase of code size, but more depends on the complexity of code structure. In general, experiments show that *TFFV* is feasible, efficient and correct.

5 Conclusion and Future Work

This paper designs *TFFV* to translate EOS smart contract for formal verification, and describes a method of language transformation based on abstract syntax tree. The formal verification code generated by this method has clear structure and *TFFV* based on this method has features of scalability, adaptability and efficiency. *TFFV* solves the problem of translating EOS smart contract into formal verification language and shortens the period of formal verification. At present, *TFFV* performs well, and it provides an effective idea and technology for the translation of blockchain smart contract.

In the future, we can propose a more efficient translation action mode based on the *Sugar* module of *TFFV*, we can also try layered design to make *TFFV* support the translation of various code based on C++ and realize the translation into various formal verification languages.

References

1. Crosby, M., Pattanayak, P., Verma, S., et al.: Blockchain technology: beyond bitcoin. Appl. Innov. **2**(6–10), 71 (2016)
2. Baliga, A.: Understanding blockchain consensus models. Persistent (2017)
3. Zhao, Y., Zhang, S., Yang, M., He, P., Wang, Q.: Research on architecture of risk assessment system based on block chain. Comput. Mater. Continua **61**(2), 677–686 (2019)
4. Li, C., Gang, X., Chen, Y., Ahmad, H., Li, J.: A new anti-quantum proxy blind signature for blockchain-enabled internet of things. Comput. Mater. Continua **61**(2), 711–726 (2019)
5. Deng, Z., Ren, Y., Liu, Y., Yin, X., Shen, Z., Kim, H.J.: Blockchain-based trusted electronic records preservation in cloud storage. Comput. Mater. Continua **58**(1), 135–151 (2019)
6. Michael del, C.: The DAO attacked: code issue leads to $60 million ether theft, 2016, 2 Dec (2017)
7. Wohrer, M., Zdun, U.: Smart contracts: security patterns in the ethereum ecosystem and solidity, pp. 2–8. IEEE (2018)
8. Bhargavan, K., Delignat-Lavaud, A., Fournet, C., et al.: Formal verification of smart contracts: short paper. In: Proceedings of the 2016 ACM Workshop on Programming Languages and Analysis for Security, pp. 91–96. ACM (2016)
9. Yang, Z., Lei, H., Qian, W.A.: Hybrid formal verification system in coq for ensuring the reliability and security of ethereum-based service smart contracts. arXiv preprint arXiv:1902. 08726 (2019)
10. Yang, Z., Lei, H.: Formal process virtual machine for smart contracts verification. arXiv preprint arXiv:1805.00808 (2018)
11. Yang, Z., Lei, H.: Lolisa: formal syntax and semantics for a subset of the solidity programming language. arXiv preprint arXiv:1803.09885 (2018)
12. Yang, Z., Lei, H.: FEther: an extensible definitional interpreter for smart-contract verifications in Coq. IEEE Access **7**, 37770–37791 (2019)
13. Zafar, M.A., Sher, F., Janjua, M.U., et al.: Sol2js: translating solidity contracts into javascript for hyperledger fabric, pp. 19–24. ACM (2018)
14. Levine, J., Flex, B.: Text Processing Tools. O'Reilly Media, Inc (2009)
15. Blazy, S., Dargaye, Z., Leroy, X.: Formal verification of a C compiler front-end. In: Misra, J., Nipkow, T., Sekerinski, E. (eds.) International Symposium on Formal Methods, pp. 460–475. Springer, Heidelberg (2006). https://doi.org/10.1007/11813040_31
16. Larimer, D.: Introducing EOSIO dawn 4.0 (2018)
17. Ullman, J.D., Aho, A.V.: Principles of Compiler Design. Addison Wesley, Reading (1977)
18. Levine, J.R., Levine, J.R., Mason, T., et al.: Lex & Yacc. O'Reilly Media, Inc (1992)

FVIL: Intermediate Language Based on Formal Verification Virtual Machine

Weiru Zeng[1], Yong Liao[1], Weizhong Qian[1(✉)], Zehui Yan[1], Zheng Yang[1], and Ang Li[2]

[1] School of Information and Software Engineering,
University of Electronic Science and Technology of China, Chengdu, China
qwz_617@163.com
[2] Chengdu Hucheng Online Technology Co., Ltd., Chengdu, China

Abstract. As the software scale continues to increase, the software development cycle becomes more and more compact, which takes more time to the software test. How to test the software and ensure its safety efficiently and accurately is an urgent problem to be solved. The formal verification virtual machine (FSPVM) [1] developed by Coq [2] assistant verification tool can effectively verify programs with formal method. However, its widespread application is heavily restricted by the compliant syntax of the formal specification language Lolisa [3] and the mechanism of generalized algebraic types GADTs [4]. This paper proposes a more user-friendly intermediate language (FVIL) based on FSPVM, which changes the hierarchical structure of Lolisa and expands the type of Lolisa, makes the formal verification of software easier to be applied in practice. The experiments show that the intermediate language can make the formal method easier to understand, apply and expand.

Keywords: Intermediate language · Coq · Formal verification · Software security

1 Introduction

With the continuous expansion of software application field, software is increasingly being used in areas where software security is critical [17], such as medical treatment, aviation, economy, big data [5, 6, 16]. Software vulnerabilities have caused great loss, such as economic losses caused by block chain leakage [7] [18], malfunction of Mars probe [8] and so on. This makes the significance of software testing in the whole software engineering more and more obvious. An efficient and accurate software testing method can improve the security and stability of software, and reduce the cost of software maintenance.

Compared with the traditional case testing, the formal method [9] is based on the strict mathematical definition, which is a technique for formalizing, developing, and verifying computer soft-ware (hardware) system. There are two kinds of formal methods: model checking and theorem proving. Model detection has a state explosion problem when

© Springer Nature Singapore Pte Ltd. 2020
X. Sun et al. (Eds.): ICAIS 2020, CCIS 1254, pp. 664–675, 2020.
https://doi.org/10.1007/978-981-15-8101-4_59

verifying a system with a high degree of concurrency; and model checking generally cannot verify an infinite state system. These result in the failure of model checking methods to formalize complex systems. Formal verification based on theorem proving takes the assertion that "the system satisfies its specifications" as a logical proposition, and proving the proposition by deductive inference through a set of inference rules. The first order logic cannot model the complex program, so the formal verification method of the higher order logic becomes an effective way to formally verify the complex software. Traditional formal verification of higher-order logic is mostly completed in a semi-automatic way, so there are a lot of auxiliary theorem proving tools, such as Coq [2]. In the first VSTTE (verified software: theories, tools, experiments) conference held in 2005, some plans for verifiable software were proposed, one of the them [10] was to establish a set of automatic verification tool set which can be applied in the industrial field. Therefore, the automation of formal validation of high-level logic will be an important direction of software test.

Recently, Zheng Yang [1] proposed a formal symbolic process virtual machine (FSPVM) and an extensible formal specification language Lolisa based on Coq. This work built a set of formal verification tools that can automatically model and verify the program. At present, the syntax of Lolisa is complicated, which makes it difficult to be widely used. There are [11, 12] and other work which have simplified other formal modeling methods, these works include using syntactic sugar and establishing an intermediate language. This paper proposes intermediate language FVIL to optimize and expand Lolisa's formal syntax based on Coq. Specifically, FVIL adds some new types and optimizes the hierarchical structure of Lolisa to make the formal verification language more user-friendly. The present work makes the following contributions:

1. Propose an intermediate language to optimize and expand the Lolisa, so that Lolisa built by Coq can be better applied to high-level programming language program verification;
2. Simplify the syntax of formal specification language Lolisa, enhance the use friendliness of formal specification language, and promote the popularization and application of formal verification of high-level logic;
3. Implement an intermediate language mechanism that enables to support the formal verification of different high-level language programs.

In the second section, the background of FSPVM is introduced. Section 3 describes the specific design of the intermediate language, including the extension of the type of Lolisa language, the simplification of syntax and the support of multiple high-level languages. In Sect. 4, the experiment compares C++ source code, FVIL code, Lolisa code. Section 5 summarizes the whole paper.

2 Background

Architecture of the formal verification virtual machine (FSPVM) is shown in Fig. 1. The application program is translated into the formal program described by Lolisa. The formal program is interpreted by the formal verified interpreter FEther [13] and the

FEther changes the formal memory state [14]. In this process, the formal kernel of Coq performs the execution and verification. The final result of program execution will be compared with the post conditions to determine whether there is a bug in the program.

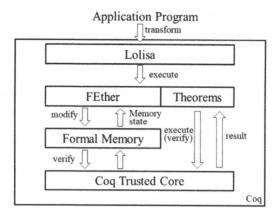

Fig. 1. Main structure of formal verification virtual machine (FSPVM)

This paper focuses on Lolisa. The program logic of Lolisa is similar to Floyd–Hoare logic which contains *Pre* condition, *Post* condition and program *P*, the form is as follows:

$$\{Pre\}\,P\,\{Post\} \tag{1}$$

It is different from the traditional Floyd–Hoare logic, the *Pre* and *Post* conditions of Lolisa based on Coq conform to the high-order logic. The *Pre* and *Post* are formal description of the user requirement or the properties that the program needs to meet. For a large number of verification requirements described in an informal way, at present, *Pre* and *Post* conditions are defined manually. So a user-friendly specification language is required.

Lolisa formal syntax is divided into four levels: *type* level, *value* level, *expression* level and *statement* level. The following Table 1 gives meaning of each level.

The *value* level, which lies next to the *expression* level, is usually encapsulated in *expressions*.

The *value* and *expression* of Lolisa based on Coq are defined by GADTs:

$$T : \tau_0 \to [\ldots] \to \tau_n \to Type \tag{2}$$

The *expression* or *value*: *T* belongs to *Type* of Coq, their *Type* is specified by the static *type* τ_i. This mechanism makes it impossible for Lolisa to construct the wrong type, also prevents type errors in the source code.

Most of Lolisa's syntax conforms to the hierarchical relationship (see Fig. 2). The *expression* and the *value* are designed using GADTs, so that they require a *type* level. The *expression* needs the *value* to construct complex objects, the *statement* is based on *expression* and the parameter list (*pars_list*), *pars_list* is mainly used to store corresponding parameters in function-related statements. Because Lolisa defines kinds of *pars_list* for different *statements*, syntax of *pars_list* is quite complex.

Table 1. Levels of lolisa

Level	Meaning	Element
type level	Type declaration, such as int, bool, string, pointer type (variable pointer, function pointer, etc.), structure type, etc.	τ
value level	All possible values in the program, such as the element or member of the array or structure, value of bool, integer, float, point, etc.	*val* τ
expression level	The value or expression being manipulated in *statement*, including mathematical expression and variables, constants and parameters in function calls	*expr* τ_0 τ_1
statement level	Statements directly constitute a program, including loop, if-else, variable declaration, assignment, function related statements and class related statements, etc.	*stat*

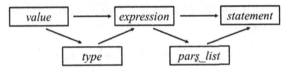

Fig. 2. Level relationship

3 Intermediate Language

This section introduces the specific design of the intermediate language and its characteristics. FVIL is the expansion and simplification of the formal specification language Lolisa, it is based on Coq, and the structure of docking for different high-level languages is pre-designed. Formal specification is a system model or a property that the system needs to satisfy, it is strictly described by formal specification language.

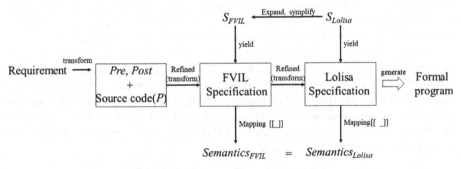

Fig. 3. Procedure of formal verification

The model specification of a program can be gradually refined by the source program, and the property specification is given by *Pre* and *Post*, which are manually defined by the user according to the user requirement. Then we get FVIL speciation which will be transformed to the specification of Lolisa according to the relationship between FVIL and Lolisa, the final generated formal program is interpreted and executed on the FSPVM. The specific procedure is shown in Fig. 3. S_{FVIL} denotes syntax set of FVIL which yields FVIL specification, S_{Lolisa} denotes syntax set of Lolisa which yields Lolisa specification. Because of the restrict corresponding relationship between FVIL and Lolisa, the FVIL specification semantics are equal to the Lolisa specification semantics.

There are two contributions: 1. For the redundant syntax caused by Lolisa's hierarchical structure, this paper simplifies syntax set S_{Lolisa} by the syntactic sugar, and generates $S_{simplify}$; 2. For the redundancy of types caused by GADTs. this paper designs new types to integrate and simplify the original types, and generates syntax set S_{expand}. The syntax set of FVIL is the union of the $S_{simplify}$ and S_{expand}:

$$S_{FVIL} = S_{simplify} \cup S_{expand} \tag{3}$$

FVIL is expansible and concise because of this construction.

Lolisa is able to support the formal verification of many different high-level languages. In this paper, the FVIL is divided into many subsets to be compatible with different high-level languages.

$$S_{FVIL} = S_{general} \cup (\cup_{i=0}^{n} S_{special\_i}) \tag{4}$$

Where $S_{general}$ denotes the generic syntax set which can be applied to all high-level programming languages. and $S_{special\_i}$ denotes the syntax set which just applies to a particular high-level programming language. $S_{special\_i}$ corresponds to the specific interpretation logic in FEther. This design enables FVIL to support a variety of different high-level programming languages.

3.1 Language Expansion: S_{expand}

Motivation

The Lolisa stores all kinds of parameters in the *pars_list*. The following Table 2 gives a summary of *pars_list*s. The *pars_list* difference increases the difficulty of formalizing the target program. In this section, Lolisa is expanded to hide the *pars_list* difference, and then improving the user friendliness of formal specification language.

τ, τ_0, τ_1 (*Tpid oα*) $\in$ *type*, *expr* (*Tpid oα*) τ_1 is used to indicate the formal parameter, *oα* denotes the parameter name or memory address of parameter (memory address is parameter name in FSPVM), the τ_1 denotes the parameter type, and the expression *expr* $\tau_0 \tau_1$ is used to denote the actual parameter or the default parameter. *str_name* and *type* in *struct_mem* denote the member variable name and its type. The Sect. 2 introduces that the *expression* of Lolisa is defined by GADTs. Specifically, the *Type* of *expression* conforms to the EXPR-TYPE [3] rule:

$$expr : \tau_0 \rightarrow \tau_0 \rightarrow Type \quad (EXPR - TYPE) \tag{5}$$

The *Type* of *expression* must be declared by two concrete type identifiers τ_0 and τ_1, and $\tau_0, \tau_1 \in$ *type*. The *expressions* with different type identifiers τ are regarded as different *Type*.

Table 2. Parameter list of different application

pars_list	Application of list	Types of elements
pars	Parameters in function declaration (without default parameters)	expr (Tpid oα) τ
capture_pars	Capture variables required in lambda	expr (Tpid oα) τ
struct_mem	Member variables in a structure	type str_name
fun_init_pars	Parameters in function declaration or function definition (default parameters are optional)	expr (Tpid oα) τ_1 expr τ_0 τ_1
fcall_pars	Parameters required in function call	expr τ_0 τ_1
call_pars	Parameters required to create class objects	expr τ_0 τ_1

Our work uses *list* to store *pars_list* elements. The *list* in Coq conforms to the rule POLY-LIST:

$$list : T \to Type \quad (POLY - LIST) \tag{6}$$

The *Type* of *list* must be defined by T, and $T \in Type$. All elements in the *list* defined by T should belong to T. This leads to two problems: 1. In one *pars_list*, because of the difference of τ_0 or τ_1, elements which belong to *expr* τ_0 τ_1 may have different *Type*. These elements which contrary to POLY-LIST cannot be stored in one *list*. 2. Elements in different kinds of *pars_list* shown in Table 2 belong to different *Type*, result in the problem that elements of different kinds of *pars_list* cannot be stored in the same *list*.

New Type and Structure

Our work defines new data structure and data type to integrate different *pars_list*:

1. *expressions* which could be default parameter or actual parameter are integrated into a new type: *par_expr*:

$$par\_expr : Type \tag{7}$$

The abstract syntax of *par_expr* type is as follows:

$$pe :: = pEfun(o\alpha, \tau)|pEvar(o\alpha, \tau)|pEop(\varepsilon)|pEauto(o\alpha)|pEconst(val)|$$

ε denotes *expression*, $o\alpha$ denotes variable name or function name, and *val* denotes *value*. Compared with the *expression* in Lolisa, *par_expr* removes the limitation of GADTs, but *par_expr* preserves the necessary information of *expression*. This makes it possible to restore the Lolisa *expression*. According to the relevant rules in [3], this paper constructs rules PAR-EFUN, PAR-EVAR, PAR-EOP, PAR-EAUTO AND PAR-ECONST to define function, variable, operation, auto type variable and constant which could be actual parameter or default parameter.

$$\frac{\Sigma, \Theta, \Lambda \vdash \tau : type \quad \Lambda \vdash oa : option\ L_{address}}{\mathcal{F} \vdash pEfun:option\ L_{address} \to type \to par\_expr}{\mathcal{F} \vdash wf\ (pEfun(\tau,oa)):par\_expr} (PAR - EFUN) \tag{8}$$

$$\frac{\Sigma,\ \Theta \vdash \tau : type \quad \Lambda \vdash o\alpha : option\ L_{addres}}{\mathcal{F}/\Phi \vdash pEvar:option\ L_{address} \to type \to par\_expr}{\mathcal{F} \vdash wf\,(pEvar(\tau,o\alpha)):par\_expr} \text{(PAR - EVAR)} \tag{9}$$

$$\frac{\Sigma,\ \Theta \vdash \tau : type \quad F,\ \Phi \vdash e : expr\tau\tau}{\mathcal{F}/\Phi \vdash pEop:\forall(\tau:type),expr\tau\tau \to par\_expr}{\mathcal{F} \vdash wf\,(pEop(expr\tau\tau)):par\_expr} \text{(PAR - EOP)} \tag{10}$$

$$\frac{\Lambda \vdash o\,\alpha : option\ L_{addres}}{\mathcal{F}/\Phi \vdash pEauto:option\ L_{address} \to par\_expr}{\mathcal{F} \vdash wf\,(pEauto(o\alpha)):par\_expr} \text{(PAR - EAUTO)} \tag{11}$$

$$\frac{\Omega \vdash v : val\tau}{\mathcal{F}/\Phi \vdash pEconst:\forall(\tau:type),val\tau \to par\_expr}{\mathcal{F} \vdash wf\,(pEcosnt(v)):par\_expr} \text{(PAR - ECONST)} \tag{12}$$

Σ, Θ, Λ, F, Φ, Ω denote structure information, structure pointer set, memory address set, formal system space, function information, value set, specific information of them could be find in [3], *option* $L_{address}$ denotes the virtual memory address. $F \vdash wf$ (*x*):*par_expr* denotes that the *x* is well-formed in space F, and x belong to *t*. $A \vdash x$:*t* denotes that *x* is exiting in space A, and *x* belong to *t*. F/Φ denotes the space including F but excluding Φ. The formulas above mean that if the condition above the line is true, the conclusion below the line can be deduced

2. *list_ tetrad* is used to store four different *list*.

$$list\_tetrad : Type \tag{13}$$

This structure conforms the rule TETRAD-TYPE:

$$LP : list_1 \to list_2 \to list_3 \to list_4 \to list\_tetrad \text{ (TETRAD - TYPE)} \tag{14}$$

The *list_ tetrad* consists of four *list*s, The *Type* of each list is shown in Table 3:

Table 3. Element types in the *list_ tetrad*

list	*Type* of *list*
$list_1$	*list* (*oa, type*)
$list_2$	*list* (*type, oa, par_expr*)
$list_3$	*list* (*type, str_name*)
$list_4$	*list par_expr*

list (*type, str_name*) in the above table is used to store structural member, *type* denotes the type of structural member, and *str_name* denotes the name of structural member. $list_1$ is used to store information about *capture_pars* and *pars*, $list_2$ is used to store information about *fun_pars*, $list_3$ is used to store information about *struct_mem*, and $list_4$ is used to store information about *fcall_pars* and *call_pars*. Each *list* is used to save the basic information of corresponding *pars_list*, so that *pars_list* can be restored.

When *pars_list* is needed, just building the corresponding element $list_i$ (i = 1, 2, 3, 4) in *list_ tetrad* according to Table 3, and the other three elements are set to the empty list. because of the correspondence of *list_ tetrad* and all kinds of *pars_lists*, it is easy to restore the specific *pars_list* in Table 2. In the aspect of syntax, all the *pars_lists* are given in the unified form of *list*, and then reducing the difficulty of using formal specification language, and facilitating simplification of Lolisa.

3.2 Language Simplifying: $S_{simplify}$

Motivation
The syntax of Lolisa designed in levels makes the program of Lolisa complex. The program is built level by level. User has to take all the components and the keywords in each level. This greatly improves the difficulty of coding.

The complexity of Lolisa syntax is illustrated by the follow code of 3 being assigned to a:

Assignv(**Evar**(Some a) Tuint) (**Econst**(**Vint**(**INT** I32 Unsigned 3))) $\equiv a = 3$

the syntax of Lolisa is on the left. The derivation of *expression* " constant 3" is as follows: first, using *expression* syntax: *expr* :: = **ECONOMY** < *val* > ; then using *val* syntax: *val* :: = **VINT** < *int* > ; in the end, using *type* syntax: *int* :: = **INT** < *intsize* > < *signedness* > < *z* > , and there are other three non-terminals which need to be computed. The constant *expression* 3: **Economy** (**VINT** (**INT** I32 unsigned 3)) is used as the operand ε_2 of assignment statement **ASSIGNV** ε_1 ε_2. The boldface is keyword of Lolisa. The construction rule of stat in Lolisa is:

$$stat ::= p_{stat}\left(p_{expr}\left(p_{type}(), p_{val}\left(p_{type}()\right)\right), \left[p_{stat}\right]\right) \tag{15}$$

where p_{stat} (), p_{expr} (), p_{val} (), p_{type} () denote syntax in *statement* level, *expression* level, *value* level and *type* level in Lolisa, p_x (p_y) means that p_y is the non-terminal in syntax p_x (), and [p] denotes that the non-terminal p is optional.

Simplifying Levels
Syntax of Lolisa is verbose, and syntax of each level is closely related, so the complex syntax of Lolisa can be expressed succinctly in a familiar way. The sugar [9] defined by notation [2] is used to simplify syntax of Lolisa and generate the syntax of FVIL. Notation is a symbolic expression denoting some term or term pattern in Coq. Syntactic sugar encapsulates highly relevant Lolisa syntax components. We will now illustrate the main ideas of sugar with a few examples.

Specifically, because the *statement*s of Lolisa correspond to the statements of high-level programming language, we design syntactic sugar for *statement*, this sugar is the statement syntax in FVIL, it encapsulates the syntax of *statement*, *expression* and *value* in Lolisa. There are syntactic placeholders in sugar, they are corresponding to the non-terminals of high-level programming language statement. For instance, syntactic sugar of function declaration statement:

$$\textbf{FUN\_DEC}[ac](t) \; addr[fip1; ..; fipn] \equiv$$
$$(\textbf{EOS\_Fun\_declaration} \; (\textbf{Some}ac) \; (\textbf{Eexecutable} \; (\textbf{Some}addr)t)$$
$$(\textbf{list2pars}(\textbf{getLpars} \; (\textbf{LP nil} \; (\textbf{cons}fip1..(\textbf{cons}fipn\textbf{nil})..)\textbf{nil nil}))))$$

The placeholders include access permission: ac, function return type: t, function name: $addr$, parameters: $fip1,\cdots, fipn$. The boldface is keyword of syntax. Syntax of FVIL on the left, Syntax of Lolisa on the right. The syntax of Lolisa contains many rules, **EOS_fun_declaration** in *statement* level and **Eexecutible** in *expression* level, **LP** is rule of *list_ tetrad* and **list2pars**, **getLpars** are type transform operations of S_{expand}, all of them are cumbersome. FVIL's syntax style is similar to that of C++, it is concise and easy to understand.

Placeholders contain *expression*s, *type* related syntax, numbers, parameters, variable names, and other non-terminals like access permission. Expression placeholders $p'_{expression}()$ include most of the *expression* of Lolisa, and encapsulate some of the *value* syntax which are closely related to *expression*. For instance, syntax of integer constant expression placeholders:

$$\textbf{SINT} \; n \equiv \textbf{Econst}(\textbf{Vint}(\textbf{INT} \; \text{I32 Signed} \; n))$$

Syntax of FVIL on the left, keyword **SINT** identifies the expression, number n denotes the value. Syntax of Lolisa on the right, which includes *expression* rule: **Econst** and *value* rule: **Vint**. The expression of FVIL can obviously simplify the syntax of *expression* and *value* in Lolisa language.

The FVIL can simplify most of the Lolisa *statement* construction to:

$$stat' ::= p'_{stat}\left(p'_{expr}(p_{type}()), \left[p'_{stat}\right]\right) \tag{16}$$

There is no *value* syntax, it is merged into FVIL expression syntax: $p'_{expr}()$, The FVIL *type* syntax $p_{type}()$ is the same as the syntax of Lolisa *type*, FVIL statement syntax $p'_{stat}()$ simplifies the $p_{stat}()$, FVIL expression syntax $p'_{expr}()$ simplifies $p_{expr}()$ of Lolisa, in addition, $p'_{stat}()$ encapsulates $p_{stat}()$ and part of $p_{expr}()$ which is closely related to the *statement* level, $p'_{expr}()$ encapsulates the $p_{expr}()$ and part of $p_{val}()$ in Lolisa. The FVIL simplifies the entire Lolisa syntax according to the similar principles. And generating the syntax of the intermediate language.

3.3 Multiple Languages Supporting: $S_{special\_i}$

FSPVM includes general virtual memory and extensible formal specification language Lolisa, these enable formal verification of high-level programming languages. For this reason, FVIL also needs support different high-level languages.

The scope [2] is a set of notations for terms with their interpretations in Coq. The FVIL is divided into multiple unrelated scopes. The syntax in each scope is based on the corresponding high-level programming language. The syntax in different scopes corresponds to different interpretation logic. We generate multiple intermediate language scopes, where $S_{general}$ contains general syntax for all languages, $S_{special\_i}$ contains special syntax supporting the specific language, and the relationship of the syntax in each scope is described in formula (4). When expanding the support for the new language, the syntax in $S_{general}$ will be used to support the general part in the language. For the special syntax, $S_{special\_i}$ will be added. In each scope, the relationship between FVIL and Lolisa will be defined by notation.

FVIL uses stable and simple syntax, and can support a variety of different high-level languages. Such a design is the base of the framework of translator-FVIL-interpreter, this framework supports the formal verification of different high-level program languages and further realizes the automation of the formal verification of program. The framework is shown in Fig. 4. Different high-level language programs are translated into program of FVIL by a translator. This FVIL program corresponds to a specific interpretation logic, and is finally interpreted and executed by FSPVM.

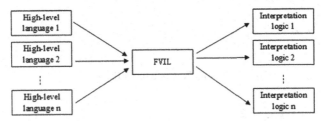

Fig. 4. Overall framework of translator-FVIL-interpreter

In this framework, if a new programming language needs to be support, just building a corresponding translator to translate the high-level language into FVIL. If there is new syntax, expanding $S_{special\_i}$, and adding corresponding interpretation logic in FSPVM. As the number of supported languages increases, this structure will become more and more complete.

4 Experiment

This section shows the program block of FVIL and its corresponding source code and Lolisa code. In this case, C++ source code (see in Fig. 5) and Solidity source code (see in Fig. 6) are converted to the same FVIL code (see in Fig. 7). The FVIL code is converted to corresponding Lolisa code of C++ (see in Fig. 8) or Lolisa code of Solidity [2] (see in Fig. 9). When C++ program or Solidity program is converted to a FVIL program, all variables are converted to numbers which identify the addresses of the corresponding variables in the virtual memory of SFPVM.

Intermediate code (see in Fig. 7) and source code (see in Fig. 5, 6) are basically consistent, the main difference is that all variables of FVIL have corresponding type identifier, this is because FVIL retains the nature of GADTs. Most statements are based on the *type* level, *value* level and *expression* level like the code in Fig. 8, 9. Lolisa is inconvenient to users owing to the complexity and diversity of keywords and the hierarchical structure. From the above experiments, we can find that FVIL can simplify

```
bool fun_cplus(bool a){
  if(a == true){ return true;  }
  else{ return false;  }
}
```

Fig. 5. Code of C++

```
function fun_solidity(bool a) returns bool {
  if (a == true){ return true; }
  else{ return false; }
}
```

Fig. 6. Code of solidity

```
Definition test_FVIL:=
(FUN_EXP ( Tbool ) 1 [Tbool:14 := PFALSE] ){{
(IFE(TRUE b(==) EVAR(Tbool)14 ){{
  RETURN TRUE ;;
}}ELSE {{
  RETURN FALSE ;;
}} );;}} );;
END.
```

Fig. 7. Code of FVIL

```
Definition test_Lolisa_c_plus:=
cons.
( EOS_Fun_expression None (Eexecutable (Some 1) Tbool)
    (list2finitpars (getLfinitpars (LP nil
    (cons (pair3 Tbool (Some 14) None )
    nil) nil nil ) ) )
(cons (If (Ebop feqbOfBool (Evar (Some 14) Tbool) (Econst (Vbool true)) )
(cons (Return (Econst (Vbool true))) nil)
(cons (Return (Econst (Vbool false))) nil) ) nil))
nil.
```

Fig. 8. Code of lolisa corresponding to code of C++

```
Definition test_Lolisa_solidity :=
Seq.
(Fun (None) (Efun (Some 1) Tundef) (pcons (Epar (Some 14) Tbool) pnil) (nil)
      (If (Ebop feqbOfBool (Evar (Some 14) Tbool) (Econst (Vbool false)) )
      ( Seq (Return (Econst (Vbool true))) Snil )
      ( Seq (Return (Econst (Vbool false))) Snil ) )
  Snil.
```

Fig. 9. Code of lolisa corresponding to code of solidity

the formal specification language program, and make it easy to translate a high-level language program into a formal program.

5 Conclusion

Formal verification can ensure the security of software, but it is difficult to implement. The intermediate language and related concepts proposed in this paper can effectively reduce the difficulty of using formal techniques, so as to promote the application of formal technology and ensure the security of software. Future work will focus on refining the intermediate language to support more high-level programming languages.

Acknowledgements. The authors wish to thank Chengdu Hucheng online Technology Co., Ltd. for its generous support during the research process.

References

1. Yang, Z., Lei, H.: Formal process virtual machine for smart contracts verification. arXiv preprint arXiv:1805.00808 (2018)
2. Yang, Z., Lei, H.: Lolisa: formal syntax and semantics for a subset of the solidity programming language. arXiv preprint arXiv:1803.09885 (2018)
3. Xi, H., Chen, C., Chen, G.: Guarded recursive datatype constructors. In: ACM SIGPLAN Notices, vol. 38, no. 1. ACM (2003)
4. Wang, J., Zhan, N.J., Feng, X.Y., Liu, Z.M.: Overview of formal methods. Ruan Jian Xue Bao J. Softw. **30**(1), 33–61 (2019)
5. The Coq proof assistant. https://Coq.inria.fr/. Accessed 3 Nov 2019
6. Yang, Z., Lei, H.: FEther: an extensible definitional interpreter for smart-contract verifications in coq. IEEE Access **7**, 37770–37791 (2019)
7. Yang, Z., Lei, H.: A general formal memory framework in coq for verifying the properties of programs based on higher-order logic theorem proving with increased automation, consistency, and reusability. arXiv preprint arXiv:1803.00403 (2018)
8. Yu-kun, X.U., Shu-fen, L.I.U., Bing, L.I.: Research of text concrete syntax analysis methods in modeling language. Appl. Res. Comput. **25**(3), 791–794 (2008)
9. Beer, I., et al: The temporal logic sugar. International Conference on Computer Aided Verification. Springer, Berlin, Heidelberg (2001)
10. Berthomieu, B., et al.: Fiacre: an intermediate language for model verification in the topcased environment. In: ERTS 2008 (2008)
11. Hoare, C.A.R., et al.: The verified software initiative: a manifesto. ACM Comput. Surv. **41**(4), 1–8 (2009)
12. del Castillo, M.: The DAO attacked: code issue leads to $60 million ether theft. https://www.coindesk.com/dao-attacked-code-issue-leads-60-million-ether-theft/. Accessed 2 Dec 2017
13. Sha, L., Rajkumar, R., Lehoczky, J.P.: Priority inheritance protocols: an approach to real-time synchronization. IEEE Trans. Comput. **39**, 1175–1185 (1990)
14. Zheng, D., et al.: An assertion graph based abstraction algorithm in GSTE and Its application. Integration **63**, 1–8 (2018)
15. X-Y, Li., et al.: Machine learning study of the relationship between the geometric and entropy discord. EPL (Europhys. Lett.) **127**(2), 20009 (2019)
16. Centonze, P.: Security and privacy frameworks for access control big data systems. Comput. Mater. Continua **59**(2), 361–374 (2019)
17. Zhang, Q., Liang, Z., Cai, Z.: Developing a new security framework for bluetooth low energy devices. Comput. Mater. Continua **59**(2), 457–471 (2019)
18. Zhao, Y., Zhang, S., Yang, M., He, P., Wang, Q.: Research on architecture of risk assessment system based on block chain. Comput. Mater. Continua **61**(2), 677–686 (2019)

Author Index

Printed in the United States
By Bookmasters